PALAWAN

SULU
SEA

MINDANAO

Davao

NE ISLANDS

NORTH
BORNEO

CELEBES SEA

SARAWAK

MOLUCCA PASSAGE

B O R N E O

STRAIT OF MACASSAR

MOLUCCAS

CERAM SEA

CERAM

Amboina

Banjermasin

CELEBES

BANDA
SEA

Macassar

SEA

FLORES   SEA

Bandjoewangi

BALI

FLORES

SUMBAWA

LOMBOK

SUMBA

SAWU SEA

TIMOR

Koepang

EAN

TIMOR
SEA

To
The Waleys,
this very dull biography
by Emily Hahn (Boxer)

with best regards.

England
Sept. 8, 1947

RAFFLES OF SINGAPORE

BOOKS BY
EMILY HAHN
RAFFLES OF SINGAPORE
HONG KONG HOLIDAY
CHINA TO ME
MR. PAN
THE SOONG SISTERS

EMILY HAHN

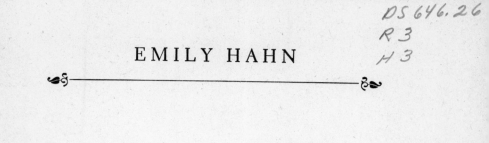

Raffles
of
Singapore

A BIOGRAPHY

1946

GARDEN CITY, NEW YORK
DOUBLEDAY & COMPANY, INC.

With much affection to
GEORGE AND KATHARINE SANSOM

ACKNOWLEDGMENTS

Many thanks are due the Explorers' Club of New York for their generosity in allowing a free use of their excellent library during the preparation of this text. The same is true of the British Library of Information in New York, with special reference to the kindness of Mrs. Mary Burke of that organization. The writer also wishes to express her gratitude for the practical help given her by Dr. James Chapin of the American Museum of Natural History.

Dr. Bartholomew Landheer, of the Netherlands Information Bureau in New York, was kind enough, during the writer's absence in England, to check the book in proof for the spelling of the many Dutch names which occur in the text, a tedious job and one which she sincerely appreciates his having done.

LIST OF ILLUSTRATIONS

APOLOGIA

"The volume is too cursory for the specialist and too detailed for others. . . ." (From R. O. Winstedt's review of Vlekke's *Nusantara* in the *Journal of the Royal Asiatic Society*, 1944.)

Cruel words which, though they were not inspired by this book, might well have been. The author of *Raffles of Singapore* hereby offers a brief apology for her unorthodox treatment of an exceedingly conventional subject, knowing that biography and history used customarily to be written in a special style, dry and pedantic. That, in her opinion, was a fault. She feels that her own generation while growing up was frightened away from history by this stupid tradition, which masked Clio's beauty and drowned the music of her voice in dull, pedestrian language. The old fashion was deliberately to steal from the story of men and nations all excitement and even interest. History we understood to be a dreary list of wars and coronations, appended to a catalogue of dates.

If in following the new fashion the writer exaggerates, leaning too far in the other direction, she hopes that her facts at least are fundamentally sound and that she has avoided sloppiness in recounting them.

Her hope and purpose in producing this book are not to contribute to our knowledge of Raffles; for excepting that she had access to Dutch sources which are not commonly known to English readers, she has nothing new to offer. She meant it rather for the ordinary person who, like herself, was cheated at school by bad teaching and never learned of history's true deep pleasures until he was able to dispel his early false impressions.

Those readers who are already well grounded in the period are asked to refer to the Bibliography before reading the book. They may then feel that the writer has at any rate tried to avoid being included in the category of those so scathingly condemned by Lord Curzon as "either not having read what has been written by better men before, or reading it only in order to plagiarize and reproduce it as their own, . . . misunderstand, misspell, and misinterpret everywhere as they go." The desire to avoid this pitfall for the hack writer turned historian also explains why the author has refrained from the temptation to paraphrase or modernize the older writers whose works she has consulted.

The interest we all feel today in Indonesia as well as the general topic of imperialism appears to her to lead as a matter of course to England and, particularly, to Raffles's period. What is happening today in Java has a definite relationship with the past in which he played so large a part.

It has been difficult to keep to a consistent spelling of Malay and Javanese names, particularly as they occur many times in direct quotations where they must be left untouched in whatever form the original writer preferred: Dutch, English, or purely arbitrary. Sticklers for accuracy are referred to the Glossary and Index, where these variations are properly listed.

Acknowledgment is made elsewhere to those individuals who have helped in various ways to locate or secure the information included in this book; but it should be stated here that Major C. R. Boxer was responsible for all of the translation and much of the selection of the Dutch material used. Naturally this responsibility does not extend to the writer's interpretation of the facts thus supplied. On a number of occasions Major Boxer's views did not coincide with those of his wife, which is one of several reasons for his firm, consistent refusal to accept more credit for his help than is herewith given.

EMILY HAHN

RAFFLES OF SINGAPORE

CHAPTER I

Had Mrs. Benjamin Raffles been able to hold out one more night her son would have been born on the *terra firma* of Jamaica instead of seeing his first daylight from the cabin of the *Ann*. Not that it mattered to anyone. Even the captain was complacent, a rare state of affairs for a man of his calling when a baby gets itself born under his command. But then the circumstances were unusual, for he was Benjamin Raffles, father of the infant, who was the first male child his wife had produced; what man under such circumstances would complain, even though he was captain? Not the father of Thomas Stamford Bingley Raffles, in any case.

The eighteenth century was altogether more philosophical about such facts of nature than is the twentieth, due in large part to the difficulties of travel. When a ship's sailing schedule is liable to be knocked galley-west by a change of seasonal wind, it seems unduly captious to take exception to some feminine mistake of a month or so. Today the shipping companies are not so amiable about maritime deliveries. Ticket agencies have been known to refuse ladies all too evidently close to their hour of travail when they try to book passage on long sea voyages. But such practice is generally frowned on and will probably not become general. There is a good deal of old-fashioned prejudice still to be found in our hearts: we are still hopelessly in favor of reproduction, and it goes against our instincts thus summarily to discourage women big with child, however inconvenient their company aboard ship. We are extraordinarily kind, for some reason, to any woman who, like Mrs. Raffles, gives birth on a ship at sea. Be she steerage passenger or millionairess, half-witted or famous, malodorous or attractive, sweet or bad-tempered, everybody loves her for a day. She is esteemed, petted, and spoiled; she is considered a creature of noble fortitude rather than just another feckless female who can't count.

Since this is the case in 1946, one can see how much less reason Captain Benjamin had to complain, back in 1781 on the fifth of July. He wasn't an exception. English sea captains who liked to have their wives about them used often to take them along on voyages like this journey aboard the *Ann*. The ship was making a routine run, London to Port Morant and back with fresh cargo, so while she was loading Mrs. Raffles had ample time to recover and to slip ashore and register her babe properly, before the *Ann* pointed her nose toward home.

Our information on this subject is meager, but since we learn from Raffles, in letters which he wrote years later, that his father was chronically unable to support his family without aid, we can guess that the bright warm islands of the West Indies gave the captain's wife an unusual taste of luxury, after living frugally in London most of her life. We must be satisfied, however, with conjecture, because Sir Stamford has never been generous with descriptions of his childhood's difficulties. Doubtless he was reluctant to dwell on his own trials and troubles partly because he was modest, partly because of pride.

Fortunately for us, writers like Thackeray, Hickey, and their contemporaries have been less self-contained, and so we have a clear picture of the London in which Raffles grew up, whether or not he ever wished us to know the worst. We can make a close guess at what his home was like: it must have been dark and inconvenient, for even the wealthy residents of London lived in gloomy buildings in those days. Nobody knew any better. The Raffles family was poor, but not abject with the poverty that knows no pride. Such a state would have been, in many ways, easier to support philosophically. Raffles came of gentlefolk, poor boy, and he was taught never to forget to be genteel, no matter what misfortunes he labored under. When he went out into the world, a weedy boy of fourteen, he had learned his lesson well and knew how to keep the true state of affairs at home decently hidden. So did his parents, so did his sisters, with a fierce pride that cost them God knows what in privations which were never admitted, then or later, when circumstances became easier.

It is difficult, indeed, not to lose patience with the long-suffering clan of Raffles. Life could have been much pleasanter for all of them if they had possessed a little less fortitude, a little more humility. If only Captain Benjamin Raffles and Mrs. Raffles (nee Lindeman of the Herefordshire Lindemans, also sister of the Rev. John Lindeman, a respectable clergyman), and the young Misses Raffles, and Master Thomas Stamford Bingley Raffles—if only they hadn't been so tiresomely genteel and decent it would have gone better for everyone. But they couldn't help it: they were victims of the time and the system. Far more than she is today, England was rigidly divided into classes, and the Raffleses belonged irrevocably to the respectable middle class. Had they been low-class cockneys, they could have relaxed. A poor cockney with no education, heir to no social position, was able in the late eighteenth century to settle back in his dirt with his wife and ragged brats; he got a little fun out of life. He took it easy. He could beg or steal, he could even do a menial job and earn some menial money, which goes as far as the other kind. Nobody expected him to entertain ambitions for his children's betterment; he wouldn't dream of it. He took no more thought for his offspring's future than an animal of the fields. So long as they pigged it with him and were willing to share his lot he was not unkind to them, unless he happened by some accident to achieve drunkenness. Then he might possibly beat up his dear ones, unless they were wary enough to stay out of his path. Anyway, one way or another, life for the genuine low-class poor was not too terrible to contemplate, back in those dark ages before England was modernized by machinery.

It was the shabby-genteel who were in pitiful condition, so

3 ଓ

that one is divided, when contemplating them, between exasperation and reluctant respect.

It is genuinely a relief to know that the captain's wife went down to Jamaica once, at any rate, for a sort of holiday. There were other mitigations in the Raffleses' lot too: their father the captain could at least tell them about warmer climes, where slaves were plentiful and everyone had leisure and every day was like a dream. They would probably become ambitious to see all this for themselves. At the end of the eighteenth century more than one English heart yearned toward the romance of "the Colonies." Hundreds of British men and women were out in India or Malaya, finding compensation for the discomfort of the long voyage in a marvelous manner of life unknown to the home island.

English minds were full of oriental visions just then. We citizens of the United States used to learn at school that the loss of the American colonies and the revolution leading to it were heavy blows to the British. We were taught that the English were plunged into the depths of despair by our defection, and that George's throne practically tottered when his subjects realized how he had wantonly lost this pride of the Atlantic for them. For all I know, our children are still hearing this nonsense. In actuality the ordinary Briton of the late eighteenth century was scarcely aware of America, either before or after our war of independence. The quality of the troops the Crown sent to put down the insurrection was a fair sign af England's contemptuous opinion of us; only a handful of men were spared for the job. When they failed in their mission, the English, far from feeling astonishment and terror, didn't experience much emotion at all, with the exception of a few businessmen who had invested heavily rather than wisely in the new western colonies. No ordinary Briton could have guessed how the United States were to flourish in the next couple of centuries. The only important effect our Revolution seemed to have on the mother country was to turn public notice more completely toward the Indies, West and East, which had long held most of their attention anyway. And British above all— it was so new, so glamorous, so full of possibilities! It was convenient, too, as a wastebasket: India in those days fulfilled the function of Australia in the next century in accommodating the wild youngsters, the problem children, and the younger sons of England. She also offered tempting careers to solid citizens. The ports of India were already well-established cities, with an aristocracy composed of British men and women who kept dozens of native servants, lived in a sort of fairyland, and were too happily busy to remember their more humble origins at home. A lady writing a friend from Madras in 1783 makes none of the mention we might expect of political difficulties or of housekeeping problems, but she speaks briefly and ungrammatically of the trials of sea travel, as one sufferer to another, before turning once and for all to the engrossing topic of dress. A lady who at home would have been absorbed in domestic topics, in India has learned to chatter like a lady of fashion, of high degree, and of no earthly use to anybody.

"I have received your letter and am very happy to hear of your safe arrival in Bengal after so uncommonly bad and disagreeable a passage as you had, but you was most fortunate in meeting with such a man in the command of the ship as Captain Serocold. I make no doubt but you will like your situation, as I hear the inhabitants of Bengal are much more sociably disposed than we humdrum Madrassars. To add to your society there are a great many ladies arrived here whose final destination is your quarter. Many of them are single, and some very pretty, really beautiful. I have not yet been to see them, being, as you well know, a sad visitor. I hear nothing talked of now but *the fashions!* It is reckoned the height of indelicacy to show the ear or any part of it; the hair is therefore cut in such a manner as wholly to cover that part of the head, not even the tip must be seen. For my part I am very well satisfied with the old custom, and too sedate to adopt every absurd and preposterous innovation. . . ."

A glorious vision had taken hold of the British. True, England was not the empire she was to become when Queen Victoria sat on the throne and Disraeli taught her to be an empress, but she was already the country which had produced the East India Company, and her people were cashing in on that fact.

5 &

Colonization was not yet a political matter. It was not even primarily the affair of the government. The colonies were off-shoots of trade, the be-all and end-all of the average Briton. If an Englishman went to far-off lands and wrestled with the natives for existence, and finally produced something worth sending home to sell, he was not thinking so much of his country's glory or of his King as he was of his record with the Company. He was always, if he lived in India, connected with one of the "factories," and through his very languid efforts petty trading was done to such a degree that a thousand such small transactions made up an important figure for the annual accounting back home, in Threadneedle Street.

Remember, it was a disparity of opinion as to the nation's duty toward British colonists which finally led to that revolt of America. The colonists of North America had come to think of themselves as settled residents of the new country, rather than temporary commercial travelers out to exploit a strange land. In India the mentality was different.

Stamford Raffles was born during the Revolutionary War, and there is a definite link between our history and his. A comparison, though farfetched, is amusing. Our nation was born at the same time he was. We didn't know to what heights our destiny was to take us; neither did he. (Though we all felt premonitions of glory.) The children being born in the American provinces when Thomas Stamford Bingley Raffles put in his appearance were dedicated to the new experiment of a republic. Raffles, on the other hand, was an empire builder, dedicated to empire from the cradle. He didn't know it. Until just a bit before the end he thought of himself as a servant of the East India Company first, and second as a loyal and not unworthy subject of the Crown, doing his best for the nation by way of trade. But he was an empire builder nevertheless, perhaps the first genuine one in England. Clive and Hastings came before him and played their parts against the same backdrop, it is true. But both of these men, particularly Clive, were individualists and careerists first: their work was only fortuitously constructive of the British Empire. Raffles, a younger man, saw the Company, and himself an integral part of the Company, all a

§ 6

part, in turn, of the great divine plan of empire. He never doubted the final rightness of empire; he merely doubted the Company's interpretation, sometimes, of Divinity's intentions. Then he tried to set them right again, back on the path leading to the right true end—a greater empire.

As a result he was not half the "character" Clive was, nor did he want to be. In his world a man didn't stand alone on the stage, posturing. A man who could choose his part didn't play the hero: he preferred to be stage director. He stood offstage and told the mob what to do—yes, and the hero too.

The relations which had existed through two centuries between the East India Company and the Crown seem simple enough in retrospect, a long record of charters granted, renewed, held back, and then granted again as new monarchs came to the throne and felt kindly disposed or covetous toward the merchant adventurers. Closer inspection breaks up the orderly pattern. A conscientious student of history can easily spend a lifetime tracing the East India Company's strange Siamese-twin existence, side by side with the British Government through the years; still he will not have unraveled it. What at first seems obvious becomes obsure under the reading glass. For example the chief article of trade for many years, the staple industry which provided the lifeblood of the Company, was not an Indian product at all but a Chinese one—tea. And though we speak nowadays a good deal, loosely, of England's conquest of India, as though it were a simple tale of armed expansion, the British Government was not India's conqueror. The East India Company, John Company, was. The conquest of India was primarily commercial; it was carried out by commercial agents. It is true that they were Englishmen, and their military wore English uniform, but they were acting for the Company. For generations the British rulers of the Indians and all their petty officials were East India Company agents, and nothing else. This does not mean the Indians were mistaken in laying the actions of the white men at the door of the British Crown. By the time Clive made his name famous

7 ॐ

there had been so much mingling of interests between government and Company out in Asia, and so many hundreds of British soldiers dead on Indian soil, that it would be an impossible task to extricate the single strands of either agency's story from the tangled record. The responsibility must be shared. John Company is dead, but his soul goes marching on. We find it in a thousand places: in a tradition, for example, surviving today in the Belgian Congo, where the leading commercial agent for the most important British firm in any sizable community there is *ipso facto* British consul for the town.

Eighteenth-century England was not a nation of shopkeepers. She was a nation of traveling salesmen, who carried arms as well as goods in their sample cases.

It all began in 1581, when Queen Elizabeth granted a charter to a group of merchants who wanted to seek foreign countries with which to trade. That group was not the original East India Company, but many of the members went over to our Company in time. They were all possessed with a dream of the East, that land of gold and emeralds and rubies and spices which beckoned to any adventurer worthy of the term. It was not until 1600 that the true East India Company received a charter, and that was first limited to fifteen years and allowed simply for operations by ship between the Cape of Good Hope and the Strait of Magellan.

In 1600 the Company's offices opened in Philpot Lane, in the home of Sir Thomas Smythe, their first governor. From the beginning competition was fierce, not only with the Portuguese but also with the Dutch, who had their East India Company too. The first and second British voyages were made to Sumatra and Java, and though they were profitable enough to satisfy the stockholders and to sway capricious royal prejudice toward granting the new charter which was soon to be requested, a good deal of the profit can't honestly be laid to the address of Trade. Piracy pure and simple brought in those good returns, at least one "prize ship" being towed into an English harbor, the cause of great and joyful excitement.

 8

The first English factory of the Company was founded at Surat. That word "factory," which persists through the decades and is found with the same connotation in African posts, owes its existence to the Portuguese word *feitoria*; early commercial agents were always called "factors," a word derived from the same root. The Surat station, small and unpretentious though it was, angered and affrighted the alert Portuguese. But the Company's real competitor was not Portugal, as the British soon learned: it was Holland. The Dutch had begun to supplant the Portuguese everywhere, and though the English were willing for a while to maintain peaceful relations in the East Indies with these determined traders, such a state of affairs could not continue forever. Not, at any rate, in the minds of those traveling merchants and pirates from England, flushed with success and flush with profit. They were in a grabby mood.

By 1621 the Company group had outgrown their offices in Philpot Lane and had moved to Crosby Hall in Bishopsgate. Altogether it would seem that as a commercial venture it had proved itself solid.

The future was to bear out appearances. What other stock company can claim to have lived more than two hundred and fifty years?

Those days in which John Company matured and reached his giant stature were to see a strange paradox, something that seems to happen wherever commercial-minded Englishmen, having led the way, are followed by more Englishmen, wanting more trade. That was all they were after. None of these men consciously aspired to responsibility, but they got it, and this duty was to weigh heavily upon the shoulders of their successors. It is a sort of curse on England that her people should always get so heavily involved in governing the lands they set out merely to exploit. It happened at that time too; the traders didn't ask for all that authority in perpetuity, though there is no doubt, later, that the British made a virtue of convenience, and even miscalled convenience by the name of necessity. Who at the beginning could have guessed that England would one day rule India? Not the British, not the Portuguese, and certainly not the suspicious Dutch, who still held the advantage in Far Eastern commerce. Nor, for that matter, did the Indian rajahs know what future they were preparing when they haggled with the foreigners. Some of them had an inkling, perhaps, of what lay in store, and they were the stubborn ones, the unreasonable ones, the troublesome, narrow-minded ones who resisted the encroachment of strangers on their lands and steadily refused the blandishments of promises and gifts from the Company.

Of course we can hardly consider Clive a simple trader, a pawn of Fate, or a dark horse. He knew what he was doing, and he liked it. Clive's advent marked the real change in Britain's approach to India. Had it not been for his stormy career, the Company's records would probably have been wound up in the middle of the eighteenth century instead of the nineteenth. It was Clive who gave the story of India a new twist, unveiled the figure of Politics which had always been shrouded in the Company's warehouse, and with his ruthless swift decisions committed his country to the role of British Raj. One could go further back and lay the blame, when it be considered blame, at the door of the French, who by threatening English supremacy in India brought out Clive's military genius in opposition to themselves, thus sacrificing any permanent French interest there.

Robert Clive's career is an imperatively necessary study for anybody interested in Sir Stamford Raffles and his motives. Clive more than any other of Raffles's predecessors made definite the relationship between the Crown and the Company, and showed how inevitable was the final solution of any real difference between them, in the government of India. Clive saw early in his life in the East that the Crown would one day have to take on the Company's work.

"See what an Augean Stable there is to be cleansed," he wrote from India. "The confusion we behold, what does it arise from? Rapacity and luxury; the unreasonable desire of many to acquire in an instant, what only a few can or ought to possess. Every man would be rich without the merits of long service, and from this incessant competition undoubtedly springs that disorder to which we must apply a remedy, or be undone, for it is not only malignant but contagious. The Court of Directors must supply the Settlement with young men more moderate or less eager in their pursuit of wealth, and we may perhaps be reduced to the necessity of drawing some senior servants from other Settlements."

In 1765 Clive obtained from the "Great Mogul," in exchange for his support of the ruler, the most important treaty ever made between India and the Company. By its rules, the Company ceased to be merely a lessee of property and commercial rights in India, and instead supplied armies to police large areas as well as to protect the Emperor. This arrangement led to a great influx of Englishmen aside from the soldiers, not the earlier, adventurous type, but the civilian, the predecessor of today's civil servant. Besides these good bourgeois, we see the development of the special soldier who made India and only India his career. One such youth bequeathed us his lively memoirs. William Hickey at the age of nineteen, in 1768, had got into so many scrapes that his father, upon the death of William's mother, took a step which was evidently considered desperate and "procured a situation" for his problem child as a cadet in the East India Company's service. The young man first went to interview the director who had nominated him:

"He said he had appointed me for Madras in preference to Bengal. . . . I then went to my father's tailor, Anthony Marcelis, of Suffolk Street, Charing Cross, to order regimentals, but not knowing to what corps I should be appointed, I conceived the best thing I could do would be to have a suit of each description, which I directed accordingly. Upon my way from Marcelis I met in the street a dashing fellow in a scarlet frock, with black waistcoat, breeches, and stockings, which in my eyes appeared remarkably smart. I therefore returned instantly to the tailor to bespeak a similar dress, as I was then in mourning for my mother. Marcelis suggested an improvement, which was to have the coat lined with black silk, and black buttons and buttonholes, which not only looked better than the plain red, but was more appropriate as military mourning.

"Mr. Walter Taylor, a very old friend of my father's, presented me with a beautiful cut and thrust steel sword, desiring me to cut off half a dozen rich fellows' heads with it, and so return a Nabob myself to England."

Here is a chance to grow sententiously indignant about the young man's attitude toward India, which was evidently typical of his times. But what would we prove? Hickey was no monster: he was the logical result of the system. (And incidentally he was usually charming and always drunk.) To the eighteenth-century mind those natives of faraway India were not real living creatures at all. They were part of the fairy tale of the mysterious East. It was a Never-Never land of adventure, and young Hickey thought of decapitating those "rich fellows" in the same spirit in which our little boys go outdoors to collect imaginary scalps from redskins. We shouldn't condemn the Hickeys for their dreams as long as they do their dreaming in England. It is later on that danger lurks, when they meet up with real flesh-and-blood natives, genuine people they must live with. With such preparation as they had in the 1780s, one could scarcely hope the Hickeys of England would be particularly imaginative or understanding representatives of the British Raj when they disembarked and found themselves surrounded by "natives." It was high time, however, that the young men learn the strange truth: that the world outside England was simply swarming with natives. The world was far bigger than one had realized. It was made up in large part, one now discovered, of potential colonies for England, wherein Englishmen governed natives, traded with natives, and were waited upon by natives.

It was very good for the young men to get out and work for the Company: it was good for them to travel. Travel, if I may be permitted to coin a phrase, broadens the mind.

CHAPTER II

"I am a bad Englishman," said Horace Walpole, "because I think the advantages of commerce are dearly bought for some by the lives of many more. But . . . every age has some ostentatious system to excuse the havoc it commits."

Measuring with that yardstick, Walpole would have called Raffles a good Englishman. So, of course, do the good Englishmen of today. But though there are more bad Englishmen in this generation than there were in Walpole's, even they don't dislike Raffles too much. What saves him is the large proportion in his make-up of humanitarian principle. He provides what excuses there are for the imperialist pattern. His appearance coincided more or less with a merging of the Crown and John Company's interests. Perhaps because of this he was a departure from the type of man who, before him, enlarged the influence of the East India Company abroad.

As a youth, however, he was evidently Type incarnate. If we are to believe his biographers, Thomas Stamford Bingley Raffles was the prototype of every success story they told schoolboys of the past generation. He was the Alger boy himself, *if* we are to believe his biographers, and if we are not—for we must consider the source and the times that produced it—then there isn't much to tell about Raffles as a child. All the material that might have singled him out and given him individuality has been suppressed, ignored, or lost. When Raffles became a great man and people began to write biographies and memoirs about him (his greatness was commensurate with that of Singapore, and Singapore waxed great just as her founder died) the fashion was all for Alger boys. The word "debunk" had not been invented. Neither, alas, had the practice, or, if it had—we must not forget Rousseau—England was not yet amused by it. Even if Raffles had been an unpleasant youth, even if he had flouted his parents, or robbed an occasional bank, or slain a little baby for the coral round its neck, you wouldn't have found anyone to say so, least of all the worthy Demetrius Boulger, who wrote the standard biography of our hero. "Worthy" is the word for Boulger, and for Boulger's boy Raffles.

No Alger hero ever started life as a rich boy. There, immediately, at the threshold of his subject's life Boulger leaves us in the dark on an important point. He gives us no explanation whatever as to why the family of a sea captain should have been so strapped for money that they couldn't afford the poorest education for their only son. Young Thomas had only two years of schooling, under a Dr. Anderson of Hammersmith, before his parents took him out and put him to work. He was then fourteen. Success-story heroes are usually fourteen when they begin life, unless they are fifteen. Freud was yet to be a power in our civilization, and no one would have rebuked Raffles for getting started so late on his career, as Ben Hecht is reputed to have rebuked Jascha Heifetz when the violinist said, "I first appeared on the concert stage at the age of six."

"I suppose before that," said Hecht, "you were just a bum?"

Raffles, according to the story, was grief-stricken at being taken out of school, and though that item, too, sounds as if it needed a little salt to improve the flavor, it may well have been true. A normal boy would have been overjoyed, but young Thomas couldn't have been normal .Only a strong, precocious sense of responsibility could have made a fourteen-year-old work as hard as he did when they put him to wage earning, and his sense of bitterness is easy to perceive. Recollected in his later life, when he wrote his confessions, it is obviously the stimulus that kept him at his books after hours, when he tried at night to make up for the schooling of which, he felt, Fate and his parents had robbed him.

So seldom does he mention his father that we are apt to forget the elder Raffles. Reading the Boulger biography, it comes as a shock when Captain Benjamin's death takes place, the reader having long since assumed from this neglect of his name that he was already dead. What could have been the trouble? He may have been a disgrace to the family because he drank or bet on dogfights; something like that would account for their silence, and very little else would. Perhaps the captain was simply so ineffectual that he drifted while still alive into what amounted to oblivion. At any rate he couldn't support his wife, three daughters, and one son, and though his father's pension helped them out until Thomas was three, the old man died in 1784. So at the age of fourteen Raffles went to work in the East India Company's offices in Philpot Lane, as an "extra clerk," or in our language an office boy.

For these services he earned a guinea a month. It is doubtful if India House ever had another office boy as studious or as hard-working. As soon as he was given duties that called for a little initiative, something better than polishing the handles of the big front door, he tried to do them better and more quickly than anyone else—according to the tradition of success-story heroes. But it was the work he did at night that interested him and prepared him for the career he was evidently determined to have.

It is difficult to believe that his studies of French, Latin, and science were not organized and channeled by some older person, but that is evidently the case. Raffles never speaks of anybody who offered sympathy or advice during that time. His mother and sisters thought of him as their only hope: they spoke, when they mentioned him, of the happy day when his earning power would increase. His mother, indeed, grudged him the candle he used for a reading light: he wrote in later years of the struggle he had to keep up against her gentle tyranny and soft, insistent miserliness. She watched his room

15 ॐ

like a hawk for any sign that he was at it again, wasting expensive candles on his foolishness.

Since History is so stingy with us, we will have to make out in roundabout ways to fill in the gaps of our knowledge. As a detective, I deduce that Raffles's relations with his parents and his three sisters, Mary Anne, Leonora, and Harriett, were unusually pleasant to begin with, or they would have given way before he grew up. There are not many family circles whose members can long maintain a civilized politeness among themselves, under poverty's erosion. Of course Alger mothers are always sweet, but Alger mothers let their sons use all the candles they want—Mrs. Raffles didn't quite play the game. For the Raffleses it must have been especially hard to carry on, because of that tiresome tradition of gentility, their pride, and their sense of superiority. The strain of keeping up appearances, and being ladies and gentlemen even when they weren't well fed or warmly clad—well, many relatives have come to blows under those conditions. Anyone but a success-story hero would bear a grudge. It was because of his mother's decision that Raffles had been taken out of school, and his mother made his difficult study periods at home much more difficult with her complaints, yet he was unfailingly sweet and courteous about her name; we can't doubt that in the face of evidence. And as soon as he could afford it, even sooner, he contributed money to help her out and make her comfortable. Again, the inert weight of responsibility which, as a gentleman, he had to carry for his sisters cut short his youth because, as they were ladies, they couldn't work or help him out in any way: they just sat at home, keeping up appearances, and waited for a miracle to bring them husbands, portionless as they were. Yet Raffles shouldered that responsibility without blaming them, at least publicly. Moreover, as soon as he possibly could he worked the miracle, and took them East, and found them husbands— good husbands too.

From this we deduce that they were nice people. The only other alternative I can see is that young Raffles was a true saint, and in the light of later developments I don't think he was. His second wife, Sophia, whom he married in 1816, would have us believe it, but I almost never believe Sophia when she estimates her husband's excellence. Unfortunately for those of us who have to depend largely on her memoir, everything she says about Raffles's merits sounds distant, unreal, phony. Often we are misled by this trait: we defeat ourselves with too much suspicion. She is certainly reporting accurately, for example, when she says, "His affection for his mother was always one of the strongest feelings of his heart. At this time, with that self-denying devotion to the happiness of others, which was his distinguishing quality through life, he deprived himself of every indulgence, that he might devote to her his hard-earned pittance: and in after-days of comparative affluence he delighted in surrounding her with every comfort." Yet we hesitate to swallow it whole. It sounds too good to be true. Nothing could be more praiseworthy than these sentiments. There is nothing wrong with the grammar either. Nevertheless the passage sounds—doesn't it?—like a funeral oration. The impression left with us is unfair to Raffles's memory. Evidently in spite of all this he actually *did* love his mother; he really *did* deprive himself for her sake; he *did* do his amiable best to spoil her, the minute he could afford it. Let us not yield to temptation, then, let us not try too hard to be clever.

When Lady Raffles says, ". . . the early youth of Mr. Raffles was a period of obscurity and labor, without friends to aid him, as well as without the hope of promotion: his family only searching for that mode of life in which he was most likely to acquire the greatest pecuniary success, without regard to the natural bias of his mind, or to the talents he possessed"—when she says that, we will not be wasting our emotion if we allow ourselves to pity him. The boy Raffles could not have had a very good time from any point of view, even the modern, even when he has been debunked.

Still, though Lady Raffles speaks of "his dull routine of duty," it may not have been so bad after all. The scene of his labors was East India House, one of the most romantic places in London, and the workings of the great Company must have held considerable fascination for a boy of Thomas's

17 &

tastes. He saw the important men of the day, working in their offices; he heard the names of far-off lands, names which were new to English ears; he learned the importance of such exotic commodities as spices, tea, and silk. Why, even the great ladies of London wore woolen gowns before his Company began importing silk! Young Raffles swept floors muddied by the boots of Clive himself. He must have heard exciting gossip centering around Clive's name.

The atmosphere of India House sharpened his appetite, already keen in a boy his age, for better things. He picked up enough of trade secrets to learn valuable lessons about what he must study in those extracurricular hours of toil at night. The correspondence clerks taught him the value of French, and so he went home and learned French with such assiduity that all his life he was to be thankful for it. In the offices he acquired the technique of map making; at home he perfected it. He learned that his scientific tastes were not merely those of a schoolboy, and so with a clear conscience, priggishly sure he was not wasting time on mere enjoyment, he indulged his love for natural history—geology, zoology, and most especially botany. That knowledge even more than the "humanities" was to help him to be an educated man in the Company's special sense. Then of course there was Latin, without which no gentleman went out into the world. And German, for good measure.

Naturally during those weeks and months and years the boy made friends among the other young fellows who took care of all the odds and ends of Company routine. He maintained a careful reserve, however. That fatal Raffles gentility kept him from getting overly familiar with boys who were obviously going to be menials all their lives, but he was afraid of becoming too intimate with the other sort, the sons of rich merchants or professional men who were learning foreign trade (even in those days foreign trade was much more acceptable socially than the domestic kind) from the bottom. Thomas Raffles knew he couldn't keep up his end of any social relationship; not yet. He was confident, I am sure, of someday belonging to the choicer crowd without feeling any necessity to keep his private life a secret, but the day was not yet arrived, not nearly. (And wasn't there the possibility that he wanted to keep Captain Benjamin hidden away in life, as he was later in history?)

Therefore, among the young sprigs of sixteen and seventeen with whom he mingled in the early years, Raffles kept his distance. Never once did he invite a friend home with him. Maybe that shocks our American code of simplicity, but by the lights of the English he was entirely reasonable. And of course many Americans would act likewise but never admit it. His one good friend was young William Brown Ramsay, whose father was secretary to the Company, but even he never saw the inside of the Raffles home. Mr. Boulger mentions this fact in what would surely, if he were speaking it, be a commending tone. One knew one's place, in Old England!

It is really too bad, that lack of material. The imagination easily conjures up half a dozen scenes, but the truth, alas, is what we want in biography. If it were not, we could listen in, for example, to many a lively exchange of words between young Thomas and Mrs. Captain, his mother. Thus:

T: "I'll be late tonight, Mother. They want us to help copy a few dispatches."

M: "Very well, Thomas. Is that nice young Chapman helping too?"

T: "I dare say." (Disapprovingly.) "Why, what do you know about Chapman?"

M: "His mother sits next to me sometimes in church. Thomas, why don't you bring him in someday for tea?"

T: (Freezingly.) "Because our acquaintance doesn't warrant such an invitation. Anyway, why should I do such a thing? Chapman's not at all my style."

M: "Perhaps not, dear, but you needn't be so self-centered. He may very well be nearer Mary Anne's style than yours. It's high time you give a little thought to your sisters; they sit here night after night, and it's not interesting, poor things. And such good girls too."

T: "Really, Mother. I'm sure the girls already have all the amusement that's good for them—Chapman will never be more than a petty clerk anyway."

19 &

M: "Half a loaf's better than no bread, my dear, and it's about time you realized it."

T: "My dear mother, you forget who we are. What would your great uncle-in-law, the baronet, say to such a philosophy? Would you sacrifice your daughters' birthright for such pottage as Chapman?"

Or else, "But how could you guarantee Dad wouldn't come home stinking drunk?"

Et cetera, et cetera, as the Victorian novelists would say. It's good fun; it's a pity I'm not allowed to do it once in a while. Now let us return to the whole-wheat bread of truth, guiltily wiping the crumbs of fiction from our lips. . . .

Lady Raffles says fondly of her husband-to-be, speaking of the adolescent years, "His was a master mind and soon burst its shackles, and manifested a high and noble resolve to devote itself to the good of others, and a yearning to obtain the station for which it felt itself best fitted."

There was, however, a grave drawback to the stimulating atmosphere of East India House, even if we do not accept Lady Raffles's "dull routine." Raffles in his teens may or may not have had a master-mind; he evidently did, Sophia's affirmation and our immediate resistance notwithstanding. But his physical constitution was not that good. Considering the general hygiene, or rather the lack of it, obtaining in eighteenth-century London, it is scarcely surprising that a boy who habitually overworked during the day and studied half the night should drive himself into tuberculosis. The only wonder is, once he acquired a "chest," that he should have been able to throw it off again. But Raffles always had plenty of common sense. The minute he knew beyond doubt that his chest was affected, he stopped everything he was doing and went out into the country. As an incident, this is not much, but his biographers have always been hard up for things to say about Raffles's childhood, so they played it up. They talked so much about it that we feel unreasonably let down to discover that the whole business lasted only a fortnight. Fifteen days was what he was allowed from his duties as extra clerk; fifteen days charitably bestowed on the little clerk, merely in order to recover his health! Sir Stamford Raffles lived longer than anyone who knew him as a boy would have expected, but he died without having heard of trade unions. And as for guilds, they were not for the ambitious individualist. Raffles made his way alone— all alone. Even when it came to fighting Death he went alone. Whatever you may think of empire builders in general, I say that the young clerk with his tainted chest went into Wales as to a peculiarly terrifying battle. I see him as a soldier, and as gallant a warrior as any in His Majesty's Army.

Free of India House, he set out on foot from London, aiming for Wales because there, he had heard, the mountains were everything he expected mountains to be. For the entire fortnight the thin, intense youth walked, simply walked, with grim concentration. He did as much as forty miles a day sometimes; he often covered thirty. It was a kill-or-cure treatment, and it was sheerly by luck that he cured himself instead of dying. Or perhaps the vigor of ambition did duty for physical vigor too. He also got to Wales, which probably seemed as important a triumph as the other to a boy his age. When it was time to go back he was recovered and anxious to start overworking again.

Boulger offers the theory that this boyhood vacation supplied the training for long, arduous trips he made on foot through the jungles of Sumatra and the Archipelago. Perhaps, but I doubt very much if two short weeks during a man's adolescence could be considered permanent "training." Whatever special muscles Raffles developed in those two weeks had ample time to become flaccid again in the long years before he reached Sumatra. More likely getting to Wales, as well as to the Eastern post he was aiming for, called for mental stamina, and he had that. Some people have another word for it: they call it stubbornness.

In the ordinary sense Raffles never was a sportsman. He didn't care for games, probably because he never attended one of the orthodox boys' schools. He hated the pastime of shooting, because he was thoroughly sentimental about wild animals. The upper-class Englishman considers himself an animal lover and the rest of the world has always accepted his evaluation

21 ༄

of himself as such, but I have never understood why. In English society it is de rigueur to be fond of dogs and horses and it is not too eccentric to extend this affection to cats. But no conventional British sportsman is truly fond of foxes, bears, lions, elephants, or any of the other quadrupeds which are considered trophies of the chase. As for pigs or cows or chickens, they don't tug at British heartstrings in a really poignant manner. Raffles may have come of gentle stock, but as a sportsman he was an oddity.

Worse, he gloried in his unconventionality. Otherwise why did he say in his later years, "I have never seen a horse race, and never fired a gun"? Less courageous men would have sought to conceal these shameful facts, not reveal them. Again I am tempted down strange bypaths of conjecture, reading this item. If Raffles had lived today, would he have followed the conventional pattern of the colonial official: would he have been a good bridge player? Probably not. And if he were not a good bridge player, would he have become governor of Java, as he did? Probably not.

Yet he was a very good governor. At least the British think so. The Dutch, naturally, do not. It was a long time ago, but Holland has not forgotten her prejudice against Raffles. In a way that is a tribute; Raffles would certainly consider it one. You see he was really Walpole's good Englishman: one of the best.

CHAPTER III

Much of the literary comment on the current events of Raffles's period sounds nervous. The writers appear anxious to prove a point to themselves as well as their readers, to establish beyond doubt or challenge the Deity's favorable attitude toward commercial expansion. One understands their apprehension; after all this is not an easy thing to do. Military apologists who claim God for an ally definitely have something: the Old Testament bears witness that Our Lord does occasionally go to war. But one searches the Scriptures in vain for any reference to Him as traveling salesman.

And to date, the only generally accepted authority on such matters is the Bible.

Historians of the time ultimately worked it out, however, in a manner satisfactory to everyone, nor did they have to put too great a strain on logic. The Lord their God was zealous in battle; trade follows closely in the footsteps of war; the connection between divine Providence and British foreign trade was not, after all, so very tenuous. After peace was achieved the Lord naturally would want the English to civilize and convert the vanquished heathen. Only the most naïve or willful Oriental, therefore, could fail to perceive God's will back of the East India Company.

One person not at all beset with doubts was Sophia, Lady

Raffles, who survived her husband and wrote a Memoir of him. She vouches personally for Raffles's religious spirit, assuring us of his faith in heaven and India House. The two institutions, he firmly believed, were intimately connected. Lady Raffles admits with reluctance that he was not an orthodox worshiper in the Lord's house, but this was no fault of his. The blame, she says, lay with his parents, who neglected to instruct him when he was a child.

"Little is known of his religious feelings on first entering the world," says Lady Raffles. A careless glance at this statement rather startles the reader until he realizes that she is speaking not of the newborn infant Raffles but of a later phase, when he was a young fellow just entering into man's estate.

As a child, Thomas didn't attend church or Sunday school ("Early religious instruction was not then, perhaps, so general as at present") but he turned toward Christianity in time; as soon, in fact, as he began to have a little luck collecting this world's goods. That's what Lady Raffles says. "As he advanced in life, prosperity warmed his heart towards the God who led him forward in his course of usefulness." No mere fair-weather worshiper, in adversity he pinned his hopes for compensatory happiness on the afterlife. "He acquiesced in every privation, as the wise purpose of an Almighty Father working for His own glory. . . ." God, as usual closely collaborating with the East India Company, kept a protective eye on Raffles, whether in prosperity or adversity. "Beginning life under the influence of such principles and feelings," Lady Raffles says, "it will not be a matter of surprise, that his own exertions proved his best patron, and procured him friends, whose good opinion was at once honourable to his talents, and favourable to his advancement. Such friends, at a very early period of his connections with the East India House, he had obtained: for a vacancy having occurred in the establishment, his peculiar qualifications were allowed to secure his accession to it, notwithstanding the claims of others, who possessed an interest of which he could not boast."

Is the foregoing paragraph rather a lot to take in, all at once? Sometimes this writer finds it helpful to translate Lady Raffles at her most overpowering into colloquial American, like this:

"His character was just the sort to appeal to certain of the directors, so, in view of his special talents, they put him first on the list for the next vacancy. Thus, in spite of the fact that other young men in the Company had friends at court, our Raffles got the job."

What is left out of my version is Sophia's implication that God himself, personally, recommended Raffles for the job. My skeptical mind seizes on the presence of one William Ramsay in the secretary's office as a more logical reason for Thomas's good luck. Ramsay, as I mentioned in the last chapter, was the father of Raffles's best friend and contemporary in the Company. Not that I wish for a moment to suggest that God's Son, too, wasn't a good friend of our hero . . . but they were on more formal terms.

At any rate whether God or Ramsay acted as patron (and probably they both helped), Raffles was definitely the beneficiary and a very fortunate young man too. Think of it: only nineteen, without any official mentor among the older men, with no fortune behind him, and no regular schooling; and yet he was written down on the books of India House as a junior clerk, "on the usual terms." Nobody knows today exactly what these terms were, but they must have been a great improvement on the office-boy wages Raffles had hitherto received, for on April 7, 1801, according to the books, he was given an extra sum, a bonus of twenty pounds. Twenty pounds at that time was a lot, and a bonus was then, as now, calculated according to salary. Then in 1802 we come across Thomas's name again on the books, this time as the recipient of another bonus (thirty pounds), and a fixed salary of seventy pounds per annum. It is no use thinking of these sums in today's terms, for there is no comparison. Seventy pounds was enough to make a big difference to the family. Brother Thomas must have been able to buy new dresses for Mary Anne, Leonora, and Harriett, with a bit of 'baccy for Captain Benjamin thrown in. Perhaps even a bottle.

Lady Raffles, writing that Memoir many years later, was meticulously careful not to mislead her public, nor to claim more of religious fervor for her husband than she really thought he experienced during his life. It is obvious that she wasn't quite happy on that score. Raffles was not the psalm singer she wished he had been. It must have cost her a pang to include in his correspondence a certain letter he wrote to his uncle in Liverpool a few years after he left England the first time. Though he wrote it in 1807 when he was all of twenty-six, and so it has no right to be included here, chronologically speaking—for he was still married to his first wife and had not yet dreamed of a second marriage, nor of investing any wife, first or second, with a title—yet I feel that it should be quoted in this place or not at all, because it is our only detailed evidence of his religious convictions. We haven't much reason to suppose that he changed them fundamentally, later on. He did become more kindly toward missionaries, and in the adversity of which Lady Raffles speaks, during the truly horrible trials he underwent in Sumatra, he did seek comfort in prayer; he found it, moreover, but Raffles was too clearheaded to find a disproportionate amount of consolation in specific hopes of an anthropomorphic afterlife. We can see in this letter of 1807 that the poor man was cursed with a scientific mind as well as just enough detachment to keep him levelheaded in grief, but not enough to spare him any of its keenest anguish. All of that phase, however, is not for our eyes just now. We are occupied only with the letter of 1807, a charming letter, and one which must have sorely troubled and worried the humorless Sophia when she came across it, years later.

Penang, 15th January 1807

To Mr. Wm. Raffles.

My Dear Sir,—I had the pleasure to receive a letter from you some months back, and beg leave to return you my sincere thanks for its contents. Be assured I shall ever be happy to hear from you. The accounts of your son Thomas are very satisfactory. By this time I imagine him firmly fixed in the pulpit, and expect shortly to hear of his continued success. I must confess to you that I should have been much better pleased if his inclination had turned towards the Church of England [Cousin Thomas was a Dissenting clergyman]; but as he has taken that path which the light of the gospel pointed out to him as the best, he must ever be respected for the choice he has made. Tell him that I shall be very happy to receive letters from him, and that I look forward to receive much benefit and instruction from his correspondence. He need not be afraid of writing on religious topics, although he looks upon me as a heathen; it was the cant of Methodism that I detested, and that only. Wherever there is cant there must be hypocrisy. I respect the religious of every persuasion, and am sorry my experience draws from me a wish that Christians did as much justice to their Redeemer as Mahometans do to their Prophet.

As I know that religious topics are those principally brought forward in the society which you have selected for yourself, it may be more entertaining to dwell upon them in this letter than any other. Of the Christian religion I fear there is more said than done, and therefore shall not add to the numerous useless and foolish remarks upon it. I ever considered it as the simplest religion on earth, and for that reason the best. But of the Mahometan religion, on the contrary, as much, if not more, is done than said. We are here surrounded with Mussulmen, and I find them very good men, and by far more attentive to the duties and observances of their religion than the generality of Christians—even Methodists. No religion on earth is so extensive, and though in many instances it has been extended by fire and sword, it has in equally many others found its way without such means. Their religion, which you know is called Islâm (faith), would, in its general principles, be very good if divested of its corruptions, superstitions, and ridiculous observances. The great doctrine of the Koran is the Unity of God—to restore which point was the main object of Mahomed's mission, and to be candid, I think Mahomed has done a great deal of good in the world. I amuse and instruct myself for hours together with the Mahometans here, who to a man all believe in the Scriptures. They believe Jesus Christ

27 &

a prophet, and respect Him as such. Mahomed's mission does not invalidate our Saviour's. One has secured happiness to the Eastern and one to the Western world, and both deserve our veneration.

I wish you would instruct Thomas to send me out a Hebrew grammar and dictionary, as well as a Greek dictionary. I am applying myself close to the Eastern languages, and must obtain a general knowledge of these ancient languages before I can finally decide on many points.

East India House had become aware of Raffles. Now that he was earning a salary more suitable to what he was worth to them, his superiors decided to trust him with tasks that were a little above the level of the ordinary clerical work which his friends did. They gave him the Asiatic Annual Register, in his own words, to "revise and improve." It was a long, difficult job and he never did finish it, as a matter of fact, because he was interrupted later by the unprecedented promotion Fate was fattening up for him.

The recognition of his excellence which the directors had indicated in such a practical way may have increased Raffles's self-esteem. Indeed, it's possible to see the first stirrings of modest pride in his own account of his early career, written from the Indies many years later to his Liverpool cousin, the Dissenter. He had gone through the worst of his early struggles and conquered them while yet in his teens. The soreness and sorrow of that disappointment in the matter of school was at last forgotten—almost. We shall see that he never quite lost it, as I said before.

In the meantime Raffles would have been no more than human, and certainly no different from other very young men, if he had relaxed a bit on his uphill climb to success just at this point. There were plenty of other boys who would have thought they had done enough for life if they achieved a salary of seventy pounds per annum so early in the game; certainly his father, Captain Benjamin, never bettered that record in his whole life. But Raffles wasn't like other young men. He carried on in the same intense way as he had done before, when he was just an ambitious office boy instead of a well-paid clerk. Perhaps he felt encouraged to work even harder at his extra-curricular studies, if that were possible. Certainly he made a resolution to that effect. He decided that he would "appropriate eight hours in each day to study, reading, or writing, and that the loss of time on any day should be made up on another. My object in making this memorandum is that I may hold the rule as inviolable as I can, and by frequently recurring to it revive my sleeping energies should I at any time be inclined to indolence. I should not, however, omit to add that all reading and study on a Sunday is to be confined to the Bible and religious subjects. The Greek and Hebrew, however, as connected, may nevertheless form a part of the study of that day."

A formidable youth, Raffles. If he had gone on for many years at such a rate, under such an austere, self-imposed program of improvement, he might very easily have dried up and lost all his human, emotional qualities. He would probably have turned into a sort of dried fig, without a drop of sweet juice in him. Luckily for himself, for his family, for his friends, and for the slaves of Java and Sumatra, Fate arranged an interruption. What the novelists of the period called, archly, "the gentler passion" was just about to take a firm grip on India House's prodigious young genius. The fig was not yet, after all, completely devoid of juice.

Mrs. Olivia Fancourt walked into the secretary's office of India House looking the perfect lady she was. One would have guessed, regarding her, that she was not accustomed to such a masculine atmosphere, that she had been recently bereaved, that she was completely self-assured and not scared to death. The last premise was incorrect; Mrs. Fancourt was rather a worried lady at that period, preoccupied by financial difficulties. But she was a stately person, one of your poised, dignified sort: she did not show her perturbation. Her beauty was particularly noticeable in England, being of a type the British consider Latin; she was dark-haired and dark-eyed. Tall and distinguished-looking, Boulger calls her, with flashing black Italian eyes. People said she was handsome, but as she was now thirty-three they probably spoke of her as a passée beauty, definitely out of the running. This was 1804, when women were forced by public opinion to age early.

Her maiden name was Olivia Mariamne Devenish. Her husband, Fancourt, up until his death had been assistant surgeon of the India Company's Madras Establishment. Long residence in India probably lent his widow a quality out of the ordinary, an aura of glamor which added to the effect she had on Raffles the minute he saw her. The clever, industrious junior clerk was now twenty-three, and he may have been fortunate enough to interview the pretty lady himself, but that detail hasn't been handed down to us. No such personal, trifling bits of gossip about his courtship have been preserved in the Raffles letters, partly because the couple were exceedingly sensitive on the subject of Olivia's age. When Raffles wrote of the marriage and of the events leading up to it he maintained an austere, distant style which is definitely misleading. Royalty's archives could scarcely sound more severe and less romantic. Somebody must have been very unpleasant about that ten years' hiatus, to have had such an effect on the young lover. Could it have been Raffles's mother? The ladies of his family, depending as they did on Thomas for nearly every penny they had, could not have been overjoyed when he fell in love and planned to marry. At twenty-three, too, and to a widow old enough to be—well, scarcely his mother, but I don't doubt the Raffles ladies used the well-worn phrase just the same.

The biographer Demetrius Boulger has gone to a good deal of trouble to find out what he could about Olivia and Fancourt. He was led astray by the one mention of the first wife Lady Raffles allowed herself, but after he ran the inaccuracy to ground he managed to dig up plenty of well-annotated information. The husband was named Jacob Cassivelaun Fancourt, he married Olivia in 1793, in Madras, and he died at Ryacotta in 1800. Though Boulger couldn't prove it beyond the shadow of a doubt, he makes out a strong case in favor of

Olivia's being Irish, the daughter of a Devenish who had left Ireland and settled in India.

She came to India House that day when Raffles saw her to present a petition. "Young Raffles saw her," Boulger writes, "and it may even have been part of his duty to receive her petition, to instruct her as to the correct form in which it should be drafted, and, perhaps, even to add some literary flourish of his own." (Pure conjecture, of course, but it is pleasant to find that someone before me has also fallen victim to this habit.) "Her application was not an uncommon one. It was the petition of the widow of an officer on the Military Establishment of Madras for assistance from the compassionate fund, which was long known by the name of Clive, who founded it out of Mir Jaffir's gift. . . . In accordance with custom, it lay on the table for a week, and on the 12th of September Olivia Fancourt was granted a pension of one shilling and threepence a day, and in addition the sum of twenty-five guineas. This was entirely according to rule. The matter followed a prescribed course. If she had been any other assistant-surgeon's widow, old or young, remarkable for her plainness instead of for her beauty, the result would have been precisely the same."

The rather waspish, defensive tone of this passage is due to certain unpleasant hints which Raffles's enemies put into circulation when they attacked Olivia some years later. We shall come across the whole story in due course.

Raffles met Olivia about August 1804. In the absence of any written word from her, or any confidential remarks from him on the subject, I don't really see why we can't assume they fell in love. I realize I am going against the popular theory in saying this, but I can't understand why Boulger and Co. won't agree with me. I certainly have no intention of agreeing with them. Boulger gives the strangest picture of all—since Thomas Raffles was going a long distance off, he says, and since he wouldn't be back, in all probability, for years and years, and since he was going to a place where he wasn't likely to meet anyone who would serve as a "helpmeet"—Mr. Boulger boggles at the sentimental word "wife"—what more natural,

31

he says, than for Mr. Raffles to take to himself a—er—a help-meet before he left? I don't quarrel with what Mr. Boulger says, exactly; I quarrel with what he doesn't say. He gives the impression that it was a case of *faute de mieux*, as if Olivia Fancourt had been the first and only woman Raffles met, outside the family circle. One feels, reading his version, as if Raffles got word of his appointment and reacted like this:

"What's this in the mail this morning? It comes from the office. That's funny—you'd think they would tell me anything they had on their minds, instead of—— Oh, I say! What do you know about that? Mother, look here—I'm going to Penang! Penang, I said; it's a colony out East. Well, that's all I know about it myself. No, not India. It's another place, much smaller. . . . Now let's see. I'd better take my lightweight suit and plenty of white socks. I shan't be needing more flannels. . . . Well, I shan't. . . . No, Mother, I tell you this place is tropical. . . . No, nor mufflers either. But I'll be wanting asafetida. . . . And let's see . . . oh yes, a wife. A wife, now let me think a moment. Where on earth am I to find a wife? What was the name of that woman who came in last week after a pension? Yes, of course she was unmarried, Mary Anne, don't interrupt. At any rate she must be a widow; it's her dead husband's pension she was after. H'mmmm. Olivia, that was it—Olivia Fancourt. I could do a lot worse. I'm sure we've got her address somewhere in the files. What's that, Harriett? Meet your girl friend? Well, I don't care if I do, but wait until I've seen this Olivia Fancourt first. There's no sense going to a lot of *trouble* over this."

I simply refuse to accept it. After all, Olivia was very handsome. Just because Raffles was customarily thoughtful and judicious doesn't rule out the chance that for once in his life he acted on impulse, because people do behave oddly when they fall in love. Besides, Olivia wasn't at all an eligible *parti*. She had no dowry; she was older than he; she was completely the opposite of the sort of wife he would be expected to choose if he had gone by his head rather than his heart. I'm sure I'm right. He fell in love at sight, and so did Olivia. They must have done; I insist on it.

They married rather in a hurry, too, because from August until March, when he had news of his appointment, is not long for an eighteenth-century courtship.

We don't know all about it, but we can be sure that the appointment didn't come as a complete surprise to Raffles. He had himself sown the seeds of it, probably with this job in view, or an allied one, when he mentioned to William Ramsay, whose protégé he was by way of being, that he would not in the least mind going to the East to make a career. Nowadays plenty of young men have similar hopes and ambitions, but in 1805 it was sufficiently unusual for Raffles to make a point of it when he talked to Ramsay. People didn't go far afield in those days just for pleasure cruises, and adventure-seeking young men could find plenty of excitement much nearer home than the Indies. A long trip by sailing ship was no joke. It was a hazardous undertaking, but Raffles knew what he was doing. He had somehow to make more money. Even his generous salary was not enough for the family, for Captain Benjamin seems to have grown progressively less effective at breadwinning as the years went by. Raffles was a student of trade and he could see that England's future was in foreign lands, not at home. He realized, too, that the world was shaping toward a boom out East, and he wanted to be on the spot when it happened.

William Ramsay understood all this, and he knew how matters stood at Thomas's home. Besides, the East India Company always needed strong, willing men for those Eastern posts. He duly put in his word for Raffles with the chairman, Sir Hugh Inglis, as soon as the new development in Penang cropped up in directors' meeting. The word "new" does not mean Penang was a recent British acquisition. On the contrary, the little island represented the first British occupation of the Malay Peninsula. They had moved in on Penang back in 1786, when the Dutch were forced to realize the existence of an impending competitor for trade in the East Indies. England had at first been content to leave the island in an ambiguous state of government. The Rajah of Kedah ceded Pulo Penang to a Company officer, Captain Francis Light, as dowry for his daughter, whom the captain allegedly married. (One of his sons later denounced this tale of marriage as a complete falsehood, which it was, according to the best evidence.) The island was not a gift outright; Light paid rent on it. Because he took possession on the birthday of the then Prince of Wales, George, he called the island Prince of Wales Island and the main town on it George Town. Along with the island proper, a strip of territory on the mainland was included in the bargain Light made with the Rajah, and this strip of land was known as Wellesley Province.

Penang, or Prince of Wales Island, is fertile and productive, and because of its mountainous nature and high relief white men found it a pleasant health resort. Later they changed their minds about its salubrity, but whether this change was due to superior knowledge, or the conditions actually did become bad, historians have not been able to decide. One theory was that a bad drainage system poisoned the water. The harbor of George Town, too, was good. As long as Francis Light lived he ran the colony under the title of superintendent of trade, but he died in 1794 and his place was taken by a lieutenant-governor, who had other duties concurrently and so let things slide. In 1800 the Company made another arrangement with the Rajah and bought the island outright, but nothing else was done about this promising little possession until 1805, the date which interests us on Raffles's account.

The Company decided to do something definite now, to the advantage both of themselves and of Penang. (The name "Prince of Wales" had somehow failed to supplant the old original title.) They elected to raise it to the rank of a presidency, hoping it would serve as the leading trading center of the island group. Mr. Philip Dundas was sent out as governor, with a council, and Raffles was named assistant secretary. His nomination was ratified at a meeting of the Court of Directors, on March 8, 1805, and he was granted the rank of junior merchant as well, with a salary of fifteen hundred pounds a year.

This was It. This was the break for which he had waited all those joyless busy years. Now, all at once and by virtue of one stroke of the Company's pen, Raffles was handed recognition, a promising career, and the security of a really big salary. He could provide for his family, marry, and still start out for Penang comfortably well off. He could take with him the eldest of his three sisters; he could set to work immediately on the important task of finding her a husband, so that the way might be clear for the other girls.

The thought nearest his heart must have been that he could marry Olivia immediately. What a staggering affair an appointment can be! One brief hour in the committee room of the Court, a little discussion, a ballot, and the thing was done; the universe had been broken up into tiny pieces and made over completely, according to the Raffles plan. What a plan, what a day, what a world! Thomas Stamford Bingley Raffles must have been drunk, for the first time in all his worthy short life, on nothing but triumphant joy.

Five days after he was appointed Raffles took out at the vicar general's office a license for marriage between Thomas Raffles, Esq., bachelor, twenty-three years old, and Olivia Mariamne Fancourt, widow, no age given; to take place in the parish church of St. George, Bloomsbury, London. The day after that, March fourteenth, they were wedded by the Rev. A. P. Poston. Richard S. Taylor, Thomas Raffles's business agent, and Charles Hammond, his cousin, attended the wedding ceremony, as well as two girls whose names do not turn up again in any of the Raffles papers. Mariamne Etherington and Maria Welthew were probably friends or relations of Olivia's.

Fairy tales always end with a wedding—"and so they were married and lived happily ever after." But this was a true-life marriage, so everything was different. It marked the beginning of a true-life tale, not the end. Nevertheless, the old nursery tag would have answered for that portion of time which remained of Olivia's story. She did, indeed, live happily ever after. Nor was it her fault, poor gracious lady, that she could not keep pace with her beloved husband, step by step, until he too reached the end.

CHAPTER IV

Vanity Fair, required reading in our United States high school classes, gives most of us the first mention we encounter of the East India Company. Though the name of India House may have faded from memory by the time we grow up, the figure of Jos Sedley almost certainly has not, for any of us. Jos, you will remember, was Amelia's fat brother, object of Becky Sharp's first matrimonial hopes. Just by being there in the book, he is proof of how closely the Company affected middle-class England at the turning point of the century. India House was a fixed landmark in the world of the Sedleys and the Osbornes. Stupid, fat Anglo-Indian Jos must have been so familiar a type that Thackeray's readers were delighted to encounter him in black and white, after meeting him so often in the flesh. "He was in the East India Company's Civil Service, and his name appeared . . . in the Bengal division of the East India Register, as collector of Boggley Wollah, an honourable and lucrative post." Jos was "a very stout, puffy man, in buckskins and Hessian boots, with several immense neckcloths, that rose almost to his nose, with a red-striped waistcoat and an apple-green coat with steel buttons almost as large as crown pieces." He liked his curries very hot and could be depended upon to give expert advice as to their preparation. He brought his sister Cashmere shawls from India. "He described the balls at

Government House, and the manner in which they kept themselves cool in the hot weather, with punkahs, tatties, and other contrivances; and he was very witty regarding the number of Scotchmen whom Lord Minto, the Governor-General, patronized; and then he described a tiger-hunt, and the manner in which the mahout of his elephant had been pulled out of his seat by one of the infuriated animals."

I think I am not alone in feeling lost, when I read a biography, until I have some idea of the appearance of my hero and his friends. I want to know what they wore, and how they furnished their living rooms, and in what sort of style their meals were served. Thanks to Thackeray we know that Olivia wore bonnets and shawls, and that her best dress was probably made of muslin. We are vividly reminded that men in those days could indulge their fancy in dress. We have one portrait of Sir Stamford, by G. F. Joseph, which hangs in the National Portrait Gallery, and there is also a bust by Chantrey, evidently idealized out of recognition and therefore worthless. The painting is pleasant; Raffles, in an enormously high neckcloth, regards us out of wide-set, grave eyes. His face is full and youthful in appearance, and his chiseled lips wear the look of a man who smiles often. Though this may be too much to read into an indifferently well-painted portrait, Raffles seems to be eagerly interested, habitually, in the world outside him and not in himself. One can imagine him talking to the painter as he sits, asking questions about technique, pigment, and light, all his attention and interest focused on Mr. Joseph rather than on the execution of the picture.

Raffles, his wife, and his sister Mary Anne traveled out to the East in the *Ganges*, a Company ship commanded by Captain Harrington. Luckily for the novices, the voyage was uneventful, though it was long, as trips must be in sailing vessels. It is hard for us to imagine the extreme discomfort which those travelers took for granted. We would complain loudly if we had to journey through the tropics, nowadays, in a ship without refrigeration or electric fans, a ship which gave way to the mood of the ocean and felt every wave, rolling and slipping across the surface of the sea even in good weather, and in bad tipping at such an angle that the passenger must make his way along deck like a monkey, holding to everything solid that he can reach. Sailing, as in races, is all very well for a hobby, but not many of us in this pampered world would care to go on sailing for months on end, without a chance to relax. The food was progressively worse as they passed more and more time out of harbor, and usually by the time they put in to another port and could provision afresh such victuals as they had left were decayed and wormy. Salt pork and biscuit were the staple diet, no matter how well they had supplied themselves at the beginning with superior delicacies. Then there was the matter of water. They had to use it sparingly, washing in salt water, naturally, and going easy with the drinking supply. After a few weeks it smelled and tasted stale.

But there was one bright spot, if not more than one, on this gloomy canvas. Olivia and Mary Anne were at least comfortably clothed. Seldom have women been as sensibly yet prettily dressed as they were at that time in Europe, when the Empress Josephine had her portrait painted in her favorite pseudo-classic draperies, and a gathering of fashionable beauties in Hyde Park resembled a collection of Greek statues suddenly become animate. Olivia daily wore a gown of which the waistline was exceedingly high, under the armpits; of which the neckline, even in the morning, might be cut so low that it barely covered the lower half of her bosom. On cold days it was permissible to fill in that wide, bare display of neck and breast with swathed silken shawls or high boned collars, but the favored décolleté, which nowadays we would consider too daring for any costume but a nightgown, was then perfectly respectable and worn by everybody, even fat old ladies. It was the period when everything "classical" was good. Imagine the two ladies in flowing robes of sheer muslin, with short puffed sleeves, shawls, and heelless soft slippers, and large mobcaps or deep bonnets to protect their hair, which they wore à la Grecque, or cut short, again after the manner introduced by Josephine Bonaparte. I defy today's designers to evolve anything more suitable to a tropical climate. Those lucky ladies were even permitted freedom in regard to underclothing. The world of fashion in Europe had gone over completely to hygiene and nature nearly unadorned.

In this sudden triumph of simplicity Raffles was the loser. He grew up just when men were sacrificing their position as the peacocks of the human race. He came along after fashion condemned the extreme color and fussiness men had hitherto enjoyed. The splendid striped coats and silken breeches worn by the gentlemen of his father's day were now passé. It is exceedingly doubtful if Raffles ever possessed or wore a wig, though a few older dandies still availed themselves of the grudging permission given them by custom. (Ramsay the secretary probably wore one, after the style of George Washington's, and sometimes clubbed his own hair.) Definitely Raffles lost out, aesthetically speaking, when men gave up their fine colors and silks in an ill-considered sacrifice from which their clothing has never recovered. But like his wife he gained in comfort from the new styles. His trousers, cut reasonably tight at the knee, were worn tucked into high boots or confined by gaiters, and gave him freedom in walking. His coat was tailed and long in back, but ended at the waist in front, a sober dark version of its glorious, heavy, satin and gold or velvet predecessor. For color and dash he had to depend, now, on waistcoats, of which he could wear as many as he liked, and on the many gold seals which hung and clanked at his watch chain. His collar was fantastically high, but at least it did not meet in front, and so he was spared the torture of modern neckwear. His shirt was ruffled, but the ruffles were smaller than they had been in the old days, and were simple starched affairs, not the waterfalls of lace that now seemed old-fashioned. He wore a tall curly-brimmed beaver hat, and a cape in cold weather—a "cloak." The famous Raffles statue represents him in Roman toga, flourishing a classically rolled document of the sort all such statues seem to carry, but that was merely the customary formality of sculpture, not a lifelike portrait. It is a pity he never tried it out in actuality. In this garb he would have been a fit companion for the draped Olivia, but the men, shy as ever, stopped short of adopting the clothes of those ancient times which in other respects they imitated enthusiastically.

39 ৰ৯

We need not pity Olivia Raffles on her wedding trip, then, as we might have done if she had made the journey later, when gowns were instruments of torture even in the Temperate Zone, and the crinoline and hoop made their extraordinary appearance. She could walk the deck easily and gracefully in her soft slippers, hoping for a rare tropical breeze to flutter her light muslin draperies, and trying, ever vainly, to get away from the smells of the ship. Some of these were so much a part of everyday life that she soon ceased to notice them, but as the weather grew warmer other unpleasant smells grew insistent.

We hope for Olivia's sake that Mary Anne Raffles was pleasant company. Probably she was; she was bound to feel happily grateful to her brother's wife, without whose chaperoning presence she could never have gone with Brother Raffles on this exciting adventure. Without Olivia she would still be crowded in at home with her mother and sisters, and no prospect of freedom. Now that Thomas had married, anything was possible for Mary Anne—or, if not anything, at least she could hope for marriage, which was the only ambition allowed a young English girl in 1805. And in this delicate matter of husband catching, Olivia was the all-important factor, *in loco parentis*.

Indoors in their cabin, even though they must have been crowded, the ladies were much more comfortable than they were on deck. This matter of cabins was so entirely foreign to today's arrangement that we must pause for a glance at the ships, usually East Indiamen, in which Raffles and his family made their voyages. Parkinson explains that what the passenger bought from the captain or perhaps the purser—and the purchase sum was not fixed, but had always to be arranged beforehand—was deck space. In peacetime this was enclosed by light wood frames or panels; in time of war by canvas screens, fixed to beams overhead and laced down underfoot to battens nailed to the deck. The "great cabin," just below the roundhouse, was usually assigned to unmarried army officers if many of the army were traveling. Passengers, if there were only a few of them, dined in the roundhouse; if there were many they ate in the "cuddy," under the fore part of the poop.

The East Indiamen were the most comfortable of all ships for passengers, but even with these the selection of one's cabin was not a choice of comfort so much as a choice of evils. Hickey, who on his first journey out selected the starboard side of the great cabin, speaks feelingly of the noises he had to endure: sailors working the spanker boom, the feeding of poultry which was kept there in coops, with the pecking noises that resulted, every day, twice a day, children crying or playing in the steerage, perpetual creaking of the bulkheads. But if one slept on the gun deck there were various other discomforts: stinks, heavy seas which occasionally forced their way through the seams of the canvas, pouring over one's bed, and similar joys. For this cabin Hickey paid a thousand pounds!

Many travelers wrote in great detail on this absorbing subject, often giving helpful advice, like the lady who published an article in the *Asiatic Journal* for 1835:

"Notwithstanding the noise which is the invariable accompaniment of a cabin on the poop, old sailors will always make choice of this situation, as more light and freer circulation of air can be obtained there than in those below. But, as some of the party must inevitably take the second deck, they should endeavour to guard against the possibility of injury to things of value in the event of shipping a sea. In the most exposed parts of the cabin, the boxes should always be raised a little from the floor, in order that the water may run under them; or it is a good plan to dispense [with] boxes, altogether, and dispose of their contents in canvas, or other bags, suspended from the ceiling."

For any man unable to get a cabin at all, even an inferior partition shared with one of the ship's guns, there was the common dormitory, either in the great cabin or in steerage. Cadets and other youngsters usually braved such accommodations because they were cheaper.

Official passengers like Raffles were allowed baggage in volume proportioned to their rank. All passengers furnished their own cabins, the minimum outfit consisting of a table, a sofa or two chairs, a washhand stand, and bedding. If one was very luxurious one brought a carpet, too, and most people added to this list more chairs, bookshelves, a lamp, a coffee machine, and some swinging "cots," rather like stiff hammocks, to avoid the sea water when it got in and flooded the deck. One always brought tobacco, soap in bars, and brandy to bribe the sailors with, in the hope that they would then help out with odd jobs in their leisure moments.

As soon as the passenger embarked he set to work fastening down his furniture and boxes, nailing and roping them securely. Then he swung his cot, fitting cleats for the purpose if there were none already in place. He had to do all these things himself, for the ship's carpenter was busy.

Setting sail was a noisy, rackety affair, for the ship was always crowded then with a party for friends and well-wishers of the captain. The noise of this kept up until the moment of sailing, in perpetual open house. The traditional ship's farewell party was for most passengers one of the worst features of sailing.

Parkinson quotes the diary of a lady who traveled out East in 1805, the same year Olivia Raffles went out with her bridegroom. This Mrs. Sherwood and her husband were very late embarking; it was, in fact, at the last moment.

". . . When Mr. Sherwood hurried to the ship to make what preparations he could, every cabin was already taken with the exception of the carpenter's, and had he not been able to secure this I must have stayed behind.

"No woman who has not made such a voyage in such a cabin as this can possibly know what real inconveniences are. The cabin was in the centre of the ship, which is so far good, as there is less motion there than at either end. In our cabin was a porthole, but it was hardly ever open; a great gun ran through it, the mouth of which faced the porthole. Our hammock was slung over this gun, and was so near the top of the cabin that one could hardly sit up in bed. When the pumps were at work, the bilge water ran through this miserable place, this worse than dog-kennel, and, to finish the horrors of it, it was only separated by a canvas partition from the place in which the soldiers sat and, I believe, slept and dressed, so that it was absolutely necessary for me, in all weathers, to go down to this shocking place before any of the men were turned down for the night. But, wretched as this place was, I was not to have it till I could be truly thankful for it, for according to some rule which I did not understand, the carpenter did not dare to let us have the use of it until the pilot had left us. . . .

"During the whole of that day our fellow-passengers were coming in. We had on board eleven of our officers, nineteen cadets, and several gentlemen of the Civil Service, Madras. There were in the state cabins two families—Colonel and Mrs. Thornley and an infant, and Colonel and Mrs. Carr. In the great cabin below were our officers on one side, and, on the other, partitioned off, three daughters of a well-known Dean of Bristol, Dr. L——.

"I watched all these persons coming on as I sat on my gun-carriage, and thus that miserable day wore out. At night we got our cabin, not before I was thoroughly thankful for it. After a wretched night in our cot, which was slung over a gun, I awoke, as it were, to renewed misery. . . .

"Our cabin was just the width of one gun, with room beside for a small table and single chair. Our cot, slung cross-ways over the gun, as I have said, could not swing, there not being height sufficient. In entering the cabin (which, by the way, was formed only of canvas) we were forced to stoop under the cot, there not being one foot from the head or the foot of the cot to the partition. The ship was so light on the water that she heeled over with the wind so much we could not open our port, and we had no scuttle. We were therefore also in constant darkness. The water from the pump ran through this delectable cabin, and I as a young sailor, and otherwise not in the very best situation for encountering all these disagreeables, was violently sick for days and days, the nights only bringing an increase of suffering. The cabin could not be borne during the daytime. . . ."

Olivia had more reason than most brides to worry about making her cabin habitable, because Thomas Raffles, unlike most husbands, spent most of his time there. Other men hurried out in search of male company to alleviate the boredom of sea travel, when they weren't taking their wives for constitutionals, or eating meals, or taking part in other communal

43 ᴣᴇ

activities such as concerts. But Raffles, as soon as courtesy permitted, made for his books like a bee heading for the hive. Day after day, hour after hour, he sat in the cabin studying Malay, and Olivia and Mary Anne, knowing well they must not disturb him, sewed or read quietly to themselves, pretending not to be there at all. Raffles was accustomed to picking up languages in this way, as we know. By the time the family arrived in Penang he was able not only to speak Malay but to read and write it, though his friend Travers must certainly have exaggerated in saying that Raffles had acquired "a perfect knowledge" of the language before the end of the voyage. Captain Travers, who knew Raffles throughout his Far East existence, kept a journal which—unlike the diary Raffles himself kept, alas—has survived the years. He writes:

"It was in the year 1806 I first became acquainted with Mr. Raffles, at the Island of Penang. He was then deputy-secretary to the new government, which had been recently sent out to that place. At this time, which was soon after his arrival, he had acquired a perfect knowledge of the Malay language, which he had studied on the voyage out, and was able to write and speak fluently. . . . [His heavy daily program] did not prevent his attending closely to improve himself in the Eastern languages: and whilst his mornings were employed in his public office, where at first he had but little assistance, his evenings were devoted to Eastern literature."

Today the British bride who starts out for India with her husband is considered fortunate by the women who watch her go. The name "India" or its cousin "the Indies" may have lost during the past years a certain luster of romance, but there is still a glow over those magic syllables for the housewife who drudges along at home on a middle-class income. In spite of all the grumbling we hear from Anglo-Indian colonials about the high cost of living and the dear dead days, a white man is better off in the East than in England, and his wife has the greatest benefit of the change. The famous lure of the tropics is the houseboy. That retired planter who sits in his Piccadilly club with a dream in his eyes, longing for the mysterious East, is thinking about horses and how easy they were to keep in Kuala Lumpur. Don't believe the girl who says, "There's something about India, I don't know what it is, but I'm longing to go back." She knows perfectly well what it is. It's the way she can say to her Indian head servant, "There'll be ten for dinner tonight," and then go out shopping for a hat.

If Olivia had any hopes that life on Prince of Wales Island would be quite as simple and civilized as she had found it at Madras, she was disappointed. It is more likely, however, that she was not so ignorant as all that: the Company had acquainted her husband with most of the important facts about living conditions, and any woman who had been once married could scarcely have failed to look up and question some veteran female, some Company wife, who knew Penang of old. The town was being filled with a greater number of people from England than it had been planned to accommodate. It was a one-horse city, suddenly pressed into service for a full-dress presidency. No doubt the *Ganges* had carried other officials bound for Penang, as well as Raffles. They were lucky when they found comfortable lodgings straight off.

On the other hand it would be an exaggeration to say that the young newlyweds had to struggle at first. Such a word simply cannot be applied to white people in the Far East, especially a hundred years or more ago. The very armies of conquest took their ease. Thus, though the Raffles couple and Miss Mary Anne were probably worried to find a suitable house, and though they may have been puzzled at first to set a proper European table, and though they must have been hard put sometimes to meet their bills promptly, they didn't work hard at housekeeping. Raffles was not the leading official in Penang by a long shot, but he would have had to be far lower down in the social scale before he would have gone short of servants.

We find proof of their difficulties in the Company correspondence files. The governor, Dundas, and the council complain in their earliest dispatches that they have insufficient housing, both for living purposes and office space. Houses

45 &

were hard to get and very costly when you could find them. Raffles had to pay three hundred thirty pounds a year for the rental of Runnymede, which he and Olivia occupied the whole of their Penang term. Other living expenses were comparatively high, so that he remarked ruefully that he had been a lot better off in England than he was now. The fact was, all the Europeans were suffering from a local inflation which was not common to the other Eastern colonies, and they had the bad luck to be stationed at a place which did not stimulate the Court of Directors to generous treatment, either then or later. If ever a British colony was run on pinched pennies, that colony was to be found on Prince of Wales Island.

We are giving an unfair, gloomy picture of the life that met Olivia however. There were compensations for these pecuniary difficulties. She must have been well pleased with her first sight of the harbor: it would have been a strange woman who was not. These tropical places are not glaringly bright, as so many people imagine; the sultry heat of the climate usually adds a mist or fuzziness to the landscape which softens the sunlight and gives a tender, soft appearance to everything. Seen from shipboard, Prince of Wales Island was all blue and purple, with silvery layers of mist floating about the hills. The town lies between two ranges, not so close in that any of the valley is in gloomy shadow. People of the country, Malays, came out to meet the boat in their little craft; some of them clambered aboard with fruit to sell. They were small, brown people with liquid brown eyes and a charming childish expression that went well with their soft speech. Olivia, accustomed to the darker, more sophisticated natives in Madras, must have lost her heart to them immediately.

Like most of the native dwellings in the Archipelago, these were airy structures of light wood, standing on stilts where they were built in swampy districts. But the British-built houses were of a type which is found from Hong Kong south, through all the places where the English have settled. Largely planned, of white stucco, they are tropical variations of the country houses of home. Save that the early builders raised their ceilings a little higher and built their verandas a little deeper, any of these dwelling places could have been carried back to an English suburban town and set down there overnight without attracting comment on the outlandish appearance. Those were the houses they were used to, and they were the houses they wanted, and never mind the way the natives liked *their* dwellings. A less rigorous adherence to convention might have led to more comfort; the Spanish style, for instance, would have been cooler and easier to keep clean . . . but British architects have seldom been imaginative.

The furniture and decoration of these houses was always as aggressively British as the owners could afford. Everything possible was brought out from home. Carpets, pictures, chairs and tables, silver, were just what one would find in a Kensington or Russell Square mansion: Axminster carpets, heavy dark oil paintings in deep gold frames, dark brown chairs, ornate, massive silver plate, linen that was the pride of the housekeeper's heart—and, for a few very fortunate women for whom the triumph was worth all its deterioration in the tropics, the pianoforte. Pianos did very poorly in the Indies. The humid salt air relaxed the strings, and always within a week or two the instrument was badly out of tune. (Today a piano tuner comes every month to your house in Singapore, automatically, on a yearly contract.) But owning one gave the colonial bride a special cachet, nevertheless, which was much prized by the ladies.

There is no documentary evidence to support my theory, but I am willing to bet against the chance of someday acquiring proof that the Raffles house alone in the entire island numbered native wood carvings among its decorations, and found a place for the Malay figurines and puppets and pictures which today are considered prizes in our drawing rooms. Most of the settlers were miserably homesick and showed it by closing out of their private lives and houses any trace of the Archipelago's culture. That accounts for the Belgian carpets, Irish linen, and English walnut they cherished with such pride, and the few English flowers which they brought and planted and tended lovingly among the alien corn. That alien corn—those tropical flowers—with what un-English vigor and vulgarity did they

47 ᘓᗢ

flourish! That teeming, foreign soil! It must have frightened the junior and senior clerks and their wives all the more because they had had no warning of it. Strange lands in those days were really strange, truly unexplored.

Be certain, at any rate, that Raffles was satisfied with his Runnymede. Back home he would have toiled for a lifetime without being able to shelter his family in a large house with spacious gardens and more than enough servants to run it.

The tempo of life, Olivia found, was not unlike that of India. That is, nobody except her husband worked as hard as he would have done in London, in the home offices of India House. The climate, soft and enervating and actually very unhealthy, was an excuse, if an excuse had been necessary, which it never was. There were dinners to attend and to give. There were fruit trees to watch over and discuss. There were the difficulties which always attended transportation by horse —in Penang the favorite vehicle was a tiny two-wheeled affair, but grandeur and government service called for the larger, heavier sort of carriage. There was the constant struggle for fresh meat, in which all the wives of the colony cried out for their share whenever a beast was slaughtered, and Mrs. Smith of this house knew what portion of the late cow she would dine off when she was invited to Mrs. Jones's across the way. Everyone was a little less brisk, a little sleepier, a little slower as time went on.

Life with Mr. Thomas Stamford Raffles called for more exertion than this. All the newly arrived officials complained of the pressure of work, getting things started, all, that is to say, except Raffles, who was still staggered by his good fortune and not yet sophisticated enough to grumble. Yet he alone had good reason to complain, because he worked like a horse. This was because he was accustomed to do it, and also because it was expected of him, in his position. The climate never slowed up Thomas Raffles. He fell victim to his own virtue; the more work he did, the more the others piled on his shoulders, and once he had set his pace he had to keep up with it.

I always see him, in my mind's eye, sitting at a desk with his coat off, with his elaborate shirt front and high collar looking all the stranger, to my modern eyes, in deshabille. He is writing with a quill pen—whether my mind is correct on this point of costume or commits an atavism, he is writing with a quill pen, very rapidly, throwing the sheets of paper aside as he finishes them, and pulling fresh ones toward him without having to glance up. There are books piled around him and the desk is not perfectly neat, either, in other respects. In Penang the disorder must have been particularly picturesque. I imagine one or two botanical specimens drying out on their plates, waiting for overdue attention; a small monkey's skull serves as paperweight until its owner shall find time to identify it; a hunk of crystalline substance that looks like gold has been brought to him by an excited, overhopeful friend, and left to add to the modest litter. But all this is anticipating: in London there were no monkey skulls. I see him writing like this first as a young man in London, with pink cheeks and thick hair, against the dark-papered walls of his mother's house, that flicker in the stolen candlelight. Then in Penang I see him in the same attitude, still writing rapidly, but with hands finer drawn, with hairline sketchier than it was in the past, and linen better. The background is changed too: it is lit with the cheerful brightness of his study at Runnymede. The woodwork there is light. The shades are drawn tight against the warm, heavily fragrant night air, but his lamp is surrounded by great insects that have stolen in somehow, and the little white night moths of the tropics try in vain to kill themselves against the lamp chimney. Everything is different except the look on Raffles's face, the earnest, withdrawn, purely unself-conscious expression of the scholar.

Captain Travers was much impressed by the manner in which Raffles was able to keep up with his work, which was of a crushing weight, and yet not neglect his true enthusiasms. The Travers Journal enumerates the different duties he carried out as assistant secretary—details of the new government proceedings, compilation of almost every public document, public dispatches, drawing up and keeping the records. "Being of a cheerful lively disposition, and very fond of society, it was surprising how he was able to entertain so hospitably as he

49 ತ

did, and yet labour so much as he was known to do at the time, not only in his official capacity, but in acquiring a general knowledge of the history, government, and local interests of the neighbouring states; and this he was greatly aided in doing by conversing freely with the natives, who were constantly visiting Penang at this period, many of whom were often found to be sensible, intelligent men, and greatly pleased to find a person holding Mr. Raffles' situation able and anxious to converse with them in their own language."

It is small wonder if the natives were "greatly pleased" with him. Penang is not British India, but the colonial Englishman is pretty much the same no matter where you encounter him, and there is no doubt that the "sensible, intelligent men" native to the district had expected a Jos Sedley rather than a Raffles when they heard that the East India Company had sent them a new man. When the assistant secretary evinced his delightful, eccentric interest in the history, government, and local customs of his Malay neighbors, he started something that did not die with him. Today no other country belonging to the British Empire is so well documented or its language so carefully studied as the British-occupied parts of the Malay Archipelago. The average Briton, when he goes out to live in Singapore or Kuala Lumpur, is still affected by Raffles's example. He begins as a matter of course to learn Malay, even though he be the type who can live thirty-five years in China without trying to speak Chinese, and then goes out of his way to boast of his ignorance.

Penang had first been occupied by the British as a precautionary gesture for the benefit of the Dutch. The Netherlands East India Company had been much put out by this action; it was the first time they took seriously the hint that England was likely to become a formidable rival to their sovereignty in the East Indies. Now as Raffles conversed with the native gentlemen who came in from neighboring states to see what he was about, he gathered much useful information about the Dutch and their habits in colonizing. Penang had always stood as a lone British colony on the Archipelago. But shortly before the new government was formed there were many changes in the surrounding territories, and all of them were directly related to Penang's welfare.

"We hear of a Javanese prince," B. H. M. Vlekke writes in his *Story of the Dutch East Indies*, "who had been exiled to Ceylon and who on his return to Java was considered a great expert on dealing with Europeans. He tried to explain to his countrymen the characteristic differences between the Dutch and the British. . . . 'The British,' he said, 'are like the strong rapid current of water; they are persevering, energetic, and irresistible in their courage. If they really want to obtain something they will use violence to get it. The Dutch are very able, clever, patient, and calm. If possible they try to reach their goal rather by persuasion than by force of arms. It may well happen,' he concluded, 'that Java will be conquered by the British.' Thirty years later it happened. . . ."

The Franco-British-American war of 1780, in which the Dutch were also involved, was particularly disastrous to the Dutch East India Company because their Indian possessions were blockaded by the British, and before communication could be re-established things were hopelessly tangled. In 1784 Holland sealed the Company's fate by signing the peace treaty, thus sacrificing forever their monopoly.

In the meantime there were stirrings of revolt at home (1780–81) in Holland—unsuccessful at first, but 1793 saw the fruition of the attempt. Holland became vassal to the new French Republic and remained in this curious and difficult position until 1810, when it was annexed outright by Napoleon.

What then of the Dutch Company's Indian possessions? Prince William of Orange, refugee in London, arranged that. In an attempt to rid the colonies of the French, never mind how, he wrote a letter to all the governors of all the Dutch territories and told them to hand everything under their control over to the English, who had promised to turn it back after the war was finished and the Prince back in Holland where he belonged, or thought he did.

"Batavia had to choose," says Vlekke, "whether it would follow William V or the States General. The slogan, 'Liberty, Equality, Fraternity,' had no appeal to them. On the other hand, the prospect of surrendering the administration of Java to the British had little more. Batavia, therefore, decided upon a middle course, namely to maintain at the same time its allegiance to the government of the Hague and its independence in internal affairs.

"Nevertheless, as soon as news came from Holland that a new government had been established upon a democratic basis, things began to move in the Indies. First a group of citizens and employees of the Company composed a petition to the High Government, written in the pompous style that seems to have been an unavoidable evil in that period: 'If the pretense of liberty that masked until now the most burdensome oppression of the people had succeeded in making the Netherlands into a republic of fame so great that it was envied by the whole of Europe, what may now be expected once freedom has been established here on the unshakable pillars of equality and fraternity?' They hastened to make clear what was expected: a celebration of the 'liberation' of the Netherlands, the abolishment of all outward distinctions of rank among the employees, and the organization of the defense of Java against counter-revolutionary—i.e., British—attacks."

The directors refused to take the petition seriously, but it scarcely mattered, for after 1798 they were out of a job anyway—the Dutch Company was no more. Its affairs were put in the hands of a committee, which asked, since Holland was now free, what about Batavia? To which the authorities replied ambiguously:

"We must state that we can hardly imagine in what way a revolution based on the system of liberty and rights of the people could be introduced into this country without destroying its value for the home country.

"Of course we are not well informed on the special principles of the new system . . . but we trust that we may declare that the revolutionary change will not be applied to our relations with the native princes and peoples, for, as the whole existence of the State is founded upon the moral and political conditions actually existing among these princes and peoples, such a change would cause a revolution in this State itself.

"Therefore we assume that it is your intention that the new system shall be applied only to the Government of the Company, to its servants and the Dutch citizens. The number of these citizens is, however, very limited, and only a few of them are capable of forming a sound judgment on affairs of importance. The interests of these few citizens can not outweigh those of the Company and they must never jeopardize those more important interests."

The new rulers of the Netherlands decided to consider these special interests in a special way.

"We persist in the opinion," wrote the committee, "we have always held that the doctrines of liberty and equality, however strongly they may be based on the inalienable rights of men and citizens and however thoroughly they may be introduced into this commonwealth [the Netherlands] and some other European countries, can not be transferred to nor applied to the East Indian possessions of the State as long as the security of these possessions depends on the existing and necessary state of subordination [of the Indonesians] and as long as the introduction can not take place without exposing these possessions to a confusion the effect of which can not be imagined."

The committee went on, expressing in the kindest manner its compassion for the "miserable fate of the slaves, men and women, born free like us and the rest of mankind," but declared that the abolition of slavery would have to wait "until a higher order of general civilization will permit the amelioration of their fate under the cooperation of all European nations that have overseas possessions."

That last bit makes peculiarly good reading today, side by side with the morning newspaper. It is doubtful if any other nation since then would express this point of view (a fundamental one for all imperialists) as frankly or with such freedom from cant, always excepting the late lamented Fascists, who didn't number cant among their vices. But it was an ordinary enough philosophy for that time, not peculiar to the Dutch. Even as it shocks us, it is a relief for that reason. Since yesterday's defeat of the Nazi party no one save perhaps Churchill has dared to speak out so clearly, without pulling punches or muffling diplomatic utterance with pious nothings and excuses. Considering that this attitude was held by the Dutch (among others) so openly at the end of the eighteenth century, one realizes how much happened in the years intervening, that we idealists of the United States, in this generation, were brought up to think them model colonizers for the world. That idea started early in the twentieth century.

There is always a reason, however obscure, for the opinions popular among the citizens of the great American Middle West. For example, ten years before the Japanese attacked China by planting a bomb on the South Manchuria Railway, the school children of the United States believed that all Japanese were delightful, clean people, who wanted only to be exactly like us—or anyway as like us as possible. Of course we liked that, and were convinced that the Chinese by comparison were a dirty people without taste or manners. None of this misunderstanding was accidental, though perhaps its origin was not obvious; and today we know why and how we were taught to believe it. It would be interesting to know why and how we grew to be so heartily in favor, at that particular time, of Dutch imperialism. Today's newspaper headlines are, of course, a different story. Another government supplies today's schools with today's propaganda.

One of the drawbacks to being a man like Raffles, brilliant and ambitious, is the loneliness of existence. As a boy drudging for a guinea a month, he had never had the leisure to make friends or the wherewithal to keep them even if he became acquainted. The long day was full of work and the night was all too short for his studying. Even when he became a man he was still too earnest to attract other young people like himself, and we have seen how his pride kept him from becoming intimate with anyone of his own class, because of his poverty.

The one exception had been William Brown Ramsay. Among his colleagues at India House in London he had always inspired respect, but until he won his spurs and gained the heights, social life was one of the luxuries he did without. Most men taste the sweets of friendship first, as bachelors, and later experience love and marriage, but with Raffles it was the other way about. He was a settled benedict before he met his good friend Leyden. After that life was never quite the same for him. Leyden led to others. Through him, his first good friend of the adult world, Raffles found more of his own sort of companions.

John Caspar Leyden, though he was only six years older than Raffles, had achieved fame in the world of letters before he came to take up his post in India. He was a many-sided, many-talented person. Though it is Stamford Raffles who has lived in the memory of mankind, and Leyden is known only through being his friend, it was a different story at the time the two young men first met. Then it was Leyden who was the great man, Leyden who condescended to the friendship, Leyden who was the lion of any social occasion. A Scot of humble origin, his boyhood bore no similarity to that of Raffles except that he too received no formal education. But he made up for it later by matriculating at the University of Edinburgh when he was barely fifteen. Lockhart, in his *Life of Sir Walter Scott*, gives us a romantic picture of John Leyden at the university, confounding the learned doctors with his store of knowledge. He was first intended for the Church, but he soon discovered that he much preferred science to theology, and medical science to any other kind. He studied—and learned—Hebrew and Arabic at Edinburgh; at St. Andrews where he continued his studies he took an M.D. degree. But his real aptitude (if Sir Walter Scott is any judge, which some of us doubt) was for poetry. Encouraged by Scott, Leyden wrote and published many poems and was best known for his collaboration with his mentor, the master, in the *Border Minstrelsy*.

It is not clear just why this young man, as soon as his feet were set on the road to success through letters, should have elected to become a doctor instead, and to practice out in

India instead of England. He did just that, however; in 1803 he asked for and got an appointment to the Madras Establishment, where Olivia Raffles's first husband had been working when he died, three years earlier. It could have been a romantic impulse of course. Whatever Leyden's reasons may have been, it was obvious that he and Raffles should become friends as soon as they met, if only because they had so many interests in common.

The meeting took place shortly after the Raffles family arrived in Penang. Leyden had been ill ever since he landed in Madras two years before, and though he managed in spite of his poor health to study the local languages and to do a certain amount of scientific work, he was sent to Penang on sick leave. Penang was believed, "very erroneously," as Boulger says, to have a healthy climate for white men, which is why Leyden's medical adviser chose it. Probably the climate did not benefit him, but his meeting with Raffles was the best thing that could have happened to either man.

Although the following amusing passage, by Lord Minto, was not written until some few years later, just before the expedition to Java, I am quoting it here.

"Dr. Leyden's learning is stupendous and he is also a very universal scholar. His knowledge, extreme and minute as it is, is always in his pocket at his finger's end, and on the tip of his tongue. He has made it completely his own, and it is all ready money. All his talent and labour indeed, which are both excessive, could not, however, have accumulated such stores without his extraordinary memory. I begin, I fear, to look at that faculty with increasing wonder; I hope without envy, but with something like one's admiration of young eyes. It must be confessed that Leyden has occasion for all the stores which application and memory can furnish to supply his tongue, which would dissipate a common stock in a week. I do not believe that so great a reader was ever so great a talker before. You may be conceited about yourselves, my beautiful wife and daughters, but with all my partiality I must give it against you. You would appear absolutely silent in his company, as a ship under weigh seems at anchor when it is passed by a swifter sailer. Another feature of his conversation is a shrill, piercing, and at the same time, grating voice. A frigate is not near large enough to place the ear at the proper point of hearing. If he had been at Babel, he would infallibly have learned all the languages there. . . . I must say to his honour that he has as intimate and profound a knowledge of the geography, history, mutual relations, religion, character, and manners of every tribe in Asia as he has of their language. On the present occasion, there is not an island or petty state in the multitudes of islands and nations amongst which we are going, of which he has not a tolerably minute and correct knowledge."

Following the charming fashion of the times, Leyden kept a journal. He was amused by the hectic atmosphere of George Town, which was in a tremendous bustle, what with the arrival of the new government staff and the departure of former officials who were being relieved of their posts. The poetical doctor remained nearly three months in Penang, most of the time as Raffles's guest. While Olivia nursed the invalid, the men studied Malay together and thoroughly enjoyed themselves.

CHAPTER V

Olivia, ah! forgive the bard,
  If sprightly strains alone are dear;
His notes are sad, for he has heard
  The footsteps of the parting year.

For each sweet scene I wandered o'er,
  Fair scenes that shall be ever dear,
From Curga's hills to Travancore—
  I hail thy steps, departed year!

But chief that in this eastern isle,
  Girt by the green and glistening wave,
Olivia's kind, endearing smile
  Seem'd to recall me from the grave.

When far beyond Malaya's sea,
  I trace dark Soonda's forests drear,
Olivia! I shall think of thee—
  And bless thy steps, departed year!

Each morn or evening spent with thee
  Fancy shall mid the wilds restore
In all their charms, and they shall be
  Sweet days that shall return no more.

Still may'st thou live in bliss secure
Beneath that friend's protecting care,
And may his cherish'd life endure
Long, long, thy holy love to share.

Leyden wrote and presented the *Dirge of the Departed* Year when he said good-by to the Raffles home, starting back to his professorship in Calcutta. Raffles was deeply moved, made happy, doubtless, by that peculiarly satisfying emotion which comes to a man when his best friend falls (hopelessly) in love with his wife. There is no setup more pleasant, all the way around, than that design for living which seems to take shape oftenest in the warmth of tropical colonies. Perhaps this is because white women are at a premium and native women are not, so that the bachelor member of the trio need not be under too much of a strain, preserving a high-minded worshipful adoration of his friend's missus.

This is a flippant generalization, definitely *not* to be applied to Olivia Raffles and Leyden. We may see the colonial design for living in that relationship, but the reader's impressions of the Raffles household will be distorted if he doesn't remember that Olivia was not the usual wife of the colonies. She was no more the brisk tennis-playing, cocktail-drinking good sport (or whatever its equivalent was back in 1806) than she was the overvivacious girl who "could just dance all night," and who usually does on Saturday at the club. We have proof of Olivia's special quality, though not from Leyden. Leyden was a man of taste too good to write his impressions of Mrs. Raffles even in his private journal. Writers know in their hearts that they cannot insure true privacy for any of their writings, particularly diaries. So the proof lies not with him, nor with the second wife of Raffles, Sophie, who was one up on Olivia in sharing her husband's title, and possessed countless other advantages as well, but who never forgave her predecessor just the same for having existed.

We get no help from Raffles himself. That agile pen which was usually able to surmount even the difficulties of contem-

59 ॐ

porary style, so that he was readable in spite of regulation pomposity—that accomplished pen faltered when its subject was Olivia, and the unhappy widower was driven to taking refuge in stilted phrases to express his vanished happiness. "It gave me domestic enjoyment," was the way he described his first marriage. It is scarcely a vivid portrait.

Lord Minto has bequeathed us a few lines in a gossipy letter to his wife, which we will quote in its proper place. But the best, most detailed picture of Olivia which we will ever find is that one which Abdullah, a young teacher of Malay who first met the Raffleses in Malacca, was to write in his autobiography some years later. Perhaps we ought to save Abdullah for the Malacca chapter, but since no one else comes to our rescue, we must break the chronological order and borrow a little bit from him in advance, if only for Olivia's sweet sake.

"She was not an ordinary woman," says Abdullah, "but was in every respect co-equal with her husband's position and responsibilities; bearing herself with propriety, politeness, and good grace. She was very fond of studying the Malay language, saying, What is this in Malay? and what that? Also whatever she saw she wrote down, and, whatever her husband intended to undertake, or when buying anything, he always deferred to her. Thus, if it pleased his wife, it pleased him. Further, her alacrity in all work was apparent; indeed she never rested for a moment, but she was always busy day after day. In this diligence which I observed there is a very great distinction between the habits of the natives [of Malayan countries] and the white people. For it is the custom of the Malayan women on their becoming the wives of great people to increase their arrogance, laziness, and habitual procrastination. . . . But to look at Mrs. Raffles, her hands and feet were in continual motion like chopping one bit after another. Then there was sewing, which was succeeded by writing, for it is a real truth that I never saw her sleep at mid-day, or even reclining for the sake of ease, but always at work with diligence, as day follows day. This the Almighty knows also. And if I am not wrong in the conclusion that I have arrived at, these are the signs of good sense and understanding, which qualify for the undertaking of great deeds. Thus her habits were active, so much so, that in fact she did the duty of her husband; indeed, it was she that taught him. Thus God had matched them as king and counsellor, or as a ring with its jewels."

Raffles was doubly proud of Leyden's *Dirge*. Poems which are written to us, or to people who belong to us, always seem much better than similar effusions which have no personal interest, and Leyden was so well known then as a poet that one could truthfully call him famous. No doubt it was because of this fame that his ex-host thought himself justified in his coyness when he gave it to the world without signature.

There is no obvious reason why this *Dirge of the Departed Year*, blameless as it is in sentiment, destined as it was for publication under the author's name in a posthumous collection, should have appeared first in such mysterious style, without any signature. The fashion of the times, though, decreed these harmless, meaningless little masquerades. It was thought to be the essence of refinement, to avoid giving a person's name outright, and yet to indicate it so that the thickest understanding must know who was meant. No wonder Thackeray used to make fun of the custom; when writing of someone like Prince George, for instance, he would spell the name thus: PR-NCE G-RGE. Byron, too, was impatiently scornful of so much exaggerated caution and "good taste."

"The following lines on the departed year have too much merit not to find an acceptable place in your paper," wrote Raffles to the editor. "They were written by a friend who, after travelling far and near in pursuit of knowledge, was at last driven to our Eastern Isle for the recovery of his health. He has now quitted our shores, but his distinguished talents and enthusiastic feeling must ever endear him to those who knew him sufficiently to estimate his worth and value his friendship. 'The stranger is gone, but we cannot forget.'"

The British colony of Prince of Wales Island was not large enough to be anything but intimate, and sometimes, probably, it was uncomfortably so. Thus it is significant that neither Raffles nor his wife made other close friends in the community during their first term of foreign service. Their chroniclers of past days were afraid of current conventions and never spoke directly about this, but now there seems to be no reason to maintain such anxious secrecy about what was in truth trivial. The whole thing seems to have been that there was gossip about Olivia Raffles, from the moment she set foot on the island; perhaps aboard ship, too, on their way out.

It was cruel that such a very small tale, inspired to some extent by jealousy of Raffles and his rapid advancement, should have made any difference at all to Olivia. Perhaps it didn't. We will hope so. She may have been perfectly happy with the company she did have, her husband and a few others. There was nothing Stamford Raffles could have done about it even if he had known, and he probably did not, because nobody would have dared repeat the gossip to him. It was the usual thing that springs up whenever someone gets ahead faster than the rank and file, in whatever society he may be. One hears similar tales today, in theatrical circles and large business communities as well as in the drawing rooms of the diplomats. The burden of the legend was that Olivia Fancourt had long been mistress to some big shot in the Company—some said it was William Ramsay, others named the chairman— who, when tired of her, bribed Raffles with the assistant-secretary post to marry her and take her to Penang. For corroborative detail the scandalmongers cited Raffles's youth ("Why otherwise would such a good post go to such a young man?"), Olivia's ten years' seniority ("Old enough to be his mother, my dear"), her social obscurity ("After all, who was she? How otherwise could they have met? I'm sure I never heard of her"), and, of course, the suddenness of the marriage ("They say his people never set eyes on her until he brought her home from church").

Much later, after Olivia had died and Thomas was made a knight and Java had been taken from the French and then given back five years later to the Dutch—much later, in 1819, Raffles came upon the story, boiled down to one catty little paragraph, in the Biographical Dictionary of the Living Authors of Great Britain and Ireland, edited by a man named Henry Colburn. "Mr. Raffles went out to India in an inferior capacity, through the interest of Mr. Ramsay, Secretary to the Company, and in consequence of his marrying a lady connected with that gentleman." Alone and to our modern eyes this may not seem as bad as it was intended to be, but Sir Stamford understood the insinuation. His state of mind was like that of Browning when he wrote his famous sonnet to Fitzgerald, the one beginning, "I chanced upon a new book yesterday,—" But Raffles was too angry to stop and think of rhyme schemes and meter. He sat him down and wrote Dr. Raffles, that cousin in Liverpool who for years served as an exhaust to his feelings when Raffles felt one to be necessary. Originally, no doubt, Sir Stamford's intention was merely to retort to the biographer's insults with a speedy, smashing statement, giving the lie to Mr. Colburn. Then his pen ran away with him. Once embarked, he didn't stop; perhaps he could not. He told the whole story of his career, and the remarks destined for Colburn's address were only a small part of the missive. But that is the portion in which we are particularly interested just now.

"This work, from its nature, must be in general circulation; and the mention it makes of one who is no more, as well as the general tendency of the article altogether, is as disagreeable to my feelings as discreditable to my character. My first wife was in no manner connected with Mr. Ramsay; they never saw each other; neither could my advancement in life possibly be accelerated by that marriage. It gave me no new connections, no wealth, but, on the contrary, a load of debt which I had to clear off. It increased my difficulties, and thus increased my energies. It gave me domestic enjoyment, and thus contributed to my happiness; but in no way can my advancement in life be accounted owing to that connection. My resolution to proceed to India, and my appointment to Prince of Wales's Island were made before the marriage took place; and, when I was about to quit all other ties and affections, it was natural that I should secure one bosom friend, one companion on my journey who would soothe the adverse blasts of misfortune and gladden the sunshine of prosperity—but what have the public to do with this? What right have they to disturb and animadvert on my domestic arrangements? What right have they to conclude that interest and not affection was consulted by me? . . ."

Only one man seems to have recorded in writing the overt insults and obvious snubs aimed against Mrs. Raffles in Penang. Raffles's position was not high enough to defend his wife against spiteful demonstrations of that sort. If Prince of Wales Island had an average group, then the gossip was probably held just within bounds; the women of such a colony are no worse than those at home, but the monotony of the lives they make for themselves, the unchanging dull routine, sends them pelting in full cry after the smallest excitement. And spite, of course, can be exciting. Scandal has a low boiling point and a long life in the colonies.

Besides, Olivia was probably a little too individual for their taste or understanding. It is difficult to imagine her joining the other women in their feasts of malice on toast, with tea. She had unusual interests, which made her suspect from the beginning. Evidently the punishment was not drastic—a gentle, tacitly handled exclusion from all social life but the large official functions would be the size of it, nothing so gross as out-and-out snubs. Perhaps she noticed, perhaps not: it is most unlikely if, noticing, she suffered acutely. Olivia and her quiet, studious husband nevertheless did their share of entertaining. Boulger proudly produces a notice from the *Prince of Wales's Island Gazette* of "the elegant dinner given by Mrs. Raffles" on the King's birthday in 1807, and from the same sheet of a later date that year reprints a society column in full:

THE BEAU MONDE

We have the pleasure to congratulate our numerous readers upon the happy return of the gaieties of Penang.

On Thursday, being Lord Mayor's Day, Mr. Robinson en-

tertained a select party of friends at his mansion on the north beach. In the evening a most elegant fête was given by Messrs. Clubley and Phipps. It is impossible for us to convey any idea of the style and manner in which everything was concluded.

The Honourable the Governor, together with the whole of the beauty and fashion of the island, assembled at an early hour.

The ball commenced between eight and nine. Mr. Clubley had the honour of leading Mrs. Raffles down the first dance to the tune of "Off she goes."

The supper rooms were thrown open precisely at twelve o'clock. The tables were covered with every delicacy that India can produce. The wines were of the most delicious quality; and that nothing might be wanting to render gratification perfect, several ladies and gentlemen entertained the company with songs, displaying on the one part the utmost delicacy of taste, and on the other true original comicality.

Dancing recommenced with increased life immediately after supper, and continued until an early hour in the morning, when the party separated with every appearance of regret,

> "That time should steal the night away
> And all their pleasures too—
> That they no longer there could stay,
> And all their joys renew."

In addition to the musicians of the island, Captain Harris was so good as to allow his band to attend. They played several pieces in a very superior style. One of the performers danced a hornpipe à la tamborina, which bore strong marks of his being a perfect adept in the art, and called forth loud and reiterated bursts of applause from his fair beholders.

But we have on the other hand the evidence of one Mr. Thomson, a teacher in a college at Malacca, who, if not quite a witness of the newly wedded Raffles's social fate in Penang, was nearly enough contemporary to be plausible. If he says there was gossip, there is your gossip in itself. And he does. (This is

65 ॐ

all in a footnote to his translation of *Hikayat Abdullah*.) After a few sarcastic remarks in which he rightly rebukes Lady Sophia Raffles for ignoring the existence of Olivia, he continues, "Why Mr. Raffles, a poor, half-educated clerk, should have been promoted suddenly to a position that would give a salary of £2,400 a year (knowing the mercenary nature of the Leadenhall Street Directors) was always an anomaly to me, till I had the cause explained, and which I will repeat in as gentle a manner as possible. The fact of the matter is, that young Raffles got a precious woman to wife and a good salary from the same dispenser of patronage, whose name I need not mention. This gave such umbrage to the ladies of Governor Dundas's suite, that both were sent to Coventry. Thus Nature, true to her principles, in young Raffles' humiliation opened the road to his future elevation. Had he been carried away by the gaieties of society he could never have studied the native languages deeply, nor could he have mixed with the chiefs so as to gain their confidence. . . .

"Thus also was it with his wife. . . ."

Sir Stamford was dead when Mr. Thomson (Dr. Thomson, perhaps?) wrote this "gentle" passage, and I think from the tone of it that his own indignant repudiation of the story had not reached this gentleman's notice. This sounds as if the scandal hadn't been imparted to Thomson by means of the phony Biography either; rather, Thomson seems to have got it from somebody in person, possibly after lunch in a historians' club. It is, of course, that sort of item which always lives most tenaciously, traveling by word of mouth, and no amount of denial like Raffles's, though it appears in print, can stamp the thing out. It is a sad fact that people like such stories, and they like repeating them, even when they aren't sure they are true.

For this reason alone, even if it hadn't been for the significant records dug up by Boulger, which prove that Olivia actually did petition for her pension, I would be inclined to disbelieve it. It is much the kind of thing one hears today in colonial communities, wherever rank or position counts a great deal and where people are not overworked; that is, where the tendency toward jealous spite is strong and chances to indulge it offer themselves a dozen times a day. Anyone who has lived more than a week or two in places like Peking, Hong Kong or British East Africa, will recognize the type and will admit that in these communities there is always an immense amount of smoke stirred up by disproportionately tiny fires. In other words, it could be true, but the chances are a hundred to one against it, because a hundred pieces of false gossip must have been told in Company social circles to every one piece which was founded on truth.

Besides, Boulger's disclosure of the records indicates how unlikely it was that Olivia should have filed her widow's petition if she were actually under the protection of Ramsay or any other Company official. Even if her hypothetical sugar daddy had been mean enough to allow her to need that small bit of money, the last thing he would permit, surely, would be that his mistress should appear in the Company offices, and on such an errand. It would have been madly indiscreet, rendering him liable at the very mildest to accusations of using undue influence for his girl friend.

In his curmudgeonly way, Mr. Thomson goes so far as to admit, however, that Olivia must have been extraordinarily charming to have had the effect she evidently did upon Leyden, Minto, and the humble Abdullah. (From his point of view, of course, that charm makes the gossip all the more convincing.) Abdullah indeed, says Thomson with characteristically delicate irony, must have been considerably smitten to burst into verse as he does when he speaks of her. I shall quote that verse presently: here I shall say only that Abdullah's tribute doesn't sound in the slightest immoral to me. On the contrary it is so virtuous as to outstuff the stuffiest of Leyden's literary offerings.

It follows that part of Abdullah's description of Olivia which I have already quoted, and if the Malay's style seems suddenly to have changed, that owes itself to the fact that I now take my text from a different translation—Mr. Thomson's, rather than the Rev. Mr. Shellabear's.

"Thus it was fit that she should be a pattern and friend to those who live after her time," wrote Abdullah, after likening her to a "jewel set in a ring." "Such were her habits and deportment as above related, and of which I have composed a *pantun* as below."

There follows the poem, which Mr. Thomson refers to, sneeringly, as evidence of Olivia's charm. (A pantun, by the way, is a Malayan form of poetry in which each stanza uses for first line the second line of the stanza preceding. The only similar form to which one can compare it in English, and that a very farfetched comparison, is the triolet.)

> *The quail 'tis certain is the name,*
> *The pool 'tis certain is its place:*
> *Beautiful indeed and sweet his mien,*
> *Combined with charming wit and grace.*
>
> *The pool 'tis certain is its place,*
> *Her loving chief her only guard;*
> *Sweet indeed her mien with grace,*
> *While prudence claims its best reward.*

Well, Coventry or no, tea parties or none, the dark-eyed lady must have kept busy enough. There remains one mystery on that score which I admit I have been powerless to solve. What of Olivia's children? Raffles does not mention them in his letters. Not only does he avoid speaking their names; he never announces any births in the family, at least in any of the letters we know about. There is one place where he refers to his "family," but that word could apply quite correctly to Olivia only, or to Olivia with his sister or sisters (for at one time all three of them visited him at once), living together in his house. Then there is one jovial mention in a letter by Leyden of Mrs. R. and Miss R., which might be interpreted as Mrs. Raffles and a young daughter, but again it is much more likely to have meant Mrs. Raffles and her youngest sister-in-law, who became engaged to Leyden. I would be inclined to dismiss both these hints and decide once and for all that Olivia's and

Thomas's was a childless marriage, except that Boulger is definite: "The death of Olivia Raffles did not stand alone among domestic afflictions, for about the same time he lost in quick succession the children she had borne him."

Now what can we say? It is easy to understand Raffles's silence upon the subject after these children had died, but what about his natural pride and happiness before the tragedy? How reconcile his silence on that score with his triumphant announcements of later days, when, every time his second wife Sophia presented him with a child, which was not an infrequent occurrence, he wrote all his friends about the happy event?

Leaving aside this one mystery, we have a fairly detailed, accurate picture of the Raffleses' domestic life during this first term in the East. It was a quiet, cheerful, productive sort of existence, with Raffles's success in the world of letters and science running a close second to his mounting popularity among his official colleagues. And in these triumphs Olivia kept her place by his side, for she had her modest success too. Whether or not she bore those children Boulger speaks about, she did her duty as a good sister-in-law—she married off Mary Anne! Yes, within six months of their arrival the eldest Miss Raffles made an excellent match, and became the bride of Quintin Dick Thompson, sub-warehouseman and deputy paymaster of Penang. Little is known about him save that his salary equaled that of Brother Thomas, which is a good mark for Mr. Thompson, and that he died three years later after having begot a child a year—one mark against Mr. Thompson, because their care rested on their uncle's already overburdened shoulders until Mary Anne married again. But in 1806 that was all in the future.

All we see is the pleasant scene of Mary Anne's wedding, which eliminated for her once and for all the danger of giving up this dream which she was privileged to share in the glamorous East, with brilliant Brother Thomas and clever sister-in-law Olivia. No more of London as an underfed maiden of good blood but poor parents! Couldn't Leonora and Harriett, too, be saved? Brother Thomas started to think, and save, and make plans toward that happy end. They were candid in those days, franker than we are about marriage, sometimes really brutal, though the British were apt to put on airs and to preen themselves for being better than those disgusting French, with whom marriage was just a business contract.

"What causes young people to 'come out', but the noble ambition of matrimony?" asks the author of Vanity Fair, like the sentimental moralist he is. "What sends them trooping to watering-places? What keeps them dancing till five o'clock in the morning through a whole mortal season? What causes them to labour at pianoforte sonatas, and to learn four songs from a fashionable master at a guinea a lesson, and to play the harp if they have handsome arms and neat elbows, and to wear Lincoln Green toxophilite hats and feathers, but that they may bring down some 'desirable' young man with those killing bows and arrows of theirs? What causes respectable parents to take up their carpets, set their houses topsy-turvy, and spend a fifth of their year's income in ball suppers and iced champagne? Is it sheer love of their species, and an unadulterated wish to see young people happy and dancing? Psha! they want to marry their daughters."

Harp playing has gone out with toxophilite hats of Lincoln green, but the sentiment of that passage applies to colonial society today as well as it did when it was written. With first one and then two more young ladies to launch, Raffles was put to considerable extra expense, though his salary, as he said, had been inadequate from the beginning. Because of his special talents, he always had extra work to do, but he didn't draw extra pay for it. For example, the new government had not been long at work before it was obvious that the official Company translator, a Mr. Hutton who had held the post for years, was by way of being a fake. Not only did he employ a large number of native clerks for the actual work, but the translations he produced were untrustworthy. Either through ignorance or by design, he sometimes altered the text in transcription. Raffles soon knew Malay well enough to watch Hutton, and in four months he was able to tell the governor that he could not only correct the translations of Hutton's department but was able himself to put English letters into Malay, or, as he then spelled it, "Malayee."

"I have been at much expense," he wrote, "in retaining in my service several natives whom I have selected as persons whose ability, and perhaps integrity, might be depended upon from their not being engaged in trade or other pursuits wherein the occasional knowledge they might obtain of the affairs of Government might be improper. These men were engaged by me, and have hitherto been maintained at my expense.

"But I have now to regret the narrow limits of my income will not longer admit of continuing so expensive an establishment on my own account, and more particularly so as I had reason to expect from them considerable assistance in explaining and commenting upon the customs and laws of the adjacent States, which I am endeavouring to collect, in the hope of laying a fair translation thereof before your Honourable Board.

"I cannot, however, omit adding that I was in a great measure induced to engage those men, from the circumstance of the *full* appointment of Translator to Government not having been yet granted to any person at this Presidency, conceiving that it was thereby intended to leave an opening for such who might prove themselves best qualified for the situation. And I trust that whenever the Honourable the Governor and Council shall take this appointment under consideration that I shall be honoured with their favourable notice, being willing to undertake, if necessary, to write all letters in the Malayee language that may be deemed of a secret nature in my own hand, and in many other respects to prevent, by my personal application, the affairs and interests of Government being intrusted in the hands of a native."

The government duly forwarded this matter to London, with Raffles's estimate of what his assistants cost him and a recommendation that something be done to help him out. As a result, Mr. Hutton was relieved of his duties and Raffles took over. He was graciously allowed sixty dollars a month for his native staff, but as for himself—let the record speak.

"We have derived much satisfaction," wrote the Court,

71 ॐ

"from the representation made of the conduct of Mr. Thomas Raffles, your Deputy-Secretary, in the great proficiency he has acquired of the Malay language, in the short period of five months after his arrival at Prince of Wales's Island, and desire that he be informed, that we entertain a high sense of his laudable exertions, and that a perseverance in that line of conduct will ensure our approbation and support. The establishment of natives at an expense of sixty dollars per month, which you have allowed Mr. Raffles to employ, and from whom he expects to derive great assistance in explaining and commenting upon the laws of the adjacent States (a work which Mr. Raffles has commenced), has our entire approbation. We trust, however, the establishment will be abolished on the completion of the work."

Not a word, you will observe, about boosting Mr. Raffles's salary.

It might be in order here to put in a word about the salary system, or rather the lack of it, obtaining in the East India Company in Raffles's time. It seems to have been understood that the Company servants should all dabble in the game of profiteering, and because the gains were so great from this corrupt practice, they were willing to take low salaries. Strange and shocking as it may seem to us, they all did it, without exception, so bribery and unrecorded commission taking must have been less immoral than they sound today—that is, if we consider morality as based on custom rather than social influence. One might say that racketeering today is equally widespread; an important point of difference, however, is that the government didn't frown on the eighteenth- and nineteenth-century rackets; everyone benefited too much. After all, in an age when commissions in the regular army were bought and sold, it is unlikely that much public indignation would have been called forth by any so-called exposé of the Company's methods. Says Furnivall:

"Governor Pitt was drawing a salary of about Rs.200 a month when he paid Rs.200,000 for the Hope Diamond; a writer drawing £5 a year could not live on less than £5 a month; princes were overset, populations sold and towns annihilated in the ordinary course of business, and for every rupee of profit gained by the English Company its servants made a hundred; anyone who could obtain an appointment was a made man, and a place on Rs.30 a month was actually worth some Rs.30,000 a year. In other respects also the position of the English Company resembled that of the Dutch. While the servants of the Company were amassing colossal fortunes the Company was rapidly advancing towards bankruptcy. In 1772 the Directors had to borrow over £1 million to meet the necessary payments of the next three months. In 1783, when the debts of the Dutch Company were some £55 million, the liabilities of the English Company exceeded its assets by Rs.80 million. And the accounts of the English Company were as involved as those of the Dutch Company, and for the same reason; they were kept in such a fashion that in 1813 it was impossible to ascertain whether the actual trading balance showed a profit or a loss. Finally the corruption in London exceeded, if possible, that in Amsterdam; for the stock of the Company, though worthless as a commercial asset, was keenly sought as a title to patronage, and a Nabob might return ten members of Parliament."

Raffles must have taken his whack too. This circumstance may not excuse John Company all his sins, rather on the contrary, but it explains, at least, how he got away with treating his servants in such niggardly fashion. They still made out, some of them more than fairly well.

Penang was not the health resort everyone had thought it would be. Pearson, the secretary, like many other government members, soon began to suffer from ill-health. For eight months he was away, and Raffles did his work as well as his own, already more than enough for one man. It was a formidable task they set him. Even if everything had been in good order it would have been formidable, and it was not: the correspondence had fallen far behind. Raffles found it necessary to hire extra clerks, and when the Court characteristically cautioned him against such extravagance he had to defend his action, explaining that his office was understaffed. Frequent illness of the writers, failure of paper supply, a multitude of difficulties made it absolutely essential to use more men. The Court retired its claims, grumbling but undefeated.

Dundas, the governor, died in 1807. There were other deaths too. In an all-round promotion Raffles was appointed full secretary with an increase of five hundred pounds over his former pay. Many of his colleagues considered this sum too little. Being on the spot, personally acquainted with Mr. Raffles, they naturally felt more sympathy for him than did the Court of Directors back in London, whose chief function, seemingly, was to find fault with their agents out in the colonies, and mechanically to refuse all requests from places like Penang. When his new appointment went into effect, Penang decided that Raffles should in all justice receive more than two thousand pounds a year. This, they argued, was fair not only because he would give superior service in the post but because the new assistant secretary was inexperienced and so could not help Raffles very much. Therefore it was resolved that the secretary's salary be augmented by two hundred extra rix-dollars a month, this fund to be taken from the salary of the new assistant secretary. All the local government approved this decision (with the possible exception of the new man), and Raffles drew his extra pay for two years. And then, but not until then, the Court in London signified their disapproval of the plan and ordered Penang to call the whole thing off! It was, of course, their privilege to do so, but one wonders why they took so long about it. A full year elapsed *after* they heard of the plan, not to mention the year the suggestion was en route, before they replied and ordered the arrangement to be canceled, in the following words:

"We are not aware of any objection to the appointments of Mr. Thomas Raffles and Mr. W. Clubley to the offices of Secretary and Assistant-Secretary to your Government, in consequence of the succession of Mr. Pearson to a seat at your Council Board; we, however, highly disapprove the arrangements you have adopted with regard to the salary of the former.

§ 74

"The salary established by our Orders of the 18th April 1805, for the Secretary to your Government, namely [rix] dollars 8000 per annum, we consider in every respect sufficient; and although the addition you have granted is to be provided by a corresponding reduction in the salary of the Assistant-Secretary by which no additional expense was to attach to the Company, yet we can never admit that because the salary of one office will bear reduction, another is therefore to be increased in a proportionate degree.

"Mr. Clubley being a writer of only two years' standing, you very properly restricted his allowances to dollars 2000 per annum; but upon the expiration of three years' residence in India, we agree with you that 3600 dollars per annum will be an adequate allowance, which we accordingly authorise you to allow to him.

"With respect to the salary of the Secretary to your Government, we desire that it be reduced to the sum originally fixed by us, and that Mr. Raffles be called upon to refund the amount which he may have received over and above the sum of dollars 8000 per annum."

If that isn't clear, this is what it means. No raise for Raffles, although the cut in the other chap's salary was to stand. Furthermore, Raffles found himself faced with the extraordinary problem of repaying more than sixteen hundred pounds in one blow, though it was money which he had never requested in the first place. Naturally he protested the injustice, and the Penang officials backed him up in his protest. The Court at last waived its claim, but in that, too, they were dilatory. Not until 1810 was it decided that Raffles need not repay the sum. He was returned to his original salary nevertheless, and besides, he had suffered much mental turmoil during the years of argument. The amount of work he had to turn out, and the number of extra duties and titles he now held, were fantastic. One wonders sometimes why their outpost people were so patient with the Company, but after all, where else could Raffles and his sort have worked?

The true explanation for the Company's niggardly attitude, though not for their inefficiencies, is that none of these possessions in the vicinity of Penang was paying off. Like most boards of directors, the Court was made up of businessmen of average intelligence, and to every one who had foresight and judgment enough to see that the East Indies might one day mean a good deal to the Company, there were four or five reactionaries who saw only as far as their own noses. Raffles's schemes and plans terrified them, and they resented the expense to which he was constantly putting them. Besides, there was more than a hint that the government in England, on whose promises the directors had gone in for that new establishment at Penang, was now backing down on the agreement. In 1809 the Court commanded a reduction of Penang's government, because the ministers of the Crown had not, in spite of former agreements, used the island as a site for an important naval station. Raffles and his pals were simply the innocent victims of higher politics, though the Court, naturally, pretended it was their own fault.

Nevertheless somebody loved Raffles—nearly everyone, in fact, who dealt directly with him, loved him. He was elevated by Penang's governor to the rank of senior merchant sometime in 1809 or 1810, and the Court of Directors, however they may have grumbled, confirmed this promotion.

We should never close a chapter on the gloomy note of official business if we can possibly help it. Private life in Pulo Penang offered many compensations to these petty, humiliating matters—and there was always the beloved Leyden, whom Raffles would not have met if he hadn't come out to Prince of Wales Island.

"My Dear Madame," wrote this Playboy of the Eastern World as he sat on deck, Calcutta-bound after his vacation with Thomas and Olivia. "We have now lost sight of Pooloo Penang, more, I am sorry to say, from the darkness than from the distance, and while our Portuguese friends are recommending themselves with great fervency of devotion to their patron saint, I have retired to pay the devoirs which I owe to her whom I have chosen my patroness for the voyage. I cannot help congratulating myself a good deal on the superiority of my choice of a living saint to a dead one, and am positive if you choose to exert yourself a little you have a great chance of rivalling his sublimest miracles, among which none of the least is his preaching on a certain day with great zeal and fervour to divers asses till their long ears betrayed powerful symptoms of devotion. Now, without wishing to cast any reflections on the wisdom of the islanders of the modern Barataria, I am perfectly of opinion that this miracle, doughty as it is, may be rivalled in Penang.

"There is, however, another miracle which I should be glad you would first try your hand at to enliven the dreariness of a voyage which bids fair to be one of the most tedious and insipid I was ever engaged in, as, if Providence do not send some French privateers or others to our assistance, we have not the least chance of an adventure. Most travellers by land or sea are of a different way of thinking, and maintain that no adventure is a lucky adventure, just as no news are reckoned good news by all our insipid, half-alive, half-vegetable acquaintance. I confess honestly I like to see some fun, and to see every possible variety of situations as well as of men and manners. However, if it be possible to overcome the irksomeness of light gales, a heaving cradle of a sea, and a barren, sweltering, tropical voyage, I flatter myself that I have adopted the best possible method by associating with all the pleasant recollections which I hoarded up at Penang in the society of you and your amiable husband. It is a terrible circumstance, after all, that there is little real difference between the recollections of past pleasures and of past sorrows. Perhaps the most we can make of it is that the memory of past pleasures is mournful and pleasant. I remember to have read of some such distinction in a volume of sermons, but I will by no means vouch for the accuracy of the quotation, as on second thoughts the epithets, I imagine, might be reversed with equal propriety. However this may be, the recollection of the pleasure I enjoyed in your society is by no means so vivid as my distress at losing it, and the little prospect I have of soon recovering it. I need not now request you, my dear sister Olivia, to think of me kindly, and never to believe any evil you may hear of me till you have it under my own hand, for whenever I have the courage to become a villain,—scoundrel and rascal are too pitiful to be mentioned,—but I say, whenever it shall be possible for me to become a villain, I shall have the courage to subscribe myself one, which I am in no danger of doing while I have the honour of subscribing myself your sincere friend."

A JAVANESE RENGGENG OR DANCING GIRL
(From Raffles's *History of Java*)

A JAVANESE IN COURT DRESS
(From Raffles's *History of Java*)

CHAPTER VI

The beginning of the Java affair found Raffles in exclusive company. Only he himself and his confidant Leyden, as far as he knew, had any designs on that large island with the interesting past. Nobody else in the Company had the slightest intention of such a thing, or so he thought. He was wrong. Gilbert Elliot, who was Earl of Minto and currently governor general of Bengal, had been thinking for a long time about Java, not as a seducer but as a suitor with the most honorable intentions. After all, England had a sort of claim on Java because the Prince of Orange had given his promise. All the French-held colonies of Holland were England's to borrow, he said.

Minto was something new among expansionists, a man who thought colonizing ought to benefit the natives as well as the agent. He now wanted to benefit the Javanese as well as England.

Raffles was to see a good deal of this Lord Minto. (He was, by the way, on John Company's pay roll, not the Crown's. John Company was still running British India.) But until 1808 the Java expedition was nothing more than a gleam in Minto's eye, and less than that with Thomas Raffles, who was feeling ill and not at all enterprising. The Court of Directors were not ripe for any suggestions along the line of expansion. They were heartily fed up with the East Indies, afraid of their commitments in the territory they already had, and far, far from wanting any more.

Somehow we modern Americans have fallen into a grossly mistaken idea of how the British Empire came to exist. This is true regardless of our attitude, whether we approve or disapprove of Great Britain. We take for granted that the Empire was acquired by direct methods of piracy or armed assault, by soldiers or sailors of the Crown led by aggressive empire-minded commanders. Venturing out overseas and overland, these armies, we mistakenly assume, wrested the land from such hapless natives as lived on it and took whatever territory they thought worth acquiring.

In truth the acquisition was seldom accomplished so simply or in such crude fashion. The armies came, all right, but they were always somehow a by-product of political or commercial activity; they were sent out to protect the moral principles of the state or to defend their native island from some threat—"some ostentatious system to excuse the havoc," as Walpole sadly said. Even when they were only mercenaries for the East India Company, the soldiers were all worked up. You can't send men into battle without a battle cry to stir the blood; not, that is, if you want to see real action. The Japanese in their late bid for the Pan-Asiatic Empire appealed to their public in the name of Greater East Asia, but it didn't work until they dropped that comparatively intellectual concept of simple gain. Though the Japanese leaders felt no necessity for justification, the truth was not enough. They had to picture England and America to their people as personal enemies, gross, overfed bloodsuckers who were attacking Japan's sacred race by cutting them off from the wherewithal to live. Japan was good, the States and England were bad; Japan was white, the United Nations were black; Japan was Virtue, the soldiers of the United Nations were frightful creatures who had to be fought and conquered and stamped on as a desperate necessity. And if, as an incidental, accidental result, Japan should find herself owning all the territory in Asia after the war, why, that would be very nice, but it wasn't what she went out fighting for.

Now the interesting point of all these scarcely original remarks is this: that nowhere in Japan, after the war was under way, would you have found a cold-blooded man directing public thought processes. Nobody, however deliberately he had made propaganda at first, remained detached. All the militarists and the government officials actively mixed up in the war were believing their own speeches before the end. Even the intelligent ones, though they may well have started out with cynical intentions, couldn't stand the strain; it was a matter of joining in or falling out of line, minus your sanity as well as your job. The picture painted by some extreme pacifists, of wars being finagled and strings being pulled by sinister, omniscient monsters in high places, is as unreal and oversimplified as the picture of those sinister communists painted by the extremist Red-baiters.

The Court of Directors was a group of average higher-ups in the business world. With one or two exceptions they entertained no dreams of conquest for glory's sake. Even when Lord Minto persuaded them, a year or two later, into taking Java over, they never thought of this step as an empire-building action, or as anything bigger than a clever stroke of business. Even Raffles went into the project as a practical man and no dreamer. His visions came later, after he occupied a position of responsibility, but they were always modified transports, even at his most extreme moments. And the thing was typical of all the Empire's expansion. England in the nineteenth century was no 1939 Germany; no British Mussolini could have led her into a glorious armor-clanking campaign. Her martial ardor was working overtime, but working on the European problem and Napoleon; France at home on the Continent was the enemy to consider, not France or anybody else in some far-off Pacific island, the other side of the globe. He was a wise man who said Britannia's Empire was acquired in a fit of absent-mindedness.

Official England, left alone, always followed a policy of appeasement in the face of trouble, and stagnation in the absence of a crisis. That is the way democracy seems to work out, internationally; ambition is a foible of the individual, not the

81 ॐ

crowd. For instance, take this Javanese campaign. It was a case of conquest in spite of home opposition; conquest by reluctance; conquest which was intentionally and in practice temporary. Its immediate and only object from the general point of view was strategic, to put a stop to Java being used as a base by French privateers, like Mauritius and Bourbon. But Java could have had another destiny. Raffles and Minto dreamed it up between them, and Raffles, particularly, lost his way in the end. So did England. They both, England and Raffles, lost Java. It was relinquished deliberately and by default in England's case, but not in Raffles's; he nearly broke his heart when England gave Java back to Holland. The wonder is that he was successful at all, dabbling in the game of conquest. After all, he was a civilian. He was no fire-eater who loved war for fighting's sake, though he was certainly a perfect example of Walpole's good Englishman and was more than willing to lose soldiers' lives in the cause of commerce. Never once has Raffles left for posterity any suggestion, any hint that he might have had qualms about those dead men. He didn't have any. It was their duty, as he saw it, to die in order that England be great. He never grudged his own life to the cause: why should they?

In justice to Raffles, however, I must point out that England's sojourn in Java is still memorable not for military achievement—it was a cheap victory throughout—nor yet for any permanent effect. Java, after all, was a dead issue as far as that British expedition was concerned; the annexation of the French-occupied isle was wiped out five years after it took place, when Holland regained possession of her valuable colony. But Raffles as administrator is the factor we will not forget. He is remembered by the Javanese and by the descendants of the slaves he helped there to achieve freedom. His hand is still evident in some of the reforms he had put into effect. Whatever Walpole might have thought of Raffles, Abraham Lincoln would have liked to know him.

A visit to Malacca was the beginning for Raffles of the big adventure. It started as a pleasure journey. Olivia went with him: joyfully they planned a sight-seeing tour to refresh him, body and soul. The secretary had actually broken down at last. Many of his colleagues had long since given in to Penang's "healthy" climate, but Raffles, though he was supposedly delicate, was always a lion for work under difficult conditions. We have seen how the tasks of his appointment multiplied out of all proportion to the rewards, as soon as he took up his duties in Penang. Now in 1808, as secretary to the Penang Presidency, he was really snowed under. He hired clerks to help him but there were never enough of them, due to the penny pinching which the Court of Directors practiced more and more intensively. He had to fight for every man on the pay roll. All Company or committee minutes and everything else that was recorded had to be done in quadruplicate (in longhand, of course), but that was only the beginning of his tiresome routine labors. There was in addition to that a tremendous amount of writing, every average day. The translating, for which he had early volunteered his superior talents, increased with his proficiency in Malay, many such documents being far too important to trust to anyone but himself. He was evidently the kind of man who attracted responsibility, whether or not he consciously wanted it. Now, however, he really had carried too far his usual indifference to ordinary precautions. Travers's Journal gives some idea of the amount of daily work done in Raffles's office and at home:

". . . whilst his mornings were employed in his public office, where at first he had but little assistance, his evenings were devoted to Eastern literature. Few men, but those who were immediately on the spot at the time, can form any idea of the difficult task which he had to perform, in conducting the public business of such a government as existed on the first establishment of Penang as a Presidency. . . ."

From Lady Raffles's Memoir:

"The fatigue and responsibility attaching to the office of secretary, in the organization of a new government, in a climate which in a very short period proved fatal to two Governors, all the Council, and many of the new settlers, brought on an alarming illness. The attack was so severe, that for some time little hopes for his life were entertained." Somehow Lady Raffles manages to render her husband obnoxious even on his bed of pain—and all merely by using conventional phrases which are almost certainly untrue. The italics are mine. "*Throughout sufferings,*" she writes, "by which his strength was nearly exhausted, he evinced the *utmost patience and resignation.*" He must really have been pretty badly off, poor fellow, but somehow it is difficult to pity him, even so, "When the disease abated, and he could be removed without danger, (1808) he was recommended to go to Malacca for the recovery of his health." Lady Raffles says nothing about Olivia's accompanying him.

Raffles had several reasons for choosing Malacca for a holiday, out of all the unknown East. One depended not on Malacca's past but on her future. The East India Company had lately decided to do away with the city: not merely to abandon her but actually to destroy her, building by building. This extraordinary project was already under way. Raffles speaks his mind on the subject better than we can paraphrase his report, but before we come to that let us read a romantic story —Malacca's.

It begins in the thirteenth century. Malacca existed before then, but only as a little fishing village. A thirteenth-century Javanese prince, having got into trouble at home, fled to the Archipelago. He stayed a little while in Singapore, which was then just as much of a one-horse town as Malacca, but his foes caught up with him and he ran away again, following the coast line. In Malacca he settled down, perhaps because he could recognize the advantages of the town's position. His crowd of followers, rich and sophisticated in comparison with the local population, increased Malacca's size to that of a considerable city. By the fifteenth century the language of the inhabitants had been adopted by most of the Archipelago peoples, and everybody visited Malacca, the center of commercial activity, to trade.

China, at the height of her power, got into the way of using Malacca as a stopping place for her fleets on their way to India and Ceylon as they passed through the Straits. Under Chinese protection the town flourished. It was the chosen rendezvous of pirates and traders; they came not only from the rest of the mainland but from the many islands round about. The official religion of the Malays was now Moslem.

Then the Portuguese arrived. As usual they sought wider horizons, for trade as well as piracy, and they did more than that. Mingled with their practical ambitions was a strong urge to save heathen souls. They had come as far as Malacca because they sought new directions from which to attack the Moors of Africa, in order to conquer Mohammedanism. Finding that the Malay Archipelago, though it wasn't in Africa, was also in the grip of Islam, they were more than willing to make war upon this country as well, fitting it into a general allover campaign for the Cross. We come across familiar names among the crusaders: Vasco da Gama and Albuquerque. It was Albuquerque who took possession of Goa on the Indian coast for Portugal. From Goa he went to Malacca, where he demanded permission from the Sultan to erect a fortress. As they expected, the Sultan refused, and the Portuguese promptly attacked, quickly driving the Malays into the interior; they built their fort as soon as they were in possession. (This is the accepted version, though the Malays tell the story with a slight difference.)

We already know the history of the Portuguese Empire. They lost out, ultimately, in the East Indies as well as everywhere else, giving way to Holland's superior sea power. The Dutch took Malacca in 1641; the story from then on is uneventful from the viewpoint of the native Malays until the British took their town away from the Dutch in 1795.

It was the new establishment at Penang which nearly brought her doom upon Malacca. In order to remove all possible competition to the projected presidency, in the same year that Raffles came East—1805—Malacca was ordered abandoned. Her staff, stores, and part of the population were to be moved to Prince of Wales Island, and the old fortress razed, in order to prevent its being put to use against Britain, in the future, by some rival European power. The commandant, a man named Farquhar, not unnaturally was horrified by this naïvely drastic program. It is easy enough to speak of picking up and moving the entire population of a town, especially when one is at considerable distance from the people involved. But Farquhar, being on the spot, knew that one cannot summarily uproot a whole town's population and expect the people to like it or even to obey the command unless they are forced. Either the Court of Directors had been misinformed about Malacca or they had somehow misunderstood the facts. Malacca was a far larger place than they considered it to be, and the people affected by their summary order were much more numerous than was indicated by statistics in hand. Farquhar strongly protested his orders and even sent the Court a petition against the project, signed by the most important men of Malacca, the list headed by his own name, but the directors in reply reiterated the original message and in addition scolded him for stirring up the populace to send the petition. Farquhar could do no more. In 1807 he began the painful task, and the fort was pulled down immediately.

In 1808, however, before more mischief could be accomplished, the Marines arrived: that is, Raffles paid his momentous visit to Malacca. It wasn't as long a vacation as he had hoped for. Almost immediately his holiday was cut short because George Town had discovered after his departure that they couldn't do without him, even for the brief time which had been promised him for furlough. "We shall not be able to make up any despatches for the Court without your assistance," the governor wrote, and though he added many apologies to his summons, it was clear that Raffles, rested or not, must return to work in Penang immediately. He argued not at all: he stayed not upon the order of his going; he didn't wait for a proper ship but took advantage of the presence in Malacca's harbor of a small vessel, what was called a "country boat," and by embarking on that he arrived back much the sooner at his desk. Nobody has recorded Olivia's reactions to this summary disposal of her husband's holiday, his first in some years' service. As it was also supposed to have been "sick leave" because he had nearly died of his breakdown, we hardly need written evidence of what his wife's feelings must have been.

Still, one aspect of the matter must have comforted her and quieted her shrill words of protest. If Raffles had used the rest of his sick leave which was so rudely snatched from him in the same way he evidently employed the free time he did have, I don't see how he could possibly have survived the rigors of his rest cure. Nowadays we laugh bitterly at those hit-and-run journalists who visit a country for ten days or two weeks and then go home to write a book about it. But the speediest foreign lecturer, summing up America in three days after a quick tour through the corn belt, or John Gunther, who got under Asia's skin in four months, or even Brooks Atkinson, who in one visit saw down to the middle of the Chinese-Communist situation as if it were a flawless crystal—all these modern lightning-flash reporters will have to cede the title to Raffles. On coming out of Malacca he sat himself down and produced a report on that city, addressed to his chiefs and aiming to prove that they had all been completely wrong in advocating its destruction. The bare facts are not staggering, but the report is; first because of its length, for he wrote thousands of words without padding, and second because it is such a beautiful example of logical argument. One is left incredulous that he could have collected such masses of information in less than several years of work. It is certain that he must have had plenty of help from Farquhar and that he turned the government offices upside down in Malacca, using the trade and government statistics that had been collected through years, but these are tasks anyone could have done. He needed a special advantage, and he had it, simply in being Raffles. It was his well-known gift for talking with the Malays that gave his report its extra something. He must have spent most of his research time looking up natives who could answer his questions. The Court had fallen into error for want of just this sort of information, and now Raffles was determined to make good the hiatus in their knowledge of Malacca. He deserves special credit because the original mistake was as much his as anyone's. He had been as loud as the next man in demanding the town's destruction; his name was signed to one of the Penang missives addressed to Farquhar, the one which commanded for the second and more peremptory time that Malacca be wiped off the map. Raffles had a largeness of spirit which is lacking in most of us, or perhaps it was rather a scientific detachment: he was willing to admit having fallen into a foolish error and was anxious to repair the damage as quickly as possible, regardless of appearances.

Briefly the report's content was as follows:

The plan to destroy Malacca has two objectives: first, to discourage any European power from wishing to develop it, in case they should move into the neighborhood, and, second, to improve the settlement at Prince of Wales Island by adding to it Malacca's population and trade. The Court, having been misinformed, believes that Malacca has no natural advantages in produce or in inducement to trade, and thus is not worth the considerable expense involved in keeping it up. However, twenty thousand people live in the town and its near neighborhood. More than three fourths of this number were born in the community of families which have been settled there for centuries. Even the Chinese emigrated there at a very early period. The Malays are very good citizens. Besides this fixed population there is a constant flow of traders from the East and near by, Malacca being the center of native commerce in the Straits. The country is well cultivated and valuable buildings have been erected. No common advantage will persuade the natives to abandon their family tombs, their temples, their independence, and their land. The inhabitants are decidedly not as they have been pictured to the council. Three quarters of the population of Prince of Wales Island, for example, might be induced to remove, but Malacca people are entirely different. The adventurer class long ago cleared out and went to Penang; those who remained are landed proprietors or their employees, a class not willingly converted into artisans. They have determined to remain by Malacca no matter what. The offer made by government to pay the passage of such Malaccans as would embark for Penang was not accepted by a single individual.

Owing to various designated sources of food supply, the inhabitants are self-supporting and won't need government help.

Of course they won't move to a new place where they must either buy land from earlier settlers or clear unhealthy jungle. They remember certain promises made by the English when the settlement fell into their hands and consider British faith pledged to protect them. They are willing to make great sacrifices for this protection and pay heavy duties cheerfully. The tax revenues of Malacca are never in arrears.

Indemnifying the European inhabitants who move to Penang is going to be particularly costly. Is it worth it?

There follows an exhaustive discussion of Malacca's market: what tribes came to take part in it, what articles they bartered, and when they came, with special reference to the problems of navigation which faced the native traders. Raffles argues that many of the prows going to Malacca found the added journey to Penang too much to attempt. Only the rich and well equipped made it. He also points out that if the duty at Malacca were lowered to Penang's level, Malaccan trade would vastly improve. One of the most important items of trade was evidently opium, and Raffles ascertained that it came from Bengal either on commission or that it was bought from Bengal ships returning from unsuccessful journeys eastward.

"The great object in fixing the commerce of Prince of Wales' Island, is to establish it as an entrepôt between Eastern and Western India; . . . Great delicacy is requisite in keeping the duties at Penang (and, perhaps, at Malacca, for the smaller prows) sufficiently low to prevent the merchants in Bengal from fitting out vessels direct for the Eastward. It should be more to their interest to be satisfied in leaving it at Penang; and the uncertainty and length of an Eastern voyage will always induce them to put up with less profit there."

In like detail the report examines every other item of trade and discusses the chances of improving British interests through the proper use of Malacca's position. But the real bite of the report comes at the last. The warning implicit in these lines is familiar strategy, the most emphatic argument an empire builder (or keeper) has in his arsenal. It was all the more emphatic when Raffles used it because he was quite sincere, then and later. He was always afraid of the Dutch. When they were powerful he was justified by the evidence, and when they were down he watched them anxiously, fearing a comeback. The Dutch East Indies were always far too Dutch for Raffles, and they didn't like him either.

"Thus far it has been my object to explain the difficulties that will arise in transferring the present population and trade. It is now necessary to view the subject as to the dangerous consequences likely to ensue to Penang in the event of the garrison being withdrawn.

"Malacca, having been in the possession of a European Power for three centuries, and even previously to that period considered as the capital of the Malay States, has obtained so great an importance in the eyes of the native princes, that they are ever anxious to obtain the friendship of the nation in whose hands it may be. Its name carries more weight to a Malay ear than any new settlement, whatever its importance. This preeminence ensures constant respect from the traders to and from the neighbouring ports: at least it has done so till very lately; and by this means affords a considerable check to piracy. Were Malacca in the hands of a native prince, however respectable, or supported by us, this check would not only be lost, but fleets of piratical vessels and prows would be fitted out, even from its shores, whose depredations the enterprise of our cruisers would find it difficult to keep under. . . .

"But to look at the subject in a more serious point of view still,—for I am far from thinking it would ever remain in the hands of a native Power,—although the permanent fortifications and public works of every description may be effectually destroyed, the possession of Malacca will ever be a most desirable object to a European Power and to our enemy. Prince of Wales's Island, though advantageously situated for commanding the bay and the northern entrance of the Straits, has by no means the same advantage and command within the Straits that Malacca possesses. Every ship that passes up or down must be observed from the latter place, and should this station ever be held by an enterprising enemy, not only Penang, but our more important China trade, would be materially endangered. We have now the command. Why give it up, unless we are forced? and I trust we are not reduced to that extremity. . . .

"It is well known that the Dutch Government had in contemplation to make Malacca a free port, with the view of destroying the English settlement at Penang. Should the place ever fall into their hands again, or into that of their now superior authority, which it no doubt will if evacuated by the English, a similar, or more active policy must be expected. . . .

". . . I am enabled to assert with correctness that any European Power possessing Malacca would, in a very short time, be able to intrench themselves nearly as securely as they could have done within the old walls, and that we should find the greatest difficulty in again obtaining possession of the place. . . .

"The garrison and establishment at Malacca appear to have been reduced to the very lowest state consistent with the honour of the British Flag and the internal safety of the place; and no further reduction can, I think, with safety, be attempted."

The paper had immediate results. A copy was forwarded to Lord Minto at Calcutta as soon as it was ready, and he was immensely impressed. Aside from the intrinsic interest of the work, a special factor added to its effect on Minto. As we know, John Leyden was in India, at the University of Calcutta. He got ready to put in his two cents' worth as soon as Raffles notified him that the paper was on its way to the governor general. Minto had struck up a close friendship with Leyden: he too was a Scot, an ardent one, and Leyden's reputation among his countrymen was especially high just then because he had collaborated with Sir Walter Scott on the *Border Minstrelsy*. It may seem a far cry from the Scottish border to Malacca, but it wasn't, as long as Gilbert Elliot governed Bengal for the East India Company.

Leyden had already found occasion to call Minto's special attention to Raffles. In a speech the governor general made during some scholastic junket at the university he had awarded honors to Raffles *in absentia* for his Malay translations, putting him in a class with the learned Marsden as an oriental scholar. In this opinion he was to be enthusiastically supported by

Marsden himself. Raffles, writing the elder man indirectly through Governor Dundas of Penang, had done his usual excellent job of collecting and imparting information about the natives. It was the beginning of an important friendship between the scholars, though they didn't meet personally until 1816, when Raffles visited England.

Some great men award these university honors easily, for political reasons, without reflection beforehand, and completely forgetting the entire affair afterward. Not men of Minto's caliber, however. A true Scot, he was predisposed toward scholarship, and now, through seeing so much of Leyden, he had begun to take a personal interest in oriental studies. But until now it had been more as a hobby than as a part of his career that he kept an eye on the Malay world. Raffles's Malacca report was not a scientific essay to be noted, praised, and filed away under "Native Affairs." It showed a grasp of possibilities that was statesmanlike. It was a clear exposition, besides, of Raffles's own attitude toward the position of England in the East, and this was so closely akin to Minto's ideas that his full attention was immediately captured.

It goes without saying that Malacca was to be spared. This was not only Minto's reaction; the men in whose hands the city's fate rested were convinced of it as soon as they had read and grasped the paper's import. Not one objected to Raffles's conclusions or disagreed with him. Malacca was saved, and that was the end of that chapter. But Raffles's career really began when Minto read the Malacca report.

Those were good days, exciting days for the world's intellectuals. The situation in Calcutta must have been something like Franklin Roosevelt's ideal society. When our President started his "Brain Trust," he frightened the life out of the politicos of Washington by attempting to bring scholarship out of the cloisters of education into the white glare of American government. Lord Minto was more fortunate than F.D.R., a hundred and forty years ago. Then nobody was surprised or alarmed that he selected scholars to be his advisers and surrounded himself with men whose common passion it was to investigate the culture of the people they governed. The earl actually thought his behavior natural rather than eccentric! Yes, they were happy days.

They were happy for another reason too. In these our times everything is specialized. We inherit and collect so great a store of information that we are forced to divide it into compartments. Our young researchers must decide which compartment they want to work in, or they will never get anywhere; they will be diffused. Those must have been better days when a colonial official could combine his duties with language study, ethnology, botany, art, and yet be home in time for dinner. Nobody knew very much about any of these subjects in Indonesia, so investigation became a duty as well as a pleasure. Every day afforded a new discovery, every discovery added to the world's wisdom, every piece of wisdom was hailed with joy not only by the professors and scholars of England but even by their merchants, the shopkeepers of the nation. Never in those halcyon days would an office manager have administered a rebuke like one the writer recalls in her wage-earning experience: "Trouble with you, Miss Hahn, is too much *education*." Imagine Dundas or Minto saying such a thing to Raffles!

After all, not many stock companies can claim to have given the world dictionaries, museums, and a national zoological society. Put it down to credit in the ledgers of empire.

The specific job which inspired Lord Minto's flattering reference to Raffles in that Calcutta University address was a paper the Penang secretary wrote about the Malay nation. It was the first piece of the sort which he had attempted, and in it he made a great stride forward for the cause of Malay civilization by proving all these people to be members of one race. Until then Malays had been studied piecemeal and considered, group by group, as a lot of small scattered races rather than one large one which has spread out and split up, which we now recognize as the fact. As always when reading something by

Raffles, one wonders where on earth he found the time to prepare it, to ask the necessary questions of his native friends, patiently trace their families, visit ancestral places, et cetera. And then there is his easy style, which triumphs over the fashion of his day and makes us, comparing them, less patient than ever with Sophia, Lady Raffles, and her misguided, genteel, overpunctuated diction. Hitherto the reader has had only his letters from which to judge Raffles's writing, so I herewith reprint for an example a piece of translating which he included in the Malay-nation paper. Remember and compare, while reading it, the lame, jerky productions we usually get from well-meaning people when they translate prose from oriental writings into so-called English.

"The following is a translation of the Malayan history of the first arrival of the Portuguese at Malacca:

" 'Ten Portuguese vessels arrived at Malacca from Manilla, for the purpose of trade, during the reign of the Sultan Ahmed Shah, at a time when that country possessed an extensive commerce, and every thing in abundance, when the affairs of government were well administered, and the officers properly appointed.

" 'For forty days the Portuguese ships traded at Malacca; but still the Portuguese commander remained on shore, presenting dollars by the chest, and gold; and how many beautiful cloths did they present to the illustrious Shah Ahmed Shah, so that the Sultan was most happy!

" 'After this Sultan Ahmed Shah said to the commander of the Portuguese, "What more do you require from us, that you present us such rich presents?" To this the commander replied, "We only request one thing of our friend, should he be well inclined towards the white men." Whereupon Sultan Ahmed Shah said, "State what it is that I may hear it, and if it is in my power I will comply with the request of my friend." The Portuguese answered, "We wish to request a small piece of ground, to the extent of what the skin of a beast may cover." Then said the Sultan, "Let not my friends be unhappy, let them take whatever spot of ground they like best, to the extent of what they request." The captains were highly rejoiced at this, and the Portuguese immediately landed, bringing with them spades, brick, and mortar; the commander then took the skin of the beast, and having rent it into cords, measured out therewith four sides, within which the Portuguese built a store-house of very considerable dimensions, leaving large square apertures in the walls for guns; and when the people of Malacca enquired the reason of the apertures being left, the Portuguese returned for answer, "These are the apertures that the white men require for windows." The people of Malacca were satisfied and content.

" 'Alas! how often did the Bendahara and Tumungungs approach the Rajah with a request that the white men might not be permitted to build a large house: but the Rajah would say, "My eyes are upon them, and they are few in number: if they do any wrong, whatever it may be, I shall see it, and will give orders for their being massacred (literally, I will order my men to *amok*, or, as it is vulgarly termed, run a muck among them)." Notwithstanding this, the Bendahara and Tumungungs remained dissatisfied in their hearts, for they were wise men.

" 'After this the Portuguese, during the night, conveyed cannon into their store-house, and they landed small-arms, packed in chests, saying their contents were cloths; and in this manner did the Portuguese deceive and cheat the people of Malacca!

" 'What the Portuguese next did, the people of Malacca were ignorant of, but it was long before the store-house was completed; and when all their arms were in order, then it was at midnight, at a time when the people of Malacca were asleep, that the Portuguese began to fire all their guns from the fort of Malacca!

" 'They soon destroyed all the houses of the people of Malacca, and their Nibong fort; and it was during this night, when the Portuguese first attacked the people of Malacca, that Sultan Ahmed Shah, with his people fled in all directions, for no one could remain to oppose the Portuguese.

" 'Thus did the Portuguese take possession of Malacca, whilst Sultan Ahmed Shah fled to Moar, and from thence in a short time, to Johore, and afterwards to Bentan, to establish another country. Such is the account of the Portuguese taking the kingdom of Malacca, from the hands of Sultan Ahmed Shah.

" 'During thirty-six years, three months, and fourteen days, the Portuguese were employed in the construction of the fort, and then it was completed.

" 'From this time the Portuguese remained in quiet possession of Malacca for about nine years and one month, when the country once more began to flourish, on account of the quantities of merchandise brought there from all quarters. Such is the account of the country of Malacca under the Portuguese.

" 'After this period, a Dutch vessel arrived at Malacca for the purpose of trade; the vessel's name was Afterlenden, and that of the captain, Ibir. The captain perceived that Malacca was a very fine place, and had a good fort; therefore, after the Dutch vessel had traded for fifteen days, he set sail for Europe, and arriving after a considerable time at the great country, he gave intelligence to the great Rajah of what he had seen, of the country of Malacca, the extent of its commerce, and the excellence of its fort. On this, the Rajah of Europe said, "If such is the account of Malacca, it is proper that I should order it to be attacked." Twenty-five vessels were thereupon ordered by the Rajah of Europe, for the purpose of attacking Malacca, and troops being embarked in each, they first set sail for the kingdom of Bantam, in the country of Java, where the Dutch were on terms of friendship.

" 'At Bantam they found two Dutch ships, and a ketch, and after having taken on board buffaloes, and provisions for the use of the persons on board, the vessels then sailed for Malacca.

" 'As soon as the fleet arrived at Malacca, the Dutch sent a letter to the Portuguese, telling them to hold themselves in readiness, as it was the intention of the Dutch to commence the attack on the morrow, at mid-day. To this the Portuguese replied, "Come when you please, we are ready."

" 'On the next day the Dutch commenced the attack, and the war continued for about two months; but the country of Malacca was not carried, and the Dutch returned to Bantam, where they remained quiet for some time, in the intention of returning to Europe; all the great men on board feeling ashamed of what had happened.

" 'The great men in each of the vessels, having afterwards held consultations respecting another attack on Malacca, they proceeded against it a second time, but it did not surrender. The Dutch now sent a letter to Johore, in terms of friendship, to the Sultan, requesting his assistance, in the attack of Malacca. With this the Rajah of Johore was pleased, and an agreement was entered into between the Rajah of Johore and the Dutch, which was swore to; so that the Dutch and Malays became as one, as far as concerned the taking of Malacca. An agreement was made, that the Dutch should attack from the sea, and the people of Johore from the land. If the country surrendered, the Dutch were to retain the country, and the cannon; and every thing else that might be found within Malacca was to be equally divided between the Dutch and the people of Johore.

" 'When these terms were agreed upon, the men of Johore and the Dutch sailed for Malacca, and after attacking it for about fifteen days, from the sea, many were slain, as well Portuguese as Malays and Dutch. The Malays then held a consultation and began to think, that if they fought against the white men according to this fashion, Malacca would not fall for ten years. It was therefore agreed upon by all the Malays, that fifty men should enter the fort of Malacca, and run a muck or meng-amok.

" 'The Malays then selected a lucky day, and on the twenty-first day of the month, at 5 o'clock in the morning, the fifty Malays entered the fort, and commenced amok, and every Portuguese was either put to death, or forced to fly into the interior of the country, without order or regularity.

" 'On this, the Malays exerted themselves in plundering Malacca, and the whole was divided between the men of Johore and the Dutch, according to their agreement.

" 'The men of Johore then returned to the country of Johore, and the Dutch remained in possession of Malacca.

" 'This is the account of former times.' "

CHAPTER VII

Up to a point, real-life success stories follow the simple lines of cause and effect, virtue and reward, which have been laid down by Horatio Alger. Then, I regret to observe, everything comes to pieces. Farewell to H. Alger, and all that. In order to keep style consistent with matter, a cynic should now take over and complete the story of Thomas Stamford Raffles. (He had dropped the "Bingley" by the wayside, somewhere in his teens.)

The moment had come when the maxim of "early to bed and early to rise," as well as an infinite capacity for taking pains, simply was not enough. Something extra had to happen or our promising lad would have had to stay just where he was for the rest of his life, getting up early, taking pains to an infinite degree, and interrupting his labors only to get to bed early again. Raffles, you will remember, had reached a similar point once before, though then it would not have been quite so nearly fatal if he had failed to find William Ramsay. We saw how a timely recommendation from that gentleman cut short the long apprenticeship to glory, and how, perhaps through his influence (which is my theory) or perhaps through God's (Lady Raffles's bet), Thomas became the boy wonder of the year. It was a triumph that he should have gone as he did to Penang, a married man earning a high salary, at twenty-four. This time, though, the occasion was far more important, bringing him as it did many steps closer to his goal; close enough to realize to some extent what that goal was. This time he met Minto.

Let us play our game of conjecture. One imagines the earl still a bit dazed after reading the entire Malacca report at one sitting, but not too dazed to say, "Who is this man Raffles?" One need imagine only a little further to bring John Caspar Leyden into the scene, leaning forward in his chair, eagerly ready to answer the question. Then, alas, one must throw the whole thing out, because we remember that Minto was already favorably aware of Raffles. The Malacca report did, however, serve to confirm an opinion he had formed some months earlier, and indirectly it accomplished more than that, for without it the governor might never have thought to invite its author over to Calcutta for a chat. Writing to his Liverpool relative, Raffles tells this part of his story for himself:

"As a reward for my labours [his translations in service of the Penang Presidency] and on account of my peculiar qualifications for the office, I was appointed Malay translator to Government . . . [But he does not say the appointment carried no salary with it: here, perhaps, his usually admirable memory fails him, though discretion does not.] and the Earl of Minto, then Governor-General of Bengal, thought fit to honour my name and exertions with notice in one of his anniversary addresses to the College of Calcutta. This was the origin of my acquaintance with Lord Minto, and the commencement of that intimacy and confidence to which I am proud to say that I owe the whole of my subsequent advancement and prosperity in life.

"Encouraged by the flattering notice thus unexpectedly taken of my humble exertions by the first authority in India, and by a nobleman whose attainments and virtues had never been surpassed, I was induced to submit to him the considerations which occurred to me on the impolicy of the measures pursued by the Government of Prince of Wales's Island toward Malacca, once the emporium of the East, and still a place of great commercial intercourse. This policy went to raze to the ground every public edifice, and to drive from the land of their forefathers every remnant of population. The object was, of course, to aggrandise Prince of Wales's Island, a small and insignificant spot, which in its greediness to devour the resources of this more important neighbour reminded me, in some degree, of the fable of the frog and the ox. In these considerations I took a general view of the nature of the Eastern trade, and the conclusions were so obvious that the Governor-General in Council, without waiting for any explanation on the part of the subordinate Government, at once put a stop to the devastating and desolating system which had been adopted, and acted without reserve on the propositions I had submitted.

"It happened that, not long after this interference on the part of the Supreme Government, the conquest of the Moluccas was unexpectedly achieved by a small naval force which had been merely sent to plunder them. The Governor-General refused to take charge of these islands on account of the Company, and the Naval Commander hardly felt himself warranted in establishing a king's government; but as the decision was left with him, he proposed to the Governor-General, who was then at Madras, that I should be nominated to the charge, and a provisional administration established pending a reference to Europe. Lord Minto immediately replied that I was not unknown to him, that he was perfectly satisfied of my fitness and claims, and that he would immediately appoint me if the Admiral would undertake that I should accept the office; for it occurred to Lord Minto that, being a family man, and of high pretensions, I might be unwilling to sacrifice a certainty for an uncertainty. My advancement at Prince of Wales's Island was secure, but the Moluccas were only a war dependency, and it was not known what measures regarding them might be taken by the Government at home. The Admiral did not like to take the responsibility, and the arrangement dropped on an understanding that my assent was alone wanting; but, as the Governor-General was about to return to Bengal, he would, of course, feel himself at perfect liberty to bestow the office on another, should an immediate arrangement or the claims of others require an early attention.

Lord Minto went to Bengal, and the Admiral despatched a vessel to give me the earliest intimation of what had occurred, hoping he had acted for the best in declining to take on himself the responsibility. Some months had now elapsed, and it was feared that arrangements for the administration of the Moluccas were already in progress. Yet the chance of being in time, and the expectation of still further advancing my interests with Lord Minto, weighed with me in the resolution I took of proceeding in person to Bengal. . . ."

This account he gives of the conquest of the Moluccas is really too brief for our ignorance, but it will be confusing to speak more about it just here, so we will discuss it in a later chapter.

We come now to the crucial moment, when Raffles goes to Calcutta in order to meet Lord Minto in person and talk things over. The governor general's first suggestion after reading the Malacca report had been a change of jobs for Raffles, but for various reasons, as we have seen, nothing came of this project. However, Raffles went to meet the earl anyway, so eager for a personal interview that he traveled in a small boat and nearly drowned.

"My attention had long been directed to the state of the Dutch possessions to the eastward; and, as rumours were afloat of a projected armament going against the Isle of France, it occurred to me that the information I possessed respecting Java might be useful, and possibly turn the attention of our Government in that direction. I accordingly left my family, and proceeded to Calcutta in a small and frail vessel—the only one which offered, but in which all my future prospects had well-nigh perished. This was in the month of June 1810. On my arrival in Bengal, I met with the kindest reception from Lord Minto. I found that, though the appointment to the Moluccas had not actually taken place, it was promised to another. I, in consequence, relinquished all idea of it, and at once drew his Lordship's attention to Java by observing that there were other islands worthy of his Lordship's consideration besides the Moluccas,—Java, for instance. On the mention of Java, his Lordship cast a look of such scrutiny, anticipation, and kindness upon me that I shall never forget.

101 ઈન્

" 'Yes,' said he, 'Java is an interesting island. I shall be happy to receive any information you can give me concerning it.'

"This was enough to encourage me, and, from this moment, all my views, all my plans, and all my mind were devoted to create such an interest regarding Java as should lead to its annexation to our Eastern Empire; although I confess that I had never the vanity to expect that, when this object was accomplished, so important an administration would have been entrusted to my individual charge; that I should be entrusted with what Mr. Marsden emphatically observes was 'as great a charge as a nation could entrust to an individual.'

"It is unnecessary to enter on the detail which followed. The fall of Bourbon, and the anticipation of success at the Isle of France, encouraged a plan for the conquest of Java. As it in a great measure originated with me, and as it was almost entirely on my information that the decision was taken, I naturally took a conspicuous part, although little or nothing met the public eye—perhaps no secret was ever better kept than the projected scheme against Java."

It is not a startling coincidence that other biographers besides this writer have seen in the Calcutta visit the most significant step in Raffles's life. The meeting was noteworthy, even in the opinion of Minto's chroniclers, but the earl had a more varied career than his protégé; his life was pitched on a higher social plane, he started out with a more important appointment because of this, and Java never loomed as large in his summing up as it was to do for Raffles. Even so, the Far Eastern chapter in Minto's biography, too, is of special importance. His reputation with posterity would have been good in any case, but when the Java campaign was added to his list of accomplishments he crossed the line that divided the good diplomats from the exceptional ones. He was a man of vision, one proof of this being that as soon as they met he recognized a valuable assistant and disciple in Raffles. Minto himself is a fascinating subject, but Boulger was preoccupied with Raffles rather than with the governor general, telling the story of Java, and so should we be as biographer to Raffles. We must stick to our last and treat the earl, however respectfully and admiringly, chiefly as an important agent of our hero's fate, the man who furnished a niche worthy of Raffles's statue, nobly immortal in a toga. The name carved over the niche is "Java."

Possibly Boulger's zeal carries him further, however, than we are willing to go. In the following quotation, for example, he credits Raffles with the *entire* original idea of annexing Java. He implies that the conquest was practically a new conception to Minto, though he gives the governor general full marks for his sympathetic reception of the suggestion. In modern language, Boulger "spotlights" Raffles in the *affaire Java*, and it is somewhat of a question whether he had the right to do so, considering certain letters of Minto's regarding Java and England's chances of supplanting the French there, which were written before he met the Penang secretary. Since Raffles's name is honored enough by the unadorned truth, it seems a pity that Boulger should have claimed even more credit for him than was his by right. It seems particularly futile in this case because Java did not long remain a jewel in the British crown. She was prised from her setting after glittering there only five years. Surely there is no need for the devotees of these two talented Englishmen to squabble over what used to be but is no more. Fortunately there has been no squabble. No one took issue with Boulger, and Raffles as well as Minto had already died when the book appeared. For the rest, Boulger was fair and gave Lord Minto his just due.

"At Penang or Malacca," says Boulger, "he [Raffles] might never have become famous. Commercial prosperity shunned those stations, and the East India Company had no love or regard for places that did not contribute to its coffers. Malacca was doomed to exalt Penang; Penang itself did not realise the expectations formed of it, and was accordingly reduced. The Company had no policy at all in the Malay peninsula and the Archipelago, where a knowledge of the Malay language was alone of practical use. Nor had any of the Governor-Generals who wielded its power any clearer views in this direction, with one exception; and that was the very ruler whose notice Raffles had attracted, and whose close confidence and favour he was now about to obtain. Lord Minto was the one Governor-General who had grasped fully the secret of maritime supremacy, and who believed that security in India depended as much on the control of the seas and the possession of the isles along our ocean highway as on military achievements within the peninsula itself. Raffles must be pronounced supremely fortunate in the fact that such a statesman held the reins of power at the moment of his going to Calcutta with the set purpose of inducing the Government to conquer Java. It may even be said that if he had come in the time of any other ruler than Lord Minto, his errand would have been bootless; but the recent conqueror of the isles of Bourbon and France was naturally sympathetic to a scheme which would entail the expulsion of French influence and authority from the one remaining island east of the Cape where they still survived.

"In everything he had undertaken Raffles had shown an earnestness and elevation of spirit which gave him a title to success. His uppermost feeling must have been one of benefiting his country rather than himself, for he could not have foreseen that his personal reward would have been as great as it proved."

Well . . . Here seems to be the moment to insert one of those parenthetical grunts of skepticism, thus: (sic). Although there is plenty of reason to credit Raffles with benevolent intentions toward other recipients as well as himself, he must surely have been aware, even if he couldn't foretell the dimensions of his reward, that the Java scheme would scarcely impede his progress. We can meet on common ground, however, by remembering that he really did believe it was good for his country when he, Stamford Raffles, had power to run things for England. A more likely commendation would be that his ambition to acquire Java for England was based on a simple, fervent faith in India House's good intentions (or at any rate his own) toward Java's natives. Raffles was positive that English administration would be welcomed by the Javanese, and that in any case they longed to be liberated permanently from the Dutch, with or without the French overlords who had been on the scene since Holland became a vassal state. He was completely sincere in his belief, and he was probably correct. In my experience subject peoples usually long for liberation, and the grass looks very much greener to them over the fence.

As for Minto's particular individual willingness to outguess Napoleon, and the fact that he alone of all possible governors general was the recipient of Raffles's confidence, surely it is an extremely elaborate reason to thank Lady Luck for this chance? "This country," as Boulger says, "was only able to fulfill her part [in the struggle against Napoleon] because she commanded the seas, and because she wrested from her rival the island that Napoleon's genius would have made the base of his designs on our Eastern possessions. It must not be supposed that these designs exist only in the imagination of English writers, or that Napoleon accepted his defeat in Egypt in 1798–99 as the termination of his dreams of Asiatic dominion." To call this setup peculiarly, fatefully fortunate for Raffles is rather the same sort of reasoning followed by my old geology professor, who struggled manfully to combine his religious faith (Southern Methodist) with the theory of evolution, and succeeded only after working out this line of reasoning: "If the Age of the Great Lizards had not just then happened to come to a close—a mysteriously sudden close, I grant you—and if the Age of Mammals hadn't just happened to begin then, the mammals wouldn't have had a chance. The first mammals were tiny, weak creatures, which the lizards in their heyday would have stamped out of existence. As it was, the difference of a paltry few millions of years gave the mammals their chance to survive, and as a result, MAN appeared on earth. I say that this was not just luck. I say that GOD arranged for the lizards to die out just then. I say that man exists by divine prearrangement. In fact, I consider evolution PROOF of divine intention."

It is always salutary to hear what the other side has to say, and the voice of the Dutch is loud and clear in the works of Bernard Vlekke. His opinions of Raffles are not like those of the British. Though Raffles's direct intervention did not begin until 1811, he had been watching the Dutch possessions in the East Indies covetously, from the beginning of the century. He was acutely aware of them as soon as he arrived in the East.

Holland had held control of the Archipelago more than a century, but her rule of Java, after about 1750, differed in certain important respects from her treatment of the natives in the other Dutch-held islands. The Dutch East India Company introduced drastic curtailment of the production of spices, and in Vlekke's words (*Story of the Dutch East Indies*): "The system was evil and the effects horrible. . . . The population of these villages rapidly diminished and grew apathetic under the suffering caused by this constant oppression that afflicted them as heavily as the internecine wars of the old days. . . . The Directors of the Company were punished for their misrule by the evil consequences of their own system. When finally the demand for spices in Europe rose, and prices went up, production could not be increased. The resistance of the inhabitants to establishing new plantations . . . could not be overcome."

At the start of the nineteenth century there were still sporadic revolts against the Dutch on Java, particularly if the man in charge was a bad egg, and some of them were. Nicolas Hartingh wrote in 1756, "Apparently the Javanese prefer being skinned by their own people to being vexed by foreigners." There was reason to suppose, however, that relations between Indonesians and Europeans—Dutch and English—were improving a little, however slowly.

A coincidence suddenly put Java on the map, economically. The West Indies, owing to the revolt of the slaves in Haiti, abruptly disappeared from the coffee market and left Java holding a monopoly, so that after five years of steady selling there was not a pound of coffee left in the Javanese storehouses. The boom period, as Vlekke says, came to an end as suddenly as it began when the American Embargo Act in 1808 put a stop to American shipping, but Java had filled her money chests in those prosperous ten years. "When Governor-General Wiese surrendered his high office to his successor, there were two million guilders in the treasury of Batavia.

"This successor was Herman Willem Daendels. A Bonaparte had come to power in the Netherlands, and from now on military considerations took the first place in the colonial plans of the Hague. Daendels had never been in the Indies, but he seemed to be the right type of man to clean the Batavian stables of Augeas, a new man who stood outside the cliques and gangs, who knew what he wanted and had an iron hand. . . . Immediately after his arrival he decided to leave the unhealthy and desolate city of Batavia and move to Buitenzorg. Then he set to work, slashing at corruption, tearing down and building up the administration, constructing roads and fortresses, in short, doing everything which a self-styled dictator might be expected to do. He accomplished a great deal but incurred the deadly hostility of many whose interests he hurt, with the result that his silver-tongued successor, Thomas Raffles, was able to take all the credit for the reorganization of Java's government for himself alone while Daendels' memory was burdened with the discreditable aspects of the affair."

These readjustments and counterclaims are inevitable as long as historians preserve any nationalistic fervor at all. Boulger is of the past, Mr. Vlekke of the present, and though the modern historian obviously tries to be just, and to tell the true story without showing the influence of his Dutch nationality, he is defeated by something else: a very natural desire to even things up. In his attempt to balance the scales of past opinion, unconsciously, perhaps, he piles the weights too high on Holland's side. But he does really evaluate Daendels's work, giving a much better, more realistic picture of the man than we get from either Raffles or Boulger, who make him out a complete villain. Vlekke says that Daendels's dictatorial behavior turned the Dutch themselves, as well as the Javanese, against him. Daendels snubbed the Javanese princes deliberately, stupidly believing that the policy of politeness which had been followed by his predecessors was injurious to Dutch prestige. He was in favor of compulsory cultivation: he wrote to the Minister of Colonies, "The only way to collect taxes from the poor Javanese peasants is to make them work." It is to his credit that he tried to get the peasants their legal share in the price of coffee, but the market wasn't profitable enough to render that question anything but academic. As a result Daendels committed the worst mistake in his entire generally unfortunate career in Java—the sale of land. He sold land right and left, whether or not it was owned by natives, and like all such desirable territory the land was, of course, thickly settled.

We quote Vlekke directly: "The Batavian government possessed merchandise to a value of several millions, but no cash. As a last expedient, Daendels resorted to the sale of 'government domains.' From Daendels' standpoint the whole of Java, except the territory of the princes, was 'government domain.' . . . Daendels actually sold enormous tracts of land west and east of Batavia. Fortunately he did not rule long enough to carry out his plans to their full extent which would have resulted in half the population of Java being reduced to a state of bondsmen."

But he never for a moment forgot that his chief reason for being in Java was to improve the "deplorable state of the defense of the colony." He set to work "in feverish activity," increasing garrisons, improving communications, and otherwise disturbing inquisitive, alert observers for the British. The forced labor he put on the highway, which was swiftly completed, cost an immense number of lives. "That invasion would come soon was inevitable, for Daendels' measures for defense made it imperative for the British to destroy this Dutch-French stronghold before it was too well organized. Daendels, however, was not permitted to conduct the defense. In 1810 Napoleon Bonaparte deposed his brother Louis, the king of Holland, and annexed the Netherlands to the French empire. Daendels hoisted the French flag in Batavia, although . . . [it] caused great discontent among the old Dutch Indian settlers. Shortly after the annexation . . . Napoleon decided to recall Daendels and to replace him by a man of more moderate character. He sent Jan Willem Janssens, who had formerly been governor of the Cape Colony, which he had reached just in time to fight a British invasion and to surrender the colony to the enemy. The same fate befell him once more when he had come to Java."

We are not surprised, but we are amused at another discrepancy which here occurs between the Dutch and British versions of the Java campaign. It is typical of their general differences. Vlekke pictures Daendels as very busy, knowing that "invasion was inevitable," feverishly throwing up defenses and building roads, working against time. Boulger, on the other hand, seems to think the British preparations were shrouded in deepest mystery, "kept a close secret," so that the invasion came as a crashing surprise to the Dutch, or perhaps to the natives round about. As for the natives, however, Abdullah, the clerk who worked for Raffles in Malacca, records in his memoirs that two or three months before Raffles came to town, where he was to await Minto in order to start the campaign, "the news came that the English intended to attack Java." He speaks as if it were the commonest bazaar rumor, as it undoubtedly was. From whom, then, was the plan kept in secrecy, as Raffles fondly believed?

The English at home, perhaps. All they did, after all, was to supply army and funds, and that gave them no claim at all to advance information. They knew their place, in Old England.

A crisp, unimaginative report is usually better for the seeking biographer than loquacious discussion, and it must be admitted in fairness to Lady Raffles that her Memoir usually supplies it. Her editorial comment is admirably brief; in fact there is only one grave fault in Sophia's book, once you have learned to ignore her piety and to forgive her for the various omissions that are due to her customary squeamishness. But that one fault is truly grave. She has maintained an icy silence on the subject of her predecessor, Olivia, and this is an inexcusable display of jealous spite. Only once, in a footnote, does she take cognizance of Olivia's existence at all, and the information supplied in that footnote is erroneous.

Fortunately for truth we have been able through other sources to follow Olivia's modest career. Besides being interesting, it is sometimes really important for us to know when she accompanied her husband on his voyages, for example, especially during this period. It is certain that she came with him when Raffles, after the plan arranged "in secret" between Minto and himself—and probably reported to Daendels by native spies within the next fortnight—moved to Malacca. Olivia had to go with him this time, though the change was not publicized; this move was definite and final. Raffles gave up Runnymede, his Penang house, and took along most of the household. In Malacca he became agent to the governor general and, not quite incidentally, was in a far better spot than Penang would have been from which to collect information useful to the approaching campaign.

Toward the end of 1810 the move was complete. Raffles and Olivia were finally installed in Malacca, with their customary army of clerks and translators, in the midst of an atmosphere somewhat strange, doubtless, to both of them. The visit they had paid before to the city, exhaustive as Raffles's investigation had been, must have warned them, to a point, of what to expect. But now they were a part of the community rather than visitors collecting material for a report, and they found it very different from Penang. Nor could Olivia have observed many details reminiscent of Madras.

The differences were mainly due to the contrasting histories of these colonial possessions. British India and Penang had both been taken over direct from oriental natives when the British moved in. Such traditions of civilization as had been built up by Europeans in those colonies, therefore, were the traditions which Raffles and Olivia found natural and logical, stemming as they did from the same root as the couple's own. But Malacca, an ancient town which had passed through many hands before the British got hold of it in 1795, had belonged to the Dutch for a long time, and the Dutch had left the strong imprint of their own very dissimilar culture on the

A Madurese Petty Noble or Mantri

(From Raffles's *History of Java*)

A HOLLANDER AND HIS JAVANESE SLAVE

ELEPHANT SENT BY RAFFLES
TO THE SHOGUN OF JAPAN IN 1813

(From a Japanese woodcut by Araki Jogen dated 1815; author's collection) place. In fact there were still many Dutch settlers there, as well as half-caste descendants of their earlier compatriots.

In many ways the two sorts of Europeans differed far more than any two white races do now, in our era of international standardization. We will see details of this difference more vividly when we accompany Raffles to Java; but even in Malacca more than a few things must have surprised the British Olivia when she started to keep house. For instance there was the matter of wives. British colonials either brought their women out from England, though that was not customary practice as it is today, or they entered into irregular relationships with the native women, carefully keeping such liaisons hidden from the public eye. Only a brazen, exceptional sort of British bachelor would have flaunted his native mistress or admitted fathering the children of such a union. The Dutch, on the other hand, ignored race distinction. In those early days it was seldom that a white woman would come out from Holland to be married and live in Java, but it was common indeed for a Dutchman to marry a woman of the people. He considered his half-caste children quite as much his own offspring as any Englishman would feel about his full-blooded white children at home. Naturally the daughters of such unions married Dutchmen rather than the native men, because they would be wealthy and in a higher social sphere than most of the Javanese or Malay males. Their fathers disposed of them arbitrarily, keeping the customary continental eye out for profitable matches. Dutch children born in the colonies, whether or not they had native blood, were known by the slang name "liplaps."

As a result, in a Dutch-Indian colony the so-called Dutchwomen were nearly all black-haired, dusky ladies, who dressed in the native style. More than one traveler of the time speaks of these wives, who never accompanied their husbands to parties but who mingled with each other in daylong idleness, placidly chewing and spitting betel nut and depending down to the tiniest, most trivial matter on their many slave girls. It can be imagined, therefore, that Olivia, however picturesque she may have found these "European ladies," scarcely felt as if she could indulge in ordinary social intercourse with them. They would have been the last to welcome unusually friendly overtures from Mrs. Raffles. But there must have been at least a few other English ladies in Malacca to keep Olivia company.

The young boy Abdullah, the clerk, watched the new household with a bright-eyed interest in its smallest affairs which every scholar of the period now has reason to bless, because he wrote it all down and left it to posterity, i.e., to us. Thanks to Abdullah, we know, for example, that Mr. Raffles and his wife stayed in the Banda Iliar quarter, in the plantation of one "Capitan China," evidently a rich Chinese of the district called by Abdullah and the other Malays "Baba Chang-lang." ("Baba" is Chinese for "Papa.") We know that Raffles brought in his luggage "numerous European goods, such as boxes of guns and pistols, satin cloth of great value, and prints with plain flowers, and many implements of which I had never seen the like."

These articles were intended as presents for native princes. The satin must have been Chinese, the prints from England. "Also woollen cloth of soft texture," continues Abdullah, "with clocks and watches, and paper for writing letters thereon to Malay princes, on which were printed flowers of gold and silver, besides many articles intended as presents for them." That writing paper was a sort much favored by the princes for their royal correspondence, so the Dutch had always been careful to use the richest-appearing paper they could find for their proclamations and letters.

In addition, Raffles was given a considerable amount of money to dispense as he thought best for his job, which included among his other duties an undercover assignment much like that of a modern intelligence operator. He was to make valuable contacts, find out what he could, prepare such people as he was sure would be friendly throughout the operation, and all the rest of it. Minto had no doubt that the author of the now famous Malacca report would do this work better than even a trained spy would have done. The new agent's existence must have been busy and complicated in the next few months, particularly as ordinary work had to go on at its normal feverish pace regardless of the extra assignments relative to the Javanese adventure. Being in new surroundings, he plunged deep into his hobby, making natural history collections. Everything he could get hold of in the way of insects, snakes, plants and flowers, shellfish, et cetera, was collected alive; more of them were catalogued and preserved in alcohol, or dried. The botanical specimens and marine animals and shells, of course, were immortalized in sketches and paintings as well. Raffles put the best native artists he could find on the job, but his own executive was often as good as theirs if not superior. He indulged in flower painting as a sort of recreation, after the more austere pastime of map making. And then of course there were his wild animal pets.

Along with various lesser simians he acquired two live young orangutans, called by the Malays mawas. They were a pair, and from time to time Raffles gave in to an impulse which seems to be universal among ape fanciers and dressed them up in suitable clothes. They had the run of the house and the young Abdullah was fascinated by their playful antics. When after four or five months the female orang died, the male moped for several days, refused to eat, and soon followed his wife to the grave, plunging the household in sorrow.

There was a tiger cub, too, which was usually the center of a crowd of natives.

One special lesson in botany—or shall we call it orchard culture?—was not relished by the enthusiastic master however. One day a peddler brought some durians to the house. The durian, as most people who have visited the Indies know, is a fruit with a smell so foul it can only be described as obscene. If you can forget the smell long enough to take a bite of it, your prejudice is supposed to vanish, for it really does taste good, but the first whiff is terrific.

The moment the peddler appeared poor Raffles grabbed at his own nose and speedily, in Abdullah's words, "made off upstairs." From a safe height, after a gasp, he called down in a rage, "Who brought those durians? Show me that Malay!" he shouted.

The unhappy peddler, much mystified, was hustled out

of the house and put on his way, earnestly assisted for several hundred paces. Raffles came down after a time, claiming that he still had a headache from the stench.

"It is most nauseous eating," he said, whereat, according to Abdullah, "Everyone was much astonished."

Raffles asked Abdullah one day to take him visiting at a Malay school. Once arrived and poking about in his usual amiably inquisitive manner, he soon discovered that the students, though they were taught most assiduously to read the Koran, never had to study Malay at all. He was surprised at this, even shocked, and asked the schoolmaster why it was so. Because nobody thought Malay necessary, replied the master: the boys learned it at home anyway to some extent; the Koran, he said, as everybody knew, was of first importance to anyone with a properly religious spirit. Malay was sometimes studied later on, he admitted, by those few scholars who wanted to continue with their education after they grew up. His reply seems to have been somewhat defensive, even indignantly surprised, for Raffles had to hurry with an implicit apology.

"Very good, O master!" he said. "I want to know only; don't be angry with me, O guru."

As they walked down the road away from the school, safely out of earshot, he told Abdullah, "If I live I shall have a school set a-going for teaching Malay. I am most anxious about this, as it is a beautiful language; further, it is of great utility."

Raffles was always asking Abdullah questions about every subject in the world—the methods of government among the Malays, what they liked best, their customs of marriage and death, the names of the hills and other places in Malacca Territory, what were the pursuits of the people, and what merchandise they produced; also he wished to find out "whether the Malacca people liked the government of the Dutch or the English."

In regard to that last question, Thomson observes dryly that it was a very silly one, aside from being unworthy of a great man. (Thomson must have been an internationalist.) He says that if the truth were known the Malays probably disliked the Dutch and the English equally, and wanted to govern themselves. He was evidently a man far ahead of his time in some things, if not in all respects.

Undoubtedly Raffles enjoyed himself thoroughly in Malacca. It must have been all the better because he had never experienced a normal boyhood. This life was a true boy's paradise, not only because of his animals and his collections but because he was playing what Kipling calls "the Game." What is the strategy of war and statesmanship, anyway, but an elaborate game of skill for grownups?

At last everything was set. Lord Minto wrote:

"The Mauritius and all the French islands being now in our possession, there is nothing to retard the execution of our further views to the eastward. The expedition, comprising 4,000 European infantry, with a suitable proportion of artillery, and 4,000 Bengal infantry, with about 300 cavalry, will sail from India the beginning or middle of March."

Then came a bombshell, but it was a welcome one. "I am now to acquaint you with my own intention to proceed in person, at least to Malacca, and eventually, I may say probably, to Java. . . .

"I count upon meeting you at Malacca: and then, in communication with yourself and Sir Samuel Auchmuty, the final plans, military and political, will be settled.

"I have no doubt that the communications you will have opened with the Island of Java and adjacent countries, will have furnished authentic knowledge of the disposition we shall meet there, and enable us to place our enterprise upon a footing which will ensure the concurrence and co-operation of the native states, if it does not procure the acquiescence of the Dutch themselves in our views."

As a matter of fact many of the Dutch were glad to exchange their French conquerors for the British when the time came. Minto was no amateur diplomat.

The following passage should be carefully read, especially if the reader has hitherto been inclined to give the Court of Directors credit for normal intelligence. The italics are mine.

"I must tell you in confidence, that I have received the

sanction of government at home for this expedition, but that the views of the Directors do not go beyond the expulsion or reduction of the Dutch power, the destruction of their fortifications, *the distribution of their arms and stores to the natives, and the evacuation of the island by our own troops.*"

Difficult to credit, is it not? At times like this we are forcibly reminded that the British were still fresh at this game of colonization: the projected destruction of Malacca was one illustration of their inexperience and the incredible commands here quoted by Minto are another example. Today no government of any civilized nation would consider such an action, unless they meant deliberately to invite disaster, as the United Nations did, for example, when they armed the Thais during the recent World War. Obviously the political world as well as nature abhors a vacuum. Any community too weak to defend itself is snatched up by the nearest powerful neighbor the minute it is left without leadership. The directors no doubt felt that Java's fate was not their affair, once the French had been kicked out, yet even so it was difficult to credit them with so much naïveté. There was, first, a strong possibility that the French would move back in as soon as they could muster the necessary men and weapons. Next there was always the chance that Holland would have a try at regaining what she still considered her own by force, for she had no confidence in England's earlier promises.

Since the directors, after Lord Minto persuaded them to see the situation, had wished to move the French out of Java, because they were so uncomfortably close to England's own station at Penang, then why leave the way open for them to return? What was the sense of letting everything slip back into the old arrangement as soon as the battle was over? Even knowing it is so from the records, one can scarcely believe the directors' message was meant to be taken seriously.

That would be Minto's first reaction as well as Raffles's, but the second would come fast on the heels of the first. Java set free, with the natives all freshly armed and supplied with food, might become a scene of massacre as soon as the English were out of sight. Though it was not absolutely certain, such things might well happen. The Dutch settlers would be the first victims, and after all the whites had been killed the natives would battle among themselves, and it would be a bloody affair before one party or another was admitted to be lord over the rest. High-minded men among the directors might argue that what the Javanese did among themselves should be their own affair, forgetting the white settlers for the moment. I myself, though I do not claim to be high-minded, would be among the first to say so. But it is one thing to leave a nation of natives alone from the beginning, and quite another to give them all the latest paraphernalia for killing each other, show them how to use it, leave everything in confusion and leaderless, and then simply walk out of the scene.

This point is particularly important because on it hangs Minto's claim to being a *justified* empire builder. Just as the benevolent despot is his own best argument, so the apologists for the Empire can point to Lord Minto without words. The same justification covers Raffles, the two men being fully agreed, always, on matters of this sort. They probably decided to consider the two obvious arguments against the directors' projected policy as of equal importance, the first (that Java would be occupied by someone else) on practical grounds, the second (that the natives might turn to violence) on humanitarian. That would be their official opinion, though in private they may have differed. It is not for me, so much later in the game, to decide which argument loomed up first, really, in Raffles's estimation, but if I am allowed to hazard a guess, without being called on for any reason or proof, I would say that the first argument was nearest to his heart, just as the second was the one favored by Minto.

Merely as a small matter of interest is Lady Raffles's comment on the question. She could scarcely have been ignorant of the political implications of the situation, but she is too much a creature of her time to mention those. Instead, with all the fervor at her command (which is not very much), she speaks of the second danger. People who are fond of the Javanese will be indignant at her choice of adjectives, who can call the Javanese "uncivilized" while referring to the Dutch as "their *ancient* masters." I quote her because this passage is an excellent example of that kind of propaganda, and probably one of the first of its kind, which was later to become familiar to all of us.

"The mere object of destroying the ascendancy of an ancient [sic] European colony," says Sophia, suddenly becoming very fond of the Dutch if it's a choice between them and the natives, "however legitimate in itself that object might be considered, as a means of weakening a declared enemy, could hardly be justifiable, if it were to be followed up by a transfer of that enemy's power to the hands of millions of uncivilized people, who would instantly annihilate the whole population of their ancient masters."

"I conclude, however," said Minto in his letter, "that the destructive and calamitous consequences of this plan to so ancient and populous an European colony, the property and lives of which must fall a sacrifice to the vindictive sway of the Malay chiefs, if transferred suddenly and defenceless to their dominion, have not been fully contemplated; and I have already stated my reasons for considering a modification of their orders as indispensable.

"The points on which I have been able to form a judgment, with any confidence, are: first, that we must establish provisionally an administration to supply the protection which will have been lost by the abolition of the Dutch authority:— this applies more particularly to Batavia:—That the Dutch may themselves be employed, in a great and principal proportion, in this new administration, under the control of a presiding British authority . . . To the native princes and people the abolition of Dutch power would alone afford a gratification of rooted passions, and a prospect of substantial relief and advantage, which may be expected to withdraw them from the Dutch and unite them to our cause: and a system of connection between them and the English Government may be founded on principles so manifestly beneficial to the people of the island, as to attach them to our alliance, and ensure tranquillity between us."

That last passage is particularly interesting, sounding as

it does the keynote of Lord Minto's benevolent imperialism. It would have made Daendels, with his anxious love for prestige, snort like a buffalo. Even though the earl himself had been governor general of Bengal for some time this program marked a departure from government policy in British India. It sounded as if the ex-Dutch East Indies might be going to serve as a proving ground, an experimental laboratory, for these humanitarian gentlemen. It sounded good. Borrowing a phrase from Vlekke, we might call Minto, Leyden, Raffles, and Co., "the silver-tongued salesmen of St. George."

It remained for them to open up their new market. Java still flaunted her new flag, the unpopular banner of the French. In the spring of 1811 the Earl of Minto cheerfully started out with his entourage, bound for the Raffles residence in Malacca.

CHAPTER VIII

"In preparation for his expedition against the Netherlands in Java, Lord Minto gathered around him a group of men with genuine interest in Indonesian affairs, in the Malay languages, and in native history and customs; men who certainly shared his humanitarian views but who knew that their sole chance of promotion lay in gaining the favor of the prominent Whig politician who was their direct chief. This does not detract from the merits of these men as promoters of the study of Indonesian affairs, but it does explain their great display of moral indignation at the injustice committed by others while their own actions were often far from blameless."

This, of course, is the voice of Vlekke.

"A burning ambition and a brilliant intelligence combined to make Raffles the right man to execute Lord Minto's plans for the East Indies. Raffles was not a man of great character, but he was ambitious enough to prefer a reputation in history to an immediate material award. To build that reputation, he worked all his life, first by serving the leading humanitarian statesmen, then by creating, through his writings, an historical legend about his administration in Java, and finally, by a daring but unscrupulous policy of expansion which led to his greatest achievement, the founding of Singapore. And he wrote so well, in such an attractive form, that for a century

120

after his death people continued to judge Raffles by his words instead of his deeds. His little publicity tricks tend to irritate the historian who otherwise will gladly concede to Raffles the honor of having been one of the most intelligent and active governors that ever ruled in the Indies."

A hundred and thirty years have not sweetened those grapes for the Dutch. Mr. Vlekke tries hard, but in the foregoing passage he really did go off the rails to a considerable distance, as the wryness in those words testifies. There are men, admittedly, who are clearheaded and coolhearted enough to make far-reaching plans for themselves and then carry them out, but there has never, surely, been a successful man who entertained such insanely complicated ambitions. The historian even suspects Raffles of having supernatural powers. Certainly he credited the Penang secretary with the gift of prophecy.

It is only natural to exaggerate the strength of one's enemy. The mind boggles at admitting that anyone but a superman could be superior to one's own compatriots. It is a case of "We weren't so stupid; it was just that Raffles was damn clever." But only the Antichrist himself could be as clever as this Dutch version of Raffles.

Besides, Mr. Vlekke commits an error which is uncharacteristic of his usually clear style and logical thought processes. Emotion does confuse people, even historians, who of all scholars can least afford the emotion of patriotism. (Yet without the urge of patriotism would Mr. Vlekke have troubled to write this particular book?) Among the paragraphs which follow on the portion we have just quoted, he scornfully calls Raffles a "crusader." But he can't have it both ways. Either Raffles was a crusader—i.e., he gave up material gain for his cause—or he was a cold-blooded schemer, interested only in personal fame. Vlekke makes both statements, accusingly, and they cannot be reconciled. Which, Mr. Vlekke, is your choice?

The answer is that Vlekke, like Boulger in another discussion of Raffles's ambition, is dogmatic, though he errs on the opposite side from Boulger's. Nowhere in the writings of Raffles himself, who is our only unassailable witness for his private hopes, and nowhere among the records of his intimate

121 ॐ

friends and relatives, do we find any proof of an inordinate desire on his part for posthumous fame. Most public servants have that desire to a certain degree. After all, who hasn't? It is one of the universal stimuli that keeps mankind at work. But it is scarcely permissible to point scornfully at a public servant whose crime lies in a lively literary style, and to say that this style is conclusive proof of his perfidious designs, to achieve fame with the next generation! Or does Vlekke really mean to show himself a complete cynic: does he really think that men who reform abuses always do it only to attract attention?

Only a prig would argue that Raffles was not sometimes actuated by motives less than sublime. He had plenty of self-interested motives in desiring a reformed administration for Java, aside from a pure desire to do good. Of course he wanted such reforms to be credited to the British East India Company rather than to the Dutch Company; to England rather than to Holland; to himself, if you will, rather than to Daendels. Of course he wanted to hold Java for England and not give it back to Holland. It is not impossible that he was gratified at making his mark on the pages of history. But these facts do not prove much to his discredit; he is not for this reason a whitewashed monster. The British Company deserves the credit he won for them; England's rule aimed at improving the lot of the Javanese and the Dutch have tacitly approved some of the British reforms by keeping them: Raffles was indubitably a better administrator than Daendels had proved himself. Possibly he exaggerated Daendels's faults and underrated his virtues when he made his reports and wrote his account of the matter, but he was far less guilty of such exaggeration than Mr. Vlekke, for example, has been, and he had a better excuse. It was a personal matter for him. It shouldn't be for the historian Vlekke.

This leaves us the last statement, that Raffles until the end fought to hold Java for Great Britain. He did, most decidedly. Certainly, too, he dreamed, as Vlekke accusingly declares, of a great British Empire in the Indies, with Java as the center, though he realized the difficulties such a program would face at the very outset, in the opposition of his own directors. He always said that Java or some other station with an equally central position was vitally necessary for Britain's commerce. In the light of some modern experts' opinion he was not correct in that belief. He overrated the power of the Dutch to sever Britain's lines of supply, and he underrated British power to keep those lines open even without grabbing a port halfway to Far Eastern points. Were these errors of judgment insincere? Was he deceiving himself or the Court of Directors when he kept after them to keep Java or, failing that, to take another station in the Indies?

Probably he was doing both—deceiving himself and misleading the Court as well, with his dire warnings and gloomy prophecies. It is every man's own guess; mine is that Raffles was an empire builder in spite of himself. His urge to create a great empire around England was an emotional one, and his reasons for doing so, sometimes good and other times specious, were all secondary rationalizations of this emotional desire. Even if you wanted to go further than that into his motives I should have to beg off. I don't know enough about the inner Raffles to do it. There is an obvious connection between his urge to acquire, to build up subsidiary British colonies, and his "crusading" desire to improve the lot of the natives coming under British jurisdiction, but I can't claim that I know how to figure it out. It is the egg and the chicken all over again: did he want to take the land in order to do good to the natives, or was he good to the natives so that England could keep the land? Or, to go further, was he good, et cetera, in order to justify England's keeping the land and taking more whenever she got the chance? Unlike Vlekke, I don't think for one second that Raffles would be able to answer that question any better than I could. Of course he would have *thought* that he knew.

Never mind all this layman's conjecture. Our job is to see the situation clearly as it existed, not merely to guess at why it all happened that way. The visible facts are these: Raffles was fortunate enough to meet Lord Minto, the only powerful Company official who shared his humanitarian principles; and

123

between them they wrote a new chapter in the book of British imperialism. The novelty of their outlook is summed up in Minto's letter, quoted in the chapter before this. Let us continue, then, with the factual story of how Java came to be borrowed by the British and what her people experienced under Raffles's administration.

Abdullah was one of the translating staff which Raffles built up in Malacca as soon as he and Olivia were settled into the old town. We know a good deal about Abdullah because he wrote his life story and it was published in England, as well as in Singapore, under the title, *The Autobiography of Munshi Abdullah*. His father had been tutor to Marsden, the oriental scholar and historian of Sumatra. They were a Malay family by adoption and Malay was their language, but Abdullah was descended from an Arab, his great-grandfather, who came from Yemen. His tribe, however, was not that of Asra, "who in loving ever perish." On the contrary they were hardy, fecund folk, to judge by the records, and they had a tradition of scholarship which they were careful to maintain.

The Arab's son became a merchant in the interior of Malacca Territory, but he was well educated, he had read the Koran, so after a time he drifted into his father's profession. His son, Abdullah's father by the merchant-preacher's Malay wife, was born in an upcountry village, and his mixed ancestry, rather than these surroundings, was responsible for his wide range of knowledge. Although he was well versed in Hindustani he was naturally more proficient in Malay, "as regards hand-writing," says Abdullah, "and composition, and writing letters to Malay princes." In Malacca city he met Marsden and served as his Malay teacher. "This gentleman gave him a letter to show that he had been his teacher," writes Abdullah. "I found this letter in my father's writing case, and showed it to the Rev. Mr. Thomsen [sic], for at that time I could not speak a word of English, much less could I read it. . . . Mr. Thomsen . . . said, 'This letter is called in English a "character," and it was given to your father by Mr. Marsden, who wrote the

Malay-English dictionary. Your father taught him for a year and eight months in the town of Malacca.' "

Abdullah's father settled in Malacca town under the Dutch, with a wife and a rapidly increasing family; he worked for the harbormaster for a bit. Then the English came and took Malacca from the Dutch, and he turned to trading, sailing between Malacca and Siak. "Malacca was a great seaport and had a fine trade, and merchandise was collected there from all directions, the town of Penang not having been founded at that time, so that the harbour of Malacca was full of traders of every race, and they came right up into the river. That was the time when most people became rich in Malacca." It was at that happy time, no doubt, that Marsden studied with Abdullah's father and gave him the letter of recommendation. Abdullah was just growing up when Major Farquhar moved in as engineer to the resident, and he saw Farquhar succeed in time to the residency. He saw the scare when the fort was razed, and the relief when the orders were revoked. When Raffles came over from Penang, his staff probably sent out word that they needed more clerks. They always needed more clerks. The young Abdullah, with two uncles, was made welcome in the office and soon, because of his superior education, he became a special sort of clerk who spent a large part of his time helping the great man. All the natives knew that Raffles was the man who had saved their city.

"When I first saw Mr. Raffles," wrote Abdullah, "he struck me as being of middle stature, neither too short nor too tall. His brow was broad, the sign of large-heartedness; his head betokened his good understanding; his hair being fair, betokened courage; his ears being large, betokened quick hearing; his eyebrows were thick, and his left eye squinted a little; his nose was high; his cheeks a little hollow; his lips narrow, the sign of oratory and persuasiveness; his mouth was wide, his neck was long; and the color of his body was not purely white; his breast was well formed; his waist slender; his legs to proportion, and he walked with a slight stoop. I observed his habit was to be always in deep thought. He was most courteous in his intercourse with all men. He always had a sweet expression towards

European as well as native gentlemen. He was extremely affable and liberal, always commanding one's best attention. He spoke in smiles. . . ."

If the observant little teacher had stopped here, the impression he left would have done nothing toward disproving Vlekke's sinister, scheming, prophetic figment. But he did not stop. After giving Olivia a similar microscopic examination, which passage has already been quoted in full in Chapter IV, Abdullah returns to the study of Raffles. Nothing is more revealing than these observations by men of different racial birth and a language far removed from our own. They are not impeded by our customs or blinded by our habits. Deaf people see things about speakers that we who hear them cannot, because we are distracted by their speech, and it works out in a similar way for natives of foreign lands on first dealing with us, the outlandish strangers. Abdullah was quick to notice characteristics in Raffles which Englishmen would never have thought worth observing. The man he paints in the following paragraphs is not Vlekke's Raffles. He is another man entirely, and an extremely attractive one.

Not everyone in Malacca agreed with Abdullah, however. Note the sentence about the Dutch in the munshi's final paragraph. If the Dutch were objects of unreasoning prejudice to Raffles, they returned his compliment with interest. Vlekke didn't dream up his villain. The portrait was painted by a contemporary, back in the nineteenth century, and Mr. Vlekke only inherited it.

"Now I observed," wrote Abdullah, "his habit was to be always deep in thought. He also was an earnest inquirer into past history, and he gave up nothing till he had probed it to the bottom. He loved most to sit in quietude, when he did nothing else but write or read; and it was his usage, when he was either studying or speaking, that he would see no one till he had finished. He had a time set apart for each duty, nor would he mingle one with another. Further, in the evenings, after tea, he would take ink, pen, and paper, after the candles had been lighted, reclining with closed eyes, in a manner that I often took to be sleep; but in an instant he would be up, and write for a while, till he went to recline again. Thus would he pass the night, till twelve or one, before he retired to sleep. This was his daily practice. On the next morning he would go to what he had written, and read it while walking backwards and forwards, when, out of ten sheets, probably he would only give three or four to his copying clerk to enter into the books, and the others he would tear up. Such was his daily habit. Now Mr. Raffles took great interest in looking into the origin of nations, and their manners and customs of olden times, examining what would elucidate the same. He was especially quick in the uptake of Malay with its variations. He delighted to use the proper idioms as the natives do; he was active in studying words and their place in phrases, and not until we had told him would he state that the English had another mode. It was his daily labour to order post letters [sic] to various Malay countries to support their good understanding with his nation, and increase the bond of friendship —this with presents and agreeable words. This gained the goodwill of the various Rajahs.

"Now Mr. Raffles' disposition was anything but covetous, for, in whatever undertakings or projects he had in view, he grudged no expense, so that they were accomplished. Thus his intentions had rapid consummation. Thus loads of money came out of his chest daily in buying various things or in paying wages. I also perceived that he hated the habit of the Dutch who lived in Malacca of running down the Malays, and they detested him in return; so much so, that they would not sit down beside him. But Mr. Raffles loved always to be on good terms with the Malays—the poorest could speak to him; and while all the great folks in Malacca came to speak to him daily, whether Malays or Europeans, yet they could not find out his object of coming there—his ulterior intentions."

We must now go back to pick up the thread of that other story which we deliberately dropped some pages back—the conquest of Mauritius and Bourbon. Lord Minto, you remember, felt himself free to discuss the projected Javanese expedition only because of the unexpected victory of the Moluccas, which, by putting several nearby islands in the hands of the British, inscribed on the map of the Indian Ocean certain arrows clearly visible to people of Raffles's persuasion, pointing suggestively toward Java.

Mauritius and Bourbon, two islands not far from the southern tip of Madagascar on a small-scale map, were in the hands of the French in 1807, when Lord Minto first came out to the East. French privateers, using them for bases, inflicted heavy losses on the Company's shipping in the Indian Ocean, and so the governor general had instructions to keep his eye on them as well as on any other islands which the French held, but he was unable to do more than keep his eye on them, much as he would have liked to take action, because he was an agent of the East India Company and they kept him short of funds. John Company was keeping everyone out East on short commons in 1807. Minto had ships though. The fleet was at his command, even though he had no money to spend on conquest, and he was deep in plans regarding those two strategically tempting little islands, figuring out ways to take them first and then pay for the war on the installment plan, when the Court of Directors got the wind up. Lord Minto received orders countermanding the original directions. He was to take his eye right off Mauritius and Bourbon. He was also to take to heart and remember that the directors were expressing "a positive prohibition of any expedition to Java and other places eastward of India." With a deep sigh Minto obediently turned around and faced west for a while.

Three years later the vigilance of the directors relaxed. At any rate they were not angry when Bourbon was invaded, perhaps because it was such a *little* invasion, such a small one that from London you would scarcely notice it at all. Admiral Bertie landed three thousand men on July 8, 1810, and after what was merely a token resistance Bourbon surrendered. The British paused only long enough to station troops on the little island and then turned their attention to the larger Mauritius, where French garrison troops under the command of General

Decaen were waiting for them. Mauritius wasn't as easy as Bourbon had been: she cost the British four ships during their first, unsuccessful, attack, on August tenth. She surrendered, however, in December. Presumably the company felt that the cost of these two victories had not been excessive, for they were now amenable, as we know, to Minto's more ambitious designs on Java. But in justice to him we should say that his unflagging attempts to persuade the Directors during the years may have had at least as much effect on them as did the victory over those strategically placed specks on the map.

The indefatigable earl did not receive word that the attacks on Bourbon and Mauritius had succeeded until the end of January. He was pleased though not surprised, and started immediately, of course, to prepare for Java. In a letter to his wife written the following month he spoke to her for what seems to be the first time of his new protégé: "I have had Mr. Raffles, Secretary to the Government of Prince of Wales's Island, a very clever, able, active and judicious man, perfectly versed in the Malay language and manners, and conversant with the interests and affairs of the Eastern States, in advance for some months past, to collect recent intelligence, to open communications with the Javanese chiefs, and to prepare the way for our operations. I carry with me good assistance of every sort, though few in number. Among these are . . . Dr. Leyden, a perfect Malay; . . ."

He evidently felt it incumbent upon him fully to explain his decision to go himself to Java. Probably he felt just a bit guilty for enjoying the expedition so much instead of sitting in his close Fort William office, being an orthodox governor general. In 1811 in the first letter of the year he says to his wife, "We are now in the agony of preparation for Java; and I will whisper in your ear that I am going there myself, not to command the army, but to see all the political wars done to my mind.

" 'Modeste' is to be my state coach." (That is, his ship.)

"Calcutta, February 25, 1811
"I am to embark in a few days for Madras. I shall then, I hope, proceed to Malacca on board the 'Modeste'—My going

129 ᘐ

in person upon this service is not a very usual measure, and my motives not being generally understood, many ingenious conjectures are, as usual, in circulation. The first notion was that I was going home, and that my touching at Madras was only a cover for my retreat; others reported that I was going to the Mauritius, and from thence to visit Bencoolen and all the other outlying settlements. A third conjecture was that some great fault had been committed at Madras, and that I was going to set things right there. My own reasons are that there are many important points, regarding our future relations with the Dutch, and with the native States in Java, which ought to be adjusted at the moment of the attack; that . . . [it would be] impossible to get complete information at a distance, that modifications may be necessary. I think Admiral Drury is fond of acting for himself, and M. would have no security for the execution of his plans. Upon the whole, I am of the opinion I should not perfectly discharge my duty without going. . . .

"The object we have in view is of the greatest national importance, and it is of infinite consequence that the first political arrangement should be made on the right principles. For this I should have been equally responsible if I had remained at Calcutta, but I could not have made an adequate provision for it by any other course than that I am now pursuing. It is not matter of taste or choice, but of duty, or rather of necessity, that I am going to friskify in this manner, although I confess, since it is right, that I never engaged in any affair with greater interest or more pleasure; and you will easily conceive what a gratifying break this kind of adventure must make in the monotony of my not less laborious life at Fort William."

Things were moving toward Java at a good rate of speed. A letter from Leyden gives us some feeling of the excitement that must have prevailed in Raffles's Malacca home, the hurried preparations for the great man's visit, the whisperings and elaborate precautions which were deemed necessary even then, for the expedition was still, officially, being kept secret from France. Just as though a secret like that could be kept, one week, in the Orient! I often wonder why Raffles pretended to believe it could, and why he played the pompous game so solemnly. Probably he enjoyed the play acting.

Lord Minto wrote to Raffles from Calcutta, in March, "I still hope we may take our final departure from Malacca in April." He must have set out a few days after this letter was posted, and one wonders why he took the trouble to write at all, when he was so soon to be with Raffles in person. But perhaps he did it deliberately so that he could thus informally place the following promise on record: "It is proposed to style you Secretary to the Governor-General when we come together: . . . secretary is the highest office below the Council. I hope you do not doubt the *prospective* interest I have always taken, and do not cease to take, in your personal views and welfare. I have not spoken distinctly on that subject, only because it has been from circumstances impossible for me to pledge myself to the fulfilment of my own wishes, and, I may add, intentions, if practicable. The best is, in truth, still subject to one contingency, the origin of which is earlier than my acquaintance with you; but I am happy to say that I do not expect an obstacle to my very strong desire upon this point; and if it should occur, the utmost will be done to make the *best attainable situation* worthy of your services, and of the high esteem I profess, with the greatest sincerity, for your person."

The governor general and his retinue arrived in Malacca on May 18, 1811. Raffles was undoubtedly in a tizzy about it, and Olivia must have been fairly busy herself with housekeeping cares, preparing for their august guest. Nobody watched the pageant more appreciatively, though, than Abdullah. He recorded it all with enthusiasm, beginning with the salutes which were fired as the ships approached, a few every day until the roadstead was crowded. He noted with joy the regimental uniforms of the British soldiers, the many Indians, Malays, and other Orientals who made up the greater part of the army and rendered life difficult with their religious dietary taboos, and of course the navy with its British officers. The army tents were surrounded constantly by thousands of staring Malaccans.

H. S. Banner, in a novel about Java and the conquest, goes

131 {≈

into details about those colorful British uniforms—the Bengal native infantry wore scarlet coats faced with the different colors of their regiments; the Madras Horse Artillery were all red and blue; the Madras Pioneers were comparatively sober in gray and black; but the Royal Marines outshone them all— they wore red coatees with blue facings and shiny steeple hats.

It is no wonder that Abdullah had naïvely expected the Great Lord Minto to look like an Indian nabob, weighted down with brilliant silks and satins and jewels. The bigger the official the more splendidly he would be attired, Abdullah told himself, and so the governor general, who held a higher rank than the little scholar had ever yet encountered, must be of dazzling, blinding gorgeousness. One feels the mounting excitement in the town as the *Modeste*, the flagship, sails into view, last of all the fleet to arrive. Everyone in Malacca who could walk was down on shore to watch the great lord disembark.

Effectively Abdullah described the actual appearance of Minto. The humanitarian statesman was "middle-aged, thin in body, of soft manners, and sweet countenance; and I felt that he could not carry twenty cutties [catties: about thirty pounds that would be] so slow were his motions. His coat was black cloth, trowsers the same, nor was there anything peculiar."

After the first surprise Abdullah was soon scolding himself for having felt disappointment. He need not have worried about the august visitor's failure to provide excitement, for from that moment when Minto landed on the beach the town was whipped into a whirlwind of rumor, the wildest of which was founded on fact.

For example, the day after he arrived, Minto set out to inspect the town prisons. At the first one, which was evidently an ordinary jail for malefactors of a less serious sort, the culprits were all allowed to come out of their cells to pay him homage in greeting. A ragged, pitiful crew, they ran in a small mob toward Minto, swiftly approaching him as he came on foot; they fell on their knees or on their faces, clutching at his garments, all crying out together, begging for attention, for mercy, for pardon, for justice. Abdullah saw tears in Minto's eyes. No doubt the demonstration and greeting had all been arranged beforehand between Raffles and his chief, but the prisoners didn't know it, and I doubt if those tears were part of the preconceived plan. Minto gave the word in Hindustani: "Don't you worry, in a moment everyone will be set free," and the promise was kept, as a sort of good-luck gesture on the eve of the expedition, and also no doubt to win the good will of the natives for the British.

Scarcely had the populace ceased to marvel at the fortune of those prisoners when Minto, next day, paid another visit, this time to a special sort of dungeon reserved for extraordinary criminals. This was a really nasty pesthole farther out from town, well furnished with the efficient implements of torture which the Dutch had used.

"When Lord Minto saw all these appliances," wrote Abdullah, "he looked very cross, and he spat several times, and said to the man in charge of the implements, 'Take these down below and burn them; don't let one of them remain.'"

The prisoners themselves took part in the ceremony of the burning, and meanwhile Minto gave orders that the prison should be entirely destroyed. A model new one was later put up in its place, and Abdullah takes time off to sing a hymn in its praise. It must really have been a great improvement. Our Abdullah was particularly impressed that visitors were allowed to call on their relatives in the new jail. It was the most noteworthy gesture the governor general of Bengal made during his entire stay at Malacca, and we are fortunate to have Minto's own account of the memorable day, a passage in one of his letters to Lady Minto.

". . . One of the pleasantest parts of the celebration took place privately after the levee. I released all the Government slaves at Malacca, presenting to each with my own hand a certificate of their freedom and four dollars to provide for their immediate subsistence till they can get into some way of life. They have also the option of resuming their former state if they find a difficulty in maintaining themselves. They are only nineteen in number, male and female, of all ages, from infants in arms to old helpless people. Most of them are *born* slaves to the Dutch Company, some to the English, and all their children would have continued slaves. Slavery is established in all these countries to a shocking extent. An insolvent debtor, however small his debt, is condemned to be the slave of the creditor. Some have been slaves for life for 100 or 200 dollars, and if the sum is considerable the whole family shares the same fate. Men may gamble their children, their wives, and lastly themselves into slavery, in satisfaction of bets upon fighting cocks, or any other gambling debt; nothing is more common. If a criminal is condemned to slavery, his whole family goes with him; or if he is put to death, the wife and children, young and old, after witnessing the execution, are sold into slavery—the mother to one master, the children to others. I speak now, not of Malacca, but of other Malay countries, including Java. I hope something may be done—partly by authority, partly by influence—to mitigate these horrors; in the meanwhile the people of Malacca have been told and have seen that the English think no man should be deprived of his liberty except criminals. Another proof has been given to them that we dislike cruelty. Finding some instruments of torture still preserved, although they have been long disused, I had the cross upon which criminals were *broken*, and another wooden instrument that had served as a sort of rack, burnt under the windows of a room from which executions are seen by the magistrates, where I and the magistrates were assembled for the purpose; at the same time various iron articles for screwing thumbs, wrists, and ankles, and other contrivances of that diabolical sort, were carried out in a boat by the executioner into the roads, and sunk in deep water, never to rise or screw poor people's bones and joints again."

The lady who edited her distinguished kinsman's letters has found the following footnote by Thomson, one of Abdullah's translators, and appends it, as is fitting, thus:

". . . as a memento of the deliverance of the prisoners and of other high-minded acts at Malacca, Lord Minto's portrait was procured and hung up in the resident magistrate's office, where he is represented as breaking the shackles of cruelty.

When I saw it in 1848, I viewed it with great curiosity. The climate had so destroyed the colours that it might have served for a black Madonna."

Abdullah was there when Minto called on Mrs. Raffles at home, paying his first ceremonial visit. The great man chatted a little with the clerk, shook hands with him—"His hand was delicate and soft as a woman's," Abdullah remembers—and then passed on to the interior reception room. Raffles, of course, called on Minto daily at the earl's quarters. Writing to his wife, Minto spoke of Olivia, and we learn from the same letter that the Raffles household was now augmented by all three of the sisters. (Two of them were shortly to depart under the protection of their newly married husbands, Mary Anne as Mrs. Captain Flint and Leonora as Mrs. B. Loftie.)

"Mrs. Raffles," wrote the earl, "is the great lady with dark eyes, lively manner, accomplished and clever. She had a former husband in India, and I have heard, but am not sure of the fact, that she was one of the beauties to whom Anacreontic Moore addressed many of his amatory elegies." Lord Minto's informant must have been mistaken, for as it has since been pointed out Olivia and the Irish poet were not contemporaries. Unless he wrote his elegies at the tender age of twelve or thereabouts, he didn't write them to Olivia Fancourt, because he never saw her again. "The sisters are all fair," Minto's letter goes on, "one a very pretty woman. You need not smile, Anna Maria, for George says so." George was Minto's son, commander of the ship he traveled in. "She is the wife of Captain Flint of the Royal Navy; the other two, to avoid sneering, I shall say, are honest-like. I have exchanged dinners with them, have breakfasted and visited there."

Thus the shadowy Olivia once more takes on substance for us, in spite of Sophia's determination to blot her out. "Dark eyes, lively manner, accomplished and clever." Obviously the earl meant it sincerely when he used the word "accomplished": he was not saying it with the delicately scornful connotation of Jane Austen's young clergyman from Northanger Abbey.

The coming battle for Java did not cast a shadow over the spirits of Malacca's white population. On the contrary, the great man Minto's visit was the excuse for a whirl of parties such as had not been seen since white men first moved into the city. Besides, people usually do feel gay and excited at the beginning of important military events, however they may feel afterward. Look at the ball held by the Duke and Duchess of Richmond in Brussels, just before Waterloo, and the parties given in Hong Kong to honor the newly arrived Canadian troops just when Pearl Harbor was brewing; look at the social columns in any city during all the wars, except, perhaps, this latest one. We seem to have discovered, somehow, since Pearl Harbor, that war is not such a junket after all. Or perhaps it is just that we have cut the gold trimming off our modern battle dress. Even in mess kit our gallant warriors aren't such beautiful dancing partners as they used to be.

However, there was plenty of gold braid around in 1811. The governor general of Bengal was frankly in high spirits, and the agent for the government of Malacca saw small reason to conceal his transports either. His dear friend Leyden had arrived with Minto. Everyone he loved best was there, under his roof. The penniless office boy of 1795 was playing host to the aristocracy of England in Asia. The great ones of his world were proving to be men very like himself, men who shared his tastes, his opinions, his dearest hopes. One of the most cherished of his plans, the acquisition of Java, was coming to fruition under the happiest auspices. The frosting on the cake, for this soldier in blue stockings, was that the Asiatic Society held a meeting while the Earl of Minto was in Malacca, in special honor of their distinguished visitor, and of course it was a meeting de luxe, with everyone showing off his best paces and his lordship himself presiding.

Dinner parties, soirees, card parties, amateur theatricals, all the pageantry of colonial life at its most secure was there. The men's uniforms vied with the ladies' best gowns in brilliancy and glitter. It was all very exciting and amusing, taking Java away from the French. Never had Malacca been in so much of a bustle, though in truth the ancient town had seen the start and finish of other expeditions. And of other empires too.

CHAPTER IX

If in the last chapter we were a bit hard on the Dutch, too much attention to Mr. Boulger's account of the Java expedition rather throws us in the other direction, and might very likely start a prejudice working in our minds against the British. Human nature is like that. Great Britain's righteous indignation with the Dutch in Java makes me want to ask Mr. Vlekke to move over and make room for me. His Dutch ire (which incidentally he does not claim to be righteous) is very natural.

For Mr. Boulger really does overdo it. In his own words and also with a carefully chosen quotation from the *History of Java* (author, Thomas Stamford Raffles) he draws, first, a picture of Paradise which he calls Java, and then—but here is the picture. The climate of Java, though varied, is delightful. The cottages of the natives are charming, airy, sunlit, and placed so cunningly against the verdurous background as to be invisible to the untutored eye, though why this should be desirable Boulger does not explain. The fields of crops are lovely in every phase, but most particularly do they take the breath in beauty during the harvest season, when the crop is golden yellow. . . . And now, let's look at what the Dutch did to all this.

"The island might have been an earthly paradise; it became, wherever the contaminating power of the Dutch was felt, a long scene of misery and smothered discontent. Fair and fer-

tile provinces, once peopled by a happy peasantry, were turned
into vast farms or factories of sullen bondage, worked by a
rapidly diminishing race," et cetera, et cetera.

It was the Dutch;
It was the Dutch . . .

Now all this is true enough, as Vlekke readily admits. It's
the way Boulger says it that seems unfair somehow. What ir-
ritates us is probably the unctuous tone and the emphatic suggestion, so constantly repeated, that all this is peculiarly the
fault of those Dutch; that the Netherlands always, and only the
Netherlands, ruin the paradises of the world. It betrays a lack
of moderation in reporting which one usually finds only in
daily newspapers, and only during wartime. It is so very biased
that to come across it in a standard book of history is startling.
This work was intended for use as a reference book, and for all
time, whether in peace or war. Any unsuspecting Dutchman,
reading it, will probably be more than startled; he is fairly certain to be infuriated, particularly if he knows that many of his
compatriots, settled in Java at the time of the British invasion,
were heartily pro-British at first and helped the English to the
best of their ability in driving out the French. [Oddly enough
Boulger some years later wrote a book which was as much in
favor of the Dutch as *Raffles* is prejudiced against it.]

However, once Mr. Boulger has assuaged his conscience and
feels satisfactorily convinced that the invasion was justified, he
becomes again a careful and accurate historian, and a better
source of information for our purposes than a military expert's
technical report might be. We need not use all the material he
offers so lavishly, for Raffles had done his usual job and snowed
his superiors under with data. He knew exactly which rulers
among the many petty princes would work for him, which
would support the defense, and which preferred to remain on
the fence until they were sure of the safe side on which to
jump down. He made an ally of a powerful Sumatran prince
and arranged that this ruler should supply the troops regularly
with fresh meat. He thought of everything. Considering his

civilian status, he really did do a good, military job of intelligence. His informants estimated the garrison to be twenty thousand strong; it proved afterward to have been seventeen thousand.

One of Daendels's many sweeping reforms was to move the government from Batavia, which was low and marshy, to Buitenzorg in the healthier hills. The Dutchman also gave signs of expecting help from outside; at least it was reported that he seemed cheerful and confident, a state of mind which his existing defenses did not seem to warrant. Raffles wrote, "The fall of Mauritius has no doubt fully confirmed his apprehensions of the nature of the intended attack. It seems currently believed in Java that the Marshal expects almost immediate assistance from France."

We owe Abdullah thanks as usual; this time it is for a glimpse of our hero in a refreshingly unheroic dilemma, upon one occasion when he fell down on the job and, along with England and the Company, was had for a sucker. This is how it happened:

Two weeks or so before Minto was supposed to arrive in the flagship, and very shortly before the early birds among the fleet were due in Malacca, Raffles held an audience with the King of Siak, whose name was Těngku Pěnglima Běsar. This petty King had come to Malacca to be there during Raffles's stay: Abdullah, who usually knows everything, confesses that he is not sure in this case whether Těngku was actually summoned by Raffles or simply turned up on his own, in order to show his loyalty. At any rate he was there, living at the expense of Raffles's "expedition fund": his house, his servants, his carriage, and his pocket money were all provided by the Company, for that was part of the great game Raffles was playing. Siak is a small state between Java and Malacca.

One day Raffles told Těngku that he very much wanted someone he could trust to carry a letter to one of the sultans in Java, the Susunan of Bantaram [probably Mataram], in order to feel this chief out, "that I may get reliable intelligence as to conditions there, and as to whether he intends to side with the Dutch or not. If I can get a trustworthy man who can keep a secret, to take my letter to Java, I shall be very much pleased."

Dramatically the King of Siak leaped to his feet and brandished his kris, one of those curved daggers which are carried by almost every Malay. "What is the good of this kris?" he cried. "As long as I have 'Si-hijau' [his pet name for the weapon], wherever you go, sir, I will be in front of you; and I must die first before you can be killed. Write your letter, sir, and I will take it to the Susunan of Bantaram."

Abdullah, who anticipated the technique of modern novelists by always being behind a nearby curtain or outside an adjacent window when interesting things were happening, saw Raffles's face light up at this. With sincere emotion he thanked Těngku Pěnglima Běsar, shook both his hands and assured him of England's everlasting (and practical) gratitude. For the next few hours they discussed elaborate arrangements, and finally Těngku brought to the Raffles house one Pengerang, the son of a Javanese chief, who declared himself able and willing to show Těngku the proper place to land with his message, when they should have arrived at Java. Raffles prepared his letter for the Susunan and put together presents to the value of two or three hundred dollars. He paid Těngku four hundred dollars for expenses and gave him for himself two boxes of valuable opium and two hundred dollars more. (Oh, Abdullah and his greedy sharp eyes!)

Most important, according to Těngku, was the letter of safe-conduct which Raffles wrote for him, through which he could be sure of the freedom of the seas on his way, permitted by British ships to go where he liked. "Hurry back," was Raffles's last order, often repeated, "because the Lord Minto will arrive in a fortnight and we must sail soon after that. Don't stop anywhere on the way."

He sent the men in his own fast cutter and watched them away, standing on the beach. Then he turned to pressing duties of preparation for the expected arrival.

Time passed. The messengers should have come back, but they didn't. They were due, then overdue. Raffles was worried, and so was Lord Minto, learning how important the matter was. But the expedition couldn't wait, even on the Susunan of Bantaram; everything had to go on according to plan. Some of the fleet set sail, more ships departed, and still no Tĕngku came. All of the fleet, save the very last few with the *Modeste* herself, had gone when a government signaler brought news at last: the long-awaited cutter was in sight. Just in time, too: the *Modeste* was to sail in a week at the outside, some of her officers did not want to wait even that long, and Raffles was very eager for the information he had sent for.

Tĕngku and Pengerang landed and came straight to his house, carefully and proudly carrying a letter wrapped, native fashion, in a yellow cloth.

"Well, what is the news, Tĕngku?" asked Raffles. "Are you well?"

"Quite well, sir: I was very nearly killed by being stabbed; but only two of my men were killed, being stabbed as they went ashore to take the letter."

"Don't worry, Tĕngku," said Raffles; "the English Company will adequately reward all your labor. If we succeed in taking the island of Java I will ask Lord Minto to let you govern a province, whichever one you like. Now what about the letter?"

With a flourish Tĕngku produced the yellow bundle, and Raffles eagerly grabbed it. "Did you yourself meet the Susunan?" he asked.

Tĕngku said, "I did, sir, at night; and he told me that whenever the English wished to come and take the island of Java, he was ready to come and help on shore." He went on to describe the dangers he had run, and the fierce fight they had had with Javanese who surprised them in the interview. Oh, he was fluent, and Pengerang, standing there, had no chance to talk, but he kept confirming his superior's words. At last the travelers took their leave and went back to town, to their houses.

That afternoon Raffles sent again for Pengerang, as the only Javanese handy, to read the Susunan's letter to him, and to interpret as he went. Pengerang obediently did so. After the customary compliments to the Company and to Raffles himself, the missive continued, said Pengerang, "The letter and the things sent me have been received, and as for our friend's request to us, we are ready waiting and whenever our friend comes to Java, we will come to his assistance on shore."

As Pengerang ceased reading, Raffles gazed at nothing for a long time, sunk in thought. Pengerang waited a bit, hesitating, then took his leave.

It was plain—at least it was plain to Abdullah and no doubt to others as well—that Raffles was uneasy somehow. He seemed "unsettled," the clerk noted. Every now and then he would take up the letter, look at it, and put it down. That afternoon he changed his usual habit and didn't ride out in his carriage to take the air. He didn't seem to want to leave the house at all. All night he was like that, restless and worried and thoughtful, and the moment Abdullah saw him the next morning at nine o'clock he knew that his chief was still in the same frame of mind. He was leaning back in his chair, holding the letter in his hand. In the course of the morning's work in the office he carried it with him everywhere.

Suddenly he ran downstairs, still carrying the letter, to the big workroom where several clerks were writing.

"Ibrahim," he said, "bring me four or five sheets of the paper that is in the cupboard."

He took the fresh paper and the Susunan's letter and held them out together to the secretary, saying, "Is the number of this paper on which this letter is written the same as this paper, or not?" (His words were probably, "Is the quality the same?" but Abdullah evidently uses some local idiom, some office language, which in translation is not clear.)

All the clerks answered together, without hesitation, "Exactly the same; there is no difference, except that it is a little crumpled by the hand which wrote it."

Raffles immediately sent a policeman to fetch Pengerang. He arrived, pale as a ghost. Raffles let him stand outside on the veranda while for a long time he marched up and down, up and down. About twenty times he did this, ignoring the Javanese. Suddenly he turned, still holding the letter; he rushed at Pengerang, and very nearly struck him—nearly, but not quite. Abdullah, peeping through the window, fully expected to see a blow.

"Did the Susunan of Bantaram really give this letter?" Raffles shouted.

Pengerang, his face corpselike, was silent.

"Don't you hear what I ask?" yelled Raffles. "If you don't tell the truth, I will have you hanged this moment!"

Pengerang, his feet and hands shaking, still remained silent. Abdullah says that Raffles's face grew almost blue with anger.

RAFFLES: "You won't tell the truth?"

PENGERANG: "Sir, what can I do?"

RAFFLES: "What is that? Tell the truth."

PENGERANG: "Sir, I was a subordinate under the orders of Tĕngku Pĕnglima Bĕsar, and I obeyed whatever he ordered; if I had not obeyed, he would have killed me."

RAFFLES: "What is that? How did it begin? Tell the truth; if not, it will be the worse for you."

PENGERANG: "How can I tell it? For I have sworn on the Koran not to reveal this secret."

RAFFLES: "That is no use, you must tell it."

The sorry, sickening story came out piecemeal, in painful fashion. Cut down to essentials, the mission hadn't gone to Java at all. They had put in first at Siak, because, as Tĕngku said, the wind was too strong for sailing. There he took some of the valuables ashore straight off and probably gambled them away, piece by piece. At any rate he seemed to be in a vile temper when he came back empty-handed to the cutter. He took all the rest of the stuff that time. Before long he was openly practicing piracy—piracy, in Raffles's own cutter, using Raffles's safe-conduct! When the time came to go back to Malacca, he pondered long, evidently, and at last decided that not to turn up at all would be fatal. A King of Siak couldn't simply disappear, after all; someday he would surely be caught if he tried that. And so . . . and so he made Pengerang swear secrecy on the Koran and write that phony letter, and . . .

Abdullah says that Raffles, as the long story of treachery was disclosed by Pengerang, gnawed at his finger, and at the end he

143 ॐ

stamped on the floor. His face was flushed as he said, "You go downstairs."

Alone—or anyway thinking he was alone, for Abdullah remained discreetly concealed—he acted like a man in great trouble, sighing from time to time. Abdullah understood. It was the day he was to take his luggage and go aboard the *Modeste*. All of this could not have been less opportune or more worrying an omen. Every remaining ship but the flagship was sailing that very day, and the *Modeste's* date of departure was now put ahead and scheduled for the next day.

Still, the news had to be transmitted to the other heads of the expedition, and so he sent out word. At three in the afternoon their carriages began to roll up to his door, all the men anxious to hear what news had come from Bantaram. Raffles, his clerk thought, was suffering cruelly from humiliation, but I don't think so, as I said before. Still, it is possible. He might very likely have felt that Těngku's defection reflected on his judgment of character, and of course the financial loss was his responsibility, and the use of his private cutter as a pirate vessel was no more or less than a wicked joke on him. . . . Yes, Raffles probably did feel humiliated. But first and foremost he must have been a badly worried man. Now the expedition would have to set out without that important information as to the Sultan of Bantaram's true intentions.

Minto's arrival was the signal for assembly, and when they were ready Raffles sent for Těngku Pěnglima Běsar, giving private orders to the sepoy on guard not to let him bring any of his retinue into the house. They were to remain outside the door while their chief entered alone.

As soon as he appeared before the assembly Raffles shouted at him: "Go away! Don't stand in front of me any longer! I do not want to see the face of a liar and a pirate." If Těngku didn't get out immediately he would tie him at a cannon's mouth and shoot it off; and if the party had not been sailing so soon, he added, he would certainly see that Těngku should hang.

Abdullah's private opinion was that Raffles meant to convey a hint in his angry ravings, and it does sound rather like it. He said, "The small boat is leaving at four-thirty"; without some such explanation this ambiguous statement doesn't make sense at all. Raffles must have been telling Těngku in this round-about manner that the prince had better get out of town instanter, and would if he knew what was best for him, otherwise the speaker, Raffles, would have no recourse but to punish him as he deserved. There is small doubt that Raffles didn't really want to carry vengeance as far as all that against a native king. No matter how much he may have longed, personally, to hang the man, he knew such an action would reflect adversely on the British and would have harmful repercussions. Therefore, even while he screamed and raved and abused Těngku Pěnglima Běsar, he was warning and directing the prince at the same time. It is a nice picture, the worthy British officers in righteous wrath assembled, nodding as one in approval while Raffles ranted and roared, and all the while, subtle as any Oriental, transmitted his message to the craven prince at the top of his voice. It is a very nice picture.

Těngku Pěnglima Běsar duly escaped that night by sampan, probably going straight back to Siak. What the British gentlemen said among themselves Abdullah doesn't report. After all, there was very little that could be said at that late stage of the game.

We learned at first hand in the recent war that the chief problem facing the invader is always how to get there. When the invasion is to take place on another continent or an island, the task is doubly formidable. The United Nations, when they made their celebrated landing in North Africa, planted the seed of victory then and there. But they had the resources of half the world at their disposal. To the earl and his aides, contemplating the transportation problems involved in moving their little army from Malacca to Java, the job must have looked at least as tough as that which the United Nations dealt with in 1942.

Two sea routes were possible, neither of them particularly inviting. One voyage, round the northern tip of Borneo, would take at least two months, with luck and barring accidents. The navigation was risky though. And if they elected to go this way, they would have to put off the whole thing, because otherwise the rainy season, due in a month or six weeks, would overtake them about halfway even if they started immediately.

The other route by the southwest was known only by hearsay, but its reputation was bad. Navigation was supposedly far worse that way than by the North Borneo passage.

Raffles, backed up by Minto as usual, refused to accept these vague accounts, which if they were believed would have discouraged everyone from attempting to do anything whatever. He dared not take a risk with the whole fleet however. Though time was precious, unless he were to decide to hang around Malacca for months with the entire expedition, waiting for the end of the rains, he allotted three weeks for research. At his suggestion the efficient, intelligent Captain Greigh took his ship ahead to explore the unknown channel, with the understanding that he was to make his report within twenty days at the most. The point to be considered was not the advisability of going by the southwest; Raffles and Minto had decided already that they had no choice and must use it. What was still unsettled was whether they should go by the Strait of Macassar or the Karimata Passage.

In twenty days, as he had promised, Greigh returned, and with welcome news. The Karimata Passage appeared quite feasible. Moreover, it was his opinion that the voyage could be accomplished in a month, or six weeks at the very outside.

Many of the officers wagged their heads dubiously when the plans were announced, and no wonder. From start to finish the thing was unorthodox. These naval and military men were not only mercenaries hired by the Company, a good many were soldiers of the Crown, which was sharing in the venture with the government's Siamese twin. It was Lord Minto, the good Englishman, who had arranged that. Now they found themselves in a most unconventional position, in the hands of a youthful civilian who was not even in government, a merchant with no claim to experience in the field of naval or military campaigns, a self-confessed amateur, even in navigation. And failure on the field of battle was not the chief thing that the soldiers had to worry about, for once. The tropical waters of the Indies are infested with sharks. . . .

What could they do when the governor general himself was always on Raffles's side? Nothing; not even hint. Pity the officers of His Majesty's Army and Navy whose fate had sent them on the Java expedition. But pity Raffles, too, for the weight of responsibility he was carrying. A less imaginative man would only have enjoyed his brief, extraordinary authority, but for Raffles it was as if he were worrying with the combined anxieties of every man in the party. He wasn't used to it. I wonder how many nights of good unbroken slumber he enjoyed after the expedition set sail with him from Malacca. He probably counted ships instead of sheep—one hundred ships, and eleven thousand men, a lot of ships and a lot of men. And the man on whom they depended, the agent who had brought them all to Malacca and was now leading them to Java, the one single solitary thirty-year-old dreamer who had brought it all to pass, was Thomas Stamford Raffles.

A century later Raffles would certainly have developed stomach ulcers. Fortunately for him and his associates, stomach ulcers hadn't yet been discovered.

History says the expedition started out from Malacca on June 11, 1811, but that is because History is an orderly muse, strongly prejudiced against anything vague or indefinite when it comes to dates. The fleet did not set sail on any one day, because Minto forbade this and made them divide the ships (fifty-seven of which were transports) into groups in order to avoid bumping and crowding. The troops, eleven thousand, were a mixture of white men and natives. There had been more at the beginning, but twelve hundred were already casualties left in the Malacca hospitals, victims of the ordinary tropical complaints, probably for the most part dysentery.

Pride of the fleet was the *Modeste*, commanded by the Hon. George Elliot, Minto's son, and naturally she was the earl's choice for flagship. The *Modeste* carried himself and his closest friends, of whom Raffles was of course numbered. She made much better time than the others, so Elliot kept her in port a week beyond the day the first of the fleet sailed. In no time, however, she was leading, and Lord Minto, his high spirits continuing, wrote his wife: "Commodore Broughton, who is the most cautious navigator that ever wore a blue coat, was not satisfied to abide by Greigh's report, but ordered the *Modeste* to go ahead and reconnoitre the whole passage, thinking, very properly, that I had better drown than he. As I was entirely of the same opinion, I accepted the service very thankfully. In reality I knew that George was much fitter to perform this duty than any other officer in the fleet, and I thought it would be amusing to myself."

It has been a long time since we depended on sail. We simply do not realize the difficulties of such navigation even while we are claiming that we understand. Nobody could, who hasn't lived with it. They really were giants in those days, who went out in such small force, in such cranky craft, to make war on foreign shores. Beset with disease—and remember, every fever was a mystery, and every recovery was pure luck—not knowing most of the fundamental rules of hygiene, those officers and such men as were not natives, but British, had yet another unofficial foe to conquer. The name of it was Discomfort. Those Company quartermasters were too new at empire building to realize the need of special uniforms for the tropics, so the unfortunate British set out under the blazing skies of the East as heavily caparisoned as they would have been in chilly, gray-skied Europe.

Lord Minto has noted in a brief account some few of the problems faced by his son and the other naval officers.

"The difficulty was this. As soon as what is called the southeast monsoon in the eastern seas sets in, the wind blows hard and pretty steadily from the east along the channel between the north of Java and the south of Borneo; it blows to the north-west along the east coast of Sumatra, and between that coast and the Malay Peninsula; it blows to the north between the west coast of Borneo and the Straits of Malacca. So that, starting from Malacca, the wind was directly contrary in every part of the course to the northern coast of Java. Besides this difficulty there is a current in the same direction as the wind throughout. To carry a great fleet of transports, not famous in general for working to windward, a long voyage directly against wind and current, did not appear promising. It was known, however, that with a little patience, a fleet can at that season make a passage down the Straits of Malacca by any one of the several passages which lead to the eastward. This is done by the help of squalls, which generally blow from the northward; by occasional shifts of wind, and by alterations of tide or current, which afford a favourable start to the eastward. . . ."

Captain Greigh's estimate had been accurate. The full fleet glided up Java's coast just six weeks after setting forth—though the *Modeste*, of course, could have arrived a week sooner, according to proud Papa Elliot, Lord Minto. They assembled on that part of the coast opposite Batavia.

"I will not attempt to say what my feelings were on the occasion," wrote Raffles (in his autobiography). "We had separated from the fleet for a few days, and it was only when we again joined them that we saw all the divisions united at the close of one of the finest days I ever recollect, and this in sight of the Land of Promise." But even if it had rained, hailed, and snowed, it would have been fine weather for the happy Raffles that day. "Lord Minto, while at Malacca, had communicated his intention of appointing me to the government in case of success; and, as I had nothing to do with the military operations, I now looked upon my part as completed—perhaps a greater responsibility was never for so long on the head of a single individual, and the relief which I felt was proportionate." Yes, for a moment the *Modeste's* sails must have been filled with the heartiest sigh of relief ever heard in the history of the Indies.

From now on the leader of the expedition would be the commander of troops, General Sir Samuel Auchmuty, a good friend of Lord Minto's and a talented officer. He had started out with troops numbering just short of twelve thousand. A tenth part of these, remember, was left ill in Malacca. Fifteen hundred more fell ill en route to Java: this left him with nine thousand against the Dutch General Janssens's seventeen thousand. But those are customary odds in an invasion.

The name of the place along the Javanese coast where the

troops disembarked, on August sixth, is Chillinching Bay, and there in a small village the British troops prepared for the march on Batavia. "The troops were so well behaved," wrote Minto proudly, "that they did not even kiss an old woman without her consent." It doesn't sound like war in Asia as we know it. Today (February 4, 1946) is marked in the news by a few developments in the trials of the Japanese "war criminals" Yamashita and Homma. What kind of letters, I wonder, did the Japanese commanders write to their wives from the victorious battlefields of Manila and Singapore, four years ago? Proud, small doubt of that; burstingly, overweeningly proud, and with reason. They had lived up to their traditions as Minto lived up to his. Today at their trials they seem bewildered by our code of honor. Spiritual heirs to the Earl of Minto, we are placing emphasis on what seems to the Japanese generals the most utterly trivial matters. So their soldiers were cruel to their prisoners? So a few thousand women were raped, an occasional civilian got himself bayoneted? So what? A truly courageous army is the only virtuous army. What, they wonder dully as they stand in court, and plod back to the cells, and plod out again for the next day's inexplicable proceedings, what is the idea of going over and over these boring details? To try a man in court because he surrendered, that is a different matter and it makes sense. To kill Yamashita and Homma only serves them right, think Homma and Yamashita. They should have killed themselves first, before falling into the hands of the enemy. They are worse than dead right now, and death will be a welcome escape. Oh, bitter humiliation, to have met defeat at the hands of these masqueraders, these civilian sheep in wolves' clothing, these uniformed eunuchs who place value on the worthless lives of cowards and talk mystifying nonsense about forcing women, just as if women were not created to be forced!

The entire passage from Minto's letter, which is practically a journal of the first three days, is as follows:

"The disembarkation took place without any kind of opposition. All the troops, a few field pieces and part of the stores were landed that evening and in the course of the night. The horses, ordnance, and additional stores were put on shore next day. . . . This village is principally Chinese. They made us welcome; and brought their articles out for sale with very flattering confidence. This was justified by the exemplary behaviour of the troops, who paid their way and did not even kiss an old woman without her consent. There has been but one drunken man in two days.

"*August 7.* As everything has been quiet, and the army remained at Chillinching, where the general [Auchmuty] occupied the only gentleman's house, I have continued on the 'Modeste' and go on shore when I like. Yesterday I took a ride with the General to the advanced post, about four miles, and then returned to the 'Modeste.' The country is like Chinese paper on a wall. Canals, tanks and narrow ways between; here and there a little dry ground, and these spaces are in a state of high cultivation. Every now and then we found a gentleman's house with no appearance of splendour, but always marked by the characteristic neatness of the Dutch. Our road ran westward parallel to the sea; the right of the line of the troops on the sea, the left inland. I had an opportunity of observing what may be deemed, I believe, a pretty nearly unexampled degree of discipline in the troops. They do not use tents, and have as yet had only their salt provisions. They are posted in gardens and orchards with cottages and houses of a better description, surrounded with poultry, fruit and vegetables. No fresh beef or pork was to be procured, the cattle and pigs having been very generally removed by order of the Government. In these circumstances we saw the peasants living as quietly in their own houses and carrying on their usual occupations with as little annoyance, apprehension, or even notice of an invading army in the midst of them, as if we were all their near relations on a visit. You see the trees laden with cocoa, nuts and plantains, acres of onions, cabbage and many tempting things, not one taken, nor the slightest offence given to a single inhabitant. Not a duck or a hen made free with, money offered and given in every instance for what the people are willing to spare. . . . The gentlemen's houses and other habitations of a middling kind being deserted, with some old slave or servant left behind to look after them, the officers have astonished these guardians by refusing to occupy the houses with clean beds and neat furniture, and sleeping sometimes in the verandah, sometimes in a separate pavillion, and never in the house; and the cocks are seen fighting, the hens and chickens pecking about, and the ducks gobbling and dabbling, just as if they were our own fellow-subjects. I observed yesterday to the General, as we were passing the house of the Dutch Paymaster-General, that a battle which we saw between two of his cocks was the only thing like war I could perceive in our invasion.

"*August 9.* The advance of the army having moved forward to a place about three miles from Batavia, the General sent a summons to the city which was immediately acknowledged by a surrender at discretion. The enemy, in order to concentrate their force at a place called Cornelis, had withdrawn the troops on the 6th, and set fire to some public stores and to the citadel; the town was therefore glad of our protection against a disposition to plunder and disorders manifested by the slaves and lower class of Malays. We were thus in possession of the metropolis of the Dutch East Indian Empire the fourth day after our landing. Not a gentleman, not a person of any note was left in the city. The Dutch, that is, the French Governor, had required them under pain of death to quit their houses and repair to the headquarters of the army, where they are narrowly watched. They had left their houses, however, richly furnished, their wives, children, and slaves to the safe-guard of the invaders' generosity; and we are all Scipios. The deserted women were in terror, not of us but of their own slaves, who have a slavish trick of using the opportunity of public disorder to gratify their private passions by rising on the defenceless whites and murdering those they rob. . . . Everything portable of public property had been removed from the town, but much valuable public property was consumed and much plundered. In some streets people walked during the first days of our occupation over their shoes in sugar, coffee, spices and rice. But much had been preserved. In that great city were found only six horses (ponies) and not one head of cattle.

"I sent a letter yesterday to General Janssens, the Governor-General, containing a summons, and distributing at the same time a sort of manifesto to the Dutch inhabitants to remove their apprehensions and invite their cooperation. The summons was refused and I received the answer that night."

Two proclamations, signed by the earl and countersigned by Raffles, were posted in the town. One was addressed to the Dutch, in their own tongue, and the other was written in Malay and Javanese for the natives. The Dutch were reminded that France was their enemy, and as for Holland, "Their country has expired." England offered them refuge: England, "champion and defender of Europe . . . His Excellency . . . offers friendship and protection during any contest which it may be necessary to maintain with those who would adhere to France."

The address to the natives was not so brief. After the customary reassurances and promises of liberation, they were warned not to take up arms against the French or the Dutch, "except when expressly called upon to do so by an English officer." Take note of this, because it is interesting in the light of Minto's orders, which you should remember as being of an opposite nature. He had been commanded to "subdue the Dutch Government, to destroy the fortifications, to distribute the ordnance, arms, and military stores, amongst the native chiefs and inhabitants, and then to retire from the country."

Minto was a humanitarian, and he had all the excuse of his principles in annexing the territory he "liberated," instead of retiring from the country as he had been ordered to do. Remember his letter. He argued that the Company could not ignore its moral obligation to protect the Dutch settlers from retribution at the hands of the natives. From there to the next argument, that England was equally obligated to protect the natives from the aftereffects of this disrupted system, was a short step. It was a very short step then, and it is shorter nowadays, when we face the same problem in other parts of the world as well as in Java, though at the moment of writing it crops up in Java again today.

There are echoes of this argument everywhere. They resound deafeningly from the shores of India. They thunder from Japan. We have heard them for years in Hong Kong. And the commissions and committees of the victors are not silent even in Europe.

As for Java in 1811, Lord Minto was there on the spot and the Court of Directors was not. Minto could be stubborn when his Scottish conscience was involved, along with his Scottish foresight. Thus their moral obligation was recognized by their representative, and the meeting of it became a *fait accompli*.

Meantime the war continued, though not in Batavia. Janssens held a position in the hills where the climate was comparatively healthy, and he felt that the British, occupying as they did the swamps and fever-ridden, low-lying locality of Batavia, would soon be decimated by nature, without any effort on his part. Auchmuty's methods, however, were not of such a passive character. He attacked Janssens and captured his position two days after the occupation of Batavia, then he waited at ease in those superior hill entrenchments until heavy artillery could be brought up from the ships. Janssens's losses in men were great; Auchmuty's were not. To tell the truth none of these encounters, save Cornelis, was more than a skirmish.

The battle for the fort of Cornelis was definitely a brilliant victory, credit for which lies with Colonel Gillespie. Then the worst was over. After that it was a matter chiefly of time, though there were still the battles of Samarang, Sourabaya, and Fort Ludowyck to win. Java was obviously soon to be surrendered to the British, at least those portions of Java which the white men held. (The island had never yet been completely conquered.) Though fighting was rumored still to be going on in several obscure localities, Lord Minto felt himself justified in issuing his proclamation of victory September eleventh. Java, after a very short term under the French, was now in the hands of the British—"added to the dominion of the British Crown," as Minto said in his dispatch to the Court of Directors, "and converted from a seat of hostile machination and commercial competition into an augmentation of British power and prosperity."

Raffles had done it. There he was occupying a position that rivaled a boy's wildest dreams of power. He remembered dreams like that. Filmy stuff they had been, reveries to comfort a frustrated, undernourished, overworked youth in London, fairy tales to allay his adolescent disappointments. Now they had come true, and he, Thomas Raffles, who had been too poor even for a rotten little Hammersmith school—Raffles had done it. He had paid his way, and he had got there.

" 'What will you have?' asked God. 'Take it, and pay for it.' "

Raffles had paid a high price. Leyden was dead.

When the expedition started out from Malacca, John Leyden had been as integral a part of it as Lord Minto himself. It was John Leyden who first interested the earl in Malays as humans, with a literature and a morality of their own. It was Leyden who spoke warmly to the governor general of Bengal, time and time again, of his friend Raffles, until Minto began to watch out himself for communications from the remarkable secretary of Penang. Leyden had sympathized with Minto in his enthusiastic plans, at the very beginning, when Java first crept into their talk. Leyden it was who had invested the expedition with charm and turned it from a political maneuver into a golden adventure with his eager plans for the Javanese and his intuitive appreciation of his friends' special quirks and loves and hates. He somehow took from the undertaking the curse of most military projects—saber rattling in society—and invested it with a scholarly flavor that was piquant and original. Leyden was the first to dash ashore when the fleet weighed anchor on the Java coast; he rushed through the surf at Chillinching and stood on dry land in advance of the army. He was a happy man when they moved into Batavia, eager to touch and to read the Malay manuscripts there. The Dutch offices had been closed since the administration moved to Buitenzorg: Leyden hurried to open them up and examine such archives as had been left there. According to the accounts they gave Raffles afterward, he must have been struck down in one of the "godowns"—the warehouses—where such papers were stored. He had broken into the little room, ignoring the fetid atmosphere, and begun immediately to go through some official papers stored on the shelves. He came out shivering with the ague and died two days later in Raffles's arms.

That happened in August. A few months later and he would have married Leonora Raffles, the youngest sister of his best friend. But even that marriage could not have brought him closer to Raffles than he was already, and had been for years.

His enemies called Thomas Raffles an overly ambitious man. Perhaps he was. But if anything is certain it is that on this, the occasion of his greatest triumph, he was completely indifferent to all his success. It is doubtful whether he knew what his friends were celebrating, or cared. In the center of the joyous hubbub of victory he was silent, trying to appreciate his loss and foolishly, futilely missing the closest friend he had ever had or was ever again to find.

CHAPTER X

Scenes sung by him who sings no more!
His brief and bright career is o'er,
    And mute his tuneful strains.
Quenched is his lamp of varied lore,
That loved the light of song to pour;
A distant and a deadly shore
    Has Leyden's cold remains!

What amazingly bad poetry Sir Walter Scott wrote, to be sure.

Lord Minto helped Raffles at Leyden's funeral. They were pallbearers, if that is the correct term. His closest friends, who were together because of him, buried him in Batavia cemetery. The greatest honor Raffles was able to pay Leyden he had to keep until he published the *History of Java*, and that was not until five years later. He paid due tribute to Leyden in the Introduction. But though the words are correct and thus sound cold, he must have been acutely aware of his loss all the while he was writing his book. No occupation could have been more calculated to remind him hourly of how much he could have profited by Leyden's advice and how they would have enjoyed doing that work together. "We have lost in him a host of men," he wrote Marsden soon after the event.

Whatever his private feelings, however, it was now time, when Leyden had been buried, to take over Java and the immense lot of work that accompanied the island's possession, after the final victory. The day of the proclamation was also the day Lord Minto kept a promise he had never quite voiced but only hinted: he commissioned Raffles lieutenant governor of "Java and all its dependencies." It seems impossible ever to award a diplomatic plum like this clean and clear. There is always some other claimant who must be disappointed, and Lord Minto, whose career included many projects beside his favorite Java, had evidently led someone else to expect the governorship. The man's name has never been put on record. Boulger thinks it was probably Robert Farquhar (not William), formerly of Malaya, now a knight and the new governor of Mauritius.

I mention it because I would like to make a guess myself. Could some one of Minto's circle possibly have given Colonel Gillespie any idea of hoping for the job? Gillespie was an excellent army officer and his part in the campaign for Java was an important, honorable one. Perhaps he dreamed a few dreams of his own while the battle was going so well. Later developments indicate that his was not a subtle nature, nor an overly modest one. Even though he had no right, logically speaking, to feel aggrieved when Raffles got the appointment, he must have experienced a pang of resentment that the youthful civilian had done so well out of the venture. Military groups relinquish the prizes for which they have fought very reluctantly, and there have been cases when they wouldn't relinquish them at all. (MacArthur's men held onto Manila jealously for a long, long time.)

It is not difficult to understand this. Consider the matter from the soldier's viewpoint. He feels that he carries the whole burden of the undertaking. If he didn't think of this for himself, everybody assures him of it, and praises him, and pets him—before the battle. When the war is over and everyone is happy and the prizes are being given out, it must be hard to watch some civilian, who, as far as the soldier can see, has done nothing but send other men into danger, step up and become the big boss. A high-ranking officer has even more aggravation than that. His men, if they like him, are more than ready to help him feel aggrieved and to assure him of their support. In Java things must have been hard enough for these army people all the way along, for Raffles was with them from the beginning to the end—Raffles the outsider, the tradesman, governing their lives, telling them what to do—them, soldiers of the King! Every time an unpopular direction came from Minto, the younger officials probably muttered curses on Raffles's head for having put the old man up to it. It was obvious that he carried a lot of weight with the governor.

If, added to this normal resentment, Gillespie had reason or even thought mistakenly he had reason to hope for the big appointment, it is no wonder that he hated Raffles bitterly from the day the new governor general took office.

Ignoring all such spiteful jealousies, as he had long since learned to do in his career, Lord Minto was happily certain that he had been just. The words of the appointment included a statement that he could not "conscientiously withhold it from the man who had won it." Exactly, grumbled Colonel Gillespie in his secret heart; and who, he would like to ask, *had* won it? When he was told that he would remain in Java as a council member and as commander of the garrison, his transports were moderate. He was one of three councilmen, and the only Briton. The others were H. W. Muntinghe and J. P. Cranssen, Dutchmen who had served before with the Javanese Government, under Dutch rule, and who were favorably disposed toward their British conquerors, the self-styled liberators of Java.

Minto wrote his wife, after the campaign, about the ill-fated Janssens, his number one prisoner of war, recommending the Dutch general to her courteous attention in the unlikely possibility that she might meet him. The passage is quoted here because of an interesting reference to Daendels. It should be mentioned that this concept of Daendels, though Minto was thoroughly sincere, in the light of later evidence appears to be exaggerated and unjust. Witness the fact that Raffles in his Javanese post actually learned to admire the

"Thundering Marshal" for some of his works, and did not scruple to admit it.

"This letter goes by transport, the 'Countess d'Harcourt', which carries General Janssen and his suite to England as prisoners of war. If you should by any chance come their way, *Palm, be civil* [a phrase frequently addressed by Lady Palmerston to her lord]—for he is one of the best and most estimable men I ever knew. He has suffered a great and severe reverse, which he has felt so deeply as to affect his health. His predecessor was a wretch in every imaginable way, one of the monsters which the worst times of the French Revolution engendered, or rather lifted from the mud at the bottom to flounce and figure away their hour upon the surface. He was greedy, corrupt and rascally in amassing money for himself, and equally unjust and oppressive in procuring public supplies. He was cruel, and regardless of men's lives beyond most of the revolutionary tyrants in the Realm of Terror. He forced the Javanese to cut a road through a morass at the expense of 6000 lives for this short space. He ordered two Javanese Princes, confined by him as state prisoners, to be privately murdered, and became savage from the delay which arose from the scruples of the officer in whose custody they were; a providential delay, for Janssen arrived in the interval, and passing through the place on his way to Batavia saved the victims. D'Aendels was as great a brute and tyrant in his pleasures— no man's family was safe. . . . In short, none of the worst of the Roman pro-consuls ever vexed and scourged the provinces, too distant for control, with more extortion and cruelty than this villain. His successor is his opposite in every point—a virtuous, just, and humane man; a brave and good officer! and I think, from his conversation, a wise and even enlightened statesman.

"Bonaparte certainly did one good action in sending a character so respectable to supersede D'Aendels at twenty-four hours notice; for he was peremptorily ordered to resign the government in that time, and to embark immediately for Europe. As soon as the ship was under weigh, it is understood here that the captain produced an order to carry him to France as a prisoner. The attachment of all sorts of men to Janssen is remarkable; and he certainly deprived us of the support which, if we had found D'Aendels in the government, the Dutch particularly of this colony would have given us. So pray be civil to my virtuous predecessor in Java, if you have the opportunity."

Minto could not stay more than a month or so, after his proclamation indicated that the war was over. In October, Raffles, now officially in residence at Ryswick in Batavia, gave a large dinner party and ball in honor of Lord Minto and General Sir Samuel Auchmuty, who were sailing for India on the nineteenth with most of the troops. It was the grandest affair over which he had ever presided, with fireworks and all the trimmings. A heavy rain spoiled the fireworks, but then nothing is ever quite perfect, and without that trifling annoyance our Raffles might have felt too proud to stay on the ground like ordinary mortals; he might quite possibly have discovered the power to fly.

Minto seemed equally elated, as his gay letter to Lady Minto testifies.

"George sent you the history of my orgies at a dinner given by me to Sir Samuel Auchmuty and the army. The army has since given a ball and supper to Sir Samuel and me promptly; and we entered hand in hand, like the two kings of Brentford smelling at one nosegay. This festival was at the residence of the former Governor-General, and the decorations had been all or nearly so in a state of preparation for the celebration of Napoleon's birthday, which we disturbed like *trouble-fetes* as we were, by landing and getting possession of Batavia, Government House, decorations and all, a few days before the grand occasion. . . . It is impossible to give you anything like an adequate notion of the total absence of beauty in so crowded a hall."

It is said by the novelist Banner among others that the Dutch guests at this dinner—many of them were invited, even General Janssens and two of his generals—were shocked by British levity. The fact that toasts were drunk to music startled them, and they were further amazed and dismayed when

Raffles was "chaired" around the room, to the accompaniment of great cheers and hunting halloos.

It would not be so very strange if that were true. One could scarcely expect to find Janssens entering into the spirit of the party with genuine gusto.

For the several years preceding the climax of Java, everything moved so quickly for Raffles that the account has been confusingly crowded. It would have been one more extraneous detail in an already overdetailed canvas, and so I have purposely postponed, until now, speaking of a letter Raffles wrote to England in 1809, just before he went to India and met Lord Minto, and settled his fate.

He had not yet met Minto, but he evidently had premonitions of grandeur. Or perhaps it would be better to say simply that he saw which way things were shaping, for the word "premonition" is a rather silly one to use in connection with the scientific Raffles. One may as well claim he had been entertaining premonitions ever since as a boy he fought for his right to an education. Let us rather call it an "intimation" that led him to write the following request to his uncle William:

My Dear Sir,—

The above extract [it was from a book of heraldry] will in part show the purport of this letter. The only circumstance relative to our family to be traced in the Heralds' College is, as far as I could learn, that about the time of James the First, or Second, there was a Sir Benjamin Raffles created Knight-Banneret, and I recollect to have heard you mention that, after some troublesome search for the arms of the family, this information could alone be obtained.

Now, as Knights-Banneret were next to Barons in dignity, as appears by statute made in the fifth year of King Richard II, statute 2, chap. 4, and by the foregoing extract, their heirs male are entitled to precedence, and consequently the title, *it is of some importance to me to trace this more particularly, not that I am anxious at present to obtain the title, but I have reason to think that hereafter it may be of consequence. I have therefore to request of you, as a particular favour, that you will make the most diligent enquiry for me into every particular to be found in the Heralds' Office, and communicate the same to me with every particular you know respecting the family of my grandfather, and back from him to the date in which the glorious Knight-Banneret, Sir Benjamin, strutted his hour.*

Whatever expense may attend the inquiry will be cheerfully defrayed by my friend Mr. R. S. Taylor of Gray's Inn. If you are successful, send out attested copies of every particular in duplicate by the first opportunity, and oblige, your affectionate nephew,

Tho. Raffles

Prince of Wales's Island
24th Feb. 1809.
P.S.—At all events get the arms drawn and emblazoned with their supporters, etc.

The situation was not definite when Raffles began his Javanese administration. Put in plain language, it amounted to this: Minto and Raffles hoped, strongly, that the home government would agree with their urgent advice to keep Java as a permanent acquisition. They were under no illusions however; they knew that many influential men were against the idea and that their opposing counsels would in all likelihood prevail, sooner or later. So much for the new ambitious plan Raffles had evolved, to use Java as a center of a great Eastern empire, from which to spread out not only to the Archipelago but farther and farther, to the gateways of India and China. "No man better than yourself," he wrote Marsden, "can appreciate the value of this new acquisition to the British empire—it is in fact the *other India*." Knowing that his chances of carrying out his plan grew slimmer every time his opponents were confronted with evidence of his attempts, Raffles embarked on a campaign of quiet, independent preparation. He concealed nothing which it was vitally necessary to report to the home group, but he did a good deal of feeling around, and thinking, and talking things over with his ally Minto, which was kept from the others. He went further than this in many small ways. Boulger is blunt about it: "As he was fearless of responsibility, he prosecuted his own measures without reference to the superior powers, because he knew that the delay caused by reference would make them useless and out of date, and was actuated by the conviction that the success and result of his proceedings would be their best and sufficient justification."

In doing this he was following the example of Minto, who deliberately disobeyed every one of the Company's injunctions when victory was achieved in Java. Minto hastened to explain his disobedience and to ask forgiveness and support, as we can see if we read the dispatch he sent back on the heels of his proclamation of victory. In modern language we would call the dispatch one long alibi. But even though he may have made his point, and though the Company did not act fierce about it, or demand his resignation (he had never feared they would do that), they reserved the right to persist in their own policy. It was a tug of war in the next few years, with Minto and Raffles trying on one side to persuade the Company and the government to continue carrying out the action they had forced, and the Company and the government silently waiting for the best way to get back without fuss on the path they had determined to follow. In the meantime Raffles went ahead piling up his bets, making ready for the eventuality of Minto's carrying the day. He governed Java, deliberately, as though the British were there to stay. But between himself and the earl there was no need of pretense, and several times in their correspondence we come across some reference to the true situation. The two men felt that even if Java failed they still had some secondary choice. There was the island of Banca near Java, which had never belonged outright to the Dutch, though they had some vague claims of suzerainty over it, as usual. It couldn't be compared with Java in convenience for their purposes, but it would do, failing better, and Minto was quite certain that Banca at least would be retained by the big bosses, even if they did give Java back. There were other possibilities too. Raffles never closed his eyes to new ones.

He found his policy of independence all the easier to follow because he had extraordinarily full powers bequeathed to him by the departing governor general. He needed such support for two reasons. One was the fact that Java was still incompletely under control, to put it politely, and the second was that Gillespie, smarting with a sense of injustice and temperamentally predisposed to chafe under Raffles's direction at any time, started making trouble in camp.

Java had never been entirely conquered by any European nation. Two chiefs reigned over the unoccupied portion, and until the time the topic of Holland's colonial possessions became the tennis ball of Europe, the Dutch had been preparing to give nominal independence back to yet more of the island's inhabitants. Raffles found himself up against a formidable job of subjugating nearly half of Java, before the strains of the victory ball died out on the air.

The Emperor of Java, called the Susuhunan, and the Sultan of Jojocarta were the two chiefs who held most power on Java.

Two months after British occupation Raffles started out to follow his instructions and to settle the situation, or at least to establish relations with these kings. On the east coast of Sumatra there was another territory, Palembang, which had been a dependency of the Dutch in Java; that too had to be rounded up. Therefore in November a commission set out from Batavia for Palembang, to take over the factory in the name of the British, and to pay a call on the Sultan just to see how the land lay. A Dutchman was included in the party as one of the commissioners.

The arrival of the commission had a disastrous effect on the Sultan's temper. He gave his orders, and his subjects promptly massacred the local Dutch settlers and would have done the same to the British commission if they had got hold of them.

As soon as the news arrived in Batavia, Raffles sent out

troops, under Colonel Gillespie, to subdue the peppery Sultan, and the affair was soon settled. Gillespie's account was vivid and informative, though scarcely like a modern communiqué from the front.

". . . In my inquiries, I have been occasionally so bewildered by falsehood, guilt, and prevarications, that I have experienced considerable difficulty in selecting the evidences most worthy of attention," he said. He decided to believe the following story, and threw away masses of taller tales.

Pangerang Ratoo, the then Sultan's eldest son, was the villain responsible for the massacre. "The crimes committed by this barbarous and sanguinary assassin, since the period he has been enabled to indulge his abandoned inclinations, have been distinguished by circumstances of such aggravated cruelty and guilt, that the inhabitants of the kingdom have beheld him with one common sentiment of horror, hatred, and indignation. . . .

". . . Among other pursuits that were followed by him with great avidity, was that of spearing the unhappy and defenceless wretches whom he accidentally encountered in his lawless excursions, or of sacrificing their wives and daughters to his abandoned cruelty and passions. . . ."

Attracted by a Chinese woman, he made her husband help him accomplish her rape, upon which the outraged man, who lived near the Dutch garrison, shouted to them for help. "An armed party was detached to his aid, and pursued the Pangerang Ratoo to his prow on the river, without being sensible of the dignity they were so successfully routing; the discovery of this unpleasant truth was made by himself before their separation. The boat was moored several yards from the shore, and in consequence he was compelled to swim a considerable distance before his escape was complete. No sooner, however, had he gained his canoe than he turned to his pursuers, and cried with the most callous effrontery, 'You are ignorant,' said he, 'of the influence and power you have so audaciously defied; know, to your confusion, that it is the Pangerang Ratoo himself, and rest assured that in three days you shall all of you be murdered, and your present habitations rendered such a scene of desolation, that they shall only be fit for birds to build their nests on.'" Rather foolishly, it seems to me, considering the warning, all the officers of the garrison soon afterward accepted the father's invitation to meet him at the palace for some affair or other. While they were absent, his troops got into the fort and easily massacred the whole lot of foreigners. There was plenty of reason, averred Gillespie, for believing that some of the townspeople joined with the Sultan in this business, in particular the principal magistrate. "I have, therefore, stipulated most expressly with Adipattie," said the colonel, "that all the prompters and abettors of this inhuman massacre shall be treated with great severity; that their property shall be sequestered the moment they are known, and a portion of it laid aside for the support of the wives and orphans who have been so cruelly deprived of their natural protectors.

"There was one European [female] among the unhappy victims thus sacrificed by the Sultan. She was embarked on the boats, and after suffering every violence and pollution her abandoned murderers were capable of offering her, she was inhumanly butchered and thrown into the river with the rest of the garrison.

"The remaining women were sent as slaves up the country, and the relation of distress, starvation, and misery they encountered in their bondage, is calculated to excite such sentiments of horror and indignation against the whole race, that at times I can with difficulty hold intercourse with people allied to such monsters of barbarity. . . .

"Their joy on emancipation is proportioned to the severity of their former sufferings, and their gratitude to the government is animated and sincere. Except the one previously specified, they are nearly all of them under my protection, and I shall take the earliest opportunity of either forwarding them to their friends on Java, or permit them to remain on the Island of Banca until some further arrangements may be made respecting them.

"I have endeavoured to ascertain, as correctly as I can, the primitive source of the Sultan's inhumanity, which is clearly to be attributed to the unbounded indulgence he has always bestowed on the vices of his son. He appears to have tolerated him in the pursuit of every evil, and protected him in the accomplishment of every object to which his unruly passion or violent inclinations hurried him forward, and to have been but an instrument for the protection of his son's wickedness. He has discovered too late, by his own overthrow, the melancholy consequences that ought always to attend so unprincipled a departure from every sacred law and moral obligation."

On May twenty-ninth Colonel Gillespie was here referring to the punitive measures adopted by him when he settled up, in placing Sultan Ratoo Ahmed Nujm-ood-deen on the throne in the room of his brother Mahmud Badruddin, who had been deposed. After describing the ceremony, the coronation, or whatever the proper term is when a king is deposed and his brother put on the throne in his place, Gillespie spoke of "the treaty":

"I shall have the honour to forward to you all the public documents that were either proclaimed or ratified upon this important occasion. You will see by the stipulations of the treaty, how completely they have been dictated with a view to our interests, and you will perceive that the cession of Banca and Billiton is unlimited and complete.

"In establishing the British authority at Minto (previously called Minta by the natives) I declared the Island of Banca to be named after his Royal Highness the Duke of York; the capital town after the Right Hon. the Governor-General of all India; and the fort now building there after his Excellency the Commander-in-Chief."

That affair marked the beginning of the high hopes Raffles placed in Banca as a second-string center for his empire.

At the same time that the commission to Palembang was running into such stormy weather, Raffles was paying his respects to the Sultan of Jojocarta. It was a dramatic occasion, one on which the new lieutenant governor had his first opportunity to show what he was made of. Was he going to live up to tradition as befitted a representative of the great white race? Or would his inferior education now show up? Raffles, as the angry Gillespie never allowed himself (or the world) to forget, was not the orthodox diplomat with years of international poker playing to give him that poise so necessary at such moments. But the bulldog breed didn't let England down. Raffles during the interview behaved exactly like all his predecessors in history, and all his successors on the stage.

What made it so tense was a matter of arithmetic. Raffles had only a handful of retainers, and the Sultan brought along the entire military force of Jojocarta to witness the meeting in the hall of audience. Since there had been no preliminary correspondence between them, it was touch and go whether the Sultan should become as capricious as his royal colleague over in Palembang (though that news had not yet been brought to Batavia) and suddenly command a massacre. However, he didn't. They talked and made an agreement which was soon to be forgotten by the Sultan, and then they said good-by, very politely.

"The Sultan was accompanied," says Lady Raffles in one of her infrequent bursts of personal narrative, "by several thousands of armed followers, who expressed in their behaviour an infuriated spirit of insolence, and several of his own suite actually unsheathed their own creeses to indicate plainly that they only waited for the signal to perpetrate the work of destruction; had this been given, from the manner in which the English were surrounded, not a man could have escaped."

One of my favorite phrases in all the literature of Raffles is included in this quotation—that "infuriated spirit of insolence." I can well imagine the Sultan's favorite wife writing her memoirs, inditing her version of the same incident: "The hirelings of the rascal Englishman, traitors to their own breed, stood about in the royal hall and imitated in their behavior the incredible impertinence of their white master. He, at least, had the excuse of his own infidel ignorance, whereas they knew better. Picture the scene: the puny potato-sprout creature without so much as a Ceylon ruby anywhere about his dingy clothing, exhibiting the most barbarous bad manners when he addressed the Lord of Creation, the monarch of our mighty Java. Though to give the devil his due, at least he did speak a civilized language, which is more than one can say for most of the pests."

Boulger actually tried his hand at it: ". . . in the centre of this disturbed and threatening scene the far from stalwart but energetic and impressive form of Raffles, calm, unmoved, stilling with eloquent Malayan phrases the storm, and convincing Sultan and vassals alike that in him they had a friend, perhaps, but certainly a master."

As a passage this has a nice ringing fall, but Boulger must have been fairly carried away by his own eloquence thus to forget in how short a time the Sultan and his vassals denied their certain master and perhaps friend. A very short time indeed elapsed before Raffles had to accompany Gillespie, scarcely off the ship from Sumatra, to remind the Sultan of Jojocarta all over again of his existence. This time it was really serious, for the Sultan had got in touch with the Susuhunan and made peace with him for the first time in history, and the two newly made allies with all the smaller Javanese princes immediately determined to band together and get rid once and for all of the whites.

This exciting event in Raffles's early Javanese days has been incorporated in Travers's Journal in a vivid passage which combines daily life with an extraordinarily grave struggle, in a cockeyed sort of way, the way these things really happen. "After the expedition to Palembang had sailed, Mr. Raffles' attention was again directed to the courts of Djocjocarta and Couracarta, where disturbances were recommencing, particularly at the former place, and he, in consequence, determined on proceeding to Samarang, when he took his family with him. On his arrival at Samarang he obtained such information as led him to suppose that it would be difficult to bring the Sultan of Djocjocarta to pacific terms. He accordingly deemed it prudent to collect such a force in the neighbourhood as would enable him to dictate such terms as he deemed advisable for the safety of the Island.

"At the time these operations were carrying on, Mr. Raffles was availing himself of every opportunity of gaining local knowledge. The native chiefs were constant guests at his table, and there was not a moment of his time which he did not contrive to devote to some useful purpose. The only recreation he ever indulged in, and that was absolutely necessary for the preservation of his health, was an evening drive, and occasionally a ride in the morning. He was not, however, at this time an early riser, owing to his often writing till a very late hour at night. He was moderate at table, but so full of life and spirits, that on public occasions he would often sit much longer than agreed with him. In general the hour for dinner was four o'clock, which enabled the party to take a drive in the evening; but on all public days, and when the party was large, dinner was at seven o'clock. At Samarang the society of course was small in comparison with Batavia, but on public occasions sixty and eighty were often assembled at the Government-house, and at balls from 150 to 180. Mr. Raffles never retired early, always remained till after supper, was affable, animated, agreeable and attentive to all, and never seemed fatigued, although perhaps at his desk all the morning, and on the following day would be at business at ten o'clock. In conducting the detail of government, and giving his orders to those immediately connected with his own office, his manner was most pleasing, mild, yet firm; he quickly formed his decision, and gave his orders with a clearness and perspicuity which was most satisfactory to every one connected with him; he was ever courteous and kind, easy of access at all times, exacting but little from his staff, who were most devotedly attached to him. The generosity of his disposition, and the liberality of his sentiments, were most conspicuous and universally acknowledged.

"As a public servant, no man could apply himself with more zeal and attention to the arduous duties of his office. He never allowed himself the least relaxation, and was ever alert in the discharge of the important trust committed to him; and it is astonishing how long his health continued good under such great exertions both of mind and body.

"Whilst remaining at Samarang, a fleet arrived at Batavia from England, bound to China, and at the same time a vessel was reported ready to sail from thence to Batavia, which determined Mr. Raffles on proceeding there without delay, to receive the despatches; on which occasion, Mr. Assey, Secretary to Government, and myself, accompanied him. We embarked on board a small vessel, the Hamston, and had a very quick passage of only seventy-two hours; during which time he drew up the Report on the capture of Djocjocarta, entering into a full and clear account of the circumstances which rendered this measure absolutely necessary for the preservation of peace on the Island. We landed at seven o'clock in the evening, when a grand public ball was given at Weltervreeden, to celebrate the anniversary of the Prince Regent's birth-day. At this entertainment Mr. Raffles, to the astonishment of all present, attended, as it was supposed he was at Samarang. He was the life and spirit of the entertainment. Not less than three hundred persons were assembled; and, indeed, on all similar occasions, which were always duly celebrated under Mr. Raffles' government, he contributed greatly to promote and encourage the gaiety and amusement of the party. After remaining a short time, he returned overland to Samarang, where he was most actively employed in completing the arrangement attendant on the capture of Djocjocarta, which of course brought an accession of territory to the Government, and which called for local knowledge and personal observation, to render profitable and advantageous. After obtaining all the information within his reach, Mr. Raffles and his family returned to Buitenzorg, at the close of 1812, where, of course, some arrears of public business awaited his arrival, and to which he devoted the most zealous assiduity."

Not all the army had come back with Gillespie, but there was no time to lose in waiting, so they did as well as they could with the troops at their command. On June 20, 1812, it was all over; the Sultan had been captured and Java could be called pretty well under control at last. Gillespie was slightly wounded; nothing serious. Five days later Raffles wrote Minto about it, and joyfully summed up the profits of the expedition. "A population of not less than a million has been wrested from the tyranny and oppression of an independent, ignorant and cruel prince; and a country yielding to none on earth in fertility and cultivation, affording a revenue of not less than a million of Spanish dollars in the year, placed at our disposal. . . . The Craton having fallen by assault, it was impossible to make any provision for Government to cover the expenses of the undertaking; consequently the whole plunder became prize to the army. It is considerable, but it could not be in better hands; they richly deserve what they got. I cannot speak too highly of the conduct of the army."

(One of the most highly execrated customs of the Japanese is that of turning over any town which they have just conquered for three days' plunder by the army. The commanders feel that the men richly deserve what they get. Barbarians!)

Compared with these exciting affairs, the matter of piracy suppression was not as impressive as it may sound. These pirates worked from the islands fringing Borneo on the side nearest Java, and some of their centers were on the mainland as well. They would descend suddenly on one of the seacoast towns, plunder it, and retire to the maze of straits which only they knew well, whither no stranger dared to follow. They also set up a lucrative business of attacking the trading prows of the natives, and sometimes did so well at this that trade came to a standstill. It became obvious in time that Raffles as a good administrator owed it to the people to put a stop to the whole thing.

Two elaborate campaigns made by the fleet did the trick. Raffles followed up the destruction of two most important repair centers on small islands, where the prows had been in the habit of putting in after battle to be refitted and readied for more mischief, with a delegation to Borneo. Through a messenger he assured the natives there that the anti-pirate campaigns were just what they were alleged to be, and that he had no slightest desire to annex more territory for Britain, either from the Borneo mainland or their islands. (Though he left small posts on the refitting islands.) He was aware that the pirates drew their forces from the seacoast villages and that it was likely most of the men his delegate addressed were themselves guilty of part-time piracy now and then. The natives took the political agent's promises in such good faith and respected

173 ૐ

the British fleet to such an extent that piracy in Java ceased almost completely. It is interesting to reflect that it still exists along the coast of China, and in very similar form.

All of this took up more than a year. It was not until the beginning of 1813 that the first overt sign of resentment was made by Gillespie, who had been giving an excellent account of himself in the military actions of the past year. It happened during a dispute on a matter of policy. Raffles felt that all important warlike activity was at an end, such operations as might still be necessary calling for less material and men than had the battles of 1811 and 1812. His was the viewpoint of the all-round governor, with an eye to economy—his apprenticeship in the Company's service had taught him the value of that quality—and he now proposed to reduce the garrison. Major General Gillespie, as he now was, declared himself strongly opposed to this suggestion. Raffles summed up the difference in a dispatch to Papa Minto. He, the lieutenant governor, had been directed by the Supreme Government of India to keep Java's forces down to a size only just big enough to maintain "internal tranquillity and security against any predatory attack on the part of the enemy," the enemy, one supposes, being his word for the local sultans. It was "a defined and limited purpose," and called for defined and limited numbers. "The Commander of the Forces, on the contrary, has been always in expectation of attack from Europe, and would prepare accordingly."

It was the old, old story; any official who has ever served a term in a colony will recognize that argument. The military always want the lion's share of funds to build up their defenses, and the civil government is always trying to hold them down and turn the funds to some peaceful purpose. The military are ambitious: they *want* serious trouble, and they want to prepare for it. A similar argument raged in Hong Kong for years before the Japanese attacked at Pearl Harbor; at least one governor, it is rumored, was bumped out of the Crown Colony for refusing to spend anything on preparatory measures. After that the army crowd got their way to a certain degree, but it all came about too late, and the funds available were insufficient anyway, and what happened after Pearl Harbor gave the military group a working argument for the future which may yet cause the civil government many a headache. In Java, though, back in 1813, Raffles had no intention of letting Gillespie give him a headache. He called for help from Minto, who had never yet let him down, and Minto backed him up as usual, and Raffles had his way, and Gillespie hated him more than ever.

CHAPTER XI

The thunder of the Javanese campaign slowly diminished and came to a halt, with only an occasional threatening rumble sounding in the distance, and the British hastened to settle into their newly won territory. Olivia Raffles brought her household from Malacca, but she didn't occupy the house, Ryswick, which had been the Dutch governor's official residence. The English nearly all followed the example which Daendels had already encouraged, of living outside town, and Raffles's new home was in Buitenzorg, on the higher ground toward the Blue Mountain, about forty miles south of Batavia. He transacted as much business there as he could, though once or twice a week he had to ride into Batavia to take care of matters which had collected in his absence, and sometimes he slept a night or two in Ryswick. Leyden's tragic death must have strengthened his prejudice against the canal city.

In those days people didn't know about malaria and its insect hosts. They knew only from experience that swampy, low-lying ground was unhealthy. Every traveler who wrote of his visit to Batavia, then or earlier, told the same story. Of the canals which ran through the town, they said, many were practically stagnant most of the time, and all of them were full of the filth of sewage. Thus the air which they exuded was unhealthy, fetid, poisonous stuff, which it was probably fatal to breathe. And worse, there were the trees which bordered the canals; they looked pretty, yes, but they had a harmful effect on that air, because they offered so much more opposition to what should have been a "healthy movement of the atmosphere." It was necessary that breezes carry the air away to offset its poisonous influence, but except in the season of the "good monsoon" this was impossible in Batavia, because of the trees along the canals. Abandoned houses, too, exuded bad air. (All these factors, of course, would account as well for mosquitoes.) Everyone accepted Batavia's reputation as a deathtrap, never for a moment supposing that anything could or ever would be done about it.

Major William Thorn, in his *Conquest of Java*, actually grew lyrical on the tragic subject. "Death's shafts fly thickest at the breaking up of the Monsoons, which is the most sickly period of the year. Then

> *Gaily carousing,*
> *Calling for joys beneath the moon,*
> *Next night, Death bids them sup*
> *With their progenitors—He drops his mask,*
> *Frowns out at full,—they start, despair, expire!*"

In no other country, says Thorn, did people hear of the death of a friend with more nonchalance, or less surprise and concern. They were too much used to it. During the "sickly period" the sight of a funeral was an ordinary thing, so that even the hired mourners smoked cigars or pipes as they marched along, and they chatted with each other openly, cheerfully disregarding the conventional behavior for funerals.

The traveler John Splinter Stavorinus, rear admiral in the service of the States-General, whose translated memoirs appeared in London in 1793, in his exhaustive descriptions of social life in the Indies, also speaks of the "noxious exhalations" of the swamps, morasses, and marshy woods of the locality as being the cause of so much disease and death. He calls Batavia one of the most unwholesome spots upon the face of the globe, where preventive medicines were taken as

177 &

regularly as food. "The European settlers at Batavia commonly appear wan, weak, and languid; as if labouring with the 'disease of death'." Few strangers stay long without getting the "fever." First it appears as a "tertian ague"; after three or four such paroxysms the fever turns to a double tertian, then continues in remittent attacks which frequently carry off the patient in a short time. The "Peruvian bark" (quinine) was seldom prescribed, or was taken in a quantity so small as to be no use whatever, most Batavians preferring to dose themselves with camphor in spirit of wine. Sometimes the patient survived and simply got used to his fever. Stavorinus cites the example of one gentleman who, while talking of how many friends he lost each year, though he continued, himself, to enjoy "excellent health," kept mopping his face, and explained that he was perspiring from the aftermath of a bad attack of fever. Oh yes, he said, he had had a shocking fit only that morning, and knew that in time he would probably die of it, but he hoped to be able to make his pile and retire to Europe before that sad event came to pass. Stavorinus estimated a fifty per cent death rate among newcomers every year. When an acquaintance of some Batavian burgher died, the citizen would only say calmly, on hearing the news, "Well, he owed me nothing," or "I must get my money of his executors."

Stavorinus had a very low opinion of the typical Batavian Dutchman and his Eurasian wife. Evidently the company of the inhabitants offered no compensation for the climate. The island itself, however, was so beautiful, and there were so many lovely gardens around the rural residences, that it was difficult to believe any land so attractive could be as unhealthy as Java was. A young man just arriving exclaimed as he looked his first on the island, from the boat:

"What an excellent habitation it would be for immortals!"

There are many absorbing accounts of social life in Batavia, through the eighteenth century and for some years of the nineteenth, before the arrival of the British. Styles and customs changed slowly in those days, and we can accept the accounts of travelers through several decades as if they were contemporary, remembering only that the British arrivals did in time have a certain indubitable effect which will be mentioned in due course. Dutch and Eurasian society in Batavia before the British came makes fascinating reading. One doubts, though, if it was equally fascinating to experience.

Stavorinus had a most emphatically unfavorable opinion of the Europeans in Java. The people there, he says, quickly learned to care only for riches. Whatever ideas of virtue or honesty they may have held when they arrived were lost in record time. Very few men could resist the temptation in Batavia to indulge in petty graft and dishonest practice. Yet few of them got together enough wealth to satisfy themselves, and they became disappointed, discontented, melancholy, dejected souls. Added to the effect on their spirits of the noxious climate and the want of their customary food, all of this rendered them easy prey to death. Most of the people looked dejected, he observes, even the rich burghers. Their only resources were tobacco, dull conversation, drinking, and cards. They were bored to death. Stavorinus blames this *ennui* largely on their attitude toward marriage, of which the "normal happy intercourse" was unknown, for the Dutch kept their women, slangily called "liplaps" (India-born girls, usually Eurasian) in a world of their own, and that world too was damnably dull.

Opinions seem to vary as to the position these women occupied in Batavian society. As Stavorinus's picture is that of the town as it was in an early phase while still completely under Dutch influence, we had better start with it.

The governor general, head of the government, was aided by a council made up of a director general, five ordinary councilors, nine extraordinary councilors, and two secretaries. Nevertheless his authority was almost unbounded. He was a man to respect and fear, for he could get jobs for your relatives or send you back to Europe at the slightest prompting of his whim. He usually lived in the country, at his seat at Weltevreeden, a superb mansion where he would hold public audience every Monday and Thursday. On Tuesdays and Fridays he held sessions in his second country seat, which was nearer town. On all other days he was inaccessible in his official capacity, save for really urgent business. Nobody was allowed or expected to pay him visits of ceremony during office hours: he was bothered only for business affairs. The hours of audience were from 5 A.M. to 8 A.M. Everyone waited in the open air, in a courtyard before the house, until his name was called in due turn by the bodyguard.

When the governor rode out in his carriage he was accompanied by horse guards. One officer and two trumpeters preceded him. Anyone who happened to meet him and who was also in a carriage had to stop and get out until he passed by. Some of the most important councilmen also had this privilege of being a nuisance to the public. A visiting British sea captain, a man named Carteret, ran into a little excitement because of this, in 1768. He had been in Batavia several days, blithely ignoring the stop-carriage custom, until one day his landlord brought him word from the governor that he was to step out of his carriage like everyone else whenever he met the governor's equipage, or that of any of the councilmen. Captain Carteret replied warmly that he had no intention of so doing. When the landlord discreetly hinted that in that case the governor's armed slaves might take action, Carteret replied meaningly that he would know how to deal with *that*, and he nodded toward his pistols as he said it.

After an absence of a few hours the landlord called on him again, saying that His Excellency, after due consideration, had pronounced that the captain might do as he pleased. From that time on no visiting Englishman got out of his carriage for anybody, unless he wanted to. (But Raffles revived the custom for a bit, later on.)

All the distinctions of precedence and rank were minutely observed, and life in old Batavia must have been most disagreeably complicated. "Every individual is so stiff and formal, and is as feelingly alive to every infraction of his privileges, in this respect, as if his happiness or misery depended wholly upon the due observance of them. Nothing is more particularly attended to, at entertainments, and in companies, than the seating of every guest, and drinking their healths, in the exact order of precedency. The ladies are particularly prone to insist upon every prerogative attached to the station of their husbands; some of them, if they conceive themselves placed a jot lower than they are entitled to, will sit in sullen and proud silence, for the whole time the entertainment lasts." Ladies would be like that in a colony. They always are.

Stavorinus tells of a scene which took place before his eyes, in the street. Two ladies riding in carriages happened to meet in a narrow road, and neither would give way to the other. It happened to be a difficult matter to settle according to precedence because their husbands were both clergymen! For fully fifteen minutes they sat, both inexorable, "during which time they abused each other in the most virulent manner, making use of the most reproachful epithets, and whore and slave's brat, were bandied about without mercy. . . ."

To prevent such occurrences, which sometimes dragged out to a couple of hours' duration, the Netherlands East India Company in 1764 drew up a remarkable set of rules, ascertaining the respective ranks of Company servants. They laid down regulations as to the pomp of funerals proper to each rank, what sort of dress could be worn, i.e., who could wear embroidered or laced clothes, and everything else which could possibly be imagined. Most of the rules were broken every day, but some were faithfully observed, such as the prohibition of the wearing of velvet coats by any man of less rank than senior merchant. The act related to one hundred and thirty-one articles in the most minute detail—carriages, horses, chairs, servants, dress, and so on. Little hand-drawn chaises for children, for instance, were not to be gilded or painted unless the exact rank of their parents permitted it, and even then there were restrictions on the styles of decoration allowed. No one lower than a merchant could carry a parasol or umbrella unless it was raining. Jewels worn by ladies whose husbands were of less than councilors' rank must not be worth more than six thousand rix-dollars. Ladies of the higher ranks could go abroad with three slaves, and the slaves could wear earrings of single middle-sized diamonds, gold hairpins, petticoats of cloth of gold or silver, or of silk, jackets of gold or silver gauze, chains of gold or beads and girdles of gold, but they couldn't wear pearls or diamonds or any other jewels in the hair. That was for the slaves *only*; the mind faints at the thought of how many other details were considered and decided before the Company officials were through with their commands!

There were also stringent rules regulating the number of musicians permitted in the slave bands which customarily played at mealtimes, or in the early days accompanied the carriages during the evening outing. Some high officers could have trumpets, clarions, and drums in their orchestras; others, lower in rank, couldn't. In Surat (for all the Dutch Company's colonies came under these same regulations) the director when he went out in state was especially permitted to carry four fans, made of bird-of-paradise feathers and cow hair, with golden cases and handles. Why fans, and why four? Why not three, or five, or ten? God alone knows, now, but the solemn committee which perpetrated all this incredible silliness must have had their reasons.

Here is a contemporary description of an evening's festivity in Batavia, when Reynier de Klerk, one of Daendels's predecessors, was governor general:

"The General does not keep a table, at least not what can be properly termed such; the evening company is received every night about 6 o'clock. This company consists of those ladies and gentlemen who have been invited 2 days previously by cards of invitation. The company is received by the host sitting on the verandah porch, in a black shirt [*kamizool*] with a linen night-cap on his head, and when everyone is finally assembled, the host says, 'Friends, take your coats off,' whereupon everybody takes off his coat, hat and sword. Everyone then sits down on the chairs which have been placed in a row along the verandah, everybody in order of seniority, and if it should so happen that somebody inadvertently fails to observe this, the Host says to him,—'That is not your place; you must sit there.' A glass of beer is then served to everybody with the formal toast, 'A good evening to you,' then next a pipe of tobacco, and conversation then begins, but in such wise that everybody only speaks with his neighbors, without seeming to talk so loud that the Governor-General can hear him; this latter talks only to the individual next to him, who is the senior in rank amongst the guests, and the only things that the general says in a voice loud enough for everyone to hear, are toasts such as 'The health of the Ladies.' As soon as he says this, everybody jumps up from his chair holding a glass of wine, and all together form a great half-circle, and with heads bowed low, they all call out 'To the health of the General's Lady.' Next follows a series of toasts drunk to the health of each one of the guests in turn, each individual standing up and bowing deeply when his own health is toasted. These toasts continue until 9 o'clock, when everybody gets up, takes his coat and sword again, and hastens to drink the Host's health, who answers briefly, 'Thank you for drinking my health.' The Company then takes its leave, and in such wise does the East India General pass the time every evening.

"The ladies are received by the General's Lady, and stay apart from the gentlemen. They also sit in order of protocol according to their husbands' rank, with the General's Lady at the top. In accordance with the Indian custom, tea is served by slave girls on silver platters and in Japanese cups with tops."

Stavorinus describes the town in careful detail. Batavia itself, he says, was in the shape of a "long square." Before Daendels came it was enclosed by a stone wall, but the marshal caused this wall to be pulled down and used the materials again for new buildings. It was thought, of course, that by doing this he improved the air of the city and reduced its unhealthiness. Certainly he reduced the heat of the place. Buitenzorg, however, was already in favor as a healthier residential district, for it is sixteen Dutch miles to the south, on the way to the Blue Mountain, on ground higher than Batavia, so that the mornings are always pleasantly cold. The seashore bounds Batavia on the north.

In town the foreigners' houses were built mostly of brick, stuccoed white. They were all alike, narrow-fronted, with floors of large, square, dark red stones. No one used hangings, probably for the sake of coolness. The furniture consisted of some armchairs, two or three sofas, and a good many looking glasses. Several chandeliers and lamps hung in a row and were lit up at night. There were no gardens in town, and though some of the houses were glazed, other residents preferred windows of latticework instead.

The Chinese quarter, down in the oldest part of town, was the scene of a horrible massacre in 1740 when the other residents, whose resentment against the industry and prosperity of the Chinese had long smoldered, took advantage of a false rumor involving a Chinese to rise up and create a race riot. Since that time the Chinese had rather avoided that quarter, called the "Chinese Kampong," preferring to live outside of town if they could, where escape would be easier in case of another race riot.

The Europeans followed this schedule, more or less: rise at five and wear a light gown like a sleeping garment for breakfast of coffee or tea, then dress and go to business, by about eight o'clock; knock off work at eleven or eleven-thirty, dine at twelve, nap until four in the afternoon, and then either work until six or drive out in a carriage to take the air of the country. At six the people assembled in companies to play cards or converse until nine o'clock, then they either went home or stayed for supper where they were; anyway they were in bed by about eleven. Though the married men occasionally took their wives to these parties, they ignored them once the couples had arrived, and tried to keep them generally under the marital thumb. The ladies didn't join in the parties as the men did, but had their own assemblies in other rooms.

"Convivial gaiety seems to reign among them," writes Stavorinus of the men, "and yet it is mixed with a kind of suspicious reserve, which pervades all stations and all companies, and is the consequence of an arbitrary and jealous government. The least word which may be wrested to an evil meaning, may bring on very serious consequences, if it reach the ears of the person aggrieved, either in fact, or in imagination. Many people assert, that they would not confide in their own brothers in this country."

Stavorinus goes into considerable detail about the liplaps. To put it politely, he did not admire them. He said you could always guess at native blood to the third or fourth generation, because the eyes of Eurasian girls were smaller than those of the whites. (Presumably he meant "narrower" rather than "smaller"—the Mongol obliquity.) Though Javanese and Dutch offspring would, after a few generations, if they consistently married white men, fade out to an ordinary white complexion, those with Portuguese blood would always remain dark [sic].

The girls were ready to marry at twelve or thirteen, sometimes even younger. They seldom waited longer, if they were at all handsome and had money or expectations, or powerful relatives. Though colonial Dutchmen did not usually legalize their unions with the native women they chose to live with them, they had no objections to marrying the children of other such liaisons. The fathers, when they went back to Europe, often took such children along with them. These liplap wives, having married extremely young and never having had the slightest education, could seldom read or write, nor did they "possess any ideas of religion, of morality, nor of social intercourse," said Stavorinus. Because of such early marriage, he thought, they didn't usually bear many children, and at thirty they were already old; women of fifty, in Europe, looked younger than these women at thirty. They were delicately made, very fair in complexion, but pallid—a "deadly pale white," he called it—and he said that the handsomest among them would scarcely be thought middling pretty in Europe. They were very supple in the joints, what we would call double-jointed, "but this they have in common with the women in the West Indies, and in other tropical climates." They were listless and lazy, no doubt because they had far too many slaves attending on them.

They would get up at seven-thirty or eight and spend the forenoon playing and toying with their female slaves, who were never absent, laughing and talking with them at one moment and yet at the next having the poor creatures whipped unmercifully for the merest trifles. They would loll in loose, airy dress on sofas, or sit on low stools with their legs crossed under them, native fashion, and they were never without pinang, or betel, to chew. Some of them also chewed Java tobacco. Betel chewing made their spittle crimson and in time left a black border along the lips, and also blackened the teeth. Their mouths were very disagreeable, always, although it was claimed by betel apologists that the custom of chewing purified the mouth and protected the teeth from decay. (Even today foreign men complain that Indonesian women spoil their beauty by chewing betel, thus blackening their teeth.)

In Stavorinus's opinion these women were ruthlessly spoiled by the system then in vogue, which gave them no chance to develop themselves mentally, so that though they were "not deficient in understanding," they grew up lazy and stupid as animals. The mother abandoned her child, as soon as it was born, to some female slave, who suckled it and reared it, having complete control over her charge until the child was nine or ten years old. Naturally the children showed the results of this training. They were reared with no more education than any of the natives had, but they were taught to think themselves vastly superior to the natives in station, and such a combination cannot but show bad results.

It is only fair to say that a few travelers report exceptions to this rule. The outstanding one is Maria Wilhelmina Engelhard-Senn van Basel, a half-caste girl who at the age of eight, on August 3, 1778, received as a school prize the *Brieven Van Mevrouw de Chapones*, being the Dutch translation of a standard English work on morals and manners entitled *Letters of the Improvement of the Mind*, by Mrs. Esther de Chapones, née Mulslo, an English authoress. There must have been occasional schools, then, and a certain degree of education possible for a few of the girls.

These Eurasian girls were reported by Stavorinus as being *remarkably fond* of bathing, because they used to immerse themselves in large tubs of water, capable of holding three hogsheads, and they did this as often as *twice a week*. Considering the bathing habits, or rather the lack of them, in Europe at that time, it is no wonder that Stavorinus found this practice worthy of surprised comment. Another traveler, however, says that to his knowledge they bathed twice a day. In that hot, humid climate even this excess of cleanliness does not seem too unnatural to us Western folk, but it was a shock to the eighteenth-century European mind.

The Eurasian ladies were very jealous, especially of the female slaves whose beauty and constant presence around the house must have been a chronic threat to domestic fidelity. Often when the jealous wrath of the mistress was aroused in this manner she put the offending slave to torture, and she knew various subtle and unusual ways of doing this. One particular passage of Stavorinus can scarcely be paraphrased, so I shall quote it, as many a nineteenth-century traveler has done before me:

"Among other methods of torturing them, they make the poor girls sit before them in such a posture that they can pinch them with their toes in a certain sensible part, which is the peculiar object of their vengeance, with such cruel ingenuity, that they faint away by excess of pain."

Turning her attention next to her husband, the outraged lady of the manor uses a very different torture on him, according to the same writer. To him she administers an aphrodisiac which has this one quality in common with Iseult's love-potion —his passion will be aroused by the first woman his eye lights on, after drinking the stuff, and he will have eyes for none other but her. His wife must be careful to stick around at that time, if she knows her stuff, and she keeps the slaves out of the way. Unlike Iseult's potion, however, the aphrodisiac keeps on working—this is the story; I don't say I believe it implicitly—until the unfortunate husband dies of exhaustion. The tale has evidently been current for many years in Java: a very pretty example, to my mind, of wishful thinking.

There are other tales told of the jealousy of Javanese girls. Stavorinus says, "The women are proportionately more comely than the men, and are very fond of white men. They are jealous in the extreme, and know how to make an European, with whom they have had a love-affair, and who proves inconstant, dearly repent his incontinence and fickleness, by administering certain drugs which disqualify him for the repetition of either." Just the other effect, in sum, than Stavorinus's aphrodisiac.

In the past century and a half the Dutch have not lost their fear of the subtle revenges practiced by native girls. Only ten years ago a Dutchwoman told me about a young man she knew, a Dutch naval officer, who after living with a native girl several years in Java threw her over in order to come back to Europe and marry his white fiancée in Rotterdam. Foolishly he allowed the Javanese to know his plans. Nothing happened to him before he left Java: the girl went on being pleasant, keeping house for him, cooking his favorite curry, et cetera, until he kissed her good-by and sailed away. But when he reached home he fell ill with a painful stomach-ache. He vomited repeatedly, and nothing the doctors gave him had any effect on the pain, until they discovered that he was voiding countless tiny lengths of *hair*. The girl in Java had mixed cut hair in all his food, and it was so stiff and bristly that it penetrated his intestines in a thousand places before he could get rid of it. He died of course. My Dutch informant's eyes sparkled and her face was pale when she told me this story; there is no doubt that she, at least, believed it, every word.

The Eurasian ladies wore native dress, a very light and airy costume. A piece of cotton cloth was wrapped round the body and fastened under the arms next to the skin. Over it was a shift, a jacket, and a chintz petticoat, all covered by a long gown, the *kabay* or *kabaja*, which hung loose, the sleeves coming down to the wrists, where they were fastened close with six or seven little gold or diamond buttons. For state occasions, such as a meeting with a councilor's wife, they wore a fine muslin kabaja made like the other but much longer, hanging down to the feet, whereas the ordinary everyday garment came only to the knees. Great importance was attached to this matter of a kabaja's length, just as we speak of formal and informal evening dress.

They always went about with their heads uncovered. Their thick, sleek black hair was worn in a wreath, fastened with gold and diamond hairpins, which was called a *kondeh*. The front and sides of this headdress were stroked perfectly smooth and shining with coconut oil. Sometimes they also wore chaplets of flowers. It was a beautiful fashion, often copied by the

European ladies who saw it. For that matter, all the Dutch, both men and women, adopted native dress for indoor, informal attire in Batavia.

On Sundays the Eurasian ladies sometimes put on European dress, but they didn't care much for it. (Later, under the British, unfortunately they did start liking European clothes, and the British thought that was just fine.) A lady going out would take four or five female slave attendants along, one to carry the inevitable betel box. They all, mistress and slaves, wore a lot of gold and silver, and loved it. The ladies seldom mixed with men socially, except at marriage feasts, according to Stavorinus. The title "My Lady" was kept exclusively for councilors' wives, and those who could use it were very proud of their privilege.

The ladies loved to ride out in their carriages in the evening. In earlier days they were also fond of riding along the surface of the canals in pleasure boats, with slave orchestras playing music as they went, but this practice was discontinued in the latter part of the eighteenth century, presumably because the water was growing too odoriferous. The coaches used in Batavia were small and light, and glass windows in them were permitted only to government members, as were painted or gilded wheels. A slave had to run ahead of each carriage with a stick, to give warning to the people in the street of their approach. Sometimes ladies would ride out in a *norimon*, a sort of sedan chair in which one sat cross-legged like a Buddha, invisible to the public.

A passage by Victor Ido van de Wall, describing social life in Batavia around 1812, differs in certain respects from all these accounts, perhaps because the coming of the British had already in one year made considerable difference to the atmosphere. According to the records he studied, the Eurasian ladies evidently played a far more important role in daily life, and mingled much more freely with the men of their acquaintance, than some other commentators have led us to believe. This description I am about to give, of daily life in a wealthy family's country house where guests are staying, is taken from the book by that Van de Wall who discovered a mention of the extraordinary half-caste girl, Maria Wilhelmina Engelhard-Senn van Basel, the student who actually won a prize at school. The family of whose country estate he writes are these same Engelhards; we come across the name Engelhard more than once in the later annals of Batavia.

They got up very early, at daybreak (about five o'clock apparently, summoned by five strokes on the gong). The company assembled dressed in sarong and kabaja (both men and women), to drink coffee and admire the view; later the house gong called the servants to work and the guests to their morning bath, which they took either in the river or in the bathroom in the attached building, using only cold water. Next came a big breakfast on the back veranda, of warm rice, curry, fish, beefsteak, *dendeng* (dried meat), Makasas fish, bacon, peppered small chow, greens, roast chicken, lavishly washed down with red wine, beer, Madeira, Rhine wine, brandy and seltzer water. The day at Pondok Gedeh (a country house at Buitenzorg which was the favorite visiting place of the Batavian beau monde) began with this Lucullan meal.

When the meal was over and the hostess had risen from the table, the guests scattered in all directions, so that the great house seemed deserted. The gentlemen went with Engelhard to see his new indigo plantation and horse stables, or they went horseback riding, or in a chair (sedan chair), in the latter case with a slave to hold a parasol over their heads to keep the sun off. The ladies, led by the hostess, went to the outbuildings, watched the female slaves at work, the seamstresses, embroiderers, et cetera, and listened to the birds singing. They squatted or lounged around on low stools, benches, and long easy chairs or even on mats on the floor, gossiping busily. The hostess and her dearest friends smoked, usually, the finest Manila cigars, but others had a good quid of prime Puerto Rico tobacco to chew, with the inevitable cuspidors close at hand.

The chat became very animated when it veered round to the topic of wearing the troublesome European clothing which Mrs. Raffles, in an unfortunate moment, had introduced for daily wear. The new fashion caused much comment in the

Java Government Gazette and was a burning topic with the Indian ladies. Although an English poet had taken up the cudgels for this airy clothing, wherein the English ladies came off rather badly, a lady calling herself *Njonja toea* felt herself obliged to break a lance on behalf of the much criticized kabaja wearers, and wrote the following Malay poem in which she twitted the English preference for roast beef and beer:

> Tra Tahon minoem sehari hari
> Port, Madeira, Brandy, Beer
> Tra Ton Makan Beef en Curry
> Makanan Böesoek, English Heer!

which may be translated freely as—

> To do nothing but drink, every day of the year,
> Port, Madeira, brandy, and beer;
> Naught accomplished save beefsteak and curry bitten,
> Is a very bad thing indeed, Mr. Briton!

How fiercely the battle raged is evident from the fact that even the men could not forever bear the taunts cast at their womenfolk. A certain Lopes gave vent to his poetical spleen as follows:

De Vrouwen al te zaam op eene leest te schoeien
En's Lands gewoonten op het bitterst te verfoeien
Is dat het werk eens gans of van eenen jongeling
Die ooit een wijze les in al zyn tijd entving?
Is spraak en vrouwen dragt in't eene deel van London
Als die ter zelver tijd in't andere werd gevonden?

To condemn all women together, in a fashion most uncouth,
To place the customs of a country in the worst conceivable
    light;
Is it a goose who does this, or just a callow youth
Who has never in his life learned how to be polite?

Tell me, do all ladies speak alike in London town?
Do they all appear like copies in the same design of gown?

After hurling this dirty crack in the direction of the autocratic British, he concluded with the reproachful advice:

Wilt van een Indiaan dees korte les onthauwen;
Schimp nimmer zonder reden op mannen of op vrouwen,
Houdt U tbij roast beef, bij Madeira, port and beer,
Want dat is, wel beschouwd, uw grootste, Uw waar pleizier.

Let an Indian teach you a lesson short and sweet:
Never without reason scoff at other folk you meet.
Just stick to your roast beef, your Madeira, port, or beer,
For after all that's the only joy Life holds for you out here.

The ladies' world likewise at Pondok Gedeh was divided into two sides, the pro-kabajas and the anti-kabajas. The hostess naturally belonged in the first category and was just arguing heatedly for its retention, what time many a puff of cigar smoke curled in the air, and many a gob of betel juice was spat into the cuspidor, when heavy steps were heard, and the shouting of slaves in the garden. Some moments later the gentlemen entered, tired and sweating, plumped themselves down on the long easy chairs in the hall, and indulged in some glasses of "particular old and very [choice] Madeira." The arrival of the gentlemen brought the ladies' lively conversation to an end. It was now about 1 P.M. and therefore the hour of siesta. Everybody went to their bedchambers and soon went to sleep. For the old hands, the grumbling, retired old gentlemen of over a score of years' service in the tropics, this was probably the best time of the day. These could not drop off soundly to sleep unless they were first properly massaged by suitably trained slave girls. There were several forms of this massage. The younger men also enjoyed these welcome attentions of the slave girls. . . . About four o'clock everyone was waked up from the midday siesta, and after a fresh bath in cold water sat down to the welcome midday dinner. There was an overflowing amount of fish, greens, and fixings, both fresh and preserved, and alongside each plate was placed a plate of rice and a finger bowl of white or blue crystal. The finest wines were served on a kind of dumb-waiter, wrapped round with a damp napkin to keep them cool. The rice was eaten with the fingers, but the meats and vegetables with knife, fork, and spoon. Conversation became general and the gaiety reached its height when the house slave orchestra began to play lively tunes, until finally the ladies thought it time for them to withdraw and to continue elsewhere their arguments over the kabaja problem. The gentlemen remained at the table, smoking either a *hooka*, a *kabaalpip*, or a good Manila cigar, and took their ease with their legs stretched out on the table.

When the company had had enough, the carriages were summoned and they went for a ride in the neighborhood. By the time they returned, the evening shadows were falling and the evening breeze had tempered the heat of the day in house and grounds. In the hall card tables were ready, while tea, pale ale, porter, claret, and grog were served to the guests. Those who did not care to play cards sidled along the wall to have a look at the dancing, which was participated in by old and young alike. There was usually first a round dance, then a gallop, with three, four, or more couples, called the "*Haagsche Officieren*," ending in a general free-for-all when many of the ladies lost their slippers and pocket handkerchiefs. When this was over, the hostess gave the signal for a collation to be served, consisting of rice and some Indian dishes, which were enjoyed with equal gusto. About 11 P.M. the lights were put out, and everyone went to bed, well pleased with the enjoyable day. Such was the daily life at Pondok Gedeh when there was a large house party.

The kabaja seems to have been largely discarded by the Indian ladies as an outdoor costume, judging by the following quotation from the *Java Government Gazette* of May 2, 1812: "At the entertainment recently given at Batavia, it was remarked how great an improvement has been introduced in respect to the attire of the Dutch ladies since the British authority has been established. The 'Cabaja' appears now

193 ह

generally disused and the more elegant English costume adopted. We congratulate our friends on the amelioration of the public taste because we see in it the dawn of still greater and more important improvement." This very readable and exceptionally attractive *Gazette* contains many amusing verses, contributed by the supporters and opponents of the kabaja, who give full rein to their ironical and bantering humor. The weekly journal forms a most important source for the knowledge of the local social life during the period of the English occupation.

Portuguese influence on pre-British social life was evident in many little details: an occasional Portuguese word was used as commonly as a Dutch one, and songs of a rather corrupt Portuguese were very popular in old Batavia. These were usually love ditties, sung to the accompaniment of the viola da gamba, zither, or flute. Here are a couple, in translation:

> Bastiana, Bastiana,
> Bastiana, my very dear:
> Bastiana's handkerchief
> I keep as hostage here.

> Laugh, rejoice, my Bastiana,
> Don't cry alas, alack.
> One day soon
> You'll get your kerchief back.

> Here's a golden ring, Margarita,
> With seven stones, you see.
> Whoever wants this ring, Margarita,
> Will have to marry me.

> When you are married, Margarita,
> When you pass my door,
> Then will I give you, Margarita,
> A rose my rose tree bore.

They drank heavily, if we are to judge by the number of toasts which it was *de rigueur* to honor at their assemblies and marriage feasts. Here is a typical toast list on the occasion of a high society wedding:

1. A hearty welcome to the feast.
2. The bride and bridegroom.
3. The first best man and bridesmaid.
4. The second best man and bridesmaid.
5. The boy and girl pages.
6. The boy and girl trainbearers.
7. His Excellency the governor general.
8. Other relatives and friends of the bride and bridegroom.
9. The ladies and gentlemen of the government here present.
10. The absent ladies and gentlemen of the government.
11. The married ladies here present.
12. The married gentlemen here present.
13. The unmarried ladies.
14. The unmarried gentlemen.
15. The good success of this present marriage.
16. The welfare of India under the rule of H.E.
17. The East India Company.
18. Their High Mightinesses.
19. The prosperity of the House of Orange.
20. The Lord Masters.
21. The welfare of the Fatherland.

As a signal that the party was breaking up, the company sang the following song:

> Strew posies and flowers:
> The Bride must to bed.
> Escort her, prepare her,
> For now she is wed.
> Then kiss her good night
> And when she's undressed,
> Be careful that no one shall hinder her rest.

The last admonition was scarcely necessary, as by that time none of the guests, let alone the husband, was capable of hindering anybody's rest. They were all too busy getting a spot of rest themselves to worry about the bride.

These weddings were always celebrated on Sundays, according to Stavorinus, and the bride was not supposed to appear again in public until the following Wednesday evening, when she attended divine service: "to be sooner seen in public would be a violation of the rules of decorum."

It seems to have been quite true that death was not taken as seriously in old Batavia as it usually is elsewhere. At least the typical Batavian widow did not spend much time repining: the law expressly forbade her to remarry until *three months* after the burial of her previous husband! A rich widow never lacked for suitors. Stavorinus speaks of one lady who lost her husband while the traveler was visiting Batavia. In the fourth week of her widowhood there was a candidate duly come a-courting her, and she would surely have married him before the three months were up had the law allowed it. Probably in this particular case it was her wealth which attracted the suitor, but Stavorinus seems to think that the lady herself, like most of her Eurasian sisters, was chronically of a passionate temper. "The warmth of the climate," he explains, "which influences strongly upon their constitutions, together with the dissolute lives of the men before marriage, are the causes of much wantonness and dissipation among the women."

Among the pages of Stavorinus's *Voyages* is a reference to another Dutch naval man's report on his Motherland's colonists, circa 1722. This man, Commodore Roggewein, gives a ludicrous account untempered by mercy, saying that his crew were contaminated by their example. All the lower classes were "as profligate and lewd as it is possible to conceive people to be, insomuch that the first question many of them asked of strangers arrived from Europe is, whether they have not brought some new oaths over; and whether they cannot teach them a more lively and extravagant method of swearing."

In the opinion of Major William Thorn, somewhat pompous chronicler of the conquest of Java, Batavians could scarcely be called Europeans, "so completely are they intermixed with the Portuguese and Malay colonists. The same may be observed of the other great towns along the coast, and of the Dutch Settlements in general throughout the East. With very few exceptions, that which is emphatically called the Mother Land, or Mother Country, is only known by name; and this is particularly the case with the Batavian women, few of whom are Europeans by birth. . . ."

The Dutch colonists did not seem to be of a mind to resent this opinion, for when speaking or writing they often referred to themselves as "Indians" rather than as "Indo-Europeans" or some similar name, even when they were of white, unmixed ancestry.

But of all the people who visited old Batavia, it remained for a Dutchman to put on record the most vicious description of his colonial compatriots that has ever, I dare say, been set up in print. So violent is Mijnheer de Graaff that if he were an Englishman, a Frenchman, or of any nationality but his own, I wouldn't dare quote him. Since he is Dutch, however, I feel the use of this quotation to be excused, at least, though I most decidedly don't claim that it is justified. Not justified, let us say, but lively and amusing, like some other sorts of hysteria. Mr. de Graaff fairly sputters.

He defines Batavian women in the following fashion:

(a) *Holland women*: those come out from Holland (where they were born) in ships to the Indies.

(b) *East-India Holland women*: those born in the Indies of pure Dutch parents, usually called *liblabs* on account of their accent (cf. the Anglo-Indian *chichi*).

(c) *Kastisen* (from the Portuguese *castiço*): the children of a Dutch father and a Eurasian mother.

(d) *Mestisen* (from the Portuguese *mestiço*): Those born of a Dutch father and a native mother; these were usually called "spotted nobility" or "unbleached dungarees," as they were neither black nor white, but in varying shades of color.

"All [these classes of women] are so garrulous, so proud, so wanton and lascivious that from sheer wantonness they scarcely know what to do with themselves. . . . They are waited on like princesses, and have a great many slaves of both sexes at their beck and call, waiting on them like watchdogs, night and day, and watching their eyes closely in order to catch their slightest whim; and they are themselves so lazy that one will not stretch out her hand for a thing, not even to pick up a straw from the floor, even if it be just at her feet or beside her, but will call a slave to do it. And if they do not come quick enough the women will scold them for a 'lousy whore; negress whore; son-of-a-whore; son-of-a-bitch,' [these words are written in Indo-Portuguese in the 1703 original] and sometimes worse than this. And for the very least fault, they have slaves tied to a stake or a ladder, and cause their naked backs to be mercilessly flogged with a cat-of-nine-tails, till the blood pours down and the flesh hangs in tattered strips, which they then rub with salt, pepper and pickle, to prevent the wounds' rotting or smelling. These women are often too lazy even to walk . . . and cannot rear their own children, but as soon as they are born, leave their upbringing entirely to a slave nurse, or whore, or any kind of slave in their entourage; which is also the reason why their children would rather be with their slave nurses than their own parents, and why they are brought up with the slaves' own ideas, and speak as good Malabar, Bengali, Guzerati and Bastard-Portuguese as the slaves themselves, and can hardly speak a single word of Dutch when they grow up, and that little with a strong Indo-Portuguese accent.

"Still worse than the Dutch-born women are the *Kastisen* and *Mestisen*, who know nothing, and are fit for nothing, except to scratch their arse, chew betel, smoke cigarettes, drink tea or lie on a mat or a carpet; in this wise they sit the whole day, idle and bored, without turning their hands to a thing; and squatting for the most part on their heels like an ape on its arse; because they cannot even sit on a chair properly, but they must needs tuck their legs under the body, which is the common use amongst the Asiatics. Their usual topic of conversation is about their slaves,—how many they have bought, sold, lost, etc., or of a tasty curry or rice dish. They also dislike eating at table with anybody save each other; seldom eat with their own husbands; but invariably with some of their own cronies and girl friends, their table conversation being limited to such remarks as, 'A good chicken soup is not so tasty as an appetizing curry sauce.' And they don't eat nicely like other folk . . . but mix their chicken or fish with the rice, and gurgle and suck it up through the fingers like pigs from a trough, and then stick their hands and fingers in the mouth so that the juice runs down between and slops over them. . . . And if these Liblab or half-caste women should occasionally chance to be invited to a gentleman's table or a wedding, they have no idea how to behave, and seldom dare to speak a word save to their own kind, lest they make fools of themselves in public. As happened on a certain occasion when one of these ladies, sitting at table with a number of other ladies, was served by one of the gentlemen present, as a compliment, with a piece of roast chicken: when she took the same very ungraciously from her plate and put it back in the dish, saying, 'I don't want to eat a bit of hen's arse.' [This quotation is in Indo-Portuguese in the original.]"

De Graaff also accuses these unfortunate females of another vice, namely, lasciviousness. "I can give you more than one example," he says, "of those who have had to do with their own slave boys or men, for which the latter have subsequently been hanged." There follows on this a tirade against Dutch employees of low rank, soldiers, sailors, clerks, workmen, et cetera, "who marry stinking negresses and black canaille and are invariably had for cuckolds by their wives, who would rather sleep with a native or Eurasian than with a pure European."

This strikes a familiar note. Just so do suspicious Flemings speak of their women in the Congo; just so do the gossips accuse European ladies who live alone in Peking. "It was by no means unknown," says William Plomer (Double Lives), writing of his childhood in Johannesburg, "for a native house-boy to complain that when his white employer was out at work in the daytime his employer's wife had been making excessive demands on his virility—a remarkable circumstance in a country where the colour-bar is supposed to be rigid." De Graaff obviously suffers from one of those mass jealousies which stimulate such beliefs.

"The most astounding thing in Batavia is the great pomp and ceremony which prevails, not only amongst the Hollanders but also amongst the Eurasians, particularly in going to and coming from Church on Sunday, High-Days and Holidays. For everyone is then tricked out in her best finery, in silk and brocade, cloth, damask and gold-thread work, or heavily embroidered and decorated cloth of gold, striped and flowered stuffs with gold embroidered borders, etc. Their headdress is decorated with costly pearls . . . necklaces and earrings of fine pearls and diamonds, others on their breast and so forth. Thus they sit by hundreds in the Church, decked out in their finery like dolls in a row,—the meanest of them looking like a Princess or a Burgomaster's wife or daughter, so that Heaven itself blinks; And what is more, when they go to Church or come home, the least of them is accompanied by a slave who holds a sunshade over her head, some of which have large hanging silken embroidered borders. So that when the Service is beginning and ending, the Church doors and courtyard are so crowded with a throng of sunshades, slaves, slave-maids, body-guards and lackeys, that one can scarcely push through them, to say nothing of those that are waiting outside with their coaches and carriages to bring their masters and mistresses home. . . . This ridiculous pomp and ceremony is the rule not only in Batavia but throughout all Asia wherever Hollanders live or are settled; because nobody will give way to anybody else, or take a small step aside, each one wishes to play the fine lady, even if it should be on the steps of God's altar."

[Then there is more about the folly of "keeping up with the Joneses" anno 1701.] He further points out how these women who are so high and mighty in the Indies are very small beer in Holland, being usually of very low origin, like kitchen maids, dairymaids, et cetera, and if they try treating their Dutch maidservants like their Indian slaves on their return, they are speedily disillusioned and find themselves without any. Hence the majority prefer to stay in India, where they are so much better off.

Space doesn't allow us to cite examples of life in other Dutch colonies at this time. But in Malacca and so on conditions were very similar. The women of these communities were brought up in the same careless way, and though the habits they learned from the natives varied, of course, with the different races, the Dutch veneer seems to have produced over all this part of the world something like a special type of woman.

CHAPTER XII

No survey of old Batavia before or during the British occupation would be worth a penny if we did not take a special look at the slaves of Java. The subject of slavery is of particular interest to us. Raffles, while he was lieutenant governor of Java, committed the outstanding act of his career in declaring the slave trade illegal in the colony, though his claim that he was merely enforcing litigation which already existed is justifiable.

He was, of course, encouraged and even put up to this action by his patron Lord Minto, who wrote in one of his first letters from Java:

"The state of slavery has attracted my serious and anxious attention. That monstrous system prevails to a calamitous extent throughout these Eastern regions of India, and produces, as it cannot fail of doing, most of the miseries incident to that mode of procuring the service of men. But it is too general to be suddenly suppressed by any one Power in so many separate and independent countries. In Java it is fortunately not grievous to the slave; servitude being wholly domestic or menial. I hope something may be done immediately for modifying this evil, and I propose that Government should set the example in this report by abstaining entirely from the future purchase of slaves. A return is preparing of the public slaves of Government now existing, and if the number should prove inconsiderable, as I hope it will, I have in contemplation to hazard an anticipation of your approbation, which I shall surely receive, by emancipating all those to whom that change would be advisable. The importation of slaves may also be checked, although it cannot yet be abolished." '

By our modern lights, this bit of administrative detail outweighs all Raffles's other activity. Many of his contemporaries, however, would not have agreed with us. They may have held various opinions concerning slavery, but they were united in their failure to recognize the far-reaching effect of his decision.

To begin with, Raffles hit some of the highest-ranking people of his Company where it hurt most—in their pockets—by putting a stop to the buying and selling of slaves. Those gentlemen made no secret of their grievance; they were loud and shrill in their condemnation of his behavior, which they interpreted simply as a reckless disposal of other people's rights; theirs, for example. It is true slave traffic had already been outlawed in British India, but most of the interested parties had hoped this law would shortly be forgotten and allowed to fall into desuetude, as anti-slavery laws have done more recently in certain non-British African districts for example. Raffles, they felt, was tactlessly pressing a point best forgotten.

Besides, the average stay-at-home Englishman who had no personal interest in colonial life didn't have much personal interest in slavery either. England was no place for the dusky Oriental or blackamoor; save as an occasional curiosity, few natives of tropical climes were ever brought to the fogbound islands of Great Britain. Londoners, true cockneys, heard about slaves, read about slaves, envied or criticized slaveholders of their own nation, and characteristically suspected slaveholders from other lands, one and all, of being monsters of cruelty. But unless they profited directly from slave dealing, as they did if they happened to be relatives of the British blackbirders, or unless, like Robert Browning's father, they themselves held property abroad where slave labor was used, it was a question which didn't hold the attention of the public in England. The man in London's streets was not interested in the problems of the far-off Indies, East or West.

There were exceptions, naturally, or the legislation which Raffles ultimately had to cite in support of his unpopular action would never have been passed. A few wealthy people like Browning of Jamaica felt that their principles forced them to take action. Browning himself was one of the first plantation owners in the West Indies to free his slaves, and he made himself unpopular doing so, though he was very proud of that record.

Travelers who reported on conditions among the slaves of Java are by no means unanimously agreed. Reading their arguments pro and con, one is inevitably reminded of the flood of dispute, of defense and accusation, which followed on our early public discussions of slavery in the United States. In Raffles's time, however, in the East Indies around 1812, the question of principle was not yet uppermost in people's minds, or there would have been far more discussion of it than there was. Most people accepted slavery, in Stockdale's words, as "a necessary evil," if they entertained any misgivings at all. The main query was simple and oft repeated: were the slaves in Batavia well off in general or were they usually victims of bad treatment and cruelty? That is a question, of course, which could be answered with perfect truth a hundred times over, in every possible manner, and it was. Like the African slaves of our own South, a Batavian slave depended for his welfare upon the temper of his individual owner. Stockdale comes nearest to drawing a general conclusion when he states that the slaves of Batavia were better off than those of the West Indies, because they would not support too much harsh treatment. In the East a bad master was usually assassinated, sooner or later. Considering the dangerous tendency of Malays to "run amok," the slaveholders of the Archipelago and its environs no doubt tempered their discipline with a certain amount of discretion.

J. Olivier in 1836 claimed that the slaves at Batavia were better treated than any others elsewhere in Asia, and that in some respects they were even better off than ordinary servants in Holland. In 1825 there were, according to him, 12,419 slaves at Batavia, and the total was slowly decreasing every year. If this be compared with Stockdale's figures for 1778, in which year he says there were 20,072 ordinary slaves and 4,873 "mardykers" (manumitted slaves of all nations), Olivier's claim of a steady decrease in slavery certainly seems to be true.

Stavorinus declared himself in favor of harsh treatment of slaves whenever it seemed necessary. Necessity as he saw it meant self-protection against dangerously insane slaves (those running "amok"), by means of unrelaxing vigilance and a regularly severe punishment for grave crimes such as murder. He does not, however, reconcile his description of slaves running "amok," in which he admits that a madman of this sort is not responsible for his actions, with his faith in severe punishment as a warning and a deterrent. Evidently Stavorinus was not troubled by doubts, as I am. I should like to be told why, if nothing on earth can stop an "amok" native, the example of some fellow slave, writhing in the agony of disciplinary torture, should have a salutary effect on the behavior of a man incapable of seeing him, or rather of appreciating what he sees.

We learned in the preceding chapter that the Dutch and liplap ladies of Batavia were not always kind to their slaves, to put it mildly. Raffles was shocked but not astonished when he came across an example of his predecessor Daendels's brutal notions of discipline. On one occasion Daendels ordered hanging as punishment for nine native thieves, and he threatened some Dutch magistrates who protested against the severity of this command with a similar fate if they did not carry out the sentence forthwith.

Yet Thorn thinks that we are generally inclined to be too hard on the Dutch in this respect. In his *Conquest of Java* he says they "have been unjustly accused of adding unnecessarily to the evils of slavery; but the fact is, that the imported slaves, and those who have been made free, with their progeny, are the only domestic servants that can be procured. The Javanese are naturally too indolent for employment, and they have besides an unconquerable aversion to servitude in families, in which dislike the Chinese participate with still stronger feelings of repugnance.

"In the selection of female slaves for the respective duties of the house, great attention is paid to their personal appearance and musical accomplishments, as well as to those qualifications, which seem to be their principal recommendation. Here the slaves are valued for their beauty, their skill in playing on the harp, and their melodious voices. This peculiarity of Asiatic luxury is carried to such a height, that in some of the houses of the more opulent Europeans, as well as of the wealthy natives, some dozens of these enchanting female slaves may be found, as if the owners thought of realizing the promise of the Mahommedan paradise in this world."

Doesn't one hear in this passage a note that is definitely wistful? The good Thorn obviously has forgotten, for a moment at least, to weigh the strictly moral aspects of slavery, when the slaves are beautiful women. He has lost himself in a dream of beauty, ignoring for a space such crass matters as commerce and private ownership of these Mahommedan houris . . . until, with a start, he returns to his sheep.

"The condition of the slaves in Java," he says with a fresh burst of austerity, "is far from being uncomfortable; they are well fed and clothed, and by no means hard worked or severely treated, except perhaps where they are made to experience the resentment of female jealousy; which passion is not confined to the European ladies, as many instances are mentioned of some favoured slaves having taken revenge on their masters for their inconstancy, by different kinds and degrees of poison." It seems a rather odd sort of freedom at which to point with pride—life, luxury, and the pursuit of poison.

"Since the Conquest of Java," continues the cheerful Thorn, "the act of the British Legislature for the Abolition of the Slave Trade, has been published and enforced in these seas; in consequence of which, several vessels conveying slaves have been seized by our cruizers, and this has not a little conduced to enhance the value of those at present in the Island."

This last item of information was hardly, one supposes, the end Raffles had in view when he enforced the Abolition Act, any more than the high price of scotch in the States, during the period of the ill-fated Eighteenth Amendment, could have rejoiced the hearts of W.C.T.U. members. Still, it was an evil only to be expected, and if events proceeded according to his plan it was only temporary pending complete emancipation.

Van de Wall, in the description of Batavian country life which we have already noted, speaks of the large number of slaves always found in such a household. It was not all ease and luxury, either, when a housewife had to deal with her slaves' disputes, for they were apt to dislike each other automatically unless they belonged to the same race, and one usually found a great mixture of races among these people. Timor versus Nias, Nias versus Borneo, et cetera—they all quarreled with each other. Most of the Java slaves came from the coast of Coromandel, Van de Wall says, and from Bengal; the next largest number were from Sumatra, the Moluccas, and all parts of the Archipelago save Java itself, Javanese being forbidden by law to be enslaved—(though this law did not apply to children born of slave parents on Java). Slaves from Bali and the Celebes were most feared as being liable to run amok, and for this reason the Company periodically forbade their use.

Illicit amours between slaves were numerous, which is only to be expected, and it is not surprising, either, that masters and slave girls were often lovers. Occasionally even mistresses and their male slaves were guilty of cohabitation, though this variation on a familiar theme always raised a fearful scandal.

Johannes Olivier stayed in Batavia in the early years of the nineteenth century, during a part of the time which particularly interests us, and he wrote as follows: "I had heard and read so much of the brutal mis-treatment which the poor blacks were forced to endure, that the mere mention of the slave trade sent cold shudders through me. But here now, I saw on the contrary, that the slaves were considered and treated not merely with great humanity but even with great consideration, with mutual concern, with friendliness, and as members of the same patriarchal family. The orders were given in the most considerate fashion. If a slave, male or female, or one of their children fell sick, strengthening soups and other delicacies were sent them from the master's table, and often given them by the hand of their charitable mistress. Who can be surprised that slaves who were treated in such wise, often remained faithful to their master and mistress unto death? Look, for example, at the Dowager Lady de Klerk, who on her death in 1786, in her will freed over 50 of her slaves with their children, and left them in many cases a sum of money varying between 25 and 500 Rixdollars."

Other writers, however, such as Noble (1762), Haafnei (circa 1800), and Dirk van Hogendorp (circa 1800) bitterly criticize the mistreatment of the slaves at Batavia, which an earlier French traveler, De Biervillas (1736) nevertheless contrasts very favorably with that meted out to the slaves at Goa. However, Olivier, like everyone else, does admit that the lip-laps treated their slaves very badly.

The governor's private orchestra, around 1786 or so, consisted of seventeen slaves, playing without other members; their instruments included a flute, clarinet, violin, horn, trumpet, castanet, bassoon, and various others. Olivier (circa 1810) states that the house-orchestra slaves were well taught, had good ears for music, and gave a good performance. The orchestras usually played during meals, at required intervals and for dancing, this last category including kafarinja, an old Portuguese dance, as well as gallops like the plow dance. Generally speaking, the Dutch at Batavia were very keen on music. Cooks were the most valued and highly priced slaves, but musicians were next in importance, whereas female embroiderers and seamstresses came third.

Classical names were favored by their Dutch masters foi slaves: names like Achilles, Castor, Andromeda, Theodora; they also liked biblical names, such as Joseph, Daniel, oi Jacoba. Occasionally the slaves were called simply by native names—Ismail, Sapto, Lesarda. The ungallant C. F. Noble, in 1762, wrote, "Europeans that reside at Batavia, buy or keep as servants the most beautiful Malay women. There are a few Dutch white women in the City, but so sickly and weak, that were I to reside amongst them, I would sooner chuse one of the natives than one of them." Well, after all, to paraphrase the modern American colloquialism—who wouldn't?

Other categories of slaves were gardeners, maids of various kinds, including some whose duty it was merely to serve tea and refreshments, grooms, grocers, sandal makers—everything, in fact, that one might find in a village of freedmen, among the shopkeepers of the town.

"It later became obvious to me," writes Olivier, "that the vast majority of the Europeans treated their slaves with the greatest consideration and kindness, and I am the better pleased to state this fact since it indubitably rebounds to the credit of my countrymen. This observation does naturally not apply to the Liplapps or Creoles, whose upbringing, hitherto, has been most sadly neglected in India. But it seems a natural conclusion that the generous spirit of the Netherlands Government will finally exert its beneficent influence over the character of this pitiful race. The way has already been pointed to the improvement of the worst habits and customs of the female section of the Liplapps (one cannot count many among the fair sex) by the establishment of a Governmental educational institute, in which they will at least be able to attain a certain degree of moral and cultural civilization."

Notice the date when Olivier wrote that—1827. The British had been and gone, long since, but they had left their mark at least on the liplaps, if not on Javanese politics. The bad old days were slipping backward, fading out, drawing nearer and nearer to oblivion. Perhaps this is a good place to remark that the attitude toward the Javanese at home, in Holland, was changing too. The government was beginning to urge European ladies to go out to the colonies. In 1933, as a matter of fact, young government servants going out to the East from Holland had to be either engaged or married before they started on their voyaging; and to home-grown Dutch girls, too; none of your liplaps! Some of those portly old eighteenth-century merchants must be looking on cynically from the other world, sneering as they draw on their pipes; pausing in their sneers only long enough for a good old-fashioned Batavia fever chill. (From habit, naturally—nobody is really ill in the after world.) White women, *real* white women, from Amsterdam or The Hague? The old boys snort lustily. What good would such chits be in a climate like Batavia's? The new project (Operation Caucasian?) must look terribly impractical, from the viewpoint of a real, genuine, eighteenth-century Dutch ghost. But of course from his viewpoint the colonies have been going to the dogs anyway, for a long, long time; for almost as long as they have been living among the other shades of antiquity.

Here, however, it must be said that in the opinion of at least one Dutchman, Dr. F. de Haan in his *Oud Batavia*, Raffles was a hypocrite, for he himself was guilty not of owning slaves but of importing them, during a later and different administration. De Haan says that Raffles brought Balinese slave girls into Singapore for the benefit of the Chinese of that city! Since he does not give the name of his authority for this statement, we cannot refute it, and speaking from the scholar's scientific viewpoint, we should ignore the story.

On other points, however, De Haan is more generous with data, and many of his observations are well worth noting. According to him, during the period when the English were in Java, 1811–16, three quarters of the total number of slaves at Batavia were not born there but had been imported to keep up their numbers, as their mortality rate was very high. He implies that their death rate was even higher than that of the ill-fated Europeans, probably because of their even less sanitary housing. The total number of slaves in Batavia and its neighborhood in 1816, he says, was about twelve thousand, and the largest number in a single owner's hands was 165.

"That one could do without slaves, and that one could get better and cheaper service from free natives, was first made clear after the English conquest. The English officers and officials brought their own free servants with them and did not like to use slaves." In contradiction to this general rule, however, we must remember that Gillespie at least once bought slaves—three dancing girls—during his residence in Java. It became a *cause célèbre* after Raffles heard of the transaction. "This must have had some effect," says De Haan, speaking of the more usual behavior of the British in eschewing slave labor. "Moreover, the times were such that people did not feel inclined to invest much money in possessions which involved so much risk." A slave's purchase money was too high a sum to be considered lightly, and the high mortality rate among them rendered slave buying a bad investment. "And also the realization that slavery is as demoralizing for the master as for the servant must gradually have gained ground. Fortunately the abolition of slavery proceeded by very easy stages in Java, and it was not until 1860 that the last slaves were freed, to their great disgust."

Generally speaking, the treatment of slaves in the Dutch Indies was better in the eighteenth century than in the seventeenth, and better in the nineteenth than in the eighteenth, partly owing to the growth of religious tolerance. (This is still De Haan.) Up to 1782, a slave woman who had children by her Dutch master could be sold by him, together with their children, whose status was that of slaves like their mother, but this practice was then prohibited, and a man could not sell either concubine or offspring. (Slavery did not legally exist in Holland, and therefore the law was based on the old Roman Law in this respect.)

Typical auction announcements are as follows: One, in 1814: "Household furniture, gold and silver work, some dancing-girls, wagons and horses," for sale by a Chinese.

Another, in 1816: "For sale, a perfect cook who can bake pastry as well as anybody in Batavia."

Chinese were reputed to be the harshest taskmasters, De Haan says, but does not name his informant(s).

Obviously De Haan was correct in describing the abolition's progress as going by easy stages. As late as 1816 the *Java Government Gazette* reported a case where a young slave girl had been shut up for some months in a vat, and another where a smith's slaves had been chained to their workbenches.

The practice of sending slaves to prison or to the stocks for punishment obtained in Java, according to De Haan: it was evidently much like conditions in contemporary Cuba, described in the book *Anthony Adverse*. He adds that Raffles used to put natives and Chinese in jail if they did not show his own servants proper respect, citing chapter and verse for one

211 ৡৰ

occasion. That was evidently at the beginning of Raffles's term in office, and it may well have happened that once, as an example. But it could scarcely have been Raffles's habit.

De Haan's final comment on slavery versus the use of free labor is an explanation as to why the slaves weren't better workers. In a big household, he says, there would naturally be a lot of them, and so no one slave had very much work to do. Even that he usually did badly. In other words, slavery is not only demoralizing to the master, but it also spoils a slave's own working capacity. The average wealthy slave owner in Java, when the English arrived, had about forty slaves, or perhaps fifty or sixty; somewhere thereabouts. Such a number of workers didn't really leave much for anybody to do on his own, nor could these conditions have done very much for a man's sense of responsibility.

The good old days, then, were not so very good after all, and Raffles didn't really do anyone much of a disservice when he insisted upon putting slave traffic out of action. For, after all, it does no good to argue whether or not this slave was happy, and that slave better fed than his free cousin in the backwoods. Slavery asks a deeper question than these. We humans have gone over the border and sipped the intoxicating wine of Principle; it's too late, now, to answer critics by telling them that we have, on the whole, been pretty good to our slaves. Among all the Nazi practices which are now coming to light, the one which shocks us the most is that they enslaved thousands of people, inhabitants of the conquered territories of Europe. They dealt in human flesh and bone and muscle, just when we thought slavery was finished and done with. That was the great outrage.

It is no use to talk of patriarchal households; that phrase does not explain away the dreadful possibilities which always lurk behind the word "slave." Look for a few minutes at the punishment they meted out to a Macassar slave in Batavia back in 1769, at that same period when many writers were satisfied and smug about the situation, convinced that the slaves of Java were better off than a good many freemen.

This man from Macassar had murdered his owner, and so

they condemned him to death by impalement, which was a punishment concocted deliberately, by the council, especially in order to discourage such slaves as may have felt a natural urge now and then to murder their masters.

The slave was taken to the execution place and made to lie down on his belly. Four men took hold of him and held on while the executioner made a transverse incision at the lower part of his body, as far as the sacrum. The executioner then took a spike of polished iron, six feet long, and introduced the sharp end of it into the wound, so that it passed between backbone and skin. Two men drove it up, forcibly, along the spine, the executioner holding on at the other end and steering it properly, until it came out between the neck and the shoulders. The lower end was now put into a wooden post and riveted fast, the whole contraption lifted upright, and the post driven into the ground. At the top of the post, about ten feet from the ground, was a kind of little bench on which the body rested and was kept in place.

Stavorinus, who witnessed the affair, said that the slave's fortitude was incredible, or perhaps it was not fortitude as much as insensibility. He did not utter the least complaint except at the point in the proceedings when the spike had to be riveted to the post: the hammering and shaking caused by this did make him bellow out. Also he uttered loud complaint when he was lifted up with the post and it was set into the ground.

The slave from Macassar did not die until three o'clock the next afternoon, and then, according to the bystanders who talked to Stavorinus, it was because a light rain fell that he was thus released from life. In dry weather such victims could last much longer than that, they explained, as long, sometimes, as eight days, and without food or drink. The reason they gave for such slow death was that no vital parts of the body were injured by the impalement. Water in the wounds, however, brought on an immediate gangrene, they said.

The only complaint the slave made was of insufferable thirst, for he was out in the burning sun and no one was allowed to give him water to drink (for fear of hastening death and curtailing the punishment). He was also, of course, tormented by thousands of stinging insects.

Up to three hours before his death he conversed, quietly on the whole, with the bystanders. He would relate the manner of his crime and express repentance, doing all this with great composure, yet an instant later would break out in bitterest complaints of his thirst, and he raved deliriously, begging for a drink.

That happened in 1769, but the date doesn't matter. It is a thing which can happen any time, anywhere, to any slave, as long as slavery exists. Don't talk nonsense about patriarchal households, then. There were probably a few patriarchs in Nazi Germany too. It's beside the point. Raffles and his friends knew that, back in 1814.

CHAPTER XIII

It was with deliberate intent that until now I have avoided as far as possible mentioning British influence in Java after the conquest in 1811. Rather, I have placed emphasis on conditions in Batavia before the British interregnum while she was exclusively Dutch, for there is no doubt that the island's administration under Raffles, and the influx of British officials and a few English wives, produced an impact from which the Indies staggered for a long time afterward.

There were many elements in this situation which contributed to its explosive nature. Some were political, some social, and a good many more were a combination of both. To begin with, there was of course the inevitable resentment a conquered people feels against its conquerors. The setup in Batavia was complicated; it had not been a simple matter of England versus Holland, and so in a way Raffles was given an out from the customary embarrassment which besets the overdog. He and his assistants tried manfully to maintain from the beginning of their residence on Java the polite fiction that they were welcome as flowers in May to the Dutch, and that the Hollanders in turn were their favorite neighbors too. The English proclamation on landing day had been worded as tactfully as Minto, out of his wide diplomatic experience, had been able to make it, to imply that Great Britain and Holland were allies in the campaign, banded together against their common enemy France toward a common end, British sovereignty on Java. Carefully planning for an amicable, just future, the earl and Raffles arranged that out of the administrative council of three which they decided upon, two members should be Hollanders. Now that peace was achieved, during the four and a half years of British occupation, the English and the Dutch to all outward appearances were living on equal terms, like the usual big happy European family. Both sides realized that this appearance of unity was vitally necessary because of the native princes, who were always on the alert for any sign of trouble between their ill-assorted masters.

There were many small matters which contained the seeds of importance, and Raffles was a subtle soul who understood such things almost too well, so that his career in Batavia was complicated by countless little questions which must be carefully weighed before decision. For example there was that vexatious problem of carriage stopping. It will be remembered that a certain Captain Carteret while visiting Batavia under the Dutch had insisted that he need not follow the Dutch law in that case, and he had won by his resistance an exemption from the rule, for all English who came after him. No Englishman had to get out of his carriage when he met the governor or a councilman riding along in the opposite direction—under the Dutch. Now, however, Raffles changed all that. De Haan says, "But Raffles, who in the matter of state and dignity, followed as far as possible in the footsteps of his Dutch predecessors in order to prove that he was not their inferior, still ordered the natives and the Chinese that on meeting his coach, they should dismount from their horses and/or step out of their vehicles, and that nobody could overtake him from behind and ride past him, on pain of arrest; a coachman who dared to do this was imprisoned for a month. On the other hand, employees addressed him in private letters as 'My dear Sir. . . .' "

As anyone with knowledge of international diplomacy will agree, social relations in a situation of this sort count a good deal. For this reason Olivia Raffles too had an important role to play, unofficially. As lady of the lieutenant governor she was the acknowledged leader of Batavian society; it behooved her to make all the nice adjustments and to pay the subtle courtesies demanded of that position. Her deportment at official parties would be only a part of it; the real test would come in her dealings with the world of the ladies.

Did any other woman in all the history of diplomacy inherit such an outlandish society to govern? Olivia's problem would have been complicated enough even in an ordinary Dutch city, for the position occupied by women in England was immeasurably higher and more dignified, in those days, than that of the typical household frump of Holland. On Java things were even worse, much worse. The few Dutchwomen who had come from Europe were not numerous enough to make a dent in the system. Most wives of Batavian Dutchmen were either half-castes or women who had been brought up in a *milieu* of half-castes, and had in consequence taken on their habits and attitude, which might be described in some as a combination of betel chewing and ignorant laziness. The Dutchmen of Batavia were of no mind to let any outrageous English notions of women's rights enter the minds of their usually bovine wives, and they presented an unbroken front of resistance to Olivia and her feminine compatriots. In the end the English ladies probably agreed to drop all attempts at intercourse, no matter what hopes Olivia may have entertained at the beginning. They stayed with each other and with their men, while from afar the Dutch watched them and made scathing comments. In this tendency they were not alone; the English were not always silent on the subject of their neighbors either. Lady Anne Bernard wrote of the Dutch girls at the Cape, about 1800, that "what they want most is shoulders and manners."

But of all English commentators, none exceeds in vividness and bluntness of expression Lord Minto, who in a letter to his wife described his first view of the cream of Batavian society. It was at that ball which the army gave, honoring Sir Samuel Auchmuty and the earl.

"It is impossible to give you anything like an adequate notion of the total absence of beauty in so crowded a hall. There never is a dozen of women assembled in Europe without a few attractions amongst them. Here there was no difference, except in some few varieties of ugliness and ordinariness of dress and manner. The Dutch did not encourage, nor indeed allow freely, European women to go out to their colonies in India. The consequence has been, that the men lived with native women, whose daughters, gradually borrowing something from the father's side, and becoming a mixed breed, are now the wives and ladies of rank and fashion in Java. The young ladies have learnt the European fashions of dress, and their carriage and manner are something like our own of an ordinary class. Their education is almost wholly neglected; or rather no means exists here to provide for it. They are attended from their cradles by numerous slaves, by whom they are trained in helplessness and laziness; and from such companions and governesses, you may conceive how much accomplishment and refinement in manner or opinions they are likely to acquire.

"In dancing the young beauties seemed lame in English country dances, of which they knew neither the steps nor the figures; but in their own dance, which was to a very slow valse tune, the figures much the same as ours, with a valse embrace, however, instead of an allemande, they were at home and not without grace; while our English damsels and cavaliers were all abroad and about as awkward and crippled as their Dutch fellow-subjects had been before. Mrs. Bunbury, the wife of an officer, a young pretty Englishwoman, stood up in the dance; but seeing, when the first couple reached her, the Dutch gentleman take his partner fairly in his arms and hug her, as it appeared to her, as a bear does his prey, she fairly took to her heels and could not be brought back again, by any means, to see or share such horror. The Dutch valsers certainly deal in very strict embraces, but our English gentlemen, to their shame be it said, appeared so entirely unpractised in that art that their Dutch partners gave the point up as a bad job, and were forced to content themselves with merely taking hands and swinging the loobies about. The chaperons and older Dutch ladies are a class not yet described in Europe. The principal mark to know them by is their immense size. The whole colonial sex runs naturally to fat, partly from over-feeding—partly from want of exercise. The morning air is the grand pursuit of the English Orientalists; the Dutch of both sexes have a horror of it and prefer their beds. In the rest of the day nobody can go out; and in the evening they think a drive in a carriage too great an effort. . . . Suppose an immense woman sitting behind a stall with roasted apples and we have an old Dutch lady of the highest rank and fashion. Her upper garment is a loose coarse white cotton jacket fastened nowhere but worn with the graceful negligence of pins and all other fastenings or constraints of a Scotch *lass*, an equally coarse petticoat, and the coarsest stockings, terminating in wide, thick-soled shoes; but by standing behind her you find out her nobility, for at the back of the head a little circle of hair is gathered into a small crown, and on this are deposited diamonds, rubies, and precious stones often of very great value. It is well with this if they can speak even Dutch, many knowing no language but Malay."

The English never quite accustomed themselves to the custom, prevalent even among Dutchwomen without Asiatic blood, of wearing the native dress. For example there was Madam Couperus, who "was dressed in a mixture between the Malay and the Portuguese, her outward garment being made exactly like a shirt. She looked as if she reversed the order of her dress altogether." This was in 1795.

Yet little by little these Englishwomen's manners and tastes did have an effect on the local ladies. This naturally showed itself first in dress, with the liplaps leading the way in the adoption of English fashions. Thorn speaks of it with customary smugness in his brief description of Batavia's social life:

"After the arrival of the English, the younger ladies, and those who mix much in society with them, adopted the fashionable habiliments of our fair countrywomen, and in their manner as well as dress they are improving wonderfully. . . ."

Like many other writers, Thorn mentions the Harmonie, that club which before the conquest had been the center of Dutch social life and which under Raffles's government continued to be important in a different way. In the old days the Dutchmen had used the building for their smoking, drinking, dull, conversational evenings; their women were brought along sometimes, but rarely, and then merely as an afterthought. When the English moved in, however, they brought their own amusements with them and followed their usual custom of joining parties in company with their wives. Thorn said, "The higher circles, however, have to boast of ladies as well as gentlemen of rather superior acquirements, who are for the most part Europeans, either by birth or education. These meet frequently in convivial parties, entertaining themselves with sprightly dances and elegant suppers."

It was the English who first popularized dancing at official parties. It was the English who taught the Dutch burghers to have music with their toasts rather than merely to recite them, when they were drinking. Someone with a sense of humor selected the tunes on purpose for their titles. To the toast, "The Queen and the royal family," the appropriate tune was "Merrily Danced the Quaker's Wife and Merrily Danced the Quaker." When "The Company" was toasted, the tune was "Money in Both Pockets." When the company drank to "The ladies of Batavia," the band played, "Will You Come to the Bower?"

New festivities were introduced after the British pattern: for example, every year during his tenure Raffles held a New Year's reception. Today an average international gathering in the Far East would probably greet with amused incredulity the statement that a *British* government, of all groups, should have had a lightening, gay effect upon any society whatever, but so it was in 1811. In those days and by comparison with the slow Dutch, the British looked like tearing, merry madcaps.

What did these English ladies wear *en grande tenue*, and how did they amuse themselves? It is rather a pity that they should have happened to become models of fashion for the Batavian ladies just at that particular time. It is a shame that this political development didn't take place ten years earlier, when European clothes were really pretty and simple. Now, in 1811 and after, the graceful pseudo-Grecian simplicity, with its light draped muslins and its freedom of movement, was going out. The women of Europe were entering on a phase of ridiculous overelaboration. Olivia and her intimate friends were probably a little later in getting around to it than were her fellow women in England and on the Continent, but she was no unnatural monster; she tried to keep up with the styles, like everyone else. And, also like everyone else, the half-caste wives of Batavia obediently trotted along in the footsteps, those long English footsteps, of Raffles's lady.

Both nymphs and goddesses now went out of style, and the costumes which appeared instead were distortions of the human body.

In European centers of fashion, about 1817, dresses were now entirely bodice-less, and hung straight from the neck to an embroidered hem on a comparatively short skirt. Pantalettes were clearly visible beneath usually heavily trimmed in lace. It was a peculiarly hideous style, concealing as it did all natural shape of the figure. The only favorable thing about it was the continued absence of elaborate corsets, but for almost a decade European women went about looking like nothing so much as bifurcated piping.

Shawls were much in evidence, in all materials and for all possible prices. Women in every walk of life had their shawls. It is said that the Empress Josephine, much to Napoleon's disgust, owned four hundred English cashmere shawls, each costing at least fifteen thousand francs—a far cry from the poor cockney's printed cotton of the same shape and name. So important an article of dress was the shawl that a lady's entire reputation for taste depended on the way she arranged this, her most important garment. You didn't say that a woman was well dressed, in 1810; you said she was "beautifully draped."

Hair styles underwent a similar change. One's hair was worn pressed flat to the head, either netted or arranged in small tight curls over the brow; or plaited. Farewell to the luxuriant wind-blown tresses of the pagan deities!

As for the men's clothing, it did not change so quickly. It never does. Knee breeches, however, went completely out of style about 1815. The redingote, which earlier had sported tails so long they were carried by their wearers as a lady carried her train, settled down to its final shape. Already men who longed for the old color and gaiety were reduced to wearing color only in their waistcoats and neckcloths. Little did the poor creatures realize, as they complained, that they would shortly be reduced even further, and would have to depend for relief from their drab suits solely upon one pathetic little scrap of silk, called a cravat or necktie. "By about 1815 . . . [the vest], and the other two articles of man's attire, the coat and the trousers, were essentially the same as they are now, all extravagance of style having been discarded." Men, hapless creatures that they are, had stopped emulating the peacock, and forever. Gone forever, too, were the velvets, plumes, and laces of the good old days.

Travel books of the period speak more than once of the extreme cleanliness of the Malays. Tourists tell in accents of wonder and fright how the native women actually went *bathing,* some of them every day. So, one supposes, did their men. We need not wonder that white travelers considered this fact worthy of comment, when we look at the personal habits which prevailed among the "civilized" nations of the world. In 1775 an order of the Batavian High Government forbade forcing the soldiers of the garrison to take a bath once a week! A few advanced souls had recently been driven to producing tracts on the subject of cleanliness, begging their compatriots in France and England to bathe at least once in a while, and to change the underclothing of their children if not of themselves. The French were evidently worse offenders than the English. Anyway that is what the English said. It was one of the things you understood, without saying it aloud, about French ladies of high society: that they were charming to look at, but it was better not to get too close to them.

Now as to the parties of Batavia and Buitenzorg. We saw away back in the columns of the *Prince of Wales's Island Gazette* that Olivia was not above joining the dance now and then. What were these dances like? Back home in England, in France, and in Vienna, the waltz had become so popular by 1810 that ball program cards were predominantly given over to waltz numbers. The remaining dances were the usual gavottes, minuets, et cetera. The waltz was the only "round" dance. We must remember when we read about styles in clothing, dancing, and so on, that there was a time lag in receiving news about fashion changes for people who, like Olivia Raffles, lived in out-of-the-way places such as the East Indies and British India. Even today, in our world of air mail and fast liners, the white women who live in India and China are nervously aware that they aren't quite up to the minute in such matters, so one can imagine the pangs of impatience and anxiety suffered by the ladies on Java back in 1815, who had to wait the best part of a year for their Paris styles!

Public sentiment about the English was not always good-natured, unfortunately, though we can scarcely be surprised at this. It was a prejudice of long standing, an old story stretching back through two centuries. Stavorinus mentions the British repeatedly and usually in anger; he repeats a long tale from Surat, for example, setting forth the complaints of a lady there who claimed she had been forced by an Englishman (around 1770) to sell to him a pair of horses which she had not at all wanted to give up, and at his price too. Stavorinus said that wherever these haughty conquerors went trade declined sharply. The English wouldn't pay the native workers enough, and that was one of the chief reasons for the deterioration of colonial economy. "The decay of Surat is not a little owing to the superiority which the English have attained there since the last revolution," he says. "The arrogant and arbitrary conduct of that nation, makes the merchants averse to engage in extensive enterprizes of trade, and the capitalists are afraid of putting out their money to interest, or of risking it in the operation of commerce."

Moreover, he complains, those English would always spoil bargains for others if they couldn't trade; in proof of this allegation he describes how he himself experienced their "selfish conduct" and suffered by it. An English councilor named Sitton, conspiring with the local nabob, prevented the native merchants from buying any commodity of Stavorinus, especially sugar, in private trade; so that the traveler had to sell everything at the British fixed rates if he wanted to sell at all.

The English even kept brokers from purchasing of him, Stavorinus said bitterly. "Thus the trade of a formerly flourishing emporium is running to decay."

He adds that one of the Dutch directors, one Senf, had suggested that the Dutch take possession of some other place near Bombay in order to steal trade away from the British again. (This of course was fifty years before the conquest of Java.) They had evidently gone so far as to send a committee to a place called Goga, in the Gulf of Cambay, about 1765, who, "under the appearance of a party of pleasure [i.e., picnic], surveyed the places in that neighborhood, and the island Peram. But nothing resulted therefrom. . . ."

That "party of pleasure" brings memories to us, as an early example of the German and Japanese "tourists" who, it will be recalled, flooded their neighbors' territories for months and years preceding the recent war, surveying whatever places interested their governments, and taking photographs as well.

On the general topic of British in the Far East, Stavorinus made a few additional spiteful remarks. Domestic peace and tranquillity could only be kept in English homes out East by "enormous expenditure." The women would rise between eight and nine, and spend the rest of the forenoon paying visits to each other or "lolling on a sofa, with their arms across" (probably that means "with arms folded"). Dinner was served at one-thirty, after which the ladies slept until four-thirty or five. "They then dress in form," he writes—does he mean in formal attire? Probably—"and the evening and part of the night is spent in company, or at dancing parties, which are frequent, during the colder season.

"Both men and women generally dress in the English style. The ladies affect, for coolness, to wear no covering on their necks; and leave none of the beauties of a well-formed bosom to be guessed at. They are friendly and affable toward strangers, and certainly do not deserve to be called either coy, or cruel. They are fond of parties of pleasure, which are frequently made both upon the delightful banks, and upon the pleasant waves, of the Ganges."

When the British took possession of the Dutch colony of

Java they were quite as shocked by their predecessors' habits as the Dutch were by their conquerors.

Dr. de Haan, who has already contributed so largely to these pages, comes to our help again, describing details of Dutch colonial life which must have been viewed by the British with horror and alarm. The beds of Batavia were large and spacious and provided with as many as ten cushions or pillows, including the "stomach-pillow," which was used to protect the lower part of the body against cold. (Most of the Belgians and many of the French in tropical Africa still wear a "cholera-belt," a wide strip of woolen stuff, around their bellies at night for the same reason. The famous "Dutch wife," a bolster provided the traveler most places south of Singapore, is a different thing entirely, designed for coolness.) There was such a general horror of catching cold, partly because of a fantastic notion that this originated beriberi, that the sleeper not only surrounded himself with a mass of pillows but often wore a "night neckerchief" and a woolen nightcap. "When it is added that the bed curtains were not usually made of gauze or muslin but of cotton, linnen, or costly thick textiles, and that the bed room was on the ground floor and was therefore very stuffy due to the absence of ventilation, then one begins to get some idea of the ambrosial nights passed by the well-to-do in Old Batavia, whilst those of the poor, spent on a bench without curtains, must have been little else than a hopeless fight against the swarming mosquitoes."

Then there was the question of a proper diet for hot climates. The ideas of the old-fashioned Dutch on this subject were not ours, to put it mildly. The Europeans at Batavia as much as possible avoided eating rice until well on into the nineteenth century, and they always preferred their costly, difficult-to-get, half-sour or rancid, ill-preserved and unsuitable European foodstuffs, together with local poultry, green vegetables, butter from the Cape and Bengal, all of which were very plentiful. There is no mention in Raffles's day of the now so famous *Rijsttafel*. From Holland came pickled meats and salted bacon, butter, cheese, ham, smoked or salted salmon, Bologna sausages, herrings, smoked tongue and meat;

225 &

from China, Persia, and India came dried and preserved fruits like apples, chestnuts, persimmons, and apricots; from Persia currants and jams.

About 1625 Jan Pieterszoon Coen wrote, "Our nation must drink or die," and for hundreds of years after that his nation seems to have done its earnest best to go on living. The Dutch consumption of alcohol was increased, if that were possible, during the eighteenth century, by the idea that spirituous liquor was a protection against malaria and all other fevers. Thus in a bad malarial epidemic of 1732–35, the government issued the soldiers extra rations of arrack against "the striking hand of God."

For that matter, during some similar malarial epidemics in the 1840s, in Hong Kong, the British garrison there was issued extra sherry and bitters rations, as a precaution against malaria and "the damp night airs and exhalations."

In Batavia everybody drank a bottle of wine a day as a matter of course, quite apart from the beer, sake, spirits, and so on which were consumed on the side. Heavy drinking was customary at parties. Visitors were given a toast with each glass of wine, principally no doubt to compensate for the lack of intelligent conversation. Official parties were punctuated with a numerous and lengthy official toast list, sometimes accompanied by cannon shots and three cheers. The widow of Governor General van der Parra, about 1780, who according to contemporary witnesses was an exceptionally sober and strait-laced man, died long after her husband but still left forty-five hundred bottles of wine and over ten thousand bottles of beer. Dutch, German, and English beer were all imported in large quantities, and wine came from Persia and the Cape as well as from Europe. It was so cheap and plentiful that it was sometimes only six stuivers a bottle (that would be about six cents).

Shortly after the capture of Malacca in 1641, J. Schouten recommended that owing to the high death rate there among the Hollanders "we should follow a more healthy way of life, as is exemplified by the good example of the Portuguese, than is customary with our own people, principally in washing the whole body clean each morning, and utilizing the early morning and late evening cool in order to take walks or other forms of exercise, and avoiding the heat of the burning sun, the strong drinks;—and particularly to use a fit and proper dietary regime in food and drink."

Nevertheless bathing remained the exception rather than the rule, at least among the men—the women, under the Indo-Portuguese semi-harem regime, seem to have been more particular about washing—until the English interregnum, when the English habit of taking daily baths (in the East) took a firmer hold. Minto said, in the long letter already much quoted, which he wrote his wife from Batavia: "There is a canal opposite to every door on the other side of the road. Each house has a little projecting gallery supported by posts in the canal. The lower part of this, that is to say from the level of the road down into the water, is made in some degree private, by upright bars at a little distance from each other, and with this bath the road communicates by wooden steps. Here the lady of the house, her relatives and female slaves, lave their charms, and here you may behold the handmaids of Diana sporting on and under the wave in sight of all passing Actaeons. This is the morning scene. In the evening they have chairs brought out in the gallery above, and sit with their beaux in conversation and repose."

The charm of this description is somewhat damaged when one recalls that Raffles's secretary Addison calls the canals "mere ditches," and that all writers agree that the local practice of dumping the city's sewage and refuse into the water gave it a noxious odor and an unpleasant "exhalation." Captain James Cook saw a dead ox lying for days in one of the canals.

As we know, the world had long accepted Batavia's proud claim of being the unhealthiest spot on earth. About 1795, Lord Macartney, remarking on this, said that in its mortality Batavia "resembles a field of battle or a town besieged."

Now, however, the British were about to issue a counter-claim. "It was the English," says De Haan, "who first objected to the bad name given to the sea breezes. They opined that the winds from seaward must necessarily be healthy, and that the faint smell of coral-reefs and pools were of no significance." This because it was generally believed that bad smells carried disease. "On the whole it can be said that the best account of the reasons for the unhealthiness of Old Batavia are those given in the *Java Gazette* of 1815,—with the exception of course of the malaria infection due to the mosquito, which nobody did or could have surmised—by Robert Tytler under the pseudonym of *Benevolus*. The English in their colonies followed an entirely different way of life than our Batavians, gave light and air free circulation in their dwellings and took much exercise. Hence Tytler was at once able to see various unfavourable factors which the people at Batavia had ignored through custom or ignorance. . . . Batavia might well have been built, to show exactly how *not* to live in the tropics."

He continues with the usual description of the city, but his emphatic observations of the effects of some of this on the public health are novel. The city was built on marshy land, with the houses built close to each other on the edge of muddy ditches and canals. In the dwelling places light and air were excluded as far as possible. As if this were not enough, the doors and windows were kept closed the greater part of the day, curtains were hung to keep the sun out, and even then one often sat behind a screen. To crown everything, the mode of living was the worst possible. Exercise was almost never taken, and baths only occasionally, while it was *de rigueur* to overeat grossly of heavy foods and to regard alcohol as a splendid and indispensable medicine. Morning, noon, and evening, said Benevolus, the Hollander drank gin, rum, and cognac. Only too common were pale, wan, and bloated faces, shaking hands, red and watery eyes, a foul breath. In the evenings it was customary to sit smoking and drinking gin by the side of a stinking ditch or canal, after which an unnecessarily heavy supper was taken, after which one passed out, half seas over, behind thick curtains in a stuffy room.

All this was in 1815, but as late as 1856 an Englishman wrote that "Gin and brandy have killed five-sixths of all Europeans who have died in Batavia within the last twenty years."

This is probably the reason why the women as a rule lived longer than the men and why, frequently, persons of weak constitutions lived longer than the robust individuals who fancied themselves strong enough to resist any excesses.

The appalling mortality at Batavia at the end of the eighteenth century is shown by the following examples. In June 1775, C. P. Thurberg dined with a party of fifteen, on the eve of his departure for Japan. On his return at the beginning of 1777, he found that eleven of the thirteen were dead. Von Wollzagen found in 1792 that all his friends had died within a period of sixteen months. Of one hundred and fifty soldiers who arrived with the ship *Morgenstern* in 1770, only fifteen were alive four months later. Dysentery, typhus, typhoid, and malaria were the principal diseases.

As might be expected of Raffles, one of his first actions in an official capacity was to revive the moribund Batavian Society of Arts and Sciences. The origin of this society, the first of its kind in the tropics, was due to the efforts of J. C. Radermacher, councilor-extraordinary and son-in-law of the Governor General Reynier de Klerk (1777–80). It is interesting to note that one of his reasons for suggesting the formation of such a learned society was that education must necessarily precede the propagation of the Gospel, "in the same way as the Renaissance had preceded the Reformation over 200 years ago." Radermacher's pet project, after lying fallow for some years, finally resulted in the founding of the society on April 24, 1778.

The society was inevitably too closely tied to the East India Company's governmental setup (for instance the governor general was automatically president and the directorships were limited to members of the governing council) but, thanks to the presence of earnest seekers after knowledge and well-educated individuals such as Radermacher himself, Willem van Hogendorp, Joshua van Iperen, and Isaac Titsingh, the first three volumes of its Proceedings which the society printed at Batavia in the years 1779–81 contained a number of interesting essays. It was also fairly well endowed thanks to the generosity of some members, who were lavish with gifts in kind and cash, the former including, *inter alia*, a house, garden, and "a white Papuan girl," not as a lady's maid but as a curiosity!

Moreover, the very fact that at the ordinary meetings the members and even His Excellency the governor general met common folk on a more or less equal footing made the foundation of this society an almost revolutionary deed. The program had a marked Masonic flavor and, as might have been expected, was obviously influenced by its founders' reading of the works of Rousseau, Voltaire, the Abbé Raynal, and other French humanitarians—and Encyclopedists of the time. It dealt as much with social questions as it did with purely historical and scientific matters, the early volumes containing queries on such varied topics as:

"1. What are the chief edible plants used by the East-Indian natives in their food, and what are the best ways of preparing and cooking them?

"2. What is the best way of rendering useful to the Community, the children of the common people who now aimlessly roam the streets?

"3. What reasons are there to prove that the children's death-rate in the East-Indian colonies can be reduced to a level similar to that in the countries of Northern Europe? [W. van Hogendorp offered a prize of one hundred gold ducats for the best answer to this question.]

"4. What means have been employed by the Imans and other Mohamedan priests, teachers and missionaries, to convert to and retain in the fold of Islam, the peoples of many islands and localities in the East Indies? [Radermacher offered a prize of a hundred gold ducats for the best answers to this, but (as Raffles observed later) found no takers although the society expressly stated that they would welcome answers from native Moslems.]

"5. Why is sitting in the moonshine more dangerous here than in Europe? What are the real ills that are derived therefrom and what are the best means of curing them?

"6. How can one fruitfully undertake to improve the moral character of the Javanese, so that they may live lives more happy for themselves and more useful to the community?

"7. What are the best means for improving the practical and moral upbringing of the [Dutch and Eurasian] children in this colony; and what is the best way to ensure that these children speak Dutch as their mother-tongue from their earliest years?

"8. What are the best means to get the household work in Batavia done wholly or in part by free native Christian servants instead of by slaves?"

One is inevitably reminded of the minutes from the early meetings of the Royal Society in England, when large amounts of time and reams of paper were devoted to essays proving such points as "It is determined that no oaks do grow but from acorns." All the same, De Haan's acidulous observation that there was something irresistibly comical about the society should not be allowed to obscure the fact that some of its founder-members were able and disinterested men.

Hofhout, nevertheless, was not far wrong when, shortly after the opening in 1778, he expressed the fear that the society would not last long. In fact, as De Haan points out, all the requisites for a healthy career were lacking: public interest; freedom of speech and writing; ability, knowledge, and character in the leading personalities, with the exception of a few like Radermacher and Titsingh. Although three volumes of its *Transactions* were published in the first four years of its existence, the society then fell into a state of decay, owing to various factors of which the chief were (1) impossibility of impartial investigation of controversial subjects due to its dependence on the government; (2) the death of many of its leading members and the absence of others in outlying establishments like Chinsura and Canton; and above all (3) the disastrous English war of 1782–84 and the outbreak of the French Revolution in the last decade of the eighteenth century.

Between 1785 and 1792 only three volumes were published and in the twenty years from 1792 to 1812, the society was virtually moribund. From this state of stagnation it was revived by the enthusiasm and drive of Raffles, who took a great interest in its affairs and injected new life and vigor into its proceedings. "To him was due the free and unpaid use of the Government Printing Press, the presentation of a collection of important books from the Government Library, and a fit and proper building for housing its meetings, library and Collections. The Rules of 1800 were revised under his presidency, and partly modelled on those of the Asiatic Society founded at Calcutta in 1784. The activities of the Society were resumed with a flourish on its 35th anniversary, 24 April 1813, with an inaugural address by Raffles, reviewing its past, present and future functions. The 7th volume of the Transactions was published in 1814 [the sixth had appeared in 1782]."

Contributors included himself (Raffles), the American Dr. Thomas Horsfield (who had also been connected with the society in 1802–10, but whose botanical and other works had not been printed for lack of a printing press), Colonel Mackenzie, and John Crawfurd, all of whose names are still honored in the learned world. The seventh volume of the Transactions, and also the eighth, which was printed in 1816, were both largely the work of these men, and the society thereby acquired a fame and reputation which affords a striking contrast to the deplorable situation in which it had stagnated for the previous two decades.

"But," writes Bleecker, "this flourishing period likewise proved of short duration. After 1816, the Society again relapsed into a state of inactivity, largely through the departure of so many outstanding members after the change of government from England to the Netherlands. When Raffles left for Europe, there was enough material on hand for the publication of a 9th volume, but Raffles's promise to secure publication of this material in Europe remained unfulfilled, neither did the Society receive back from him the manuscripts which he had taken away,—the reason for all this being probably connected with the important political events which transpired in the Archipelago after the handing-over of Java." Another temporary revival of activity occurred in the years 1821–

26. From 1830 onward the society got fairly into its stride, and for the last half century has been renowned throughout the learned world for the high scholarship of its output and the wide range of subjects covered, thus fulfilling the aim expressed by its original motto *"Ten Nut van het Gemeen— The Public Weal."*

The first number of the *Java Government Gazette* made its appearance on Leap Year Day, 1812. It was in a completely different style from that of the pompous official mouthpiece of Daendels; it had character, a zest for life and freedom, which had been completely unknown hitherto in the Indies, and has seldom been equaled since. It is hard to believe that such cracks at the government, even good-natured ones, would be permitted to appear as, for example, the complaint that all the prizes in a government lottery had been drawn by senior members of the government. "The government has got them all," mourns the sender of a sorrowful poem.

This old paper, with its curious sidelights on colonial life of those days, on the prevailing antipathy between the English and the Dutch, and the struggle between progress and reaction, is one of the most interesting Eastern products of the grim drama that was being played out in the West— Napoleon's march on Moscow, Leipzig, Elba, and Waterloo. But there are no leading articles. The editor did nothing but reprint snippets and cuttings from other papers. For his news he was very dependent on the good will of the public. Agents or correspondents were unknown. Even the British-Indian papers only occasionally published leading articles, but contributors were gladly welcomed and treated with great hospitality. There was a separate "Poet's Corner," and whoever could write an indifferently good verse could probably find a place in that corner. (Cf. almost any modern number of Hong Kong's *South-China Morning Post* or Shanghai's *North-China Daily News*. British journalism out East doesn't change very quickly.)

The European news came only intermittently and very tardily. No consecutive accounts were received for ten months after May 10, 1812. In the number of May 1, 1813, the latest news is of mid-September 1812. On one occasion the latest (European) news is that received from Constantinople via Bagdad; and on another it comes via Koepang in Timor from an Australian pearl-fishing vessel which had touched at that port.

Though a national attitude toward race difference is a thing not easily defined, it can give rise to endless arguments between representatives of different countries, such as England and Holland, when they meet in a land foreign to both. So it was whenever some incident pointed out the difference between the way the Dutch had always treated the Asiatic natives and the way the English who accompanied Raffles felt about them. Though American readers will be skeptical about this, the British showed far less severity than did the Hollanders in these white versus Asiatic relationships. The attitude of the Batavian Dutch toward the Javanese and Indonesians of the island who were not slaves is exemplified by Admiral Cornelis Maatplief's remark, which has become famous: "So long as the Dutch knife is sharp, the natives will show us respect."

Raffles accused the Dutch East India Company of treating their Javanese subjects with less consideration than a West Indian planter did his slaves. This was true up to a point, but it should be remembered that the Company showed equally small consideration for its humble European employees. Admiral Verhuell, who was at Batavia in 1784, wrote that "Experience has shown that the sick [sailors] recover quicker and better in the fresh air and aboard a hospital-ship. But this makes no difference. The Hospital Directors are often favorites of the Governor-General and must have their profits. Therefore the poor sailors are sent thither, often at the cost of their lives."

No European on Java, according to Raffles, understood the native languages "except the Overseers in the forests or coffee-plantations, whose duty obliges them to a constant intercourse with the people of the interior." It is amusing, in the light of the customary reproaches aimed today by Americans at the British, to find an Englishman accusing some other national of the same fault: ignorance of the language used by the natives he is governing.

This question of languages, by the way, becomes less and less simple as we study the situation on Java more closely. At the time of the English occupation free Javanese were relatively few in Batavia and its immediate neighborhood. More numerous were Balinese, Amboinese, Bugginese, et cetera. The Chinese were by far the largest colony of all, with the exception of the Dutch, and this in spite of that cruel massacre and race riot in 1740. The "Mardykers," children of freed slaves, were those of pure Asiatic origin, whose parents came mostly from Arakan, Bengal, and Coromandel. By the end of the eighteenth century they had merged under the term "Portuguese" though they had no Portuguese blood at all, because they spoke the bastard Indo-Portuguese tongue found at Batavia, Malacca, et cetera. This Portuguese language was slowly replaced by the Malay tongue during the years between 1790 and 1820, after which period no Portuguese was to be heard in Batavia.

The Mardykers had a bad reputation, according to Vlekke. Because they were Christians, they didn't have to follow the law which forced all other Asiatics to wear their native costume. One of the Dutchmen of the period said of them, "They wear so-called European costume, but without shirt, socks or shoes. They parade, dressed up like a quack's monkey at a country fair, and are the shrewdest and most self-conceited of Batavia's inhabitants."

One of the strangest products of this fantastically mixed population of Batavia was the language spoken by Batavian children, especially the hundred per cent Dutch infants who were born on the island. A few schools were maintained for such boys, but, as we have already seen, the girls seldom got the chance to learn anything. They grew up among slaves: they were trained by slaves. Often they didn't even learn to speak Dutch. "They picked up a mixture," says Vlekke, "of

Malayan, Portuguese, and Dutch, which remained their only means of expression for the rest of their lives."

The English stayed only four and a half years on Java. How much longer would have been necessary, one wonders, before their tongue added itself to this rich bouillabaisse of dialects?

CHAPTER XIV

It is not often that History presents us with surprises, but through the Dutch East Indies she has done just that. At the end of the eighteenth century there appeared in Delft a pamphlet wherein one Dirk van Hogendorp actually praised Great Britain's colonial policy! What is more, this Van Hogendorp, in spite of being a Dutchman, proceeded on the strength of this unorthodox admiration to recommend reforms in Java which bear a remarkable resemblance to the actual changes Raffles was to put into effect a dozen years later, while the British were occupying the island.

England was wealthy and prosperous, said Hogendorp, chiefly because her government officials administered their laws with impartiality and justice. The laws themselves were probably no better than those of many other nations, but they were enforced as a matter of course in England. Hogendorp ascribed this impartial justice to four causes. The first was the independent position enjoyed by British judges, who could not be removed from their posts for any reason but misconduct, and who were paid such large salaries that they need not fear poverty and were not subject to ordinary temptation by bribery. The second was the trial-by-jury method—a jury, remember, actually composed of "good men and true." The third reason was the assumption made by English law that a man is innocent until he is proved guilty and until sentence has actually been passed on him by the judge. The fourth was the fact that cases of law were always tried in open court, with admission granted to all and sundry.

In comparison with this British state of affairs, all open and aboveboard, the writer pointed scornfully to Dutch Java, where, he asserted, there existed not even the shadow of justice, and a fair trial was unknown; Java, where the Council of Justice, the Bench of Magistrates, and all subsidiary judicial officials were part of, appointed by, and entirely dependent on the local government, consisting of the governor general and his council. These men could transfer, dismiss, remove, or replace anyone they disliked at a moment's notice and without referring to Holland for confirmation or approval, putting in their own creatures to take the place of the banished victims. The august members of the judiciary of Java were badly paid in the bargain: consequently they indulged in smuggling and bribery quite as an understood thing.

It can be imagined how little chance any Hollander of that time stood, under such circumstances, of receiving a fair trial in Java, if he happened to do anything which might annoy the government. Needless to say, matters were still worse as regarded the Javanese and other local natives. Owing to the want of subordinate courts outside the urban centers, Batavia and Samarang, cases involving natives might have to wait as much as a year for trial, and since both witnesses and accused were confined in noisome, unsanitary jails pending trial, many hundreds simply died from neglect and starvation before they were called into court. Of course this rule didn't apply to rich natives, who could easily buy themselves off when they got into trouble. The poor, however, whether guilty or innocent, usually had to hang, as the cases were investigated and tried in the most summary manner imaginable.

Van Hogendorp strongly advocated scrapping the whole of the Company's feudal system of forced labor and deliveries, replacing it by a small head tax, a land tax based on yearly production of crops and extent of cultivated land, import and export taxes, and taxes on salt, on firewood, on the seals on stamped documents, on the hire of open markets, and so forth. These revenues, he asserted, would produce far more than the Company's actual oppressive system. His claims were justified, he added, by the example of the English in Bengal: they raised more than sixty million guilders a year, simply by similar means.

He also suggested a redistribution of land ownership among the peasants who actually tilled the soil or, in other words, the common Javanese. Van Hogendorp's distribution plan included both the rice fields and the ground on which their houses stood. Of course this rearrangement would have called for an accurate land survey, and written proof of ownership would have had to be given to each peasant-proprietor to start out with. Under this (theoretical) system, the native regents and the large landowners who had heretofore battened on the toil of the tenant workers were to be compensated with tracts of unoccupied land suitable for clearing and rice planting. Any land that might remain was to be given to European, Chinese, or native settlers, no more to one man, however, than he was capable of planting and operating productively. All woods, forests, and jungles were to become the property of the State.

Van Hogendorp stressed the vital importance of giving the Javanese peasants proprietry of the soil and the fields they tilled, just as the peasants of Europe had at last come to enjoy ownership of their land, after centuries of serfdom and feudalism.

According to his estimate, "The Chinese possess ten times the amount of wealth on the Island that the Europeans do, whilst their yearly profits are in about the same proportion." The Chinese under the Company's jurisdiction in Java, he said, numbered around one hundred thousand.

Considering the reforms put into practice by Raffles as soon as he got his administration into working order, all of this is surprisingly modern and anticipatory of things to come. However, on second thought one realizes that anyone of the then new school of thought, which embraced an advanced idea of the value of humanity no matter what the race, would of course come to this sort of conclusion. The humanitarian spirit was abroad in the land and Van Hogendorp's theories were the only logical outcome. Nevertheless it is more than surprising to find so much bitter criticism of Holland, with such enthusiastic praise of perfidious Albion, appearing over a Dutch signature, especially when we reflect that Raffles's land-tenure reforms were severely criticized not only by the Dutch but also by certain of his own superiors.

Moreover, Van Hogendorp's was not the only Dutch voice raised in Raffles's praise. We must admit that they are small voices indeed to be heard among the loud chorus of criticism, even vituperation, which resounded from Holland's shores after the British interregnum on Java, but they are noteworthy for that very reason; their rarity makes them at least twice as interesting as they would be without competition. One Jan Samuel Thimmerman Thijssen, a merchant in the opium trade and a magistrate, during the festivities which marked the Dutch holiday and celebration in 1814 at Batavia (the liberation of the Netherlands, August twenty-fourth), paid the lieutenant governor eloquent tribute:

"The most fortunate moment which Java had ever known was that on which Lord Minto selected Mr. Raffles for its future Governor." Thimmerman Thijssen had a good word for Lord Minto as well: "His Sovereign has conferred on him the dignity of an Earl, but the Almighty has recorded his name in the Annals of Philanthropy and at a future period we may expect to behold our Noble Benefactor in the Mansions of Heaven decorated with the emblems of sincerity and virtue."

Bread-and-butter appreciation, you may say; a natural but insincere speech from an unwilling subject who in his heart wishes he had never been "liberated" by the British and sighs for the good old days when Holland could call the East Indies, as well as her soul, her own. But the Dutch didn't behave like that. We can expect hollow manifestations of loyalty and love from discreet Orientals, but in Java as well as Europe, Netherlanders have always been remarkable more for blunt, ungracious honesty, even toward their conquerors, than for tact. I think we can allow ourselves to believe Mr. Thimmerman

Thijssen, just this once. God knows he didn't have much compatriate company in his affection for that humanitarian but British pair, Minto and Raffles; let us give him credit, then, for the moral courage he showed in thus making a speech which was sure to be unpopular.

One of the weightiest witnesses for the defense of the Dutch administration, it will be recalled, is Dr. Bernard Vlekke. Dr. Vlekke claims that many of Raffles's reforms on Java were actually merely a continuation of plans made by Daendels, who had no time to carry them out before the imminent threat of British invasion brought about his recall to Holland. Raffles had a positive genius, says Vlekke sourly, for making himself sound big, without seeming, of course, to boast unduly of his own excellence. He skimmed the cream off Daendels's projected renovation of the Javanese Government, and then collected all the praise that was forthcoming for the resulting success.

A study of the records provides some evidence in favor of his idea; things had certainly been in a nasty mess in the Dutch East Indies, particularly on Java, and Daendels's appointment, even if Great Britain had not offered complications, would doubtless have meant better days for the Javanese, or at least some slight improvement. But at the very best these reforms would not have been nearly so clean-sweeping or effective as Raffles's. That wasn't the motive behind Daendels's presence on Java. He had been sent out primarily to prepare a defense against the English. It is exceedingly unlikely, even given the good will such work calls for, that the marshal would have been allowed to devote much of his time to social reform, and he didn't have an overpowering amount of good will to start with. Not to put too fine a point on the matter, the welfare of Javanese natives was *not* closest to Daendels's heart. His best friend would not have accused him of humanitarianism and his worst enemy would not have dared. Daendels was hard-boiled. Even among his compatriots there were few who claimed to like him, though many were willing to bear witness to their admiration.

D. J. A. Collet says the marshal can be described as a man

"whose name can be spoken with enthusiasm or with hatred, but never with indifference or contempt." His defense of his own acts can be summed up in the words "Necessity knows no law," and he himself maintained the familiar maxim, "The end justifies the means."

It is a moot point whether Daendels could have put through any reforms, anyway, considering his one great mistake—a mistake in judgment, in economy, and in policy. It was more than a mistake in fact; it was a crime against the population of Java. I refer (again) to the sale of public lands, an act of which Daendels was certainly guilty, and I refer to it a second time herewith, in preparation for our account of the next phase in Raffles's career, when he was accused, with reason, of having done the same thing.

Before we leave the subject of Daendels and start on Raffles's administration, however, we ought in fairness to report the rest of Collet's defense of him. The book *L'Ile de Java sous la domination Française,* by Collet, is a convenient, reasonable discussion of the marshal from the pro-Daendels point of view. Most of his defenders are either personal friends or ardent Dutch patriots who overstated their case and allowed their emotional bias to become too obvious, and even the scholarly, convincing defenses are embedded in so much other paper, hidden away in such heavy tomes, and scattered so profusely, that Collet with his neat, small, concentrated book is a welcome relief.

Daendels, "the thundering marshal," was certainly not perfect, but neither was he the unmitigated fiend which Minto thought him. Raffles himself said, "A much more regular, active, pure, and efficient administration was established by Marshal Daendels than ever existed before." He had his merits, and one of them was a superior brand of courage. Collet cites for example the story of how the marshal, single-handed, dealt with the rebellious Sultan of Bantam. He cowed and deposed the Sultan, seated himself on the throne, subsequently annexed his dominions to the Crown (which was then a combination of French and Dutch, it will be remembered), and exiled the disgraced prince to Amboina.

In appearance he left the Indies a very different man to what he was when he arrived. Before going out to Java his portraits depict a striking figure of a soldier, stocky, strong, and virile. Unfortunately the easy life of Batavia and perhaps the excessive drinking then in vogue did the dirty on Daendels and after a time he became monstrously fat and gross. Like other Dutchmen in the islands, he often wore the Malay sarong, but he went the rest of them one better by wearing it even when he entertained, and sometimes did not stop short of appearing à la Malay at his office. The effect of so much avoirdupois thus lightly clothed, with his enormous hairy arms and chest bare to the elements, can be imagined.

Nevertheless Daendels's qualities as military leader did not seem to have been impaired as was his manly beauty. After being recalled to Holland, with Janssens taking his place on Java, he was made divisional commander and as such participated in the early stages of Napoleon's ill-fated Russian campaign, in 1812. He greatly distinguished himself by his fifteen-month defense of Modlin (October 1812 to December 1813), which he surrendered only after all food and munitions were used up. After the Dutch Restoration of 1814 he offered his services to the new government and was appointed governor of the Dutch settlement of Elmina, on the Gold Coast, where he died in 1818—of piles, incidentally. Piles are fatal, usually, only to very fat people; Daendels's fat was acquired on Java; it is not too awfully farfetched, then, to call him a Javanese casualty.

Now for Raffles and the New Deal of 1812.

The situation will not appear clear to us unless we keep in mind constantly the complicated state of affairs which existed regarding Java's ownership. Day after day would have seen Raffles hopelessly hampered as he tried to make decisions, completely inhibited in all his administrative measures, if he had accepted as final his superiors' dictum that England was not always going to maintain her hold on Java. For the space of several years Java's future was ambiguous, and the Com-

243

pany didn't make a positive statement one way or the other. As long as it seemed likely they would decide against it, Minto didn't press them for their decision: he hoped he might yet be able to dispel their doubts and persuade them to see things his and Raffles's way. Raffles therefore went ahead on the assumption that his dearest wish would be gratified and that Java would become in fact, as he saw her in his visions, the center of a great British Oriental Empire. He couldn't have been sure of it really; there is not much doubt that he tapped on wood a dozen times a day, but in public he kept up the pretense of believing everything was going to go just as he wished.

Not for one moment, however, did he set to work digging Dutch influence out of Java or attempting to banish it. On the contrary, he was careful to retain, whenever it was at all feasible, every appearance of the original form in administrative action. The two Dutchmen on the council helped him in doing this. Chiefly in order to reassure them of his friendly intentions, the first measure which he caused to be put into operation was an outright adoption of the Dutch legal code, and it was, in truth, an adoption rather than an adaptation. In only one respect did Raffles alter this code, though that was an important alteration: he stripped it of its fangs by outlawing the former methods of torture and other penalties involving extreme cruelty which had until then been in force. He also added a new feature shortly afterward, just about the time Lord Minto took his departure: trial by jury.

Dutch opinion of this latter innovation has been variously interpreted. Boulger maintains that they looked upon it with favor; Vlekke says it was not a success. The contemporary Dutch could not have resented it too much, for it was one change which they retained after Holland took back possession of her East Indian territory, though only for a short while. Afterward, on the grounds that the Javanese didn't like juries, they abolished that much of Raffles's judicial administration.

Next and most pressing problem was the ever vexatious one of revenue. Seventy years later the Anglo-Saxon world was to be stirred to its depths when Morel "exposed" His Belgian

Majesty King Leopold's methods of exploiting his Congo. It was stated in various British periodicals at that time that never before had history seen a like example of downright robbery; never before in the memory of man had nation or monarch gone so cold-bloodedly to work, taking everything out of a colony and putting nothing in, as Leopold was accused of doing when he squeezed the Congo. If this was a sincere statement it proved one thing at least: the extreme forgetfulness of all mankind and of newspaper writers in particular. Java was as obvious a case of exploitation as the Congo ever proved to be.

The Netherlanders who had a share in the government of the Eastern colonies never pretended that they had any other intention, when they formulated their policies, than to profit as much as possible and as directly as they could from these possessions. It is an interesting difference and one which we should not forget, for it is the keynote of all international disputes over imperialism, now as well as in the early nineteenth century. The British take their cue somewhat from Minto's school of thought and never forget to mention their duty to subject peoples, even when, like Churchill, they speak bluntly of what they want out of their empire. Kipling merely expressed the attitude of imperialism's harsher exponents; he did not originate it, as some people evidently believe, when he spoke in *Recessional* of the "lesser breeds without the Law." The Kiplingites are not one with the followers of Minto; they are less altruistic and claim to be more realistic than the humanitarians of England. But even these British Junkers have never hit bottom, never stood firm on the bedrock opportunist philosophy of Holland in the East.

Muntinghe, one of the two councilors chosen by Raffles from the Dutch community of Batavia to govern the colony, side by side with Gillespie, had plenty to say about the new era and Raffles's humanitarian methods of raising money. Commenting on the new land revenue system as opposed to the Dutch Company's forced labor and delivery, he observed that its main object was improvement of the native population's lot. This in itself was a noteworthy innovation, of course, and Muntinghe acknowledged that it was a great task and one worthy of the British nation.

". . . And there is no doubt," he continues, "but the result of it must be an increase of the happiness of the inhabitants and consequently of the future wealth and prosperity of the colony. The amelioration however of the condition of the natives on this island, though undoubtedly a consideration of the highest moment in the eyes of humanity, seems to me to become only a secondary object from a political point of view, and, with the exception of every measure contrary to the principles of justice and equity, it appears to me that the safest principle which can be adopted to judge of the propriety of any colonial regulations or of any changes and alterations to be introduced therein, is that every colony does or ought to exist for the benefit of the mother country."

Nothing could be franker, could it? In thus expressing himself, Muntinghe was reiterating the opinion of the state commissioners of 1803 (Nederburgh and Co.) in their *Report*, that they had taken it as a fundamental maxim that "all injustices apart, the Colonies exist for the Motherland and not the Motherland for the Colonies."

Even General Janssens, of whom Lord Minto became so very fond after whipping the daylights out of him on Java, even the general felt that way. In a letter of July 23, 1811, he wrote "*Les colonies sont pour la métropole et non la métropole pour les colonies.*"

In order, then, to work out any sort of reasonable program, and to find some ground on which they could meet, Raffles decided that it was a matter of agreeing to disagree, and he let it go at that. After all, for as long as he was boss on Java he would be able to interpret the British policy rather than the Dutch. Out of the ensuing four and a half years the government archives offer a mélange of languages and attitudes, but Minto's policy, at any rate, reigned supreme. De Haan feels himself called upon to make an odious comparison between the Dutch and English styles, in which the English come out definitely ahead, which occurred to him as he turned the records over. He contrasts "shamefacedly, as a

246

Hollander, the long-winded, trivial, sloppy and cringing reports of our countrymen in the Archives, with the brief, clear and correct documents of their English colleagues."

De Haan is too severe on his compatriots. At least part of the inferiority manifest in their writings is due to the fact that several of the best-fitted and most patriotic Dutch officials either refused to serve under the English administration or were not employed by it, owing to their close association with Daendels. Any conquering invader can tell the same story about the difficulties of government, once victory has been achieved. The true leaders of the people have a way of going underground at such a time, and the triumphant governor has to make out with the community's second best officials, if he can get anything better than third class.

We had better get down to particulars on the reformed laws. To begin with, Raffles found that one of the worst taxes borne by the natives was a heavy, direct one on all native produce. This shortsighted, stupid arrangement had the same effect that such a tax always has had and always will. The natives immediately became so discouraged that they simply stopped producing anything in excess of their immediate needs, in order to avoid being taxed. At the rate they felt themselves being pushed, it was cheaper not to work at all.

Things had been going on in this sorrowful manner for a long time, and it was impossible to come to a quick decision as to the best method of reforming it all. Raffles went to work carefully and set his best men to studying conditions as they had been both before and during the recent (and worst) period of Dutch rule. The Dutch council members, Muntinghe and Cranssen, were each put in charge of two other compatriots, with orders to collect and register all public records and plans. A British colonel of engineers was attached to this commission to compile statistics. They were all five kept busy for two years, merely collecting and organizing their material. That deliberation and the scientific approach were typical of Raffles. No impending political change was going to hurry *his* administration into making mistakes. According to Furnivall, however, it wouldn't have mattered how long he

247

studied the picture: he would always find what he expected, and it wasn't, alas, always there.

First, last, and in between, the Javanese problem for Raffles was the same old one which faces all colonizers: namely, how to make the project pay for itself. The Dutch system, because of the monopoly on produce, had not permitted the levy of export duty on anything. Now, however, under the British, the government claimed monopoly on nothing except opium; and by "farming out" on such items as tollgates, gambling houses, arracks, et cetera, they instituted free trade on everything else. (The Company hung on to that one opium monopoly until 1833, when the China trade was declared open. In Hong Kong the government maintained an opium monopoly until 1941, when it was taken over by the Japanese conquerors of the Colony.) Now under the Raffles system, export duty of three per cent was collected on sugar, indigo, arrack, and such native produce, whereas the new import duty was six per cent. The system began to show good results immediately, and revenue increased in a way to bring joy to Raffles's heart and credit to his financial acumen. It wasn't enough though: the money was coming in too slowly. The government needed a large lump sum to put them on their feet and get everything under way.

For a long time the Dutch system had been stifling native enterprise. Large numbers of the populace were constantly migrating, leaving deserted areas which in former days had been busy, thriving communities. They were all searching for some land where they could be safe. Everywhere natives were on the move, in flight from the crushing taxation imposed on them by greedy Dutchmen who had evidently never read of the goose and the golden eggs. Quick action was needed.

For a long time, moreover, there had been no silver in the treasury. The Dutch issued paper currency, but it decreased in value as fast as it was printed. Daendels on his arrival in Java dealt with this difficulty by issuing another million in paper, to float which he calmly sold three of the best provinces on the island (one of which was Probolingo) to certain rich Chinese residents of Java on condition that they buy up fifty thousand of the paper currency every six months. Immediately the money was dubbed "Probolingo paper": nobody showed the sudden fondness for it which Daendels had expected. Whereupon he issued a proclamation, ordering everyone to accept the paper as hard money, but that was no good either. Currency is one thing you can't be highhanded about. It doesn't take kindly to dictatorship.

When the time came for the Chinese to pay for their first fifty thousand they paid in that same Probolingo, or toilet, paper, and blandly cited Daendels's recent proclamation ordering it to be honored, in defense of their action. Daendels was fairly caught on the horns of his own, home-grown dilemma. It was a good joke on him, but the unfortunate Malays who lived on the land of the betrayed provinces were caught in a much more painful fashion.

One need drop no tear for the Dutch governor over the Probolingo paper fiasco, because he didn't lose out in the end. He had also appropriated for his private use one half the proceeds from Birds' Nest Rocks, a highly profitable area which, it is said, produced forty thousand pounds in good years, whereas the Probolingo paper, when the British moved in, was selling at only sixty-six per cent of its face value.

Another cause of the trade depression on Java was that the Dutch had neglected the local coffee planting and had suppressed the vineyards so as not to compete with Dutch wines from the Cape.

Not even Vlekke denies that Java's economy was a mess in 1812. Present and future revenues were sold to alien taxgatherers, trade in the interior was at a standstill because of heavy import duties levied between provinces and districts, and the natives, beaten down by poverty and continued discouragement, in larger and larger numbers fled into "free" territory until the best districts were practically depopulated. As Raffles expressed the task before him, he had to strike a delicate balance by improving the lot of the Javanese without quite giving them power to throw off European control; he had to collect revenue enough to support a government and garrison which they started out by not liking; and he had to invest them with pride in being part of the British Empire. That third item, one supposes, might or might not happen by itself, as the mechanical result of success in the other two projects. But unless those two should be successful, the last one was a hopeless proposition.

It must be said that we cannot always accept Raffles's claims for his accomplishments. As far as he knew, his plans worked out and were based on accurate understanding of local custom, but an unbiased observer such as Furnivall maintains that some of his reforms were introduced too hurriedly and led to confusion in practice. In some cases they remained merely reforms on paper, because they were too ambitious. Sometimes the surveys were not really made, and as regards his abolition of forced labor, it was claimed this applied to the entire island, "except that in the Preanger he introduced a new system which made the burden heavier," says Furnivall, "in Batavia replaced the old arrangements by new arrangements to the same effect, and elsewhere left matters as before, apart from neglecting roads and allowing public buildings to fall into decay."

As for his land reforms, Furnivall is similarly skeptical, doubting that the common man experienced much benefit—"the arrangement by which he was required to pay his taxes in money merely handed him over from the regent to the money-lender."

Nevertheless Furnivall admits that Raffles's work was justified by its results. The Dutch took over his administrative and judicial organization, although with certain large modifications, and they also carried on with his system of revenue administration. The subsequent yield proved that Raffles's expectations had not been wrong, merely overly optimistic. The Dutch liberals who so admired him summed it up thus:

"Though his reforms were hastily introduced and often on paper rather than in practise, still he must be honoured for the great philanthropic ideals on which they were based."

Boiled down to simplest terms, Raffles's method was as follows: he abolished the practice of forcing natives to cultivate crops they didn't want; he did away with all forced labor except the minimum number of workers necessary for road building, and even those laborers were at least paid for their work, whereas on the old terms they had not been; he bought out the Chinese who had been speculating in land sold to them by Daendels (just in time, incidentally, to keep the entire population of Probolingo from running out).

Unfortunately it was then that Raffles blotted his copybook, and in the same way Daendels had done. At least that is what it looked like, though there were many minor points of dissimilarity. He didn't sell public lands for private gain and he made no secret of what he was doing; he had the approval of the council as well as the more cautious agreement of Lord Minto (who wasn't asked to express his opinion, however, until after the *fait accompli* because time was pressing). But the fact remains that he did just that: he sold some of the public lands.

According to Boulger, always his firm defender, Raffles's action had an excellent effect on Java's finances, relieving the government from having to continue operations on worthless paper revenue. First of all, obviously, something had to be done about all the paper money that was in circulation. Probolingo paper was only a part of it. As soon as British rule began, these various notes took a further downward rush, partly because all the troops had to be paid in silver, which meant a drain of thirty-six *lakhs* annually. Raffles decided (and, Boulger says, every sagacious statesman would have agreed) that it was "imperiously necessary to remove this paper currency from the market, and to replace it with such a circulating medium as could be supported in its credit, and rendered available for the public disbursements." The council decided to recall all the currency, partly by this sale of land and partly by an issue of treasury notes at six per cent. The Lombard Bank, a respectable institution which had some time since fallen into disuse, was re-established in order to circulate notes as loans for security deposited, taking nine per cent for advances and paying a small interest on its notes.

Boulger insists that the public remember, in the light of later happenings, that General Gillespie actually gave his assent, in December 1812, to this sale of land. Gillespie was also fully aware at the time that one of the principal purchasers was Muntinghe, the more outstanding of the two Dutch councilors. "It should also be stated that a sale of lands for the benefit of Government was one of the recognized modes in Java of replenishing the Exchequer," says Boulger. "Sanctioned by usage, carried in its early stages into effect with the unanimous assent of the Council, and in its later with the approbation of the Dutch members, Raffles might reasonably assume that such a step would never be challenged, provided it accomplished the purpose that dictated its adoption. That it did accomplish that purpose is beyond the shadow of dispute."

As far as one can make out from the quarrel which broke out later over this piece of high finance, the delicate point was not so much that Raffles sold the land as that he bought it too. His excuse, that he did this simply in order to give the sale a push in the right direction, makes sense, and he managed to prove also that he didn't profit from the transaction. At first glance, however, it does look odd, undeniably.

Himself, the lieutenant governor was haunted by no doubts at all, and he wrote Lord Minto of his action not because he wanted his patron's permission—after all, he had already done it—but because he always did tell Minto what he was doing, and he knew that this complicated maneuver would need explanation. The effect of the news on Minto must have surprised the innocent Raffles. The earl saw more clearly than his protégé what might be the result of this measure, which is why he sounds a little worried in his reply of November 22, 1813. No doubt some part of his misgivings were due to the fact that he was just about to resign office and return to England, after which he knew Raffles would need an amount of protection which would no longer, perhaps, be forthcoming from Calcutta. How right he was will shortly be evident.

Minto started out by assenting "without reservation" to the urgent necessity which was the motive and the justification of Raffles's action. Raffles was left with no option but to withdraw the depreciated paper from circulation, and quickly:

that much must be admitted, said Lord Minto. Also, since the only resource in sight had been the sale of public property, Raffles could count himself lucky that he had public property on hand to sell.

The urgent necessity of a prompt remedy, said Minto, was the essential, indeed the indispensable, ground for what had been done. (What he meant was that it was Raffles's only excuse, and so would have to be good enough.) An extensive "alienation of the public domains" was not in itself good, ever, and particularly at such a time. In the first place it was too important a measure to have been adopted during a provisional government, the duration of which was more than precarious. (That was the rub of course. As usual he was reminding Raffles that Java might not be British forever, and that it therefore behooved the government not to forget its temporary nature.) Secondly, the measure should have received the previous sanction of the Supreme Government of Bengal—as of course it would if only there had been time, he added tactfully. Third, though Minto himself always approved the transfer of public territory to "the management of individual industry," he felt that it could not be done suddenly in such a place as Java, which contained at the time neither capital nor capitalists enough to afford a sufficient knowledge of market values in land. Minto himself would have inclined to small and partial sales of land, if outright sales were necessary at all, but he preferred short leases at first. He cautioned Raffles that the sentiments prevailing at home were divided on this question of permanent settlements. Though his own system in Bengal, which had in a great degree been carried into effect during his administration, was gradual, even so it was more sudden than was approved at home. Since Java was in a state infinitely less favorable to perpetual alienations—i.e., outright sale of territory—Raffles might be sure that such measures as his, if he hadn't had the excuse of urgent necessity, would be disapproved, even disavowed and annulled, by the authorities in England.

Raffles wasn't at all worried by this gentle warning. He went over the situation again, surveyed the resulting conditions, and felt more justified than ever. He wrote confidently to Minto in Europe, saying so. The effects were so obviously good, he felt, that he need have no fear at all that the authorities would fail to approve what he had done. This was still during the period when he hoped Java would remain in British hands, evidently, for in the same letter (February 13, 1814, from Buitenzorg) he prattles on lightheartedly about reforming the laws more radically and definitely getting rid of the Dutch institutions, the retaining of which for such a long period has already brought upon the English, he feels, "much odium." (From whom?)

By this he was referring to the comparatively gentle way in which the newly arrived British had handled the whole delicate matter of working law, two years before. Raffles need not have been in such a hurry to bring in yet more reforms. Judging from his record, a good deal had been accomplished since then. For instance, with the council's approval he revived the old village system of maintaining law and order, according to which the village chief, who was chosen by election, decided most disputes. Those cases too big for the chief to handle were referred to a higher tribunal composed of a British resident, a native regent, a chief priest, and a Moslem law officer. Criminal cases which involved only natives of Java were tried by this court, but the sentence had always to be confirmed by Raffles. The resident's court was held at different times, in different places, as convenience dictated. There was a circuit court for capital charges, with a jury of foreman and four members. The circuit judges, members of the old Dutch courts, made tours at regular intervals.

Raffles claimed that the system was immediately successful and that crime fell to a minimum. Perhaps, he said, this happened in part because the inhabitants were better satisfied now than they had been in the old days, but most probably it was chiefly because the British had called in all the guns and ammunition in the colony, besides which it was declared against the law to carry arms in the street. Furnivall, on the other hand, maintains that crime increased, because the times were out of joint.

After several years had made it fairly evident that Raffles's methods were meeting with satisfaction (though most Dutch commentators will not admit this), he wrote a long report to the Court of Directors on the subject of the Javanese, in which he asserted that as a race they were much maligned. He pointed out a few general truths; for instance, that no people in the world can be expected to work when they are penalized instead of rewarded for their industry, which is exactly what the Dutch system of taxation was doing to the natives of Java. Only exceptional human beings, moreover, will continue trying to accomplish anything after they have been discouraged and pushed down again and again; this, too, happened constantly to the Javanese under the old Dutch regime. Raffles pointed with pride to the effects, which he declared were already visible, of his reform measures. Under the new conditions the recovery of Java's internal economy was proceeding at a strikingly swift pace.

Nevertheless some of his superiors remained skeptical. The land-tenure reforms were too sweeping to suit their taste, and they looked with dubious and restrained rapture upon "so sudden and so general a change in the system of revenue-administration in Java, while the information possessed by this Government [in Bengal] with respect to the resources of the island, the nature of the tenures, the rights of individuals on the soil and other points of high interest and importance was necessarily so imperfect." Some people alleged that the new Lieutenant-Governor was superimposing an Indian pattern on the Javanese social structure, and that he was not justified in doing this.

A man who knew Raffles at least as well as any of his colleagues was John Crawfurd, who succeeded the first appointee, Farquhar, in the government of Singapore. Crawfurd in his *Dictionary*, after highly praising Raffles's abolition of monopolies, forced deliveries, and corvée labor in 1811–16, continues, "The financial system which he adopted, however, was not so happy. Insofar as the land-tax was concerned, the elaborate, vexatious, scourging, and impracticable system which proceeds on the principle of the States entering directly into an arrangement with each individual occupant of a few acres, in the case of Java probably not fewer than half a million, was at the time in vogue with the authorities in England, and he attempted the establishment of this pernicious innovation. Under this system, the tax was paid either in money or in land [kind?] at the option of the occupant; and being generally paid in the latter, it followed that the government was converted at once into a warehouse-keeper, and a corn-merchant. As in our own Territories on the continent of India, the new system was found mischievous and impracticable. The land was over-assessed, and the hypothetical tax could not be realized.

"After a two years' trial, the Dutch commissioners who received charge of the island, judiciously abandoned the Ryot-warrie system of 1814, and arranged with the heads of the village corporations for the land-tax, leaving its distribution among the occupants, to these corporations themselves. This natural and simple system, the only one suited to such a state of society as that of Java, after being in operation for 14 years, was partially relinquished in 1832, and the old system of forced deliveries of certain agricultural products, and of corvée labour in raising them, was to a certain extent restored."

I venture a guess that some of these critics were the men who were so shocked and chagrined when Raffles, backed up by Minto, began to stamp out the slave market of Java. There is the same note of unemotional business sense, the tacit disapproval of Minto's sort of sentiment, the scarcely concealed desire to find fault with humanitarian Raffles and his works, no matter what he might be doing or how he did it. For, after all, Raffles's knowledge (and consequently the government's information) concerning "the nature of the tenures, the rights of individuals on the soil and other points" was *not* "necessarily . . . imperfect." As we know, for some months Raffles had devoted the entire working time of five Europeans to a meticulously careful investigation of all those points, and of his five European investigators at least one of them, the British officer of engineers, had been especially trained to do that work. I venture to say that never did any colonial administration approach its job with a greater eagerness for knowledge.

"Activity, industry, and political courage were the most remarkable endowment of his character," said Crawfurd of Raffles. "In the transaction of public business he was ready, rapid and expert,—partly the result of early training, but far more of innate energy and ability. He was not, perhaps, an original thinker, but readily adopted the notions of others—not always with adequate discrimination. Thus, without much time for examination, seeing it lauded by its partisans, he adopted, and at once carried into execution among the then five million inhabitants of Java, the fanciful and pernicious Indian revenue system called the Ryotwarry, and saw it break down even before he had himself quitted the administration of the island."

As long as we are sounding the hostile note, it seems in order to glance at the opinions of one of Raffles's most redoubtable critics, the Netherlander H. S. Levyssohn Norman. Mr. Levyssohn Norman damns with faint praise and kindly forgiveness rather than with blasting and bad temper.

To begin with, he excuses Raffles many of his (alleged) mistakes on the grounds of the difficulties which are likely to be encountered by any conquering nation during the first uneasy days of peace. "One cannot expect too high a standard of government in cases where a land is captured in wartime, so long as its ultimate fate has not been settled by a peace treaty; because in addition to the inevitable difficulties of administering territory that has been acquired by the uncertainty as to its fate on the conclusion of peace. This is the reason why the whole government usually has a purely administrative character, the administration is usually carried on in the same way as before, and, if the government wishes to deal with the situation fairly and squarely, it is usually content to avoid misusing its temporary authority and power.

"This natural line of conduct was the one applied by the English to the greater part of those Dutch possessions in the Archipelago which fell into their hands, successively, after 1795. At Malacca, as well as in Sumatra and the Moluccas, everything that was not otherwise directly affected by outside matters of greater import was left as far as possible on the old footing. It was not so much a matter of governing, as of limit-

257

ing activity to the maintenance of the administration, and even that was done in the most slovenly manner. In Java, on the other hand, an entirely different line was taken, in spite of the fact that it was the most important colony of all, and was regarded as ripe for great reforms; and despite the fact that it was first captured after all the other possessions had fallen, so that the prospect of peace was then more formidable than elsewhere.

"The British government of Java was chiefly characterized by its zeal to institute reforms which would overthrow the existing order of things. This zeal was revealed in innumerable rapidly drawn-up plans which, however, were too weak to attain the wished-for goal. Lord Minto had previously given the start to such a line of policy, because, although he realized that the ultimate fate of Java was as yet uncertain, he took the viewpoint expressed in the phrase which is attributed to him, 'but in the meantime let us do as much good as we can', as also in his *Instructions* to Raffles, to broaden the scope of a narrow and limited administration and if necessary to introduce far-reaching changes in the seat of government."

It might here be mentioned that Mr. Levyssohn Norman's accusation of "zeal," which he declares led Raffles to change everything possible for the sheer joy of throwing away whatever was born of Dutch statesmanship, is a very natural reaction. Most reformers call down this criticism on their unlucky heads, and of course the harder they try to reform things, the more resentment they elicit from their predecessors. Witness the paragraph directly before this last one, wherein the writer dubs the British administrations of Malacca, Sumatra, and the Moluccas "slovenly," on the grounds that no changes were rung in by the incoming governments if they could possibly be avoided. Raffles wasn't governor in any of those places, it is easy to see. Yet when the British actually did start moving, as Raffles did on Java, Levyssohn Norman was cross just the same. The truth of the matter is that you can't win when you're the winner of a war. Nothing in this attack is surprising save that Levyssohn Norman has not em-

ployed the expression, "throwing the baby out with the bath."
He continues:

"From this point of view, it is understandable that a man
like Raffles should have thought it possible to succeed as a brilliant statesman where he failed to possess the requisite qualities of an administrator. If Lord Minto had confided the
government of Java to a routine official, things would probably
have gone on in much the same way as previously, and this
five-year British supremacy would undoubtedly not have provided sufficient material on which to write a monograph.

"There was too much government and too little administration. No difficulty was made about destroying much of the
existing structure, but the inevitable ensuing disadvantages
were further increased by a lax and muddled administration.

"Although it can be regarded as creditable to the British
administration that it sought in all sincerity and inspired by
good intentions, to inaugurate a completely new state of affairs, yet it must be admitted that it deserves no admiration
for the way in which it carried out the other part of a ruler's
task, that of the actual administration, which it seems to have
neglected and regarded as comparatively unimportant. It seems
to have been regarded as sufficient to lay down policy and
laws, and assumed that the execution thereof followed automatically upon their promulgation. . . .

"The enthusiasm for trying to accomplish a great deal in a
short time with inadequate means was clearly discernible in
the political sphere. It was hoped to plant the British influence, not only on Java but all over the Archipelago, and on
a broad and firm foundation. It was thought that with the
destruction of the Dutch rule, the work of two centuries had
been obliterated. It was thought that under the influence of
British victory, complete submission would follow. This expectation was likewise far from justified, and the comparatively
little trouble experienced by the Dutch in subsequently renew-
ing their control, conclusively proved that British Diplomacy
had failed in this respect likewise.

"It was a great mistake on the part of Raffles, that he did
not realize the importance of a powerful administration. He

did not realize that the Governor of a possession like Java must take quite a different viewpoint than that of a colony like the Cape or Canada."

Well, maybe. Since the "lax and muddled administration" wasn't permitted to carry on, either to prove or disprove itself, since it was cut short before it was five years old, we shall never know whether England could have muddled through or not. Furnivall thought she would have, but only after a very long time. According to Levyssohn Norman, she couldn't have; according to Raffles, proud papa of British Java, she had already rolled up a good record and would have gone on to better things.

The testimony of Crawfurd, forty years later, holds great interest as a candid, detached piece of observation. "In Java," he wrote, "Sir Stamford found the government still conducted on the old and vicious principle of commercial monopoly and forced labour, and intrepid innovator as he was, he overthrew the whole system. But he was not so successful in the more difficult task of reconstruction. Many errors were committed both by himself and by the officers who served under him, of whom I was one. The changes from one scheme to another were too frequent, the draughts on the treasury of British India became burdensome to it, and Sir Stamford, after an adminis tration of four years, was removed by the government of the Marquess of Hastings. . . ."

Minto, at least, was pleased with his bright young man, and felt that in Java his pet principles were vindicated. Unfortunately for Raffles, though most of the directors were willing to praise him and his work as much as anyone could want for glory's sake, they continued to be adamant on the subject of a permanently British Java. Little by little the stubborn hopes of Raffles faded.

CHAPTER XV

Of all the plans, fulfilled or abortive, which occupied the clever, restless mind of Stamford Raffles, the modern reader will probably find his Japan project most absorbing. Following the journalistic fad of the day in using "secret" army language, such as Churchill's "Project Habakkuk," or the name given by the British to the invasion of Italy—"Gibbon"—I am strongly tempted to name this chapter "Operation Pachyderm."

Japan was almost completely cut off from the Western world. This was by her own desire; she was well satisfied with things as they were and would probably have been even better satisfied if her insular immolation had been quite complete. But by an arrangement made in the seventeenth century with Holland, the Dutch had a foothold in Nippon. It was a precarious one, but still, there it was. The Dutch were ahead of the British by one foothold in Japan. It can be imagined how that fact rankled with Raffles.

The Hollanders were not allowed access to the chief islands of Japan, except once a year, to pay homage at the capital, but they had a factory on the tiny island, Deshima, off the coast of Kyushu, a part of the town of Nagasaki, and there a few Dutchmen were permitted to live, year in, year out, under most humiliating conditions and under constant surveillance of Japanese interpreters. One might compare the situation with that of the British traders and factors in China, before the Opium War, who were confined to a small segregated area, a sort of ghetto, in Canton, from which they had to do their work as best they could. But the Dutch in Japan were confined even more stringently. It is true that they alone among Europeans could share in the Japanese trade, but all that amounted to was permission to send two ships a year to Nagasaki, which carried cargo in and then carried other cargo out. Before the British moved in on Java these ships were dispatched from Batavia as the nearest important Dutch port, a fact which was, no doubt, partly responsible for Raffles's idea of opening Japan to British trade. His orders were to take over all subsidiary holdings of the Dutch in the Far East, and he understood the phrase "subsidiary holdings" to include the Deshima factory. It wasn't a brand-new idea, anyway, to trade with the Nipponese. Japan's exclusive attitude had not always been so extreme. Before the middle of the seventeenth century, while Holland was still battling for the supremacy of trade in the Archipelago which she ultimately won, there had been an English factory in Japan, at Hirado. Also, though there isn't much concrete evidence of this, it is difficult to believe that most European nations with interests in the Orient didn't sneak in by the back door sometimes, getting some of their products into Japan by way of the Chinese, who were able to enter and leave the stubbornly mysterious islands even when all white men's efforts failed. There was always, throughout the seventeenth and eighteenth centuries, plenty of traffic between China and Japan, though the Chinese trade, like that of the Dutch, was strictly confined to the port of Nagasaki.

We see the beginnings of Raffles's interest in the part of his speech, entitled "Japan," which he delivered to the Society of Arts and Sciences at Batavia on September 10, 1815. He was president of the society at that time, and the discourse was a noble piece of work, of truly staggering length. Speaking of the Japanese, he draws the customary courteous comparison between his own homeland and the "imperial island" in a few conventional words. The information he is about to divulge, he says, has come to him verbally, from Dr. Ainslie. Ainslie is an interesting character in this drama. He had just spent four months on Deshima; by what means he overcame the Japanese prohibition of Englishmen is an interesting story. This is what Raffles reported from Ainslie's description of the Japanese. It is quite an experience to read this and then to turn to more recent literature on the same subject.

"They are represented to be a nervous, vigorous people, whose bodily and mental powers assimilate [approximate?] much nearer to those of Europe than what is attributed to Asiatics in general. Their features are masculine and perfectly European, with the exception of the small lengthened Tartar eye, which almost universally prevails, and is the only feature of resemblance between them and the Chinese. The complexion is perfectly fair, and indeed blooming; the women of the higher classes being equally fair with Europeans, and having the bloom of health more generally prevalent among them than usually found in Europe."

Yes, puzzled reader, these are Japanese he's talking about.

"For a people who have had very few, if any external aids, the Japanese cannot but rank high in the scale of civilization. The traits of a vigorous mind are displayed in their proficiency in the sciences, and particularly in metaphysics and judicial astrology. The arts they practise speak for themselves, and are deservedly acknowledged to be in a much higher degree of perfection than among the Chinese, with whom they are by Europeans so frequently confounded; the latter have been stationary at least as long as we have known them, while the slightest impulse seems sufficient to give a determination to the Japanese character, which would progressively improve until it attained the same height of civilization with the European. Nothing indeed is so offensive to the feelings of a Japanese as to be compared in any one respect with the Chinese, [?] and the only occasion on which Dr. Ainslie saw the habitual politeness of a Japanese ever surprised into a burst of passion was, when, upon a similitude of the two nations being unguardedly asserted, the latter laid his hand upon his sword!"

It should be mentioned here that Raffles until some years later maintained an unfortunate and ill-founded prejudice against the Chinese, perhaps owing to some personal experience, some unpleasant encounter he had during his term of residence in Penang or Batavia. In these early days he did not appreciate their valuable qualities as citizens, but after he founded Singapore, if not before then, he learned his mistake.

There follows here a paragraph embodying opinions familiar to anyone who has been exposed, as Raffles so obviously was, through Ainslie, to Japanese self-advertising; a hundred and thirty years have not changed international propaganda methods, whatever may happen to our opinions. Raffles asserts that the Japanese people have an extraordinary liking for foreign ways, and blithely casts aside any possible adverse criticism of their awkwardly inflexible prohibition from their island of non-Japanese, such as the British. He goes further than that and actually manages to find something praiseworthy in their "extraordinary decision" to exclude the world from their shores. Say what you will, Raffles implies, but to carry out a decision like that takes energy.

In another comparison with the Chinese to the derogation of China—China, where all individuality has disappeared, says Raffles, broken down by the government until one Chinese is the counterpart of the other—the Japanese do not exhibit uniformity. And, again unlike those tiresome Chinese, "the women here are by no means secluded—they associate among themselves, like the ladies of Europe." Dr. Ainslie was very much mistaken on this, either about Japanese ladies or the ladies of Europe. "During the residence of Dr. Ainslie, frequent invitations and entertainments were given; on these occasions, and at one in particular, a lady from the court of Jeddo [Tokyo] is represented to have done the honours of the table with an ease, elegance and address that would have graced a Parisian. [Actually this "lady" was indubitably a tart, as only such women were ever allowed on Deshima. The Japanese made it a habit to palm off prostitutes on the innocent foreigners as great ladies. Their real ladies never appeared before such people.] The usual dress of a Japanese woman of middle rank costs perhaps as much as would supply the wardrobe of a European lady of the same rank for twenty years.

"The Japanese, with apparent coldness, like the stillness of the Spanish character, and derived nearly from the same causes, that system of *espionage*, and that principle of disunion dictated by the principles of both governments; are represented to be eager for novelty, and warm in their attachments; open to strangers, and, abating the restrictions of their political institutions, a people who seem inclined to throw themselves into the hands of any nation of superior intelligence. . . ." Here, too, Raffles cannot resist the temptation to cock another snook at the Chinese. "They have at the same time a great contempt and disregard of everything below their own standards of morals and habits, as instanced in the case of the Chinese."

A Far Eastern expert has lately dubbed the Japanese, of whom incidentally he is very fond, "professional charmers." In Raffles's case at least his description proves amazingly apt, the charm they exerted having been strong enough to carry through a third party, and Ainslie did a magnificent job of conducting an impression as it was intended to arrive, unchanged.

"This may appear to be contradicted," says Raffles, referring to the admiration allegedly felt by Japanese toward any nation of superior intelligence, "by the mission from Russia in 1814, under Count Kreusenstern; but the circumstances under which that mission was placed should be considered. From the moment of their arrival they were under the influence of an exclusive factor, who continued to rain upon them every possible ignominy which can be supposed to have flowed from the despotism of Japan, through the medium of an interested and avaricious man, who dreaded competition or the publication of his secret." The wicked Dutch, of course, were responsible for every unpleasantness which overtook the Russian mission, and the Japanese, equally of course, were utterly innocent.

It is not true, says Raffles, as has evidently been said by prejudiced people, that the Japanese are not liberal in religious matters.

Speaking of a former unsuccessful attempt on the part of the British to start negotiating with the rulers of Japan, he sounds a note of hope for better luck next time, because the failure of the previous attempt was of course due to the machinations of *those Dutch*, who could now be expected to sing but very small. For the past seven years, moreover, the younger members of the College of Interpreters had been assiduously studying the English language, in obedience to an imperial edict.

"In a word," he summarizes at last, "the opinion of Dr. Ainslie is, that the Japanese are a people with whom the European world might hold intercourse without compromise of character. . . . In the same spirit let us hope, that now, when

> *That spell upon the minds of men*
> *Break never to unite again—*

no withering policy may blast the fair fruits of that spirit of research which has gone forth from this hall; nor continue, under any circumstances, to shut out one half of the world from the intelligence which the other half may possess."

If this seems to us rather excessively flowery language for a simple ambition to sell printed goods and woolen cloth, remember that Raffles really felt that way about the sacred cause of Trade. Trade to him was synonymous with Civilization. No words were too harsh for him to use in speaking of those dastardly Dutch who stood in England's way when she wanted to civilize Japan. We have seen how his honest anger carried him to what other people probably found embarrassing extremes in his speech; it must be remembered that his audience was predominantly Dutch. But Raffles had long since convinced himself that the Dutch settlers of Batavia were now his friends and allies, which placed them automatically on the side of the angels and against the Nagasaki Dutch. As far as Raffles was concerned, there was no reason in his discourse for embarrassment on anyone's part.

The story carries on in the pages of *Raffles's Report on Japan to the Secret Committee of the English East India Company.* In a long preface the British consul for Osaka, Paske-Smith, sets the stage and explains the rest of the volume, which is that part of the correspondence between Raffles and the Secret Committee dealing with his attempts to reopen trade relations between England and Japan. Twice similar attempts had been made, once in 1673 (the Hirado trading station was closed in 1623) and once again in 1792. The first effort consisted of the actual dispatch of a loaded ship, the *Return*. Perhaps its failure was due to the *Return*'s name, which was certainly ill chosen; at any rate the Japanese simply turned her away. Another attempt in 1792 was not so definite; it was merely a part of Viscount Macartney's instructions when he was sent as first British ambassador to the Chinese court. He was told it wouldn't be a bad idea to look in on Japan, where tea as good as China's was produced, and where "the difficulties of trading . . . are now said to have almost ceased." They hadn't ceased by a long shot, but Macartney never found that out, because war broke out with France just as he was about to start for Japan, and his ship was called over to Canton to carry out English cargo.

Paske-Smith emphasizes the fact that Raffles didn't intend merely to transfer to the Company the privileges which the Dutch had held for so long at Deshima; for he considered those too insignificant to worry about. What he wanted was a real life-scale Anglo-Japanese commerce, "based on principles of equality, leading to an exchange of commodities between England, China, India and Japan under the wing of the East India Company."

The first excerpt quoted in the book is of special interest to us because it comes from a report written by Raffles from Malacca, in June 1811, before the final chapter of the Java expedition had even begun. The date proves that Raffles's plans for Japan were already well matured before the British occupied the important central post of Batavia. His knowledge of the history of Japanese-Dutch relations was surprisingly thorough, then, even though he had not yet gained access to the archives in Java.

The Dutch enjoyed these special benefits, he explains, because of a favor they did for the imperial family during the Portuguese war of the seventeenth century. For these reasons the Dutch originally "procured the Imperial Edict by which they were permitted to trade with Japan to the exclusion of all other European nations. This public act of their ancestors, the Japanese have repeatedly declared that they will not cancel, but they have done everything but formally cancel [it] for a more limited and less free trade never was carried on by one rich nation to another."

He thought that if the Japanese fully understood what had recently happened to Holland, and if they knew that the British were shortly to occupy Java, they would immediately terminate all intercourse between themselves and Europeans in general. "The Japanese conceive that they have entered into engagements with the Dutch only while they exist as a nation and there is the utmost reason to think in the event of the Dutch merging in any other nation, they would by no means consider these engagements as of any force."

Therefore, said Raffles, the only chance the Company had to retain the Japanese trade would be to gain to their interest the present Dutch resident at Japan, "at whatever price it may cost." He planned to insert, quietly, an English agent into the Dutch institution on Deshima, "and to make the transition as imperceptible as possible from the Dutch to the English. The last Japanese invoices of articles required by the Board of Trade will be found at Batavia and may be answered exactly and it will be requisite for the English Agent, if received at all, to reside at Japan till the return of the ships next season, according to the Dutch ceremonial, and if in the interim he could acquire the Japanese language and ingratiate himself with the Bonzes of religions of the Buddhist sects, much might probably be done to open the Japanese trade on a more liberal scale. . . . With regard to the present Japanese trade, it certainly is by no means equal to that of many neglected countries in Asia, but the principal inducement to make efforts for its continuance is the prospect of it being opened on a more extensive scale, an event which is very likely to be accelerated by the aggressions of Russia on the Kurile Islands which properly belong to Japan, and several of which the Russians have already reduced."

Later, from Batavia, he speaks of a slight change in his plans. He now proposes to send as agent a Dutch gentleman "of character and proper principles," with two ships carrying cargo under his superintendence. "I shall avow openly the change which has taken place in Java, but with the view of avoiding any objection to the English as a nation, make use of the term 'Bengal Company' which change in the term I am led to expect may remove many difficulties. . . ."

Other details as they occur make the plan seem more and more feasible. "In 1797 the Dutch at Batavia compelled by the lack of Dutch shipping chartered the English ship 'Eliza,' Captain Stewart, to visit Nagasaki, where she passed as an American because the Dutch feared to announce her as English. As the results of the information obtained on this voyage, Captain Stewart returned to India where he persuaded the East India Company in 1803 to send a ship to Japan. Sailing from Calcutta he entered Yedo Bay [Nagasaki Bay] in the East Indian Merchantman 'Frederick' with a rich cargo, but was refused admittance. . . ."

Naturally as Raffles lived longer and longer on friendly terms with the Batavian Dutch, or at least with some of them, he was able to pick and choose and finally to select men who seemed eligible for his proposition. His choice lighted on a Mr. Wardenaar, who had formerly been one of those resident agents who lived at Nagasaki and "who is understood to have possessed very considerable influence with the leading persons there. . . ." He promised Wardenaar a generous reward for his services, excusing this seeming extravagance to the Company on the grounds that the enterprise was speculative and unpleasant, and that Wardenaar was a man of high rank, habit, and years to be involved in such doings. "For [so] delicate and precarious a trust very few men can be considered as perfectly eligible or possessing that suavity of manner, evenness of temper, spirit of enquiry, extensive knowledge of mankind, habit of privation and high notions of enterprize, calculated to meet the personal insults, local prejudices, inconveniences and disappointments to be expected from a haughty and overbearing people so completely secluded and distinct from the rest of mankind and so exclusively the arbiters of their own conduct and behavior.

"Your Lordship not having pointed out to me any person to be employed on this particular mission [as companion emissary with Wardenaar, though Wardenaar was to be the permanent agent] my choice has fallen on Doctor Ainslie, a gentleman of very superior talents and education, in whom I place the highest and most unlimited confidence, for the delicate situation in which it is possible he may be placed, on the one hand from the extraordinary disposition and regulations of the Japanese, and on the other from the not impossible want, notwithstanding the confidence placed in Mr. Wardenaar, of that full and cordial cooperation of the Dutch establishment and interpreters, which may be eventually necessary. . . ."

In other words, Wardenaar was just what the doctor ordered for the job because he was Dutch, aside from all his other good qualities. But just because he *was* Dutch there would be a slight flavor of mistrust, so Ainslie's services for a certain side of the work seemed preferable to Raffles. Ainslie was to go along as surgeon, as he was actually an M.D., and Raffles summed up the arrangement at the end of his letter as follows:

"For admission to the port and the commencement of the intercourse, I rely exclusively on Mr. Wardenaar, but the ultimate settlement and proceedings will be entirely at the discretion of Mr. Ainslie."

In reply to these letters, the government secretary, Mr. Grey, replied that Mr. Raffles's appointments of Wardenaar and Ainslie met with their entire concurrence, and that Wardenaar's cut of twenty per cent, which Raffles had promised him, though certainly it was high, seemed reasonable considering everything. This reply should be kept in mind because of what followed later.

In a memorandum on the general situation, drawn up for the convenience of the Secret Committee by one Mr. Breton, there is mention of the "irreconcilable hatred" supposedly felt by the Japanese for all European nations excepting only the Dutch. It would therefore be advisable, suggests Breton, to keep England out of the picture and to "send thither a ship that would hoist Dutch colors on her arrival and during her continuance at Japan"; also, as an added precaution, the captain should be at least "nominally Dutch," if possible, a man familiar with Nagasaki. The crew should be as largely Dutch as would be practicable, and such of the crew as were English should pretend to be American. The English seamen should also be, in general, "mild and peaceable men, in order to obviate disputes between them and the Japanese which may give rise to unpleasant circumstances." All written transactions between the Japanese and the people of the expedition, of course, would be in Dutch according to custom, and so there would have to be a person aboard who could take care of all that, if possible a man formerly in the service of the Dutch Company, and in a situation of respectability. The Japanese, Mr. Breton cautions the committee, are very tenacious and particular on this point, especially if the person has never visited them before, knowing by their books and documents the names of the different persons who have been among them; they are also touchy as to the rank of such a person, who should be of such high grade as to render them honor. (Raffles's suggestions had not yet arrived when the memoir was written, but Wardenaar and Ainslie were well fitted to these descriptions.)

An important point made by Mr. Breton was that such trade would be advantageous. Many members of the Company were dubious on this point, but Breton declared the advantages to be sufficiently important to invite cultivation of this trade, "even on the condition of great sacrifice. The exports to Japan consist of the 2d. sort of Java brown sugar, and of the manufacturers and other merchandizes of Europe and India; and the returns are made in Japan copper and camphor. These are the only articles in which the [Dutch] company deal exclusively. All the other productions of Japan, such as porcelain, silks, lacker, and other articles, are left to individuals who carry thither such articles of merchandize in which the Company do not maintain an exclusive trade. And as the Company's ships are in general only ballasted with a cargo of copper, they allow their servants and seamen to fill up the ships free of freight." After a few further details of the former trade, the memorandum states that a recent inability of the Dutch Company to satisfy Japanese demands had greatly diminished the trade. The Japanese wanted sugar chiefly, and a single ship could not carry enough of sugar and other things to pay for one cargo of copper. The Japanese would not accept money, so the Dutch were always in their debt. As a result, the Chinese had been cutting in; they were the only other foreigners allowed to trade with Japan and had been able to supply the wants of the Japanese by means of articles received from the English at Canton. The English would have to overcome this opposition, but as they had plenty of the necessary merchandise, which the Chinese had been getting from them secondhand to pass on to Japan, that would not be difficult.

Altogether the early correspondence on this subject pointed to complete agreement between Raffles and the Company, a situation which never seemed to last very long, under any circumstances. There is, however, an obscure point here which has never been cleared up, at least in print. Raffles and the higher-ups, as well as Ainslie and Wardenaar, everyone, in fact, who was in on this plan, were agreed that the Japanese should not be notified of the changes that had taken place in Holland's position among the nations of the world. Also the Japanese were not to know that the British were in possession of Java. The plans were discussed and changed and discussed and changed again, as to the best lie to tell which would effectively cover up the truth. This desire for concealment was Raffles's reason for smuggling the English Ainslie into Deshima, and for sending Wardenaar in under false colors, as a Dutchman representing the old government of Holland. They were all agreed, evidently, that it was possible thus to keep the news of the world from Japanese ears. Their belief was based on the fact that Japan deliberately and painstakingly kept herself cut off from every outside influence.

However, there was one channel of information which they forgot. The Chinese were not excluded from Japan. The Chinese came and went more freely than the Dutch of the old regime had ever been permitted to do, and they were fully informed as to political changes in Europe, at least in 'so far as they affected the Far East. Therefore it seems incredible that the Japanese should not have had word from them of Holland's recent annexation by Napoleon. It is possible that the Dutchmen marooned on Deshima should not have got the news; indeed, it seems to be true beyond a shadow of a doubt that they didn't know, though even that lack of information is difficult to credit. But the Japanese authorities couldn't possibly have remained in ignorance indefinitely. Nobody has spoken of this in the discussions of Raffles's plans which took place at that time and in the articles and comments which have been written since about the situation, but the facts remain.

Why, then, hadn't the Japanese already cracked down on the Dutch factor and his compatriots on Deshima? The only explanation possible is that Raffles's supposition, which he expressed in his first letter on the subject, written at Malacca, was an error. He thought, it will be remembered, that if the Japanese knew what had happened to Holland and what was in the act of happening to Java they would immediately terminate all intercourse between themselves and Europe in general—i.e., they would throw those two Dutchmen out on their ears. Because, said Raffles, the Japanese felt that they had entered into engagements with the Dutch, and were favoring them, only while they existed "as a nation." Well, Raffles must have been mistaken. The Japanese must have known, and they must have felt that it didn't make any difference to the Shogun's edict whether the Dutch were their own masters or subject to other nations, to France or England. There is no other explanation. Considering this, however, the spectacle of everyone tiptoeing melodramatically about, taking elaborate precautions to keep the truth from the Japanese, becomes slightly ludicrous.

Trouble reared its head in May 1812, when Raffles wrote the committee that the adventure would have to be postponed to the next season, owing to some delay in getting the required trade goods from Bengal. Even at the end of October of the same year a delay until the next year was necessary. The articles for trade were being got together, however, and the first sailing was finally set for June 1813. In January of that year Raffles's secretary, Assey, made a list of the presents and goods destined for Japan, for His Imperial Majesty the Emperor. It is a fascinatingly varied array, including an almanac of Batavia, two catties of Egyptian mummy [sic], one day and night spyglass [telescope?], four civet cats, ten "Glattig" birds, twenty sheep, ten polished liquor decanters, a carpet, a piece of magnet stone, a table watch, many sorts of cloth, Persian leather, et cetera. There are various smaller groups of similar articles, evidently belonging to private deals in the names of different burghers of Batavia and, perhaps, members of the crew.

Of overwhelming importance, however, was the chief present of all, the magnificent gift intended as the *pièce de résistance* for His Imperial Majesty the Japanese Emperor [that is, the Tokugawa Shogun]. It was nothing less than a real live *elephant*. A very special elephant too: a white one from Siam. Contemporary Japanese sources, on the other hand, differ as to whether it came from Ceylon or Sumatra. No one need be told in these enlightened days, surely, how very special a white Siamese elephant was supposed to be, at least in Siam. Raffles assumed that the reputation of the species must surely have reached even to the august and protected ears of Japan's Divine Ruler, the Son of Heaven.

Now you know why that particular voyage should be known to history as Operation Pachyderm.

Two ships, the *Charlotte* and the *Mary*, were selected for the voyage, the cargo being made up to look as much as possible like Dutch cargoes of former days. Mr. Wardenaar's orders were to proceed to China and sell the stuff there if the Japanese caught on to the trick or for some other reason would not let him in.

Replying to various reports and letters sent by Raffles to Bengal at this time, the government of India, on January 29, 1814, sounded the first sour note of the proceedings. It was sour enough, however, to make up for any amount of delay. The governor general professed ignorance of Japan's state at the time, and so declared his inability to estimate the difficulty of the undertaking or to appreciate the advantages of a successful outcome. This beginning was rather ominously stately and sounded suspiciously like the makings of an alibi, but worse came along right after it. The governor general, furthermore, was suddenly appalled at the expense involved, which was "far exceeding the amount which this Government would have thought it prudent to sanction for the purpose of making an experiment, the success of which appears to be so uncertain independently of the cost of the goods, of the hire of the ships, and of the monthly salaries. . . . His Lordship in Council observes that the Lieutenant Governor has undertaken to grant eventually a very large gratuity (50,000 Dollars) to Mr. Wardenaar. . . .

"The Governor General in Council is disposed, therefore, to doubt whether the expense is not disproportioned to the value of the object contemplated; and although His Lordship in Council has great confidence in the prudence and judgment of the Lieutenant Governor, he cannot concur altogether in the propriety of his engaging in so expensive an undertaking without having more satisfactory grounds for assuming that the experiment was likely to succeed and that the advantages to be derived from an intercourse with Japan, were likely to be such as to justify great pecuniary sacrifices . . . et cetera, et cetera. . . .

"The Governor General in Council is of opinion that without some such assurance, it would have been more prudent to have confined the undertaking to a very limited scale, and that it would have been sufficient to have sent, in the first instance, a single Vessel, with a cargo of small value, for the purpose of ascertaining the disposition of the officers of the Dutch Factory, as well as the disposition of the Japan Government to admit a commercial intercourse with Java under the circumstances of the late change in the administration of that Colony."

He goes on to make the point that the Dutchmen at present on Deshima would very likely object strenuously to the English proposals, which in the end could not possibly be advantageous to them, and that their alarm and jealousy might inspire them to betray the whole plan to the Japanese. The governor general thinks a greater degree of confidence and a "more open and candid proceeding toward the Dutch Factory" would have been better.

Also, he says, if the Japanese find out about the trick, they will resent the imposition and refuse to carry on with the arrangements. The governor general "is of opinion that the attempt to establish an intercourse should have been open and avowed, that it should have been in the first instance at a small expense, and that if serious obstacles were found to exist the idea should for the time have been relinquished."

However, his lordship in council would be happy to find that his apprehensions were not justified, and that the enterprise had been productive of advantages fully sufficient to indemnify the government for the very heavy expenses attending it, et cetera, et cetera.

It is this sort of lightning-stroke development which used to turn subsidiary governors' hair white in a single night. Needless to say, the governor general in question was *not* Minto; Minto had just retired and been succeeded in office by Lord Moira, who started out on his new job with a strong prejudice against Minto's white-haired boy over on Java. Even that prejudice, however, scarcely explains the sudden change of sentiment expressed in this letter, on reading which one would suppose that none of the previous correspondence had ever existed. Forgotten are those cordial reassurances to Raffles that Wardenaar's salary, considering everything, was not excessive. Gone with the wind are all the happy agreements which came from Bengal as to the advantages of trade relations with Japan and so forth. All of a sudden Calcutta is frigidly washing its hands of the affair, and indeed behaving as if the entire thing were a new, unpleasant suggestion.

It wasn't in Raffles's power, either, to make the retort discourteous which must have sprung hotly to his lips. He couldn't remind his lordship that his doubts were very late in occurring, considering that the entire matter had been discussed over and over during the period of the past eighteen months, or that it had been agreed in Bengal, months before, that the gamble was well worth taking. He could not call his lordship a silly ass for suggesting so long after the event that a small vessel with a cheap cargo would have been sufficient the first time, or point in explanation to his original plans, which made clear just why the ships and cargo must approximate as closely as possible the ships sent annually by the Dutch. He could not suggest that his lordship rub his honorable nose in the past correspondence and take note of Raffles's early-made suggestion that the Dutchmen on Deshima be adequately compensated for their co-operation, in which event they would presumably be willing to further the English plans, rather than give way to fruitless alarm and jealousy. He could not make the most obvious retort of all, that to have followed his lordship's advice (always supposing it had been proffered in time, which it wasn't) and to have been open and aboveboard with the Japanese would have been the equivalent of asking for complete rejection from the very beginning. Anyone with more brains than a moron knew that the Japanese would never have even begun to accept a ship that was openly British. They had always turned down such attempts. To have gone about the project as the governor general described would not have been a gamble, that much is evident. It would have been something worse: an outright waste of money and effort. It would be far better to abandon the idea completely, from the beginning, than to take his lordship's suggestions seriously. But Raffles couldn't say that. He could only accept the unpalatable fact that his beloved pet project, his Operation Pachyderm, was all of a sudden unpopular in India.

He could only do what he did: write a polite communication in which he reiterated all his earlier statements without calling attention to the fact that he was repeating himself. Patiently he said, "Our object in negotiations with the Japanese Government is the free admission of the British Trade to that Island—while the interests of Java only would be accomplished in being able to resume the Trade on the exclusive privilege heretofore attached to it—but it appears that this cannot be effected in any way suitable to the honor and dignity of the British Government." That is, he didn't want merely to reaffirm Java's rights of trade, for that would revert to the Dutch if Java did. He wanted to clinch the deal for England. "It must either be carried on under false colours," he said, carefully simple and clear for his lordship's benefit, "or abandoned—and if it be possible to take advantage of the communication which through Java is open to Japan for the purpose of establishing a British connection—is such a connection to be considered an appendage to the Colony? . . . Necessity, honor and policy therefore require that in whatsoever light one may regard our connection with Japan, the general interests of the British Empire be considered rather than the local interests and advantages of the Colony which I am appointed to superintend. . . .

"We are gradually undermining the exclusive administration of a Dutch Factory and may possibly be able to supersede it by an English one—but this cannot in the present uncertain state of Java be effected by the Chief authority of that Colony, unless he acts on more enlarged views than the immediate interests of that Colony may require." For the moment, he adds, the nature of the business necessitates that the ships sail from Java, where they are outfitted, but in future, if British trade is extended as he expects, eight, ten, or even more English ships a year would be sailing to Japan, from whatever port the supreme British authority might designate.

In February 1814, Raffles was able to report the successful return of the two ships, *Charlotte* and *Mary*, and he enclosed the reports of the commissioners. On their arrival they found the commercial director, Mr. Doeff, "averse to acknowledge the British Government, and steadily refusing to deliver over the Factory; it was deemed impracticable, consistently with the safety of the Ships and Crews, to avow the grounds on which they had come, and to enter the harbour under British Colours; but it was agreed that the Annual Trade might be conducted under the usual forms. . . ." So much for that part of his lordship's apprehensions.

Dr. Ainslie brought better news, too, in one way. Not only

was all the business part of the voyage satisfactorily accomplished and arrangements made for the next trip, but it looked as if in the course of time the Japanese might actually accept the English traders under their own flag. At any rate much of the violent prejudice hitherto felt in Japan against "the English Character" had been done away with; moreover some of the chief interpreters who dwelt at the factory, as well as other officers of the Japanese Government, had been entrusted with the secret, and although they knew the true state of affairs perfectly well long before the English departed, they did nothing to hinder the success of the plan. As Ainslie said, "This tacit participation on their part was the surest pledge of our safety." So much for another part of his lordship's apprehensions. Indeed, though there had been few opportunities to communicate with these sympathetic Japanese, Ainslie was so certain of the ultimate success of Raffles's ideas that he suggested obtaining a short letter from His Royal Highness the Prince Regent to the Emperor of Japan, something as follows:

"His Royal Highness communicates to the Emperor that the Dutch nation has been destroyed and annihilated by the French, and that Batavia and all the Dutch possessions in the East are now placed under the British Protection. The East India Company will send an agent to Japan to explain these circumstances and to enter on the subject of the English Ship of War which formerly put into Nangasacky [sic] in distress."

Even if the prince regent or his government should object to writing such a letter, a similar message transmitted verbally would have a good effect, said Ainslie, for the Japanese Government set great store by rank and would look with more favor upon any word from the English if they were sure the highest authority had inspired it.

Among his own comments Raffles includes one to the effect that not the least encouraging among the aspects of this first expedition to Japan was the manner in which the Emperor had been graciously pleased to accept all the gifts which had been so carefully selected. The fact that he took them all was significant; he didn't always do that. Only the *white elephant* was sent back to Batavia, and this was not because His Imperial Majesty didn't want him, but only because there was no way, evidently, to unload the animal safely in Nagasaki Bay. The ships were not alongside any dock, but rode at anchor in the middle of the bay. No craft anywhere along that coast was capable of ferrying an elephant ashore, and so this one superspecial mark of esteem had to stay aboard and make the long journey back. (Could this incident have been the origin of the familiar phrase, "a white elephant"? It seems a logical theory.) At any rate it was evident that the Emperor would, if he could, have accepted the elephant as well; his acceptance of the other articles was regarded, says Raffles, "as a very flattering testimony of regard."

It seems that after Messrs. Wardenaar and Ainslie returned to Java they dispelled in great part the foolish notion that Japan was in ignorance of Holland's ignominious position, at the beginning of the nineteenth century. Though the Japanese may not have known all the details and didn't mention the matter to the factor, Ainslie admitted that ignorance on the part of many Japanese seemed highly improbable. Therefore, since the presents had been accepted and arrangements for another voyage made in advance, as usual, the Japanese persons involved would do their best, when the whole truth became known to the highest authorities, to persuade these authorities to look with favor on the mission, even though it should be known to be British.

Mr. Doeff, the Dutch factor, had shown great anxiety to get the direction of trade into his own hands. He tried more than once to open the matter with Wardenaar and to secure some sort of engagement to that effect. Doeff evidently felt quite sure that trade would continue to be carried on in British ships, prejudice or no prejudice. In his report Ainslie gives a close description of the factor, "an able, intriguing Character disposed to secure an ample Fortune for himself in the present moment, when he thinks the Colonial Advantages of the Japan Trade to Java would induce great sacrifices for its preservation." Neither Ainslie nor Raffles seemed to think he would be any great loss to the Company if he should leave Deshima, neither did they insist upon his departure. I mention this small matter to show how the persons involved since the return of the mission had become so certain as to the feasibility of British trade relations with Japan that they were discussing the smallest extraneous details of day-by-day business, presumably to go into effect after everything should have been settled.

Throughout most of his letters and comment Raffles plays variations on the same old tune; he is anxious to establish England firmly in Japan, come what may to Java. And of course there is another familiar old tune too: "The Character of the Japanese," says Raffles, "has evidently been subject to the misrepresentation which the jealousy of the Dutch has industriously spread over the whole of their Eastern possessions—it is observed by Dr. Ainslie . . . that they are a race of people remarkable for frankness of manner and disposition, for intelligent enquiry, and freedom from prejudice— they are in an advanced state of civilization, in a climate where European Manufactures are almost a necessary comfort, and where long use has accustomed them to many of its luxuries."

Ainslie writes in a letter to the government that the recent limiting of the trade carried on by the Dutch was due in large part to the conduct of their officers, who were getting so greedy that they took too much commission on articles of trade, thereby limiting the already limited amount they were able to bring in in their two ships annually. In his opinion the Japanese were ripe for the introduction of new manufactures: they were eager for more of what they already knew, and would welcome variations. And though the returns from Japan had hitherto been limited in the main to copper, camphor, silk, lacquer, et cetera, there were many other things which could easily be brought away—tea, beeswax, pitch, borax, gamboge, asafetida, cinnabar, iron, linseed oil, whale oil, pit coal, and flour.

The Chinese trade, like the Dutch, was limited strictly, though the limits allowed of more scope. They were permitted to send ten junks a year, and these vessels, fitted out from Nanking, brought sugar, chiefly, and a few trifling Chinese products, as well as a lot of English woolen material, for which they took back in payment a thousand piculs of bar copper per junk, lacquered ware, dried fish, soya beans, and whale oil. The Chinese were allegedly treated badly by the Japanese, and their intercourse was allowed chiefly because they had certain drugs which were much prized in Japan. If the English could supply these, then it would be easy to supplant the Chinese completely.

Raffles wrote his old friend Minto in February 1814, in England, acquainting him with what had passed. This letter is of interest to us because here again he admits that the Japanese must be at least partially aware of Holland's plight, and cites this certainty as encouraging for Britain's future relations with Nippon. (Minto died before the letter reached him.) But he adds that at the moment it would be fatal to send out any ship which was openly English, as the very sight of such a vessel, of any description whatever, would put the seal on future chances of a *rapport*. In accordance, however, with his policy of going gently, slowly, but steadily toward the goal, Raffles would have the Company start working on the knotty problem of Mr. Doeff, the Dutch resident at Deshima, who had stoutly refused to lower the Dutch flag or to further English aspirations in any way. He says as much in a letter to the committee, as well as to Minto. Doeff's refusal to acknowledge British authority (which the fortune of war and the rights of conquest had given England a right to expect) afforded a fair, just, and honorable plea to open a communication with the Japanese Government direct, and Raffles proposed that an embassy be sent to Japan with authority to state openly the political events which had taken place and the consequent dependence of the Dutch factory at Deshima.

The embassy should offer presents as a proof of friendship and show specimens of England's various manufactures, the main object being to negotiate for the establishment of a British factory *wholly independent of the commerce hitherto carried on between Java and Japan*, and calculated to introduce the British on the footing of the most favored nation. He realizes that the whole mission must be carried on with the greatest delicacy, and that even then the first attempt is almost certain to fail. He repeats that the ships which go to Japan must continue to sail from Batavia, as any sudden change in routine would be likely to alarm the Japanese and defeat their object. Everything must be introduced by degrees, allowing some consideration for the habits of centuries and time for the subsidence of the prejudices which the Dutch had endeavored to excite.

"The intercourse of last year [1813] has broken the ice. . . . If the attempt be not made while we have possession of Java the opportunity once lost may never be regained. . . . It is my intention to send one ship to Japan at the approaching season in June next upon the same footing as last year and to relieve Mr. Doeff from his situation; according to established usage . . . two of the Honorable Company's Cruisers should be sent to Japan at the favorable season in 1815, not for purposes of commerce, but to convey an agent charged with authority as above mentioned and with positive orders not to enter the harbour unless a friendly communication is agreed upon, but to inform the Japanese Government that if this offer is refused the commerce between Batavia and Japan is to cease."

Space forbids too much attention to detail on this fascinating study, which throws a valuable sidelight on Raffles's style of reasoning and his powers of persuasion. It was after some thought and reluctantly that I left out the story of the *Phaeton*, reference to which occurs again and again in Raffles's letters. The *Phaeton*, Captain Pellew, was an English frigate which sailed into Nagasaki Bay in 1808; the unfortunate governor of Nagasaki was so much ashamed of this forcible entry that he committed hara-kiri. His fate was a vivid warning to those who came after them, and the name of the *Phaeton* lived on as a sort of symbol of the misfortune that was supposed to accompany any English endeavor to establish intercourse with the Japanese. Doeff referred to this incident when he was approached by Wardenaar, declaring that the Japanese would most certainly put a stop to all intercourse with Batavia if they should discover that the British were in power there; he also professed to be gravely worried for fear the Japanese might put all the visiting English to death and confiscate ships and cargo, if they were to discover the imposition being practiced upon them.

Wardenaar, however, was skeptical, suspecting Doeff of deliberately fomenting trouble and of maintaining an artificial level of suspicion among the Japanese. He could not accuse Doeff outright of all this trickery, nor could he insist upon taking over the authority of the factory. Patience was indicated, and patience won out. For the duration of the visit no further communication was entered upon with the Japanese Government than had been the custom when the Dutch sent their ships in. Mr. Doeff was to continue in his position as director for the coming twelvemonth, at the very least. There was a flurry among the rest of the people connected with the factory, who wanted to be assured of their jobs under the new management, and Wardenaar and Ainslie were busy for a long time answering all the applicants, saying that their affairs would have to be discussed and decided in Batavia upon the return home of the two ships.

Ainslie's written report took a slightly different point of view from Wardenaar's, in that he gave more credence to Doeff's warning. He made an observation which even today sounds plausible: "In Japan the Government pervades and animates every fibre of the frame of society, it identifies itself with its Subjects, and every Individual of its numerous population moves by its pulse. . . . The consequences of the *Phaeton's* visit to Nangasacky, were in themselves sufficiently distressing, and it may be reasonably presumed, that the occasion they presented was not neglected by the Dutch Factory of directing against the nation whose influence they were chiefly apprehensive of, that jealousy of foreigners indiscriminately, which so strongly possessed the Japanese Government."

The question of direct introduction of the English, they decided, was consequently at an end for the present. (What would have happened to Moira's project of sailing up to the Emperor's front door and gaily demanding audience?) The ships therefore remained at anchor under Dutch colors.

It seems only fair, since we have it on record, to give Doeff's own account of all this hubbub at Nagasaki. He is by way of being one of Holland's favorite heroes because of this incident, as according to him he was motivated throughout the proceedings by a patriotic desire to keep his country's flag flying. It must be admitted (and it is admitted, admiringly in the bargain, by Paske-Smith in his preface) that Doeff succeeded in his aim, if this be true.

His story follows the one told in Batavia pretty faithfully, with the addition that he was indeed deliberately playing on the fears of Wardenaar when he invoked the affair of the *Phaeton*, and warned them that they might be executed forthwith. He persuaded them, and they in turn persuaded Ainslie (who according to the Dutch was a frightful drunkard), to let him manage everything, so that the ships should pass for American-freighted Dutch vessels, and enough of their cargoes should be sold to pay the factory's debt, secure a return cargo of copper, and thus maintain the fiction of Dutch authority. This was duly done according to signed agreement.

Doeff now tried to put one over on Raffles and sent his representative, Jan Cock Blomhoff, on one of these ships to Batavia with a proposal to Raffles to make a trade agreement whereby the Batavia-Nagasaki annual trade ship should be resumed, but under the Netherlands flag, pending a general peace in Europe and Asia. Blomhoff failed to achieve this; on the contrary, Raffles offered him a bribe of fifteen hundred Spanish dollars to head a second attempt on the same lines as Ainslie's. Blomhoff rejected the offer, whereupon he was placed under arrest and later sent to England, whence he was released and made his way to Holland.

Raffles gave as his reason for rejecting Doeff's proposal that Janssens's capitulation of 1811 included Java and all the Dutch dependencies, of which Deshima was *ipso facto* one. Blomhoff denied this and pointed out that the English had never tried to take over the Dutch factory at Canton, which presumably held the same status as Deshima. Raffles persisted in his attitude and sent another ship to Japan in 1814, under the command of Cassa and Captain Vrooman, despite the fact that he was already aware of the revolt of the Netherlands in 1813, the recall of the Prince of Orange and his accession to the throne, the treaty of peace and friendship with Great Britain, and the protests of Blomhoff. The ship reached Nagasaki Bay on August 8, 1814, and was recognized by the Japanese interpreters as being one of the same English ships which had appeared the previous year. In consultation with them, Doeff gave Cassa the alternative of trading under the Dutch flag, as had been done with Ainslie's ships in 1813, or telling the Japs he had been sent by the English. Cassa chose the former course, and the trade was conducted under these conditions.

No ship came in 1815 or 1816, but two arrived in 1817 with Jan Cock Blomhoff (accompanied by his wife, child, and Dutch nurse) aboard, sent as relief for Doeff. Both Doeff and Blomhoff were decorated by King William I for their patriotic conduct, as the result of which Deshima is commonly alleged to have been the only place where the Dutch flag flew in the years 1810–13, but the same actually applied to the Netherlands Consulate at Tunis, the Fort of Epmina on the Guinea coast, and the factory at Canton as well.

Among the papers forwarded to the government of India after the first voyage in 1813 Raffles included the list of articles which were ordered against the next voyage, by Japanese who were still supposedly under the impression that the ships were Dutch. It does bear out his contention that there was a large demand for European manufactures, but it came to nothing, ultimately, for the next communication that arrived from Bengal, dated August 5, 1814, was calculated to dash Raffles's hopes of Japan once and for all.

It appears under the title, *Extract of a colonial general letter from the Government of India to the Court of Directors, dated the 5th August 1814 reviewing the reasons for prohibiting further efforts to trade with Japan.*

The first paragraph makes the strange statement, "as the Lieutenant Governor anticipated the greatest advantages from such an intercourse, and we were not aware that the Dutch had acquired any rights to an exclusive trade, which the British Government were bound to respect, we did not in the first instance discourage the project of opening a communication with the Dutch Factor in Japan although we saw reason to disapprove of the means which the Colonial Government had resorted to for its Establishment."

The second paragraph says that Raffles had "unquestionably much overrated" the "real value" of the objective.

The report of the accountant general left the government in no further doubt as to the value of trade with Japan, which in their opinion was nil. "That the Japanese, as well as other Nations, can justly appreciate the excellence of our manufactures may be readily admitted, and that they would gladly consume them, if they possessed the means of procuring them, is perhaps equally true, but it does not follow that this preference will occasion an increased demand for an article, highly valuable and desirable as it may be. It must first be shown that the supposed consumer possesses the means of giving some article equally valuable and desirable in exchange." Japan didn't have anything England couldn't easily do without, was their sentiment.

Actually the mystery and concealment observed by the Dutch in regard to this exclusive trade had had the effect of producing extravagant notions of its importance, the government suspected.

Finally, Japan evidently didn't have any gold and silver.

Raffles did not give in immediately. He sent Bengal another report which he hoped would cause them to change their minds, but as there is no copy of this extant, we have no way of knowing whether or not his hopes were justified. At any rate the minds of the government were unchanged. There was a slight flurry in May 1815, when the East India Company wrote the government of India expressing their favorable attitude toward continuing trade relations with Japan, if it were at all possible. In February 1815 some firm in Batavia called Skelton & Co. put in for permission to join in the next expedition, in case one happened to be going out, but because of a shipping shortage they had to recall their offer in September. Skelton & Co. still wanted some assurance of being able to join the expedition of the following year, but after a few exchanges of letters the government in Bengal politely and firmly put a stop to all hopes in that direction.

As we have already learned from Doeff and the Dutch, even this emphatic discouragement from India did not stop Raffles however. The ship which returned in 1814 (on the seventh of July, Doeff says) was their old friend the *Charlotte*, and trade continued, still under the Dutch flag—surely the strangest transaction seen on those seas for centuries—until she left on the return trip for Batavia, on November sixteenth of the same year. That voyage was really the swan song of John Bull in false whiskers though. The next ship sighted by Doeff, as he has told us, was his relief ship, a real Dutch one, in 1817, by which time Raffles and all the other British had long since left Java. Doeff must have been happy to get all the news of the past three years, at that. Imagine how he and Blomhoff swatted each other on the back! Picture the celebration they held, and the mighty laughs they laughed, talking it over!

So ended a gallant attempt on Raffles's part to set the clock of History ahead by about forty years. When Japan was at last opened to the world it was not the English who did it, but though Raffles failed, we can rest assured it was not for want of trying.

If we again indulge in the indoor sport of speculation, and wonder how things would have gone if Raffles had not been subservient to the government of India, we would not be the first to play with that idea. Many a student of history before us has looked at this record of the Secret Committee and then at the date Commodore Perry sailed into Tokyo Bay. Of all sad words of tongue or pen, the saddest might be those spoken by Lord Moira—Lord Hastings by that time—in the afterworld when Raffles confronted him with whatever newspaper they have there, on July 14, 1853.

Come to think of it, there is another date which should interest us, related as it is to the same subject—December 7, 1941. On that day it was probably Moira's turn to brandish the *Afterworld Gazette* triumphantly in front of Sir Stamford Raffles's nose.

The last word has not yet been spoken.

CHAPTER XVI

The student of Raffles's life and times, if he be of an optimistic habit of mind, thanks Providence for such observant gossips as Munshi Abdullah and Addison, who for a while worked as secretary to the lieutenant governor on Java. A pessimist is more inclined to grumble that Providence couldn't have seen her way clear to granting a bit more of the same help. Why, for instance, couldn't Abdullah have gone along with Raffles to Java and Sumatra? Why did Addison, after proving his worth as Raffles's Boswell, have to die at such an early age, and after writing such tantalizingly profuse letters too? However, it can't be helped. Providence must take the blame that our information is spread so unevenly, so that we have long periods of our subject's life which are only sketched lightly, in the barest outlines; and then suddenly find ourselves snowed under by a flood of detailed knowledge, an avalanche of well-annotated anecdotes and manuscripts and contemporary comment.

The Javanese chapter of Raffles's life is like that. Not only has History taken such a fancy to the years 1811–16 that she keeps her brightest light trained on Raffles and Java during that time, but humanity seems to have followed her lead. We know a good deal about a lot of people who were connected with Raffles during his four and a half years in Batavia.

One fact has been mentioned by several people we have come to know in that half-world frequented by biographers, where the dead and the living meet to shake hands and swap stories. Everyone seems agreed that the British Government in Java was inexcusably understaffed and overworked. No doubt the explanation is the same one offered by the Company's apologists when, for the time, the young man Raffles was overworked and underpaid at Penang: the Indies, in John Company's opinion, weren't worth too much expenditure.

Their miserliness seems strange just the same, considering the importance of the Eastern situation in Napoleon's world, especially when we contrast the list of British officials with Raffles's domestic pay roll, for example. He employed a fantastic number of servants and outdoor workers. At Tjipanas, a country place with hot springs, he kept on the resident's estate two mandoors (foremen or overseers) and fifty men for general work, three mandoors and forty-eight men in the vegetable gardens, three mandoors and thirty men for the flower gardens and fruit orchards, one mandoor and ten men at Barntarpeteh (another country place), one mandoor and twenty men in the cow and deer paddocks, seven men in the rice mills, twenty-seven in the dairy, five in the sheep pens, two in the smithy, thirty-three in the stables, sixty grass cutters, four watchmen, fifteen sweepers, four water carriers, four white-washers, two cooks, two washermen, nine men for the poultry, two in the dispensary, three lamplighters—a total of three hundred and forty-seven people. The mandoors were paid one and a half Spanish dollars a month and the coolies one dollar.

At Batavia, Buitenzorg, and Tjipanas altogether, according to a pay roll dated March 1814, he employed three European servants, twenty-three free Indians and Javanese, plus seventy-seven government slaves at Buitenzorg (nine musicians, twenty-five house servants, seven cooks, one baker, one washer, three shoesmiths, three coachmen, six grooms, one saddle maker, six seamstresses, eleven maids, three bleachers, and a cowman), as well as eight personal slaves, which made a total of four hundred and fifty-eight. If this figure fails to stagger you, reflect that Daendels probably employed more people than that in his time, for he was even keener than was Raffles on maintaining prestige or, as the Orientals call it, "face."

Now let us turn to the government offices and look at the men there. Our invaluable friend Mr. de Haan has made a good many comments on this situation, for he took the trouble to study each one of Raffles's Englishmen and tame Dutchmen separately.

Referring to an action on the part of the British which met with his disapproval, De Haan thought he had the answer to his complaint, and he was probably right, when he ascribed it to understaffing in the government offices. "These stupid mistakes bear witness," he writes, "to one of the many difficulties of Raffles' government—the lack of trained personnel. While one finds relatively few British-Indian employees (Hope, Blagrave, Lawrence, Robinson, Macquoid) one meets correspondingly more military men of high and low mark, some of them King's Officers (serving in the regiments temporarily stationed in India), others in the service of the East India Company, either in a European regiment or in a Sepoy one. The King's Officers, amongst whom men of birth and wealth were by no means few and far between, with their ladies set the tone for social life, and thus strongly opposed the 'indianization' of the original army of occupation. Above all we have been struck by the Army Medical Officers, who, under Raffles, carried out administrative functions; strong personalities such as Assey, Crawfurd and Hopkins, likewise John Leyden. Finally there is the class of fortune-hunters, with Admiral Stopford, who got rid of his share of the loot, at their head, and others like Barrett, Bingley, Addison and so on, who looked to feather their own nests; whoever spoke fair English, like Francis, could easily earn his bread.

"Next to all these English employees the Dutch officials cut a poor figure. It is a lucky thing that the splendid gifts of Muntinghe were so well employed and fittingly rewarded by Raffles. Other capable men, like Van Haak, Van Sevenhoven, and the two brothers Veeckens, he would not make use of, owing to their political views. Rothenbuhler and Van Isseldijk appear to have been entirely worn out. Nicholas Engelhard kept himself aloof, and there was a great deal of deadwood amongst the rest of them. The Dutchmen who stayed continuously in the English Service as Residents, Doornik and Van Naerssen, did little more than draw their salaries. That the English personnel also was not free from deadwood is obvious: two examples are Heyland and Roxburgh.

"But the shortage of personnel was astounding. There was naturally a Resident in each Residency. He had to support him an Assistant Resident, who was often commonly termed a 'writer,' and who was in fact principally employed on clerical duties, but who also represented his chief in the latter's absence. Sometimes there was, besides, a European Warehouse —or Harbour-Master, and that was all, save for some native clerks, foremen and overseers. The Resident, frequently an English officer, naturally understood neither Malay nor any other native language used on Java; his assistant likewise was no linguist, and with these two he nonetheless arranged all the taxation of the land rent in that whole area, first like a 'dessage', later the individual tax. In this connection a surveyor was sometimes ordered to map a whole Residency. And it was done. But that was not all. A Resident might be ordered to undertake [public] works outside his own area; he might serve in one Residency and see the taxation done in another. No sooner did a man begin to find himself somewhat at home than he was shifted elsewhere. If one adds to this the complete lack of English literature about Java, of maps, of dictionaries, the lack of means, the prevailing ignorance amongst the Hollanders on Java of both the English and Javanese languages, then one is forced to the conclusion that either the native governmental employees did a colossal amount of work, or else (and this seems more likely) that everything went to pieces while the French [English?] were in charge. We also find curious things in the financial sphere. The salaries of the employees were discounted in bills of exchange, which gave rise to much capriciousness and a burdensome control.

"The higher functionaries were well paid, in Spanish dollars at sixty-four stivers and Javanese rupees at thirty, sometimes also in Sicca rupees at thirty-one and a half. If the lavish pay of a military officer were added to this, one could live like a prince. But one also finds a 'Resident' of Banjoewangi at eighty Spanish dollars, and of Bawean at thirty. Whilst Dalgrains as Sub-Treasurer received two thousand Java rupees a month (equal to three thousand guilders), Muntinghe as a Councillor only received five hundred Spanish dollars, or sixteen hundred guilders. Above all, the extraordinary bonuses dished out to Hope show gaps in the supervision of finances. The numerous insolvent households show the effect [of the setup] on the *bourgeoisie* society in the same way. In the slovenly and delayed execution of given orders, a spirit of *laissez-faire* is sometimes obvious. Raffles was personally ceaselessly busy, and he worked very fast; the lengthiest missives flowed successively from his pen, and the *personalia* of Addison shows how busy he kept his immediate entourage. In order to reduce written work, he ordered that all documents addressed to him should be written in duplicate. He then wrote his decision in the margin of one copy which was duly copied into the margins of the duplicate for return to the sender. This compendious correspondence had the result that many things which should have been filed in one bureau were filed in another, and the tracing of any *retroacta* is not thereby made easier. Similarly, Raffles' decisions during his numerous journeys did not invariably come to the knowledge of the Council and Accountant."

It is certainly refreshing to take a look once in a while at the reverse side of the medal, isn't it? After Raffles's naïvely glowing accounts of the progress he made, Mr. de Haan's fulminations remind us of so many that can be heard today in any colony: that they are usually loudest in British communities may possibly be due to the fact that British colonies are run worse than any other, though after seeing the way various other colonies are managed in different parts of the world, I doubt it. It is more likely that because England possesses a lot of colonies, and because her officials enjoy the game of baiting their own governments, doing it with a will and a loud gusto, not to mention uninhibited free speech, the volume of complaint and abuse swells out louder than that of any other nation. De

Haan's reporting is indubitably accurate, but the picture it presents is not as horrific as he seems to think.

Proceeding with his study, he gives us a few brief descriptions of the men who were close to Raffles in the government of Batavia. First comes George Augustus Addison, a young man who will have occasion to speak for himself shortly. De Haan quotes from his letters to prove how he was rushed into the job of acting secretary to Raffles the minute he landed on Java; we shall also read the original context with a few additions which give a more rosy picture of the background against which he worked, until his early death from fever.

The next, Dr. Daniel Ainslie, our friend from the Deshima adventure, was originally surgeon of the horse artillery at Madras, and he first came with this unit to Java. Raffles calls him "a gentleman of high talents and abilities," but Doeff, the Dutch chief at Nagasaki, had, as we know, a different opinion, and states that Ainslie's taste for liquor "rendered him totally unfit for everything." In 1816 he was voted fifteen hundred Javanese rupees for secret service money expended during his trip to Japan. He died at Weltevreeden on July twenty-second of that year. De Haan mentions that Crawfurd hated Doeff, probably merely because Doeff had attacked his fellow Scot, Ainslie.

Charles Assey, of whom Addison wrote a warm commendation, was another surgeon originally, with the 3d Bengal Volunteer Battalion. He became secretary to Raffles in 1812 and held many concurrent posts because he was efficient and hard-working. In April 1814 he went to Bengal to refute the allegations Gillespie had been making against Raffles. He was back in Java by the end of September of the current year. One of his many talents seems to have been for journalism. He published a brochure in 1819, when he was again with Raffles, *On the trade to China and the Indian Archipelago; with observations on the insecurity of the British interests in that quarter.* He was always Raffles's right-hand man when he was with him. For a time he edited the *Java Government Gazette,* a considerable recommendation for anybody.

Then there was W. Barrett, a friend of Raffles from the

Penang days. He was made assistant accountant in 1812. On April 17th, 1812, he married Jacoba Maria Goldman, the daughter of J. C. Goldman, a resident of Batavia. It was the first wedding of an Englishman with a Dutch girl after the conquest, and as such it was regarded as a great affair. The couple had a son in 1813, but Barrett died in '14, well before the British had to get off Java, thereby escaping being involved in one of those international marital quandaries which can be so awkward.

Hugh Hope, resident, deputy civil commissioner, and so on, was the lucky winner of sixteen thousand dollars in the Java lottery of 1812, and the inspiration of that poem which so amazed De Haan in that it appeared openly in the *Java Government Gazette*:

> As for the prizes great and small,
> The Government has got them all,
> God knows what they've been doing.

When at Samarang on official residence he seems to have played unwilling host to at least one very gay party. We read the following in his requisition for more housekeeping allowance:"Fifteen officers with their concubines lodged there for about a month; many articles in the house were in consequence lost or broken, as the house was crowded every day." That is all we know about Mr. Hope and, perhaps, all we need to know!

William Thorn, chiefly known to me heretofore as the author of *The Conquest of Java*, does not stir Mr. de Haan, who knows him better, to any transports of admiration. "An unimportant person and not over-trustworthy as a writer; for instance the plates in his History, are largely the old illustrations of Rach, enriched with British flags (Campbell has taken over these plates wholesale in his book); the Chinese Captain whose funeral is reproduced 'as drawn on the spot' had died as long ago as 1784."

We have already encountered Jan Samuel Thimmerman Thijssen, the opium dealer, general merchant, and magistrate.

It was he who made flattering references to Raffles and Minto in his Liberation Day address, in 1814.

George Augustus Addison was born in India, in Calcutta, but his British parents sent him home for a certain amount of schooling, so that he didn't live in the East until his return at the age of sixteen. His tastes were in the direction of letters rather than the rougher pursuits. He was, for example, a good Persian scholar and a poet. No doubt the army circles called him a sissy, or whatever may be the nineteenth-century equivalent, though his writings show no hint of homosexuality. He associated with women for choice and had no liking for sport or politics. Perhaps these qualities were the reason he got on so well with Raffles from the beginning; Raffles too had no love for sport, and certainly disliked politics, though, unlike his young secretary-poet, he had to play them just the same. Addison was twenty-one when he got the job of acting secretary to Java's lieutenant governor. He was a copious letter writer, corresponding with several ladies, very good friends whom he had met during his various attempts at a career in India in the five years he was there before Raffles gave him a chance. One of his correspondents edited and published a selection of his letters after his death. We owe her a vote of thanks for having thus preserved a fresh, vivid portrayal of Raffles's household in Java, and of his intimate aides.

Evidently young Addison had had a try at the indigo business just before 1813, but his prospects failed, and he had never entertained much love for indigo anyway. His father and friends who lived in India advised him to go to Calcutta, where it was hoped their pull might be able to procure him a better, or at least a more congenial, post. Some influential people at the presidency, interested and attracted by the boy's general intelligence and unassuming manners, made arrangements for him to go out to Java in the hope that Raffles could use him. One of the first letters in the book, written from Calcutta, tells us that Lord Minto was at that time just on the verge of leaving for home, having at last resigned his post after a long, arduous, but very honorable career. Lord Moira, his relief, was on his way out, and the excited speculations and chatter surrounding his name whenever it was mentioned at parties can be imagined.

"Nothing is talked of but Lord Moira," wrote Addison in September. "I hope his lordship may be detained a little, however, at Madras and elsewhere; for it is said, that having so many gentlemen to dispose of, fifty at least must be sent to seek their futures to the eastward, and I wish to anticipate them." As was customary, the change of governors was the signal for an army of job hunters to descend on Calcutta. They were feverishly anxious times. "Three or four of his *Aides-de-camp* are here. Nothing can be more splendid than their dresses. The other poor *moosahibs* are quite eclipsed—gold lace, ostrich feathers, and mustaches in profusion.

"There is an ———, too, here, whose imagination has been sufficiently heated with the tales of Indian wealth, as to have made him give up between two and three thousand pounds per annum in England, to come out under Lord Moira's auspices."

Soon the youth's early cheerfulness evaporated, owing to a slight but definitely unpleasant development. He kept putting off his departure for Java because Moira, through some friend, had allowed him to understand that the new governor would give him a letter of introduction and recommendation, which he could present to Raffles on arrival at Java. Though Addison had many other letters, such a one from Moira himself would of course carry tremendous weight. With that letter he could be practically sure of getting a post, whereas without it things would not be nearly so certain. Naturally therefore it was well worth putting off the trip, just so that he could be sure of getting the magic document in the end.

Unfortunately for Addison as well as for Raffles, this Moira seems to have been of a far less benevolent nature than was Minto, his predecessor. Having promised that letter, for instance, any really agreeable person in such a high position would make some effort, no matter how busy he might have been, taking office, to keep the promise quickly rather than let the boy dangle about the residency in an agony of impatience and incertitude. It was an easy promise to keep, after all. But he didn't. He let the days go by, during which time poor Addison had thrice to present himself in the ante-chambers, to go through the humiliation each time of making his request and reminder all over again. In this letter the young man frets and fumes and threatens to go off in a huff, without waiting longer, but he realizes that such an act would be childish and would harm only himself, and so he grits his teeth and waits. It is exceedingly disagreeable, he complains, to keep him running like that, asking again and again. Feelingly he quotes a Persian proverb, "Who gives quickly, gives twice."

At last there appears a postscript: Moira's letter has arrived, and Addison is off.

His next is from Java, dated December 1813. The boy is happy and relieved, for all his apprehensions appear to have been idle. "At length I have the pleasure of addressing you from my journey's end—this dreadful island of Java; dreadful, however, only in report, for I never saw a more beautiful country, or experienced a more agreeable climate. Batavia alone is unhealthy, somewhat from its mean vicinity to a large mud-bank along the sea-coast, but very much more from the habits of its inhabitants, the Dutch; who, living most grossly as they do every where, sleep after every meal, shut their houses closely up during the day, and sit in the evening drinking drams of their own country liquor by the side of vile dank ditches, dignified by the name of canals. This is the regular routine, and with such it is hardly to be wondered at that three out of five was the average annual mortality. The English, by adopting quite an opposite system, preserve their health now as well as in Bengal; there is hardly any sickness among them. Batavia itself is certainly a low, unwholesome spot; and, so strong its ill repute, that no Englishman ventures to sleep there a single night—they all reside at Weltevreeden and Ryswick, pleasant towns at about six miles' distance; and if they are obliged to have offices in the city, visit them in the morning, and come out in the afternoon. But I am speaking of customs, etc., very decidedly, when I have seen so little that I have no right to advance any opinion on the subject. The city of Batavia itself, is,

I think, very handsome; and particularly striking to a new-comer, as being totally unlike any thing either in Bengal or England. The streets are broad and clean, mostly with rows of trees at the sides, and canals in the middle; and the houses, which touch each other as in England, are particularly neat—all red-tiled, abundantly glazed, and many with facings of the Dutch painted small slabs, and marble floors, forming altogether an odd, but very pleasing appearance. . . ."

April 1814: "You will laugh at my being so mightily occupied; but recollect into how new a situation I have thus suddenly fallen;—every thing to learn—and yet to proceed at once, as if every thing had been learned. The best proof I can give you of my diligence, is the not having read a single novel, a single poem, or played three games at chess since I have been with Mr. Raffles,—but, above all, my omission [of a letter] by the late cruiser says every thing.

"I have some little ambition, and, being placed in a situation so far above my expectations, I will at least strive to the utmost to acquit myself so as to justify, in some measure, the partiality that has been shown me.

"You will have been astonished to hear of my appointment. It is one of the most respectable, and certainly the most pleasing to myself; for had I had free choice of situations, I should have selected this—that is, consulting my inclination only—ability will come by and by; at least I will try hard for it. My salary has been fixed at twelve hundred Rupees per month, which also has exceeded my expectations—but Mr. Raffles, General Nightingale, and Mr. Hope, are all more kind to me than I can express.

". . . They keep me as closely to my desk as even D. in his busiest time is kept. Indeed, I generally begin at daylight, and, with only such gross intervals as breakfast and dinner, keep at it till eleven at night. I unluckily was appointed at the worst period in the year for business, when despatches were to be framed both for England and Bengal. . . .

"I have now, from my window, a prospect of the most beautiful picturesque scenery. The descent from the house almost precipitate—in the bottom a valley filled with rice, with a romantic little village on the banks of a stream, which rushes down by twenty torrents, and roars, foaming, over rocks innumerable; in the background, a majestic range of mountains, wooded to the top, and capped in clouds, the nearest not more than twenty miles off; nothing, indeed, can exceed the beauty of the scene. . . .

"In speaking of Mr. Raffles, you will think me, perhaps, biassed by his kindness to me; but really, setting this aside, and judging impartially from what I have seen of him, and I have now seen and *marked* him closely three months, I do not hesitate to say, that I think most highly of him. He is a superior character—perfectly the gentleman—of the most polished manners—and of a suavity of disposition I have not seen exceeded. This, perhaps, is his foible; he is rather *too* good-natured; and, as a governor, might have had a squeeze of acid mingled in his composition with advantage. He is possessed of considerable information on most subjects; and is at once the gentleman, the scholar, and the man of business.

"In the latter way he has few equals. I never saw anyone more indefatigable, nor one who performs it in better or more rapid style. From morn till night he is employed, and scarcely the minutest detail on any point escapes him. This is warm panegyric, but it is sincere. To you I would not utter a sentiment I did not feel. He is no cold plodder, no calculator of merely his own interest, but possesses a highly energetic mind, an ardent imagination, and I could pledge myself for his even chivalric honour; in short, for myself, I truly not merely like and respect, but love him, he appears to me so amiable."

I would not for a moment carp at or criticize a scholar like Mr. de Haan, but I would like to point out that he never quotes this sort of passage when he makes his selections from the records.

"In size he is a little man, but has a very pleasing countenance, quick, intelligent eyes, and the *tout ensemble* of his features reminded me, at first, of Colonel H———, which you will admit to be good, *à la Lavater*. . . .

"Next comes our chief secretary, Mr. Assey. I cannot say enough of him, and like him very much indeed. He is an excellent second to Mr. Raffles, quite as indefatigable, and as capable. With two such examples before me, it is impossible to shrink from any toil. Assey is uncommonly clever, quick, and well-informed; and, what is better, joining to an amicable disposition a fine manly independence of character. He is, in short, universally esteemed, and fit for any thing. It is no slight proof in his favour that General G. [Gillespie], though cordially disliking him as a friend of Mr. Raffles, did not in any of his attacks—and he spared few—venture a syllable against Assey.

"Of course there are constantly a crowd of visitors in the house; but the above, with a doctor, a Dutch secretary, and myself, are the only permanent members. The doctor, Sir Thomas Sevestre, is an original too; but I have not time to describe him; . . ."

Buitenzorg, April 1814: "Mr. Raffles invited me in the kindest manner to live with him while on the island. Of course nothing could be more agreeable than such an invitation, and me voici regularly domesticated.

"This place is near forty miles from Batavia, most beautifully situated, and has what is called a fine, cool, bracing climate; the season almost always the same—never sufficiently warm to make a punkah necessary, yet cool enough to make a blanket agreeable—for me; but I am quite heterodox this way. It is very chilly and damp, and not one tenth so pleasant as the Bengal gentle heats. There is a great deal too much rain, owing to our close vicinity to the mountains. The clouds come rolling down then, and favour us with a shower every afternoon; and I detest rain—it makes both body and spirits uncomfortable."

Young Addison's experience of Java grows and deepens. He goes out on the constant travels which the British officials had found necessary, and is in raptures over the richness of life in the countryside. "Plays, ombres-chinoises, antiquities, pageants, tiger, buffalo, hog, goat, dog, and quail fights, etc. etc. etc. . . .

"The hog and goat fight was vastly amusing. A wild hog and beautiful goat were turned into a small arena, a stool being allowed the goat to leap on occasionally. . . . Next followed a battle-royal—three wild hogs, six dogs, and the victorious goat. The hogs were torn to pieces, most of the dogs in the same state, but the goat as fresh and frolicsome as ever."

Here, for the first time since young Addison's letters have appeared in these pages, I must admit a lack of sympathy with him. Inevitably one wonders: did Raffles join him in watching this sport, and did the lieutenant governor, too, find it "vastly amusing"? Most probably not.

About this period the acting secretary's mentions of the Gillespie case grow so numerous and frequent that we are reminded it is high time to look at this matter and follow it through. When last we spoke of Gillespie it was to mention that his relations with Raffles were showing a deal of friction, in spite of the good will each ostensibly felt toward the other just after the day of victory. Raffles's correspondence with Minto shows his side of the affair, and in these letters as well as from many other records it is obvious that Gillespie at last took his leave of Java and repaired to India in a very cross frame of mind. He had no other course left open to him, for things had reached a point where it was impossible for him to go on being polite to Raffles, whom he now hated; and Minto always backed up his enemy.

The first person who commented on the row which was to cause so much excitement in Anglo-Indian circles is rather disappointing in the light of later information. Major William Thorn, a personal and loyal friend of Gillespie's, has written a Memoir of him, evidently just after his death, in which he talks feelingly of what a villain Raffles was, but never goes into details. He is so very discreet that he never even mentions names, and often it is only because we already know the story pretty well from other later sources that we have any idea of what the estimable major is talking about.

One gathers from the following, for example, merely that the work done by the British in Java is excellent, but that it would have been a lot better if Gillespie had been running things. Thorn takes a roundabout way of expressing this sentiment. "But though a very elaborate view has been exhibited, and, no doubt, justly, of the ameliorated situation of the country, by the institutions that a liberal policy has adopted, and of the rapid progress which industry and civilization have made under our government, little, if any, notice has been taken of the obligation due to the man, who, by his vigorous measures and undaunted courage laid the foundation of the great moral change thus wrought in the character and circumstances of Java.

"It was peculiarly the hard lot of General Gillespie to be called to the execution of very perilous enterprizes at the imminent risk of his life, and to endure afterwards the mystification of seeing his glory acknowledged as a matter of course in public, and of having his good designs impeded and rendered ineffectual in private. Having extended the European power in Java and its dependencies to a state of unrivalled greatness, it was perfectly natural and just that he should have looked for honourable confidence and dignified repose, as some compensation for the difficulties which he had removed, and the benefits which he had secured. Instead of this, he found, that without compromising his principles, and yielding to measures which he disapproved, it was impossible for him to remain free from provoking slights, or unannoyed by petulant opposition. All this, however, he endured much longer than his private feelings would have permitted in any case where the public service was unconcerned: but such was his patriotic spirit and sense of duty . . ." et cetera.

No doubt a part of the major's ambiguity can be explained by the date of publication of this Memoir (1816). The charges against Raffles were preferred by his ex-commander in chief Gillespie in 1813, and the matter was decided, to some extent, at least two years before the book was written, in Raffles's favor, though not definitely enough to satisfy him. Thus the general lost considerable face over the matter. Any good friend would have done just as Thorn tried to do—played down the whole thing and taken refuge in muttered, vague complaints. Thorn is saying what amounts to this: "The whole thing has been grossly unfair, and posterity will realize it as

303 &

long as I give them something to go on, so, though I know and respect the laws of libel, and can't say half of what is in my heart, just remember this: I hereby put it on record that Gillespie was a hero, and Raffles just a low-down common adventurer with a talent for getting on in the world. Discretion forbids that I speak further."

CHAPTER XVII

We saw the beginnings of the trouble back in 1812, when Raffles wrote that letter to Minto in which he told about the sale of the public lands. Or rather, that wasn't the true beginning, but it was the one Gillespie took for the start of his revenge. Just when he and Raffles discovered for keeps how much they did not like each other isn't clear, but my guess, which I have already expressed, is that it probably was soon after Gillespie first resented being ordered around by a civilian. The characters of the two men were thoroughly antipathetic. Gillespie was used to being a hero. He made a name for himself during the Vellore Mutiny of 1806, courageously getting into a besieged fort by climbing a rope, and then persuading the soldiers there to hold out; he also did very well in the Java conquest; he was indubitably an excellent soldier. He was the epitome of the soldier. But it was precisely as such that he could not be expected to appreciate the points of Raffles's more subtle excellences. And though Raffles could appreciate Gillespie's qualities he didn't relish being stood up against, constantly, by a man whose brains as he knew were not equal to his own. A clever man hates to be balked by stupidity, especially when the stupid person doesn't recognize his own inadequacy.

Gillespie was named one of the three councilors of the Java Government, the other two being Muntinghe and Cranssens.

He did not take his work as seriously as they did; rather, he often pleaded ill-health and stayed away from the meetings. After he and Raffles became unfriendly he showed up more often, evidently in order to make as much trouble as he could: at least that was the interpretation of his behavior supplied by the exasperated Raffles. The really serious break between them, it will be remembered, occurred in the spring of 1813 when Raffles decided to cut down the European garrison and Gillespie was furious at the idea. Minto stood by Raffles. By that time things were so bad that the tactful earl transferred Gillespie to another post in Bengal, putting General Nightingale in his place on Java. It was too bad for Raffles that all this should happen just as Minto was retiring, for Moira, as we know, took a dislike to Raffles immediately on entering office, sight unseen, and was more than ready to listen to Gillespie's innuendoes.

Perhaps the word "innuendo" is too much an understatement for what Gillespie did, after he warmed to his work. From his post in Bengal he charged Raffles outright with misbehavior in that 1812 matter, the selling of public land. Yet he had condoned the act, definitely, at the time the government made the decision (hastily, remember, on account of the acute depreciation of the paper currency). The general first had sent his objections by letter—he had not been at the meeting when the decision was made. He wrote that in his opinion a measure of such magnitude should not have been decided upon without previous reference to the supreme government, and gave as his chief reason the usual one, that no one knew at that time how long Java would be British, or whether the occupation was to be a permanency. These objections were always reasonable, whether it happened to be Gillespie or Minto who expressed them, but after Raffles had made further representations to the general, as he also did, later, to Minto, and explained the limits of the proposed action, Gillespie agreed to its necessity and assented to the sale. That agreement is on record, and was Raffles's best point of defense later.

An additional complication in 1812 had been that Gillespie

flatly refused to pay his sepoys with the phony paper money, ignoring the fact that it was forbidden the Java Government to draw bills on Bengal. Thus he had consistently aggravated the financial troubles with which the Java Council was wrestling, though at that early time neither Raffles nor the other councilmen could well accuse him outright of doing this deliberately. It is possible, of course, that he didn't, and created these difficulties out of ignorance, not spite. Gillespie never pretended to be a financial wizard.

Now, however, nobody was trying to be polite any more. All gloves were off. Not only did Gillespie charge Raffles with misbehavior and shady practice in regard to the land sale, but he called the lieutenant governor "indelicate and discourteous," in a counterattack to one of the most serious accusations Raffles ever had occasion to level at anyone. That particular affair was supposed to have been fixed up and forgotten before the general left Java, but Gillespie's memory was long, he had time to brood over his wrongs on the sea voyage, and so the reconciliation was washed out long before he got to British India. What had happened was as follows:

Because of his continued ill-health General Gillespie had gone to live at Tjipanas, a popular mountain resort on Java which featured mineral hot springs. There he acquired a house, to which was attached a coffee plantation. Soon after moving in he started building a new house on his estate. He refused to pay taxes on any of this property, and he also failed to pay any of the Javanese laborers and gardeners who worked for him. Since this sort of thing was exactly what the British blamed the Dutch so bitterly for doing, the other government members were grievously shocked and angry, feeling themselves let down by one of their own number. Raffles, however, didn't allow himself to be carried away by the prevailing mood of righteous indignation. He wanted to be sure first of his grounds: probably he was even more careful than usual because he disliked Gillespie so, and he checked the story meticulously before taking the matter up in person with the general. Boulger says he sent a responsible man to report privately on the state of affairs, and when the time came he

307 ⮒

administered the necessary rebuke as quietly as possible; at any rate Boulger thinks he did. Unfortunately for his own position, which should have been completely unassailable in a matter of this sort. Raffles's indignation, at last let off its lead, carried him past the limits of scientific caution, so that he believed a companion story to this unpleasant account without being quite sure *it* was true before he accused Gillespie of it. According to the other story, Gillespie, well known for his susceptibility to women, had demanded of a native mission school at Samarang that they send him a certain student orphan—a virgin, according to the narrators—threatening the woman in charge with dire punishment if he didn't have his way. The tale grew until Gillespie was accused of carrying off a hapless maiden by force. Raffles's indignation knew no bounds when he heard of this rascally atrocity, and no doubt it was this part of the quarrel which gave Gillespie the chance to use the word "indelicate." For, alas for purity, when it came right down to cases Raffles could not substantiate his complaint. Evidently there was no virgin, there had been no abduction, and though Gillespie's house had been occupied at times by more than one dusky maiden, none of them claimed to have been dragged there against her will. Moreover, obviously it didn't occur to any of the lasses to claim virginity either. From the legal point of view the nonexistence of that virgin was too bad for Raffles, though in the end he triumphed on all other charges. It was a point in Gillespie's favor, not only because it made Raffles look "indelicate," as Gillespie had charged—though the major general's champions were not foolish enough to claim that he was any Galahad—but it also made the lieutenant governor out to be a hasty-headed prig. Added to the hint of sharp practice which still clung to the settled case like a bad odor, the way these things do, the picture remained in the mind of the uninformed public as a contrast between a bluff, good fellow military man, a trifle sensual perhaps, a bit slow on the uptake, but admirably brave, and a *gentleman* too, sir, placed in the arena against a sly, hypocritical, nest-feathering, clever, pious sort of fellow who wasn't out of the top drawer anyway.

Let's look at De Haan's report, another excerpt from his *Personalia*. It has special value because De Haan goes into a detailed study of Gillespie's life, and there are significant points in that. To begin with he was nineteen years older than Raffles, of a "smart Scottish-Irish family in Ulster, as an only son; very wild in his youth; became a Cornet of Horse in 1783 against the wish of his parents, led a debauched life and developed into one of those typical heavy-drinking, roistering and riding, but simultaneously foppish dandies of the days of the Prince-Regent, 'our abstemious Monarch' as Raffles sarcastically termed him later, when he gave orders for a cask of Batavian arrack to be earmarked for H.M.

"Gillespie secretly married in 1782 (at twenty) a young girl of good family of whom we subsequently hear nothing, but his biographer (Thorn) sometimes lets hints fall about his many mistresses. A few months after this wedding he fights a duel over a pocket-handkerchief (with each of the opponents holding a corner of it), shoots his enemy dead and flees; a price was placed on his head; he was arrested and acquitted. All typically Irish; what is still more Irish is that some years later he brawled in the Theatre at Cork, indulged in fisticuffs, and again had to flee, this time dressed as a woman! He took part in the campaign in San Domingo (West Indies) where he proved himself a tough fighter. On one occasion he was attacked by eight people in his house, whereupon, although only a small man himself, he laid out six cold. In 1805 he journeyed overland to India, had all kinds of adventures on the way, and at Baghdad was given by Ali Pasha an Arabian horse 'which became well known afterwards in India by the name of the donor.' In 1806 he showed his leadership and courage in the suppression of a dangerous sepoy mutiny at Vellore. One can easily understand that such a man, with such a past, a hunter who for sport could attack and kill a tiger on horseback with a lance, a dragoon with all a dragoon's love of wine, women and song, who could preside at a drinking bout commemorating the capture of Meester Cornelis,— 'where his toasts were as rapid as his movements in the field,—' and moreover a man of good family and breeding, should

309 ॐ

look down on the obscure and fifteen-year younger [sic] clerk, who had been suddenly placed over him by the favour of Minto,—a man who boasted (*horribile dictu*) that he had never been present at a horse-race and never fired a firearm, who never played cards and who never drank too much, who always was taking lessons or poring over a book, who showed an amazing predilection for associating with niggers, but who likewise had a disconcerting ability to profit from others' weaknesses, keeping himself in the background and playing a noble rôle, thus winning friends and knowing how to keep them,—a man who never lost his temper and who was always and eternally too slippery for him. And one can surmise how the hot-blooded dragoon boiled, when Raffles smilingly set a foot in his way, or in his official capacity complimented him on his proven courage and leadership, when he well knew how that pen-licker and his patron at Calcutta chuckled together over his own excesses. Whereto it must be added that Minto had no great reason to love the military. At any rate there had been, for a number of years, particularly at Madras, the most bitter disputes between the civil and military authorities which had nearly led to a military mutiny.

"There was thus plenty of material for a quarrel."

Unfortunately for me, Mr. de Haan does not hold with my theory, or rather with Boulger's theory which I formulated later, on my own, in ignorance of his. De Haan doesn't think it likely that anyone, least of all Minto, would have promised the governorship of Java to Gillespie, either before or after the conquest. On other points, however, we seem to be agreed, which is a relief to this writer, since no one in my experience has ever known so much about another period in history as does De Haan about the British interregnum on Java (except Van der Kemp). Though in his opinion, then, Gillespie had no reason for disappointment, "yet it must have irked him to see that Raffles . . . was placed over him, who had led the advanced guard at the landings and commanded both the assault on Meester Cornelis and the pursuit of the beaten foe. The third of September, 1811, Minto wrote to the Secret Committee in London suggesting the appointment of

Gillespie as Commander in Chief of the Army in Java. Before Minto's departure from Java, Gillespie was already earmarked for a seat in the Council. In a separate *Instruction* Minto had tried to regulate the attitude between him and Raffles; but reading between the lines of that document one can see that Minto trusted far less in Gillespie's self-control than in Raffles'.

"By proclamation of the 22nd of October he was appointed Senior Member of the Council, with rank directly after the Lieutenant Governor. Minto, in his report of the sixth of December, 1811 on his doings in Java, states that he had appointed Gillespie to this post with the idea of strengthening Raffles' [position], to show his consideration for the Army, and to secure more income for Gillespie (thus *not* on account of Gillespie's great gifts). Nevertheless Gillespie at once displayed his bad temper, by staying away from the official installation of the new government on the twenty-first of October, 1811.

"In the meeting of November first he took the oath and his seat as First Member of Council, and forthwith opened hostilities by tabling a note regarding the military arrangements and establishments in Java (a point of great difference between him and Raffles), which note was filed in the Secret Department. Some other proposals of his as to military matters were either rejected or side-tracked by Raffles,—which incident is recalled with bitterness in Thorn's *Memoir*. In the meeting of the sixteenth of November, 1811, Raffles cancelled the appointment of a certain staff officer—Gillespie now knew who was the strongest. In the Proceedings of the twenty-eighth of November, it was decided to fit up the old and dilapidated house at Weltevreden as Gillespie's dwelling. By Proclamation of the same day he was appointed Vice-President of the Council during the absence of Raffles, who left on board a ship the same day. Hardly had the latter left, when Gillespie drove through the meeting all kinds of matters which could not possibly have met with the Lieutenant-Governor's approval, particularly the establishment of the Military Bazaar in the cantonment at Weltevreden.

"However, what Boulger states . . . that Gillespie first regularly attended the Council meetings after his disputes with Raffles which marked the year 1813, is not absolutely correct. The quarrel dates from 1811, as we have seen. In February and March, 1812, he was absent five times, but before March twenty-fourth he had already left on the Palembang expedition, where he again gave proof of his exceptional courage. He returned to Batavia on the thirty-first of May, but left again on the fifth of June as an expedition against Djokja, where he was wounded in the left hand. After convalescing in Tjipanas he returned to Weltevreden August ninth for a council-meeting, but thereafter remained in the highlands. He was again present on October 19th, but absent again till the twenty-third of December, being still at Tjipanas where he took warm baths. In 1813 he came very irregularly to the meetings, the last time on August thirteenth. On the twenty-fourth of August he was appointed Vice-President of the Council in the absence of Raffles.

"In the town, he had a house at Rijswijck besides another at Weltevreden; in the highlands he had a country house at Tjinanggis, belonging to the Cantonment there; in addition he had rented Tency's house on Tjiloewar, with the slaves belonging thereto, he also bought three slave girls from this last (something very unusual for an Englishman). The quarrel with Raffles flared up again when Gillespie after the capture of Djokja arbitrarily disposed of some of the loot, which annoyed Raffles greatly, whereupon Gillespie proffered excuses.

"Due to the reduction of the garrison by Raffles against his advice Gillespie blamed Raffles for the Probolingo rebellion; furthermore he was responsible for the way the Sepoys were paid. He further disapproved of the expedition against *Sambas* and was very pessimistic over the outcome of Raffles's land taxation plans. Raffles on the other hand accused Gillespie of oppressing the populace at Tjipanas, and accused him of misbehaving himself with orphan and slave girls at Samarang and Palembang. This last is not improbable; but Raffles could naturally get the people at Tjipanas to talk as he chose; and the almoner of the institution at Samarang categorically denied that Gillespie had taken an orphan girl for himself from the orphanage—which fact did not prevent Raffles from publishing that vile accusation in his Refutation, together with the allegation that Gillespie had ordered a girl to be dragged out of a house in Batavia by his soldiers, and had behaved in a scandalous way at Palembang, according to Robison. However that may be, Gillespie was livid with rage. Already on the thirteenth of February, 1813, he had addressed a letter to the G.O.C. in Bengal, Sir George Nugent, with complaints over the sale of land. At about this time he also asked to be relieved, which was granted.

"From the Proceedings of the fifteenth of October, 1813, it is clear that he asked for and was granted leave to proceed to Bengal, whither he sailed on October tenth or eleventh. From the advertisement of the auction sale of his property we see that besides some valuable Arabian horses he had also about one hundred dozen bottles of wine to dispose of. His friend Thorn states that he finally had nothing but his pay and his share of the prize money (which must however have amounted to a tidy sum after the capture of Java, Palembang and Djokja), and that he was of quite a different type from some of his comrades who were mainly out to feather their own nests. He was even fallen into disfavour through being too trusting; had he but played ball with Raffles he could have made a fortune. It is also characteristic that in 1814 he still owed the fish-farmer of the fish-market seven or eight hundred Spanish dollars 'for the fish supplied.'

"According to Raffles there was a big reconciliation before Gillespie's departure. On July eighteenth, 1813, Minto's son, Captain the Honourable Elliot, arrived in Batavia, and effected a reconciliation between Gillespie and Raffles. Thenceforward, says Raffles, Gillespie had nothing but good words and even in his last letter he still attributed their misunderstanding to the machinations of others, but when he reached Penang he already began to talk about the complaints he would make on arriving in Bengal. Also N. Engelhard wrote in 1815, that Gillespie had written a very friendly letter from Penang to

Raffles, which occasioned all the more surprise at Gillespie's subsequent attitude towards Raffles after his arrival in Bengal. On the other hand it is worth pointing out that Gillespie received no word of thanks or praise for his distinguished services when he left Java, at any rate in the *Gazette*, although the Government was usually lavish enough in this respect. No official notice was taken of his departure save for a brief mention of two or three lines, and it is thus very problematical whether Raffles was present or not. It is true that later some verses were published about 'Rollo,' who, 'to his best friend proves a treacherous foe.' Gillespie's ex-Secretary Colebrooke wrote in 1816, that Gillespie when he returned to Bengal, expected to return to Java the following year, *i.e.* when Minto had been replaced. His friend Shrapnell had the care of his infant child, who was sent after him only in the autumn of 1816. The dispatch of this Colebrooke with Raffles' stooge Methuen to Bengal, a month after Gillespie's departure, was probably intended to counteract any action by him; in this connection it is curious to note that the Major-General made the voyage in company with his champion Blagrave.

"It is also noteworthy that Gillespie in his career had to struggle for years with the results of a complaint brought against him by one of his subordinate officers, and probably fought a battle against his better judgment, since he drew up all kinds of unfounded accusations against Raffles. Our attention is also drawn to the fact that the biographer Thorn passes over this accusation in complete silence, obviously because his hero had gained no credit among his comrades thereby, although he deals in considerable detail with the reasons for his dissatisfaction with the way things were going in Java. We will leave aside the points of the complaint (over which see *Levyssohn Norman* p. 301 and following, who has taken them from a collection of printed pamphlets on the subject, of which an extract was printed in Holland), and merely note that Gillespie landed at Calcutta on the same day as Minto left for England; that he immediately made verbal complaints against Raffles (probably on the occasion of his first meeting with Moira) and as early as the seventeenth of December, 1813, had submitted documents in support of his complaint, on the order of the Governor-General. He had already boiled these up before his arrival, probably through the suggestion of his travelling companion, Mr. Blagrave. Raffles consistently takes the line in his Refutation (in flat contradiction to Gillespie's character) that Gillespie's complaints were prompted by exceptional guile. An impartial observer however comes speedily to the conclusion that it was absolutely spontaneous; for otherwise Gillespie could certainly have obtained better material. A man like Moira, a soldier himself and one who knew Gillespie (the 'noble' Gillespie, as the knightly Nahuijs later called him), must have been unfavorably impressed by Raffles' effort to ascribe his own peculiarities to the hot-blooded soldier and to represent this latter as a consummate hypocrite."

The entire business was a headache from start to finish, involving as it did long voyages for at least two of Raffles's people, and days' worth of talk in Calcutta for many of the men concerned. Captain Travers was entrusted with the job of taking full copies of Raffles's "detailed and exhaustive replies to the charges" to London. Assey went to Calcutta as deputy for Raffles, carrying the original replies, but his ship was delayed by bad weather and he didn't arrive in India until autumn. By that time Major General Gillespie, as he was finally ranked, had met his death in battle in the Nepalese War. He never knew the outcome of the charges he had so hastily preferred against his enemy.

Everything and everyone involved in the inquiry seemed fated to be delayed. Captain Travers couldn't get swift action from the office in London, while in the meantime the government kept poor Assey hanging about India for months. It was not until May 1815 that the governor general's council turned their attention to the charges. By that time Java's fate had been decided: the British, under the Treaty of London, agreed shortly to evacuate the island. (A letter from Raffles to Marsden, just before Napoleon was captured for the second time, expressed his joyful hope that the Little Corporal's escape from captivity and his return to Europe would settle matters in Java as Raffles wanted them to be settled. However, History decreed otherwise.)

Two members of the council gave their opinions in long minutes, both of which exonerated Raffles from Gillespie's accusations, and by means of compliment and emphatic praise vindicated the British administration of Java in general, which naturally implied a direct vindication of Raffles and all his works. One of these was produced in May, the other in June, 1815. Lord Moira's opinion was not forthcoming, however, until the late date of October, and it did not follow the lines laid down by the others. The only advantageous part of it, in fact, related to Raffles's next job, at Bencoolen in Sumatra. (Minto had worked hard to make that stick) Moira said,

"With reference to that part of the Honourable Court's instructions which relates to the appointment of Mr. Raffles to the Residency of Fort Marlborough (that was at Bencoolen), the Governor-General in Council observes that nothing has appeared in the course of the deliberations respecting Mr. Raffles' conduct to authorise an opinion affecting his moral character, and although he has not succeeded in administering the extensive and important duties of the Government of Java with that degree of efficiency which is indispensable to secure the advantages held out by Mr. Raffles himself from the possession of the colony, yet there does not appear to be reason to apprehend that Mr. Raffles is not competent to acquit himself with due benefit to his employers in the less complicated duties of the Residency at Bencoolen. The Governor-General in Council accordingly considers himself bound in justice to leave unshaken the reserved appointment of Mr. Raffles to the situation of Resident at Fort Marlborough, of which Mr. Raffles is to take possession as soon as another person shall be selected for the Government of Java."

The wording of this chilly little message gives the impression, not entirely erroneous, that Raffles is getting the sack for having been complained against by Gillespie. No doubt Lord Moira wanted to give that impression outright on the general grounds that what Raffles knew couldn't hurt him, and that every bit of such unofficial chastisement was presumably good for his conceited upstart soul. In actuality, as both Moira and Raffles very well knew (and so did the other council members), it mattered not a whit who succeeded Raffles in the Java governorship, for the British were starting to move out already; also the Bencoolen post had been selected by dear old Lord Minto some time before, as the choicest plum he could offer his bright boy, from a very restricted stock of offerings; thus it was not merely a curmudgeonly gift, a bone contemptuously tossed out to Raffles for want of someone better fitted for the appointment, but the only thing he could reasonably accept.

Boulger says that this language on the part of Moira hurt Raffles's feelings, even though it confirmed his appointment as resident for Bencoolen, which he definitely did want. Accordingly he wrote the council a letter pointing out that this reserved statement did not satisfy him, as all it did was to say there was as yet nothing against his character that they were able to see, et cetera. He wanted his "personal integrity and honor . . . fully and candidly decided upon," and indicated that he was not going to stop sitting on their doorstep, in a manner of speaking, until he was satisfied in that respect.

CHAPTER XVIII

It is not particularly significant that we haven't had special mention of Olivia during these busy years. She was around, and we can find her name if we know where to look, but except for a chance mention in the social columns of the press there wasn't much to say of Mrs. Raffles. She did the honors of Government House quietly and efficiently, for if she had not, someone would certainly have said so. Boulger has taken the trouble to look up the very last contemporary appearance of her name; it occurs in a letter from a missionary protégé of the Liverpool Raffles, informing Dr. Raffles of the "erection" of "the Java Auxiliary Bible Society." Whatever may have been Raffles's private opinion of Christianity in the East, he evidently did not permit it to affect appearances, because according to this Mr. T. C. Supper, "the Governor has been unanimously chosen to the chair, as also the Governess," and the governor accepted the honor without demur. That was in June 1814. In November, very suddenly, Olivia died.

There seems to be no written account of her death beyond the brief, bare mention. There were seldom any unusual details recorded when someone died in Batavia, as Olivia did, of the fever which was for so many years thought to be mysteriously connected with "effluvia." Such a demise was never surprising. Raffles should have considered himself lucky at that, that his family had been spared to him for as long as three years, or that he himself was still alive after a full term on that island of ill repute. But there seems to be no doubt that this loss, coming as it did on top of the great worry and mental strain of Gillespie's attack and the cumulative effect of three years' intensive overwork, not to mention the shock of Minto's death, succeeded in doing to the iron man what nothing else could accomplish. Raffles broke down.

"For a long time," wrote Lady Raffles, "it was feared his life would fall a sacrifice to the keenness of his feelings." One does not forget, either, that strange, unsupported mention by Boulger of the otherwise ignored Raffles offspring—"The death of Olivia Raffles did not stand alone among domestic afflictions, for about the same time he lost in quick succession the children she had borne him." No records, no birth certificates, no names, no reference—at least, none recorded by him—in the local press to christenings, or to their funerals, and no other historian or biographer to supply even that much of a reference. . . . Where did Boulger get his information, and why isn't there more data where that came from? Today such quiet concealment could be explained by only one theory. Were these children, if any, defective in some way?

I know of nothing more irritating to the student of history than the roundabout literary style of Raffles's period. In today's terser fashion the bereaved widower, speaking of his loss, would probably say something on this order: "Please excuse me for not having written, but my wife died last month." Raffles wouldn't have dared be so downright, brief, and clear. He had to say, "As you may have heard, grievous domestic afflictions have lately been visited upon me," and that sort of thing isn't much use to the seeker after information. "Domestic afflictions" may mean the death of one person or of twenty. In Raffles's world there were floods of words, yards of cliché, to every fact. The letter writer of the early nineteenth century steps round any definite statement like a timid chicken examining a new and rather frightening insect. He goes round and round on tiptoe, cautiously strutting, an occasional gingerly peck the only approach he dare make toward his subject.

Considering everything, it is not surprising that even the location of Olivia's grave has become the subject of confused discussion. It seems that she was buried in the city cemetery at Batavia, near Leyden's grave, and that her sorrowing husband put up a monument there. Later he caused another monument to be placed in their garden at Buitenzorg, probably in memory of the many pleasant evening hours he had spent strolling with her in the cool, and on the garden monument he commanded the following lines to be carved:

> Oh Thou! whom ne'er my constant heart
> One moment hath forgot,
> Tho' fate severe hath made us part,
> I'll still forget thee not.

Olivia's successor, Lady Raffles, probably took those lines as a challenge. We will never know, now, whether she succeeded in making her husband forget his stony promise, but she has at least done her best to wipe out the general public's recollections of Olivia, if not those of Sir Stamford Raffles. The severe silence maintained throughout her Memoir on the subject of Olivia did indeed have a certain effect, for it wasn't very long after the Dutch regained possession of Java, and Raffles had died, that the Buitenzorg monument was being pointed out to visitors as Olivia's tomb. So widely spread did this error become that it was thought necessary, in De Haan's *Album*, which includes scenes of Batavia and other Javanese places, to print beneath a picture of Olivia's true resting place the explanation that Mrs. Raffles's tomb is generally but erroneously believed to be in the residency garden at Buitenzorg.

After the lieutenant governor's breakdown Raffles took the advice of his physician and got away from home for a bit. As soon as the vexatious affair at Calcutta permitted he went on a trip around the island, which could always offer something new to be discovered, examined, and pigeonholed in his files and his brain. After that, instead of going straight back to Buitenzorg, which had until then been his favorite residence, he moved farther up in the hills, to Ciceroa. Several members of his staff accompanied him, as well as a party of Javanese from the eastern districts, chosen by him for a special purpose: "With these last," said Sophia, "he passed the greater part of every morning and evening in reading and translating, with the greatest rapidity and ease, the different legends with which they furnished him, particularly the 'Brata Yudha.' His translation of this . . . curious poem will be found in his *History of Java*. . . . At this time he rose early, and commenced business before breakfast; immediately after this he went through the official duties of the day; after which he devoted the remainder of the morning, till dinner-time, to the natives who were living with him."

Not unnaturally, perhaps, this program did not have the desired effect. Raffles's health and spirits did not return as he had hoped they would after a few weeks of what he no doubt considered a vacation. It was from this mountain retreat that he wrote the letter, already partially quoted, to his reverend cousin in Liverpool, where he set forth his decisions on religion in Java. . . . "If you will consent to leave the Javanese to their own way for the present," he says, only half whimsically, "I will commute with you by recommending a vigorous conversion on Borneo, almost the largest island in the world, and thickly peopled by a race scarcely emerged from barbarism." This is tantamount to saying, "Leave my pals alone, and if you must start missions, go way over there where I don't know the people so well. These Javanese are already civilized; you can't teach them anything."

Our hero also speaks to cousin Thomas of that Mr. Supper who had been instrumental in placing the governor (and the "governess") in the chair of the Java Auxiliary Bible Society, a seat which could not have felt very comfortable to the outspoken Raffles. It is rather amusing, after reading Supper's own rapturous report of his gracious reception from Mr. and Mrs. Raffles, to see what the governor really thought about him. "The three clergymen who arrived here have been well provided for, and your friend Mr. Supper has been fixed at Batavia. He is a good, simple creature, rather silly, but amiable. He has unfortunately been in love, and as he made me his confidant I may perhaps have seen him on his weak side."

Raffles did not, however, profess a fixed dislike of the genus missionary. In the same letter he spoke with sincere warmth of Milne, of the China mission—"a liberal, well-informed, excellent man, and I cannot say too much in his favor."

It is worth noting that his recent loss did not result in any sudden rush of abnormal religious feeling, as was the case with many of Raffles's contemporaries when they lost beloved friends to the rigors of climate in the colonies. Please note, Reader, that I say "abnormal," not "unnatural." Most of the memorial writings of those times are full of pious catch phrases, but Raffles had too much taste to follow that fashion. The translation he made instead will stand through the years as a better tribute to Olivia than would any amount of insincere quotation at second hand, even from Scripture. (*An Analysis of the "Brata Yudha," or Holy War; or rather the War of Woe: An Epic Poem, in the Kawi or Classic Language of Java. The History of Java: 1817, Vol. I.*)

A more direct tribute was paid by Olivia's husband while the wounds of his grief were still fresh, when he was sailing for home sixteen months later. In reply to the regulation address and tribute paid him by his staff, he wrote them:

"You have been with me in the days of happiness and joy —in the hours that were beguiled away under the enchanting spell of one, of whom the recollection awakens feelings which I cannot suppress. You have supported and comforted me under the affliction of her loss—you have witnessed the severe hand of Providence, in depriving me of those whom I held most dear, snatched from us and the world, ere we could look around us!"

Does not the last sentence refer to his children? It is difficult to think of any other interpretation.

Until now the fullest collection which has been made of Raffles's voluminous correspondence is that which constitutes the bulk of Lady Raffles's Memoir. Reading through these pages, one begins to feel a genuine knowledge of Raffles, as a three-dimensional man rather than an astute politician, an idealist, or an enthusiastic scientific observer, all of which roles he plays in turn, according to which of his various biographers one is reading. It is not the fault of anyone that these accounts are oversimplified, the unwieldy mass of truth trimmed down to publishers' size. The same can be said of any biography which appears in convenient, compact form. But the Memoir of Lady Raffles, shapeless though it may be and irritating where my lady talks too much, has more value than the neatest modern "Life" because it is full of Raffles's own letters. It is like going through all his possessions and papers for ourselves. The picture we are able to paint from this original material, of the rest of Raffles's Javanese experience, is full of half tones and nuances; it is a living picture, not a clear-toned, flat poster. We see and understand the man who retired to Ciceroa and dived headlong into work, planning his day so that he might never be left with more than an idle moment in which to grieve and remember. Deliberately and doggedly he translated a long Malayan poem into English; collected words for a new dictionary; made voluminous notes on scientific observations; seized eagerly on the news from Europe about Napoleon's return to the scene, and his mind slipped into an activity for which it was well rehearsed when Raffles made new, stubbornly hopeful plans for his dream empire in the Pacific. Sorrow had not weakened the quality of his persistence. His days were full of letter writing, and it is obvious that during these hours of regret and lonely worry he preferred Marsden to any of his other correspondents.

The first day of 1815 he addressed to Marsden a long screed simply packed with material, as if he were crowding his mind with anything and everything to stave off thought. A long essay on the Malay character in general, the anthropological history of the different islands, the language and its derivation from Sanskrit, and a comparison of the Malayan and the Celebes natives' characteristics, seemed to be Raffles's idea of a chatty letter. Obviously the inspiration for this missive and the one which follows in the collection, also addressed to Marsden, was the extended tour which Raffles made just before he retired to Ciceroa. The second letter deals in the main with a volcano eruption; but it also includes a report on Bali and Macassar, and material gathered on an expedition made by General Nightingale to investigate conditions on those lovely islands.

"I entirely concur with you in thinking a grammar and dictionary of the Javanese language an important desideratum, and at one time I was in hope works of the kind would have been attempted.

"I can, however, assure you that however reluctantly I may attempt a work of the kind, I shall go home, whenever I leave this, prepared with the materials for breaking the ice. . . .

"In my late affliction I found it necessary to take a trip to sea. . . ."

In August that year he wrote again to Marsden, "The wonderful events in Europe [i.e., Napoleon's return] still leave some hope that Java may remain permanently English. I have, therefore, addressed the Earl of Buckinghamshire direct, both officially and in a private letter. The letters were written in haste, but I hope are to the point, and not being very long they may probably be read." Raffles's ideas of length are not ours. According to our standards the letters are very long, but the earl probably read them anyway.

"You will observe with satisfaction that the cloud which overhung our finances has been dispersed, and that the complete success of our land revenue arrangements, and the fruits of that new order of things, which could not be established without labour, expense, and risk, are beginning to shew themselves.

"A severe domestic affliction has banished for a time the hope I once entertained of an early retirement—activity and the cares of public responsibility are now almost necessary for my existence. I trust, however, that a few months more will restore that serenity of mind which will admit of my looking on the past with calmness."

Writing at the same time to his old friend W. B. Ramsay,

he expresses in almost identical words his new hopes of Java and his satisfaction with the revenue developments now that the Raffles system is working smoothly. "Whatever may have been said of former disappointments, facts now speak for themselves, and facts you know are stubborn things," he says cheerfully.

In a later passage we learn that his resolution to bury himself in work is as yet unchanged. "I have no idea of returning to Europe while any thing is to be done hereabouts. I am really too tired to write you fully; my back aches from sheer hard writing for the last two days.

"Pay a little attention to my dear sister Marianne, and her child, when you can. I am glad Flint has come out again."

The letter to the Earl of Buckinghamshire is interesting but far too long and rambling to include here. In it Raffles recapitulates briefly the former history of Java under the Dutch, the administration as it has continued with himself at the helm, and his hopes for the future, in the event that Java's disposition under the Treaty of London should after all become void. But the composition lacks the brilliant, pointed brevity of Raffles's best work and shows plainly that he is under a strain.

"I shall stand excused from the narrow views of personal interest when I declare," he says, "that I should have no inclination to accept, were it offered, the charge of such an administration as I shall venture to propose; it will require a person of high rank, either noble or military; and I have had too much experience already of the injuries which accrue from the want of that high rank."

Which is an intriguing little sidelight on the vexations which must have beset the lieutenant governor: that, too, in the course of a career which on the surface looks to have been one long sweet triumph, always excepting the humiliations of Gillespie's charges and the pinpricks of Moira's chronic carping disapproval. It is one of those remarks made only when a man feels he is standing at a crossroads and estimates the value of his past and the potentiality of his future. There is no doubt that these double finalities of his life—Olivia's death and the close of the Java term—for a time rendered Raffles, despite his frantic busyness, unusually and dangerously reflective. All of the past years, he says to himself, Olivia, Leyden, Minto, my happy years at Buitenzorg, my youthful triumphs—all are gone. Tomorrow, who knows? Only a name, Bencoolen; the rest is still mystery, and I grow too old to approach mystery with eager curiosity.

He wrote William Brown Ramsay in October 1815, "You will be anxious to know my determination as to proceeding to England; my character—my future happiness—require my presence in England. The impression on my mind is, that I shall quit this country at the close of 1816; but this depends upon circumstances not within my control. I may go earlier— I may go later. Your advice will, I think, be for the best, and I am inclined to concur in it: 'for here I am a lonely man, like one that has long since been dead;' and should any thing keep me away for one year, from friends who I am sure would be glad to receive me with open arms! I want leisure to recover from the effects of that weight of responsibility which has almost weighed me down; yet I am high and proud in my own integrity. I thank you for the warmth and attachment which breathe through every line of your letter now before me; it has roused the finest feelings in my breast: and in the test of friendship, where is the heart that would not be glad!"

Lady Raffles hints that the retiring lieutenant governor felt hurt and insulted by the manner in which his term came to an end, but she does not go into particulars as to the cause of his feelings. Undoubtedly he resented not being given the option of continuing until the end of British rule on Java; and this happened because the matter of Gillespie's charges was not yet settled to the council's satisfaction.

"Lord Minto had secured to him the Residency of Bencoolen," says Lady Raffles, "as a provision in case Java had been transferred to the Crown, when of course a Governor and Council would have been sent out from England." Java was not to belong to the Crown, but it was decided to offer Raffles the Bencoolen appointment now in any case, since he would be at liberty. However, though he accepted Bencoolen, Sophia declares that his weak condition made a voyage home an absolute necessity before he could begin to think of taking on the new post.

This tactful evasion of the truth has stirred the Dutch writer Van der Kemp to a scornful fury. So, Raffles went home for his health, did he? Had to have a rest before taking on the Bencoolen post? Stuff and nonsense! *Raffles wasn't allowed to go to Bencoolen,* snarled Kemp, until the council should declare itself satisfied that he was clear of Gillespie's charges. And Kemp knew what he was talking about—he always knew if it was a matter affecting Raffles. His life's mission, self-appointed, was to collect data unfavorable to our hero, so we need not hesitate to accept the following information as perfectly accurate.

The Company in London sent a letter dated May 15, 1815, to the governor general of Bengal (Moira) as follows:

"Whatever may be the result of the investigations of the charges preferred against Mr. Raffles, we are of opinion that his continuance in the Government of Java would be highly inexpedient, and we, therefore, desire that you would select forthwith from among the Civil Servants of the Company some person of approved talent and integrity to whom you can, with confidence, entrust the charge of that Colony, until the period should arrive for restoring it to the Sovereign of the Netherlands."

There it was, then. There remained the formality of handing over his many charges to Mr. Fendall, who came out to Java to relieve him. "Raffles felt himself aggrieved," says Sophia, "but he well knew his being so was in no way attributable to Mr. Fendall; and he wished to pay the respect and attention which he thought due to the station that Mr. Fendall was about to fill"—regardless, evidently, of the obvious fact that neither Mr. Fendall nor any other Englishman would be responsible for Java very much longer. "Mr. Raffles was alarmingly reduced at this time by the joint action of illness, and of the violent remedies which had been applied; but his spirits rose superior to his bodily strength, and he could not be persuaded to allow any personal consideration to interfere with a public arrangement." Thus he added immeasurably to the anxiety of his physician and nurses by getting up at three in the morning on the day his relief was to arrive, though he had been confined to his room the three previous days, and by insisting upon leaving Buitenzorg for Ryswick in time to receive Fendall in proper style.

Everyone was presented according to form. Fendall was polite enough to approve whatever Raffles had done and to promise that nothing could or would be changed as long as the British remained responsible. There was ample time, as it turned out, for both men to look into everything for a cursory view, before Raffles's ship was ready. The retiring lieutenant governor characteristically employed that time to prepare a memorial which he left with Fendall, setting forth a few last-minute suggestions and pleas for his Javanese charges, "to secure justice to the people whom he was leaving." He wanted various provisions in favor of certain sultans insisted upon by treaty before the Dutch should regain possession. "The question . . . arises, in how far the British Government might not be subjected to reproach, were they unconditionally to hand these princes over, thus reduced, to the mercy of their former rulers," he argued in his paper.

In the end none of this had any effect, for the island was transferred unconditionally to the Dutch, in accordance with the agreement made in Europe, and nothing Fendall or any other last-minute deputy could do would have had any opposite result. Out of his experience Raffles probably knew from the beginning that this would be the case, but he was never one to let a chance slip merely because it looked forlorn. I mention the matter here because it is a good example of the way Raffles's mind worked. He was gravely ill, so bad in fact that for several weeks aboard ship his companions were in doubt of his surviving the trip. Yet Java and the years he had spent there, and the work he had done, and his hopes, however slender, for a lasting effect, were sufficient incentive to push him into a burst of energy that would have taxed even a well man, those last days at Buitenzorg.

Raffles had been given plenty of warning: he was aware for months before his departure of the full extent of this political change. Even so, when it overtook him at last he must have felt as if disaster had come upon all the South Seas. Not only did he have to give up Java in his plans for the future of Great Britain, but even the alternative places such as Banca, which had always given Lord Minto and himself a comfortable feeling that there would be at least some port in the storm, were now out of the question. Bitterly he must have railed against the shortsighted men in England who had sacrificed so much of England's future glory, merely to achieve a peace in Europe which Raffles considered temporary and trumpery. He had spent too many years hating Holland to give up his opinions now, at the careless command of some know-nothing back home.

Raffles took his leave of Java in March 1816, sailing in a ship which by a strange coincidence bore the same name, *Ganges*, as that in which he had come out to the East. Accompanying him was that journal-keeping Captain Travers who had been associated with him for so long, as well as Captain Garnham, who with Travers shared the position of A.D.C., and his physician Sir Thomas Sevestre. The scene of his farewell was a picturesque and moving one, as can be imagined. "The Roads of Batavia were filled with boats," said Lady Raffles, "crowded with people of various nations, all anxious to pay the last tribute of respect within their power to one for whom they entertained the most lively affection. On reaching the vessel, he found the decks filled with offerings of every description— fruits, flowers, poultry, whatever they thought would promote his comfort on the voyage. It is impossible to describe the scene which took place when the order was given to weigh the anchor. . . ."

Three days out, Captain Travers presented Raffles in his cabin with a written address from the members of his personal staff. "The scene which ensued," Travers noted in his Journal, "was the most distressing I had ever witnessed. After perusing it, he became so completely overcome as to be unable to utter a word. . . ."

This was the address:

Dear Sir,—

Among the varied and distinguished proofs of regard and veneration which you have received from all classes and descriptions of people in this island, on your approaching departure, we hope you will accept from us a more silent, but not less cordial, assurance of the regret we feel at losing you; of the grateful and pleasing remembrance we shall ever entertain towards you; of the respect and affection, in short, which can cease only with our existence. We have now, dear sir, known you long; and though some of us have not had the happiness till of late years, we all equally feel that it is impossible to know you without acquiring that cordial and heartfelt attachment which binds us to you, as it were, through life, and renders us as interested in your happiness and prosperity, as we can be in our own.

Whatever may be our future destination, and however it may be our chance to be scattered, when we return to our different fixed situations in life, we can never forget the time we have passed in Java. The public sentiment has expressed what is due there to the energies and value of your administration, which the more it is examined the more it will be admired. It belongs rather to us to express what we have witnessed and felt —to bear testimony to the spotless integrity and amiable qualities which shed a mild lustre over your private life. These we acknowledge with gratitude, and these are imprinted in our hearts too strongly to be ever erased.

You will not receive these expressions of our regard until you have left us; and when, perhaps, it will be long ere we meet again.

Accept them then, dear sir, as the genuine feelings of our hearts; and allow us to request your acceptance of a small token of our remembrance, in the shape of a piece of plate, which we have requested our mutual friends, Captains Travers and Garnham, to purchase and deliver to you in England. It bears no great value among the more splendid tokens which you have received of the public esteem; but it may serve to remind you of those who are, with the sincerest regard and attachment, dear sir, your faithful friends and servants.

CHAPTER XIX

Change is bound to be salutary for a patient like Raffles; not the temporary sort of variety he found on his tour of the island, but a true cataclysm. He wanted a power outside himself, to reach down among the roots of daily existence and pull it up and transplant it. The Bengal Government's summary dismissal of their Java lieutenant governor, though he bitterly resented it at the time, may very possibly have been the saving of him, nevertheless. With every day carrying him farther from the East, from the sights and sounds and smells he had known for the past eleven years, his chances of survival grew stronger, and his companions aboard ship, as their responsibility lessened, felt easier. At first, Captain Travers said, Raffles spent most of his time sorting his papers and reading "for amusement," and he meekly obeyed Sevestre's orders, which was a bad sign. But during the leisurely days of good weather he returned to normal more swiftly than anyone had expected. Knowing that ships plying this route sometimes would put into St. Helena, he showed great eagerness to pay a visit to Bonaparte, who had lately been sent there by the British after his break for freedom.

It is worth remarking, merely by the way, that Raffles seems to have entertained the liveliest respect for the little Corsican, and never, save for a few days following the conquest of Java, did he express any sentiments of hostility toward the French nation similar to those he constantly entertained for Holland. Even that exception, which I make because of the British proclamation to the Batavian Dutch in November 1811, is perhaps invalid. The hand that wrote the proclamation may have been the hand of Raffles, but the voice was the voice of Minto. Perhaps we can rationalize this irrational prejudice of Raffles's. His whole life does seem to have been very full of Dutch trouble. The Netherlands had a tiresome way of looming up on his horizon: whenever and wherever he looked around him in the Orient the Dutch had always, always, always got there first. The French, on the contrary, were ordinary foes, familiar characters in an old story. Besides, they merely threatened the homeland, and England wasn't nearly as close to Raffles's heart as were the East Indian islands and the Malay Archipelago. (I speak merely from conjecture, and no serious historian need rise up in wrath against this dangerous statement. It is an errant impression of mine. No, I can't prove it. No, Raffles never said it outright, to my knowledge. I don't suppose he ever would have said it in any case, even if he realized, himself, that he felt that way, which I am certain he didn't.)

Raffles seems to have felt a genuine admiration for Napoleon Bonaparte, aside from his natural curiosity. Or if it was not admiration it was an emotion not far removed from it; shall we call it the vague stirrings of envy? Napoleon more than any other character in history has aroused strong feelings among the common fry who came after him, sometimes even in the hearts of men not so common. There is no doubt, for example, that he, or the idea of him, greatly influenced the monstrous Hitler, and many of Mussolini's posturings must be laid to his address. He has become so much a beacon light for small men with inferiority complexes that if we were Asiatics and Napoleon a hero of Chinese history he would now be seen everywhere in sacred effigy, with small, forlornly ineffectual men burning joss and loudly chanting their prayers to him.

Napoleon's popularity is so well known and accepted a phenomenon that H. G. Wells deliberately tweaked the public in the nose when he wrote his *Outline of History*, by giving

333 ঽ

the Little Corporal less than a page of text, a niggardly allowance compared with those he was pleased to bestow on contemporary scientists and philosophers. When the outcry came which he had been mischievously expecting, the writer explained that he had apportioned his space and attention according to the value of famous men's contributions to our civilization. He had no desire, he implied, to place a premium upon destructiveness. So much for Napoleon Bonaparte.

But in all fairness to Raffles, the attraction he felt for Napoleon was not a typical one. In the first place, this manifestation of hero worship had not yet become a general thing in the world. The wars and the escape from Elba were very recent history. Even the traditional English spirit of sportsmanship could scarcely have started working so soon after the event, and the memory of danger was still vividly with most Britons. Hence, of course, the precautions surrounding Napoleon on St. Helena.

In the second place, Raffles had far more reason than does today's little office manager to compare himself with the Corsican, even though their techniques were so widely different, for they were more or less in the same line of work, i.e., empire building. Speaking from conjecture again, I think it possible that Napoleon's slashing, dashing method was what attracted Raffles. All his life the Englishman had been hobbled and handcuffed by red tape—the red tape of diplomatic tradition, the red tape of commercial custom, the red tape that seemed to grow by the yard in Calcutta, stretching out over the sea and entangling Raffles in the East Indies whenever he tried to take a step. It was his fate to see more clearly into the future than did most of his elders and betters, without ever having enough authority to act upon this superior judgment. A man of restless intellect and large ambition, he suffered all the refined tortures of frustration and regret. Usually he was ignored; when he wasn't ignored he was scolded. It was his particular bad luck to be associated with the Cinderella of all his Company's projects. Imagine, then, the emotions of such a man contemplating Napoleon's iconoclastic career. He must often have reflected that such a life might be worth the most dismal

MALE INFORMAL ATTIRE
"Taking it easy" in Old Batavia
circa 1815

EURASIAN WOMAN
Going to church in Batavia
circa 1815

(From the *Platen-Album* of F. de Haan's OUD BATAVIA, 1919; by permission
of the Netherlands Information Bureau)

SIR THOMAS STAMFORD RAFFLES
A portrait by George Francis Joseph

(By permission of the Trustees of The National Portrait Gallery, London)

fate, even St. Helena, for the rapture, however short-lived, of carrying out one's plans freely, unimpeded by any force but the comparatively trifling one offered by the armies of all Europe.

Many a lesser man has sighed wistfully, gazing on Napoleon's picture. Raffles did not sigh, but he was so keen to pay a call on the ex-Emperor that the *Ganges* captain, Mr. Falconer, went out of his way to discover that they suddenly needed water and so would have to call in at St. Helena.

It was, they knew, most unlikely that they would get permission to interview the illustrious prisoner. The events in which Napoleon had played a central part were still recent, and the atmosphere surrounding him was full of suspicion, especially now, so soon after his daring escape from Elba.

Falconer's and his passengers' worst apprehensions were nearly realized, for as soon as the *Ganges* was spotted from shore they were brought up sharp, there to wait while a couple of naval officers came out from the admiral's ship in a small boat, to see what they wanted. These officers communicated the captain's requests to the flagship by signal—first, fresh water, and second, an interview with, or at least a glimpse of, Bonaparte. Promptly and succinctly came a discouraging reply: the water could easily be brought out to where they rode at anchor from the flagship, and definitely no, they said, to any communication with Napoleon.

Travers then sent a more detailed request ashore by letter, informing the admiral, Sir George Cockburn, that Raffles was aboard the *Ganges*, and expressing the hope that this circumstance might possibly make a difference in Sir George's decision. In the meantime Raffles was advising his fellow passengers against entertaining any hope whatever. To allay the pangs of disappointment, he said, it might be wise, rather than thronging the deck, exhibiting chagrin, and staring wistfully toward the forbidden shore, to go below to their cabins and there compose themselves to writing an account of how they felt at that moment; in other words, to compile a sort of log of the emotions. They could compare the results later on, he said, and thus relieve the tedium of their detention. Some of the others may have begun to follow his example. Raffles, carrying on with the game, did go below as soon as he had made his little speech, giving proof of his iron will by wasting not another glance at the supposedly inhospitable island of St. Helena. But after a short delay there came welcome news. Owing to Mr. Raffles's presence, the entire passenger group was granted permission, after all, to come ashore.

Raffles's party being invited to dine with the notables of the island, they slept ashore that night at Government House. After a short discussion the desired audience with Napoleon was granted, at least so far as the British authorities were concerned, with only two precautions—they must not address the royal prisoner as "Emperor," but only as "General," and if Napoleon happened to be wearing a hat the visitors must keep their heads covered too. Things did not go that easily with the French household when the petition was presented in turn to them. The ex-Emperor had little dignity left to stand on, but such as it was he and his courtiers made it go a long way. Raffles's party had to spend the morning sight-seeing in the vicinity of Napoleon's residence without being sure whether or not they would succeed in their attempt. However, when the go-between, Marshal Bertrand, heard that they were scheduled to sail that evening, he made special efforts and did, at last, get a half promise from Napoleon to receive the Englishmen.

"We found this once great man," wrote Captain Travers in his faithful Journal, "in earnest conversation with Countess Bertrand, who was walking with him in the garden; General Gourgaud preceded, Marshal Bertrand, Count Las Casas, Captain Poniatowsky, and a page followed, all uncovered. On our arrival being announced, we were quickly informed that the Emperor would receive us in the garden; and Count Las Casas added, that although it had been the Emperor's intention not to see any person for some days, yet on being told that it was Mr. Raffles, late Governor of Java, who wished the interview, he immediately consented to see us.

"On our approaching, Napoleon turned quickly round to receive us, and taking off his hat, put it under his arm. His reception was not only not dignified or graceful, but absolutely vulgar and authoritative. He put a series of questions to Mr. Raffles in such quick succession, as to render it impossible to reply to one before another was put. His first request was to have Mr. Raffles' name pronounced distinctly. He then asked him in what country he was born? how long he had been in India? whether he had accompanied the expedition against the Island of Java? who commanded? and on being told Sir Samuel Auchmuty, he seemed to recollect his name, and made some observations to Las Casas respecting him. He was particular in asking the extent of force, and the regiments employed, and then enquired if Mr. Raffles delivered up the Island to the Dutch, or was relieved by another Governor."

Such a point, of course, would have special, painful interest for a dispossessed leader.

"He appeared to be acquainted with the value and importance of the Island, but put some strange questions to Mr. Raffles, such as how the King of Java conducted himself. . . . On his making a slight inclination of the head, we prepared to take our leave, and on our making our bow we parted, Napoleon continuing his walk, and we returning to the house. During the whole time of our interview, as Napoleon remained uncovered, common politeness obliged us to keep our hats in our hands; and at no time was it found necessary to give him any title, either of General or Emperor."

This exciting interlude gave the travelers plenty to talk about for a long time afterward, on what proved to be a tedious section of the voyage. The weather was pleasant, but the winds were "light and baffling." Raffles's health now improved so rapidly that he was considered practically cured, and his spirits reacted accordingly. He read aloud to the company, from selections of literature which he was translating from the ancient Malay in preparation for his Java history, and he talked a good deal about the administration of Java, explaining this or that one of his acts in office, or speculating on the probable future of his friends the Javanese. Travers says that he was never bitter about his having been removed from office—for he persisted in his belief, probably justified, that in having removed him from office at that point Lord Moira was allowing

Gillespie's charges to influence him—and he seemed convinced, now, that justice would be done him after he should arrive in England. Practically, the recall made little difference, but the hint was unpleasant. Raffles's whole attitude, however, reflected a change for the better in his health. As everyone knows, the balance between physical and mental well-being is a delicate and accurate one, and so his friends were especially delighted with these evidences of improvement.

The *Ganges* had a narrow escape during a freak storm which snapped the three topmasts off another ship, the *Auspicious*, which had been keeping her company ever since the day of sailing. What made the occurrence so odd was the circumstance that the *Auspicious*, when the accident overtook her, was only a few hundred yards ahead of the *Ganges*, yet those aboard the *Ganges* felt only a slight increase in the breeze, whereas it was a vicious squall that attacked the *Auspicious*. Fortunately for her, her crew was able to make the necessary repairs immediately, and the two vessels continued their journey together. Raffles's thirty-fifth birthday was celebrated aboard on July sixth, and a good time was had by all. The dark days of the immediate past were gone and *almost* forgotten.

Raffles wrote from aboard ship to W. B. Ramsay: "Although I am considerably recovered, I yet remain wretchedly thin and sallow, with a jaundiced eye and shapeless leg. . . . I return to you . . . a poor, solitary wretch; and the rocks of Albion, which under other circumstances would have met my eye with joy and gladness, will not now present themselves without reflections which I cannot dwell upon.

"If the Alcyon has arrived, you will have been apprized of the result of Lord Moira's proceedings. His Lordship deemed it advisable to postpone any decision on Gillespie's charges; the Supreme Government, however, have declared my character unaffected by these charges, and further stated that they considered it but an act of justice to leave my reserve appointment to Bencoolen unshaken, this being the test by which the Court judged of my having explained my conduct satisfactorily. But the manner in which my removal from Java was effected, and the whole course of proceedings adopted towards me by the Governor-General has been such, that it was impossible for me to rest satisfied with this tardy and incomplete judgment. I therefore resolved to appeal to the authorities in England, and in the mean time quietly to go to Bencoolen; but the shock was too severe, my health has been undermined, and this injustice threw me on my back. It was the opinion of the faculty that remaining longer in India was dangerous, and I took the resolution of proceeding to the Cape, and eventually to England. . . .

"It is my intention to appeal most forcibly to the Court against the whole course of measures. I feel confident I shall obtain justice from them; this is all I shall ask for. I have a cause that will carry conviction. . . ."

The party disembarked at Falmouth, and there met with an unexpected adventure when the customs officials subjected them to a careful examination as to their state of health and asked carefully whether there had been any infection either on board ship or at the port of embarkation. "Methought the officer seemed rather doubtful as to the positive assurances our mouths were giving," wrote Travers gaily, "in direct opposition to the strong evidence of our cheeks, which . . . were of the most pale and emaciated caste. . . ." In those early days the "Anglo-Indian complexion" was still a novelty to the stay-at-home British native, though that characteristic greenish cast of countenance was to become all too familiar to England before the end of the century. Moreover, since one member of the disembarking group was Raden Rana Dipura, "a Javanese Chief," his presence must have caused tremendous excitement behind the scenes, though the customs officers no doubt were careful to retain their customarily phlegmatic facial expressions during the questioning and the orthodox baggage examination.

Safely through these formalities, one might have expected Raffles to make tracks straight to East India House, or at any rate to the luxury, such as it was, that London afforded the weary ocean traveler. But Raffles was Raffles, which means that he always took advantage of any chance that offered itself to learn about a new subject. They found themselves near to the

Cornish mines when they reached Truro, their first stopping place as they traveled overland toward London, and Raffles announced that he meant to have a look then and there at the mining industry. He did, too, going down a deep shaft and asking hundreds of questions, as was his way, until his weary companions decided he was now master of the whole routine. Raffles made no such large claim, but only said that now he was convinced of what he had only suspected before, that Javanese ore was superior by far to the domestic sort.

He announced himself at East India House the morning after his arrival in town, on July 17, 1816.

Most of us have had the experience, on a small scale, of returning home after a long absence. Perhaps it was an absence of a few months at school, perhaps a year or so at college, or even some few years in another town or country. Raffles, remember, had been away eleven years, on the other side of the world. He was a boy when he departed, and almost everything of importance that was worth mentioning in his life had happened to him in the East. For him, coming home must have been very nearly like entering a new world. There were just enough familiar names and places in London to give him a strange, unreal sensation, like that we have when we encounter some scene or hear some speech which we think we must have dreamed in the past. The greater part of his immediate family were still alive, but since his sisters had shared with him some few of his early experiences in the East they were not a part of the confusing background supplied by all the rest of London.

Raffles's instinct was not playing him false, either, in telling him that this was all new country to him. The Raffles who was now paying a visit to London, taking a house—23 Berners Street—and furnishing it, mainly with his own belongings from Java, the Raffles who walked into East India House as one of the important figures there, that Raffles was a complete stranger to this side, the top side, of English life. Eleven years ago he had been catapulted from poverty to success, but there was no time to taste the flavor of that success in his own country; he had been hustled out of London with his bride, practically in the act of pocketing his first good salary.

Now the boy was returned, still comparatively young, notwithstanding which he had become a man with an exceptional career, a famous name, and a record of which he should have been proud. He had aided the great Lord Minto and had launched the new humanitarian fashion in colonial government. He was a personality of the day. All he lacked now was someone to share the fun.

Each of us has somewhere in his past a special ambition. It is a happy moment if that ambition is realized; a happier one if there is some witness who shares our memory of the aspiration and understands our triumph when it is achieved. Raffles's youth, even his early boyhood, had been full of such ambitions. It is unhappily true that nobody in the immediate circle of the Raffles home had been sympathetic to these visions, and so he had long since enjoyed a harmless triumph over them, and shared his luck ungrudgingly with his mother and sisters, as fast as it came rolling in. The one loving heart who really knew his most secret desires was of course his lost Olivia, who had a part in his earliest Eastern adventure at Penang, and who would have rejoiced more than anyone else at the successful outcome of this journey. He didn't want to dwell on her name. So grimly and determinedly had he filled in the time after her death that it was, incredibly, a two-year-old tragedy when the Gillespie matter was declared cleared. Then at last the widower allowed himself time to breathe and look about him.

Not that the charges had been cleared to his satisfaction, even yet. He declared to the Court of Directors, as soon as he arrived in London, that the *affaire* Gillespie had been decided, and the decision imparted to him, in a "loose and unsatisfactory manner"; that if there still remained any doubt as to his character he wanted the case reopened with an immediate investigation, and if no doubt remained, then he felt that Lord Hastings (formerly Moira) had done his, Raffles's, reputation grave injury by not allowing him to come to Calcutta in person

341 ಎ

or do anything else in his own defense before the order came, recalling him from office: he prayed the Court to consider these factors and to render some public acknowledgment of his services, however belated and grudged they might be.

If the length of this last sentence had not bidden fair to rival one of Raffles's own, there would have been added to it a reference to the plaintiff's record on Java. He pointed out, with considerable justice, that the British administration of the past five years had elicited world-wide praise, with the possible, and natural, exception from the chorus of Holland's voice.

The Court, as usual, failed to come up to scratch. This time, though, it seems evident that no spite lay behind their failure to give complete satisfaction. Rather they took the attitude that Raffles's indignation was justified but that any further discussion of the charges would be giving them too much importance and making the affair overelaborate. Raffles was an injured party, Raffles quite naturally was sensitive, and so Raffles was making too much fuss over a closed incident. Raffles must take their word for it, as gentlemen, that the incident was indeed well and truly closed; besides which, Java was going back to the Dutch, so what was all the shooting for? The Court again pointed to their statement made in 1815 and said that it still stood, correct in word and sentiment.

In part the 1815 statement read as follows:

"After a scrupulous examination of all the documents, both accusatory and exculpatory, connected with this important subject, and an attentive perusal of the minutes of the Governor-General, and of the other members composing the Council, when it was under consideration, we think it due to Mr. Raffles, to the interests of our service, and to the cause of truth, explicitly to declare our decided conviction, that the charges, in so far as they went to impeach the moral character of that gentleman, have not only not been made good, but that they have been disproved, to an extent which is seldom practicable in a case of defense. . . .

"Were their [the government's financial operations] unreasonableness, improvidence, and inefficiency clearly established, this would only indicate error or defect of judgment, or, at most, incompetence in Mr. Raffles for the high, and, in many respects, exceedingly difficult, situation which he filled." (This refers to the fact, already mentioned in the complete version, that the Court hadn't had time to look over all the financial deals and so couldn't conscientiously pronounce on them as yet.)

"But the purity, as well as the propriety, of many of his acts, as Lieutenant-Governor, having been arraigned, accusations having been lodged against him, which if substantiated must have proved fatal to his character, and highly injurious, if not ruinous to his future prospects in life, his conduct having been subjected to a regular and solemn investigation, and this investigation having demonstrated to our minds the utter groundlessness of the charges exhibited against him, in so far as they affected his honour, we think that he is entitled to all the advantage of this opinion, and of an early and public expression of it . . ."

Not, you will say, completely satisfactory. One can understand Raffles's persistent desire for something a little better. It cannot be pleasant to be branded as a muddling fool, even when the brander adds as his opinion that one has been a perfectly *honest* muddling fool. Naturally the Court didn't put it quite so baldly as all that. In effect they said, "This man may possibly have been the world's biggest ass at financial wangling —we haven't taken time out to look carefully at his work, and we are far too careful ever to let slip a chance of calling a fellow a fool, so we're not going to go on record as saying he's not. Not until we jolly well have to give him a clean bill as a financial wizard. Between you and us, he probably made the most Godawful mess of the Javanese treasury. But no matter what sort of boners he may have pulled, we are convinced he pulled them from the best and purest of motives. Why, anyone can see that Raffles is too stupid—beg pardon, too honest—a type ever to try to feather his nest. So lay that tarbrush down."

Thus blandly, kindly, with the best of motives, the Court of Directors kept assuring Raffles that his record was perfectly clear and that they couldn't understand what more he wanted. In vain did he dance with rage before the door of East India

343 &

House; everyone kept on patting his head and telling him absently to go away and sin no more. The wonder is that Raffles was not dead of apoplexy before he got what he wanted at long last, but he wasn't, and he did. After all, he had served his term as apprentice to the foibles of that Court of Directors for many weary years, and anyone who survived the correspondence which Raffles used to receive from Moira should have been able to survive anything the official brain, even at its muzziest, could devise.

It is a pity that we have had to follow our subject's example, dragging the reader straight off to India House before we give him a chance to enjoy his return to his family as the complete conquering hero.

Now, however, his official duties are over, and we can indulge in a little personal gossip among relatives. Boulger is our source; he found this passage among the reminiscences of Dr. Raffles, the reverend cousin of Liverpool, who came up to London to meet Raffles and welcome him home. It is pleasant to find that the lieutenant governor had not forgotten his favorite aunt, but then one knew that he would not.

"One of his first visits was to his aunt, for they were very fond of each other. He left his equipage, which was a splendid one,—and private carriages with rich liveries were not so common then as they are now, and were indeed a great rarity in the quiet corner of London in which my father lived,—and, walking the length of Princes Street, knocked at old No. 14, and on the opening of the door went at once into the sort of parlour-kitchen where my mother was, busied as usual about her household affairs. 'I knew well,' he said, 'where at this time of the day I should find you,' and taking his accustomed seat in an old arm-chair by the fireside, where he had often sat, made her at once, by his affectionate and playful manner, quite unconscious of the elevation to which he had attained since he had last sat there. 'Aunt,' he said, 'you know I used to tell you, when a boy, that I should be a duke before I die.' 'Ah,' she replied, 'and I used to say that it would be "Duke of Puddle Dock,"' which was a proverb in London at that day, referring to a wretched locality in Wapping, and with which aspiring

lads, who had great notions of the greatness they should hereafter attain, were twitted. But he had actually attained to far
more than a dukedom, having had Oriental kings and regents
under him."

His letters and other writing prove Raffles to have been consistently gentle and affectionate toward his family, regardless
of the years and experience that might have separated some of
them spiritually from him. He never seemed to feel that he
had "outgrown" these simple folk, or lost touch with them.
I am not repeating the old cliché, always served up when Local
Boy Makes Good, that Local Boy was never guilty of putting
on airs. Raffles in keeping the common touch did something
much subtler than merely to refrain from ordinary snobbery.
He refrained also from feeling himself too complicated for the
old folks at home. He was a simple man and he remained simple; it is quite possible to be intelligent and educated without
becoming complex, and Raffles somehow managed to do this,
perhaps because he had had to deal so much of the time with
Malays, who are a sensitive, forthright people, and who recognized in the Java governor an inner simplicity like their own.

"He did not know me, nor did I for a moment recognize
him. . . . He had lost nothing of himself but his colour and
his flesh. . . . He intends to publish an account of Java, and is
very busy in getting maps, etc., prepared for the work. He has
very extensive collections of Javanese literature of his own collecting. I am amazed at his industry. In one day he wrote two
hundred letters with his own hand, and dictated to two secretaries besides."

The cousin, who now lived at Birmingham, often wrote his
wife from London, reporting fully on this his fabulous relative, back at last from Eastern parts. "My cousin has an unbounded flow of spirits; I fear too much for his strength." The
reverend gentleman gleaned what he could from his modest
kinsman about his work in Java; then when Raffles dried up
and wouldn't give him more, the parson applied to Raffles's
friends. "[The Javanese] declared that they would express their
sentiments to the King of England, and the native powers
were coming down in a body to address my cousin on the sub-

ject, and entreat him to stay amongst them," wrote Dr. Raffles after that, gently boasting. "But this he prevented by the quickness of his departure, for it was only determined that he should come to England a few days before he sailed.

"He has brought over Eastern curiosities and treasures to the amount of thirty tons weight, in upwards of two hundred immense packages," he marveled. "He has some presents for the Prince Regent."

Modesty or no, Raffles was always glad of the chance to spread abroad in England his sentiments about Java and her reversion to the Netherlands. Assuming (well ahead of his period) that advertising is always the best policy, he seized on the fact that his presence in England was stirring up an interest in the East Indies and took the chance which presented itself to publish his book, the *History of Java.*

Raffles in everything he did was a bit of a politician, and his book, though it was a sincere and extremely valuable piece of work, did double duty. Aside from its intrinsic value, the timing was perfect for his purposes, just as he had known it would be. Raffles during that period was a man with a message, and he was not ashamed to preach it in any way, in any place, according to any opportunity that offered itself. Briefly, the message was that England had made a grave error in tossing Java and her subsidiary islands back to Holland. Java was a valuable property, and the ordinary Englishman was ignorant of that fact, said Raffles, or there would have been an outcry when the Treaty of London arranged for England to relinquish her claims. If only even now the public could be brought to realize how much had been lost to them, and what a waste had been perpetrated, it might at least not happen again that so much wealth and strength should be wantonly given up. And, what was worse, it had been given up to one of England's dangerous rivals, a country which had only lately been an enemy! The soothing word "restored" was one which Raffles scorned. The British interregnum of five years, he felt, had been so obviously advantageous to the natives that it gave England a claim at least as great as Holland's to the governorship of Java; in his opinion the claim was far greater.

The production of the *History* was done with Raffles's customary amazing accuracy and dispatch. He had been working on the preparation of it for five years, collecting material, translating ancient manuscripts, and tracing legends, not to mention the valuable collection he had made in Java of paintings and drawings for the illustrations. The actual work of writing, however, and of putting it all together, was done in a magically short time, in London, at the height of his social activity. Sophia says that he would dash off a few sheets each morning for the printer, and by evening the proof was waiting for him; he would correct it the same night when he came home from his usual dinner engagement. He began writing the text in October 1816 and was finished in time for the book to be published and out in May 1817—a span of eight months. Few of today's lightning-speed writers could do as well. Moreover, there is nothing slapdash about the book. It is today, just as it was when it appeared, the best of its kind, a standard work of reference, rich in accurate information, clearly written as if the author had possessed all the leisure in the world in which to prepare it.

Those were days in which the dedication of a new book was still an important matter of diplomacy, often far more important than today's dedication, which is little more than a courteous gesture, like the conventional gift of flowers or candy. After due thought on the subject, Raffles requested permission to dedicate his *History* to the Prince Regent. As the ex-governor of Java was enjoying quite a vogue just then in society, a result of his suddenly enhanced reputation among statesmen, the Prince readily granted his gracious permission and accepted the honor.

When the book had come out Raffles was invited to attend the Prince Regent's next levee. It is hard to decide at this date which agency was the true motivation for the honor shown him—that dedication or his years of service in Java. Probably both contributed, where either one alone might not have been enough. At any rate the ceremony must have been most gratifying to Raffles, the self-made man who had incurred such scorn from Gillespie. When he arrived at the party, his host the Regent told everyone to stop what they were doing. His attendants, already prepared, formed a circle around the Prince, and in their presence "Prinny" made a twenty-minute speech to Raffles, thanking him for "the entertainment and information he had derived from the perusal of the greater part of the volumes," and commending him for the services he had rendered his country by his conduct in governing Java. (It is quite possible, as a matter of fact, that he had actually read the book. Prinny had a nice taste in literature.) Then he told Raffles to kneel, and knighted him.

It was Sir Stamford Raffles who returned from the levee. There was no need now to trace that vague relative, Sir Benjamin Raffles, knight banneret, through the Heralds' College in order to bolster the family name. Sir Stamford himself had taken care of the glory of the Raffles family, forever and forever.

CHAPTER XX

Henley-upon-Thames, 23rd February, 1817

MY DEAR COUSIN,—You will, I doubt not, approve of the
change I have made in my condition in again taking to myself
a wife; and when I apprise you that neither rank, fortune, nor
beauty have had weight on the occasion, I think I may fairly
anticipate your approval of my selection. The Lady, whose
name is Sophia, is turned of thirty; she is devotedly attached
to me, and possesses every qualification of the heart and mind
calculated to make me happy. More, I need not say. . . .

How unfailingly true is that old saying, *autres temps, autres
mœurs.* Imagine any newly wedded husband today daring to
write such a letter about his bride to a relative or, for that matter, to anyone at all. One realizes that Raffles meant well by
the lady in describing her as he did, but it certainly sounds
somewhat severe and unkind. One is tempted to ask what the
devil did have weight on the occasion, and why he married
Miss Hull at all, if she had no rank, no fortune, and no beauty.
He should at least have professed that in his eyes his bride was
beautiful. And why, too, was he so positive that those three
negatives by themselves would be enough to win Cousin
Tom's approval of his selection? Surely the British Isles could

have offered him any number of ladies with similar charms, surely ladies without rank, fortune, or beauty were a drug on the market? "Turned of thirty . . . devotedly attached to me . . . every qualification of the heart and mind calculated to make me happy." No, it is too great a strain on at least one imagination. The bridegroom was simply being coy and oriental thus to deprecate his new wife. I prefer to tell myself that the fair Sophia *did* possess a certain beauty, a reasonable fortune, and enough rank to keep her from getting an inferiority complex when her husband came home late one evening with a tingling shoulder and his brand-new knighthood. She had something. But her possession of these qualities was not the deciding factor with Raffles when he made his selection; and that is what he meant of course. He was trying to say that he had married Sophia for her spiritual superiority. She had beauty, fortune, and rank as well, but he didn't care. He was broad-minded. He married her in spite of them. He married her because she had a kind face, and a heart and mind full of quality. That is how it must have been, anyway.

Miss Sophia Hull was the daughter of T. W. Hull, Esq., of County Down, Ireland. Raffles seems to have been peculiarly susceptible to Irish ladies: Olivia Devenish, it will be remembered, was also of Irish extraction. He met Sophia at Cheltenham, probably: that is where she lived, and he went to Cheltenham for the warm baths soon after his arrival in England. (That is the time to get husbands, as any experienced Englishwoman will tell you. You catch them as they step off the boat, fresh from their lonely years out in the colonies.) With this marriage the last of the Raffles generation was once more settled in the bonds of matrimony, for Harriett, the remaining spinster sister, the youngest one, who went out to visit Olivia and Raffles in Penang back in 1809, had been married in October of the preceding year to a gentleman at Somerset House, a Mr. Browne.

Whatever may have been the accepted theory of Cousin Tom's contempt for rank, which Raffles refers to in the announcement letter, the reverend doctor doesn't himself support it with much enthusiasm. He is frankly, innocently snobbish, and dearly loves a lord. In his reminiscences of this visit to England of his distinguished kinsman he proudly lists the great people with whom Sir Stamford hobnobbed.

The people who live as Sir Stamford did in the colonies most of their lives make up a very special world. They recognize each other almost at sight, but in relation to the ordinary humans who live at home, who own houses in England and dig in their own gardens, who raise children in a temperate zone without once thinking how lucky they are, in relation to the normal world, colonials are as a race apart. On infrequent occasions when they come back, as Sir Stamford did in 1817, for an extended visit, they may act normal and look normal, so that one cannot distinguish them from the rank and file in a crowd, but they are really acting a part and they know it.

Sir Stamford was on vacation. He had become a sort of man of the hour. He was the rage, all of a sudden, and high society was enthusiastic about him, and full of questions on the subject of Java. The East Indies and Sir Stamford Raffles were altogether fascinating that season. Through it all Sir Stamford smiled and moved graciously and enjoyed himself, putting on his act, but in his heart he was counting the days before he could get back in harness, back to the old routine, fighting off fever and dealing with the recalcitrant government in Bengal. In the meantime he didn't at all mind being the rage of society. No doubt it pleased Sophia as well.

He made many cordial acquaintances with whom he passed the time for the duration of his leave, and in a few cases went further and laid the foundations for lasting friendships. Though he had passed the age where men usually find their lifelong friends, the circumstances were abnormal and in this respect Sir Stamford enjoyed a sort of rejuvenation, a compensation for the pleasures of youth which he had missed. Most influential among these new but close friends were Prince Leopold and Princess Charlotte, that lady whose unhappy fate was to be the daughter of a brilliant, erratic prince, yet to possess in her own right neither brilliancy nor an unsteady nature. She suffered keenly from her father's captious treatment, acutely needing as she did the steadiness and security of

351 ⟨⟩

conventional affection. Her mother was too unstable to provide it, and though Prinny had his virtues, they were not evident in his dealings with his daughter. That is putting it mildly. One becomes infected, inevitably, with the Raffles caution, writing of these matters—a dangerous state of mind for a biographer.

Indeed, if it were not for Cousin Tom the parson, we would never have known some of the nuances of the situation there at Claremont, or how they affected Raffles and his new knighthood. Sir Stamford was discreet to a fault, but Sophia's discretion amounted to a passion; very little but the barest facts were left when she finished screening her account of this London interim in the Memoir. Cousin Tom was more generous, and Boulger was the gainer by this generosity. Through Boulger we glean the following royal gossip.

Sir Stamford had given a handsome present to Princess Charlotte, some furniture pieces made of a pretty Indian wood called *kiabooca*, which the princess put to use in her dining and drawing rooms. When her mother, Caroline, saw the tables and chairs she was seized with the desire to have some for herself, and immediately announced, with characteristic lack of ceremony, her intention of calling on Sir Stamford at home, in order to find out how to obtain them. It was this sort of behavior which used to drive her estranged husband, the Prince Regent, wild with rage. He felt that in his own family he should have the monopoly on informality and eccentricity. This was one of his favorite poses, though as a matter of fact informality really displeased him very much from any quarter. But I wander far afield; this sort of remark is too indiscreet even for chatty Cousin Tom and cannot be blamed on any of the Raffles group. I quote from later biographies, from material in the public domain.

Said Sir Stamford when the royal message was brought to him, "Of course I could not allow the Queen of England to come to me." Instead, he suggested, he would go to her at whatever place she chose to name. This conversation was being carried back and forth by the Countess Harcourt, one of Caroline's ladies in waiting, who with her husband the earl were two more of Sir Stamford's very good friends, and so it was finally arranged that the meeting should take place at the Harcourt country seat, St. Leonard's. Modestly Cousin Tom admits that while his cousin and Lady Harcourt waited for Caroline, of all things they talked about himself, the good doctor. Sir Stamford described him as a Dissenting minister, which he was, and said he had been to hear Dr. Raffles preach at Liverpool. Upon which Lady Harcourt said, "Ah, but you must not tell the Queen that, for she *hates Dissenters!*"

Probably Sir Stamford found it more tactful to shut up at this point. He felt a strong admiration himself for his cousin, who evidently maintained his unpopular views with a sturdy independence which set at naught the fact that he was in a blind alley as far as his career was concerned. Only bona fide Church of England priests had any future, as Sir Stamford on at least one occasion pointed out to Dr. Raffles, but this unpalatable truth did not alter Tom's stand. Sir Stamford admitted he couldn't quite see the value of such a fine point himself, but the idealism which saved his own ambition from being unpleasant made him recognize its match in his kinsman. He never pretended that Christianity in its full formal panoply held many attractions for him, under one name or another, but as soon as he and his cousin had agreed to differ on this point they managed to maintain a close and affectionate relationship throughout life.

Caroline arriving at this point, introductions were performed and the little party set out for a walk in the grounds. Caroline was nothing if not direct. Almost immediately she dived straight for her object. "I hear wonderful things," she said, "of the treasures you have brought from India, and everybody is in raptures with the beautiful tables, et cetera, which you have given to the Princess Charlotte."

When he told the story to Cousin Tom, Sir Stamford said that he was then "obliged," naturally, to offer her something of the same sort for Frogmore, her house. As a result he was commanded to Frogmore, and there met Amherst as my lord was on the point of sailing to India, to which he had recently been appointed. Altogether it looked as if Raffles's future in

353 ॐ

the East was to be far less like Cinderella's early days than his past had been, and more like her career after the ball was over. Meeting your superior officer socially, as every statesman knows, makes all the difference!

Dr. Raffles had a theory that the Prince Regent rather resented Sir Stamford's intimacy with his daughter's household. Prinny was often jealous for such petty reasons, so it seems a logical conclusion to draw. Cousin Tom even dared elaborate on his first idea, going so far as to suggest that without so much Princess Charlotte and Prince Leopold in Raffles's social program he might have found himself a baronet that fine morning of the royal levee, instead of a mere knight. Perhaps. Cousin Tom was alive then and this writer was not, but it seems to me that the knighthood was a sufficiently dizzy jump for the ex-governor of Java to have made, considering that a few months before that he had been very much in Lord Moira's black books over in Calcutta, without speculating too exhaustively on lost baronetages.

"The honour of knighthood could not be very highly esteemed," wrote Cousin Tom sniffily, "by him, when he had in his own establishment a man of equal rank, as his body physician, Sir Thomas Sevestre." But after all, what's so low all of a sudden about a body physician? This grumble must have originated in Dr. Raffles's own loyal heart; for Sir Stamford would have known better than to betray any chagrin over such a matter. It's always a relative, usually a poor one, who gets delusions of grandeur like that.

It is no wonder if all this royalty did go to Cousin Tom's head a little, for he was not made of the stuff his cousin was. Sir Stamford had been rehearsing for this drama, in a way, all his life. Not without result had he lain awake as a young boy, planning great things. His shabby bedroom had been the scene for many a royal levee: often had the furniture witnessed Raffles moving effortlessly in his dream, with superb grace and perfect poise, through the glittering multitude as he gathered to himself the plaudits of England's nobility. Raffles, the great Raffles, champion of the world's poor and downtrodden, envy and admiration of all Great Britain for his successes in the military field as well as the halls of diplomacy! After such an apprenticeship the truth when he encountered it had no terrors for Sir Stamford Raffles; it would have taken a far more formidable figure than Prinny's to strike the governor of Java with genuine awe. The world has more people of his stamp than we realize. Have you never marveled at the readiness with which a girl of the people can take her place in society when she becomes a successful actress or opera singer? Hasn't it been proved for nonsense time and again, that old proverb that Breeding Always Shows? And Raffles was not exactly a newcomer, an interloper among the princes. Years in the Orient, holding audience with sultans in one of the world's most courteous, deliberate, and stylized languages, had given him a stateliness of manner which was deeply impressive.

We shouldn't, however, grudge Cousin Tom, the country mouse, his moments of vicarious glory; rather we should appreciate his wide-eyed wonder, without which he would never have troubled to record these trivia, which make the drama vivid all these years after the curtain. For the innocent parson all this excitement was the biggest thing in his life. The Dissenting pulpit in Liverpool gathered dust while he hovered about his wonderful kinsman in London, playing to admiration the part of an adoring Boswell.

For example there was the awkward moment when Sir Stamford found himself with two engagements on a single day, both of them with members of the royal family. Princess Charlotte asked him to dine at Claremont, and just after he accepted this invitation the Prince Regent commanded him to dinner at Carlton House for the same day. Knowing as everybody did that Prinny was subject to fits of jealous spite, sometimes for quite ridiculously trivial reasons, Raffles felt that he was on a spot. It called for careful handling, but after all his years dealing with the Orient the governor of Java was up to it. He wrote to Sir Benjamin Bloomfield, one of Prinny's A.D.C.s, innocently asking to know whether he should consider an invitation from Princess Charlotte in the light of a royal command, as he did Caroline's summonses, or the Prince's. Back came a prompt and pompous reply: The Prince

Regent chose to remind himself that his daughter's invitation was that of heir presumptive to the throne; i.e., Her Royal Highness's invitation amounted to a command. That made it easy for Raffles; all he had to do now was to write Sir Benjamin again, informing him that, Her Royal Highness having commanded Sir Stamford to appear on the date in question, Sir Stamford could not, much to his regret, dine with the Prince Regent, owing to a previous engagement. Prinny was hoist with his own petard.

The last time Sir Stamford was at Claremont Leopold and Charlotte gave him a diamond ring as a keepsake (worth four hundred pounds, said Cousin Tom), and made him pretty speeches of farewell. "Sometimes wear that for my sake," said the Princess. The pair did not scruple to show their scorn for Sir Stamford's mere knighthood, a sentiment they shared with Dr. Raffles of Liverpool. According to him, Princess Charlotte "thoroughly despised the knighthood which her father had conferred upon him . . . a feeling in which the Prince fully participated." Raffles reported to Cousin Tom that "the tone and manner of Prince Leopold was quite ludicrous, when, on his first visit after he had been dubbed, he [Leopold] turned to the Princess and said, 'Why, Charlotte, they have made him a knight!!!' "

This story bears the stamp of truth even beyond the source, for everyone knew how the feud between the two houses, the Prince Regent's and his unfortunate daughter's, was always blazing out in these little manifestations. Raffles was earmarked, according to Tom's gossip, for the governor-generalship of India if all had gone smoothly and Princess Charlotte had become Queen of England. But Charlotte died, and Sir Stamford was not fated to live to a ripe old age either. Even the shadowy possibility of the India post, which was as much as could be achieved during this visit to England, should serve to show us what a long way Sir Stamford had come, in the estimation of the higher-ups of his department, since he had left Java, a sick, tired, aggrieved, and grieving man. But this good fortune did not continue. After the death of the princess, her husband Leopold found it impossible to remain longer on any sort of friendly terms with her father, whose attitude toward his wife Prince Leopold had never ceased to resent, though for the sake of appearances he had concealed his feelings. The royal widower stopped attending court, preferring to remain withdrawn from all activities connected with his father-in-law, and among the projects which were consequently lost sight of were the plans the Prince and Princess had entertained for Raffles, their particular pet.

Third family among the friends made by Raffles in 1816–17 were the Duke and Duchess of Somerset. The duchess discovered in herself a great fondness for anthropological subjects, and so Sir Stamford after his return to the East made a special point of writing her the kind of letter he had always until then reserved for Marsden, under the impression, probably correct, that most people would not appreciate his scientific observations. He wrote often to the duchess from Sumatra, no doubt exulting in having found in her an intelligent correspondent, for Raffles was one of those men who worked best when he could talk about his work with somebody able to understand it, and the duchess's enthusiasm was genuine, as was her capacity to learn. Like many men of his type, Raffles was at his best and most charming when writing letters to a woman. If he had not made friends with the Duchess of Somerset he would never have found out this talent in himself. Though the duchess's age and various other obvious factors rendered impossible any likelihood of a flirtation between them, still there was between them a something. There nearly always does exist between a man of Raffles's sort and a woman of similar interests and enthusiasms, never mind what their respective ranks and ages, a sentimental bond, harmless and tenuous perhaps, but nevertheless wielding a definite influence upon the correspondence between them. He was sensitive, eager, intellectually passionate: she was sympathetic and receptive. Because it was the duchess rather than the duke whom Raffles addressed in his letters, they were buoyant, fascinating compositions with a special flavor, and made much better reading than did the missives dealing with the same subjects which he wrote to Marsden, valued old friend as he was.

All well-rounded young British gentlemen of those days made the Grand Tour before they settled down to a man's work or pastime, whatever that might be. Raffles in his new capacity now felt it incumbent upon him to make up such arrears in his early education. At the time when he should have been putting the finishing touch on his education, touring France and Germany, at the age of twenty-one, he was as we know preparing for a much longer and more important voyage. Nothing about his early education had been conventional and he never pretended that it was, but he felt now that he should make up for this particular deficiency without longer delay. It was more than merely wanting to keep up with the Joneses, this urge to take a look for himself at the Continent. Though nobody in the diplomatic service knew more than did Raffles about his particular province in the oriental world, his knowledge was limited, and he felt the effects of these limitations. A statesman ought to have a general, overall conception of what makes the balance in international politics, and Raffles could hardly claim to possess that, since he had never even paid a visit to the home countries of the colonials with whom he had been dealing. It was more than merely interesting, it was really important that he should see Europe, the Netherlands particularly. As for Paris, from which had come all the fashions of Western diplomatic society, naturally it behooved a man who was soon to be honored with a title to pay a visit to the world's center of elegance and style.

Besides all this, he and his Sophia really had a honeymoon coming to them.

Therefore in April, just before his book appeared and he was knighted, Raffles, his wife, and his eldest sister, Mary Anne Flint, resolved that in the following month they would start out on a tour of the Continent. "My plan," he wrote Cousin Tom, "is to visit Paris and Brussels, and to see all besides that I can in the space of six weeks or two months, the limit which I am obliged to fix. . . . Now, my dear cousin, if you can possibly manage to be of our party I can promise you will find it a pleasant and interesting trip, and I am sure I need not say how happy it will make us to have you as a *compagnon de* voyage. . . . My eventual plans are to proceed to India about August; but a few weeks delay will be of no importance, as my departure entirely depends upon my own convenience and pleasure."

As a result the party of four—for Dr. Raffles was easily persuaded to accompany them—used their six weeks to such good advantage that the itinerary of the journey sounds like the efficient see-all, cover-all kind of trip that might be made by some modern American tourist on the traditional roller skates, rather than an English party of pleasure, just out for sight-seeing on the Continent. France, Belgium, Switzerland, Savoy, and the Rhine were all included. The men of the party seem to have spent most of their available time keeping journals or writing letters that could be used later for publication. Dr. Raffles actually did just that; he published the letters he wrote from the journey in a book "and thus," says Boulger, "became the historian of this continental trip, one of the first taken after the Great Peace." The fact that this volume of letters, which evidently met with considerable success, in time became a standard guidebook rather gives one to think. How often is a guidebook upon which tourists trustingly depend written, as was this one, by a traveler who did the whole thing in six weeks? Of course we don't know for a fact that this was Dr. Raffles's first time on the Continent, as it was for his cousin Stamford, but even so, even supposing it was Cousin Tom's second trip to Europe instead of his first, the ease and speed with which the whole thing was accomplished is somewhat startling.

Raffles's own letters show, according to Boulger as he quotes a missive addressed to the Duchess of Somerset, "how he went to the root of things." It also answers in some part the question which, it may be remembered, occurred to us when we encountered Raffles's speedy way of doing things some time back, after his first visit to Malacca, when he wrote that enormous, long, comprehensive account of the city which saved it from destruction. At first glance it looks as if Raffles left himself open to the accusation of hasty judgment and of basing his decisions upon information too easily accepted, too carelessly gathered. On second thought, however, once again we find we have been unfair. Unless he really knew his subject he made no weighty decisions upon specific matters. It was generally an age of pontifical utterance, even among the best of writers; very rarely do we encounter anyone of the early nineteenth century who is not guilty of sententiousness once in a while. And so, though Raffles's letters are padded out with solemn observations, they are seldom startling or meaty. They are not devoid of interest nevertheless; one is sure to find something worth reading in the remarks of a white man who has never until middle age watched a normal Caucasian peasantry going about its business. The sight of the farmers of Belgium and France at work in their own fields brought home to him sharply the advantages of private ownership over the landlordism which still flourished in the feudal East.

"I was certainly surprised and delighted with the appearance of agriculture in France," reads his letter to the Duchess of Somerset, dated from Brussels on July 14, "not that the fields were as highly cultivated as in England, nor that any thing like an advanced state of agriculture was to be seen. I was pleased to observe two things, which I know are highly condemned by agriculture, the smallness of the properties, and the cultivation of the fruit-trees in the grain and hay-fields. Agriculturists maintain that capital is essential to improvement, but when it is rich, and wants little or no improvement, capital is unnecessary. For the greatness of a country it may be an object that the greatest possible quantity of produce should be brought to market; and those who are for raising a nation maintain that this can only be effected by large farms and the outlay of capital. The philanthropist, however, and even the philosopher, will hesitate before he sacrifices everything to the greatness of the nation. . . . And when I see every man cultivating his own field, I cannot but think him happier far than when he is cultivating the field of another; even if he labours more, that labour is still lighter which is his pride and pleasure, than that which is his burden and sorrow."

There is no doubt that at this time, as is perhaps natural,

France and her recent Revolution were more in his thoughts than were the natives of Java and Malacca. He felt that France was in a healthy, hopeful state even though she was undergoing the depression inevitable to an after-war period; that her new political structure provided a "foundation . . . to support a much greater nation than France ever yet was."

By far the high point of the tour, of course, was the visit paid by the party to Holland, where Raffles actually had an interview with the King of the Netherlands. He must have been the prey of many mixed feelings when he first saw the streets of the Dutch towns, so neat, so closely built, so very like the streets of Batavia. All the while, no doubt, the familiar accents of that once alien language were sounding in his ears, bringing back more keenly still the mood of his early days on Java. Needless to say, he did not go about arranging a meeting with the Dutch monarch solely to satisfy his curiosity, nor yet to make a gesture of bravado toward a government which he would never cease privately and secretly to consider as inimical to him, his country, and all their works in the Orient. In the back of his mind there seems without doubt to have been an urge to present to His Majesty the case and claims of his friends the princes of Java. Rumors kept coming from Java bearing disquieting hints of their difficulties under the new-old order. Besides that, Raffles wanted to put in a word or two in favor of the Dutchmen who had helped the British Government on Java by working pacifically side by side with the intruders, in consequence lightening immeasurably the burden of administration as well as making the take-over less painful to the public. He had heard that they were now suffering for this behavior, as alleged "Collaborationists." It must not be supposed for one moment that Sir Stamford visited the royal palace as a representative of the Prince Regent of England. He went purely as a private individual, in the hope that he might be able, simply by force of personality, to banish from the King's mind any prejudice which still lingered there against his former enemies. Who knew better than Raffles how stubbornly those feelings cling to the heart? It was only for the sake of his friends in Java that he was able to bring himself into the King's presence socially like this. Nor does it seem to have occurred to him that he was inconsistent.

It is the pleasant truth that he succeeded, at least to some extent, in this self-imposed mission. The cards were stacked in his favor; the King had heard of him before. Those Dutch authorities who followed him and his councilors in office had already sent home favorable reports on his work during the British occupation of Java, and we have seen how they saw fit to preserve many of the leading reforms which Raffles put into working action during the daily routine of administration. It will not surprise anyone who knows Raffles's character and prejudices, however, to learn that he was not so favorably impressed with the King as the King in his politeness professed to be with his guest. Raffles wrote to Marsden: "I met with very great attention in the Netherlands, and had the honour to dine with the King last Monday; they were very communicative regarding their eastern colonies; but I regret to say that, notwithstanding the King himself, and his leading minister, seem to mean well, they have too great a hankering after profit, and *immediate* profit, for any liberal system to thrive under them. They seem to be miserably poor, and the new government in Java have commenced by the issue of a paper currency from every bureau throughout the Island; formerly, you will recollect, that paper money was confined to Batavia, it is now made general, and will, I fear, soon cause all the remaining silver to disappear."

With that dinner the belated Grand Tour ended, and so in a manner of speaking did Raffles's holiday.

The reason for his exile was gone; his stubborn vigil was over, his record clear. The council had released a public letter on February 13, 1817, which took up Gillespie's charges separately, one by one, and admitted in each case that it had been unjustified. The sale of lands was completely, satisfactorily accepted, along with the one fact which had been considered particularly awkward and suspicious—Raffles's own purchase. Everyone on the council agreed with the findings, and so at last the affair could be considered closed. Raffles alone was still not absolutely satisfied, but he accepted the letter pro tem, and with Sophia on receipt of the news he prepared to set out for Bencoolen.

Thus on their return to England it became necessary to begin all the unpleasant duties connected with travel, of which packing is not the least. His bride now had a sample of what her husband was like in his ordinary workaday mood; his activity, she noted, was "incessant." He set to work collecting animals and plants to take along for experimental purposes and stock breeding. One of his favorite plans was to establish in London, against the far future, a society of natural history, the pattern for which he visualized as that of the Jardin des Plantes in Paris, which had much impressed him. It was too late, this time, to go further toward this goal than promise all his scientific friends to send more and yet more specimens from Sumatra, botanical, zoological, mineral, and of course ethnological. (He had met throughout his entire stay with the most gratifying enthusiasm whenever he produced his traveling companion, the pet tame prince, Javanese Raden Rana Dipura, but it is doubtful whether he promised to send back any more live specimens of the human native. The Raden accompanied him on the return passage.) But we must not lose sight of the society project: Raffles did not, and in the estimation of at least this biographer, the work for which Sir Stamford Raffles ought to be most kindly remembered is the Zoological Society of London, in Regent's Park. He finally succeeded in making real this wonderful vision on his next and last return trip, in 1826. From the beginning it outshone the Jardin des Plantes. Something about the British atmosphere seems to encourage zoological societies.

There were still two duty calls to be paid, one to Cousin Tom's home in Mason Street, Liverpool, and the other to Sophia's native heath in Ireland. A last visit to the Duke of Somerset, another to Sir Hugh Inglis, and the Raffles couple were ready, eager to sail for the East, where Sir Stamford was now, at last, to serve his term as lieutenant governor of Bencoolen on Sumatra.

"Oh! that this leave-taking was at an end," Raffles wrote the Duchess of Somerset shortly before they sailed. Scarcely a soul would not feel warmly sympathetic, or refuse to say "Aye," to that sentiment. "My house is filled with those who are all determined to say good-bye, and make me more miserable when it requires all my fortitude to keep my spirits calm and uniform."

He wrote to the duchess often during the next fortnight, in a sort of journal, a running commentary on the small adventures of getting off. Going through Cornwall, he again visited a tin mine; the sea trip from Plymouth to the port of embarkation for the East—Falmouth, where his party had entered England—proved that poor Lady Raffles was very susceptible to the curse of seasickness; then, just before the Raffleses departed in earnest, he received the sad news of Princess Charlotte's sudden death.

At last they were off. From the other side of the Bay of Biscay, where for once Lady Raffles can scarcely be called delicate for having suffered agonies of *mal de mer*, he wrote in gayer mood. "You will be glad . . . to hear that all the individuals of the ark are well and thriving. The cows, dogs, cats, birds, the latter singing around me, and my nursery of plants thriving beyond all expectation; the thermometer is at 70. What a waste of waters now lies between us and yet the distance daily widens, and will widen still until half the world divides us."

Though the ship, which by the way was a new one—the *Lady Raffles*—made no other port of call and went direct to Bencoolen, she was five months en route, due to unfavorable winds. She arrived at Bencoolen March 20, 1818, by which time her passenger list had been augmented; history repeated itself and Sophia discovered that ladies always take a chance aboard a sailing ship. "The beautiful little girl," as her proud father called her when writing the duchess, was born "to the southward of the Cape," and was immediately given the name of Tunjong Segara, the Lily of the Sea, by the tame Javanese prince. Her English names for obvious reasons were Charlotte Sophia.

CHAPTER XXI

Though Sir Stamford and Lady Raffles had enjoyed a great success at home in London, the post to which they were going was no prize. In fact so striking is the contrast between the treatment afforded Raffles during his leave by his friends in high places and that meted out to him by the Company as soon as he went back to work that anyone ignorant of the true story behind the scenes would be completely mystified. There is no mystery about it, in truth. Any experienced businessman knows that the gap between social and commercial success is a wide one. There was not necessarily much contact between the royal personages who had bestowed their favor so generously on Sir Stamford and the powers in the East India Company who directed his working career. It is quite probable that the leaders of the Bengal Government didn't foresee how eagerly the rejected lieutenant governor of Java would be received by London on his arrival there; it is likely, too, that none of this popularity could be said to have injured him. On the contrary, his stock in the Company went up sharply when the news of all this arrived in Calcutta. But though it was pleasant to have the opinions of his superiors so sharply revised for the better, this improvement was not sufficient completely to change an important fixed appointment like Raffles's to Bencoolen. It had stood too long, ever since Minto first arranged it. Raffles had to be thankful that he need not now take a demotion, which had been the Company's earlier plan for him, going out to Bencoolen as a mere resident. He was permitted to retain the rank of lieutenant governor.

When we survey the field, what first appears to be stubborn opposition and gratuitous cruelty on the part of the Company loses a good deal of its harshness. True, Bencoolen as a post was no plum. In comparison with Java it was an immense comedown. But after the new regime was established there wasn't really very much in hand to offer Raffles. England had given back to Holland all those possessions in the East Indies Archipelago which had belonged to the Netherlands before the Napoleonic wars. This left a very small part of the East Indies in British hands. Nothing that had taken place since Raffles's first arrival in the Orient, when he took up his post in Penang, had been of a nature to stimulate the Company's languid urge toward development and expansion in those islands. India was their particular pet; India and the trade with China was their reason for existing, as they saw it. They did not deny that Raffles had laid the foundation for a highly profitable colony in Java, if only Java had remained British, but she didn't, and according to the records then standing, a good deal of money had been expended on a project which after all was cut short in its prime.

We do not give titles to our chapters in this work, but if we did the title for this section would be "The Dead Land." That was the natives' name for Bencoolen (Malay Bankaulu), a bare strip of land along the edge of the island of Sumatra which had been in the possession of the British since 1685.

At first glance there seemed to Raffles no possible basis for comparison between the two islands, Java and Sumatra. As a scientist he may have been happy when he first saw the land: Boulger thinks he was. Sumatra is a marvelous country for people who like wild, mountainous scenery. The steep range to which it probably owes its existence—for the island is merely a ridge of mountains high enough to keep their heads above the ocean's surface—is volcanic in origin, and

MAP OF THE ISLAND OF SINGAPORE

(From J. Crawfurd's *Embassy to Siam*, 1828)

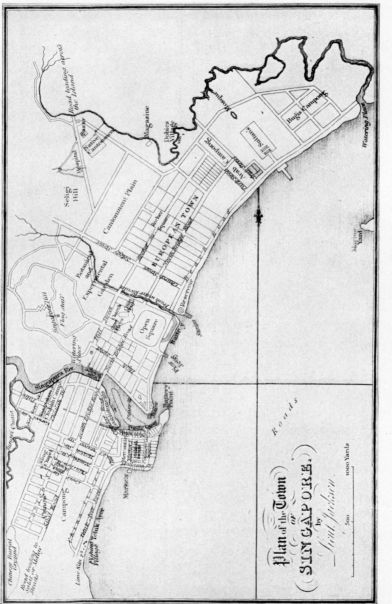

PLAN OF THE TOWN OF SINGAPORE
(From J. Crawfurd's *Embassy to Siam*, 1828)

when the Raffles family, now a trio thanks to little Charlotte Sophia, first set foot on Bencoolen there was plenty of volcanic activity going on, chiefly earthquakes. As near as Raffles could figure it from the native reports, there must have been eighteen volcanoes in the range ready to pop off at any time, and they often did. One put on a show for them the day before the ship dropped anchor. The slopes of the range were covered with thick jungle growth, in which lived wild animals and wild men. Anything less like the peaceful agricultural levels of Java would be hard to imagine.

Raffles the scientist may have exulted in anticipation, but Raffles the family man and career diplomat felt downcast and apprehensive at sight of his new domain. He was not reassured, either, by the inside information he possessed as to the financial difficulties which faced him. One of the reasons Bencoolen was not numbered among John Company's favorite possessions was that she had already cost a tremendous lot for upkeep. In the eighteenth century the station of Fort Marlborough, Bencoolen's leading settlement (founded 1714), had been a place of hope and favor. Just looking at the map, there seems to be no reason why an island of that size, so near the isle of Java, one of the same group and in the same climatic belt, should not be as profitable a place for trade as any part of the enviable and coveted Java. In fact, however, it did not work out well, though the Company lavished a lot of money, men, and material resources on Sumatra before they found that out. The chief product of the settlement was pepper; with this commodity, the directors had believed, and the position of Fort Marlborough, which appeared advantageous for trade, nothing should have stopped their progress toward wealth. In a century and a half they expended a hundred thousand pounds annually on Bencoolen. The directors' enthusiasm ebbed at a rate that was slow as well as maddeningly costly. For a century and a half all they had got out of Bencoolen every year was a few tons of pepper. The Company kept trying, in order not to have it said later that they lost the ship for a hap'orth of tar, but by 1817 they were unanimously agreed that Bencoolen had never been a ship at all, and the tar had cost them immeasurably more than a halfpenny. Bencoolen was one of those things which are found in the possessions of any large established company—an investment which has been so disastrous that it is almost, but not quite, the joke of the firm. Fifteen million pounds is a sum about which it is very difficult indeed to be humorous. Bencoolen was not the joke of the house; she was rather the corn on John Company's toe, or the boil on his neck, whichever is the more painful.

And this was the job which they gave Sir Stamford Raffles, recent toast of London: to whip Bencoolen into shape after years of mistake and mismanagement, and to shift it from the red side of the ledger to the black.

It seemed always Raffles's luck to slip into spots like that, with the one happy exception of Java. To a certain point, however, his luck could not be expected to alter unless his entire field of operations was changed. He was an East Indies expert. To John Company the East Indies was made up of a lot of islands with administrations all greedy for money, where only very occasionally some colony paid off, sufficient for itself but not for its neighbors. Raffles had been sent out to Penang at a time when the Company grudged every penny they had to spend on the place, and justly or unjustly some of that ill will had somehow clung to him personally. Now he was in a similar situation, except that things were even worse for him here in Sumatra. At Penang he had been starting out, a mere assistant secretary. His employers might have been cross with him at times, but he wasn't important enough to be the recipient of their sharpest shafts of ill-humor. At Bencoolen, though, he had grown in stature: he made a magnificent target. He was the number one. Anything that went wrong on British Sumatra under his administration would be traced to his address as sure as God made little apples. It was not a cheerful prospect, any way one looked at it. Sir Stamford needed every bit of the new-found security he had brought with him from the drawing rooms of London; the plaudits of admiring salons still made music in his ears, softening to some extent the sorrowful plaints of the howler monkeys out in the Sumatran jungle. At any rate he was starting out fresh, thirty-six years old, with new health, a devoted wife, a pretty little daughter, and a title. At any rate it was a new adventure. He took heart, and as an exhaust for his feelings sat down and wrote letters. To the Duchess of Somerset he gave a vivid picture of the awkwardnesses that met the family on disembarking.

"My arrival was not hailed by the most auspicious of omens, for the day previous to it, a violent earthquake had nearly destroyed every building in the place, and the first communication which I received from the shore was, that both Government-houses were rendered useless and uninhabitable. . . . It occurred during the night, and by the accounts given, it must have been truly awful. Every building has suffered more or less; some are quite ruins, others hardly deserving repair, the house which I now occupy is rent from top to bottom, there is not a room without a crack of some feet long and several inches wide; the cornices broken and every thing unhinged; from some houses many cart-loads of rubbish have been cleared away, and still they are inhabited, notwithstanding they rock to and fro with every breeze."

Lady Sophia in her capacity as editor does not give her personal reminiscences of that disastrous day so long ago, which is a great pity. It is difficult to imagine just what could have been the reaction of a thirty-year-old lady from Cheltenham, who as far as we know had never been farther from civilization's amenities than a six-week honeymoon tour of the Continent until her husband brought her out to Sumatra. As a foretaste of the sort of life she was thenceforth to lead, Fate had decreed that she bear her first child on board a cramped little sailing vessel instead of solid ground. Then, only a few weeks after that ordeal, she was set down with her newborn child on this strange shore, under the frowning gaze of a jungle-covered mountainside, with no home to move into and no real community to receive her, and only the rubble of an earthquaked town to reassure her. However, there were a few members of her own race living there. Presumably, then, it was possible at least to survive these trials.

"As we are not inclined to make difficulties, or murmur

against Providence," said her husband cheerfully to the duchess, "we shall, I have no doubt, contrive to make ourselves very happy." That's what he said. Sophia seems to have said nothing, anyway not aloud.

"This is without exception," wrote Sir Stamford to Marsden, "the most wretched place I ever beheld. I cannot convey to you an adequate idea of the state of ruin and dilapidation which surrounds me. What with natural impediments, bad government, and the awful visitations of Providence which we have recently experienced in repeated earthquakes, we have scarcely a dwelling in which to lay our heads, or wherewithal to satisfy the cravings of nature. The roads are impassable; the highways in the town overrun with rank grass; the Government House a den of ravenous dogs and polecats. The natives say that Bencoolen is now a *tana mati* (dead land). In truth, I could never have conceived anything half so bad. We will try and make it better; and if I am well supported from home, the west coast may yet be turned to account. You must, however, be prepared for the abolition of slavery; the emancipation of the country people from the forced cultivation of pepper; the discontinuance of the gaming and cock-fighting farms; and a thousand other practises equally disgraceful and repugnant to the British character and Government."

"If I am well supported from home . . ." That was a very big if. They were starting out under more disadvantages than he sketched in this letter, for his most influential friend, Princess Charlotte, was dead, Leopold was washing his hands of anything that smacked of government, including the Indies; and the gaming and cockfighting which Sir Stamford so slyly mentioned were the two most profitable pastimes indulged in by the Sumatran natives—profitable, that is to say, for the Company, which openly owned, operated, and supported most of them as admitted sources of revenue. It was well known, too, that the Company owned slaves in Sumatra. Had they all been the ordinary local natives this awkward fact would not have been so obvious, but there was in Fort Marlborough a group of *African* slaves who had been imported by the Company and were resultantly their special property and responsibility. It was appalling, thought Raffles, so much slavery in a colony which had been British for a hundred and fifty years and had never at any time been Dutch.

Continuing his letter, Sir Stamford outlined his plans for a tour of inspection, which would also be a journey of exploration. "Mr. Holloway seems half afraid, but, *nolens volens,* as he is Resident, he must accompany me."

Then came the familiar note, the inevitable refrain: "I am already at issue with the Dutch Government about their boundaries in the Lampoon country. They insist on packing us up close to Billimbing, on the west coast. I demand an anchorage in Simangka Bay, and lay claim to Simangka itself. . . ."

It was all too obvious even at this distance in space and time, and must have been doubly, trebly obvious then, that Raffles was up to his old tricks of empire building. These border disputes were not aimed merely at enlarging Bencoolen's domains. The new lieutenant governor, his head bloody but unbowed, was still hoping for his great Pacific-British Empire, only now in his dreams he saw Bencoolen as the center instead of Java. Scarcely there long enough to set up temporary housekeeping in a cottage cracked to the foundations, still his brain was working away as fast as ever on the old theme. He was incorrigible.

One of the least familiar aspects of this post to Raffles, who had become accustomed to Java as a typical East Indian community, was that the population was so sparse as to be downright insufficient to keep things going. Java had been just the opposite; Batavia was crowded, and even in the countryside there had always been someone to be found somewhere about, either working or living on someone else's toil. In her Memoir Lady Raffles briefly sketches this state of Sumatran affairs. The Company when first they set about forming their establishment, from which they expected only to get pepper and nothing else, had founded their ideas on India, where the population was thick and the civilization comparatively of a high degree. Bencoolen was very thinly settled; the land was new and needed a lot of preparation agriculturally as well as economically. That in itself shot the expense curve way up, as soon as the pepper production was got under way.

Then they had immediately started off on the wrong foot, using the indirect method to handle the natives, though any method of forced cultivation is bound to be bad. The Company "bound down" the native chiefs to compel their subjects each to cultivate a minimum number of pepper vines, and also insisted upon a monopoly market at which they paid the laborers at a rate far below what the work was worth. It is an ugly pattern which we have seen before—and since. The British themselves were horrified when they found King Leopold of Belgium doing the same thing with rubber in his Congo. Had the agents been men of experience they would have realized that such methods, dangerously similar to those of the Dutch, would not work indefinitely. They wouldn't even work for any reasonable length of time. The cultivators simply would not lift a hand unless they were driven to it, and the chiefs could not or would not keep on driving them, preferring to shift this arduous task to the Company agents who had introduced the stupid method in the first place.

Discouraged and faced with the necessity of retrenchment, the Company in 1801 cut down the establishment and withdrew in force from outlying districts. People were now employed by contract, each of the outlying residencies being farmed to whatever man made the best offer. As an inducement to them to force their labor to greater efforts, these residents were given a small percentage of payment for every quantity unit of pepper delivered to the government. There was also the "free-garden system" in operation around Bencoolen, wherein the natives were advanced a certain amount of money in exchange for their cultivation of pepper. Seventeen years later, when the Raffles regime came in, a little less than two thirds of this had been repaid, worked off in pepper, leaving more than one third unaccounted for. Though many of the debtors had died or run away, their children or their villages were liable for the debt, and the contractors were become "slave debtors," while the children and the village people were practically slaves. Added to this sorry crowd were the two hundred Africans, who according to Lady Raffles were considered indispensable, as they were used for the hardest work of the Company, loading and unloading their ships, et cetera. "No care having been taken of their morals," said Sophia, "many of them were dissolute and depraved, and the children in a state of nature, vice, and wretchedness."

On top of all this the attitude taken hitherto by the British toward the natives had been as bad as if not far worse than that of the Dutch toward their people on Java. Malays, they asserted with sincere belief in what they said, were an indolent, vicious, despicable people by nature, and this sort of treatment was absolutely necessary for their own sakes as well as for the sake of the community in general. No blame attached to the government for maintaining the gaming and cockfighting establishments: the Malays were bound to indulge in such pastimes anyway, and in pandering to their instincts one simply bowed to the inevitable.

Against this argument Sir Stamford, at first, could only oppose his personal philosophy, which today is widely accepted but in those days had still to be proved to a skeptical, ignorant public, that no race is inherently, irrevocably this way or that way. It was always an offense to his neatly logical mind when this kind of fuzzy argument was presented. But in any case he held the cards; he was lieutenant governor, and so, unless he feared the arguments which his assistants presented, he had only to begin putting his reforms into action. It is unnecessary to say that he did not fear the criticism of Bencoolen's old-timers. Raffles was accustomed to the whole routine, from the first appalled expostulation to the last, lingering, hard-to-prove sabotage which slowed up his programs whenever they were unpopular with his colleagues. Sooner or later he usually won them over, by a combination of personal charm and concrete proof that his ideas, wild as they may have looked, usually worked out well in the end.

Here at Fort Marlborough he found a crying necessity, as soon as he started in office, to improve conditions for the civil servants. He described the situation to Marsden in a letter which was written within the first month of his stay. Because earlier in the year their number had been reduced on order of the directors, and because no writers had been appointed for several years, inevitably a good deal of local talent had found its way into the establishment, first as a temporary measure and then little by little as fixtures. As the civilians from England dropped out or died, these local people rose in importance. Then suddenly the Court sent out eight regularly covenanted writers from England, young men who naturally thought they had a good future at Bencoolen and were not aware that they would find such strong competition from these firmly embedded people who had been hired on the spot, unofficially as it were. "At the date of my arrival," said Sir Stamford, "only two of them could be considered as holding offices of any trust, and the salary of one of them only amounted to 150 dollars a month. Some had either quitted the place in disgust, or returned to England, and the remainder were posted as assistants under the other description of servants, with an allowance of 150 dollars per month, a salary which in this place is most certainly not equal to the subsistence of a gentleman.

"If a cure for the evils that have been depicted is to be found, it is not to be sought in the simple provisional reduction of establishment. An inadequate salary given to the Overseer by Government, creates the greater motive to draw his advantage from the people subjected to him. A subsistence, and even a liberal one, he expects, and will obtain, if not by open, certainly by clandestine means. The evil is in the system of management, and a thorough change is indispensable."

As to the condition of the Malays, free and enslaved, as well as another class of native, convicts who had been transported in considerable number since 1797 from Bengal, Raffles wrote a long letter to the Court of Directors, by way of clearing the ground immediately for action. First he said flatly that it was all too common an idea among respectable people at Bencoolen as well as among the ignorant masses that the Malayan character was too despicable to be entrusted with personal freedom. "That indolence and vice prevail among the Malays on this coast, and to a considerable extent, I am not prepared to deny," he said, "but I apprehend they are rather to be attributed to the effects of the system . . . than to any original defect of character."

His own experience in the Archipelago, of twelve years' duration, he claimed, gave him the right to claim some knowledge of the matter and to assert that there was nothing radically wrong with Malays. At Bencoolen they were laboring under oppressions and disabilities, and were surrounded by temptations to vice. About these oppressions, he said, he would not at present speak, because they were connected with the revenues of Bengal, but he felt that he must point out that the gaming and cockfighting were local in nature; that as chief magistrate he asserted that their continuance was destructive of every principle of good government, social order, and the morals of the people.

The forced services and forced deliveries at inadequate rates must be abolished. The laborer would have to be allowed to cultivate pepper or not at pleasure. Radical changes must be made throughout, so that the people could distinguish the political influence of the British Government from the commercial speculations of the Company and their agents. A surprising statement to come from one of the Company agents, was it not? It was a small matter but significant of Raffles's high principles that he should think such a statement perfectly natural, regardless of his own position in the matter. He was discussing good government, and so he felt that he must state the first principles of good government, that was all. "I am aware," he said, "that the task is difficult, if not invidious, but under the confidence placed in me, and having at heart the honour and character of the nation, and of the East India Company, I shall not hesitate to undertake it."

His first public act, he continued, would be the emancipation of the African slaves. When he had done this, and abolished the gaming and cock-fighting farms, he would feel ready to call on the Chiefs to assist him in "the general work of reform, amelioration and improvement."

One other problem calling for immediate consideration was

375 &

that offered by transported convicts. About five hundred of them were alive on the island at that time. Raffles's suggestions were in line with the humanitarian school of thought, closely following Minto's pattern. Fear of punishment, he said, is not as powerful an inducement to good behavior as is hope of reward, and if you make this reward something for which your convict really yearns, you possess a truly strong power. Promise these men the restoration of their citizens' privileges, and they will exert themselves; it is axiomatic. "The prospect of recovering their characters, of freeing themselves from their present disabilities, and the privileges of employing their industry for their own advantage, would become an object of ambition, and supply a stimulus to exertion and good conduct which is at present wanting. . . . While a convict is unmarried and kept to daily labour, very little confidence can be placed in him; and his services are rendered with so much tardiness and dissatisfaction that they are of little or no value; but he no sooner marries and forms a small settlement than he becomes a kind of colonist, and if allowed to follow his inclinations, he seldom feels inclined to return to his native country."

These ideas, worked out with additional detail, were applied with excellent results to Bencoolen's transportees, Lady Raffles declares. A large body of people who had been living "in the lowest state of degradation" thus became useful laborers and happy members of society, she said with pride. In 1825 when Bencoolen, too, was transferred to the Dutch these people were sent to Penang, where they begged to be treated as they had been at Marlborough and not reduced to the status of the other Penang convicts, who were kept "as a gang, to be employed whenever their services might be thought desirable." Very unfortunately for them, the Administration at Penang found the old method too advantageous to relinquish, and they were forced to live again as unpaid laborers, in a gang. Sophia observed shrewdly that the temptation is always strong to keep ready at the disposal of the government a body of men without family ties or position in society.

Raffles's enemies usually retorted to his wife's proud claim that the *statement* of a reform is one thing, but that putting it into working order is quite another, and it was in this active part of the program that Raffles and his theories always fell down. The most determined hostility cannot stamp out all factual evidence, however, and no one has ever been able completely to discredit the work Raffles accomplished on Sumatra. The improvement he brought about was more dramatic and palpable in Bencoolen than on Java, because reform was such a crying necessity in Bencoolen. Dutch Java may not have been perfect, but natural resources protected her. She was never in the sad state of British Sumatra, when Raffles came out to be governor in 1818.

As the first step in his spring cleaning, Sir Stamford called together all the African slaves, and there at a meeting of the important native chiefs, after making an oration about slavery in general, emphasizing the British dislike of it, he set them all free, separately and distinctly. He had prepared "certificates of freedom" which he duly presented, one to each slave. It was an impressive ceremony, says Sophia. One of the Negro children, "a little bright-eyed girl" eight years old, was immediately selected by herself to rear, in order to set an example to the rest of the European community. "She proved a most docile, affectionate little attendant," said her protector. The girl was properly married off, dowry included, about the time the Raffles family went away from Sumatra.

Next the cultivation of pepper was declared free. No longer were the people forced to cultivate it, whether they wanted to or not.

Next was a special matter, closely related to native prejudice. For a long time, but in vain, the chiefs had been asking for a repeal of the dagger law, the prohibition of the kris, it being against the law, according to recent orders, for natives to wear or carry the curved Malay dagger in the city streets. Raffles understood. To a Malay the kris is more than a mere weapon; it carries a special significance which has nothing to do with everyday offense or defense, and the chiefs felt that the Malays' pride was being impugned when they had to obey this prohibition. It had been in force ever since a shocking affair at Fort Marlborough during which one Mr. Parr, a resident, had been

377 ૐ

murdered. The story behind the kris prohibition is so interesting as an example of misunderstanding between races and civilizations that it should be repeated here in all its detail. We have had occasion lately to think a good deal about these same matters, ever since the Japanese attacked the United Nations at Pearl Harbor. The ensuing war was packed with misapprehensions, wild resentments, and bitter allegations of wanton, atrocious cruelty, the results of just such mutual ignorance on the part of the combatants. It is always difficult to bear in mind that one man's pride may not be another's, and that what constitutes an insult, an act of courage, or a compliment in our society may be subject to a very different interpretation by members of a different culture, such as an oriental civilization.

We have already mentioned that the year 1801 was marked by a reduction of the establishment of Fort Marlborough. From that time on Bencoolen ranked as a dependency of Bengal. Before the change, private trade had been carried on openly and without reproach by everyone in the colony, the governor, his council, and the Company servants. The trade flourished to an extent which kept the settlement in very good financial shape. Articles were imported from western India; a few were sold in Bencoolen but the greater part went to Java, where the restrictive policy of the Dutch made such contraband trade very profitable, especially to the Bencoolen traders because they were close by, right in the road, admirably placed to intercept the flow of opium and piece goods from India. But when Mr. Parr arrived in 1801 he changed this happy state of affairs and enforced a "pure" system of administration. The Company servants stopped their trade, and the higher authorities withdrew their support, so that the private trade, which is more commonly known as smuggling, lapsed and dwindled down to nothing. Something had to be done to keep things moving, so Mr. Parr cracked down on the forced cultivation of pepper and added to that a new idea, the forced growing of coffee.

All of this naturally made Parr unpopular with the people. But added to it was another, graver factor. The drive for economy included a reduction of the public establishments, and large numbers of people were resultantly thrown out of work and reduced overnight to poverty. Naturally they associated that calamity, too, with the new governor, and hated him for it. Also Parr was used to British India, where the lower classes were docile and obedient: he behaved in Bencoolen as if he were still in Bengal, which made him all the more detested, if that were possible. Often he by-passed the native chiefs and altered procedure in the courts in an arbitrary fashion which made them fear for their ancient institutions and customs, of which they were extremely jealous. Parr was not aware of this sentiment, nor was he likely to have paid any attention to it had he been. That was not his way.

For a long time the chiefs and the people suffered under his authority. The finishing touch seems to have been Parr's boorish manners. He insulted the chiefs gratuitously, not merely once in a while but as a habit. One cannot say truthfully that it was this particular offense which sealed his doom, for at the rate he was going he was bound to bring trouble upon himself anyway, sooner or later, but there is small doubt that he hastened the end by his bad manners.

The chiefs didn't know much about English custom, but in all probability they would not have allowed such knowledge to change their intentions regarding Parr, even so. Many secret meetings were held, various plans of vengeance were discussed and discarded, and it was at last decided that what they wanted was Parr's head, *tout simple*. That was what you did to your enemy on Sumatra: you collected his head. As proof of how innocently these people went about procuring justice for themselves, according to their uncomplicated philosophy, we should take note of the fact that they carefully warned every other European in town of their plans. The entire native community, as Lady Raffles remarks, was in revolt for several days beforehand, yet Parr knew absolutely nothing about it. He was insulated by his stupid self-sufficiency. Only two anxieties seem to have beset the chiefs: first, to get Parr's head in spite of all difficulty, and second, to avoid harming any other European. The avenging Malays were explicit about this. Everyone of European race was warned to stay home on that evening: even the *date* was announced!

Of course the whites warned Parr, but he wouldn't listen. On the fatal night he refused haughtily to double his sentries and turned down the suggestion that he take some sort of weapon into his bedroom with him. His wife nevertheless carried a hog spear to his room after dinner.

Just before midnight the first blow was struck; someone shrieked, "The Malays have come!" and the fighting was on. The conspirators had probably been lying in wait, concealed in bushes near the house for some time, waiting for lights to go out in the house and for Parr to retire before they attacked. They cut down the guard and entered the house in short order, three of them finding their way to Parr's room and dragging him out of bed. Parr had been ill and was no match for even one healthy man, let alone three, so that the execution would have been swift if Mrs. Parr had not fought valiantly for her husband's life. Patiently the Malays asked her to let them proceed, explaining that they were afraid they might accidentally injure her, but the unreasonable woman persisted in interfering, throwing herself upon Parr's body and generally trying to get herself killed. At last, when she had managed to be slightly wounded in the hands, the men were reluctantly compelled to use force on her. They shoved her under the bed and went about their business. They cut off Parr's head and then, as quietly as possible, without any ill-bred fuss, they went away with it. As far as they were concerned the revolt was over, and everything was quite satisfactory.

The Malays were astonished and aggrieved when the English seemed to resent the affair. At first it all went according to a design they recognized; a reward was offered for the heads of the assassins, and that, the chiefs thought, was intended to be the customary compensation paid for murder. They only wondered why the eccentric English didn't ask them to pay compensation in turn for Parr's murder. They were perfectly willing to stump up, shake hands all round, and thereupon forget the whole business.

Unfortunately for all the wretched Malays in the near

neighborhood, however, they were wrong; they woefully mis-
judged those English. The Company authorities, having talked
it over and decided that it was unsafe to punish the chiefs
directly, went about the business of punishment in a cruel
way. A few lower-born alleged assassins were tied to the mouths
of cannon and blown up, but the matter did not stop there.
"As the danger diminished," says Sophia with ironical truth,
"the spirit of indignation and revenge seems to have increased." Orders went out to destroy every village within a certain radius of the city, and this job was done with shameful
efficiency. The fruit trees surrounding these villages are looked
upon by the Malays as protecting spirits of the place; these
were dug up and destroyed, an act of deliberate sacrilege. The
buffalo were shot or driven away. The houses were burned, and
the homeless people were turned out into the wilderness. By
the time Raffles arrived there had been some recovery, but
none of these little communities ever regained their former
size or prosperity, inconsiderable as these had been at the best
of times.

He revoked the kris law, incidentally.

It is a small matter, but worthy of mention, that Mrs. Parr
and the children of the lieutenant governor, on their way home
after Parr's death, were shipwrecked and drowned off the
Cape.

That was the general situation then; that was the legacy
handed to Sir Stamford Raffles when he arrived to start his
term of office as lieutenant governor of Bencoolen. Businessmen have an expression which they use when they are selling
out their shops or firms. The purchasers are supposed to pay a
certain sum for a mysterious intangible something called "good
will." There seems little doubt that Raffles could not have sold
the good will of the Bencoolen Malays, when he took office
at Fort Marlborough, for a plugged halfpenny.

Unreasonably sensitive people, those Malays.

The life and career of Thomas Stamford Raffles has been
until now the record of a man who advanced himself a long

way in education, fortune, and rank, though in the end his advance in wealth will prove to have lagged far behind the other items. But we haven't yet reached the end. At thirty-six we see him just at the crossroads, though he doesn't know that; a man who has done amazingly well in the summing up but is still heavily burdened with practical trouble and spiritual doubt. His progress has not been exactly steady, Fortune having led him along a most erratic path. But in justice to the goddess it must be remembered that she has never, for one moment, in morass or on mountaintop, relinquished her grasp of his hand.

We pause here that I may make a prophecy, which is one of the smaller indulgences historians permit themselves. They have advance information; they gamble on a sure thing. Nobody else is playing, so it's all right; rather like the solitaire player who cheats himself at patience.

I hereby prophesy that in the pages of this book the irregularity of Raffles's past career will sink into insignificance as his future unfolds itself. The word "irregular" will no longer suffice. The next five or six years spent by Sir Stamford on Sumatra and other points East were crazily complicated and uncomfortably crowded, so crowded, in fact, that for the first time we shall have to split the story into its component parts in order to avoid the worse confusion of chronology. It would be a pity to get mixed up at this point, because it is just at this spot on the map and at this moment in time that Sir Stamford contemplates his post with a sinking heart, fearing his talents will be buried in Sumatra, that the high-water mark has been reached.

The story falls of its own accord into two parts, whereupon the bigger portion promptly subdivides itself again, like an amoeba having a baby. The first part is the story of Sir Stamford governing Sumatra, exploring his domain with Lady Raffles by his side, producing a family of children, adding immeasurably to the world's store of scientific knowledge, clearing up the name of Sumatra and putting her on a firm basis as a proper and equal companion to Java, losing most of his children, bowing his head helplessly under the crushing weight of tragedy. That portion is the private personal history of Sir Stamford, if such a man can be said to have a private history at all, which is questionable. I propose to tell this story first, all the way through to 1828 so that we may have it ready as background for the other part when the time comes.

This divided treatment is necessary, for if we tell it all at once Sir Stamford's life outside his working hours will be smothered and lost. And then, besides, the rest of it is too much of a tale by itself not to stand alone, as it deserves. These five years following Raffles's 1818 arrival in Sumatra contain in their span the climax to his lifelong campaign for victory over the Dutch around the Malay Archipelago. Involved in this story is British foreign policy as it shaped up during the early nineteenth century. Because of Raffles, we see that policy being radically altered. The beginning of the East India Company's inevitable disappearance becomes evident during these years. But the main part of the story is Singapore, the final flowering of all Sir Stamford's efforts, all his life. Time after time he had built his empire and watched it crumble in the dust or melt away in the ocean; time after time he started all over again, like the ant whose anthill is destroyed, or the coral insect when the atoll reaches the surface of the water. He seemed indeed to be possessed of the same spirit as these laborious insects; watching him, one might conclude that he didn't build his empires so much out of conscious stubborn will power as because it was his nature to: he couldn't help himself.

> *The pledge is still the same—for all disastrous pledges,*
>   *All hopes resigned,*
> *My soul still flies above me for the quarry it shall find.*

Singapore was the triumph, the anthill preserved forever as hard rock; the coral island, strong and permanent wall of fragile tiny bones, against which the waves of the ocean batter in vain. Singapore, one more bulwark of the British Empire, fashioned in spite of all the opposition which that empire's own authoritative power could command. Singapore, founded

383

against orders, by trickery, in haste, in secrecy. Singapore, the best thing Great Britain did for herself (or had done for her under protest) in the entire century.

That is the subdivision of the story's second portion: Singapore, how she was founded and how the battle raged around her afterward. But the ant triumphed and the tiny coral survived. Sir Stamford Raffles planted the English flag on the beach and then, having added immeasurable miles and uncounted years to the British Empire's extent in space and time, he went home to die. He was tired.

In the meantime let us follow the private fortunes of the Raffles family on Sumatra, after they were welcomed by the earthquake.

CHAPTER XXII

When enough work had been done to settle in the new government at Bencoolen, with a certain degree of firmness, Sir Stamford's lively curiosity began working on the question of Sumatra's interior. True, the East India Company laid claim only to the strip of land along the coast, almost every square foot of which at one time or another had felt the effects of civilization in its less pleasant aspects. But those were early days, happy days, when a good deal of the earth's surface was still unclaimed by any nation if there seemed to be no direct reason for building fortresses on it or using it for some other sort of defensive structure. Soon enough the nations of the world would become mine-conscious, and then all the jungles and deserts which had been no man's land would be covered with eager, greedy little figures staking out claims over vast areas, just in case some kind of mineral wealth was hidden away underground, however unlikely this might seem. In 1818, though, mining fever and oil hunger hadn't yet encroached on the jungles of Sumatra, and when Sir Stamford Raffles wanted to go exploring, nobody stopped him. The natives were sometimes reluctant to accompany him, because they had been brought up on stories of angry gods living behind the peaks of the distant mountains. Likewise there were white men's legends. The local Europeans warned Raffles dolefully that no one had ever crossed the mountain range extending down the middle of the island, like the bony spine of Sumatra, and come out to tell the tale. Aside from these rather metaphysical hazards there were a number of actual dangers, chiefly from tigers, though wandering bands of elephants are not always harmless either when one meets them in thick underbrush. The Sumatran jungle was thickly populated with dangerous wild beasts, actually more so than the forests of the Congo. But to dare all that kind of thing was in the British tradition and held no terrors for either one of the Raffles couple. Even the inexperienced Sophia welcomed the chance to go out and examine the haunts of the tiger.

We have full accounts of two such expeditions, the first ever made under such circumstances by the Raffleses. For that reason they were recorded by Sir Stamford with exceptional gusto. There are references, also, to later trips in the letters Sophia saved. Probably her husband prepared these long, detailed descriptions especially for his faithful correspondent, the Duchess of Somerset, because on leaving England he had promised to tell her all about the strange people and the landscapes of this, his newest adventure. But reading between the lines one can guess, too, that he loved writing for its own sake. It is hardly accurate to say that literature lost a brilliant writer when Sir Stamford went into politics. Literature gained him as she would never have done otherwise, had Raffles embraced any other vocation. Most likely the only reason he never dabbled in fiction or wrote novels like Disraeli is that he didn't have the time, though there are a few Dutch historians, come to think of it, who would readily declare that Raffles was a fiction writer, an accomplished one at that. Raffles didn't have the time for novels, but after all he scarcely had reason to write fiction, since almost everything he recorded was more exciting than any plot he could have dreamed up.

His first journey inland was a short one, up the mountain of Bencoolen, on a sort of preliminary survey. He traveled quickly through country which he found "in a wretched state, and very thinly peopled," climbed a small range of hills, and chose on the side of the "Hill of Mists" a pleasant location for a country week-end residence, which he immediately started building, taking pleasure in the thought that no European had been there before him. The only inconvenience about the neighborhood, he told the duchess airily, might be found in the preponderance of tigers and elephants: tigers were especially thick thereabouts because the people worshiped them as sacred and believed their grandfathers' souls were contained in the animals' bodies. When a tiger visited a native village the people offered him rice and fruit and hoped he would go away without doing too much harm, but in the past year, said Raffles, as more than a hundred people had been carried off, the appeasement policy could not be said to have worked very well. "I am doing all I can," said Sir Stamford, "to resume the empire of man. . . . I hope we shall be able to reside on the Hill of Mists without danger from their attacks."

Lady Raffles accompanied him on his next trip, a far more ambitious undertaking of three weeks' length. Dr. Arnold, the government scientist, and Mr. Presgrave, resident of Manna, a small community near by, with six native officers and fifty coolies to carry supplies, were included in the party. Reading the description is enough to give one a strong nostalgia for the innocent days of the nineteenth century. We denizens of the twentieth-century world still retain a few of their hopes and admirations; we reach out pathetically for the shreds of that pioneering excitement which was theirs in lavish quantity. Over high cliffs and through thick forests they went; they came across "tracts of elephants" which must have preceded them by only a short time; they visited the alleged site of a village but could find no trace of human dwelling or cultivation, and after walking eight hours they set to work and erected "three or four sheds to sleep in, collecting the materials from the vegetation" around them. They were awakened once during the first night by a party of elephants, and were also annoyed, waking and sleeping, by leeches which got into their boots and dropped on them off the leaves at night.

It was almost with the impossible luck which characterizes the Swiss Family Robinson, that amazing castaway family who managed to find every sort of thing they needed on their desert isle the moment they thought of needing it, that Raffles made his great find on the second day out of this, his first long Sumatran expedition. However, it was evidently merely a matter of getting there first, for the *Rafflesia arnoldi* was certainly not difficult to discover, once you were in its vicinity.

The natives called it the Devil's Betel Box. It is a gigantic red flower, often three feet across from petal tip to petal tip when fully opened, though the bud before bursting open is merely a foot in diameter. I am no botanist, but from the fact that Sir Stamford describes it as a parasite on some other plant, and later says that the chemical composition is "fungous," I presume it is a sort of orchid, or a fungous growth like a mushroom. In the drawing which accompanies his description, reprinted in the Memoir, it looks like a simple flower pattern of five petals, rather like a huge cosmos blossom. The "nectarium," Sir Stamford told the duchess, could have held a gallon and a half of water, and the whole flower weighed fifteen pounds. Inside the cup it was intense purple and dense yellow. The petals were brick-red, with numerous pustular spots of a lighter color. The flower itself was at least half an inch thick anywhere, and of a "firm fleshy consistence," probably similar to that of more ordinary orchids. Soon after expansion, Raffles said, it began to give out a smell of decaying animal matter. The fruit never burst, but the whole plant gradually rotted away, the seeds mixing with the putrid mass. That, too, sounds orchidaceous. No doubt the plant is familiar nowadays to botanists, but it must have been a shock at first sight. Raffles said that there were not many of them even in their native haunts, a conclusion he drew from the fact that quite a few Sumatrans had never seen one, but he was later to contradict that statement, saying that there were lots of them. As for that first specimen, the party didn't have enough alcohol to preserve the whole plant, flower and all, but they managed to save two of the buds and sent them back to England.

"It appears at first in the form of a small round knob, which gradually increases in size. The flower-bud is invested by numerous membranaceous sheaths, which surround it in successive layers and expand as the bud enlarges, until at length they form a cup round its base. These sheaths or bracts are large, round, concave, of a firm, membranaceous consistence, and of a brown colour. The bud before expansion is depressive, round, with five obtuse angles, nearly a foot in diameter, and of a deep dusky red."

The name our party gave their discovery, *Rafflesia arnoldi*, doesn't need explaining. In Sumatra the native name is *Petimun Sikinlili*. Most specimens, they thought, were to be found near the locality of Manna, Mr. Presgrave's residency, but later this belief was corrected. The host plant is scientifically known as the *Cissus Angustifolia of Box*. Though as a rule these discoveries spell news and excitement only to scientists, there is something flashily tremendous about this particular flower which would indubitably have attracted attention even in our blasé age of sensational tabloid journalism. Imagine the color films alone!

"There is nothing more striking in the Malayan forests than the grandeur of the vegetation: the magnitude of the flowers, creepers, and trees, contrasts strikingly with the stunted and, I had almost said pygmy vegetation of England. Compared with our forest-trees, your largest oak is a mere dwarf. Here we have creepers and vines entwining larger trees, and hanging suspended for more than a hundred feet, in girth not less than a man's body, and many much thicker; the trees seldom under a hundred, and generally approaching a hundred and sixty to two hundred feet in height. One tree we measured was, in circumference, nine yards! and this is nothing to one I measured in Java. . . .

". . . The day's journey being most fatiguing, and not less than thirty miles, entirely through a thick forest, and over stupendous mountains . . . Lady Raffles was a perfect heroine."

Dr. Arnold evidently took advantage of this journey to make a sort of preliminary health officer's survey, and vaccinated as many natives as he could persuade to undergo the strange ordeal. The travelers noted that though the natives were reputed to be Mohammedans they seemed to cling to the older faith of their ancestors. "I clearly traced an ancient mythology, and obtained the names of at least twenty gods, several of whom are Hindus. . . . The utmost affection and good-humour seemed to exist among the people of the village; they were as one family, the men walking about holding each other by the hand, and playing tricks with each other like children; they were as fine a race as I ever beheld; in general about six feet high, and proportionably stout, clear and clean skins, and an open ingenuous countenance. . . . Every one seemed anxious for medicine, and they cheerfully agreed to be vaccinated. The small-pox had latterly committed great ravages, and the population of whole villages had fled into the woods to avoid the contagion. . . .

". . . The hardest day's walk I ever experienced. We calculated that we had walked more than thirty miles, and over the worst of roads. . . . The baggage only came up in part, and we were content to sleep in our wet clothes, under the best shade we could find. No wood would burn; there was no moon; it was already dark, and we had no shelter erected. By perseverance, however, I made a tolerable place for Lady Raffles, and, after selecting the smoothest stone I could find in the bed of a river for a pillow, we managed to pass a tolerably comfortable night. . . ."

The impression one gets of Lady Raffles from these lines is exceedingly agreeable, far better, we must admit, than she makes of herself. Sir Stamford's account also shows strikingly how admirable is the British convention of understatement when the topic is courage or fortitude. It is inexpressibly pleasant and novel to read someone who dismisses as nothing the courageous behavior of one of these women, many of whom quietly followed their husbands and dealt as a matter of fact with all the vicissitudes of life among the ragged outposts of Empire, taking it for granted that they should. As an American, I for one have had a surfeit of the literature which is still enjoying a vogue in our country, extolling the peculiar virtues and hardihood of the "Pioneer Woman of America." There is even, I believe, a fund to maintain statues, one for each state on the Santa Fe Trail, depicting one of these pioneer women, complete with flintlock and sunbonnet, pointing with heroic forefinger toward the West. I don't mean to say anything against the pioneer woman; I do think, though, that we have praised her enough for a long time to come. If we must praise some female let's turn our attention elsewhere, though not on the British wife, because she would only be embarrassed and puzzled. It's not that I want to detract from the glory of the American pioneer woman, but did anyone ever pause to ask himself what would have happened to her if she had not accompanied her husband to the frontier but had remained behind, alone in the wilderness?

At this point in her Memoir there occurs one of the few passages in which "the Editor," as Sophia invariably refers to herself, doesn't back out of the picture. In the ordinary way she has an annoying habit of effacing herself in ladylike fashion, no doubt just as her mother brought her up to do. It is annoying for two reasons, one being that Sophia would serve a useful purpose in her narrative by telling us directly, as woman to audience, her impressions of what was going on. It would give verisimilitude to the account, a fresh, nature-colored, eyewitness tone which is woefully lacking in her contribution to the text. Every time she calls herself "Editor" it is a chilling reminder that we are not only poles apart; somehow we are separated by one more than the usual dimensions. There is another cause for our annoyance with the unfortunate, if gallant, Lady Raffles: so exceedingly strained and careful are her exits and retirings that she distracts our attention rather than leaving it unimpaired, which is her charitable intention. One fairly sees her in the act, finger to lip in a warning gesture, voluminous petticoats rustling, floor squeaking as she tiptoes to the draped velvet curtain in the corner and secretes herself behind it. . . . "The Editor"! How many times, I wonder, have I longed to interrupt in the middle of a page and implore the Editor: "Oh, don't leave us, Sophia; draw up a chair and be friendly. Relax, girl, relax!"

I was saying, however, that in this passage for once the Editor does relax and tell us about her life as well as her husband's. Immediately we are stirred to admiration of Sophia. For once in a way she talks simply and pleasantly, like any woman who loves and respects the man she is discussing. Sir Stamford, she tells us, fell in love with Sumatra on this journey to the interior, and, though she does not say it, almost certainly a large part of his happy surprise was due to relief. The strip of land called Bencoolen was dismal, and the inhabitants living there seemed at first acquaintance to be completely wanting in hope, energy, or joy in living. Therefore the unfortunate lieutenant governor was doubly pleased when the natives of the inland forest turned out to be "ready and willing to profit by his influence and advice." "The Editor" adds, "It was Sir Stamford's extreme simplicity of mind and manners that rendered him so peculiarly attractive to them. . . .

"The Editor on reaching Merambung, laid down under the shade of a tree, being much fatigued with walking; the rest of the party dispersed in various directions to make the necessary arrangements and seek for shelter; when a Malay girl approached with great grace of manners, and on being asked if she wanted anything, replied, 'No, but seeing you were quite alone, I thought you might like to have a little bichara (talk) and so I am come to offer you some siri, (betel) and sit beside you.' And no courtier could have discussed trifling general subjects in a better manner or have better refrained from asking questions which were interesting to herself only; her object was to entertain a stranger, which she did with the greatest degree of refinement and politeness."

Sir Stamford offers further evidence of this amiability, speaking of a part of their journey which included a visit to Passumah. ". . . the country I now beheld reminded me so much of scenes in Java, and was in every respect so different to that on the coast, that I could not help expressing myself in raptures. . . . The people, too, seemed a new race, far superior to those on the coast—tall, stout, and ingenuous. They received us most hospitably, and conducted us to the village of Nigri-Cayu, where we slept.

"I should not omit to inform you, that the immediate occasion of my visiting Passumah was to reconcile contending interests which had long distracted the country. For the last ten years these people had been at war with us, or rather we had been at war with them, for we appeared to have been the aggressors throughout. I was assured that my person would be endangered, that the Passumahs were a savage ungovernable race, and that no terms could ever be made with them, and I was not a little gratified to find every thing the reverse of what had been represented to me. I found them reasonable and industrious, an agricultural race more sinned against than sinning. . . .

"During our stay at Tanjung Alem, the Chiefs entered into a treaty, by which they placed themselves under the protection of the British Government, and thus all cause of dispute and misunderstanding was at once set at rest."

Mr. Presgrave, one of the members of this expedition, again made the trip in October of that year, and kept a full journal of his progress which is good reading. He must have been a comfort to Sir Stamford, for he was obviously of the same school of thought regarding the administration of colonies: he bears the unmistakable stamp. Also his observations of the natives are fuller, more detailed, quite as sympathetic in tone, and if I may say so better expressed, than Sir Stamford's random jottings which his wife preserved from the Sumatra expeditions. With a companion of this congenial type, as was also Dr. Joseph Arnold, the medical officer and botanical expert, Raffles was not completely deserted and alone, as he had feared he would be. One's admiration for Presgrave grows with every paragraph of his journal; he was evidently an observant man and, whether or not he was especially trained for it, an excellent ethnologist. About this time, also, Raffles was in close communication with Dr. Horsfield, whose name is still associated with Java and Sumatra. The governor had need of all this stimulation and encouragement, for History was developing a tendency to be truly monotonous, and in the cruelest way, once again she decreed that death should rob him of a valued companion. This time it was Dr. Arnold who fell victim to the dread tropical fever; not as suddenly, it is true, as Leyden had been carried off, but evidently he died of the same complaint. We can only hazard guesses from this distant point in time; one is inclined, perhaps erroneously, to put all these tragedies down to malaria of the cerebral variety because that works most swiftly. Dr. Arnold was first taken ill during the expedition on which Sophia gave such a good account of herself, after a thorough wetting and exposure, and though he seemed to recover from that attack his death followed on a similar one soon after the party arrived back at Bencoolen.

These journeys, in spite of hazards and catastrophes, were so enjoyable to Sir Stamford that in the summing up he may very well have decided that his term on Sumatra was better than the Javanese episode. The luxury of writing Marsden from Menangkabu, for example, was great. Menangkabu is an ancient territory, perhaps the cradle of the Malay race. Before Raffles visited it very few Europeans had been there, though in an indirect manner that land was responsible for the beginning of the East India Company. My authority for this surprising statement is the following passage from Lady Raffles's book:

"Menangkabu had been famed since the earliest periods of history for the riches of its gold mines, its iron ores, and its mineral productions in general. It was from Menangkabu, and principally down the Siak, Sudragiri, and Sunda rivers that the gold which traders found at Malacca in remote periods was carried. It was to the gold of Menangkabu that Malacca owed its designation of the golden Chersonesus, and navigators even distinguish in their charts to this day two mountains in its vicinity, called Mount Ophir, one in Sumatra to the west, the other on the peninsula of Malacca, but nearly in the same degree of latitude with the capital of Menangkabu, that is to say, under the equinoctial line."

There you have it—the golden Chersonese. Sir Stamford, needless to say, fully appreciated what it meant to get there first, and as soon as he reached that significant spot on the map he sat down and wrote Marsden, historian of Sumatra, to announce his arrival, in company with Dr. Horsfield and Lady Raffles. His letter to the duchess a few weeks later is of more interest to the uninitiated public because there he was careful to use plain language. From a combination of facts we may conclude that the journey was not exclusively for the purpose of scientific exploration. Sir Stamford had good political reasons for investigating that area. He wanted to ascertain how far inland the Dutch were claiming influence, and he wished besides to reassure himself that the British were in good standing with the natives. Padang was the important town from that angle but a later chapter is being reserved for the politics of Sumatra. To the duchess, on September tenth, he wrote,

"On my arrival at Padang, I found, that notwithstanding the previous instructions I had given, no arrangements whatever had been made for facilitating the proposed journey into the interior. Here, as in a former instance at Manna, when I proposed proceeding to Pasumah, the chief authority had taken upon himself, on the advice of the good folks of the place, to consider such an excursion as altogether impracticable, and to conclude that on my arrival I should myself be of the same opinion. I had, therefore, to summon the most intelligent European and native inhabitants, and to inform them of my determination. At first all was difficulty and impossibility. Besides physical obstructions, the whole of the interior was represented to be under the sway of Tuanku Pasaman, a religious reformer, who would undoubtedly cut me off without mercy or consideration: but when they found me positive, these difficulties and impossibilities gradually vanished; distances were estimated, and a route projected; letters were immediately sent off to the principal Chiefs of the interior, informing them of my approach, and in three days every thing was ready for the journey."

Dr. Horsfield went on ahead of the main party in order to gain time for botanizing. Two or three days later he sent a letter back to Raffles which, as Sir Stamford says ironically, deserves to be quoted (to the duchess, naturally) as a good example of how to encourage your friends.

"Your servants, Covrington and Siamee, have just arrived at Gedong Beo, with a report that one of the Coolies was carried away by the stream, in attempting to cross the river; we have had continued rain for twenty-four hours, by which the rivers are all greatly swelled. Covrington thinks it impossible that Lady Raffles can pursue the route. As for myself, I came in just before the rain. I must inform you that there are many difficult passages; I should not, however, despair of your progress, as far as relates to yourself, but as for Lady Raffles, I almost doubt whether, in favourable weather, she could come on, as in many places a lady *cannot be carried*; if it rains, doubtless, communication is stopped. The road passes through the bed of a stream, which rapidly swells after rains; and if the rains continue, the natives are positively of opinion, that the progress forwards or backwards is impeded. I do not wish to discourage you in the attempt, but it is my duty to inform you of what your servants have communicated to me, with a request to make it known to you as early as possible.

"The further route towards *Tiga blas* is reckoned worse than that hither by far, and large packages, as a table, etc., cannot be transported."

Just as a finishing touch, it rained all that night the letter arrived. But Lady Raffles was of sterner stuff than Dr. Horsfield thought, and the couple went ahead in the morning, "fully determined to overcome every obstacle," as Raffles wrote the duchess. "The first miracle wrought was to bring the dead to life, in the reappearance of the Coolie, who was reported to have been lost; this poor fellow had truly enough been carried away by the flood, but having had the good sense to lay hold of the branch of a tree which overhung the river, he afterwards regained the rocks."

Raffles's entire letter is full of interest, but we have not the space to reprint more than the highlights, omitting descriptions of a typical Sumatran native dwelling, the primitive agricultural tools they used, and most of the trees and flowers the travelers discovered.

"It was near Simawang (toward the goal) that we first found feltspar, granite, quartz, and other minerals of a primitive formation. They were here mixed with a quantity of volcanic productions in the greatest confusion. . . . Dr. Horsfield got specimens of these, which he gave in charge to some coolies who attended him; after the day's journey he wished to examine this collection; the men produced their baskets full of stones, but on the Doctor's exclaiming they were not what he had given them, and expressing some anger on the occasion, they simply observed, they thought he only wanted stones, and they preferred carrying their baskets empty, so they threw away what he gave them, and filled them up at the end of the day's journey, and they were sure they gave him more than he collected. . . .

". . . our path, which had hitherto been narrow, and sometimes steep and broken, widened, and it was evident we were approaching the vicinity of some place of importance: but alas! little was left for our curiosity but the wreck of what had once been great and populous. The waringen trees, which shaded and added solemnity to the palace, were yet standing in all their majesty. The fruit-trees, and particularly the cocoanut, marked the distant boundaries of this once extensive city; but the rank grass had usurped the halls of the palace, and scarce was the thatch of the peasant to be found; three times has the city been committed to the flames. Well might I say, in the language of the Brata Yudha, 'Sad and melancholy was her waringin tree, like unto the sorrow of a wife whose husband is afar.'

"On our arrival at Suruasa we were conducted to the best dwelling which the place now afforded—to the palace, a small planed house of about thirty feet long, beautifully situated on the banks of the Golden River (*Soongy Amas*). Here we were introduced to the *Tuan Gadis*, or Virgin Queen, who administered the country. We were received with all the satisfaction and kindness that could be expected. It was a scene which made me melancholy, and I will not attempt to describe it.

"The extensive population and high state of cultivation by which we were surrounded, seemed to confirm the opinion I had always formed, and even publicly maintained, as you may see in my History of Java, that the Malayan empire was not of recent origin, and that in its zenith it was of comparative rank, if not the rival and contemporary of the Javan. The Malays have always excited considerable speculation from the circumstance of their being evidently in a retrograde state; but where were we to look for their history? In their literary compositions they seldom go farther back than the introduction of Mohammedanism, except to give an account of Noah's ark, or some romantic tale from which little or nothing can be gathered. It was my good fortune in Java to discover the vestiges of a former high state of literature and the arts, in poems, in the ruins of temples, in sculptured images, in ancient inscriptions. Nothing of this kind was supposed to exist among the Malays; Java was therefore considered as the cradle of the arts and sciences, as far as they had been introduced into the Archipelago. The Malays were even stated to have derived their origin from Java, from the Javan word *Malayu*, meaning a runaway; they were said to be the runaways and outcasts of Java. You may see all this, and much more to the disadvantage of the Malays, stated in the forty-first number of the Edinburgh Review. Your Grace may therefore judge with what interest I now surveyed a country which, at least as far as the eye could reach, equalled Java in scenery and cultivation; and with what real satisfaction I stumbled, by the merest accident, upon nothing less than an inscription in the real Kawi character, engraved on a stone, exactly after the manner of those which have excited so much interest in Java. Immediately opposite the house, or palace, which I have described, was the mosque, a small square building. In front of the mosque, turned up on its edge, and serving as a stepping-stone to this modern place of Mohamedan worship, was this relic of Hindu dominion. I soon traced the characters to be the same as those we had discovered in Java. All hands were immediately collected. In about an hour we succeeded in laying the stone flat on the ground, and the operation of transcribing it was immediately commenced. The evening did not pass without further inquiries. A second inscription in similar characters, was discovered near the site of the former *kudam*, or palace. This was on a stone of irregular figure, and partly buried in the ground. We had only time to transcribe two lines of this. . . .

"In quitting Saruasa we noticed several small tanks, and passed over the site of many an extensive building now no more. The only vestige, however, of any thing like sculpture, beyond the inscriptions already alluded to, was in four cut stones, which evidently had formerly served for the entrance of the city."

At the next town they made even more extensive discoveries—at Pageruyong, from where Sir Stamford sent his happy little letter to Marsden. To the duchess he was more expansive, realizing that he would not later be sending her a full scientific comprehensive account as he would to Marsden. Joyfully he recounted how he had found a Hindu image like those discovered in Java, "evidently the work of similar artists, and the object of a similar worship." Only scholars can appreciate the full depth of excitement which must have been Raffles's and Horsfield's, but one need not be a scholar to understand the thrill of such a discovery. We all feel the pull of ancient civilizations; our popular literature, even the "comics," often deals with like subjects.

At the risk of being banal I refer to Sophia's adventures. It is actually difficult to avoid cliché here—"the natives seemed friendly, so we decided to spend the night," as well as that good old chestnut about "the first white woman ever seen by the simple blacks." But that's the way Sophia wrote it and that's what I've got to repeat. The people of the Tiga-blas country, she said, were struck with amazement by her appearance. The question was not "Who is that?" but "What is that?" She put it down to a combination of two things: her fair complexion and her unfamiliar kind of clothing. At length the natives decided she must be something supernatural, and the idea gained ground rapidly that there was virtue in her touch, so that women crowded around her, holding out their young children and begging her to touch them. This became such a nuisance that a guard was stationed at the door of the hut where Lady Raffles stayed one day while the men were away. There were so many native spectators, however, that they overpowered the guard and crowded in their hundreds into the house, and there they sat down and stared, and stared and stared. They were peaceable enough, but after all . . . Lady Raffles begged them at last to go away so that she could sleep. But they wanted to watch her sleep, too, to see if she did that like an ordinary mortal. There was no way of getting rid of them until the rest of the party came back.

There is a definite note of pride, certainly a natural emotion considering everything, in the few lines the Editor's husband wrote to his friend the duchess after their return from this arduous journey:

"We are going on, I am happy to say, very well; our dear little Charlotte daily improving, and promising to be every thing we could wish. Lady Raffles is quite well, notwithstanding the excessive fatigue of the journeys we have taken; the last occupied fifteen days, and we did not walk less than two hundred and fifty miles over the very worst route, for road there was none,—at first, up the bed of a river, where we had to force our way by leaping from rock to rock; then for some days over hills covered with forest; and the roots of the trees which projected far above the ground, our only foot-path; the ascent sometimes so steep, that Lady Raffles was obliged to be dragged up by two men, often so fatigued she could not raise her foot the length of the step, having to walk some days from day-light, with one hour's rest at mid-day, when the only refreshment to be obtained was a little rice and wine, until eight o'clock at night, before we reached the shed prepared for our night's lodging."

Delicacy has evidently forbidden both Sir Stamford and Mr. Boulger, as well as Lady Raffles herself, to point out that she was pregnant when she embarked on this adventure. She was not in an advanced state, it is true, but at just that time when ladies of good breeding are apt to feel most miserable, especially early in the morning. Nobody has ever remarked on this fact, as far as I can discover. Moreover, this was not the end of the excitements which precluded the birth of little Leopold, but rather the beginning.

I have determined to tell the story of the Raffles family on Sumatra in its entirety, finishing it and then retracing steps and starting again on politics, without trying to sandwich it between chapters of the Singapore saga. For this reason we must be satisfied with the mere mention of Sophia's journeyings in company with her husband, without too much discussion as to why she should thus abandon her little Charlotte in order to visit Calcutta and Penang, at such a time. The truth was simply that she wanted to stay with Raffles, and dared not take the baby. Sir Stamford was madly busy then, and his loving wife did not keep up with him all the way, but after having visited Calcutta with him and afterward gone to Penang, she stopped there. He speaks of this in a letter to Marsden, dated January 16, 1819: "Sophia will remain at Penang, while I visit Acheen." She was within two months of her time on that date. But for some weeks before that he was speaking anxiously of his wife, mentioning her in almost every letter to Marsden which is quoted in the Memoir: "Lady Raffles has accompanied me [to Calcutta, in October]— she is quite well, but finds the climate very different from that of our Eastern Isles. . . ." In November, again from Calcutta: "Lady Raffles is quite well, and unites," et cetera. With the Duchess of Somerset at the same time he is more confidential, as is natural:

"My own health remains much the same as when I left England, and Lady Raffles is, if any thing, better. Do you not pity poor Lady Raffles and think me very hard-hearted to drag her about in her present state, but she will not remain from me, and what can I do? We are now above three months without any news of our dear baby, so that you see we have our minor as well as major separations."

It is from Sir Stamford's letter to someone who was not so constant a correspondent as the duchess that we owe our most definite information on little Leopold's birth. This is a long epistle addressed to Colonel Addenbrooke from Singapore itself on June 11, 1819—Addenbrooke was equerry to the late Princess Charlotte, and Raffles no doubt felt moved to inform the royal family in this manner that he had founded the new colony:

"You may judge of our anxiety to return to Bencoolen, when I tell you that we left our little girl there in August last, and have not since seen her. Lady Raffles, who accompanied me to Bengal, and is now with me, has since presented me with a son. The circumstances preceding his birth were not very propitious. I was obliged to quit her only four days before the event; we were almost amongst strangers, no nurse in whom to confide, no experienced medical aid; for we had expected to reach Bencoolen in time. And yet all went on well; and a finer babe, or one with more promise of intelligence, never was beheld. You will recollect that our little girl was born on the wave, under circumstances not more promising, and yet no mother and no children could have suffered less! What strange and mysterious dispensations of Providence! When I think of Claremont, and all the prospects which were there anticipated—but I must check my pen."

Claremont, remember, was the home of the princess, and no doubt Charlotte and Leopold, like the Raffles couple, had planned to have a large family. Princes and princesses usually do.

On the same day to the Duchess of Somerset he wrote, "Poor Lady Raffles! do you not pity her, to have been so long separated from her little girl, at such an interesting age, and to have been again confined among strangers, and with no one about her in whom she could confide?

"To add to our misfortunes, I was myself compelled to leave her only four days before the event. On my return, however, to Penang, I found her quite well, and one of the most beautiful boys that eyes ever beheld. Both have done well ever since, and all are in doubt which is the most beautiful, Leopold or his sister Charlotte: he is three months old this day."

In a letter written about the same time to an unknown (probably his mother) he said: "Sophia and young Leopold are in high health and spirits: our darling girl is running about and talking, but it is now eight months since we saw her. What an age!"

All these excerpts strike an unreal note to the reader familiar with modern English convention. It must be remembered, however, that the taciturn Englishman who respects reserve, who views with horror anything remotely resembling sentimentality, who likes to profess complete indifference to family affection, is a modern-style figure, the creation of writers and philosophers of only the past thirty years. That is to say he has existed as an Englishman only that long, though similar emotionless personalities have been the ideal of other nations long before England thought up the type. In China, for example, ever since the days of Confucius it has been considered bad form to exhibit much emotion of any sort, whereas the Japanese go even further and refer to their wives and children in the most unflattering terms they can think of.

When he went into transports of joy and admiration over his little ones, Sir Stamford Raffles wasn't outraging convention but was, rather, right in the middle of the swim. Times were different then. We must not forget that he lived in the period of Thackeray and Dickens, when children were supposed to be golden-haired angels of purity, adorable little imps, beautiful infants, rosy-cheeked cherubs. It was to get a lot worse, too, before it got better—though there is no doubt the pendulum has swung as far as it can go, now, in the other direction, and it will not be long before we have another reaction toward the rosy-cheeked school of thought. Before England entered the present tight-lipped phase, where children have become blasted nuisances and little horrors even to their fond parents, and everyone must pretend to hate his children whether or not he actually does—before England reached her present status, she was to live through a painful siege of the Teutonic sentimentality which Victoria's Prince Consort brought into fashion. Compared with the expressions then in use, Raffles's exultations are not too offensive but seem in comparison to be touching, simple, honest, and natural.

It is hardly fair to speak of Thackeray et al in the same breath with him, for Raffles's letters about the children are not literature. They are genuine. Fashion or not, he actually felt that way about his little ones. Few men of his time or of any other period can claim to have enjoyed the company of their offspring as much as did this self-appointed priest of empire. In the aftermath when we add up the sum of his life, when the time comes to evaluate the happiness he gained, quite aside from his success and accomplishments, there is not very much which can be declared on the credit side of the

403 ॐ

scale. His pleasures were limited and his happiness curtailed, but at any rate such as it was, what there was of it, was of a deep, strong, satisfying quality. Those people who have become fond of Raffles may be sure that for a while, at least, in his short life, so full of tragedy, he tasted the best our world can offer.

Writing again to that anonymous recipient, probably his mother, we learn in October that the family is back at Bencoolen, though the group was almost immediately to be broken up again, this time in a manner less pleasant for Raffles and his wife, as there was no room in the ship for her when Sir Stamford was called again to Calcutta.

"Sophia enjoys the best of health, and our two children are of course prodigies. The boy even excels his sister in beauty and expression, and our only anxiety is to take them to England before the climate makes an inroad on their constitution. Till they are six, seven, or eight years old, they may remain with safety; but after that period both mind and body will be injured by a longer residence within the tropics.

"Such portion of my time as is not taken up in public business, is principally devoted to natural history. We are making very extensive collections in all departments; and as Sophia takes her full share in these pursuits, the children will, no doubt, easily imbibe a taste for these amusing and interesting occupations. Charlotte has her lap full of shells, and the boy is usually denominated 'le jeune Aristote.' "

His mention here of natural history has finally decided the writer that this pursuit, a favorite hobby with Raffles, belongs by rights to his private rather than his public life. From the beginning of his career in the East, Sir Stamford seems to have selected as friends those among his colleagues who shared his passion for natural history, which accounts for the preponderance of "doctors" in the list. It was his bad luck to lose Dr. Leyden early in his official life, and a similarly unkind turn of fate took Dr. Joseph Arnold from him at the outset of the Sumatra adventure, practically at the very moment, happy

 404

as it then seemed, when they discovered the giant flower together. It was no mere convenience that had led Sir Stamford and Sophia to an intimate friendship with Arnold: "he formed part of our family, and I regret his loss as that of a sincere friend." Had this been the habit of the Raffleses, the American scientist Dr. Horsfield would have been as readily accepted in the family circle, but he was not. For some reason which Sir Stamford and his wife have not wished to place on record, they evidently did not like Dr. Horsfield. I have no authority to say this; there is nothing definite that I can quote in support of the statement, but there is certainly a feeling in the words, printed and impersonal as they are, which are used whenever Horsfield is mentioned; one feels a strain on Sir Stamford's good nature in these passages. I know nothing else of Dr. Horsfield except, of course, his reputation in the scientific world, and a long letter from him addressed to Lady Raffles after Sir Stamford's death, which praises Raffles without stint. It forms part of the Memoir's Appendix. Perhaps it was merely a matter of unsympathetic personality, but there it is—Horsfield was not accepted and loved by Sir Stamford, but Arnold was, as was the ill-fated young Addison, and the great man Marsden himself. Arnold had been recommended to Raffles by Sir Joseph Banks, who was responsible in England for the new Natural History Society, Sir Stamford's great "Home" enthusiasm. Now it would be necessary to do without him, though it is my personal opinion that Presgrave, the resident at Manna, must have been just another such companion. But as Sophia shared her husband's interests and was more than willing to train the children along the same lines, the cause of Science continued to flourish in the Raffles home and in the lieutenant governor's office.

In fact that latter circumstance was responsible for one more problem in Raffles's public life, so closely connected with his personal tastes that I think any mention of it had better be made here. About this time a botanist named Dr. Jack was hired and set to work for Sumatra; and just when young Leopold was born Raffles received an offer from two Frenchmen, Diard and Duvaucel, who described themselves as comparative anatomists, and who were perhaps of the same type as the men who today specialize in collecting specimens of wild animal life, rare plants, et cetera, in out-of-the-way corners of the earth. Just as they do nowadays, these adventurers preferred to consider themselves scientists rather than hunters, and they were actually connected with the well-known anatomist Cuvier, so they may have been justified. They wanted to hire themselves out to the East India Company in order to explore the forests of Sumatra, and their offer attracted Raffles, so that he actually did sell the idea to his employers and caused the Frenchmen to be hired as collectors for a limited amount of time. At the end of that period something evidently went sour with the arrangement. Whether it was merely the usual caution of the Company's penny pinchers, or the fact that Diard and Duvaucel didn't produce as much as Raffles thought they should, the connection was severed after the first trial period, not quite without rancor. Somehow in the course of events, as usual, Sir Stamford found himself footing the bill for the Company but if we can take the last letter of the Frenchmen's correspondence as gospel, he thought the expense justified and didn't regret it. Perhaps one reason for Raffles's initial enthusiasm was that he had a few months previously stumbled upon a discovery which bade fair to rival his giant flower in interest, and he felt that a man of his many interests could not do these things justice all by himself when they appeared on his horizon.

The discovery was an animal, the tapir. According to a letter he wrote Marsden from Calcutta at the end of 1818 (during the visit which he made in order to present to Hastings his plans for a new settlement, which turned out ultimately to be Singapore) he had first heard of this animal in Penang, when he arrived there as assistant secretary back in 1805. A short time before his arrival, the natives said, under the government of Sir George Leith, who preceded Dundas, there was brought to Penang from Kedah an animal that looked exactly like an elephant except that it was very small. Unfortunately while Leith was away this beast had died and the servants ignorantly threw the corpse into the sea, instead of seeing to its preservation. Raffles remembered the story, and when he visited Malacca (in 1806?) he made inquiries among the natives, the answers to which convinced him that the mysterious animal must be some form of tapir rather than a pygmy elephant. Any scientist will appreciate and sympathize with Raffles's gratification when he proved to himself that his guess was correct, "that the animal exists, not only on the Peninsula, but in Sumatra," as he wrote Marsden. "The head of one obtained in Malacca is now deposited in the Museum of the Asiatic Society at Calcutta; and a living tapir, from Sumatra, is now in the Governor General's park at Barrackpore. . . . It is the most docile animal I ever met with, and is more like the hog than any other animal to which I can compare it."

From Penang, short of a month before Sophia's confinement with Leopold, Sir Stamford in a letter to his duchess draws a sprightly picture of the Raffles household, temporary as it must of necessity have been, with their "dear baby" Charlotte awaiting them in Bencoolen. "Your Grace would, I think, be amused were you to overlook our present occupations. Were it not for the Dutch, I should have little in politics to interest me, and as it is, I should have much leisure if I did not devote my time to natural history, in which we are daily making very important discoveries—the lower part of our house, at this moment, is more like the menagerie at Exeter Change, than the residence of a gentleman. Fish, flesh, and fowl, alike contribute to the collection; and above stairs the rooms are variously ornamented with branches and flowers, rendering them so many arbours. There are no less than five draftsmen constantly employed, and with all our diligence we can hardly keep pace with the new acquisitions which are daily made. I can assure your Grace that while directing these various departments, we often think of the days that are to come, when quietly in Park Lane, or in the country, I may attempt to display to your domestic circle, some of the riches and beauties with which nature has adorned these Islands; but when will that day come? A year has nearly elapsed since we landed on Indian ground: that year has not been spent in idleness; but yet I must look through three or four more still longer years before I think of home; would that they were past too!"

407

CHAPTER XXIII

Of all the many letters written by Raffles from Sumatra, the most original is a long treatise, on the Batta tribe of cannibals, which he sent to the Duchess of Somerset. He wrote it during his convalescence from a serious illness which had confined him to his bed for a month in Calcutta, "forbidden," he says, "to write or even to think." He wrote as he lay on deck within sight of Sumatra, returning home, after weary long months away, in February 1820. The sight of that place which he had once feared and detested, but which now meant all the happiness life held for him, must have had the effect he declared was true. One look and, miraculously, he was almost cured: he insisted on it. His gaiety proved it. Seldom did Raffles ever rise to such heights of drollery—and on such a subject too! He must have been sure of his audience, for his pen traveled on and on, underlining every horrid detail, and all the while he kept assuring the duchess that in spite of their peculiar habits he liked the Battas very much. They were monotheists, he explained; they were warlike and fair and honorable in all their dealings; their country was highly cultivated, and crimes were few. Marsden in the *History of Sumatra* had already talked about the Battas at some length, but Raffles claimed that he had not gone half far enough, describing their cannibalism. In order then to refresh the duchess's memory, and also no doubt to start her off with the proper attitude and make the ducal flesh crawl, Raffles touched briefly on the high places of Marsden's account and repeated the worst of them.

"He seems to consider that it is only in cases of prisoners taken in war, or in extreme cases of adultery, that the practice of man-eating is resorted to, and then that it is only in a fit of revenge. He tells us that, not satisfied with cutting off pieces and eating them raw, instances have been known where some of the people present have run up to the victim, and actually torn the flesh from the bones with their teeth. He also tells us, that one of our Residents found the remains of an English soldier, who had been only half eaten, and afterwards discovered his finger sticking on a fork, laid by, but first taken warm from the fire: but I had rather refer your Grace to the book; and if you have not got it, pray send for it, and read all that is said about the Battas.

"In a small pamphlet, lately addressed to the Court of Directors, respecting the coast, an instance still more horrible than any thing related by Mr. Marsden is introduced; and as this pamphlet was written by a high authority, and the fact is not disputed, there can be no question as to its correctness: it is nearly as follows.

"A few years ago, a man had been found guilty of a very common crime, and was sentenced to be eaten according to the law of the land; this took place close to Tappanooly; the Resident was invited to attend; he declined, but his assistant and a native officer were present. As soon as they reached the spot, they found a large assemblage of people, and the criminal tied to a tree, with his hands extended. The minister of justice, who was himself a Chief of some rank, then came forward with a large knife in his hand, which he brandished as he approached the victim. He was followed by a man carrying a dish, in which was a preparation or condiment, composed of limes, chillies, and salt, called by the Malays *Sambul*. He then called aloud for the injured husband, and demanded what part he chose; he replied the right ear, which was immediately cut off with one stroke, and delivered to the party, who, turning round to the man behind, deliberately dipped it into the Sambul, and devoured it; the rest of the party then fell upon the body, each taking and eating the part most to his liking. After they had cut off a considerable part of the flesh, one man stabbed him to the heart; but this was rather out of compliment to the foreign visitors, as it is by no means the custom to give the *coup de grace*.

"It was with a knowledge of all these facts regarding the Battas that I paid a visit to Tappanooly, with a determination to satisfy my mind most fully in every thing concerning cannibalism. I had previously set on foot extensive enquiries, and so managed matters as to concentrate the information, and to bring the point within a narrow compass. You shall now hear the result; but, before I proceed, I must beg of you to have a little more patience than you had with Mr. Mariner. I recollect that when you came to the story of eating the aunt, you threw the book down. Now I can assure your Grace that I have ten times more to report, and you *must* believe me.

"I have said the Battas are not a bad people, and I still think so, notwithstanding they eat one another, and relish the flesh of a man better than that of an ox or a pig. You must merely consider that I am giving you an account of a novel state of society. The Battas are not savages, for they write and read, and think full as much, and more than those who are brought up at our Lancastrian and National Schools. They have also codes of laws of great antiquity, and it is from a regard for these laws, and a veneration for the institutions of their ancestors, that they eat each other; the law declares that for certain crimes, four in number, the criminals shall be eaten ALIVE. The same law declares also, that in great wars, that is to say, one district with another, it shall be lawful to eat the prisoners, whether taken alive, dead, or in their graves.

"In the four great cases of crimes the criminal is also duly tried and condemned by a competent tribunal. When the evidence is heard sentence is pronounced, when the Chiefs drink a dram each, which last ceremony is equivalent to signing and sealing with us.

"Two or three days then elapse to give time for assembling the people, and in cases of adultery it is not allowed to carry the sentence into effect, unless the relations of the wife appear and partake of the feast. The prisoner is then brought forward on the day appointed, and fixed to a stake with his hands extended. The husband or party injured comes up and takes the first choice, generally the ears; the rest then, according to their rank, take the choice pieces, each helping himself according to his liking. After all have partaken, the chief person goes up and cuts off the head, which he carries home as a trophy. The head is hung up in front of the house, and the brains are carefully preserved in a bottle for purposes of witchcraft, etc. In devouring the flesh, it is sometimes eaten raw, and sometimes grilled, but it must be eaten upon the spot. Limes, salt, and pepper are always in readiness, and they sometimes eat rice with the flesh, but never drink toddy or spirits; many carry bamboos with them, and filling them with blood drink it off. The assembly consists of men alone, as the flesh of man is prohibited to the females: it is said, however, that they get a bit by stealth now and then.

"I am assured, and *really* do believe, that many of the people prefer human flesh to any other, but notwithstanding this *penchant* they never indulge the appetite except on lawful occasions. The palms of the hands, and the soles of the feet, are the delicacies of epicures!

"On expressing my surprise at the continuance of such extraordinary practices, I was informed that formerly it was usual for the people to eat their parents when too old for work. The old people selected the horizontal branch of a tree, and quietly suspended themselves by their hands, while their children and neighbours, forming a circle, danced round them, crying out, 'When the fruit is ripe, then it will fall.' This practice took place during the season of limes, when salt and pepper were plenty, and as soon as the victims became fatigued, and could hold on no longer, they fell down, when all hands cut them up, and made a hearty meal of them. This practice, however, of eating the old people has been abandoned, and thus a step in civilization has been attained, and, therefore, there are hopes of future improvement.

"This state of society you will admit to be very peculiar.

It is calculated, that certainly not less than from sixty to one hundred Battas are thus eaten in a year in times of peace.

"I was going on to tell your Grace much about the treatment of the females and children, but I find that I have already filled several sheets, and that I am called away from the cabin; I will therefore conclude, with entreating you not to think the worse of me for this horrible relation. You know that I am far from wishing to paint any of the Malay race in the worst colours, but yet I must tell the truth. Notwithstanding the practices I have related, it is my determination to take Lady Raffles into the interior, and to spend a month or two in the midst of these Battas. Should any accident occur to us, or should we never be heard of more, you may conclude we have been eaten.

"I am half afraid to send this scrawl, and yet it may amuse you, if it does not, throw it into the fire; and still believe that, though half a cannibal, and living among cannibals, I am not less warm in heart and soul. In the deepest recesses of the forest, and among the most savage of all tribes, my heart still clings to those afar off, and I do believe that even were I present at a Batta feast, I should be thinking of kind friends at Maiden Bradly. What an association! God forgive me, and bless you all.

"I am forming a collection of skulls; some from bodies that have been eaten. Will your Grace allow them room among the curiosities?"

Soon afterward Raffles was restored to his family, and great was the rejoicing thereat. Though we have placed a temporary prohibition on any discussion of politics, it should be permitted to remind ourselves that the date of his arrival—March 1820—is significant. By this time the new colony, Singapore, had been settled, and Sir Stamford felt that his most important life's work was thus accomplished. The passage of more than a century since then has produced nothing to disprove that belief. It is strange to reflect at this time that Raffles was not yet forty years old. Small wonder that some of his biographers have been tempted to overrate the length of time devoted to some of the outstanding incidents of his life. Even the most overwhelming of his adventures were usually compressed into short periods. An ordinary man could not have lived at that rate of speed. At thirty-nine Raffles could look back on a life more packed with excitement and accomplishment than the careers claimed by most septuagenarians. His shade can afford to laugh scornfully at modern commentators when they talk, patronizingly, of the leisurely rate at which our forefathers ambled through their allotted span. With all our planes and non-stop round-the-world voyages and transoceanic telephone calls, we seldom accomplish as much, as quickly, as did young Sir Stamford Raffles more than a hundred years ago.

Even at begetting children he didn't waste any time, once he settled down to it, though admittedly he was late getting started. "Charlotte and Leopold are in high health and spirits," he wrote his mother when he got back to Bencoolen, "and in the course of two or three months, we hope to make up the trio." Considering that his son's first birthday had only just been celebrated and that Charlotte, the first-born, was little more than two years old, that was pretty good going.

Sir Stamford was in earnest when he announced to Sophia that he had accomplished enough to satisfy his large-scale ambitions and could do no more than he had already done for England's interests in the Orient. Only time could prove how right he was in feeling that Singapore was a big thing, and he for one was perfectly happy to leave that job to time. Now the immediate task of Bencoolen's administration would be his only public work, and he intended to enjoy himself in ways which hitherto he had longed for in vain. For two years he had intended to build a country house; now he did it, and Sophia says with fond amusement that he moved out of town and lived in it when one room was barely finished, taking with him "a part of his family," as she put it, and happily planting a garden while the workmen continued to build. There he was able to experiment with spice and coffee growing, aided in his work on the plantation by convicts who settled down and made a community near by which they modeled on one of Minto's favorite patterns. They did well with Raffles as overseer, and were far more contented and useful with this arrangement than they had been before, under the old plan.

Everything for once was exactly as Sir Stamford wanted it. He was leading a regular, healthy existence, with enough experiment and mental stimulation to satisfy him; he felt easy in his mind and heart over Singapore, from where he received only the most encouraging reports; his beloved children were growing more interesting and lovelier every day. Lady Raffles said that in the country he rose at four in the morning and worked in the garden until breakfast, always insisting upon planting the seeds himself; he wrote and studied until dinner and then inspected the plantations, where, accompanied by the children, he walked about, sometimes until very late hours. Among the items in a zoological collection which he forwarded to Sir Joseph Banks in London, described in a letter to his friend Marsden, were a tapir, a rhinoceros, a kijangs (?), and various rare animals of which at that date he was able to supply only the Malayan names. "I have thrown politics far away," he wrote another friend, "and since I must have nothing more to do with men, have taken to the wilder but less sophisticated animals of our woods. Our house is on one side a perfect menagerie, on another a perfect flora; here, a pile of stones; there, a collection of sea-weeds, shells, etc."

He told the Duchess: "Your Grace will, I doubt not, be happy to hear that our prospects, even at Bencoolen, are improving; the place no longer has that gloomy and desolate appearance of which I first complained. Population and industry are increasing; the inland merchants begin to bring down the gold and cassia from the interior, and a stranger would hardly know the place again, so much is it changed from what it was two years ago. We have a good many comforts about us, and shall really regret any political necessity which obliges us to remove from what has now become our second home. We have a delightful garden, and so many living pets, children tame and wild; monkeys, dogs, birds, etc. that we have a perfect *règne animale* within our own walls, to say nothing of the surrounding forests now under contribution. I have one of the most beautiful little men of the woods that can be conceived; he is not much above two feet high, wears a beautiful surtout of fine white woollen, and in his disposition and habits the kindest and most correct creature imaginable; his face is jet black, and his features most expressive; he has not the slightest rudiments of a tail, always walks erect, and would I am sure become a favorite in Park Lane."

Here a fellow ape enthusiast pauses for conjecture. Literally, "Man of the woods" in the Malay language is "orangutan," but orangs are not black-faced, and their children, though like this one they always walk erect, are usually apt to stand more than two feet high. I think this particular little man of the woods is certainly the other tailless Malay anthropoid, a gibbon. Raffles, man of taste that he was, was known to be fond of gibbons, and I cannot imagine any other anthropoid ape that could possibly, under any circumstances, become a favorite in Park Lane. The gibbons have it.

A few months later Raffles announced to the duchess the birth of his third child, a boy, christened Stamford Marsden—Marsden, of course, for Sir Stamford's great good friend, the historian of Sumatra. (For the same reason the baby's nickname was "Marco Polo," Marsden having recently completed and published his translation of that fascinating journal.)

"My dear little Charlotte is, of all creatures, the most angelic I ever beheld. She has those inborn graces which, as she expands, must attract the admiration of every one—but she has a soft heart, and is so full of mildness and gentleness, that I fear she will have many trials to go through in this unfeeling world. Her brother Leopold, however, will take her part, for he has the spirit of a lion, and is absolutely beautiful; but I will not tire you with any more family details. . . . My life is at present rather monotonous, not however unpleasantly so, for I have all the regular and substantial employment of domestic comfort in the bosom of a happy and thriving family; and in the daily pursuits of agriculture and magisterial duty I find abundance to interest and amuse—but I am no longer striding from one side of India to another overleaping mountains, or forming new countries—I am trying to do the best I can with a very old and nearly worn-out one, in which I hope, by infusing a new spirit, and encouraging habits of industry, and motives of enterprise, much may be done. . . . I believe I shall be sorry to change this mode of life. Allow me, therefore, to indulge my whim for a short time longer."

Perhaps, said Sophia, this was one of the happiest periods in her husband's life. One might hazard a guess that the letter just quoted shows the first stirrings of fresh ambition, a sure sign that Sir Stamford was cured and rested. In fact he seemed almost ready to think again about his vow to retire from the greater world of politics. Certainly he was making plans for future activity, but that does not mean Lady Raffles was mistaken in supposing that he was completely happy. Happiness and boredom go hand in hand, and as she herself shrewdly remarked, "The consciousness of being beloved is a delightful, happy feeling." Sir Stamford was wallowing cozily in the warm bath of popularity. For the first time since entering public life he was not in trouble with his superiors; his natives adored him; he was practically God to his family; he was feeling well; and though no doubt he was in debt, because that was a chronic state with him as it seems to be with so many other good people, he must long since have ceased to worry too much about that.

One of his greatest pleasures was to observe how his children were following in his footsteps and concentrating on nature study. "This will not be wondered at, even at their early age," said their mother, "when it is added, that two young tigers and a bear were for some time in the children's apartments, under the charge of their attendant, without being confined in cages, and it was rather a curious scene to see the children, the bear, the tigers, a blue mountain bird, and a favourite cat, all playing together, the parrot's beak being the only object of awe to all the party."

In town Raffles's daily life was not unlike his country program—up early to drive through the villages and inspect the plantations, breakfast at nine with various people working with him, and afterward "he wrote, read, studied natural history, chemistry, and geology, superintended the draftsmen, of whom he had constantly five or six employed in a verandah, and always had his children with him as he went from one pursuit to another, visiting his beautiful and extensive aviary, as well as the extraordinary collection of animals which were always domesticating in the house. At four he dined, and seldom alone, as he considered the settlement but as a family of which he was the head; immediately after dinner all the party drove out, and the evening was spent in reading and music and conversation. He never had any game of amusement in his house. After the party had dispersed, he was fond of walking out with the Editor, and enjoying the delicious coolness of the night land wind, and a moon whose beauty only those who have been in tropical climates can judge of; so clear and penetrating are its rays that many fear them as much as the glare of the sun. Though scarcely a day passed without reptiles of all kinds being brought in, and the cobra de capello in numbers, the Editor never remembers these pleasures being interrupted by any alarm.

"Amidst these numerous sources of enjoyment, however, Sir Stamford never forgot that the scene was too bright to continue unclouded, and often gently warned the Editor not to expect to retain all the blessings God in his bounty had heaped upon them at this time, but to feel that such happiness once enjoyed ought to shed a bright ray over the future, however dark and trying it might become."

Freed of its priggishness, that last paragraph carries the poignancy of truth. It is real. When time stands still for a little and fate allows him to be happy for more than a breathing space, who has not been moved to warn himself and his lover? Who has not said at least once in his life, "This is too good to last"? Because that is what Sir Stamford was saying, though in other words than ours; that is what he tried to say to his beloved, walking late, all silver in the rays of the great bright moon of Sumatra, in the delicious cool of the night wind that blew down on them from the jungle on the mountainside, lifting their hair, refreshing their faces, stirring the heavy sleeping leaves and flowers. It was all too quiet, too fragrant, too contented. It was too good to last.

417 ઠ્રજ્

If we leave out of Raffles's story everything but family affairs, we travel swiftly through the next few months, during which there occurred no important change. His two most faithful correspondents, Marsden and the duchess, were informed in the autumn of 1820 that their friend was not feeling perfectly well, and he had therefore reluctantly determined that the time was coming when the entire Raffles clan, like many other colonials before them, must pull out of the East for good and arrange to live at "home." His reasons for deciding on this course were probably more urgent than he cared to express. An occasional rheumatic twinge, a seasonal fever, would not have been sufficient to frighten an old hand like Stamford Raffles, but he knew it was more serious than these trifles. His general constitutional resilience was failing. It meant more to him now when there was a change in the climate; he confessed it.

After all, he reflected, two or three years more would be enough to realize his dearest wishes, to see his Singapore firmly established and to feel satisfied that things were going well enough in Sumatra to leave them under some other man's guidance. Then, he said, he could carry on at home, of course keeping an eye on the fountainhead of government and the head office of John Company, for not even when planning to retire could Raffles contemplate *complete* inaction. "My great object, the independence of the Eastern Islands," he said comfortably, "has been attained. Lady Raffles and my dear children continue to enjoy excellent health. Leopold is the wonder of all who see him. Charlotte speaks English very distinctly, and finds no difficulty in Malay and Hindostanee, and it is curious to observe how she selects her language to the different natives. To us or her nurse she always speaks English; to a Malay she is fluent in his language, and in an instant begins Hindostanee to a Bengaleeh: if she is sent with a message, she translates it at once into the language of the servant she meets with. She is only two years and a half old; such is the tact of children for acquiring languages. She always dines with us when we are alone, and the cloth is no sooner removed, than in bounces Master Leopold, singing and laughing, and occupying his place. Mr. Silvio, the Siamang"—aha! then it was a gibbon, and my judgment is upheld—"is then introduced, and I am often accused of paying more attention to the monkey than the children. This last gentleman is so great a favourite, and in such high spirits, that I hope to take him to England with the family, and introduce him to my little friend Anna Maria."

Throughout the year his letters from time to time mentioned various relations and in-laws. Two of Sophia's brothers dropped in sometimes to stay at Bencoolen, and one of the Raffles sisters, probably Mary Anne Flint, made an extended visit about the same time, accompanied by a little daughter. Nothing is more eloquent of the improvement in conditions brought about by the new governor of Sumatra than this series of informal, comfortable, pleasantly long visits with the family, which would have been impossible at the beginning of their term, only two years previous. Yet it was the fate of one guest to die at Bencoolen, and his death seemed to set off a veritable avalanche of catastrophe. Scarcely three weeks had elapsed after he sent the duchess this cheerful letter when Sir Stamford wrote to inform a close friend in England that one of Sophia's brothers, Robert Hull, an army officer stationed in the East, had died suddenly in their house, the fatal complaint aggravated by the hardships of a campaign in which he had recently taken part. And though it can hardly rank as a family tragedy, the death of Sir Joseph Banks, when news of it reached Sumatra half a year later, was far worse news for Sir Stamford Raffles than the loss of any brother-in-law, however amiable.

The loss of such a good friend in London was all the more of a blow because Raffles and his wife had been making their plans afresh for retirement—"if not in 1823, certainly in 1824," he told the duchess. ". . . a truce to politics: I have other reasons to urge me home. Neither my health nor that of Lady Raffles is very good; I never was strong, and during my first residence in India, the climate made a considerable inroad on my constitution. I have had two or three severe attacks since my return, and am now under the necessity of being very careful. I really do not think I could last out above two or three years more [i.e., in the Indies]; and certainly ambition shall not weigh with me one moment against life. Besides this, my dear little rogues will be rapidly expanding. Charlotte is already as advanced as most children of five years old: she takes an interest in every thing that is going forward, and is really becoming quite a companion. In two or three years both her mind and body will require a colder climate, and to send her home for her education, as people usually send their children from this country, is out of the question; we have determined to take her and all the children (for we have now four born in as many years) and to time our departure with reference to their health and happiness." The fourth child, by the way, actually appeared without fanfare—a girl baby named Ella. Even Sir Stamford's paternal raptures were capable of modification after too much repetition. Granting that one can't have too much of a good thing, he was an artist at heart, and as an artist he knew it was time to play down a theme when it occurred once too often. The Raffleses were beginning to wonder whether this were not as good a place as any to stop. "Leopold also will, in two or three years, have grown beyond my management, and it will be time to commence upon the rudiments of a better education than I can give him. I believe people generally think I shall remain longer, as they hardly suppose in such times, and with an increasing family, a man will be inclined to forego the advantages of the field before me, but they know me not. I have seen enough of power and wealth to know that, however agreeable to the propensities of our nature, there is more real happiness in domestic quiet and repose, when blessed with a competence, than in all the fancied enjoyments of the great and the rich."

In the Memoir letters there is only one more mention made of the children before the first blow fell. Writing to Marsden on July twelfth, Raffles announced little Ella's birth and assured his friend that his godson, Marco Polo, was now running about. Almost immediately after that cheerful word was dispatched Sir Stamford's pride and joy, his eldest son, Leopold, fell ill and in the space of a few hours had died.

The feelings of his father are left to our imagination. Beyond a few hurried words now and then which usually ended with the excuse that the writer must close the letter and hurry back to Sophia, Sir Stamford was unable for some months to write at all. Suffering themselves from dysentery, a complaint which was aggravated by this emotional shock, both Raffles and his wife were ill for a long time. Out of the darkness and pain of those days the mother, years afterward, recalled only one special incident, which remained so clearly in her mind, no doubt, because it marked her first change for the better and brought to her a small abatement of agony.

In the early stages, she says, overcome with grief for the loss of this favorite child, unable to bear the sight of her other children, nor even to look on the light of day, as she lay miserable and motionless on her bed, there came to her room a scrubwoman who worked in the nursery, a "poor, ignorant, uninstructed native woman of the lowest class," who took it on herself to give Lady Raffles a good scolding.

"I am come," said the scrubwoman, "because you have been here many days shut up in a dark room, and no one dares to come near you. Are you not ashamed to grieve in this manner, when you ought to be thanking God for having given you the most beautiful child that ever was seen? Were you not the envy of every body? Did any one ever see him, or speak of him, without admiring him; and instead of letting this child continue in this world till he should be worn out with trouble and sorrow, has not God taken him to heaven in all his beauty? What would you have more? for shame, leave off weeping and let me open a window."

Strange are the ways of the heart. Hearing that flood of reproach, Sophia did indeed feel shame. A ghost of her old courage came back to her, and she struggled to her feet, and opened a window, and also her bedroom door, and set out to find her husband.

Nevertheless it was four months before either Raffles or his wife could take up their duties in a normal manner. Sir Stamford confided in Marsden that they were convinced they must think seriously of going home soon, and that he was worrying about a successor to fill his place. In franker vein, he unburdened himself to his good friend the duchess in what is in my opinion one of the most pathetic letters ever written.

"My heart has been nigh broken, and my spirit is gone: I have lost almost all that I prided myself upon in this world, and the affliction came upon us at a moment when we least expected such a calamity. Had this dear boy been such as we usually meet with in this world, time would ere this have reconciled us to the loss—but such a child! Had you but seen him and known him you must have doated—his beauty and intelligence were so far above those of other children of the same age, that he shone among them as a sun, enlivening every thing around him. I had vainly formed such notions of future happiness when he should have become a man, and be all his father wished him, that I find nothing left but what is stale, flat, and unprofitable. My remaining children are, I thank God, rather superior to the ordinary run, and Charlotte is every thing we could wish her. How is it that I feel less interest in them than in the one that is gone?—perhaps it is in our nature.

"But I must leave this subject or you will have cause to regret my correspondence. You will be sorry to hear that Lady Raffles and myself have been seriously ill, and that I am still so far complaining that I hardly know whether I shall live or die. At one time I am sorry to say I cared but little which way my fate turned; but I now begin to think of the necessity of exertion for those about me, and sometimes venture to look forward; but I am too low and wretched to write much more even if my paper allowed."

He confessed to another friend that he was maintaining "but a crazy kind of existence." Since he was being doctored with mercury at the time of writing (a favorite treatment in those days for dysentery), he was probably in an abnormal mood practically all the time, and spoke truer than he knew when he used the word "crazy," mercury being a cumulative poison, extremely depressing to the spirits. Even with the small scraps of evidence at our disposal and after all these years, it is possible to notice how changed Raffles's personality became for the months following Leopold's death. He could not absorb himself in anything, even those administrative matters which had always been closer to him, one would have said, than any emotional interest. He could not make up his mind to any course of action and follow it through. He thought they must go away somewhere, but where? Singapore? But would not Bencoolen be just as good for them, perhaps better? But then they were calling out for him in Singapore, and a change was what he and Sophia stood in need of more than anything else. When, then? Immediately? He shrank from all the effort such a move would involve. Colonials were used to thinking in terms of years, as we think in weeks, and when at last he resolved to move the family outright in two years' time, no one considered him dilatory. On the contrary, everyone realized that such a program would be rushing matters, and when he had thought it over for a month, and had achieved a more normal mental state, he relented a little from his first hasty decision and said again that it might be 1824 before they could be ready to return home, and 1823 before he paid a last visit to Singapore. At that time he was beginning to sound more like his old self generally and was making plans and interesting himself in his work when suddenly Fate, hovering over Bencoolen like a bird of prey, swooped down and struck again. This time the victim was Charlotte.

She did not die as her brother Leopold did. The first attack was "a violent dysentery," and Sir Stamford was evidently without hope of her survival as early as three days after the onslaught, for he declared that their only chance was to effect "a salivation with mercury," whatever that may be. It was, he said gravely, a matter for question whether they, the parents, could support a loss like that so soon after Leopold's death. The younger two children were also ill, but they were getting better though Charlotte at first was not, and the parents, now frantic, were half resolved to send them away by the very first ship going direct to England.

"What a sad reverse is this! but the other day we were

alarmed lest we should have too many, now all our anxiety is to preserve some even of those we have."

A week later, however, he was reassured to the point of writing of their alarm to the duchess—"I cannot yet reflect on the event with any degree of calmness"—and reporting that the little girl was for the time being, at least, out of danger. But he wisely did not trust too much in this improvement. As anyone familiar with the tropical form of dysentery knows too well, it can hang on indefinitely and strike when it is least expected. Considering everything, the Raffleses were still determined on sending all the children to England without losing more time. "If our dear Charlotte lives to embark," he said, "I shall write you more particularly, if not I shall want spirits to address you, My own health still continues most seriously affected. I am seldom well for twelve hours, and always laid up for several days in the month. . . . I cannot leave my post without previous notice, and completing some arrangements which are in progress. . . . Lady Raffles is almost exhausted with continual watching, night and day."

Cruelly, the bird of prey waited to strike. A fortnight later Sir Stamford, still watchful, was nevertheless feeling reassured enough to report that Charlotte was still improving, if slowly, and that all was arranged to send the children home in the *Borneo*, about the first of March (two months later). He was busy and occupied with outside affairs again. Though he dared not say so, one can see that a weight was off his mind, and that was the moment for which Fate was waiting.

There is no word at all from Sir Stamford until the middle of January, a fortnight later. This time the dysentery had done its worst. Little Marco Polo had been buried ten days before, and Charlotte was carried to the grave that morning. Neither father nor mother, evidently, had enough strength even to express their feelings. It was all Raffles could do to record the facts and to say that they were sending the baby Ella, who was all they had left, by the same ship in which he had arranged accommodations for the other children. She was, he said, apparently well, and would be in the care of their Nurse Grimes. (Ella survived the voyage to England. She was alive and flourishing until her father's death, at least, but she died at the age of eighteen without issue.)

With cold determination Sir Stamford was looking into the matter of getting out of the East as soon as possible. It would first be necessary, he had discovered, to get permission to leave from the Court of Directors in Calcutta, under the signatures of at least thirteen of them. This meant that few of his plans could be changed. He would still have ample time to visit Singapore before turning homeward; in any case it would be nearly 1824 before that final journey could be attempted. But it was a mechanical gesture, one feels, made by a man who for the moment was in a completely anesthetized state, when he said toward the end of the letter, "Yet, severe as the dispensation is, we are resigned to it; we have still reason to thank God."

For what? one asks oneself. Sophia had not died, it is true: the indomitable woman actually gave birth to another child before they quitted the East, but it did not live, and no wonder.

Sir Stamford now found that it was his turn to be ill, this time of what they called brain fever instead of his customary dysentery. For ten days he was confined to a dark room. The fever "drove me almost to madness. I thank God, however, that I have now got over it, and am on my legs again, but I am still weak, and unable to converse with strangers."

Yet in the same letter, after touching on the magic subject of Singapore, his spirit revived to such an extent that he was able to write several animated pages about Siam and the current confused situation at Penang. He was like that hero of mythology who was on the point of collapse during a great battle with a giant until he fell down and touched his Mother Earth, when, immediately refreshed, he leaped to his feet and had at the giant with new vigor. The letter closed on a note which could scarcely be called cheerful, but neither was it heartbroken. There is only one adjective which can always be applied to Raffles, in sickness or in health, in happiness or tragedy. He sounded—busy.

425 ઠ്ᴄ

CHAPTER XXIV

As we draw near to the climax of Raffles's life and work it becomes increasingly evident that we hold in our hands that rare article among historical anecdotes, the perfect example. For historians the trouble with real life—and this applies to the life of a nation quite as well as to that of an individual—is that one can detect trends, but it is difficult to find conclusions: one can formulate opinions or hypotheses, but the wise writer avoids cut-and-dried formulas. There are few finalities in history; there is always a loophole for your adversary in an argument. That is why the game, It might have been if . . . or, It would not have been, if only . . . is perforce the historian's favorite pastime, rather than something scientific and exact, like chess. Therefore it is a satisfaction to contemplate Singapore and her history. Raffles was scientific and exact about Singapore, and for once it worked out. Raffles succeeded, by employing almost every trick which statesmen are not supposed to play, in planting the British flag on her beach, and, furthermore, in planting it deep enough to take root. He knew it was the time and the place for empire building. He said that he must plant that flag in one place or another before many more moons had waned, but his superiors disagreed with him. Nevertheless by dint of stubborn argument he managed to get the halfhearted acquiescence of one superior, and before it could be withdrawn he was off on his self-

426

appointed errand. He said that Singapore was the right spot, but they were inclined to dispute that point too. Against the will of practically everyone who had ever got into the habit of saying no to Raffles, and their name was legion, he founded Singapore. The Singapore affair tells in little the entire story of Raffles versus England in large.

Throughout this work I have said that the British Empire was not constructed in the manner we have been led to believe. The average American, if indeed the average American has learned to think of Great Britain at all as a body of men called government rather than a giantess in draperies, which I doubt —the American thinks of the British Empire adorning England as you think of your next-door neighbor's blondined hair, something she resolved to possess and thereupon went out and determinedly procured. In fact we need not become fanciful: a metaphor is not needed when we have the original pattern close at hand and can use a copy instead of a comparison. We have been brought up to think that England collected her empire as Mussolini collected his, and Hitler his, by cold-blooded planning and efficient execution. But, as I have pointed out once or twice before now, it wasn't done that way; England didn't wax fat by means of committee meetings and secret resolutions and careful campaigning. The average Englishman wants peace, even with poverty. There have always been one or two Englishmen who would like such a program as Raffles suggested, and there have always, too, been a few, built on his adventurous pattern, defiantly grabbing land for their country in spite of orders to the contrary; but except when there were more citizens than usual of that ilk, who got together and combined weights and pressed their point home, they failed. They failed because they played their hands alone: all but Raffles, who was alone and didn't fail. That is why he is extraordinary even among his extraordinary race.

I said in an earlier chapter that England, nation of shopkeepers, has always been willing and eager to send out her commercial travelers as long as their territory could be maintained without too much expense and bloodshed. But Walpole's good Englishmen do not often carry the day, despite his bitter protests that they do, and under the Regent's rule, during the time when England was expanding to the limits of what Disraeli was to hail as Victoria's empire, those good Englishmen were not easy to find. You could seek them through the Court of Directors in Bengal in vain. I grant that the Englishmen of the period were not virtuous and peace-loving for peace's own sake: rather, they were burned children. The fact was, they were tired of war, with Boney safely locked up on St. Helena, and as shopkeepers they were even more tired of throwing good money after bad, in the waters of the Pacific. The money question made them tired and sanctimonious. Greed and land hunger horrified them: it was also expensive. It boiled down to a difference in judgments, Raffles's against the Court's. He knew that it would ultimately be a good thing to own a piece of the East Indies, but they simply didn't believe him. They pointed to the long years of Company bookkeeping out East and reminded him that the columns were always written in red. They refused to look forward and hope for any different sort of bookkeeping; they didn't have Raffles's faith.

That is the skeleton of the situation. The rest of it, Minto's humanitarian ideals, Raffles's hatred of slavery, British versus Dutch methods of governing Malays, scientific exploration and its contribution to world knowledge, patriotic fervor in the hearts of Dutchmen and Britons, that is all trimming. At bottom the question was then as it is now: trade in the wide blue yonder. We could settle today's problems neatly and with dispatch if only we would all remember that. Yesterday's historians did not see any more clearly, however, than do today's statesmen.

Now seems to be a propitious moment in our story to regard with a critically comparative eye the works of two historians who concentrated on Raffles: the Dutch Van der Kemp and the British Demetrius Boulger. We have traveled a long way with Boulger, not so much because I admire him so madly as that he has written the most complete Raffles biography to date. We have also gone more than once with Van der Kemp, in part because he speaks for the other side and makes a nice change for us, but chiefly because he presents an exhaustive amount of source material. He has peered into every little nook and cranny he could find, looking for the Raffles story. One is staggered by the amount of work he has done and the intensity of the searchlight he trains on this object of his angry indignation. One is also grateful, at this late date, for the original material he offers. Furthermore, one is inclined, perhaps, to agree with him in his estimate of Boulger's faults. Not his estimate of Raffles, decidedly not. Mr. van der Kemp is too bitter and warped and far too chronically angry for even a neutral reader to trust him or agree with him, and I am not neutral; I am inclined to be prejudiced in Raffles's favor. Nevertheless I read Mr. van der Kemp with avidity. The fact that he is himself guilty of the crime which he abhors in Mr. Boulger does not cancel out Mr. Boulger's crime.

With commendable vigor Van der Kemp wrote a long article, "The Singapore Paper War [*De Singapoorsche Papieroorlog*]" from a phrase used by Raffles after the occupation of Singapore, in a letter to C. Assey: "Mynheer will probably enter into a paper war on the subject." The Dutch historian's sole intention was to oppose Boulger's views in his just-published *Life of Sir Stamford Raffles*. Van der Kemp sums up his views as follows: "The attitude of the governments in this dispute can be defined in a few plain words. Whilst the English authorities in India took drastic and active measures, the Netherlanders did nothing save write protests. How uncertain the English superior authorities were over the rightfulness of their claim to Singapore, and how much they themselves expected that they would have to climb down in face of the reasonable claims and justifiable complaints of the Netherlanders, is clear enough from this fact, *viz*.—that the definitive treaty by which the Sultan of Johore formally ceded Singapore to the English Company, was first signed on the second of August, 1824, and ratified by the Governor-General on the ninth of November, 1824, and this *only after the Netherlands Government had already formally renounced all objections to the occupation of Singapore by the Treaty of London*."

Another of his articles, "Raffles's Occupation of the Lampongs in 1818," is devoted to the same cause. Sometimes one wonders which man has most power to enrage Kemp: Raffles, the originator of the dastardly deeds, or Boulger, his adoring biographer. Certainly between them they make the unfortunate Netherlander gibber with fury. He is far from being all wind, though, and is even capable, at times, of being scrupulously fair, which, considering his obsession, is saying a good deal and places him high in the list of historians, most of whom in that era did not observe the ethics which are supposed to obtain today. His prejudice frequently carries him to ridiculous lengths, as for example in the Lampongs piece, on page 27, where, commenting on Raffles's letters of June 7, 1817, he says that they "bear the aggravating, unpleasant character with which his lying arguments are always characterized." Yet quite soon afterward, on pages 56 and 57, we find that he has quoted an amusing letter written him by a Dutch merchant at Batavia on September 21, 1898, apropos of his "Singapore Paper War," pointing out that in the long run, and even from the Dutch point of view, it was a good thing that Raffles got away with Singapore and that "one must be very ignorant of the details concerning the commerce and commercial policy prevailing in the Netherlands at that time, if one imagines for an instant that Singapore in Dutch hands would ever have attained even a part of the development which it has since achieved in such an astonishingly short space of time. It irks me as a good Hollander to have to admit it, but it would have been an obstruction to world trade if Singapore had belonged to the Netherlands Indies. It would never have been made a free port (I am naturally not *au fait* with the Archives, but even if you should be able to show me therein a declaration by King William I, or by one of his Ministers, to the effect that their object was to treat Singapore in the same manner as the English have done, then I would be so bold as to attach no concrete worth to a declaration like this made *post factum* but remain convinced that nothing would have come of it once the English had withdrawn). But I will go yet further, and state that in the event that we had kept Singapore, one of two things would have happened,—either another Singapore would have arisen close by under the English flag, or if no fit place could have been found, we, as the weakest against an antagonist who virtually regards his own interests alone, would have been obliged after a more or less honourable disputation —perhaps after an unfortunate war—to have surrendered Singapore to England. . . . In the light of world history, I can regard the occupation of Singapore by the English as indifferently as the occupation of Hanover, Nassau etc. by Prussia."

The Singapore affair began long before the date of the colony's founding. Strictly speaking, the story began when Raffles learned finally and definitely about the Treaty of Vienna, whereby Java and her dependencies reverted to their former owner, the Netherlands. The blow was none the weaker for having been expected. However, Raffles's busy intellect was at work looking for other ways and means of building his empire, long before he stopped bewailing Britain's loss. The map of the East Indies was always in his mind. During the last year of his governorship in Java, even in the midst of the battle with Gillespie, which he had to fight by proxy in Calcutta, he was always studying that mental map, wondering where next to take the flag of England. At home on leave, in all the excitement of his visit, while he got ready his *History* for publication and wrestled with recalcitrant directors of the Company and paid court to Miss Hull and looked over the land on the Continent, all that time his mind was on the Dutch East Indies, wondering where to find some little corner that was not yet too irrevocably Dutch for his purposes.

Back at work with his new knighthood, Raffles had not been long in his post on Sumatra before the Dutch appeared again on the horizon, and the diplomatic pouch for Calcutta was heavy with his warnings and complaints. The Court was in no position to object to this, exactly, for they had given the new lieutenant governor at Fort Marlborough certain definite instructions, reminiscent of Minto's before the conquest of Java:

"It is highly desirable that the Court of Directors should receive early and constant information of the proceedings of the Dutch and other European nations, as well as of the Americans, in the Eastern Archipelago. The Court, therefore, desire that you will direct your attention to the object of regularly obtaining such information, and that you will transmit the same to them by every convenient opportunity, accompanied by such observations as may occur to you, whether of a political or commercial nature. You will furnish the Supreme Government with copies of these communications. In the event of any such communications appearing to you to be of a nature to require secrecy, you will address your letter to the Secret Committee."

All of this, naturally, was perfectly agreeable to Sir Stamford Raffles. It is no coincidence that he began viewing the neighboring Dutch and their activities with alarm ten minutes after first setting foot on Bencoolen. He would have felt himself in honor bound to do so at any rate, after writing the paper he did before he left England, "Our Interests in the Eastern Archipelago," and forwarding it for study to George Canning, later Prime Minister, but the president of the board of control in Liverpool's cabinet. In this article, which is too long to reprint, he hammered on the now familiar theme of the Dutch and the threat constituted by their ambition to monopolize the oriental trade lanes. It was undeniably true, and nobody tried to argue the point, that the Dutch did hold all the advantages in that area; they held the gateways to Sunda Strait as well as the Strait of Malacca, whereas the British lacked not only their own ground anywhere between the Cape and China, but could not put in at any friendly port for water and supplies in all that distance. The differences of opinion held by Raffles and his superiors were based not on fact but on another less easily defined question. The Court was inclined to yawn and ask languidly, "Who cares about that?" Fortunately for Raffles, however, there were a few men who were not so indifferent, more of them when he left England than when he had arrived, and that was not coincidence.

The additional complaint which he felt justified in making after he arrived in Sumatra was that those Dutch, not content with holding all the good cards as they already did, were now hard at work consolidating their positions and earnestly engaged in squeezing out the few Britons who still dared hold out in the locality, though they were in possession only of vastly inferior positions. (An apologist for the Dutch might reasonably point out that they would have been mad not to do so, as being constantly on the alert was their only chance to maintain these superior positions which Raffles coveted so much. It was an open secret that the Netherlands could not have held their belongings if the British wished to wrest them out of their grasp. The British were ten times as strong as the Dutch as regards sea power alone. Had it come to war, Holland could never have held out, but England didn't want war. Holland played on that British disinclination and worked away like a colony of beavers, settling in on her islands as long as it was safe to do so.)

Raffles in his paper pulled out all the familiar stops and a few new ones, valiantly trying to wake England up and stir her to action. First one was commerce: two thirds of it, said Raffles, was held by the Dutch because they owned Java, Banca, the Moluccas, et cetera. A sixth belonged to native chiefs who were contracted to deal only with the Dutch, though Raffles questioned the validity of these contracts, or treaties. That left only one sixth which could be called independent trade. As long as England occupied Malacca she had enjoyed most of the trade, and after she moved in on Java she held all of it. Those happy days were past, but Raffles refused to give them up for lost. Even though the dastardly Dutch would not recognize any of the treaties which the British (i.e., Raffles) had made with native chiefs while they occupied Java, et cetera, Raffles refused to accept defeat. At the moment England was entirely at the mercy of Holland's good pleasure, but there were ways and means. "To these means what can we oppose? To their system of taking possession of unoccupied ports, and of making treaties of monopoly with the natives, we can oppose the same system. There are yet, at least there were when the last accounts came away, ports of which we may take possession before them, and princes at liberty to make treaties with us in favour of our commerce. To their intimidation of

433 ৪৯

the natives we may oppose a Court of Protection. To their imposition of heavy duties on our regular trade with the Dutch colonies, no resistance can be made in the islands; but, to the effect of such a measure, we can oppose the facility of obtaining our goods free of duty. . . ."

The paper continued with suggestions for defense against Dutch action in "degrading" the British in the eyes of the natives, one of which would be to keep watch and promptly to reply to any "calumnies" or "insults" which the Dutch might put forth. Raffles wanted the British to declare distinctly to the Dutch Government and perhaps also to the native chiefs that they, the British, expected the Dutch to realize they were bound to fulfill those engagements which the British, "either directly or by implication," had contracted with the native powers in the past twenty-three years, especially during their tenure of Java. "No provision was made in our agreements with the native princes for the contingency of the Colonies reverting to Holland. The language which we held out to them was that of a Government competent to make agreements in perpetuity. Without such a language, we never could have done what we have done for the Eastern islands.

"The British Government considered the native princes as independent sovereigns, and treated with them accordingly. The Dutch have refused to guarantee our treaties, and appear to consider those faithful allies to [the] British nation as mere vassals, who are now subjected to their vengeance and rapacity."

There is a good deal more to the paper, but that part is the most interesting in the light of what came after. Following up the hint about the unoccupied ports, Raffles took up one possibility after another and discussed its advantages and disadvantages. Banca was his favorite, and he thought it might be possible to buy it from the Dutch "out of the very heavy sum of money due by the Dutch Government to the East India Company in balance of the accounts of Java. . . ." Next there was Bintang. After that, Rhio. Failing Rhio, the west coast of Borneo.

One paragraph must have met with both enthusiastic response and scornful rejection. Prince of Wales Island and Bencoolen, said Sir Stamford, had long been losing establishments, Prince of Wales to the tune of eighty thousand pounds per annum, Bencoolen a mere fifty thousand. Now that Malacca and Padang were restored to the Dutch, the above-named colonies would be more costly than ever. The question was now, in his mind, whether the Company was content to go on maintaining those two losing establishments or whether they would be willing, by means of a small outlay and the acquisition of a third station within the Archipelago, to attempt the "only feasible means in their power of removing the incumbrance." To some of the Company directors that project sounded pleasantly like one of those now-or-never gambles; to others, unpleasantly like. They all, however, recognized it for a gamble. So did Canning, and he did not definitely dislike gaming. . . .

In addition to the problems already discussed, said Sir Stamford, there were others which were worth considering. America, Russia, and France were getting more and more interested in foreign trade. What was to prevent one or all of them from moving in and grabbing a few ports in this vicinity, if neither Holland nor England did it first? Too long had interested groups in England been thinking of the East Indies as a private battlefield between themselves and the Netherlanders, but there was no law, after all, that could keep the fight private. "Is not Russia extending her influence on all sides?" demanded Raffles. "Has not France, in renouncing the Mauritius . . . acquired a fresh motive for making establishments in the Eastern Seas? . . . The Americans have already a considerable trade with the Eastern islands, and are favourably looked upon. Would any of these nations be desirable neighbours?"

Now considering this paper, which had been written and studied before Raffles went out to Bencoolen, we cannot be amazed that it was only a few days, practically, before the Dutch horrified the new lieutenant governor with their rough, pushing ways on Sumatra. Nevertheless he possessed his soul in patience for a year or two, until the Palembang affair. It

435 &

may or may not be remembered that Palembang, when Raffles held office on Java, was the scene of considerable trouble not long after the British moved in across the straits. While rounding up all the dependencies of Java, Raffles as early as November 1811, immediately after the conquest, sent a commission to take possession of the Dutch factories on Palembang, a part of Sumatra less than a week's sail in good weather from Batavia. On what was evidently a sudden impulse, and egged on by his son, the Sultan massacred the Dutch who lived there at the factory, and then, realizing that the commission would not be pleased, he gathered up his skirts and his army and ran away. Upon which, you will remember, Raffles sent Gillespie (at that time they were on speaking terms) to punish the Sultan, which Gillespie did most efficiently by kicking him off the throne and placing his brother, a man named Ratoo, in his stead. It was Ratoo who in gratitude made England gifts of the islands Billiton and Banca, and for a long time the English really believed they would be able to keep those gifts, come what might to Java. Lord Minto in particular had elaborate plans for Banca, all of which fell by the wayside after 1816.

In 1819 the situation on Palembang became a little confused. Banca had reverted to the Dutch, though Billiton, evidently, was still British. But it was Palembang, the center of the original trouble, which proved again to be a storm center. It was Palembang Raffles had meant when he talked darkly of treaties supposedly in perpetuity, et cetera, for much to his indignation the Dutch, after they had got Java and its dependencies back, undid the British work by deposing Ratoo and replacing the original Sultan.

At first the full iniquity of their actions was not apparent. In April 1818, not long after the arrival of the Raffles family at Fort Marlborough, Sir Stamford wrote an interested friend in London this letter, in part:

"Prepared as I was for the jealousy and assumption of the Dutch Commissioners in the East, I have found myself surprised by the unreserved avowal they have made of their principles, their steady determination to lower the British character in the eyes of the natives, and the measures they have already adopted towards the annihilation of our commerce, and of our intercourse with the native-traders throughout the Malayan Archipelago. Not satisfied with shutting the Eastern ports against our shipping, and prohibiting the natives from commercial intercourse with the English, they have dispatched commissioners to every spot in the Archipelago where it is probable we might attempt to form settlements, or where the independence of the native Chiefs afford any thing like a free port to our shipping. Thus not only the Lampong country has been resumed, but also Pontiana and the minor ports of Borneo, and even Bali, where European flag was never before hoisted, are now considered by them subject to their authority, and measures taken for their subjugation. A commissioner long since sailed from Batavia for Palembang, to organize, as it is said, all that part of Sumatra; and every native prow and vessel is now required to hoist a Dutch flag, and to take out a Dutch pass from Batavia for one of the ports thus placed under their influence; so that whatever trade may still be carried on by the English with the native ports of the Archipelago, must already be in violation of the Dutch regulations, and at the risk of seizure by their cruisers, who have not hesitated repeatedly to fire into English ships.

"The Commanders of the country ships look to me to protect their interests, and even to support the dignity of the British flag; and it is to be hoped some immediate notice will be taken by our Government of these proceedings."

All too evidently the villains, the unspeakable cads, had outguessed Raffles and had actually got in ahead of him on all those ports he had lined up for Canning's consideration before leaving England! The slimy wretches, they had done exactly what Raffles had planned to do! Words fail us when we try to express our opinion of anyone low enough to do that, or at any rate low enough to beat us to it. . . . What price the dignity of the British flag now?

Raffles was not easily discouraged, though, and all the while he was blowing off steam in this manner he had a plan forming. (In all probability, besides, he was neither as surprised nor upset as he pretended.) The time had come, he said, when England must make up her mind once and for all whether to accept defeat or not. If she accepted it, then it was time to give up what shreds of belongings she still maintained in the Eastern seas, relinquish her last two posts, and get out altogether. If she did not wish thus tamely to submit to those villainous Dutchmen, it was indispensable that she take strong measures immediately, if not sooner—"some regular and accredited authority on the part of the British Government should exist in the Archipelago, to declare and maintain the British rights, whatever they are, to receive appeals, and to exercise such wholesome control as may be conducive to the preservation of the British honour and character.

"At present the authority of the Government of Prince of Wales' Island extends no further south than Malacca, and the Dutch would willingly confine that of Bencoolen to the almost inaccessible and rocky shores of the west coast of Sumatra.

"To effect the objects contemplated, some convenient station within the Archipelago is necessary; both Bencoolen and Prince of Wales' Island are too far removed, and unless I succeed in obtaining a position in the straits of Sunda, we have no alternative but to fix it in the most advantageous situation we can find within the Archipelago; this would be somewhere in the neighborhood of Bintang."

The rest of the letter is the familiar tune, though he admits the fact—and this is a new development—that the moment was not propitious, "at the present period, when the most rigid economy is demanded in every department of the British service." He is reassuring, however, on the amount of expenditure which would be necessary. He is not suggesting an elaborate establishment, but rather a mere foothold, here and there, a sort of staked-out claim merely, once in a while as it were, to check the Dutch from extending an uninterrupted chain from Batavia to Banca and Malacca. One must proceed with great caution and gradually. "The footing, however, once obtained in the Straits of Sunda, I apprehend all the rest will follow without difficulty."

 438

It is in this letter, also, that we get certain news of Palembang. Sultan Ratoo was still in the saddle and was appealing to his old friends and champions the British to help keep him there. He had an uncomfortable prickly sensation in the scalp, evidently, that the Dutch intended to restore the status quo which had existed in their time. It seemed more than likely that they would do just that, as it was Ratoo who had made a present of Banca and Billiton to the British, an act which had never been popular with the Dutch. Of course Raffles gasped with indignation that anyone should be so depraved as to want the original Sultan on the throne after he had slaughtered a whole community of Netherlandish compatriots, but land is thicker than blood, said the Dutch.

Raffles was sorry to say that in the present policy of Batavia there still remained much of the bad old principle of the former colonial regime—far different, he was sure, from the enlightened authorities' philosophy in Holland. "I have with difficulty," he said, "refrained from the expression of that honest indignation which every Briton," et cetera, et cetera. He was glad to reflect, however, that the British had left with the native population of Java a new love of independence which was going to make life tough sledding for the Dutch in the future. Without exactly saying so, he managed to imply a coming revolution. What he said was, "Fifty or a hundred years hence, we shall equally feel the advantage of the measures I have now suggested."

That was April 14, 1818. A hundred years hence from April 14, 1818, was April 14, 1918. Raffles was about twenty-five years off in his calculations, but what's a mistake of a few decades when you hit the ball so square in the middle in other ways?

It was not more than about a fortnight later when the news came through which he had been expectantly awaiting. Ratoo was out and big brother Sultan was back, and Raffles could slip the leash and let go of his honest British indignation any time he wanted now. "The Dutch choose to reinstate the man on the throne who has been guilty of treacherously murdering, in cold blood, the Dutch factory at that station, rather than permit the Sultan whom the English raised, in consequence of the atrocity of his predecessor, to continue on the throne; when I likewise discover that they lay claim to all the territory in the Lampong country, and oppose our forming any settlement in Samangka Bay, for the purpose of affording succour or refreshment to our ships passing through the Straits of Sunda; and that they even object to the continuance of the post station between Java and Sumatra, by which alone communication can be kept up with the Eastern Islands and Europe; I feel it to be my duty to submit to the Governor-General a statement——"

No, said the Court of Directors. There you go again, said the Court of Directors, stirring up trouble with the Dutch. It is beginning to be an obsession with you, said the Court: you become a bore, Sir Stamford Raffles. No. No. No.

In spite of this lack of enthusiastic co-operation with his general attitude, Raffles in 1819 made one of the boldest decisions of his career. He was carried away, as he later explained, by the fact that the governor general was not on duty in Bengal and so could not be consulted. It was acutely necessary, Raffles felt, immediately to stop these activities of the Dutch, who by reinstating the original Sultan were directly affecting British commerce; not merely indirectly in that a British treaty was flouted before native eyes, but because Palembang would thus cease to be what Sir Stamford knew was its most desirable destiny, a free port. The Dutch actually sent an expedition to enforce this change of rulers. When Raffles heard the full story, without consulting any superior authority he sent a small force of British troops straight across to Palembang from Bencoolen, under Captain Francis Salmond. Unfortunately for everyone who appreciated the importance of British success in this impulsive undertaking, the Sultan Ratoo was worse than helpless by the time his friends arrived; he was *out*. The Dutch promptly took Salmond prisoner and sent him with his men, under guard to Batavia, and the effect on diplomatic relations between England and Holland, back home, can be imagined.

"I have nothing to send my friend but tears, which never cease to flow," wrote Ratoo to Raffles.

The angry Raffles sat down and wrote (and published) a protest which became famous even before it was printed in the *Annual Register* the following year. Publishing the protest, even more than his highhanded dispatch of troops to Palembang without permission from Calcutta, was what got Sir Stamford into trouble. But both deeds met with harsh criticism, not unnaturally: indeed, one wonders why in the first flush of rage some outraged statesman did not go so far as to insist upon his recall. Certainly Canning, who until then had been inclined to listen to Raffles's plans with a sympathetic ear, came close to effecting this act. It was only after he had cooled off a bit that he decided to leave the matter to the Bengal Government, where it properly belonged. Today, it must be admitted, the reader is inclined to sympathize with Canning rather than with Raffles, even when the case is presented by the warmly pro-Raffles Boulger, in whose opinion there is no doubt that the government ought to have supported Raffles and upheld his protest. Personally, I can see plenty of reason for doubt. Much as I admire him in the ordinary way, nothing else in Raffles's entire history sailed so close to the wind as the Palembang affair, and I think he was amazingly lucky to get away with it. Canning ultimately forgave him, but the letter which Boulger triumphantly quotes in proof of this forgiveness is not exactly unqualified in its approval, even five years later.

"I cannot deny," he wrote, "that your extreme activity in stirring difficult questions, and the freedom with which you committed your Government, without their knowledge or authority to measures which might have brought a war upon them, unprepared, did at one time oblige me to speak my mind to you in Instructions of no very mild reprehension.

"But I was not the less anxious to retain those fruits of your policy which appeared to me really worth preserving, and I have long forgotten every particular of your conduct in the Eastern Seas, except the zeal and ability by which it was distinguished."

However, the Palembang affair is the only one which leaves us feeling that Raffles definitely overstepped the bounds. We can take his side, heartily and without reservation, in the other disputes which led up to the climax of Singapore. From our vantage point of a later century and given the clear view we now have, thanks to Van der Kemp, of the Dutch and their contemporary activities, we can feel sure that Raffles was not exaggerating either his case against them or their case against him. For example there is the report of William May, Dutch consul general in London, 1817, who wrote that "the ex-Lieutenant-Governor of Java, Raffles, was being sent as Resident to Bencoolen on Sumatra, with the principal object of observing the Netherlands trade in the East Indies, for which place Bencoolen is better situated than any chief factory on the Indian continental shore." He further advised that Lieutenant F. A. van Braam, as an old enemy of Raffles and one who had suffered much at his hands, who had shortly before returned to Batavia from Europe, should be appointed to a position where he could dog Raffles's footsteps and thwart his plans.

There was more than a little flurry in the Dutch dovecotes when it became known where Raffles was going, in 1817, for his next term. In the same paper we find a report by one Goldberg, director, to the King of the Netherlands, dealing with the exchange of the Dutch factories in India for Bencoolen, and full of reproaches and complaints against that man Raffles. It is amusing to reflect that this must have arrived at just about the same time Sir Stamford had dinner with the King, at which affair he received many pretty compliments from the Dutch.

Next to Palembang in importance and excitement was the affair of Padang, which interests us chiefly (for it follows the pattern otherwise, and is not worth too much detailed attention) because it brought into prominence the agreement of 1795, when according to Articles of Capitulation between Edward Coles, in the East India Company's service, on the part of His Britannic Majesty, and Dirk Ten Hoeff, chief of Padang on the west coast of Sumatra, the English were to be permitted on Sumatra at Padang to live and work side by side with the Dutch. Raffles's argument was that this agreement was the only one which still held water, because all those made later on were obviated by the Treaty of Vienna when England moved out of Java, et cetera. No Dutch were at Padang when Raffles visited it in 1818, and the inhabitants begged Raffles to keep them from coming.

Now, with the Dutch objecting to and pouncing on everything the English did which smacked of muscling in on their territory, Raffles was exceedingly eager to make this point. In August 1818 he wrote the Secret Committee from Fort Marlborough, just after his return from the famous exploring expedition with Lady Raffles, on which they visited Padang, incidentally: "I cannot too strongly impress on your Honourable Committee the importance of *at all events preserving the integrity of the larger islands.* Unless this is done *with respect to Sumatra,* our establishment must still continue on a ruinous footing. Could the return of Banca be negotiated, and the integrity of Sumatra be preserved under British protection, the greatest advantages might be anticipated. . . . The Supreme Government are informed of the grounds, on which I have felt myself justified in provisionally retaining possession of Padang, pending a reference to Europe. As the delay will afford an opportunity for negotiation, I trust its importance to the British interests in Sumatra will be sufficient to induce the Honourable the Governor-General to add the weight of His Lordship's recommendation in favour of its remaining permanently British, an arrangement which I have no doubt can be easily effected by his Majesty's Ministers. . . .

"To the Dutch Padang was never of any value. If, therefore, they are desirous to regain possession at the present moment, it must be more to injure us, than to benefit themselves."

In a long letter, dated June 1819, at Singapore to Sir Robert Harry Inglis we find this interesting passage: "Bencoolen has so little in itself that much can never be expected from it. The only chance was by the establishment of a post in the Straits of Sunda, or by the retention of Padang, and the extension of our influence in the interior. Had the latter been practicable, I am inclined to think the period would not have been distant when the whole of Sumatra would have acknowledged our authority, and a settled and enlightened government been established throughout."

Considering that these ideas and hopes of Sumatra had filled his brain at the very moment when Sir Stamford was indignantly accusing the Dutch of bad faith, reproaching them for wanting to crowd him out when all he admitted trying to do was work side by side with them, we can see why the Dutch Van der Kemp quotes all these documents together and fairly digs the paper with his pen as he does so. The good-neighbor policy of Sumatra certainly operated under difficulties, and they were not all of Holland's making. During this period Good Neighbor Raffles was also diligently collecting letters from the local native chieftains, who after the manner of subsidiary princes vied with each other in paying him and his government compliments, and complaining of their then masters, the Dutch. Some of them went further and put on record their opinion that England had better claim to their territory than did the Netherlands. A paper from Indrapura, signed by Menang Cabow, willingly gives the British first right to Mocco Mocco:

"I have no allegiance to the Dutch nation; I consider *myself, my heirs, successors, and subjects,* to have been absolved from it by a breach of good faith, confidence, and of treaty by their having attacked me at four o'clock in the morning (which I repelled with success) without any intimation being previously made known to me as consistent with every principle of justice and equity. In consequence whereof, I entered into a solemn arrangement with Henry Heath, Esq. on the part of the English nation, confirmed by the then commissioner for the affairs of the residency of Fort Marlborough, Walter Ewer, Es., which engagement is still valid. . . ." He went on to promise that he would strongly resist any Dutch attempt to regain possession of Mocco Mocco. "I now wish to conclude a specific engagement with the Honorable the Lieutenant Governor of Fort Marlborough and its dependencies, Sir Thomas Stamford Raffles, Knight;" et cetera.

There was a similar paper from the chief responsible for the assassination of "the late Thomas Parr, Esq.," who had evidently since then been condemned, wrongfully as he claimed, not for the murder but for receiving stolen goods. The trial meted out to him by the British who were in office at that time was unfair, he said, and besides, he now needed money. He was more than willing to say anything expected of him, about the Dutch or anyone else, if he could be extricated from his difficulties. He would be awfully grateful. . . .

All these odd treaties, promises, and vows of love and fidelity were carefully gathered by Raffles and filed against the day when they might come in handy, which day came fairly soon. This was all merely a part of the game as it was played by everyone in turn. The Dutch, too, had their sheaves of these agreements, but since the native chiefs were always ready to protest under pressure that their signatures had been granted also under pressure, and need not therefore be taken seriously, one wonders what value they could possibly possess. Of course, read in print in the morning newspapers, back home, without their companion pieces which the Dutch held, they probably looked quite impressive at that. They impressed the Bengal Government at any rate. The net result of these documents relating to Mocco Mocco, et cetera, was that the Marquis of Hastings, formerly Lord Moira of unfortunate memory and still governor general of Bengal, was sufficiently convinced to back up Raffles in his claims, and Hastings was a thoroughly honest man, if not exactly brilliant. He also received in a favorable spirit Raffles's letter to India in August 1818, which was a sort of summary of all these disputes. "The Position, I [Raffles] have taken up, is that the Dutch can have no claim to possession where their flag did not fly on the 1st of January 1803; and under this view, their claim to *Malacca* and *Padang* is at least questionable, these stations having been under the English flag since 1795."

Hastings forthwith sent a formal order to Sir Stamford, constituting him his agent to negotiate with the government of Johore, Lingen, and Rhio, and giving him full powers. If this action seems like a bewildering about-face on the part of the governor general, considering his earlier attitude toward Raffles, the only explanation one can offer is that it was just that. Hastings had been undergoing a change of heart pretty steadily ever since Gillespie's charges came to a head and were finally accounted for, while Raffles was in London. Though he was strongly prejudiced at the beginning, Hastings was actually a sincere man and had no desire to cling to his first impressions when he was convinced that he had been unjust. He probably felt guilty, too, for having listened too trustfully to Gillespie. The campaign which Sir Stamford had been carrying on ever since returning to the Eastern seas, even though many of the directors did not see eye to eye with Raffles regarding the Dutch, had the good effect of calling him favorably to Hastings's attention. The governor general agreed with much of Raffles's first protests about Palembang, though the Salmond affair later was too rich for his blood too. Shortly after his return from the first long expedition into Sumatra's interior, Raffles was delighted to receive an invitation from the governor general to come in person to Calcutta, there to talk over his various projects in regard to a new establishment, somewhere in the Sunda Straits.

Like everyone else in government, Hastings lived to see his resistance worn away at last by the constant drip of water. Raffles's stubbornness was bearing fruit.

CHAPTER XXV

Thick as the leaves on Vallambrosa are the documents gathered together by the indomitable Van der Kemp; anything, almost, that deals with Raffles's activities from 1816 to 1821. Kemp has been extraordinarily thorough. Nearly every word Raffles ever wrote about his disputes with the Dutch in Sumatra, Banca, Singapore, and the rest during that time must have been printed in his voluminous series, as are all the relevant dispatches of the Dutch governor general at Batavia, the British governor general and consul at Bengal, and the East India Company in London. Fortunately for us, there is no need to agree with all his comments pertaining to them, since he was intensely biased not only against Raffles himself but against England, writing as he did at the time of the Boer War, and sympathizing as he did, openly and deeply, with the Boers. I say "fortunately for us" because if we were to adopt his views about Raffles we would be tempted to throw this book into the nearest river, spit after it, and spend the rest of the season trying to forget Sir Stamford and all his works. Kemp loses no opportunity to compare English policy in South Africa in 1890–1900 with that of Raffles and others in 1816–24; he even wrote an article comparing the Jameson Raid of 1898 with Raffles's disastrous expedition to Palembang.

447

Of course in a way his general comparisons of Anglo-Dutch and Anglo-Boer enmity are not altogether wide of the mark, since (although he nowhere says so) one of England's real or alleged reasons for interfering in South African affairs was the brutal Boer mistreatment of the natives, both Kaffirs and Bushmen, just as Raffles's support of the natives and advocacy of slavery abolition earned him the enmity of the Hollanders. On the other hand (in my opinion) Kemp is quite justified in the strictures he passed on the pretentious work of Boulger, who was as anti-Boer as Kemp was pro, and delivers himself of all kinds of criticism of Dutch colonial methods and foreign policy, which in a person totally unacquainted with a word of that language is gratuitous to say the least.

In his "Singapore Paper War," Van der Kemp writes: "The book [Boulger's] forms no exception to the majority of English works written about our Colonies, in so far as it deals with the underrating of the Dutch rule. Superficial and minatory, its stupidity and partiality are clothed in the guise of presumption. Admittedly if one does not apparently understand anything more of the Netherlands language than the sarcastically employed word *Mijnheer*, it is difficult to compile a work dealing with the history of our colonies, without falling short of the standards demanded by serious study, knowledge and criticism. It is not so much the one-sidedness of these Jingo books that is a defect. Where the historian cannot live with his theme, shows that he has no feeling for the ups and downs of his heroes; for the land whose past is sketched therein; for the people in their greatness or in their decay,—then he is unable to infuse any spirit, life or talent into his picture; but if he must have some bias, then it should be based on an earnest study of the sources of the rival parties, before the critic himself can form his own opinion. 'The sole impartiality that one can demand of him,' as G. Valbert so justly observes in his remarks on the historian Von Trietschke, 'is this exact and scrupulous equality which does not condemn any enemy without having heard him, which does not pronounce any final sentence without having let the accused speak and listened to him patiently, and examined with care his proofs.'

"Taken as a whole, the Dutch historian stands high in this respect; the Jingo writer often deplorably low. Boulger's book forms no exception thereto. There is naturally no mention of the Bandjermassin scandal." (No more has there been mention of it in this book, but only because other matters, such as Padang, have crowded it out. Naturally, Van der Kemp considered it important because it did not redound to Raffles's credit, but that reason does not suffice us. In brief the facts are these: Sir Stamford was at first friendly with a certain Alexander Hare who lived on Borneo at Banjermasin and misbehaved considerably, in respect both to morals and politics. Later Raffles, who had been intimate enough with Hare to import for him a notorious girl friend, had to forswear all friendship for the scalawag and sever every tie, or run the risk of seriously displeasing Calcutta. But as this was Hare's scandal rather than Raffles's, I still think my neglect of it justified.)

"Of Raffles' blood-letters to Palembang," continues Van der Kemp, no doubt in a satisfied, savage kind of snarl, "one only reads (page 90) 'He entered into an unsatisfactory negotiation with the cruel Sultan of Palembang.' Oh! Come now! . . . Of Major Mulder's heroic death in the English capture of Meester Cornelis in 1811, he writes 'two gallant *French* officers . . . fired the magazine', whereon the 'Franco-*Dutch* army' fled. Of our eighty years' war, he writes (page 292) 'The Dutch did something for the cause of liberty in Europe' in the sixteenth century, but even that something was 'aided by subsidies and other support from England.' Even where the writer should be fully aware of all the facts, where he finds himself on his own ground, he prefers to give a bowdlerized version, copying one in the *Memoir* of Raffles' widow, than to put the departure of his hero from Java in its true light. Thus on page 211, there is described the handing-over of Java by Raffles to Fendall, as likwise Fendall's handing-over to the Commissioners-General, 'with the exception of Banca and Banjermassin.' Presumably the writer means Billiton and not Benjermassin, and he then adds 'At first . . . only means of saving his life.' With good or bad health, Raffles *was forbid-*

den to go to Benkulen, until he had been able to clear himself from the accusations brought against him. In his own *Statement* he notes this expressly himself. . . . The whole of Boulger's page 293 is a tirade against our colonial administration, with the Amboina Massacre of 1624 in the lead of course! Ignoring the fact that in those days the English were just as exclusive as the Dutch and other European nations, this policy is represented as an invariable characteristic of our nation even to . . . the Transvaal! 'What was true in Japan and Java . . . [is] evident in the Transvaal.' . . .

"But although Boulger's work is a repellent and in some ways an unscientific book, it is none the less of considerable importance. The writer prints several official papers which throw a new, or I should rather say, a clearer light on our history. Nothing compels us to follow his unjust considerations. We can leave those on one side and use what is true and necessary."

I crave pardon for such a long quote, but insist that any recapitulation of it would be vastly inferior. This is not all by a long shot that Kemp has to say on the subject of Boulger, but it ought to be sufficient to give a fairly representative idea of his style. It also should be enough to show us how Kemp falls himself into one of the sins he twits Boulger with; viz., confusing contemporary politics (Boer War, 1898–1902) with those of the eighteenth century. Admittedly, however, he was equally at home with French, Dutch, and English documents, whereas Boulger could read only English and French.

A strange paradox in this piece of research is the manner in which our hero Raffles stands triumphant and secure in our good opinion, in spite of all the harmful praise lavished on him by his well-nigh stupid biographer and his pathetic, admirable, but certainly not too scrupulously truthful widow; and also how he rises above the spite and hatred of his very adroit, scientific, redoubtable enemy Van der Kemp. If I had to choose between the two historians for source material I would not hesitate to select the hostile Van der Kemp rather than the adoring Boulger. And in the end I would still be pro-

Raffles. It is an axiom all too often forgotten in these days of public relations counsels, bureaus of information, and plain common propaganda, but in the end, do not forget, it is the facts which speak. You can color it up, you can butter it and pepper it, you can translate it into the foreign language of psychiatry or bury it in religious dogma, but in the end a fact is a fact is a fact. . . . And so is Raffles.

In reply to Raffles's suggestion, Hastings asked him to Calcutta. A long overdue gesture, it was nevertheless a source of joyful excitement to the lieutenant governor of Sumatra that he was to have the chance of talking over in person his disputes at home with the Dutch and his projects for the Archipelago. Though Hastings was not in the least like Minto of cherished memory, doubtless Raffles remembered how pleasant had been the outcome of his first call on a governor general in Calcutta and considered this invitation a good omen. It was more than a mere invitation; it was certainly an olive branch.

"It was painful to me," Hastings had written, "that I had, in the course of my public duty, to express an opinion unfavourable to certain of your measures in Java. The disapprobation, as you would perceive, affected their prudence alone; on the other hand, no person can have felt more strongly than I did your anxious and unwearing exertions for ameliorating the condition of the native inhabitants under your sway. The procedure was no less recommended by wisdom than by benevolence; and the results have been highly creditable to the British Government. I request you to consider yourself at liberty to carry into execution your wish of visiting Bengal, whensoever your convenience and the state of affairs in the Island may afford an eligible opportunity. The means of rendering the settlement at Bencoolen more advantageous to the Honourable Company than it now appears to be, are certainly more likely to be struck out in oral discussion."

Raffles stood not on the order of his going but leaped aboard the first ship pointing in the right direction. If the voyage had

451 ॐ

permitted time for recollection, he might have remembered the first eventful journey that he made out of Penang. Certainly never has lieutenant governor traveled in a worse ship than this dirty one-cabin vessel. Their pilot was drunk and upset the ship at the Hooghly River mouth; she had already lost a mast in the Bay of Bengal. Rescue from Calcutta was not long in coming, and Sir Stamford was ready for his first audience with Hastings only three months from the date the governor general posted his summons, which for those days was speedy.

Of the two pressing matters which Raffles had been eager to bring to Hastings's attention, the first was disposed of in disappointingly quick time. Hastings's mind was already made up not to carry the Sumatra quarrel any further, and to allow the Dutch all the freedom they were taking, without more argument. It was obvious to the observant if thwarted Raffles that his superior officer was primed for the interview with certain orders from England to hold back the offensive. Moreover, Hastings was not enough enamored of the British share of Sumatra, Bencoolen, to want an enlargement of their holdings. He was already considering an exchange with the Dutch, Bencoolen for Malacca, which actually did go through six years later.

The second half of Raffles's program, however, met with a much more satisfactory response. He came away glowing with hope, for Hastings had given him to understand that they were of one mind about the necessity for stopping any further Dutch encroachment like their surprise occupation of Palembang. The governor general approved the idea of another establishment or even two of them, provisionally at Acheen and Rhio. Though it became evident later, after Singapore had been staked out, that Hastings regretted his first cordial agreement and would have backed out if he could, fearing the repercussions at home, the first few weeks of their new relationship were better and more amicable than Raffles would ever in earlier days have dared to hope. Fortunately for his reputation, though it is not so good for Hastings's, there are in existence today documents which prove his claim that

Hastings agreed to his proposals of expansion during the early days of the Calcutta interviews. He wrote jubilantly to Marsden, of whose sympathy he could always be sure, that he had made his peace with the marquis and that "his Lordship has at last acknowledged my exertions in Java in flattering terms. This was one object of my visit to Calcutta, and on it depended, in a great measure, the success of the others. I am now struggling hard to interest the Supreme Government in the Eastern islands; and the measures taken by me at Palembang, etc., will, I doubt not, lead to the advantage of some defined line of policy being laid down for the future. With regard to the Dutch proceedings at Palembang, of which I hope you are, ere this, fully apprised, Lord Hastings has unequivocally declared, that his mind is made up as to the moral turpitude of the transaction, and that he considers this but as one of a course of measures directed in hostility to the British interests and name in the Eastern Seas."

Nothing further had been decided as yet, and Raffles evidently was not too sanguine as to the English reaction when they should find out that they would be called upon to "interfere" for the security of their trade. He was genuinely worried now about the time element. There was no trickery in him when he wrote his friend Marsden, for it was never necessary to convince the historian of Sumatra by other than straightforward methods. Therefore it seems safe, though we take the risk of calling out Van der Kemp's shade in angry denial simply on general principles, to quote his *bête noir* Boulger where he has summed up the Raffles-Hastings situation rather neatly in a couple of sentences.

"Still, while Raffles had made up his mind that he could rely on Lord Hastings—whose last words were, 'Sir Stamford, you may depend upon me,'—and quoted freely his confidential *verbal* instructions from the Supreme Authority in India, the Governor-General does not seem to have decided in his own mind anything more than that something had to be done in the Straits, and that Raffles was the only man available to attempt it. He did not give Raffles his entire confidence; and consequently he would, as will be seen, have backed out of the business altogether at the first check, only his emissary was too prompt and too strong for him."

In the meantime Raffles worked fast. He wrote Marsden a month later, still from Calcutta, that a change had now taken place. . . . "All parties are now united in opposing the grasping and excluding policy of the Dutch. . . . They now regret they did not listen to my advice at first. . . . It is determined to keep command of the Straits of Malacca, by forming establishments at Acheen and Rhio. . . . Acheen I conceive to be completely within our power, but the Dutch may be beforehand with us at Rhio—they took possession of Pontiano and Malacca in July and August last; and have been bad politicians if they have so long left Rhio open to us."

Clever as Raffles was, he didn't know the half of it! His letter further informed Marsden that he was to embark in about a fortnight's time to settle the whole thing. One can well imagine his joyful excitement as he made ready to carry out this plan, for it had been near to his heart a long time. The hurry and flurry of the affair must have been doubly welcome to a man of Sir Stamford's caliber after having lived a dull, if contented, existence for many months in sleepy Bencoolen. Raffles was not cut out to be a gentleman farmer: he was not born to rusticate. In the letter to the Duchess of Somerset, dated November 26, 1818, which we quoted earlier, that one in which he cheerfully hints that Lady Raffles is soon to give birth to their second child, we realize for the first time that his wife must actually have *followed* him to Calcutta, since she had not accompanied him. She must have made up her mind as soon as it became obvious that he would not be able to return to Bencoolen until after the conclusion of the new establishment business. Considering her advanced pregnancy, we begin to realize that Raffles's proud report of Sophia's devotion to him was certainly no idle boast. No doubt the haste of his own departure was all that saved her from sharing his ridiculous shipwreck in the Hooghly, outside Calcutta, as well.

"I have begged of Lady Raffles to give your Grace an account of the *regal state* of the Governor General, which really exceeds all I had heard of it," adds Sir Stamford, not forgetting that ladies, even when they are like the duchess and take pride in their intellect, are fond of gossip and chitchat, especially in high places. He soon sobers, however, and returns to his muttons. "I have, at last, succeeded in making the authorities in Bengal sensible of their supineness in allowing the Dutch to exclude us from the Eastern Seas; but I fear it is too late to retrieve what we have lost."

There is not much question as to what Raffles would have said if he had been informed in advance that the Dutch were already well ahead of him. He had not long to wait for this intelligence, poor fellow. In the meantime Hastings sent him a carefully worded set of instructions which left no doubt as to his duties. Only a man of Lord Hastings's eminence would have dared in later days to go back on his word so blandly and completely as the governor general did, with this document there for all the world to read someday. At much greater length, these were the duties Lord Hastings outlined for Sir Stamford during his coming voyage:

Recapitulating Raffles's own arguments quite as if the governor general had dreamed them up himself, he informed Sir Stamford that getting a foothold on Acheen was the first, most pressing job, and so it should be embarked upon without delay, or any further reference to London. After accomplishing this, in order to ensure free passage through the straits a station beyond Malacca should be established, if possible in such position as to command the straits' southern entrance. Upon due consideration, said Hastings without the smallest blush, he had decided (all by himself) that Rhio was the best locality for such a project. Aside from its natural advantages, "the Dutch possess no right, and have as yet stated no pretension to interfere with the independence of this state, which is generally acknowledged." The native chiefs were in a Barkis state of mind, according to a recent report from Major Farquhar, our old friend on Java.

Undoubtedly, though certain friendly arrangements had already been made at these posts, the Dutch would try to move in on them ultimately, and to forestall this, the maintenance of Farquhar's engagements "seem to point out the necessity of supporting the arrangements made with these states, by measures of a different character from what under other circumstances would have been necessary." Therefore, in the event of the Dutch not having preoccupied Rhio, it was up to Raffles; all details were left to his judgment. But Farquhar would be a good man to leave in charge after everything was settled. Acheen and all related interests in the Strait of Malacca should be placed under Penang's management, and Rhio and Lingen under Bencoolen's.

Lord Hastings's secretary thoughtfully enclosed copies of Farquhar's agreements just concluded with the chiefs of Rhio, Lingen, and Siack (Siak).

A week later (December fifth) there came a postscript full of new directions from Hastings. It had occurred to him on second thought that if Rhio and Lingen had really been occupied in advance by those Dutch, "Johor" might be a good substitute choice. In case Raffles were to find that the worst had happened, therefore, he was directed to go and pay a call on the Sultan of this Johor, to feel him out. The governor general had written a letter therewith enclosed, which Sir Stamford was to present to the Sultan. (Johore is the name of the state just across the bay from Singapore, on the mainland.)

This hasty little message turned out to be the most significant one among all Lord Hastings's voluminous letters to Sir Stamford Raffles. A week later the faithful Marsden was again addressed, from the *Nearchus* this time, by his friend Raffles: "We are now on our way to the eastward, in the hope of doing something, but I much fear the Dutch have hardly left us an inch of ground to stand upon. My attention is principally turned to Johore, and you must not be surprised if my next letter to you is dated from the site of the ancient city of Singapura."

Well, there it is: the first time any of our friends have spoken that name. We ought to pause here a moment for cogitation. On the face of it, everything looks straightforward enough: one day, evidently, Hastings said to himself, "There's Johor, come to think of it. Wonder why nobody else has ever thought of it? I think I'll make the suggestion to Raffles. Since he's going in that direction anyway . . ." and Raffles, receiving the letter, said to himself, in his turn, "Johore, eh? He didn't know how to spell it, but I know the place he's talking about, all right. Hmmmm. Yes, that's not at all a bad idea, Johore. I'll look into it as soon as I've got a free week end."

Only it wasn't done that way, really. Sir Stamford had already given some thought to Singapore; one reason no one else thought of it was that there was no native city on the island, though there had been something of the kind long ago. Only chance has arranged it so that none of his earlier speculations about it remain on paper. Even so, Raffles was not the first to have had the idea. At least two other people had thought of using Singapore, one more than a century before. Alexander Hamilton was one of them—Hamilton, the Scot who, because he did not belong to the Company, was called "the interloper."

"In the year 1703," says Captain Hamilton, "I called at Johor on my way to China, and he (the King of Johor) treated me very kindly and made me a present of the island of Singapore, but I told him it could be of no use to a private person, though a proper place for a company to settle a colony on, lying in the centre of trade, and being accommodated with good rivers and safe harbours, so conveniently situated that all winds served shipping both to go out and come into these rivers." There had been a town at Singapore, a flourishing one at that. But in 1818 almost no trace of it remained.

There was also the Dutchman Abraham Couperus, who surrendered Malacca to the British in 1795. He wrote, in 1808, that Malacca had no future: he advocated the Dutch founding a settlement either at Singapore or in the Strait of Banka. The government of Java for some reason ignored both suggestions.

Now for at least the third time the idea of using Singapore Island occurred to white men. This time it took root, and grew, and flourished, and bore such fruit as Aw Boon Haw the Tiger Balm King, the Singapore gin sling, and the sinking, in 1941, of H.M.S. *Prince of Wales*. It also perpetuated the name of Thomas Stamford Raffles as nothing else could have done.

457 &

CHAPTER XXVI

Experience has taught me that the sequence of events in the founding of the British colony on Singapore Island can be vastly confusing. There is so much coming and going by two people, Raffles and Farquhar, so much writing and answering and crossing of letters en route, so much commanding by Lord Hastings and then recalling of his commands, that the most satisfactory way to tell it is first to draw up a complete outline showing what actually happened from beginning to end. Then we can go back to the beginning and fill it in with contemporary comment, clothing the bare bones of the narrative with flesh. It would be misleading to leave the skeleton to stand alone, even though the facts may be all there in the outline. For one thing we would miss Abdullah's version, which would be no trivial loss. For another, there was the aftermath, the comments of the Dutch and the British reaction. Later occurrences depended on these things.

The story begins properly with Major Farquhar's adventures. He was involved in the affair just when he was leaving for a holiday in Europe. His were the preliminary investigations: he visited the ports which Raffles had suggested as possibilities, after having abandoned his personal plans for "furlough," or at any rate postponed them, because Raffles implored him to do so. He went first to Lingen, where the Sultan referred him to his uncle, Rajah Mooda of Rhio, as the highest authority in that region. Farquhar duly repaired to Rhio, and there on August nineteenth the two men signed a treaty, the Rajah on behalf of the Sultan of Johore, Pahang, and its dependencies, including Lingen, Rhio, and so on, and Farquhar for the Honorable Company.

Returned to Malacca, the major announced the news (on October twenty-second, formally by letter, though he could have walked down the street and told them in person) to Their Excellencies Rear Admiral Wolterbeek and J. S. Timmerman Thyssen, the governor of Malacca, informing them of the treaty which he had signed. (Remember Timmerman Thyssen? They spelled it "Thimmerman Thijssen" in the *Government Gazette*, in Batavia, when he praised Minto, Raffles, et al in a speech.)

Their Excellencies replied warmly (on October thirty-first) that the Sultan of Rhio was not empowered to sign such a treaty on account of a pre-existing treaty dated November 2, 1784, between that same Sultan and the Netherlands East India Company.

Next day Major Farquhar remarked in his turn that when England had taken possession of Malacca, back in 1795, Sultan Mohammed became independent; moreover, the Dutch East India Company no longer existed anyway, nor had done for a long time. The 1784 treaty between the defunct company and the Sultan, ever since then, was useless and might just as well be filed with all the other "obsolete or interrupted treaties with other nations."

Immediately the Dutch rushed pell-mell to Rhio in their turn and made Rajah Mooda cede one half the revenues and government powers to them, after writing Major Farquhar, "We will not permit either of them [the Rajah of Rhio or the Rajah of Lingen] to cede one inch of ground to the English."

That was the situation before Raffles decided to try Singapore direct.

As far as I am concerned, the story of Singapore's founding is rendered much more exciting by the reappearance of Abdullah the scholar. It may be remembered that we last saw him standing forlornly on the beach at Malacca in 1811, wav-

459 ॐ

ing good-by and good luck to his old idol Raffles and his new idol Lord Minto, as they sailed off to conquer Java. His mother had forbidden him to accompany the expedition, and great was his disappointment because of this. Which is not the same, however, as saying that life since then had been without savor for the Munshi, because he had undergone plenty of excitement, even though Raffles wasn't there in Malacca to make it. For one thing, the Dutch were scheduled to come back, empowered by the British to occupy Malacca at the same time they regained Java and all the other territories formerly belonging to them. At first, said Abdullah, the people were happy to hear this news, because they thought things would be far easier for them with Netherlanders than they had been under British rule. As the time for the take-over approached, keen-eyed Abdullah noted that the English he met in the road looked "sad and sorrowful, like people at a funeral, and every face was pale."

One Englishman still kept in touch with the colony as the painful time drew near—Major Farquhar, familiar to Abdullah and to us. In 1818 word went round that he was up to something special, and certainly he acted like it. He kept going away and coming back and sailing off again. It was said on good authority, the townspeople declared, that he was looking for an English lady of high degree who had been snatched from her ship and carried off by pirates.

Abdullah, however, soon learned that the pirate-and-lady story was no more than a piece of fiction. "It was not to look for a lady; that report was spread intentionally, so that people might not know that the English were going to search for a place to found a city." What purpose such a deception was supposed to serve, once the natives knew it was a deception, is definitely questionable. In that land where every man was a spy for the sheer fun of it, Farquhar was noted, watched, and checked up on every time he so much as spat. He must have realized it, after all his experience. First, said Abdullah, he went to Siak, then he went to Daik, then to the Carimon Islands. We happen to know from other sources that the visit to the Carimons was merely a polite gesture to Farquhar, who thought he had a good idea there, but didn't. Sir Stamford could have told him so in advance, but it would not have been tactful to insist. It was better simply to let him make the voyage and see for himself, but it wasted precious time.

None of these places was good for what Farquhar had in mind, said the gossips and self-appointed critics. Either the anchorage was no good, or the winds were often unfavorable, or there was a sound political reason for avoiding the locale. Finally he went to Johore, after which he visited no other port but sailed straight back to Malacca, and don't think for a minute that every tiny child playing in the Malaccan dust didn't know all about the affair.

About this time Farquhar placed Captain Daud in his office as deputy, indicating that the major expected to be busy elsewhere for a long time. Afterward he sailed back in the direction of Johore, this time to Singapore Strait, where he stayed at length, busily making friends with Tĕngku Long, the son of Sultan Mahmud. Shortly thereafter the population of Malacca was invited by Farquhar's attendants to share the significant secret news that Tĕngku Long had taken money in exchange for a promise that the island of Singapore should belong to the English.

Still in strictest privacy (nobody knew it, that is, but the town of Malacca and perhaps a few outlying communities) Farquhar then wrote to Raffles at Penang, and Raffles in turn wrote to the governor general in Bengal, and the contents of the letter (strictly private) as told to Abdullah in the market place were as follows: "If you wish to found a city at Singapore you can do so, and the Company does not forbid it; the Company, however, will not pay the expense of founding the city, but you and Mr. Farquhar must provide the money yourselves. When this has been done, the Company will consider the matter."

It is somehow reassuring that Abdullah and his pals got the account so grotesquely mixed up. One begins to hope that, after all, it may sometimes be possible to keep a secret, even in the Orient. With Abdullah's crowd it seems to have been a matter of any anecdote in a storm, no matter what.

461 ॐ

So Raffles came to Malacca, said Abdullah. And when he had arrived, he immediately sent Farquhar to Singapore, while he himself went to Acheen, and there settled a quarrel [sic] between two princes.

As a matter of true fact Farquhar and Sir Stamford went together to Singapore after Sir Stamford heard that a visit to Acheen would be fruitless. His forebodings about Rhio at least had been correct and the Dutch were already in residence. Though Sir Stamford had been aching with impatience to get started, he had been compelled to put in many days of delay, hanging about Calcutta. It was a case, literally, of every minute counting, and the Dutch had been wily enough to get in ahead of him in so many places already that he was gloomily convinced he would find them, if he went, sitting smilingly in Acheen and Rhio, triumphant if perhaps a little breathless. Considering this, he said to himself, the only way to beat them to it in Singapore (for surely they would think of Johore sooner or later, and Singapore was an inevitable afterthought) was to lead them astray and lull their fears by pretending to go somewhere else, then hastily to clinch the bargain with the Sultan. The thought of landing unimpeded on Singapore beach must have made the hateful smiles of the Dutch a little more supportable when Raffles thought of them in occupied Rhio.

With a couple of attendants from Malacca, Sir Stamford Raffles and Major Farquhar duly arrived at Singapore, and Abdullah's description of the scene is doubly interesting to those who know Singapore today, as a full-grown city. "They landed on the Esplanade where the Court has now been built, and found the place full of *kermanting* and *sakedudok* bushes. On the side towards the river there were four or five little huts, and there were six or seven cocoanut trees which had been planted there; and there was one house a little larger, but also built of *atap*, which was where the Tĕmĕnggong lived. [The Tĕmĕnggong, or Tumunggong, is a sort of prime minister.] Mr. Farquhar walked all round the Esplanade, and the sea gypsies (Orang Laut) came and looked at him, and then ran and told the Tĕmĕnggong.

"Immediately the Těměnggong, accompanied by four or five men bearing arms came to meet Mr. Farquhar."

Throughout any direct quotation from Abdullah which may follow, for "Farquhar" read "Raffles." Abdullah slipped badly on this very important point.

They talked, says Abdullah, for a very long time, during which the Těměnggong told Raffles all about the various princes who had a claim to the island and the neighboring territories, and how they quarreled, and how their ancestors had quarreled and they had inherited the disputes, after the immemorial manner of the Eastern nobility. He himself, he explained, was living on this desolate spot because he was in self-appointed exile; he had come from Riau (Rhio) "in a bad humour," and was presumably sitting on the beach in the sulks, with intent to remain there until he was rid of his hump.

Finally, said the men from Malacca when they told Abdullah about it later, the Těměnggong gave "Major Farquhar" a document, and "Farquhar" lost no time, but immediately put up the British flag there on the shore, driving into the sand a flagpole thirty-six feet in height. This time there must be no mistake about who got there first. Soon, Raffles did not doubt, there would come Dutchmen to dispute the claim. Thirty-six feet did not seem excessive.

The official part of the bargain completed, "Farquhar" proceeded to examine his new domain at leisure. At the mouth of the Singapore River was a large flat stone to which the sea gypsies had been in the habit of bringing offerings when they were about to set out on some profit-seeking voyage, sometimes called piratic by impolite persons.

All around this stone were hundreds of human skulls, "rolling in the sand," Abdullah said. Some were old and weathered, but others were all too obviously new and more or less fresh. Raffles was told that most of them were relics of pirates' prisoners, the custom of the trade being to bring such victims here to Singapore and kill them on the stone by way of sacrifice. Others, however, were the remains of pirates themselves, this being a favorite battle ground for rival groups. They were apt to meet one another at the stone, and one thing led to another,

463 ॐ

usually gambling, friendly competitions with weapons, cock-fighting, and such. Pirates are traditionally short-tempered, so these celebrations usually wound up with a few fresh skulls rolling about at the foundation of the sacred stone. Raffles ordered that they all, pirates' and prisoners', be gathered up in sacks, weighted down well with stones, and sunk far out to sea.

Most of the land near the beach was flat, even unpleasantly so, and covered only with a sparse sort of second-growth brush. But there was one hill close to the beach, and the name of it, known to all the natives, was Forbidden Hill. When Sir Stamford announced his intention of climbing it, everyone was horrified, and there was a mad scramble to get out of his line of vision before he should pick the men to accompany him. In vain, for he insisted that they come along, at least enough of them to drag the cannon from his ship. Once on top, when he had fired it off twelve times in all directions, public opinion veered sharply, and the terrors of Forbidden Hill became the best joke of the season. Its evil reputation had come down through several generations, for the kings of Singapura had lived up there certain seasons of the year, in a palace to which only the very elite and sacred were allowed to come, and the stories of what went on in the secret fastnesses of the palace halls naturally grew better every time they were repeated. So Raffles, who knew his history, laughed off the evil mists that hung about the place, and caused the old roadway leading up to the top to be cleared and made ready for use, because, he said, this part of the island was probably healthier than the low-lying ground.

It is alleged that "Singapura" in one of the Indian tongues means "Lion City," but the only animals on the island were rats, who made up in number what they lacked in size. So many were they that, far from fearing the cats that came ashore off the ships, they killed them by ganging up, until Raffles offered a bounty of one wang—i.e., two cents ha'penny—for every dead rat brought to him. Thousands were killed in the following days, until there was not one rat left. Then Raffles and the Malaccans turned their attention to the thousands of centipedes which were doing their little bit to render the

Lion City revolting. The bounty method disposed of them as well. And now this scrub-covered piece of unattractive land was ready, the stage was set, and the curtain rose on the drama of Raffles's Eastern empire.

Leaving Abdullah's dramatic narrative for a while, however reluctant we may be to do so, we go back a month or two to see how Raffles had worked his way around to the great moment. He had got the bad news about Rhio as soon as he arrived at Penang; it met him when he disembarked, and he said, more in sorrow than surprise, "By neglecting to occupy the place. . ." He was just in time to catch Farquhar on the wing; the major had been on the verge of leaving for Europe when he received Raffles's frantic call for help, but he dutifully turned around and hurried back. Sir Stamford sailed from Penang, caught Farquhar up as the major returned from Rhio, and went with him to the Carimons, which as we know were not satisfactory. An earlier visitor had described them accurately, evidently, as being a perfect jungle, not calculated for a settlement. So much, then, for Rhio and the Carimons. Raffles's personal hunch that Singapura might be just what he wanted grew stronger with each disappointment. Boulger did a bit of interesting research when he dug out of the Political Records of India this letter from Raffles dated January sixteenth, which is to say a fortnight before Singapore was occupied and even well before he went to Carimon. Note that his mind was already made up:

"The island of Sincapore [sic], independently of the straits and harbour of Johore, which it both forms and commands, has, on its southern shores, and by means of the several smaller islands which lie off it, excellent anchorage and smaller harbours, and seems in every respect most peculiarly adapted for our object. Its position in the straits of Singapore is far more convenient and commanding than even Rhio, for our China trade passing down the straits of Malacca, and every native vessel that sails through the Straits of Rhio must pass in sight of it.

465

"The town of Johore is, in the main, at some distance up the river, the banks of which are said to be low; but, on the score of salubrity, there does not seem to be any objection to a station at Sincapore, or on the opposite shore towards Point Romanea, or on any of the smaller islands which lie off this part of the coast. The larger harbour of Johore is declared by professional men whom I have consulted, and by every Eastern trader of experience to whom I have been able to refer, to be capacious and easily defensible, and, the British flag once hoisted, there would be no want of supplies to meet the immediate necessities of our establishment."

Abdullah has more to tell us of the matter. With the English flag flying bravely from its pole on the beach, there was no longer need for secrecy, and in a short time the people of Malacca, among whom Abdullah was eagerly waiting, heard the news that there would soon be a British city on the island of Singapore. Immediately a lot of traders became eager to take food down there to the settlement and sell it, and though they feared the pirates who infested the neighborhood, many of them braved the danger and did go. So many went, in fact, that the Dutch, already infuriated by the way they had been outguessed, declared that at this rate Malacca would soon be deserted, and they passed a law forbidding anyone from Malacca to sail to Singapore (all this is Abdullah's version: I can't find confirmation elsewhere), saying that they would confiscate any vessel they encountered that was Singapore-bound. Still they could not stop the rush southward, until at last they set cruisers to guarding the river, and after that it was necessary to use stealth to get out. But still the people fled, braving the threat of loss from pirates or Dutchmen; they kept going, eager to be free of Dutch oppression.

Abdullah painted in strong colors when he spoke of that oppression. He said the taxes were crushing and that the petty officials whose duty was to enforce the laws made matters even worse by cooking up false accusations in order to collect fine money. One of the most hated laws was that which provided for street sweeping. Each householder in Malacca was to see to it that the roadway before his house was kept clean and swept, and the people tried to keep on the right side of authority by being very careful in this respect. But there was one official whose habit it was to discover imaginary infractions of this rule as often as he inspected the streets. So often did he levy fines that the natives nicknamed him "Mr. Broom," and he became a sort of symbol of Dutch oppression; he was the most notorious and hated man in the city government.

Small wonder, then, that Malacca people found ways to slip out of the city and down to Singapore even in spite of the Dutch cruisers, and in spite of the news, which arrived soon after the planting of the flagpole, that food was scarce in the new settlement, although money abounded. Most people thought the town would exist for only a short time before the British pulled up stakes and departed. The Dutch of course helped spread this rumor. But though they thought it might be true, they still wanted to go and live there for as long as the city existed.

Then Raffles came, said Abdullah (who thought it had been Farquhar who founded the city, remember), from Bengal, with four ships and two cutters, and as soon as he had entered the harbor he sent for Těngku Long, the son of Sultan Mahmud, who had carried on earlier conversations with him. Until Těngku Long arrived Sir Stamford stayed aboard his own ship. Těngku Long, said Abdullah, feared he was being summoned in order to be arrested but he dared not disobey, so he went, though he was shaking in his shoes. Seeing that he had arrived, Raffles came ashore. All this time, Těngku Long's heart beat fast with terror.

"Mr. Raffles showed Těngku Long every honor and respect, and brought him to a place where they all four sat down in chairs. Enchek Abu Pateh sat behind Těngku Long, and Raja Embong sat a little way off. At that time Mr. Raffles was speaking with smiles and a pleasant face, and kept bowing his head, and was as sweet as a sea of honey. Not merely the human heart but even a stone would be broken by hearing such words as his, with a gentle voice like the sweetest music, in order to remove any sadness and that the doubt which might be concealed in the treasury of the human heart might also disappear,

467

and so all the waves of uncertainty which were beating upon the reef of doubt were stilled, and the cloud which threatened a squall of wind with darkness such as that of a great storm about to break was all dissipated, so that the weather became fine, and there blew the gentle breeze which comes from the garden of love, and then suddenly there arose the full moon of the fourteenth day with its bright light, so that the sincerity of Mr. Raffles became evident to Tĕngku Long. In a moment his sadness changed to gladness, and his face lighted up. As Mr. Raffles looked out of the corner of his eye, his face changed color, and he rose from his chair, and taking the hand of Tĕngku Long he led him into his cabin, and closed the door. In that cabin these two men conversed, and no one knows the secret of what they said. If I knew the secret of their conversation, I would certainly write it in this story, but God alone knows it. After a considerable time they came out smiling and holding one another's hands, and then they went down into the boat. Mr. Farquhar and the Tĕmĕnggong also went down with them. . . ."

Tĕngku Long dressed up in his regal attire, the story continues, and by the time he came back Raffles and Farquhar and the crews of the ships and all the Malacca people were ready waiting in the middle of the Esplanade, and a table was placed there with chairs right and left, and sailors drawn up ready, right and left. The Malays came marching with the sacred yellow umbrella.

"And as they were marching, by God's power there fell a light rain [hujan panas], which as the Malays reckon is a sign of blessings to come."

Sir Stamford quickly came and shook hands with Tĕngku Long, who according to Abdullah was suffering from a return of his terror, so that he said in a frantic whisper to his attendant Enchek Abu, "Don't you move from behind me."

In the tent Raffles seated Tĕngku Long in the middle, then Raffles stood on the right hand of the prince and Farquhar on the left. Every European present now took off his hat and stood with folded arms, paying respect to His Highness. The proclamation was read aloud, announcing that Tĕngku Long had been appointed Sultan by the governor general of Bengal, with the title "Sultan Husain Shah ibnu 'l-Marhum Sultan Mahmud Shah, in the town of Singapore and in the districts and shores thereof." The Europeans saluted; the guns on the ships were fired. Raffles and Farquhar escorted the new Sultan to the Těměnggong's house. Then Raffles went back to his ship and the Sultan said to the Těměnggong:

"Build me a palace, for I must ask my wife to come here from Riau and all the retinue of my palace."

Next day Raffles moved ashore, to live in an atap house which was built for him, with his brother-in-law Captain Flint, whom he appointed harbor master of the town. The house stood at the end of Singapore Point.

He gave Těngku Long a thousand dollars, a roll of black broadcloth, a roll of yellow broadcloth, and a fixed allowance agreed on between them.

Traders poured in, says Abdullah. Merchandise came from all countries like the flood tide, especially European goods. Every day auctions were being held, four or five at a time in different parts of the new town. All the houses were merely hastily built ones of atap, for there was no time to build brick ones. The first brick building was for the "police"—that is, the courthouse. When Abdullah arrived at Singapore four months after the occupation, the houses were still chiefly atap.

One day Raffles had an audience with the Sultan and suggested that he take steps to put a stop to piracy, which had flourished around this coast for many generations. What, then, asked the Sultan, would they do for revenue? Sir Stamford said that there were fortunes being made every day in trade, and he would be glad to arrange that the Sultan start out with an excellent stock of the best European goods. The Sultan was horrified at this suggestion and became extremely haughty. Good gracious no, he said; a sultan and a sultan's son couldn't trade. Whatever did the Englishman take them for?

Raffles turned red and replied sharply: "Is it better to be a petty pirate than a trader, then?"

469 ॐ

"Certainly," said the Sultan. "We have always been pirates. The pastime is inherited, and so is no disgrace. But trade! . . ."

It is not often we find Sir Stamford caught out like this, failing to see the other side of an alien philosophy. But even Raffles was vulnerable when it came to a matter of morality. The ethics of honesty were so ingrained in his character he forgot, no doubt, that they didn't obtain everywhere in the world, and that some people saw nothing wrong with piracy.

So much for Abdullah and Singapore. What was happening now among interested Dutch circles?

Plenty. Raffles's first public act when everything was settled was to issue the following proclamation:

"A Treaty having been this day concluded between the British Government and the native authorities, and a British Establishment having been in consequence founded at Singapore, the Honourable Sir T. S. Raffles, Lieutenant-Governor of Bencoolen and its dependencies, Agent to the Governor-General, is pleased to certify the appointment by the Supreme Government of Major William Farquhar of the Madras Engineers to be Resident, and to command the troops at Singapore and its dependencies, and all persons are hereby directed to obey Major Farquhar accordingly. It is further notified that the Residency of Singapore has been placed under the Government of Fort Marlborough, and is to be considered a dependency thereof; of which all persons concerned are desired to take notice.

"Dated at Singapore this 6th day of February 1819."

His private letters are naturally less reserved. He lost no time in sending the all-important news to his faithful friend Assey, to the duchess, to Marsden, and to Mr. Adam, who as secretary to the Bengal Government had written all the letters, actually, which announced to Raffles the desires and commands of Lord Hastings. It is the letter to Assey which includes the phrase made famous by Van der Kemp, "paper war":

"You will be happy to hear that the Station of Singapore contain every advantage, geographical and local, that we can desire—an excellent harbour, which I was the first to discover; capital facilities for defense to shipping if necessary; and the port in the direct track of the China trade. We have a flag at St. John's, and every ship passing through the Straits must go within half a mile of it—in short, you have only to ask any India captain his opinion of the importance of this station even without the harbour which has been discovered. Mynheer will probably enter into a paper war on the subject; but we may, I think, combat their arguments without any difficulty. They had established themselves at Rhio, and by virtue of a treaty, which they had forced the Raja of that place to sign, they assume a right of excluding us from all the islands and declaring the people their vassals. The legitimate successor to the empire of Johor is with us, and, on the ruins of the ancient capital, has signed a treaty with us which placed Sincapore and the neighbouring islands under our protection. We do not meddle with the Dutch at Rhio."

Explaining to the duchess just where his new project is to be found, he says, "Follow me from Calcutta, within the Nicobar and Andaman Islands, to Prince of Wales's Island, then accompany me down the Straits of Malacca, past the town of Malacca, and round the southwestern point of the Peninsula. You will then enter what are called the Straits of Singapore, and in Marsden's map of Sumatra you will observe an island to the north of these straits called Singapura; this is the spot, the site of the ancient maritime capital of the Malays, and within the walls of these fortifications, raised not less than six centuries ago, on which I have planted the British flag, where, I trust, it will long triumphantly wave."

To Marsden: "If I keep Singapore I shall be quite satisfied; and in a few years our influence over the Archipelago, as far as concerns our commerce, will be fully established."

The letter to Adams contains only what has already been expressed in various ways, save that to the secretary he naturally emphasizes the point, which is the most important one he makes, that the Dutch can prefer no valid claim to Singapore. Rhio, he is confident, possesses no authority over Johore, though that is the claim which the Dutch are most likely to make when they begin their protests, which he doubts not will be immediately.

471

Among these letters of the end of January and the early weeks of February it will not be out of place to mention another, though that was written much later, in June. It is the same letter to Colonel Addenbrooke, who had been A.D.C. to Princess Charlotte, in which we have already found timely news of Sophia, during our account of Raffles's private affairs. He addressed Addenbrooke, but it was Prince Leopold's ear he intended to reach when he sent the news of Singapore, for he knew it would interest the Prince because of the many talks they had had in 1817, on the subject of Eastern expansion during Sir Stamford's leave in England. Some of the statements are particularly worth remembering:

"I shall say nothing of the importance which I attach to the permanence of the position I have taken up at Singapore; it is a child of my own. But for my Malay studies I should hardly have known that such a place existed: not only the European, but the Indian world was also ignorant of it. . . . Our object is not territory, but trade; a great commercial emporium, and a *fulcrum*, whence we may extend our influence politically as circumstances may hereafter require."

Soon after the proclamation was issued, Sir Stamford hastened back to Penang, for he had still to visit Acheen and discover the exact position there. Also, it may be remembered, Lady Raffles was at Penang, awaiting her second confinement, and her husband wanted very much to get there in time for it. He missed by just four days, but Sophia was none the worse for having gone through the ordeal without his presence. The journey to Acheen was satisfactory in its way, but none of these political discussions and decisions bore the weight of the great adventure now under way at Singapore, and everyone who knew anything about it appreciated the fact.

The "paper war" started out as Raffles anticipated. As far as we know the first blow was struck by the Dutch when they held in their hands (as early as February) a letter from the Těměnggong at Singapore, describing the arrival of the English in highly imaginative terms. He implied that the occupation had been accomplished by force; Farquhar and Raffles practically burst in on him, he said, and installed their troops and stores before even announcing that they intended to stay there. Farquhar, according to this letter, had almost immediately set forth again to Rhio (which is variously spelled Riau, Rhio, et cetera) and came back dragging Těngku Long, who then, supposedly much against his will, was named Sultan Hussein of Johore and installed as a puppet prince. Sultan Hussein had already sent an apology to the Sultan of Rhio, explaining how it all came about—though it was noticeable that he did not offer to give up the title and honors that had been allegedly forced upon him, the unwilling recipient.

All of this was only natural, and did not even irritate Sir Stamford when it came to his attention, or turn him against the wily native prince and his premier. It was only to be expected that these puppets should safeguard themselves against attacks from any direction. Sultan Hussein, if the Dutch should gain the possession of Singapore, which they obviously were going to try for, would be out of luck unless he could prove, however feebly, that it wasn't his fault the English had set him there on the throne.

The governor of Malacca, full of righteous indignation, duly made a protest to Colonel Bannerman, governor of Prince of Wales Island, setting forth these facts.

Sir Stamford himself replied promptly from Penang. Addressing Timmerman Thyssen, in a letter dated February seventeenth, he wrote: "Sir! I was on the point of addressing Your Excellency for the purpose of apprizing you of the establishment of a British factory at Singapore, when I received from the Governor and Council of this island a copy of the letter which Your Excellency addressed to him on the 10th instant with the documents therein referred to.

"I have now the honour to inform your Excellency, that in pursuance of instructions from the Supreme Government of British India, and by virtue of the authority vested in me as agent to the Most Noble the Marquis of Hastings K.G. etc. etc., Governor-General, by the commission of which I have the honour to inclose a copy in this letter, I have entered into and concluded a treaty and defensive alliance in the name and on behalf of the Governor-General with their Highness Sultan

473 ᘓᔍ

Hussein Mohammed Sjah, eldest son and legitimate heir and successor of His Highness the late Sultan Mohammed Sjah and Datoo Toemengoeng Sri Moharadja Abdul Rahman, Toemengoeng of that division of the empire called Johore proper. By the stipulations of this treaty, a British factory has been established at Singapore and the port and island placed under the protection of the British flag, but as the views of our Government are strictly commercial and as I was earnestly desirous of avoiding collision with the subjects of our ally, His Majesty the King of the Netherlands, whom I understood to be established at Rhio, it has been provided by the treaty, and forms a part of it, that the British government is in no way bound to interfere with the politics of the adjacent states of Rhio, Linga etc. or to assert the Sultan's authority beyond that portion of the empire, in which it is now voluntarily acknowledged.

"From your letter to the Governor and Council of this island, it would appear you have done me the honour of addressing a letter to me, which I have not yet received, in which you make a protest against the occupation of Singapore. I have perused with attention the documents to which you refer in your letter to the government of this island, and do not find in them anything to effect or invalidate the arrangements I have made at that island: in the event therefore of any difference of opinion on this subject I beg leave to refer you to the immediate authority under which I act, and to request that you will do me the honour to transmit a copy of this dispatch to His Excellency the Governor-General of Batavia by the earliest opportunity."

Major Farquhar, now in command as Resident at Singapore since Raffles had gone to Penang, was quick to act on the news as soon as it came to his ears. On March first he addressed Colonel Bannerman.

"Honble. Sir,—Having obtained what I conceive to be authentic information that the Governor of Malacca has addressed a letter to you intimating that the British Establishment recently formed at Singapore has been effected in a forcible manner without the previous consent of the Local

Authorities of the country, and having at the same time ascertained that this information has been grounded on a letter from hence by His Highness the Tumunggong to Mr. Adrian Kock of Malacca, I beg leave herewith to transmit an explanatory document, signed by Tunkoo Long, Sultan of Johore, and the Tumunggong of Singapore, which will no doubt remove every doubt which may have arisen in your mind relative to the proceedings which have taken place.

"I must also take the liberty to request that in the event of the erroneous statement the Honble. Mr. Timmerman Thyssen is said to have transmitted having been received and subsequently forwarded on to the Supreme Government you will have the goodness to transmit a copy of the present dispatch for the information of the Most Noble the Governor-General by the first opportunity.

"ENCLOSURE

"This is to make known to all whom it may concern, that our friend Major William Farquhar, British Resident of the Settlement of Singapore, has called upon me to declare whether or not any letter or letters have been written by me to the Governor of Malacca, or to any person under his authority, or to the Rajah Mooda of Rhio, intimating that the factory which the English have recently established here was forcibly formed entirely against my will; I hereby freely acknowledge that I did write a letter to Mr. Adrian Kock of Malacca, and one to the Rajah Mooda of Rhio, to the above effect, but my motive for so writing arose solely from the apprehension of bringing on me the vengeance of the Dutch at some future period.

"But I here call God and His Prophet to witness that the English established themselves at Singapore with my free will and consent; and that from the arrival of the Honourable Sir Thomas Stamford Raffles no troops or effects were landed, or anything executed but with the free accord of myself and of the Sultan of Johore. In token of the truth whereof we have hereunto affixed our respective Seals."

The only trouble with this retort of Farquhar's to a protest the existence of which he had merely guessed, but guessed correctly, was that it did not meet all the loose-lying ends of the affair. To the British official mind it appeared that if Raffles had committed a misdemeanor or mistake his wrong lay not so much in having used force to land on Singapore Island and appoint an unwilling prince to be its puppet head as in having done this, as it were, *illegally*. That is to say, if he had merely been filling a vacuum, the British official mind would not have been shocked that he did it by a show of strength. The B.O.M. considered any place a vacuum which had not yet been occupied and claimed by some white man's government. Therefore, if the Dutch had truly, as they claimed, signed a treaty with a genuine Sultan of Johore on November 26, 1818 (as well as with the sultans of Pahang, Rhio, Lingen, and dependencies), which gave them exclusive right to establish factories at these places, Sir Stamford was out of bounds in occupying Singapore, a dependency of Johore. Definitely out of bounds. The question of whether or not he used force in so doing was secondary and unimportant.

Colonel Bannerman was inclined to believe the worst of Raffles in any case. Most exemplars of the British official mind were, it will be remembered, and no wonder. Starting out with this universal suspicion that Sir Stamford was an ever-troublesome stormy petrel, he glanced hastily at the Dutch claims, decided they were sound, and forwarded the whole matter to Calcutta along with his own opinion, most sententiously worded. His motto was, "In case of doubt, Sir Stamford is probably picking on the Dutch again."

A few days later the gallant colonel was further disturbed, in fact he was set to shaking in his military boots, by the rumor that the Dutch were getting ready to make war on the British at Singapore. Though a colonel, it did not occur to the governor to wonder at a nation so comparatively weak in sea power as Holland daring to get as belligerent as all that over what was, after all, merely a local argument. In actuality, Holland's declaring war on Great Britain at that point would have been as likely as a Maltese poodle making trouble for an

Alsatian shepherd dog. Bannerman didn't behave at all like an Alsatian. As fast as he could write and send it off he perpetrated the following letter to Timmerman Thyssen:

"Honble. Sir,—Information having reached me that the Netherlanders' Government of Java are, it is strongly believed, preparing to send up a force with orders to seize the English detachment posted at Singapore under the command of Major Farquhar, I conceive it as a duty I owe to you, as much as to myself, to apprise you immediately that the whole subject respecting the occupation of that island was referred by me to the Most Noble the Governor-General on the 17th ultimo, and that his Lordship's reply may be expected before the expiration of twenty or thirty days from this date.

"Pending this reference therefore, motives of humanity I hope you will allow, as well as the undoubted duty of preserving undisturbed the very friendly relations subsisting between our respective countries, call upon us to adopt ourselves and to recommend to the Netherlands Government of Java the same moderation and goodwill as have hitherto attended the transactions between your Government and mine. With this view I have a right to expect that you will join your best endeavours with mine in deprecating any such violent measure on the part of the Java Government as would lead to a cruel effusion of blood and excite a collision between Great Britain and Holland.

"I am the more induced to make this appeal to you as Sir Stamford Raffles is not under the control of this Government, and I am really unacquainted with the nature of the reply he may have returned to your communication of the Treaty existing between your Government and the Kingdom of Rhio, etc. . . .

"P. S.—I have the honour to add that Sir Stamford Raffles is now absent from this settlement."

At the same time Bannerman was refusing the urgent request of Farquhar, who had also heard the rumor and was equally excited by it, though why he should have credited the tale is a mystery until we remember how jittery an isolated community can become over even the most unlikely threats and perils, and this story came from a reliable source. Farquhar wanted reinforcements, because an acquaintance of his, a Captain Ross, had sailed into Singapore Harbor bearing the news that the Dutch were mobilizing over at Batavia. Bannerman replied coldly that Farquhar could take care of himself, when it became necessary, simply by moving out of the disputed territory with all his retinue, and that in any case he should remember that the whole thing had been done against his, Bannerman's, advice. The governor of Prince of Wales Island wished it to be understood without any chance of mistake that he had always kept clear of the affair. Come the Revolution, or rather the Retribution, Bannerman intended being on the safe side, no doubt about that. Probably Boulger is not wrong in attributing his attitude to another reason as well—he knew that Singapore as a British post would wipe out the importance of his Penang, leeching that city of the red corpuscles of trade until it died of anemia. Even so, Bannerman's behavior was a remarkable exhibition. One need not belong to Walpole's category of good Englishmen to feel contempt for his actions.

It was not the first effort Bannerman had made to put a spoke in Raffles's wheel. An earlier attempt was nearly successful. The governor had actually sent a strongly worded letter to Lord Hastings soon after the new year opened, when Raffles was in Penang, having just arrived there on his journey south under Hastings's orders. The idea of an establishment either at Rhio or at Singapore, declared the governor in this dispatch, was totally unfeasible. The Dutch had every bit of territory sewed up, he said; a new establishment was merely another crackpot Raffles scheme, and the governor general should not leave himself open to attack by countenancing any such attempt to embroil England in a war, for this was obviously what Raffles wanted.

Had it not been for the previous relations between Lord Hastings and Sir Stamford, the real motive behind this outburst might have been obvious to Hastings, but it played on a familiar theme, and rang a bell in the governor general's memory, and worked mischief. Besides, there was that worrisome fact of the Dutch occupation of Rhio. Supposing they were right in their claim, and that Johore was, indeed, a sort of Rhio, held under the same treaty? Hastings considered a bit and then tried to back water on his former decision. He replied to Bannerman, "Sir Thomas Raffles was not justified in sending Major Farquhar eastward after the Dutch protested; and, if the Post has not yet been obtained, he is to desist from any further attempt to establish one."

However, the post *had* been obtained, for this letter was not written until February twentieth. Raffles had got in just under the wire. He had known what he was doing when he avoided delay as much as possible and rushed headlong to Singapore!

Even now the matter was not closed, and he was to spend many anxious moments before it was. In London the faithful Assey kept a close eye on developments; he could have explained something of Hastings's nervous vacillations from his point of view there. The Secret Committee was definitely disturbed by Raffles's latest activities. Assey wrote to Dr. Raffles, Sir Stamford's cousin, early in May of that year:

"We have been under considerable apprehension lately. Ministers were most excessively angry at the publication of his, Sir Stamford's recent Protests and Proceedings with the Dutch Authorities"—referring, it will be recalled, to the Palembang affair and the protest which Raffles published later—"especially those in the Cabinet, who have had the credit of concluding the arrangements under which the restitution of Java was to be effected, and they were earnest in requiring his removal from Bencoolen." George Canning, particularly. "The fortunate arrival of intelligence, however, from Calcutta of his reception by my Lord Hastings, and his subsequent mission to Rhio under the immediate direction and orders of the Governor-General in Council, enabled his friends to interpose with greater effect, and I am happy in being able to communicate to you that the original expression of the sentiments of the authorities here is much softened, and we confidently trust that nothing will happen to his prejudice at Bencoolen, because it is left to the Government in India to determine the necessity of any change. In the meantime Sir Stamford has been apprised of the feeling of Ministers towards him, and when he is thus convinced that he cannot expect the support which he had anticipated, it is to be hoped that he will remain quiet."

Vain hope! Charles Assey of all people should have known better than to indulge in such a dream. Even as he wrote these words, Sir Stamford was landing himself in more hot water and imperiling that new understanding he had achieved with Hastings, which came in so opportunely when Canning demanded his head on a silver charger. Reading the sequence of events, one cannot resist giving thanks on Raffles's behalf that the telegraph had not yet been invented. He owes his ultimate success entirely to the delay in transit of news between England and the East to which it was all subject in those days. When Hastings was angry with him, England was not; when England was infuriated against him, Hastings had got over his peeve; by the time Hastings had swung back to anger, his temporary liking for Sir Stamford had reached the ears of the Secret Committee and saved the unfortunate Raffles once again.

"He is undoubtedly right," Assey added anxiously, for fear he had given a wrong impression of his own sentiments toward his former chief, "in principle, and the day will come when the national advantage of his propositions and the value of his active exertions will be acknowledged; but at present expediency seems to be more the order of the day,—and the secrets of European politics are opposed to him."

That they were. To give one good all-round example of what went on behind Raffles's back when Fate was really trying to do him down, I quote in its entirety the fascinating letter Bannerman, drunk with his own perfume, now wrote to Lord Hastings.

THE GOVERNOR.

I have the honour to present to the Board a letter from Major Farquhar, dated 1st instant, conveying intelligence of a very extraordinary communication which the Chiefs of

Johore and Singapoor appear to have spontaneously and clandestinely made to the Rajah Mooda of Rhio, and to Mr. Adrian Kock, the Senior Member of the Dutch Council at Malacca.

Although the circumstance mentioned in Major Farquhar's letter had not previously come to our knowledge, yet I conceive we are bound to forward these documents by the very first opportunity to the Governor-General.

It is, however, very unfortunate that Major Farquhar's present communication, instead of removing the mischievous impressions which the secret correspondence of the Chiefs may have excited, will, on the contrary, only serve to strengthen them materially in the minds of the Hollanders, and nowhere more so than in Europe, where the inference will undoubtedly be, that whilst the secret letters of these Native Chiefs were spontaneous and untutored, their recantation forwarded by Major Farquhar was written under the control of that officer.

There is one fact, however, deducible from this correspondence, and which I must notice, as it substantiates the truth of my former assertion, that the Chiefs of Singapoor and Johore are dependants of the Sultan [of] Rhio, etc. I can see no other reason why these Chiefs should have addressed the Rajah Mooda of Rhio, but that they knew they were accountable to him for their conduct, and had reason to dread his vengeance as much as that of the Hollanders.

16th March.

Since writing the above, a despatch-prow has brought me another letter from Major Farquhar, dated 6th instant, reporting, as the Board may see, that Captain Ross of the Honourable Company's Marine has given him information of the Dutch Governor of Malacca having strongly recommended the Government of Java to send up a force and seize the party at Singapoor, and requiring therefore a reinforcement of troops to enable him to maintain his post against a hostile attack on the part of the Netherlanders.

It must be notorious that any force we are able to detach to Singapoor could not resist the overpowering armament at the disposal of the Batavia Government, although its presence would certainly compel Major Farquhar to resist the Netherlanders even to the shedding of blood, and its ultimate and forced submission would tarnish the national honour infinitely more seriously than the degradation which would ensue from the retreat of the small party now at Singapoor.

Neither Major Farquhar's honour as a soldier nor the honour of the British Government now require him to attempt the defence of Singapoor by force of arms against the Netherlanders, as he knows Sir Stamford Raffles has occupied that island in violation of the orders of the Supreme Government, and as he knows that any opposition from his present small party would be a useless and reprehensible sacrifice of men, when made against the overwhelming Naval and Military force that the Dutch will employ. Under these circumstances I am satisfied that Major Farquhar must be certain that he would not be justified in shedding blood in the maintenance of his post at present.

The question then is, Shall this Government reinforce Major Farquhar, and invite him to a violent opposition against the Netherlanders? or shall it recommend him rather to evacuate the Post Sir S. Raffles has so injudiciously chosen, than shed a drop of human blood in its defence?

After the knowledge we possess of the views and present policy of the Governor-General; after the information we have obtained of the means used by Sir Stamford Raffles to obtain the Island of Singapoor; and after the intelligence we have received of the Dutch right to that territory, admitted as it is, by the secret correspondence of the Chiefs there, I am decidedly of opinion that this Government will not be justified in reinforcing Major Farquhar and inciting him to resist the Hollanders by force of arms.

I had fully stated the possibility of a hostile attack from the Dutch to the worthy Major, when he first lost sight of his usual prudence, and allowed himself to be seduced and made a party in Sir Stamford Raffles's proceedings, as it appeared to me upon the receipt of that gentleman's letter of the 1st of January, and although my advice was then little attended to, yet my duty, as well as a considerable portion of personal regard, will not now permit me to withhold from offering it to him again, accompanied as it may be with much responsibility to myself.

I beg, then, that the accompanying reply be returned to that officer by the despatch-prow, together with copies of the different papers alluded to therein; and I further propose that the accompanying temperate and firm remonstrance be immediately addressed to Mr. Timmerman Thyssen, by means of which I hope any projected violent measures of his Government will be deprecated, without affecting in the slightest degree the national honour and credit.

I also beg to recommend, as no opportunity will probably occur for several weeks, and as Major Farquhar would in the meantime be exposed to inconvenience, that one of the transports taken up for the convenience of the relief be sent to Singapoor, with another European officer and a further supply of six thousand dollars. This last I am, however, surprised to learn that he should require so soon, for his small detachment has not been forty days at Singapoor before it appears to have expended so large a sum as 15,000 dollars which was taken with it.

In proposing to send this transport to Major Farquhar, I have another object in view. I have just had reason to believe that the Ganges and Nearchus (the only two vessels now at Singapoor) are quite incapable of receiving on board the whole of the detachment there, in the event of Major Farquhar's judgment deciding that a retreat from the Post would be most advisable. If, therefore, one of the transports is victualled equal to one month's consumption for two hundred and fifty men, and sent to Singapoor, with authority given to Major Farquhar to employ her should her services be requisite, that officer will then have ample means for removing, whenever indispensably necessary, not only all his party, but such of the native inhabitants as may fear the Dutch vengeance, and whom it would be most cruel to desert.

This arrangement, the Board knows, may be executed without any additional expense and without much inconvenience, as the transport is now lying idle in this harbour, and as the instructions of the Governor-General respecting Singapoor will certainly arrive before she can be probably required. I desire, therefore, the Secretary to Government may issue the necessary directions to the proper departments, and also address the accompanying letter to Major Farquhar.

I must here fairly acquaint the Board that this measure of despatching a transport to Major Farquhar will subject us to one serious imputation, i.e. that we held out inducements and furnished means to that officer to withdraw the Establishment from Singapoor, which he otherwise would not and could not have done.

The necessity of sending another officer and more money to Major Farquhar must be allowed to be urgent, indispensable, and immediate; and as to the expediency of placing within his power means, and British means, for withdrawing from a Post whence a Dutch force may, in the first instance, induce him to consent retreat, and then compel him to embark on board one of their ships, my conscience tells me is equally indispensable and proper, and calculated to save the national character from a very great portion of disgrace. I confess the mortification to me would be infinitely aggravated if I was Major Farquhar and his detachment brought into this port under the Dutch flag. If the Netherlanders visit him, I certainly think they will never allow him to wait for any reference to this Government for a vessel, but insist upon his immediately embarking the Establishment on board of their ships.

Under every view of the case, therefore, I think it is our undoubted duty to furnish Major Farquhar with means for removing the Establishment in an English vessel if such a measure becomes indispensable.

However invidious the task, I cannot close this Minute without pointing out to the notice of our superiors the very extraordinary conduct of the Lieutenant-Governor of Bencoolen. He posts a detachment at Singapoor under very equivocal circumstances, without even the means of coming away, and with such defective instructions and slender resources that, before it has been there a month, its commander is obliged to apply for money to this Government, whose duty it becomes to offer that officer advice and means against an event which Sir Stamford Raffles ought to have expected, and for which he ought to have made an express provision in his instructions to that officer.

My letters of the 15th and 17th February will prove that upon his return from Singapoor I offered him any supplies he might require for the detachment he had left there, and also earnestly called upon him to transmit instructions to Major Farquhar for the guidance of his conduct in the possible event of the Netherlanders attempting to dislodge him by force of arms. Did he avail himself of my offer and state what further supplies Major Farquhar would require? or did he attend to my appeal and send the requisite instructions to that officer? No. He set off for Acheen, and left Major Farquhar to shift for himself. In fact he acted (as a friend of mine emphatically observed) like a man who sets a house on fire and then runs away.

J. A. BANNERMAN

I think we are safe this time in trusting completely to Boulger's historical judgment, which if one agrees with Kemp's theory is all right as long as his jingo passions are not aroused. He says two factors now militated in Sir Stamford's favor: (1) though the governor general had given orders that the project should be abandoned if the post had not yet been founded, the post jolly well had been founded by the time his letter reached Bannerman, six weeks before. Thus his orders didn't stand, according to his own word. Also, he may possibly have recollected—late it is true but not too late— that he had agreed with Raffles during their early interviews on the necessity of curbing Dutch expansion and aggression. Then (2), there was something undeniably nasty in the spectacle of a British official, a governor at that, actually taking sides with the Dutch, who had recently been at war with England and for all he knew would soon be at war again, against his own compatriot, when that compatriot was acting on orders from Lord Hastings himself. In attacking Raffles's actions Bannerman was attacking Hastings's authority, a fact which he had completely forgotten if he ever gave it a thought in his jealous haste to discredit his colleague.

Whereupon Hastings, without further loss of time, rapped Bannerman over the knuckles.

"With regard to Singapore, we (the Governor-General in Council) say that we think your Government entirely wrong in determining so broadly against the propriety of the step taken by Sir Thomas Raffles; 'the opposition of the Dutch' was not of the nature which we had directed to be shunned under the description of collision. The ground on which Sir Thomas Raffles stood was this, that Singapore was never mentioned in the Treaty between the Sultan of Johore and the Dutch. The supposition that it was included in the general term of dependencies is one of those gratuitous assumptions which merit no consideration. We fear you would have difficulty in excusing yourselves should the Dutch be tempted to violence against that Post. The jealousy of it, should misfortune occur and be traceable to neglect originating in such a feeling, will find no tolerance with Government, who must be satisfied (which is not now the case) that perseverance in maintaining the Post would be an infraction of equity, before they can consent to abandon it."

Unfortunately nobody seems to have recorded what the earnest Colonel Bannerman said on receipt of this dispatch. All we know is that he immediately, without further comment, sent two hundred troops and six thousand dollars to Farquhar at Singapore. Not, however, one supposes, with love and kisses.

CHAPTER XXVII

The official date of Singapore's founding is January 29, 1819, but not until well on in 1822 was the "paper war" finished. Not until then could Raffles breathe easily, at last assured that his beloved colony would not go the way of his other beloved colonies, into the greedy maw of the Dutch nation.

The happy British public was not forced to wait as long as Sir Stamford for this reassurance. They never had a doubt. No matter how much dirty linen may have accrued to the Company by laundry day, the directors didn't do their scrubbing and rubbing in public, and their officials allowed to pass unchallenged a joyously congratulatory leader ("editorial" to you, Americans) which appeared in the Calcutta *Journal* March 19, 1819, and was reprinted in the august London *Times* the following September seventh.

". . . We believe and earnestly hope," wrote the editor, "that the establishment of a settlement under such favourable circumstances, and at a moment when we had every reason to fear that the efforts of the Dutch had been successful in excluding us altogether from the Eastern Archipelago, will receive all the support which is necessary to its progress, and that by its rapid advance in wealth, industry and population, which in their establishment and development form the most

487

honourable monuments of statesmen, it will attest hereafter the wisdom and foresight of the present administration, and its attention to the commercial and political interests of our country.

"We congratulate our Eastern friends, and the commercial world in general, on the event which we this day report to them. They will rejoice in our having occupied the position which was required as a fulcrum for the support of our Eastern—and China—trade and from whence we can extend our commercial views and speculations. The spell of Dutch monopoly, so justly reviled and detested, and which had nearly been again established, has been dissolved by the ethereal touch of that wand which broke in pieces the confederacy that lately threatened our continental possession; and while we are indebted to the noble ruler of these dominions for the peace and security of our homes, we have not the less reason to admire and applaud the extensive foresight by which another and a nearer link has been added to connect us with China, and by which our Eastern commerce has been secured."

Very spirited, very pretty, but somewhat premature, was what Sir Stamford must have thought, in gloomy mood, on reading this effusion. It was all so much what he had been preaching until his throat was hoarse, and it seemed so true and obvious, and it was so evidently the popular trend of thought, that a stupider man than he might have gone completely off the rails at the first reading, have seen too much significance in the article, and assumed that everything was already settled to his complete satisfaction. But years of unpleasant experience had taught Sir Stamford a hard lesson. Public opinion means very little to politicians; after all, don't they mold it? So Raffles ignored the Calcutta *Journal*; he continued to plead his cause and attend to his business at Bencoolen, and at long distance he watched his city grow by leaps and bounds.

In truth its development went on at an amazing speed. Even by the time the Calcutta *Journal's* leader was reprinted in London it was becoming evident that Singapore was something unprecedented in colonial history. Paradoxically, however, the appearance in England of the enthusiastic editorial coincided with an outburst of enraged attacks upon Sir Stamford by the Secret Committee, for the news had only just arrived, at East India House as at the *Times* office. The governor general came in for his share of scolding, though they spared him abuse. No one found anything in Hastings's behavior to approve. Already the committee had expressed themselves definitely and repeatedly on the general subject of that annoying man Raffles, as for example in reply to an earlier dispatch from Hastings, about May, which signified his intention to send Raffles East in order to find a spot for a new establishment. Because such a mission was likely to bring Raffles into close contact with the Dutch, the committee had nearly scratched straight through the letter paper in their eager haste to head off that dangerous plan.

"We express our decided disapprobation of the extension in any degree to Eastern islands of that system of subsidiary alliance which has prevailed, perhaps too widely, in India," they had said firmly, back in the summer of 1810. But the message, as we know, arrived too late: all too evidently it had crossed, somewhere in midocean, Lord Hastings's rather apprehensive announcement that the nation now had a new factory on Singapore Island. To say that the committee blew its top would be understating the case. Judging from the records, one supposes that the dignified committee members fairly screamed with exasperation when they heard the appalling news. Poor Lord Hastings! He may have been vacillating and pusillanimous and all the other polite words one uses when one wants to call a man a sneaking coward politely, but his lot was not a happy one. Few of the governors general of Bengal knew how to manage the committee or dared take a firm hand with the gentlemen in London. Lord Minto was one of those few, but Hastings, to put it mildly, was not.

However, the members of the committee managed to get a strong hold on their tempers before quite burning up in the first heat of rage, and without ordering Hastings home, without even commanding that Sir Stamford be kicked out of the

Company in disgrace and Singapore dusted off and tenderly handed over to the Dutch, they agreed to wait and investigate the claims of the Netherlands before making any decision.

In the meantime Hastings himself was in an undignified hurry to back water and soothe the Dutch. On June 26, 1819, he sent a letter from Calcutta, signed by himself and two other members of government, which included certain placatory phrases:

"3. . . . The spirit of aggrandizement, evinced in the proceedings of the Commissioners-General of His Netherlandish Majesty, and their manifest endeavours to establish the absolute supremacy of the Netherlands in the Eastern seas, made it necessary for us to adopt precaution with a view to avert the injury and degradation, which could not fail to ensue from a listless submission to the unbounded pretensions displayed on the part of your nation.

"4. That our views relative to those seas have ever been confined to the security of our own commerce, combined with the freedom of that of other nations, is a position which does not need demonstration. Its undeniable truth is shown by the whole series of our conduct in the Eastern seas, during the period, when our power in that quarter was unrivalled and unassailable. We might then without difficulty have made arrangements for the establishment of our supremacy and might have stipulated for the preservation of those arrangements at the general peace of Europe. Instead of which we shunned the ready means of aggrandizement and restored to your nation its noble colonies, without having made any step towards the increase of our own power, during the long interval in which no nation of any quarter of the globe could have impeded its extension.

"5. In restoring your colonies with unlimited confidence and without any literal restriction, we had not to expect that you would assume as restored what we never received from you, and never occupied ourselves. We little thought that some of the first acts of your Government after the restitution would be to reduce to vassalage the states, which we had treated as perfectly independent, and to impose treaties on those states, having for one of their principal objectives the exclusion of our commerce from all ports, except when admitted by your permission. . . .

"7. . . . . after the designs of the Netherlandish authorities had become unambiguously manifest, we were desirous of forming precautionary engagements with the independent governments of Rhio, Lingin and Johor; and for the execution of this purpose a mission was deputed under Sir T. S. Raffles, to be assisted by Major Farquhar, who were both selected for that duty from their intimate knowledge of the affairs of the Eastern archipelago.

"8. So anxious were we at the same time to avoid the least collision with the Netherlandish authorities, that we directed Sir T. S. Raffles to abstain from further intercourse with Rhio, should he find any post established there on your part; though our previous treaty with that state gave us a right to consider ourselves as already connected with it.

"9. In the same spirit we warned Sir T. S. Raffles that, even in the event of your having extended your claims over the whole of the ancient kingdom of Johor, refutable as we should conceive such pretensions to be, we were not disposed to incur the probability of clashing with the Netherlandish Government in India on that question, but should reserve it for the decision of our respective governments in Europe.

"10. Sir T. S. Raffles, on his arrival at Prince of Wales' Island, found that the agents of your nation had anticipated him in Rhio. He therefore very properly avoided that port.

"11. He proceeded to Singapoor and there formed a treaty, with a chief, whom he describes as the rightful sovereign of Johor, as well as with the local Government, which he represents as being independent of that established at Rhio. A copy of the treaty is annexed for your Excellency's information.

"12. Sir T. S. Raffles has not sufficiently explained to us why he proceeded to Singapoor, after learning the extent of the pretensions advanced by your agents at Malacca. A strict attention to our instructions would have induced him to avoid the possibility of collision with the Netherlandish authorities on any point. And so sincere is our desire to bar the possibility of any altercations with your Excellency's Government that the occupation of Singapoor has been to us a source of unfeigned regret.

"13. In fact, after becoming acquainted with the extent of the pretensions advanced on the part of your nation, and before we knew of the establishment of a factory at Singapoor, we had issued instructions to Sir T. S. Raffles directing him if our orders should arrive in time, to desist from every attempt to form a British establishment in the Eastern archipelago.

"14. These orders did not however arrive early enough to prevent the establishment of a factory at Singapoor; and the question for our consideration now is, whether we shall maintain the establishment which has been formed, or carry a complimentary deference for the Netherlandish authorities so far as to withdraw it.

"15. We flatter ourselves that your Excellency's candour will at a single glance perceive the difficulty in which we are placed, as well as the wide difference between that state of circumstances in which we should have been at liberty to indulge our solicitude to shun any apparent discordance with your Government, and the case now before us in consequence of the actual establishment of a factory at Singapoor. . . .

"17. But that which we were so studious to avoid, has now perversely occurred; we find ourselves established by treaty with the native government on a spot from which your Excellency asserts a right to exclude us. We cannot relinquish our possession on your demand without subscribing to the right which you claim, and of which we are not satisfied; thereby awkwardly forestalling the judgment, which must have taken place at home.

"18. By the same account we should sacrifice the interests of those who have entered into engagements with us, injure our own reputation by such a sacrifice and justly suffer irretrievable loss of influence through so inexplicable a proceeding.

"19. Let us be convinced that, in establishing a factory at Singapoor, we have intruded on any right possessed by your nation or any claim which we are bound in equity to respect. In this case we should immediately withdraw our establishment from Singapoor, fully recognising your title to expect that course of conduct from us.

"20. On this point we at present entertain the strongest doubts, which we proceed to explain most frankly to your Excellency, in order that your Excellency may favour us, if it be in your power, with such proofs and arguments as may tend to remove them.

"21. Your Excellency claims Rhio, Johor, Pahang and Lingin as dependencies of Malacca. But, when our Government was established at Malacca, the Dutch authorities at that place, in pursuance of the declared intentions of their superiors, the government of Batavia, had withdrawn their establishments from Rhio, the only post in their occupation, and declared the independence of the chief of that country. On the strength of that public and conclusive transaction we have always considered and treated Rhio as an independent state, and never exercised over it any act of supremacy.

"22. When we restored Malacca to you, we could not restore that which we did not receive from you. We did not restore Rhio, Johor, Lingin and Pahang as dependencies of Malacca, because (not having obtained them from you) we did not possess them as such. We restored to you what was transferred to us in 1795 and nothing more. That transfer did not include Rhio, Johor, Lingin and Pahang, and this seems to be admitted in your Excellency's letter to which we have now the honour to reply. . . .

"25. If, as we hold to be the case, you have no just claim founded on engagements, which may have existed before the transfer of Malacca in 1795, your only right depends on the treaty concluded at Rhio on the 26th November 1818.

"26. This treaty was subsequent to the one settled by Major Farquhar on the part of the British government with the government of Batavia in the August preceding.

"27. Major Farquhar's treaty was settled with the government of Rhio, not as a dependency of Malacca, but as an independent state, purposely with a view to the validity and value of the connection, after the restoration of Malacca to your nation.

"28. The treaty subsequently entered into by your agents at Rhio, declares the treaty previously concluded on the part of the British government to be null and void. The conciliatory spirit in which we sought to avoid all differences here, and to leave all points to adjustment at home is sufficiently proved by our not having remonstrated against this most extraordinary and injurious proceeding.

"33. . . . Java was in the possession of Holland on the 1st January 1803. When Java came into our possession the only dependencies beyond the island attached to that Government, were the residencies of Macassar on Celebes, and Copang on Timor, and the factories at Palembang and Japan, and these only are we bound to acknowledge as the proper dependencies of Java reverting to your Sovereign with that colony by the convention of August 1815. When your Excellency carries your pretensions further, as we have a deep interest, so we possess an indisputable right to examine into their foundations.

"34. Malacca was not actually in the occupation of Holland on the 1st January 1803; but has nevertheless been restored with the only dependency which came into our hands along with that settlement.

"35. According to this interpretation, if we had received Singapoor as a dependency of Malacca in 1795, if at that time the Dutch authorities had made over to us any factories or establishments of any kind at Singapoor, if they had even asserted an acknowledged right to that place as a dependency, we should now, notwithstanding the lapse of so many years during which it has been independent, be disposed to recognize your claim. But the Dutch authorities which transferred Malacca in 1795 declared that Rhio and Johor, Pahang and Lingin, through the first of which you claim Singapoor, were not dependencies of Malacca.

"36. We observe in the letter of your Excellency, to which we have now the honour of replying, that you are disposed to argue that the withdrawing of the Dutch establishments from the states of Johor, Pahang, Rhio and Lingin, and the declaration by the Dutch authorities at Malacca of the independence of those states, were measures not approved by the constituted authorities of the Dutch East India Company. . . .

"39. If we could agree to consider Rhio as a dependency of Malacca, it would still remain to be shown that Singapoor is a dependency of Rhio, or of the principality of which the Government resides at Rhio.

"40. This brings us to the point where the chiefs who made treaties with us at Singapoor were competent to make those treaties. . . .

"43. In the meantime we have the honour to enclose a statement of information already received, which makes it appear that the chiefs at Singapoor are independent of those at Rhio and Lingin; and which directly contradicts the statement made to your Excellency, that some adventurer, named Tookoelon, had been brought forward as a pretender to the throne in order to sanction the procedure of Sir S. Raffles. . . .

"45. We shall endeavor to ascertain to our own satisfaction whether or not the Netherlandish nation possesses a right to the exclusive occupation of Singapoor, and if that point be decided in the affirmative, we shall without hesitation obey the dictates of justice by withdrawing all our establishments from that place. We most cordially invite your Excellency to furnish us with proofs of the justness of your pretensions. We do not seek any advantage, which is not supported by truth and equity, and we shall really feel indebted to your Excellency for putting us right, if we have erred in the view which we have taken of this question.

"46. In like manner we shall endeavor to ascertain whether or not the chiefs of Singapoor with whom Sir T. S. Raffles has concluded engagements, possessed a right to enter into those engagements; and if it should appear that the right to the government of Lingin or that of Rhio, or of any other native power, has been violated, our respect for the rights of every power will induce us instantly to abandon Singapoor, on the requisition of the injured power. . . .

"57. The measures pursued by the Netherlandish government since its reestablishment in the Eastern archipelago leave us only the choice of one of three modes of acting. To submit implicitly to all your pretensions, which our interests and our honour alike forbid. To oppose then by systematic counter-action and resistance which friendship and courtesy prohibit. Or to refer all questions for the decision of our respective governments in Europe, which is the course we have adopted. . . .

"59. If we were to imitate the policy acted by the Netherlandish authorities and seek to obtain exclusive privileges in the numerous ports and countries of the Eastern archipelago, we entreat your Excellency to reflect on the probable consequences of the continual collision of interests and disputes of subordinate authorities which would unavoidably ensue.

"60. We trust, therefore, that your Excellency will concur in our view of the expediency of mutual forbearance until we receive the orders which our respective governments in Europe may be expected to transmit for the future regulation of our relative policy and respective possessions and connections in the Eastern archipelago."

In the meantime Singapore proceeded according to plan—Sir Stamford's plan. Farquhar, now a colonel, accepted the post of resident, but only temporarily. Boulger makes a point of the fact that at first the appointment was described by Farquhar himself as temporary because his furlough was already overdue; it was therefore understood that he accept the post only as a favor, in order to give the new establishment a good start in life. But his salary and allowances were comparatively generous, and somewhere in the first months, liking his position better than he had expected, he forgot his early determination. By the end of 1820 he saw that he was onto a good thing—"Its trade," he wrote of Singapore, "already far exceeds what Malacca could boast of during the most flourishing years"—and he changed his mind about the furlough, asking to be allowed to carry on until the season of 1821–22. However, the salary and allowances, when they were considered as arranged on a permanent basis, were unjustifiably high, and so when things had settled down Raffles drew up a plan for the future in which this outlay was much reduced. He decided on a figure for salary and expenses based on the customary amount and appointed John Crawfurd to succeed Farquhar at the end of his term. (He also decided, with Lord Hastings's approval, that Singapore was thenceforth to depend directly upon the supreme government, and not on Penang or any other of the subsidiary governments.) When everything had been arranged, Raffles's secretary wrote Farquhar, asking politely when he would be ready to quit.

Farquhar merely replied in September 1821, that he wasn't ready yet.

At the risk of seeming persistent, Raffles wrote again. Again Farquhar replied vaguely, and settled down more firmly than ever in his nice comfortable post with its nice comfortable salary. At last in 1823, when England had graciously consented to keep Singapore as a permanency, Raffles went to visit his new city, and this time Farquhar was told flatly that he would have to get out and make room for Crawfurd, who was coming soon from Bengal. "Farquhar refused to resign or to recognise Raffles's authority," said Boulger, "and, on the 21st of March 1823, he was summarily removed by an official notification, intimating that his resignation, dated and tendered as far back as the 23rd of October 1820, had been accepted."

It was indeed too bad, as Boulger says, that a long friendship between the two men should thus have come to an end, but there wasn't much else Raffles could have done, considering everything. For once Lord Hastings was firmly back of Sir Stamford, declaring stoutly that Farquhar never had done very well anyway when he departed from Raffles's instructions. It is a matter for conjecture just what Colonel Farquhar hoped to gain by his behavior, aside from a few months more of high salary. There seems small doubt that he was suffering from an aggravated case of swelled head. Months of being boss evidently led him to exaggerate his importance to Bengal. He must have thought that Hastings, forced to make a choice between them, would prefer him to Raffles; no doubt he himself believed by that time that Singapore was entirely his idea and his work from start to finish. This sort of thing happens in every walk of life, every day. But Farquhar, jolted out of his complacent dream, departed from Singapore out of a job, sore and angry, and ready to make the wildest accusations against the man he now considered his successful rival, rather than his superior officer.

If it were not that I am afraid to swamp this account in statistics, I could write pages of figures to prove the rate at which Singapore grew and prospered. A few simple statements, however, are more effective. Farquhar, while still in a happy and good temper, admitted that after one year it was a common sight to count twenty vessels at one time in the harbor. Five years thence, said a Chinese merchant in conversation with him, the yearly revenue would be more than five hundred thousand dollars. Raffles wrote in 1820, early in the year, that the exports and imports by native boats alone, leaving all European trade out of the question, amounted to more than four million dollars in the year.

By this time even the thickest heads at East India House were being penetrated by a new idea, viz., that Raffles might possibly have hit on something good in Singapore. One of the directors, Charles Grant, wrote Sir Stamford to this effect: "The acquisition of Singapore has grown in importance. The stir made here lately for the further enlargement of the Eastern trade fortified that impression. It is now accredited in the India House."

As for Lord Hastings, that barometer of official opinion, he now dared to come out unequivocally in favor of the plan which he had blown on so hot and cold a year before. It was easy to see, he reminded the Court of Directors, that the Dutch would not like the appearance of such a competitive port, and would go so far in their dislike as to advance a prior claim to it even when such a claim might not be considered absolutely honest. Though such a conception seems to have been a sad shock to the Court, who had never before, evidently, entertained the possibility that one of their European neighbors would actually stoop to trickery, a few of them were moved to agree with Hastings. One sees them returning homeward after this session in India House, their heads bowed, their hearts heavy with a new realization of mankind's wickedness. One can well imagine the scene in many a director's humble cottage that evening, when the brokenhearted father of the family tells his wife and little ones that there is, after all, no Santa Claus in international relations.

"But, Daddy," cries an eager child, "you mean the Dutch told a fib?"

"Alas, yes, my child. And what is more, it seems that we have been grievously unjust to that poor man Sir Stamford Raffles. Come sit on Papa's knee and he'll quote you the net profits from Singapore at the end of the fiscal year."

There are so many documents available, chiefly in Van der Kemp's papers, that we could if we wished spend hours reading the entertaining story of the quarrel between Holland and Raffles. On one occasion, for example, Crawfurd, Farquhar's successor as resident, alleged to have discovered from a native report that the Dutch had dug up another prince at Malacca, a brother of the British-appointed Sultan, inviting him to Rhio, where he was "put in possession of what are called the Regalia *and raised to the throne of Johore.*" The regalia, and the possession of the regalia, played a large part in the argument, because the Dutch who took possession of them claimed that according to the natives no sultan could be a sultan without them.

This is Raffles's summary of the situation in retrospect, writing to Marsden about it. "You must be aware that the grounds on which I maintain our right to Singapore rested on the following facts, which it has never been in their power to disprove.

"1st. That subsequent to the death of Sultan Mahomed, which happened about twelve years ago [this was written in 1822] there had been no regular installation of a successor, nor had any Chief been acknowledged as such, with the essential forms required by the Malay custom.

"2nd. That the regalia (the possession of which is considered essential to sovereignty), still remained in the custody of Tunku Putrie, widow of the deceased Sultan.

"3rd. That the Rajah of Lingin had never exercised the authority of Sultan of Johore, and explicitly disclaimed the title, and

"4th. That the prince whom we supported was the eldest son of the late Sultan, and was intended for the succession. That he was acknowledged by one at least, if not both the constituting authorities of the empire, and that he himself stood in no way committed to the Dutch, when I formed the treaty with him.

"The Dutch have allowed nearly four years to pass since our occupation of Singapore, in trying to prove that the Sultan of Lingin was actually invested with the sovereignty of Johore; but finding our ministry more firm than they expected, and that their assertions were not admitted as proofs, they have at last given up the point, and actually proceeded to the seizure of the regalia from the hands of Tunku Putrie."

In the end, as we can see, the argument fell by the wayside, and so, one supposes, did the Dutch entry for the Johore sweepstakes.

The annals are also heavily weighted with letters from natives of high degree who have come to live in Singapore, all in flight, according to Raffles, from Dutch oppression in one colony or another. One Bugginese Prince Beluwa was in flight from more than that, said the Hollanders. He was fleeing justice, and when he had entered Singapore with all his family and retinue of five hundred the British were called upon to grant what would nowadays be termed the right of extradition. Raffles listened to the Prince's plea, however, rather than that of the Dutch, and Beluwa remained where he was, with Raffles absolutely refusing to give him up, safe in Singapore. But the incident didn't improve Anglo-Dutch relations, naturally.

Most of the anxious letters were inspired by hardy perennial rumors that England was going to give in to Holland's representations and move out of Singapore. Every time the story went around town, which was as often as a large mail came in from Calcutta, there would be fresh excitement and worry, and a flood of frightened questions from the public. As time went on, however, it became more and more obvious that the English would not be willing to give up such a profitable colony on anything less than complete, satisfactory proof that they had no right to it.

I shall content myself with very few more figures to support the tale of Singapore's prosperity, but they have been carefully selected and are as simple and as comprehensive as I can find. John Crawfurd has supplied just what we want, I think in an article he wrote not long after his residency was terminated, on the general subject of free trade.

Singapore, founded in 1819 on ground of which not ten acres were cleared and where the population was about three hundred, achieved in nine years the record of £2,875,800 value in combined exports and imports. This was the figure reported on April 30, 1828.

In 1814 England's whole trade in the Strait of Malacca was short of a million sterling. In 1829, the year Crawfurd wrote this article, it considerably exceeded four million.

That figure was achieved only seven years after the final decision was taken to keep Singapore as a part of the Empire.

Raffles's letters preceding this resolution are plentifully sprinkled with references to the settlement and his anxieties. He expressed himself at length to his cousin Tom during the period (1820) when everything looked most uncertain, in an interesting little essay on his plans for the future, and Singapore's general importance in them. "It [Singapore] is all and every thing I could wish," he said, "and if no untimely fate awaits it, promises to become the emporium and pride of the East. I learn with much regret the prejudice and malignity by which I am attacked at home, for the desperate struggle I have maintained against the Dutch. Instead of being supported by my own Government, I find them deserting me, and giving way in every instance to the unscrupulous and enormous assertions of the Dutch. All however is safe so far, and if matters are only allowed to remain as they are all will go well. The great blow has been struck, and though I may personally suffer in the scuffle the nation must be benefited—and I should not be surprised were the ministers to recall me, though I should on many accounts regret it at the present moment.

"Were the value of Singapore properly appreciated, I am confident that all England would be in its favour; it positively takes nothing from the Dutch and is to us every thing; it gives us the command of China and Japan, with Siam and Cambodia, Cochin China, etc. to say nothing of the Islands themselves. . . ."

Between the writing of this letter and the end of his anxiety, when he went to visit Singapore and help draft its laws, Sir Stamford and Lady Raffles were to pass through the horrible experience, as we know, of losing most of their children. It sometimes seems to the reader, glancing through his letters, as if Singapore and the interest Raffles took in it were the only influences that kept him in command of his sanity during his ordeal. Certainly throughout the painful missives which he produced during the worst of the period, when for the first time in his life it was an effort rather than a pleasure to write his good friends, Singapore is a motif which occurs again and again, the only fixed point in his thoughts.

We have already spoken of the case of Palembang and the wrath which Sir Stamford incurred by his action in sending Salmond and troops out on an adventure which missed fire. At least once more his behavior proved unpopular to the authorities in England, though Raffles himself never admitted that he had done anything but right in regard to Pulo Nias. This affair was, in a way, an outgrowth of his earlier activity in regard to slavery, when he set free the Company Africans immediately after his arrival at Fort Marlborough. It will be remembered that some of the Court took umbrage at this, as well as at his closing of the Bencoolen gaming houses and cockfighting establishments, on the overt grounds that he was making free of Company property. Raffles himself never backed down on the subject, however, and his fiery defense, that as a representative of Great Britain he did not see what else he could have done and yet maintained the national reputation, was never answered.

For a long time Raffles had, correctly, regarded the island of Nias as headquarters for the entire slave trade in Sumatra and nearby Java. It was there that the traders, realizing their commerce was rapidly being driven as illegal from the large islands, would meet and hold their auctions. Pulo Nias was still chief clearinghouse for the slave trade of the Indies when Raffles finally occupied it. Those who objected to this maneuver in England argued vaguely, unwilling to come out openly in defense of slavery, that Raffles had been too precipitate, that he should have waited for definite orders before attempting anything of the kind, and that he was, as usual, running the risk of trouble with the Dutch. Cheerfully unregenerate, ignoring all criticism, Sir Stamford wrote in very different terms to Marsden, in January 1821. Observe that he was not yet out of the woods in regard to Singapore when he incurred the wrath of the directors over Pulo Nias. . . . Sometimes one is inclined to sympathize with the Court of Directors, if only because they must have felt so outrageously helpless against the stubbornness of the man.

"I have much satisfaction," he told Marsden, "in reporting that the chiefs of Pulo Nias have ceded the sovereignty of that island to the Company. Our principal station is at Tello Dalum. . . . Not a vestige of primeval forest is to be found on the island; the whole has disappeared before the force of industry; the whole island is a sheet of the richest cultivation that can be imagined, and the interior surpasses in beauty and fertility the richest parts of continental India, if not of Java.

"The people, and in particular the Chiefs, are active and intelligent, rich and powerful, and, as far as we can judge of their character, are the very reverse of those we find on this coast. They have cheerfully entered into our views for abolishing the slave trade; and the people, and the country in general, promise much."

In a letter to another friend he enlarged on the ticklish subject of "black ivory." More than fifteen hundred slaves were taken from Pulo Nias annually, he learned to his horror; the

503 ❧

circumstances, he insisted, were no less "revolting" than those attached to the same industry in Africa. (It was a popular saying in England at the time that the East Indies slaves were far better off than the African. In that way the public kept their consciences quiet.)

"The unhappy victims, torn by violence from their friends and country, are delivered, pinioned hand and foot, to the dealers in human flesh, and kept bound during the whole course of the voyage. Instances have occurred, where the captives have seized a moment of liberty to snatch up the first weapon within their reach, stab all whom they encountered, and conclude the scene by leaping overboard, and seeking deliverance from their persecutors in a watery grave!"

Lady Raffles adds in her own right, "It was impossible to witness the constant scenes of rapine and plunder, to which the coast of the Island had so long been a prey, from the inroads of pirates and slave dealers, after the express injunctions of the legislature, and the principle so universally declared to actuate the civilized nations of the world. It was notorious that Pulo Nias, although for a long period of years nominally enjoying the protection of the English flag, was still the most abundant, and almost the only source of supply of slaves on the coast, and that notwithstanding the prohibition against importation at Bencoolen and elsewhere, it was impossible to prevent it entirely." The Raffleses seemed to have an idea, furthermore, that the natives of Nias were so ripe for conversion to one religion or another that if they weren't quickly supplied with Christianity they would immediately take to Islam instead.

Now this brings us to a matter which has confused desultory readers of oriental history for a generation and a half. It is often stated that Raffles abolished slavery in the Indies and even in British India. On the infrequent occasions that he and his merits are discussed—and approval of Sir Stamford is of course unanimous among the British now that he is dead, though he died under a cloud and almost wiped out by the Company besides—on these occasions, which admittedly do not occur very often, because Raffles has never been glamorized like Clive or Lincoln, he is always given credit first and foremost for this matter of emancipating the slaves. He freed the slaves, say his admirers. Sir Stamford comes in for commendatory mention on the side, too, whenever Lord Minto is discussed; humanitarian colonizing, the abolition of slavery, painless expansion of empire, it's all a part of the story written by Minto and Sir Thomas Stamford Raffles, to hear their admirers tell it.

Nevertheless one keeps stumbling, even after the "emancipation" should have taken place, over puzzling references to slaves. First of all there are the slaves listed on Raffles's expense account on Java. There were also the three slaves which Gillespie allegedly bought, for which the other Englishmen looked askance at him because it wasn't quite an English thing to do. But if slavery was abolished, how did Gillespie manage to buy those slaves, and why was Sir Stamford of all people using slaves in his gardens and plantations? Even the statistics so triumphantly produced, though certainly they prove that the importation of slaves dropped sharply under Raffles's administration, also prove, not quite so flourishingly, that slaves were imported during that period. So what price abolition?

The answer is simple, yet it has always been difficult to put across to the puzzled public. Raffles did *not* abolish slavery. Raffles put a stop to slave *dealing*, which is a different thing. Even in that he was not one hundred per cent successful but he did fairly well; the figures prove it in a roundabout way. We have noted that much already. During his tenure of office at Batavia the value of slaves went up abruptly, so that one had to pay a good deal more for a handmaiden or a good strong carpenter after Raffles's legislative measures than before. That was a simple reaction to the fact of scarcity. No more imports meant higher prices for such marketable items as were still to be found on the island. As for Gillespie's un-English purchases and Raffles's gardening slaves, those are easily explained too. Gillespie probably bought bootleg slaves, and Raffles was using government property as he had to do; he was not empowered to emancipate them without special permission from the

505 ठ❧

Court of Directors, and it is a scandalous fact that he never received that permission.

Indeed, on Sumatra he went against the rules anyway, as soon as he had summed up the situation. I refer to the first ceremony of his term, when solemnly and impressively he set free the Kaffirs, handing a certificate of emancipation to each. This caused a big stink in London, but things had gone further by that time than when Raffles first came to Java, and the ruffled directors dared not make too much of a noise about it for fear of public opinion. Raffles was a good friend, chiefly by correspondence, of the famous Wilberforce, and by 1817 the abolitionist's efforts were bearing fruit throughout the Empire.

Though the distinction may not sound logical, there it was. Under Raffles's reform measures it was still permissible to own slaves, but it was against the law to buy and sell them. Ultimately of course this amounted to the same thing, but literally one cannot say that Raffles emancipated the slaves of the East Indies, because he didn't. The following table of events will serve to explain the matter more clearly. The writer is always being called upon to produce it; only last week an English publisher after an advance reading of this book reproached her for not giving Raffles due credit as the man who did away with slavery in England. Here, then, are the facts.

The export of slaves was forbidden, by proclamation, in 1789. It was certainly on the strength of this proclamation that Raffles based his individual reforms in Batavia (1811–16) and earned for himself sundry directorial scowls and black marks in his copybook.

In 1811, no doubt providing encouragement and a spur to Raffles's activities for the cause, the import of slaves from Arabia was forbidden.

Not until 1824 was anything more done for slaves by legislature in England. This naturally leaves out of the accounting Sir Stamford's spirited antics at Bencoolen in 1818. But in the year 1824 it was at last announced that engaging in the slave trade was legally to be considered piracy, penalty for which in most cases was death. From that time on any Englishman who traded in black ivory was a blackbirder and a felon. *But still it was legal to own slaves.*

Slaves belonging to the Crown were emancipated in 1831.

Two years later, in 1833, slavery was abolished—wait a minute—*as from 1845.* Not before. Raffles by 1845 was dead and beginning to be popular. Ergo, Raffles did not abolish slavery. Is that clear?

And in any case he wasn't allowed to keep Pulo Nias. When Lord Hastings made his deal with the Netherlands and regained Malacca in exchange for British Sumatra, Pulo Nias was a part of the bargain, and slave dealing continued at a brisk rate on that fertile island.

From the letters Sir Stamford wrote, especially to his cousin Tom, we become aware around the Bencoolen period of a genuine softening in his attitude toward Christian missionaries. Until his children were born and began to grow up their father's attitude, while not exactly unbelieving, was certainly lacking in enthusiasm toward Christianity and his own church. Sir Stamford loved to write Dr. Raffles long quizzical dissertations on comparative religion, obviously with intent to tease his cousin a bit, and he sometimes declared that as far as his own opinion counted he was satisfied to see his natives remain Mohammedan. It was a religion which suited them, he implied, better than the milk and water of Christianity, even when Christianity was practiced by a courageous Dissenter like the Rev. Tom. But around 1819, after his marriage to Sophia, the lieutenant governor of Bencoolen dropped his joking attitude and became definitely helpful to the missions, interesting himself in them to the extent of suggesting missions among such difficult social problems as the cannibal Battas. The thin end of the wedge for Raffles was probably the Rev. Milne from China, a fine example of true oriental scholar. But even with other mission people who fell short of Milne's caliber, Raffles went out of his way to encourage them in their teaching.

This was a perfectly natural development. His earlier attitude, though it was the advance guard of a much later time when youth rebelled against all social forms, including the formal church, was too far removed from the fashion of the day for any man approaching middle age to sustain it. To remain an agnostic, Sir Stamford would have had to devote a part of his overcrowded life to self-defense and self-explanation, and the necessity would have grown greater and greater under his wife's gentle pressure and the soft smothering weight of public disapproval. Then too, as Raffles became a conventionally happy man, secure and content with his family and his work, he lost the desire to rebel. His intellect became less exploratory and more spiritual. Intellects have a way of doing that when they approach middle age.

By the time he so desperately wanted comfort and support, when his children died, it is pleasant to realize that Raffles was enough immersed in his church to accept what he needed. Without that little touch of guidance, small as it must have been, Stamford Raffles would doubtless have turned sour and remained sour, hard, and wretched for the rest of his life. Even a good, solid, old-fashioned atheist could scarcely object to Raffles's Christianity as long as it helped him live through those agonizing weeks. Sophia was a different matter; she had always been a conventional, practicing Christian, and perhaps that was a good thing when the children began to slip away. She seemed to draw courage from some inner source, for many another woman has gone under and never risen to the surface again, in like circumstances.

But then Sophia, like so many conventional people, remains a bit of a mystery even though she may not intend to be mysterious. We know that she was stalwart and courageous and not at all stupid, though there is no evidence of humor anywhere in her writings. We know nothing else about her: neither her tastes nor her talents. She was well brought up, and well-brought-up ladies in Sophia's day didn't talk about themselves any more than necessary. Most decidedly never did they talk about their thoughts and emotions, except in well-worn clichés.

It is late both in the day and in the book to repeat ourselves upon this subject, but these two people, Sir Stamford Raffles and his wife, were embarking upon a new phase in their career together and it seems not out of place once more to attempt an evaluation of their characters. I think the answer to the riddle of Sophia Raffles is not far to seek. She suffered agonies, it is true, when her children died, but though her salvation was not the same as her husband's she also had one. His was his work; hers was her life's interest too—her husband. She must indeed have been devoted to him, as he had once written Cousin Tom when describing his bride. Some women are first and foremost wives, and others are first and foremost mothers. Sophia was obviously a wife, and her love for her children came second to her devotion to Raffles. And so, though her heart broke when she lost her beautiful son Leopold and broke afresh when Charlotte lay dead, and must have broken yet again when little Marsden drifted off—though by that time she was too numb to suffer very much—still, groping through the darkness, she did at last encounter the hand of her husband, and she knew that she was not, after all, alone; she still had the dearest one of all. There was still work to do.

In spite of her neutral, quiet colors, then, Sophia is a person we can see clearly enough when we look at Raffles's world. There is nothing vague or shadowy about Sophia. The true Raffles mystery remains, as it has for years, undisturbed in the cemetery of Batavia, beneath Olivia's tombstone.

Sorrowfully resigned and still tottering from weakness, behold Raffles and his Sophia, in 1822, departing from Fort Marlborough with a double purpose: to get away from that now accursed island where they had spent happy years, and to do what Sir Stamford doggedly considered his most important duty, putting Singapore on a firm foundation of law and finance.

Immediately on arriving there Raffles felt better. For the first time since the approach of his tragic domestic crisis he realized that he was still alive and that he did not very much mind having survived, which was a sure sign that health was returning to his wasted body. The familiar miracle of convalescence was enacted once more. He wrote, the day after disembarking:

509 ঠ๑

"We landed yesterday, and I have once more established my headquarters in the centre of my Malayan friends. I have just time to say this much, more you shall have soon and often: in the meantime you will be glad to know that I feel sufficient health and strength to do all I wish. The coldest and most disinterested could not quit Bencoolen, and land at Singapore, without surprise and emotion. What, then, must have been my feelings, after the loss of almost every thing that was dear to me on that ill-fated coast? After all the risks and dangers to which this my almost only child had been exposed, to find it grown and advanced beyond measure, and even my warmest anticipations and expectations, in importance, wealth, and interest—in every thing that can give it value and permanence?

"I did feel when I left Bencoolen, that the time had passed when I could take much active interest in Indian affairs, and I wished myself safe home; but I already feel differently; I feel a new life and vigor about me; and if it please God to grant me health, the next six months will, I hope, make some amends for the gloom of the last sixteen."

The next line is poignant.

"Rob me not of this my political child. . . ."

CHAPTER XXVIII

Though Canning started out with the customary prejudice against John Company's problem child Raffles, he changed his mind. In fact it now seems evident that Canning was the man directly responsible for England's retaining Singapore and saving Sir Stamford's political offspring for the Empire.

C. H. Philips in an article on the Secret Committee discloses this fact and explains how it came to pass. According to him, Canning took the advice of the Secret Committee in the negotiations between England and Holland to settle disputes in the Archipelago (1820–24). Pattison and Marjoribank, chairmen, and Elphinstone and Grant, senior directors, were named by the committee as a *Select* Secret Committee to advise Canning on this matter, and he had such respect for their judgment that he let them overrule his earlier decision to relinquish Great Britain's claim to the island. There were in the Court of Directors five men who had been in office more than twenty-five years—Grant, E. Parry, Elphinstone, Cotton, and Bosanquet—and Canning bowed to their superior experience.

It seems that Canning, "conscious of the weakness of Britain's legal claim to Singapore," would have abandoned the station if the committee had not stubbornly insisted on Singapore's importance to England. That island was the only safeguard, they maintained, to the China fleet's passage through the Strait of Malacca. But Canning was still dubious that Britain could hold the new station, and he asked his advisers to suggest some other port that would do as well for England's purposes. The committee promptly retorted that there was no such place, which was exactly why Singapore "must on no account be relinquished." Canning thereupon agreed to hold on, and Raffles's judgment was vindicated.

Fate stopped just short of fashioning a Greek tragedy, with Sir Stamford Raffles and Sophia each playing both hero and victim. A veritable tidal wave of disaster had swept over Bencoolen, but afterward the waters of Raffles's life became calm and quiet. And then, so gently that one scarcely saw how swiftly it was happening, they ebbed away. It was as if the captious gods of an earlier day than his, like the nearly human deities on Olympus, after playing football with Raffles for years, suddenly felt ashamed of their sport and resolved to let him have his own way for a while at any rate, just for the few years that were left to him. Raffles didn't feel in the least, however, like a man whose career was soon to close. He was full of vigor and quiet satisfaction in his work, as well he should have been, because of all his remarkable accomplishments the framing of Singapore's laws was perhaps the most notable and praiseworthy. If for nothing else, it should be remembered as a feat of efficiency, the entire set of laws having been recorded and put in working order before their author took his leave, only nine months after arriving. But it is for more than winning high grades in a non-stop endurance run that Raffles deserves admiring praise. He drafted those laws in 1823. Until Singapore was captured and occupied by the Japanese in 1942 they still served, with a few minor changes, and served well. Today, with the British again in possession, Raffles's original outline for Singapore's laws and constitution is still satisfactory. He did not exaggerate, though he meant to, when he wrote with genial humor from the ship which carried him away from Singapore Harbor:

"I have had . . . to look for a century or two beforehand, and provide for what Singapore may one day become."

He started out, naturally, somewhat appalled by the size of the task before him. He admitted this weakness frankly to his sympathetic confidante, the duchess: "I assure you I stand much in need of advice, and were it not for Lady Raffles, I should have no counsellor at all. She is nevertheless a host to me, and if I do live to see you again, it will be entirely owing to her love and affection; without this I should have been cast away long ago."

But this melancholy mood soon gave way to the stimulation that he always felt when he had a job as well fitted to his peculiar talents as this one was to prove. Besides, life was shaping up pleasantly for various little reasons. His sister Mary Anne, of whom he had always been particularly fond, was living in Singapore because Captain Flint, her husband, was town harbor master. Together with the Flints and their offspring, the Raffleses occupied a newly built house on Government Hill, Abdullah's Forbidden Hill of gloomy and mysterious history, from the top of which Raffles had fired his ship's cannon. Not least important of Sir Stamford's tasks was coaching Crawfurd for his new post as successor to the stubborn Farquhar, who was still holding out and perpetrating his sitdown strike.

At this period the Marsden correspondence becomes delightfully informative. Raffles had evidently found that his thoughts sorted themselves out the better for the letters he wrote his old friend; and so even when he was lightheartedly describing the natural history specimens he had been collecting, the *duyongs* which looked like mermaids and the giant "potatoe or yam" which proved to weigh almost five hundred pounds, a fit match, he claimed, for his great flower, he was using half his brain, all the time, to think out the new pattern for Singapore's laws.

Raffles was in a unique position regarding that community. For five years after planting the British flag on the beach he had been solely responsible for his "political child." Farquhar, living on the spot, had acted as resident, it is true, and had certainly drawn his salary as resident. Nobody during those five years had pinned Raffles down as to the exact relationship between Farquhar and himself, but in fact, as the Bengal Government was well aware, Raffles was the one and only chief of Singapore. It was no innovation that one man should draw up the rules for a new Company factory, but the rapidly increasing importance of Singapore had already promoted it out of the class of mere factories, and nobody knew better than Raffles how important these particular rules were going to be.

"I am now busy," he wrote an intimate friend in England, "in allotting the lands and laying out the several towns, defining rights, and establishing powers and rules for their protection and preservation. I have been a good deal impeded, but the task, though an arduous and serious one, is not one that I find unpleasant. What I feel most is the want of good counsel and advice, and of sufficient confidence in my own experience and judgment to lay down so broad and permanent a foundation as I could wish." To another friend he said, "My time is at present engaged in remodelling and laying out my new city, and in establishing institutions and laws for its future constitution; a pleasant duty enough in England, where you have books, hard heads, and lawyers to refer to, but here by no means easy. . . ."

It is characteristic of Raffles, beginning the task, that one of his first preoccupations was with the college he had long wanted to found somewhere in the Archipelago for the study of Malay. Just as he had sought out and built up the moribund Batavian Society of Arts and Sciences when he came to Java, so he concentrated his first hopes and ideas for Singapore on an institute of learning. The man who had experienced such phenomenal material success never for a moment forgot the boy he had been, that boy who sat up night after night over his books, snatching an education out of the air, stealing the candle for light to read by. Nor had he forgotten that Malay class of which he had spoken to Abdullah long ago, the two of them pacing the dusty pathway near a boys' school in Malacca. It is questionable whether any other man in all the Far East would have started out on a formidable task in just that way, but Raffles knew his values. He founded his college, and he endowed it with carefully selected lands.

As is usual in a boom town, real estate was immensely valuable, and he could not have found a better way to ensure prosperity to his favorite project. Finally as an added precaution he arranged with Dr. Morrison of China, successor to the famous Milne, to bring the mission Anglo-Chinese College from Malacca and incorporate it with his new Malay College, the result to be designated the "Singapore Institution," avowedly intended "for the cultivation of Chinese and Malayan literature, and for the moral and intellectual improvement of the Archipelago and the surrounding countries."

It was not normal behavior for empire builders, but Raffles knew what he was doing. Sometimes his foresight was uncanny. Today, thanks to his activity during Singapore's early years, no other part of the British Empire is so well known through its literature and language as is the Archipelago. The oriental scholar is overwhelmed by the wealth of material offered him in this department of government. There are always on hand any number of books, translations, brochures, and dictionaries compiled by Malays and Englishmen alike, so that the seeker after knowledge in related fields, such as Chinese or Mongol, is smitten with wondering envy. The secret of this fine collection is Raffles first of all, Raffles and the promise he made to himself in Abdullah's presence, long before Singapore was founded. When he established the college he created a tradition too; both have lasted through several generations of war and peace.

Next to the college in importance, thought Raffles—most administrators would have placed it first on the agenda—came the job of assuring clear representation and careful protection for his darling concept, free trade for Singapore. Raffles made no mistake in judgment. He knew what agency was mainly responsible for his city's fantastic growth. The island's geographical position helped, it is true, and so did the contrast between systems, vividly evident in the contiguity of British and Dutch colonies there in the Straits. Naturally the natives flocked to Singapore; they would have done, anyway, because it was easy to reach and because they preferred British to Dutch government methods, but the new colony owed her life and health first of all to free trade. Sir Stamford had to embody these principles firmly in the new constitution, and it was also vitally important to protect them against attack in the future, when he was no longer there to watch over things. As he told Marsden, after proudly quoting a statement he had just sent the Court of Directors—eight million dollars turned over in Singapore's first two and a half years, and all in native trade—"It being a great object to establish the freedom and independence of the port on a solid foundation . . ." he had to be very, very careful to plug up all the holes, to make the setup absolutely foolproof.

Last, but most pressingly important at the moment, was the matter of law and order. A code of regulations was of course necessary. In the very early days when the population was still of a size to keep within bounds, a homespun, dictatorial sort of justice had sufficed, but the settlement was already so large in 1822 as to need something more formal than these methods. Besides, Sir Stamford had many theories which he was anxious to put into practice, theories full grown from Lord Minto's nebulous philosophies of the old days, which dealt with social problems. It is nonsense to talk of democracy in a Far Eastern colony of the nineteenth century, in a land over which two European empires had squabbled, and a community composed of itinerant natives, traders, and pirates from the hodgepodge of neighboring islands. Democracy is too big a word, besides which Raffles would never have been so grandiose or false as to use it. But he did have a strong feeling that the city would be all the better for a government in which the inhabitants had some voice, particularly in the dispensing of justice. There his anthropological knowledge stood him in good stead. He understood as few other Englishmen could have done that in justice nothing is ever immutably fixed in space. What looks to be obviously right or wrong to an Englishman may appear in completely opposite terms to a Malay. This was not to say that Raffles advocated self-government for his colony. He was neither so advanced nor so unrealistic as to entertain such a revolutionary notion as that. Even the mild measures he did advocate seemed violently revolutionary to some of his colleagues. Briefly, it was a suggestion that a magistracy be selected annually from among the Singapore merchants, twelve each year: also that cases be tried by jury and that the jury be composed, at times, of *Europeans and natives together*.

Oddly perhaps, certainly unexpectedly, he encountered no difficulty in persuading his colleagues to accept this idea. They were distracted by other problems and were willing to agree to this scheme in their haste to settle the other matters. The difficulty arose over a related affair however—over prevention of crime, rather than punishment. Raffles had long wanted to prohibit gambling and cockfighting outright and legally in the colonies he governed, because he knew by long weary experience how often these dissipations were responsible for serious infractions of the law as well as plain simple rioting. He always ran into trouble when he attempted to carry out this intention, however, because gaming houses and cockfighting establishments provided revenue in a quick, easy fashion, and the men directly responsible for the financing of the colony didn't want to give up this speedy profit. Raffles's experience in Singapore was similar to those of earlier occasions when he had made like attempts to reform the community. He readily succeeded this time in winning the approval of the government in Bengal and of prohibiting all such pastimes in Singapore town, but he had not been gone from the colony very long before Crawfurd, tempted by the prospect of large revenues and worried for the want of cash, once again allowed the owners of gambling houses, et cetera, to set up shop, as soon as he knew they were willing to pay fat fees for licenses. Sir Stamford's policy, however, won out in the end, for the matter soon came up for judgment before the grand jury, and they held that Raffles had been right, that Crawfurd could not reverse his decision, and that the gambling had to go.

Perhaps the question which holds most interest for us today, in this necessarily brief résumé of Raffles's last months and work in Singapore, is the recurring one of slavery. That was an evil which he grasped and grappled with firmly as soon as he had spotted it, flourishing like the plague in his city. His decision in every matter pertaining to the slave trade was one of the chief sources of trouble between him and sulky Colonel Farquhar. Farquhar himself, it appears, was a slave owner on a considerable scale, and he impeded Raffles's reforms in regard to the traffic as much as he possibly could. However, his day was over, and at any rate no one could have stood up successfully for slavery at this late date. Once Sir Stamford knew that he stood on firm ground he struck accurately and with effect. In a letter to Dr. Wallich, with whom he had lately become friendly, Raffles speaks plainly of this:

"The magistrates have commenced operations with great prudence and judgment; their first presentation was upon the arrangement of the town.

"Their second came in yesterday [that would be March 7, 1823] in the shape of a memorial against slavery—the slavemaster and slave-debtor system—which seems to have been permitted here to an unlimited extent. I have not yet finally decided upon the question, but I am much inclined to think the wisest and safest plan will be to do in this as I did in the lands, annul all that has gone before. This establishment was formed long after the enactments of the British legislature, which made it felony to import slaves into a British colony, and both importers and exporters are alike guilty, to say nothing of the British authority who countenanced the trade. The acknowledgement of slavery in any shape in a settlement like Singapore, founded on principles so diametrically opposed to the admission of such a practice, is an anomaly in the constitution of the place, which cannot, I think, be allowed to exist."

No doubt the following passage is the result of such cogitations on his part. It is rather a pity that we cannot in some way underline the words, or print them in red and gold, or employ some other method of calling attention to them, for they merit all the attention we can get for them. They mark a tremendous satisfaction for Sir Stamford, but there is more in them than one man's triumph, even when that man is Raffles. They meant freedom for hundreds of people, living or yet unborn.

"As the condition of slavery, under any denomination whatever, cannot be recognised within the jurisdiction of the British authority, all persons who may have been so imported, transferred, or sold as slaves or slave-debtors, since the 29th of February, 1819, are entitled to claim their freedom, on application to the registrar, as hereafter provided; and it is hereby declared, that no individual can hereafter be imported for sale, transferred or sold as a slave or slave-debtor, or having his or her *fixed residence* under the protection of the British authorities at Singapore, can hereafter be considered or treated as a slave, under any denomination, condition, colour, or pretence whatever."

The reader will recognize this proclamation to be extremely significant, once it has been translated into American English out of the quasi-legal jargon in which our hero was, unfortunately, so fluent. For his sympathizers it is an immense satisfaction to realize that Sir Stamford was ultimately entitled thus to settle the matter of slavery outright, once and for all, in his own special corner of the world, regardless of all those fine points in law which had held him back and frustrated his former attempts to combat the traffic. That is not to say that his earlier efforts were ever completely futile; they weren't. Raffles had managed to put a crimp in the slavery business more than once. In respect to Singapore, however, he wiped the slate clean, which is as it should be. Note that all the slave-holders in Singapore, as well as the dealers, had at last to give in. Their day was done. All property rights in "black ivory" which any Singapore resident may have held simply melted away under Raffles's proclamation. Every slave on the island suddenly owned his own body, complete and forever, without having to worry about paying for it, then or later. Thinking it over, one reflects that of all the various sensations which may contribute to a normal man's experience, the knowledge that he has been responsible for setting free some human being, no matter who, or where, or what sort, must surpass

519 ❧

all the other intoxications which a mortal is capable of feeling. Surely Raffles for at least a few days partook of divinity's food and learned the savor of it. Almost, in spite of his Bencoolen ordeal and the ceaseless irritation of his lifelong struggle with stupidity, I can find it in my heart to envy him his life, for the sake of those hours when it was given him to realize, freshly, that he had freed the slaves of Singapore.

The founding of Singapore, represented as the last great venture of Raffles the empire builder, is a godsend to a biographer. It is neat. It is nicely calculated in timing, in drama, and in significance. A journalist himself and one of the best writers ever graduated from John Company's educational institution, Sir Stamford fully appreciated the value of Singapore on the record as his final great accomplishment. Technically speaking, it rounds off the story to perfection. One can see that he was aware of this, in the insistence with which he repeats time and again to his favorite correspondents, "This is my last public work. . . . This is my final important political act; I am satisfied now. . . . After this the Dutch may do their worst; I am no longer worried."

Admittedly these are paraphrases, but they faithfully express Sir Stamford's mood throughout the closing years of his stay in the Orient. Now if ever is the time for a careful chapter in the best solemn manner of the historian, tracing the effect on world events of Singapore through the years that followed its annexation by Great Britain. Now if ever is the moment to do a conventional, searching study of Singapore the Cornerstone of Empire; Singapore, last, uttermost, outermost of all outposts. Had this book been written and published, as was first planned, before the events that closed 1941, that is just the sort of chapter with which it would have ended. Fortunately for the writer, it wasn't finished in time. The dramatic splash of Pearl Harbor intervened, and today, when one looks back and reads the periodicals current at that time, one is deeply impressed by the amount of similar writing then perpetrated.

 520

Especially is one struck, unavoidably, by the incredible sloppy-thinking silliness of most of it, in the light of what came immediately after. I defy anyone, reading the weekly *Life* which, a very few weeks before Pearl Harbor, featured an article entitled "The Ragged Outposts of Empire" to remain mirthless. The laughter may well sound bitter, but it is bound to come. Therefore I am fighting shy of the sententious pleasures of the historian. Let someone else indulge in resounding generalities: the facts are few and easy to set down in order. Until 1941 Singapore was certainly the bulwark of the Empire. What importance she maintained throughout the first hundred and twenty-two years of her existence as the gem of England's oriental possessions was manifest: the British themselves expected Singapore as a fortress to withstand Japan's most furious attacks. She didn't. The Archipelago fell, an easy victim, within the third month of the Pacific war, 1941–45. Therefore, though Singapore is British once more and I for one am glad of it—for she is exclusively a British invention and represents constructive action rather than the usual snatch-and-grab tactics of empire building—I have become wary of making weighty pronouncements on *Geopolitik*. Taking for granted the kind permission of my readers, I once more eschew the temptations of prophecy and hastily baked economics, and abandon the Significance of Singapore in favor of a simpler theme—Raffles, his story.

Unconsciously we have slipped, in the last few pages, into a habit of evaluating all the incidents and developments of the pain-filled weeks Raffles spent in Bencoolen after the flight of the good times, and of the busy months in Singapore after that, as a sort of house cleaning. We have been finishing up our accounts, as it were, mechanically clearing the decks in preparation for the end. Belatedly I realize that I have been speaking of "the end" in ambiguous phrases, quite as if Death were lurking round the corner, ready to pounce on poor Sir Stamford as soon as the unwary reader turns the next page. This is decidedly not true; Death was not in my thoughts. I must have taken on some few of my subject's ardent enthusiasms, and subconsciously have looked upon the fate of the

Fame as the true end of his career. Certainly that grotesque calamity was a gratuitous turn of the screw.

In many ways John Company was a dull fellow, though it is not nice to speak ill of the dead. Certainly he never subscribed to that nursery maxim about all work and no play. He never even cared for work of a different type from his own; anything except trade, and such politics as those upon which trade depended, was considered by the majority of the Court of Directors to be a wicked waste of their time. That fact is apt to be lost in the shuffle, for Raffles was always burningly enthusiastic about his natural history research and never allowed his bosses' grudging attitude to discourage him. His personal letters were full of the topic, especially when in the course of his duty he was removed from a familiar locality and placed in a strange settlement where the fauna and botany of the surroundings seemed worthy of close study. Sumatra as a whole was the most fascinating place, from that particular point of view, which Sir Stamford was ever enabled to visit in pursuit of his career. We have seen in excerpts from his letters to Marsden and his duchess how all-absorbing the study of nature was for him, and how happily he mingled this study with the technical details of opening new fields of trade for his Company. Already, before his final departure from the East Indies, he had almost completed important plans begun during his 1817 visit to London in conversation with Sir Joseph Banks: to set up somewhere in England, probably London, a zoological society. First necessity for the project, of course, was a collection of live specimens for the zoo; second was another sort of collection, of plants, minerals, mounted stuffed animals, and all the other requisites of a museum. The untimely death of the older man, Banks, did not put an end to Sir Stamford's favorite hopes, and the Regent's Park Zoological Gardens are today the chief reason England has to remember the name of Thomas Stamford Raffles. The man in the street would probably be hard put to it to reply if you were to pose him a sudden question regarding Singapore. He would not be able to answer quickly any of the common sort of inquiry; Raffles's connection with the Crown Colony is sadly confused in his mind, so that he will, almost without doubt, te. you that Raffles was the bloke who built the hotel out there. But if you talk to your cockney about the zoo in Regent's Park, you will get a very different reaction. "*Him?* Oh, that's different! Why didn't you say it was him in the first place? Of course, everybody knows about *that* Raffles. . . ."

The first time Sir Stamford sent home a considerable number of animals and plants from Sumatra he innocently expected the Company to share his pride and joy in having collected so many excellent specimens. One of them, it so happens, was that giant flower of his, *Rafflesia arnoldi:* at any rate the shipment as a whole was one to stir to rapturous excitement any person who had the slightest true interest in natural history. Sumatra even today is a fertile hunting ground for zoologists and botanists, teeming as it is with tropical life. But John Company received the news coldly, to say the least. The Court all but reprimanded their lieutenant general of Bencoolen officially for having wasted time and money on such foolishness, which, as Raffles would have been forced to admit, certainly did nothing in the way of developing trade for Great Britain in the Far East. He was definitely not, they said firmly, permitted to waste any more of the Company's money on that sort of thing.

Unregenerate and unashamed, Raffles went ahead with his hobby, nor would the most inimical of his superiors have dared to imply that he neglected his duties while so doing or used funds improperly. With or without natural history, the East India Company never got so much work out of any other employee as they did out of Sir Stamford Raffles, and in their very infrequent periods of being reasonable they admitted as much. The American Dr. Horsfield as well as the Company's Arnold and Jack, the ill-starred Leyden back in the early days of Penang, and the two Frenchmen Diard and Duvaucel, all were Raffles's companions in this world of science, and Marsden acted at long distance as professor emeritus, just as Sophia and the children, during those short years when the children were spared to him, played the parts of willing, eager students to his teaching.

523

Later, talking it over, he usually said that one half the entire collection he made in Sumatra was sent home in March aboard the *Mary* and arrived safe in London early in 1820. The bulk of it went to Sir Joseph Banks, of course, but a few extra-special things, as for example a dried tapir, he gave to friends: Prince Leopold got the tapir. There remained, then, to accompany Lady Raffles and Sir Stamford on their last trip home, the other half of the collection.

After the catastrophe the Raffleses made several attempts to list their losses. The natural history collection headed it, for at the time most of those plants and animals were irreplaceable. In the light of the present, however, a far more important portion of Raffles's belongings, surely, was his collection of Malay manuscripts. Throughout his long term of office in the East he had sought out these manuscripts; Abdullah said once in his Memoir that there was not, he truly believed, one old Malayan document left in the neighborhood of Malacca after Sir Stamford had lived there a few weeks, so earnestly did he look them out and buy them during the time he was studying Malay.

There was also a full set of maps, made by Raffles himself in his own beautiful style. Then too, of course, he had with him the entire file of his official papers, representing the work he had done since his first arrival on Pulo Penang, back in 1805. Aside from these articles, the loss of which means a loss to the general public, not only in England but in the entire civilized world—aside from these, there were the personal fortunes and belongings of Raffles and Sophia. Everything they owned in the world, naturally, was packed up and stored in the hold, ready to accompany them, and the estimated value of this part of the cargo was, at a moderate computation, twenty-five thousand pounds. Insured? No, of course not. One couldn't easily take out insurance in those days for such a perilous undertaking as a journey from Bencoolen to England. It would have to be done by special arrangement at home, and it wasn't. No, the thing could not have been avoided in any way. It was purely and simply Fate in her worst mood, the mood in which she always dealt with Raffles.

The voyage back from Singapore to Bencoolen, in June 1823, might have passed without remark if it hadn't been for our old friends the Dutch again. Lady Raffles and Sir Stamford, finding themselves, aboard the *Hero of Malown*, under necessity to pause in Batavia Roads for several days while the ship unloaded cargo from Bengal, decided that Sophia ought to go ashore and rest a little from the rigors of sea travel. (She was pregnant, as usual, but not in her customary blooming health. Lady Raffles's constitution must have been permanently impaired after her serious illnesses of 1822.) As Raffles reported with some amusement in a letter he wrote from the ship, it was a trifling notion at best, and one which it never occurred to them would give rise to any excitement. Purely as a formality, a polite gesture, he wrote a short note to Baron van der Capellen, the Dutch governor general at Batavia, and sent it ashore by Sophia's young brother, informing the baron that Lady Raffles would land, owing to her delicate state of health, but that it was neither his, Raffles's, "wish nor intention" himself to set foot on shore.

"Had Bonaparte returned to life, and anchored in the Downs," he commented in his account of the affair, "it would not have excited greater agitation in England."

The baron, very much upset, hastened to reply that Raffles's letter had extremely surprised him and that, considering everything which had passed, it was of course absolutely impossible for him to receive Sir Stamford ashore—it was a meeting which must be avoided at all costs. As a gentleman the baron respected the fact of Mme. Raffles's illness, and understood that the couple would have to come ashore unofficially, but he, the governor, begged to be excused from the usual diplomatic courtesies. He sputtered for a final paragraph, mentioning a few complaints which it had recently been his duty to send to Raffles's government about Raffles's behavior, and repeated that any personal interview between the two of them *must* be avoided.

To this Sir Stamford replied with calm and dignity, though he was inwardly quaking with laughter, that it had never been his intention to leave the ship, that his note had been nothing but a formality, that he was sorry the baron had been so shocked and surprised, and that if it came to a matter of complaints—well, he had in the recent past found it necessary on his own part to make a complaint or two about the baron, so they were probably quits on that. He reiterated his statement that if Lady Raffles had not been very pregnant he would not have dreamed of putting her ashore on Java, under these awkward circumstances. However, she was and he had to, and would the baron be sure she could get back to the ship as soon as she wanted to return?

During the week the *Hero of Malown* stayed at anchor in the roads, people in droves came out to see Sir Stamford. "He there held as it were," said Sophia, "a continual levée every day, people of all ranks flocking to him."

Presumably the baron kept his eyes turned in the other direction for the duration of the visit and saw naught of this. One can imagine him puffing and blowing and turning crimson whenever he thought of that fellow out there in midstream; one visualizes the stout Netherlandish pride with which he reflected that he had put that man Raffles in his place for once, at any rate!

The stay at Bencoolen was characteristically unpleasant. Raffles was still beset with doubts and regrets on the subject of Farquhar: "if a brother had been opposed to them [the interests of Singapore], I must have acted as I did towards Colonel Farquhar," he wrote Wallich, but the thought of it still harried him.

There were a thousand arrangements to be made, for which time was too short even after it was discovered that they could not leave Bencoolen that year, as they had hoped, but must wait at least until the second month in 1824 for the ship on which they had decided—the *Fame*. Meanwhile Sophia's confinement drew near; it was evident that she was in a dangerously weak state; her anxious husband reported just a week before the birth that "only last night we were forced to apply thirty leeches, and have recourse to warm baths and laudanum, to keep down inflammation." What with this worry and several sudden deaths among the members of the European staff, Sir Stamford was scarcely in a state to put his many affairs into good order, yet every moment was valuable and he couldn't waste them.

The wretched Lady Raffles had her baby, a little girl they named Flora, about the first of November, but she had scarcely recovered when she was brought down again by a severe attack of fever, and of course the child died during this onslaught. Most colonials know how cunningly chronic malaria lies in wait, attacking its victim as soon as his vitality is low. Sophia was indeed so bad that Raffles wrote that month to Wallich (my italics), "Whether I go home or not, I must, *if Lady Raffles survives*, send her home by an early opportunity."

To a member of the family he was more explicit: "The loss of an infant only a few months old is one of those things which in itself perhaps might soon be got over, knowing how uncertain life is at that period, but this loss of our fourth and only remaining child in India has revived all former afflictions, and been almost too much for us. Fortunately Sophia's fever has not returned since the event, and upon the whole she is in better health than she was preceding, but she has not yet left the house; her spirits as well as my own are completely broken, and most anxious are we to get away from such a charnel-house, but here we are detained for want of an opportunity. How often do we wish the Fame had come out direct —we might have saved this last misfortune—but we have neither seen nor heard of her, and God only knows when the day of our deliverance will arrive. Either I must go to England or by remaining in India *die*."

I doubt if we could find in all Raffles's correspondence another passage as depressed as that one, and small wonder. Few names are familiar in the melancholy roll call of the season's casualties, though we recognize that of Captain Salmond, but Raffles's reiterated comments on the death, now of this friend and now of that, give us at least some idea of the depression which hung over Bencoolen those last weeks like a miasma.

Raffles did not spend much time, however, in repining. Depressed or no, well or ill, the habits of a lifetime carry one on, and he was still able to send a long letter to Mr. Murdoch respecting his satisfaction with Singapore and his assurance that the colony was now, at last, surely, England's to keep. He hoped to write a detailed account of the new city, either en route to England or after arriving. In the meantime he was happy to have received, tardily it is true, but nevertheless welcome for sentimental reasons if for nothing else, a message from the Bengal Government expressing their approbation of all his public works. Then there was Cousin Tom; Raffles wrote Tom a sort of summing up of the state of grace to be found, or rather not to be found, among the cannibals of Sumatra. It was Sir Stamford's carelessly amused opinion that more Christian missions should be established among the natives of the interior, unless the Christian world wished to resign itself to the danger of "hundreds of thousands, perhaps millions, in Sumatra" ultimately falling for the blandishments of Islam. Shrewdly Raffles called attention to one advantage which Christianity could offer as a selling point: Mohammedans are supposed to refrain from most of the favorite vices of the Malay—i.e., opium, cockfighting, and so on. Not that Christianity exactly endorses these pastimes, but . . . In any case, he said, according to British policy, the local officials had heretofore ignored religious matters, supposing there was any religion to ignore among these savage tribes, but the Padries had lately made such headway as they carried the Crescent inland, and had overrun so much of the rich and populous country of Sumatra, that British authority felt called upon to take some sort of decisive action.

But the best will in the world cannot keep impatient people forever diverted. The ship did not come. Even with all his time-killing activity, with all his distractions, the days lagged until Raffles actually became neurotic and fanciful, which was most untypical of him. To one of his intimates he wrote irritably, after January had opened:

"We have entered the new year, and as yet no accounts of the Fame. You can hardly imagine to yourself the serious disappointment to all our hopes and plans which this occasions. We begin to think we are doomed to end our days here, and that there is something like a spell on our movements. After Sophia's serious illness and our last affliction, the delay of a day is most serious, and night and day we cannot help regretting that you have not ensured a ship on the strength of my letters to you—I relied exclusively on what you would do, and still have no other hope than that the Fame will be in time to save our lives, though we have very little confidence that this will be the case."

Raffles meant every word of this letter, exaggerated as it may sound today, in the twentieth century. After so many delays and so many deaths, he was becoming superstitious, and one can scarcely wonder at this, considering how many times during the past few years the life of a child or a friend might have been saved, if only the ship had been in time. No doubt in his innermost heart the unhappy man was convinced that Sophia, his last and dearest love, would be the next victim of dilatory shipping. Run down as he was, overworked, with frayed nerves and the emotional upset which accompanies such an important change in daily life, it is no wonder that even the gentle Thomas Stamford Raffles sounded ill-natured. The recipient of this letter, thanks to Sophia's discretion as Editor of the Memoir, remains anonymous. Considering what was to happen in the near future, it is just as well that his name was not disclosed. Whoever he was, he must have been bitterly reproached a thousand times, after everything was over, if not openly by the unfortunate Raffles couple, then at any rate by his own conscience, because his neglect cost them dear. It really becomes difficult not to believe there was "something like a spell" on the Raffles fortunes; it is almost impossible to suppose that Fate didn't have a special grudge against them. There was that matter of insurance, for instance. Mr. Anonymous neglected to see to it at his end, and at Raffles's end nothing could ever be done. The Fame, according to the rules of shipping then in force, was insured only in regard to her own cargo and the ship itself; thus the East India Company, which could easily have sustained such a loss, was never called upon to do so. The accident had no effect on the fortunes of John Company; it merely wiped out those of Raffles, who could *not* afford such an accident.

If only the *Fame* had disappointed them instead of turning up at last, it would have been far better for poor Raffles. In that case they would simply have shipped in the *Borneo* instead. The *Borneo* arrived in England safe and sound. . . . But what is the use of talking like that? If Raffles had shipped in the *Borneo*, I doubt not that the *Borneo* would have piled up on a coral reef somewhere. We may as well get on with our story and find out what did happen instead of what might have been. It's easily enough told. It happened quickly enough.

The Raffleses, with young Nilson Hull and a doctor named Bell, sailed aboard the *Fame* at dawn on February 3, 1824. What with the relief of having at last got away, and the knowledge that he had wound up his affairs creditably, and the fact that Sophia was after all still alive, even on the mend, Sir Stamford had forgotten all his troubles and was in his more characteristically cheerful frame of mind, a mood he had not experienced for some weeks. Evidently that was a mistake: Fate hated to see Sir Stamford cheerful. Perhaps she is really as she is pictured, a crotchety old crone. If this be so, one can almost sympathize with her at times, for certainly her victim Raffles was the most irritatingly resilient mortal any supernatural power ever tried to bedevil. Let her so much as turn her back on him for the briefest moment, let her relax but an instant after having concentrated on him for months and months, having sent him all the worst luck in her whole stock, and the maddening man was laughing again. It was enough to turn any self-respecting Fate into a raging harpy.

"I'll settle his hash this time," she hissed. "Where are those matches?"

The *Fame* burst into visible flame in the evening, her first day out from Fort Marlborough. According to Raffles's own discoveries, which he embodied in a carefully accurate report in due course for the Court of Directors, the ship's steward was responsible, for he carried a torch or a candle to light him on his way into the storeroom when he went to draw some brandy from a cask. The spirits took fire immediately, and—but Sir Stamford, as is usually the case, can tell the story better than I could, and at first hand. He wrote a detailed letter the very next day, reassuring such family members as were waiting for them in England.

"Sophia had just gone to bed, and I had thrown off half my clothes, when a cry of fire, fire! roused us from our calm content, and in five minutes the whole ship was in flames! I ran to examine whence the flames principally issued, and found that the fire had its origin immediately under our cabin. Down with the boats. Where is Sophia?—Here. The children?—Here. A rope to the side. Lower Lady Raffles. Give her to me, says one; I'll take her, says the Captain. Throw the gunpowder overboard. It cannot be got at; it is in the magazine close to the fire. Stand clear of the powder. Skuttle the water-casks. Water! water! Where's Sir Stamford? Come into the boat, Nilson! Nilson, come into the boat. Push off, push off. Stand clear of the after part of the ship.

"All this passed much quicker than I can write it; we pushed off, and as we did so, the flames burst out of our cabin-window, and the whole of the after part of the ship was in flames; the masts and sails now taking fire, we moved to a distance sufficient to avoid the immediate explosion; but the flames were now coming out of the main hatchway; and seeing the rest of the crew, with the Captain, still on board, we pulled back to her under the bows, so as to be more distant from the powder. As we approached we perceived that the people on board were getting into another boat on the opposite side. She pushed off; we hailed her: have you all on board. Yes, all, save one. Who is he?—Johnson, sick in his cot. Can we save him?—No, impossible. The flames were issuing from the hatchway; at this moment the poor fellow, scorched, I imagine, by the flames, roared out most lustily, having run upon the deck. I will go for him, says the Captain. The two boats then came together, and we took out some of the persons from the Captain's boat, which was overladen; he then pulled under the bowsprit of the ship, and picked the poor fellow up. Are you all safe?—Yes, we have got the man; all lives safe. Thank God! Pull off from the ship. Keep your eye on a star, Sir Stamford.—There's one scarcely visible."

They steered toward shore, shivering, and seeing their way with ease by the dreadful light of the burning ship, for the *Fame* carried a load of saltpeter, and sent up "one of the most splendid and brilliant flames that ever was seen . . . casting that kind of blue light over us, which is of all others most horrible."

Sophia, clad in a wrapper, was barefoot; Nilson Hull and Dr. Bell were coatless, but with Raffles's coattail they covered his wife's feet and made "breeches for the children with our neck-cloths." And then it rained. But, said Sir Stamford, "fortunately it was not of long continuance, and we got dry again. The night became serene and star-light; we were now certain of our course. . . ." Did you hear that, Fate? Did you hear what he said?

There are in existence several versions of the fire written by Sir Stamford, and as many lists of his losses. I have chosen the most carefully drawn up one, which he sent after a bit to the Court of Directors. But as I said before, it would be wise, reading it, to remember that time has reversed our opinions on the intrinsic value of certain of these items: today, for instance, there are few of his lamented natural history specimens, animal or vegetable, which it would not be simple to replace, what with the aid of modern mechanical inventions and scientific data. But the priceless manuscripts, and the maps which Raffles himself had drawn and never had time afterward to redraw, those are a grievous loss indeed, and it grows greater with each year that passes.

"They were carefully packed in no less than one hundred and twenty-two cases, independent of those for immediate reference, but which last are also lost, not one scrap of paper having been saved, or one duplicate left.

"*Of Sumatra.*—A map on a large scale, constructed during a residence of six years, from observations made by myself and persons under my authority, European and native, calculated to exhibit, at one view, the real nature and general resources of the country, on a very different scale to what was formerly supposed, together with statistical reports, tables, memoirs, notices, histories of the Battas, and other original races, native and European vocabularies, dictionaries, and manuscripts in the different languages, contained in several cases.

"*Of Borneo.*—A detailed account of the former history, present state, population, and resources, of that long-neglected island, already drawn out to the extent of upwards of one thousand pages of writing, with numerous notes, sketches, details of the Dayak population, their government, customs, history, usages, &c. with notices of the different ports, their produce, and commercial resources.

"*Of Celebes.*—Nearly a similar account.

"And of *Java* and the *Moluccas.*—The whole of the voluminous history, as carefully abstracted from the Dutch archives while I was in Java, with careful translations of the most valuable native books, vocabularies, memoirs, and various papers intended principally to assist in a new edition of my History of Java.

"*Of Singapore.*—A detailed account of its establishment; the principles on which it is founded; the policy of our Government in founding it; the history of commerce in the Eastern Islands; its present state and prospects; the rapid rise of Singapore; its history until I gave over charge; with all the original documents connected with the discussion with the Dutch, and every voucher and testimony which could have been required to make good the British claim, and uphold the measures I had adopted.

"*In Natural History.*—The loss to myself and to science has been still greater. The choicest, the cream and flower of all my collections, I retained to take under my personal charge, together with the manuscripts and papers of my invaluable deceased friends, Drs. Arnold and Jack. Among these also was that invaluable, and, I may say, superb collection of drawings in natural history, executed under my immediate eye, and intended, with other interesting subjects of natural history, for the museum of the Honourable Court. They exceeded in number two thousand; and having been taken from life, and with scientific accuracy, were executed in a style far superior to any thing I had seen or heard of in Europe; in short, they were my pride: but as man has no business to be proud, it may be well that they are lost. Cases of plants, minerals, animals &c. &c. I shall not name.

"Indeed it would be endless for me to attempt even a general description of all that has perished, and I will only add that, besides the above, all the papers connected with my administration of Java, as collected and arranged by my deceased friend and secretary, Mr. Assey, have also been lost, with all my correspondence.

"A loss like this can never be replaced, but I bow to it without repining."

Well, there it was. There sat Sir Stamford and Lady Raffles, she barefoot and in her wrapper, he sharing his coat with her, and holding one or two odd children close to him for the sake of such warmth as he could impart. There they sat in the lifeboat, the men with them rowing toward shore by the light of their burning past. . . . "All else was swallowed up in one grand ruin."

They were fifty miles from shore, which the two boats had to reach at one certain point, the only landing place on the island, or the refugees would certainly die of starvation, lack of water, and exposure. They made it, just, at four next afternoon. Sophia had given way by that time to a series of convulsive faints, but they made it in time.

I do not think of the daylight scene so often. I think, when I picture the disaster to myself, of Sir Stamford and Sophia half naked in the little boat, looking on at the magnificent flaming destruction of all their years in the East. The fire roars and crackles and reaches up to the black sky, and the little boat rocks gently on the waves far, far below, and Sir Stamford holds Sophia clutched in his arm, trying to keep her and the children warm, and the fire roars louder than ever, and then at last the *Fame* breaks up and goes down to the bottom of the Pacific, and there is no more fire. In the little boat they are colder than ever. Sir Stamford keeps his arm around Sophia, who knows she is soon going to faint.

One might suppose that it would now be too dark for that malignant old lady to see him. It wasn't.

CHAPTER XXIX

The encyclopedic account of Raffles's life is the first mention of him which most of us read, and at the end our reaction is always the same—"He was so young to die!" Oddly enough this impression fades as we grow better acquainted with the circumstances. The last few years of his term in the East were so full of experience and adventure, and often so painful, that one can well understand the fact which first seems strange, that Raffles, in the eighteen months he spent in England preceding his death, often behaved and felt like an elderly man. I know that I, for one, slip into the mistake of thinking of him as an old man whenever I go over his earlier letters of this period, though I ought to know better. He sounds like a person whose lifework is over and who is well satisfied to leave it like that.

We are beginning to understand better than we used to the complicated relationship between body and mind, or perhaps the expression "body and heart" is more expressive of my meaning. What is old age after all? It is a weariness of the flesh when the body has worked for a long period; sometimes this weariness carries over to the emotions and mental processes, in which case we say that our man shows his age, and sometimes it does not, and then we say that he is remarkably young considering his years. Raffles seems to have reversed the process. Doubtless we would have called him remarkably old considering his years. For a while he lost that resilience which had always seemed such an integral part of him. He took to fretting and worrying and brooding and pondering fruitlessly, where in older days he would have risen up and gone out to do battle with his enemies, and if he could not find them immediately he would have put all their doings out of his mind until he could deal with them in person.

It would be no wonder if this state had remained typical of Raffles until the end, though it did not. His system was full of malaria and dysentery, both in a chronic stage which medical science had not yet learned to vanquish. He had been subjected to grief and anxiety a hundred times over, and though a human heart can rise above its trials at the time, there is a residue after intense grief; it accumulates, and in later days takes its toll. Sophia was not so great a letter writer as her husband, and so we don't know so much about her, but I think she too must have been deeply and permanently affected by the terrible days of Bencoolen.

It is scarcely fair, however, to judge a man in a hard-and-fast way from the things he does and says when he first lives in a strange milieu, and Raffles as country gentleman in England was playing a new role. He had experience with farming, it is true, out in the Indies, but that had been on the grandiose scale of governor. Back home on a little place, scarcely more than a hundred acres, he had to learn his farming all over again at Highwood. Before retiring to the country, however, there were a few things to arrange.

Raffles had few remaining blood ties. His mother had recently died, the news having been carried to him, actually, while his ship paused at St. Helena on the homeward route. But there was still Cousin Tom, and Sophia's relatives at Cheltenham clamored for a visit, and these duties had to be attended to before the Raffleses went to London for a season, where they lived in a small house and enjoyed themselves thoroughly, and began almost to feel young again. The friends Sir Stamford had made in 1817 were all there, with the notable exception, of course, of Princess Charlotte. Socially everything was just what it should have been to make the two people forget as much as they could of their recent troubles. Otherwise, however, things were not going exactly smoothly. Raffles lost no time in presenting his claim to the Company, for he naturally felt they should make it up to him, as much as such a loss could be made good, the fire aboard the *Fame* having destroyed nearly everything he owned in the world.

The Court did not come to a decision immediately, but then the Court never did work swiftly, and Raffles had not expected an answer within the space of several months at the quickest. Another affair connected with his work intruded on his attention and was very annoying. Colonel Farquhar, the resident of Singapore who had clung so stubbornly to his post that he had to be booted out, was now taking his revenge on the man on whom he laid the blame for all his misfortunes. The method he used was simple, though one wonders what he expected to get out of it aside from being a nuisance to Raffles. In a lengthy communication to the Court he claimed that Singapore was entirely his own personal accomplishment; his had been the brain which picked out that locality above all others (he had forgotten the Carimons, you see), his the power which kept the settlement going from the beginning, his the administrative genius which worked out the details of government. Raffles he pictured as a rascally adventurer, what we would call today a "kibitzer," who had muscled in and grabbed the credit now that Singapore was the roaring success which report made it out to be.

It is exceedingly doubtful whether any intelligent director would have been taken in by this claim in any case. There was too much evidence against it in the archives, and too many independent witnesses in India who could speak up for the true state of affairs, to render a serious reply necessary. But Raffles, naturally, could not be satisfied until the matter was thoroughly cleared up, and he took it far more to heart in his then parlous state than he would have done some years earlier. He worked very hard on his reply. A thing like that, unfortunately, can never be quite expunged from the records; that is the devil of it. Even years later when Demetrius Boulger wrote his biography, he found it necessary to present some of the more obvious bits of proof on behalf of Raffles's indignant disclaimer, though the entire affair should have been ignored and forgotten from the start. The only practical harm it did was to Raffles's already sorely tried peace of mind.

But when that retort had been accomplished Sir Stamford felt rather easier about things in general. One can see this, reading his letters. There had been some preliminary haggling about money and other matters. For example Raffles had earlier—much earlier, six years in fact—requested from the Court a favorable decision referring to his administration in Java, for he wanted a clean slate. The Court had never replied. Now he pressed his request, repeating it. The money claim was another headache. The story of Raffles's financial affairs is complicated and I shall not attempt to do more than give a simplified version of the outstanding points, but before we begin to look at figures and sums, one thing should be said as emphatically as possible.

To put it plainly, the East India Company behaved in regard to Raffles's money like a carefully selected committee of highly pedigreed hogs. This fact will not surprise most students of John Company's history, for Raffles was not the only man to suffer unjustly at his hands. John Company is dead and cannot sue me for libel: the mystery of his sins remains. How did it happen, why did it happen, would it have happened again? The only answer we can give is in reply to the last question, and that is a loud, firm yes.

The Company, in the middle of the nineteenth century, was dissolved. What was left of its administrative assets were merged with the Crown. There are plenty of genuine historians, of whom I am not one, who can point without pride to incidents in the history of the British Government wherein worthy men who have given the best of their lives and talents to their country were permitted, as Raffles was, to grapple during their last years with utter ruin, usually brought on by their grateful sovereigns. But this was not the invariable fate of the great men of England. A general or a statesman who did well by Great Britain and his king, or queen, had at least a reasonable chance of his services being recognized at the end. John Company's record can offer few similar tales: John Company did not specialize in justice. Perhaps Raffles should not have been surprised at what happened to him. Indignant, yes, but surprised, no. He was, however; he was so amazed, in fact, that he died of it.

There had been a few arguments earlier on which showed the way things were going. Boulger cites a case, that of the fare for Raffles and his family, covering their journey out to Bencoolen in 1817. It amounted to fifteen hundred pounds, which Raffles paid himself and then billed the Company. But when it came time to collect from them they allowed him only a thousand pounds, for reasons best known to their own bookkeepers, and even that they didn't pay for five years. The ensuing argument dragged on, it seems, until 1825, after which Raffles was out his five hundred pounds for good. There is nothing at all unusual about this evidently. Then there were the three thousand pounds he had to pay for the second homeward passage from Bencoolen after the *Fame* was burned; he decided at last, in sheer weariness, to throw that item in with his general claim for compensation.

"What the East India Company may do is uncertain," he wrote at the end of 1825, "but if their liberality keeps pace with their delay, I ought to expect something handsome." He wrote more hopefully in February to his cousin: "The East India Company are now talking of taking up my case and granting me an annuity; but I fear it will be very moderate, and 500 a year is the largest amount I hear of. This, had I the means of living independent of them, I should not be inclined to accept; but necessity and consideration for my family must predominate. . . ." Poor devil.

He went on to say he had lost heavily by the cession of Bencoolen to Holland; his bankers had failed and carried into oblivion with them some thousands of his money. "The pressure is, I hope, only temporary, and I trust all will be right again, and that I shall not be obliged to seek a tropical clime again in search of *filthy lucre*—for nothing else would, I think, tempt me to venture."

Let us turn to more attractive aspects of Sir Stamford's life. There is no doubt that the activity which afforded him greatest pleasure at this time was the encouragement and inception of the Zoological Society. When it was successfully launched his name stood first on the list, and if his ghost has not long since quitted its old haunts on this earth in disgust, let us hope that he still comes around to Regent's Park on members' days and enjoys himself with the populace of London, with the admiring crowd who watch his favorite gibbons at play, and the children walking hand in wing with the penguins. He loved gibbons and children, did Raffles.

Highwood in Middlesex, where he retired to live with Sophia, Baby Ella, and a little cousin, was a small farm which they selected because it was next to the estate of his old friend William Wilberforce. Cousin Tom had a letter from him written the middle of June; it was very cheerful. In a postscript Raffles said, "We suffer a little from the heat, but as we hope to make our hay in the course of next week, I don't complain. Highwood is now in its best dress, and will, I am sure, please you. My neighbour, Mr. Wilberforce, takes possession to-morrow, and will previously spend the day with us." The children as well as Sir Stamford himself had just recovered from the whooping cough, and they were somewhat worried because measles were in the neighborhood.

One must give him full marks for this cheerfulness. He had already received word from the Company, just when he was expecting at least an annuity of five hundred, that they figured things another way. What with claims for pay they said he had got when he shouldn't, and rent he had paid when he shouldn't, and things he had bought which he had no justification for buying, and this and that—what with it all, Raffles owed the East India Company, they told him blandly, a little over twenty-two thousand pounds. His claim they ignored completely.

Almost immediately after this letter arrived there came word that a bank in India had closed. This, because of a note he had signed, would cost him sixteen thousand pounds more.

Thomas Stamford Raffles, Knight, was found at five o'clock in the morning of his forty-fifth birthday, July 5, 1826, lying completely insensible at the foot of a staircase in his home, Highwood. He was probably already dead. Sir Everard Home, his old friend and physician, pronounced his death to be due to an apoplectic attack. "The sufferings of the deceased must, for some time past, have been most intense."

AFTERTHOUGHT

The Court of Directors of the East India Company, perhaps to soften the shock of the financial claim they put forward on the same day, April 12, 1826, made the following decision concerning Sir Stamford Raffles's administration in the Far East. Though somewhat late in arriving, its text could not be called anything but completely satisfactory. Perhaps it might even be considered worth twenty-two thousand pounds, though personally I doubt it.

"DECISION

"Of Java.—The Court admit, that the success of the expedition to Java was promoted by the plans and information of Sir Stamford Raffles. That the representation of Sir Stamford Raffles as to the financial embarrassment of Java on the outset of his government is correct.

"That those financial difficulties were enhanced by the inevitable hostilities with Palembang and Jojocarta.

"That of the measures introduced by Sir Stamford Raffles for the removal of the financial embarrassments; viz. the sale of lands, withdrawal of Dutch paper currency, and a new system of land revenue;

"The sale of lands is considered to have been a questionable proceeding.

542

"The entire series of measures for the reform of the currency are conceded to have been well adapted to their object.

"With regard to the system of revenue introduced by him, the Court state that they would have been inclined to augur favourably of the success of his measures, and consider it highly probable that the colony would have soon been brought at least to liquidate its own expenses by the lenient and equitable administration of Sir Stamford Raffles's system.

"The regulations for reform in the judicial department and police, the Court consider entitled, both in their principles and in their details, to a considerable degree of praise.

"On the measures respecting Borneo, Banca, and Japan, the Court remark, that, under a permanent tenure of Java, and a different system of policy, the measures in question [promoting intercourse and enlarging the British power] would have been valuable service.

"*Sumatra.*—The measures of internal reform introduced by Sir Stamford Raffles are generally approved.

"In his political measures he incurred the strong disapprobation of the Court; but the motives by which he was actuated were unquestionably those of zealous solicitude for the British interests in the Eastern seas, and form a part of a series of measures which have terminated in the establishment of Singapore.

"*Singapore.*—It is allowed that Sir Stamford Raffles developed the exclusive views of the Dutch, and the measures ultimately carried into effect are to be attributed to his instrumentality, and to him the country is chiefly indebted for the advantages which the Settlement of Singapore has secured to it. The Court consider this to be a very strong point in Sir Stamford Raffles's favour, and are willing to give him to the full extent the benefit of their testimony respecting it.

"His administration of Singapore has been approved by the Bengal Government.

"The Court's opinion with regard to the general services of Sir Stamford Raffles is summed up in the following terms:—

"The government of Sir Stamford Raffles appears, with sufficient evidence, to have conciliated the good feelings of, at least, the great majority of the European and native population; his exertions for the interests of literature and science are highly honourable to him, and have been attended with distinguished success; and although his precipitate and unauthorised emancipation of the Company's slaves, and his formation of a settlement at Pulo Nias, chiefly with a view to the suppression of a slave traffic, are justly censured by the Court, his motives in those proceedings, and his unwearied zeal for the abolition of slavery, ought not to be passed over without an expression of approbation."

Lady Raffles managed, by February of the year following her husband's death, to scrape together something like ten thousand pounds which she proposed to pay the Company in installments. The Court graciously consented to accept this sum, and the matter was closed.

Nobody seems to have recorded an unimportant detail which nevertheless may interest some members of the public. It is not known just what Sir Stamford's widow and daughter used for money, after the Company's claim was settled.

Singapore, however, when last heard from, was doing very well.

GLOSSARY

Amok, amuck, amuk, to run amuck, et cetera. In Malay it means a furious and reckless onset, whether of many in battle, or of an individual in private. The word and the practice are not confined to the Malays, but extend to all the people and languages of the Malay Archipelago that have attained a certain amount of civilization. Crawfurd (*Malay Dictionary*) ascribes a Javanese origin for this word, but Yule (*Hobson-Jobson*) considers it to be of Indian derivation. The phrase has been thoroughly naturalized in England since the days of Dryden and Pope.

Bendahara. From the Malay *bandahára*, Javanese *bendárá*, "lord." A term used in the Malay countries as a title of one of the higher ministers of state, and usually applied to the treasurer.

Bonze. A term applied by European travelers in the sixteenth to nineteenth centuries to the Buddhist clergy of China and Japan. Derived by the sixteenth-century Portuguese from the Japanese word *Bózu*.

Captain China. The head of the Chinese community at Batavia who exercised certain jurisdictional rights over his compatriots.

Collector. The chief administrative official of an Indian *zillah* or district, charged chiefly with the collection of revenue, but often also holding controlling magisterial powers.

Country ships, boats, et cetera. Term used colloquially and in trade, as an adjective to distinguish vessels built or owned in Indian ports, though often officered by Europeans, from the bona fide East India Company's shipping.

Datoo, datu. From the Javanese *Datuk*. Grandfather; senior; elder; title of the head of a tribe; a chieftain.

Desa. Crawfurd (*Descriptive Dictionary*) states that this word, taken from the Sanscrit, signifies the "country," as distinguished from the "town," or rather from the seat of government, and it is also a synonym for "village." It occurs, not infrequently, in the names of places. See following word.

Dessaye. A word of Indian origin (desai) applied to a native official in the charge of a district, often held hereditarily. A native chief.

Diwani. The office of the Diwan or Dewaun, who was usually the head financial minister of a state or province, charged with the collection of the revenue; but with many other ramifications of meaning.

Factory. A European trading establishment in an Asiatic port or mart, such as the thirteen European factories at Canton, and the Dutch factory of Deshima at Nagasaki. In the early nineteenth century the English East India Company's covenanted civil servants were theoretically divided into four classes—senior merchants, junior merchants, factors, and writers, although these terms had long ceased to have any relation to the occupation of these officials. The Dutch Company had a similar hierarchy prior to its dissolution in 1798. The terms were originally adopted from the Portuguese feitoria and feitor.

Kabaja, cabaja, cabaya, et cetera. Word of Arabic or Portuguese origin commonly used in Java to describe the light cotton surcoat or "shift" worn by women in deshabille.

Kampong. A village; a quarter or a subdivision of a town. Thus, Chinese kampong, village or district where the Chinese lived.

Liplaps, liblaps. A vulgar and disparaging nickname given in the Dutch East Indies to Eurasians, and corresponding to the Anglo-Indian chee-chee or chichi.

Mandoor. Overseer or superintendent.

Munshi. A writer; a scribe; a teacher of languages.

Njonja, nona. An unmarried European or Eurasian woman.

Pangerang. From the Javanese pangeran. A prince.

Pulo, poeloe, pooloo. Javanese and Malay word for island, isle, or islet. It is prefixed to the names of all the small islands in the Malay Archipelago.

Prouw, prau, parao, et cetera. In Malay and Javanese the generic term for any vessel, whether rowing or sailing. Generally applied to small craft, and more specifically to denote a peculiar kind of galley, the so-called "Malay prow."

Raja Muda. The heir presumptive, literally "the young king."

Regent. A hereditary official belonging to the highest rank of the native civil service in Java.

Ryotwarry. Hindustani adjective, from the noun ryot (raiyat) literally, "to pasture," its specific Anglo-Indian application being "a tenant of the soil." The ryotwarry system was that under which the settlement for land revenue was made directly by the government agency with each individual cultivator holding land, not with the village community or with any middleman or landlord, payment being also received directly from each individual.

Sarong. From the Malay *sárung;* the body cloth, or long kilt, tucked or girt in at the waist, generally of colored silk or cotton, which forms the chief article of dress of the Malays and Javanese.

Sicca rupee. Silver coin weighing 192 grains and containing 176 grains of pure silver minted by the East India Company in the Bengal Presidency in the years 1793–1836.

Susuhunan, Susunan, Susuunan, Soesoehoenan, et cetera. Literally, "object of adoration"; religious title assumed by the ruler of Surakarta, or Solo, after the division of the empire of Mataram into the sultanates of Surakarta and Jojocarta in 1755.

Těměnggong, Tumunggong, Tamanggung, et cetera. The title of a public functionary; a kind of minister of the interior or director of police. Crawfurd (*Malay Dictionary*) adds that in Java it is the title of a class of nobles, and not the name of an office.

N.B. The foregoing definitions are applicable to Java and Malaya in Raffles's time, and are taken or derived from the following works;

John Crawfurd. *A Grammar and Dictionary of the Malay Language,* Vol. II. London, 1852.

————. *A Descriptive Dictionary of the Indian Islands and Adjacent Countries.* London, 1856.

H. Yule & A. C. Burnell. *Hobson-Jobson. A Glossary of Anglo-Indian Words and Phrases.* London, 1903.

S. R. Dalgado. *Glossario Luso-Asiatico,* 2 vols. Coimbra, 1919–21.

NOTES

(It should be understood that the two standard reference works, Demetrius Boulger's *Life of Sir Stamford Raffles*, London, 1897, and Lady Sophia Raffles's *Memoir of the Life and Public Services of Sir Thomas Stamford Raffles*, London, 1830, are included as part of every chapter's bibliography. They have been used so steadily throughout that it seems unnecessary to include the titles each time.)

CHAPTER I

Foster, Sir William. *The East India House*. London, 1924.

Hickey, William. *The Memoirs of William Hickey*, 4 vols., 6th ed. New York, 1923. Vol. I, 1749–75, p. 117; Vol. III, 1782–90, p. 176.

CHAPTER II

Foster, Sir William. *The East India House*. London, 1924. (Chapter on clerks.)

Namier, L. B. *England in the Age of the American Revolution*. London, 1930, p. 36.

CHAPTER III

Vlekke, Bernard H. M. *Nusantara*. Cambridge, Massachusetts, 1943.

Winstedt, R. O. *A History of Malaya*. Singapore, 1935.

CHAPTER IV

Hickey, William. *The Memoirs of William Hickey*, 4 vols., 6th ed. New York, 1923. Vol. IV, pp. 367, ff.

Minto. *Lord Minto in India: Life and Letters of Gilbert Elliot.* London, 1880, p. 253.

Parkinson, C. Northcote. *Trade in the Eastern Seas.* Cambridge, England, 1937, pp. 121, 264.

Vlekke, Bernard H. M. *The Story of the Dutch East Indies.* Cambridge, Massachusetts, 1945, p. 124.

CHAPTER V

Abdullah, Munshi. *Hikayat Abdullah*, translated from Malay by Rev. W. G. Shellabear. Singapore, 1918. Also translated by John Turnbull Thomson. London, 1874.

Furnivall, J. S. *Netherlands India.* Cambridge and New York, 1944, p. 49.

Prince of Wales's Island Gazette. George Town, 1807 (as quoted by Demetrius Boulger).

CHAPTER VI

(No references)

CHAPTER VII

Abdullah, Munshi. *Hikayat Abdullah*, translated by John Turnbull Thomson. London, 1874.

———. *The Autobiography of Munshi Abdullah*, translated by Rev. W. G. Shellabear. Singapore, 1918.

Minto. *Lord Minto in India: Life and Letters of Gilbert Elliot.* London, 1880.

Stavorinus, John Splinter. *Voyages to the East Indies*, 2 vols., English ed. London, 1798. Vol. I.

Stockdale, John Joseph. *Sketches, Civil and Military, of the Island of Java and Its Immediate Dependencies*, 2d enlarged ed. London, 1812.

Vlekke, Bernard H. M. *Nusantara*. Cambridge, Massachusetts, 1943, pp. 230, 239-55.

CHAPTER VIII

Abdullah, Munshi. *Hikayat Abdullah*, translated by John Turnbull Thomson. London, 1874.

————. *The Autobiography of Munshi Abdullah*, translated by Rev. W. G. Shellabear. Singapore, 1918.

Banner, Hubert Stewart. *The Clean Wind*. London, 1931.

Minto. *Lord Minto in India: Life and Letters of Gilbert Elliot*. London, 1880.

Vlekke, Bernard H. M. *The Story of the Dutch East Indies*, Cambridge, Massachusetts, 1945.

CHAPTER IX

Abdullah, Munshi. *Hikayat Abdullah*, translated by John Turnbull Thomson. London, 1874.

————. *The Autobiography of Munshi Abdullah*, translated by Rev. W. G. Shellabear. Singapore, 1918.

Banner, Hubert Stewart. *The Clean Wind*, London, 1931.

Minto. *Lord Minto in India: Life and Letters of Gilbert Elliot*. London, 1880.

Raffles, Sir Thomas Stamford. *The History of Java*, 2d ed. London, 1830.

Thorn, Major William. *R. R. Gillespie, a Memoir*. London, 1816.

————. *The Conquest of Java*. London, 1812.

CHAPTER X

Banner, Hubert Stewart. *The Clean Wind*. London, 1931.

Minto. *Lord Minto in India: Life and Letters of Gilbert Elliot*. London, 1880, pp. 302, 306.

Raffles, Sir Thomas Stamford. *The History of Java*, 2d ed. London, 1830.

Thorn, Major William. *R. R. Gillespie, a Memoir*. London, 1816.

CHAPTER XI

Anonymous. *Nederlandsch-India in Haaren Tegenwoordigen Toestand Beschouwd*. Circa 1780.

Graaff, Nicholaas de. "Oost-Indische Spiegel," edited by J. C. M. Warnsinck, in Vol. 33 of the Linschoten Vereeniging.

Plomer, William. *Double Lives*. London, 1943, p. 81.

Stavorinus, John Splinter. *Voyages to the East Indies*, 2 vols., English ed. London, 1798.

Stockdale, John Joseph. *Sketches, Civil and Military, of the Island of Java and Its Immediate Dependencies*. 2d enlarged ed. London, 1812.

Thorn, Major William. *The Conquest of Java*. London, 1812.

Van der Wall, Victor Ido. "Maria Wilhelmina Engelhard-Senn van Basel, 1770–1823," *Figuren en Feiten uit den Compagniestijd*, Bandoeng, 1933, pp. 261 ff.

CHAPTER XII

Haan, F. de. *Oud Batavia*. Batavia, 1919. Vol. I, p. 451.

Minto. *Lord Minto in India: Life and Letters of Gilbert Elliot*. London, 1880, pp. 312–13.

Olivier, Jz. J. *Land- en Zeetogten in Nederlandsch Indië in 1817–1826*, 3 vols. Amsterdam, 1827.

———. *Tafereelen en merkwaardigheden uit Oost-Indië*, 2 vols. Amsterdam, 1836.

Stavorinus, John Splinter. *Voyages to the East Indies*, 2 vols. English ed. London, 1798.

Thorn, Major William. *The Conquest of Java*. London, 1812.

Van der Wall, Victor Ido. *Figuren en Feiten uit den Compagniestijd*. Bandoeng, 1933.

CHAPTER XIII

Bleeker, P. "Overzigt der Geschiedenis van het Bataviaasch Genootschap van Kunsten en Wetenschappen," Verhandelingen, 1853. Vol. 25.

Fischel, Gukar, and Boehm, Max von. Modes and Manners of the Nineteenth Century. London, 1909.

Haan, F. de. Oud Batavia, 2 vols. Batavia, 1922.

———. Priangan, 4 vols. Batavia, 1912. Vol. IV, p. 753.

Java Government Gazette, May 1812 (as quoted by Boulger).

Minto. Lord Minto in India: Life and Letters of Gilbert Elliot. London, 1880, p. 305.

Staunton, Sir George. Authentic Account of an Embassy from the King of Great Britain to the Empire of China, 2 vols. and atlas. London, 1798.

Stavorinus, John Splinter. Voyages to the East Indies, 2 vols. English ed. London, 1798.

Vlekke, Bernard H. M. Nusantara. Cambridge, Massachusetts, 1943, pp. 165, 173.

CHAPTER XIV

Collet, D. J. A. L'Ile de Java sous la domination française. Brussels, 1910, p. 230.

Daendels, Herman Willem. Staat der Nederlandsche Oost-Indische Bezittingen. The Hague, 1814, p. 106.

Furnivall, J. S. Netherlands India. Cambridge and New York, 1944. pp. 64–69, etc.

Haan, F. de. Priangan, 4 vols. Batavia, 1919. Vol. IV., pp. 754, 766, Proceedings: 28, vii, 1813; and Substance of a Minute, p. 280; Report of State Commissioners, 1803.

Hogendorp, Dirk van. Berigt van den tegenwoordigen toestant der Bataafsche Bezittingen in Oost-Indien. Delft, 1799 and 1800, p. 19.

Java Government Gazette, 23, iv, 1814 (as quoted by Boulger).

Levyssohn Norman, H. D. *De Britsche Heerschappij over Java en Onderhoorigheden, 1811–1816.* The Hague, 1857, pp. 341–44.

Vlekke, Bernard H. M. *The Story of the Dutch East Indies,* Cambridge, Massachusetts, 1945.

CHAPTER XV

Doeff, Hendrik. *Herinneringen uit Japan.* Haarlem, 1833.

Meijlan, G. F. *Geschiedkundig Overzigt van den Handel der Europezen op Japan.* Batavia, 1833.

Raffles, Sir Thomas Stamford. "Japan," *The Pamphleteer.* London, 1816, Vol. VIII. (Address delivered by Raffles at the Society of Arts and Sciences at Batavia, September 10, 1815.)

———. *Report on Japan to the Secret Committee of the English East India Company, 1812–16,* edited by M. Paske-Smith. Kobe, Japan, 1929.

CHAPTER XVI

Addison, George Augustus. *Original familiar correspondence between residents in India including sketches of Java.* Edinburgh, 1846.

Haan, F. de. "Personalia der periode van het Engelsche bestuur over Java 1811–1816," *Bijdragen tot de Taal- Land- en Volkenkunde van Nederl. Indië.* The Hague, 1935. Vol. 92, Part IV, pp. 477–681.

Hope, Hugh. Article in *Java Government Gazette* as edited by De Haan, ibid., Batavia, October 24, 1812.

Thorn, Major William. *R. R. Gillespie, a Memoir.* London, 1816.

CHAPTER XVII

Haan, F. de. "Personalia der periode van het Engelsche bestuur over Java 1811–1816," *Bijdragen tot de Taal- land- en Volkenkunde van Nederl. Indië.* The Hague, 1935.

Java Government Gazette as quoted by De Haan, ibid. Batavia, 1812, I. viii.

Levyssohn Norman, H. D. *De Britsche Heerschappij over Java en Onderhoorigheden, 1811–1816.* The Hague, 1857, p. 301.

Minto. *Lord Minto in India: Life and Letters of Gilbert Elliot.* London, 1880, p. 296.

Thorn, Major William. *R. R. Gillespie, a Memoir.* London, 1817, pp. 17, 32, 51, 55, 61, 128, 139, 192, 193, 200, 203, 246, 251, 252, 273.

CHAPTER XVIII

Haan, F. de. *Platen Album to Oud Batavia.* Batavia, 1919.

Raffles, Sir Thomas Stamford. *An Analysis of the "Brata Yudha" or Holy War,* Vol. II.

———. *The History of Java,* 2d ed. London, 1830.

CHAPTER XIX

Raffles, Sir Thomas Stamford. *The History of Java,* 2d ed. London, 1830, dedication.

CHAPTER XX

Raffles, Dr. Thomas. *Letters, during a tour through some parts of France, Savoy, Switzerland, Germany, and the Netherlands.* New York, 1818.

CHAPTER XXI

Benét, William Rose. *The Falconer of God.* New York, 1914.

Marsden, William. *History of Sumatra.* London, 1784.

CHAPTER XXII

(No references)

CHAPTER XXIII

(No references)

CHAPTER XXIV

Philips, C. H. "The Secret Committee of the East India Company (1784–1858)," *Bulletin of the School of Oriental and African Studies.* University of London, 1940. Vol. X, Part III, pp. 707–58.

Van der Kemp, P. H. "*Sumatra's Westkust naar aanleiding van het Londensch Tractaat van 13 Augustus 1814,*" *Bijdragen van het Koninklijk Instituut van Taal- Land- en Volkenkunde van Nederlandsch-Indië.* Vol. 49, pp. 205–306.

——. "*De Singapoorsche Papieroorlog.*" Ibid., Vol. 49, p. 501.

——. "*Raffles' bezetting van de Lampongs in 1818.*" Ibid., Vol. 50, pp. 1–58.

——. "*Het Nederl. Ind. bestuur Het Midden.*" Ibid., 1817.

CHAPTER XXV

Hamilton, Alexander. *A New Account of the East Indies* (edited by Sir W. Foster, London, 1931). Edinburgh, 1727.

Van der Kemp, P. H. "*De Singapoorsche Papieroorlog.*" Ibid., Vol. 49, pp. 388–549.

CHAPTER XXVI

Abdullah, Munshi. *Hikayat Abdullah,* translated by John Turnbull Thomson. London, 1874.

——. *The Autobiography of Munshi Abdullah,* translated by Rev. R. G. Shellabear. Singapore, 1918.

Winstedt, R. O. *A History of Malaya.* Singapore, 1935, pp. 168–72, 213–19.

CHAPTER XXVII

Spear, T. G. P. *The Nabobs: A Study of the Social Life of the English in Eighteenth Century India.* London, 1932, Notes.

CHAPTER XXVIII

Philips, C. H. "The Secret Committee of the East India Company (1784–1858)," *Bulletin of the School of Oriental and African Studies*, University of London, 1940. Vol. X, Part IV, pp. 707–08.

CHAPTER XXIX

(No references)

BIBLIOGRAPHY

A. LANGUAGES OTHER THAN DUTCH

Abdullah, Munshi. *Hikayat Abdullah,* translated by John Turnbull Thomson. London, 1874.

——. *The Autobiography of Munshi Abdullah,* translated by the Rev. R. G. Shellabear, Singapore, 1918.
> Shellabear's version is fuller, but Thomson's is more informative and contains valuable notes. Original book is fascinating, though not always to be trusted as to fact.

Addison, George Augustus. *Original familiar correspondence between residents in India including sketches of Java.* Edinburgh, 1846.
> Useful for background, but unfortunately refers only to a limited period, Raffles's last days in Java.

Arnold, Wright, and Reid, Thomas H. *The Malay Peninsula.* London, 1912.
> Compendium of the entire Archipelago; the Java section, therefore, is limited and general.

Assey, C. "On the trade to China and the Indian Archipelago," *The Pamphleteer,* London, 1819. Vol. 14, pp. 515–43.
> Reflects Raffles's ideas and usefully condenses many on which he is inclined to be prolix.

Banner, Hubert Stewart. *The Clean Wind.* London, 1931.
> "Costume novel" written according to the old black-and-white

idea that Daendels was a fiend, Raffles an angel, but "atmospheric" detail is trustworthy.

————. *These Men Were Masons*. London, 1934.
Interesting account of Raffles's Java career as a Mason, with Dutch brothers in the bonds.

Boulger, Demetrius C. *The Life of Sir Stamford Raffles*. London, 1897.
By far the most detailed of Raffles's biographies, containing all English documents available to author at that date, including many not published before.

Buckley, C. B. *An Anecdotal History of Old Times in Singapore*. Singapore, 1902.
Refers in the main to period following Raffles.

Collet, D. J. A. *L'Ile de Java sous la domination française*. Brussels, 1910.
The best apologia for Daendels and his work.

Cook, J. A. Bethune. *Sir Thomas Stamford Raffles*. London, 1918.
Brief account from British viewpoint.

Coupland, Reginald. *Raffles, 1781–1826*. London, 1926.
Textbook; condensed biography.

Crawfurd, John. *The Present system of our East-India Government and Commerce considered: in which are exposed the fallacy, the incompatibility, the injustice of a political and despotic power possessing a commercial situation also, within the countries subject to its dominion*. London, 1813.
A 68-page pamphlet proving that for the E.I.C: "every trade, except that of China, whatever they may assert to the contrary, has, for years, been a constant and heavy loss to them."

————. *History of the Indian Archipelago*, 3 vols. Edinburgh, 1820.
Crawfurd was the second resident of Singapore, succeeding Farquhar, and was coached in his days of apprenticeship by Raffles, for whom he had a great but by no means uncritical admiration.

————. *A view of the present state and future prospects of the Free Trade and Colonization of India*. London, 1829.
A 106-page essay containing *inter alia* interesting facts and figures on the China and India trades, and on the rapid rise of Singapore.

———. *A Descriptive Dictionary of the Indian islands and adjacent countries*. London, 1856.
> A remarkably thorough and comprehensive work which may still be consulted with profit.

Egerton, H. E. *Sir Stamford Raffles and England in the Far East*. London, 1900.

Elliot, Gilbert (see Minto).

Foster, William. *The East India House: Its History and Associations*. London, 1924.
> Probably the most compact of this author's works about John Company's London setup.

Furnivall, J. S. *Netherlands India*. Cambridge and New York, 1944.
> Admirably detached point of view. Author was professor in Rangoon.

Hickey, William. *The Memoirs of William Hickey*, 4 vols. New York, 1923.
> Excellent picture of social life in British India preceding and during Raffles's period, affording striking contrast to contemporary modes and manners of Dutch colonists.

Kat, Angelino. *Colonial Policy*, 3 vols. New York, 1931, Vol. II.
> Useful for clear, textbook presentation of Dutch colonial policy in history, with explanatory comment.

Makepeace, Walter. *One Hundred Years of Singapore*. London, 1921.

Marsden, William. *History of Sumatra*. London, 1784.
> Still the standard work on the subject in English.

Minto. *Lord Minto in India: Life and Letters of Gilbert Elliot*. London, 1880.
> Very useful for background as well as for sidelights on outstanding men in East Indies.

Parkinson, C. Northcote. *Trade in the Eastern Seas, 1793–1818*. Cambridge, England, 1937.
> Excellent study of conditions in East during this period, both at sea and ashore.

Philips, C. H. "The Secret Committee of the East India Company (1784–1858)," *Bulletin of the School of Oriental and African Studies*, University of London, 1940.

Raffles, Dr. Thomas. *Letters, during a tour through some parts of France, Savoy, Switzerland, Germany, and the Netherlands.* New York, 1818.

> Travel letters from Raffles's confidant and cousin, the Dissenting minister, written while touring the continent with Raffles and his bride in 1817.

Raffles, Sir Thomas Stamford. "A discourse delivered to the literary and scientific society at Java, on September 16, 1815," *The Pamphleteer.* London, 1816. Vol. 8, pp. 67–105.

————. *Report on Japan to the Secret Committee of the English East India Company, 1812–1816,* edited by M. Paske-Smith. Kobe, Japan, 1929.

> Exhaustive account of this strange bypath in colonial history, with full correspondence from records formerly kept secret in Company archives.

————. *Substance of a minute recorded by T. S. Raffles . . . on the introduction of an improved system of internal management on the island of Java.* London, 1814.

————. *The History of Java,* 2 vols., 2d ed. London, 1830.

> Fit companion piece to Marsden's *History of Sumatra.* Beautiful plates for accompanying illustrations.

Raffles, Lady Sophia (Hull). *Memoir of the life and public services of Sir Thomas Stamford Raffles,* 2 vols. London, 1830, 1835.

> Invaluable collection of Raffles's correspondence, both personal and, occasionally, official, with running commentary, not exactly free and uninhibited, by his widow.

Renier, G. J. *Great Britain and the Netherlands, 1813–15.* London, 1930.

Say, J. B. *Historical Essay on the Rise, Progress and probable results of the British Dominion in India.* London, 1824.

> A 36-page pamphlet giving interesting statistics on the Company's employees.

Saito, Dr. A. *Doeff to Nihon.* Tokyo, 1921.

> In Japanese. The best authority for Raffles's efforts to open up trade with Japan, as he has used Japanese sources in addition to Doeff, Raffles, Boulger, et al.

Schoute, Dr. Dirk. *Occidental Therapeutics in the Netherlands East Indies during Three Centuries of Netherlands Settlement, 1600–1900.* Batavia, 1937.

This contains special information about Raffles's policy in regard to public health, including the treatment then in vogue of "social diseases."

Song Ong Liang. *One Hundred Years of the Chinese in Singapore.* London, 1923.

Spear, T. G. P. *The Nabobs: a Study of the Social Life of the English in Eighteenth Century India.* London, 1932.
Entertaining informal account, including much material not used by other historians.

Staunton, Sir George. *Authentic Account of an Embassy from the King of Great Britain to the Empire of China,* 2 vols. and atlas. London, 1797.
Sidelights on social customs in old Batavia.

Stavorinus, John Splinter. *Voyages to the East Indies,* translated from the original Dutch by Samuel Hull Wilcocke, 3 vols. London, 1798.
The original work from which most other travel writers of the time have borrowed when writing of old Batavia and the other Dutch colonies.

Stockdale, John Joseph. *Sketches, Civil and Military, of the Island of Java and Its Immediate Dependencies.* 2d enlarged ed. London, 1812.
Well-known travel sketches, which contain a good deal of Stavorinus material, but with further contributions from others.

Thorn, Major William. *R. R. Gillespie, a Memoir.* London, 1816.
The famous Raffles-Gillespie controversy colors these pages with prejudice.

———. *The Conquest of Java.* London, 1812.
Account of the conquest by eyewitness and participant. De Haan is scornful of its value.

Vlekke, Bernard H. M. *Nusantara: a History of the East Indian Archipelago.* Cambridge, Massachusetts, 1943.
Summary of the subject. Allowing for the author's prejudice against Raffles, one of the most convenient books on the Archipelago which we possess in America.

———. *The Story of the Dutch East Indies.* Cambridge, Massachusetts, 1945.
Widely used as a textbook in the United States, this is a condensation of *Nusantara* by the same author.

Wakeham, Eric. *The Bravest Soldier—Robert Rollo Gillespie.* London, 1937.

> Interesting biography, by modern writer who feels Gillespie has never had his due.

Willson, Beckles. *Ledger and Sword.* London, 1903.

> Another work on John Company, who possesses a fatal attraction, evidently, for novelists on holiday.

Winstedt, R. O. *A History of Malaya.* Singapore, 1935.

> Includes excellent detailed account of the founding of Singapore.

Wright, Arnold. "Singapore and Sir Stamford Raffles," *Quarterly Review.* New York, 1919.

> Article on Raffles's early aims for Singapore.

B. WORKS IN THE DUTCH LANGUAGE

Anonymous. *Nederlandsch-India in Haaren Tegenwoordigen Toestand Beschouwd.* Batavia, no date but circa 1780.

> Although this scurrilous but amusing little pamphlet on social conditions at Batavia purports to have been printed there, it was presumably published at an English or Danish settlement such as Calcutta or Tranquebar, in view of its contents and the strict censorship exercised by the Company.

Deventer, M. L. Van. *Het Nederlandsch Gezag over Java en onderhoorigheden Sedert 1811.* The Hague, 1891. Vol. 1, 1811–20.

> Covers the same period as Levyssohn Norman (q.v.) but contains more original documents.

Doeff, Hendrik. *Herinneringen uit Japan.* Haarlem, 1833.

> Gives the Dutch version of Raffles's attempt to open trade with Japan in 1813–14, by the man chiefly responsible for peacefully thwarting it.

Graaff, Nicolaas de. *Reisen van Nicolaas de Graaff, 1639–1687,* works published by the Linschoten Vereeniging. The Hague, 1930, Vol. 33.

> A scholarly edition by J. C. M. Warnsinck of the rare eighteenth-century original. Particularly valuable for its account of social life at Batavia as contained in the *Oost-Indische Spiegel* or *East-Indian Looking-Glass.* This accounts for the status of Batavian women in Raffles's day.

Haan, F. de. *Oud Batavia*, 2 vols. 1 album of plates. Batavia, 1922.
De Haan's magnum opus and an appropriate contribution by the Batavian Society of Arts and Sciences to the third centenary of the foundation of the city (1619–1919). He has made full use of material in the archives and supplemented it with extracts from numerous relevant historical works in Dutch, German, English, and French.

———. *Personalia der periode van het Engelsche bestuur over Java 1811–16*, printed in *Bijdragen tot de Taal- Land- en Volkenkunde van Nederl. Indië*. The Hague, 1935. Vol. 92, Part IV, pp. 477–681.
De Haan's last major work and a fitting climax to his labors. As the title indicates, it is a biographical dictionary of English and Dutch personalities of the years 1811–16. Even the most obscure nonentities are included, and there is a great deal of information about the major figures such as Thomas Horsfield, Rollo Gillespie, and Alexander Hare, derived from unpublished material in the Batavian archives.

———. *Priangan*, 4 vols. Batavia, 1910–12.
This work contains a great deal more material than is indicated by the title, which infers that it is limited to a history of the Preanger highlands. It is actually a veritable encyclopedia of the political, social, and economic history of the Dutch in Java down to and including the English interregnum. The fourth volume is particularly full of material for the years 1811–16. Dr. de Haan has made use *inter alia* of unpublished English documents (such as the *Proceedings of the Lieutenant-Governor and Council*) in the archives at Batavia.

Hogendorp, Dirk van. *Berigt van den tegenwoordigen toestand der Bataafsche Bezittingen in Oost-Indien*. Delft, 1799; reprinted 1800.
A sweeping condemnation of the Dutch East India Company's administrative measures based on his own experiences in Java and on the liberal ideals he had conceived from his reading of Voltaire, Raynal, and Rousseau. In many ways he anticipates Raffles's reforms, which would not have been needed had his own even more far-reaching suggestions been put into practice.

———. *Nadere uitlegging en ontwikkeling van het stelsel van Dirk Van Hogendorp*, etc. The Hague, 1802.

A clarification and amplification of his former 194-page pamphlet, chiefly in rebuttal of the strictures of his enemy, C. S. Nederburgh, the apostle of the status quo.

———. *Correspondentie van Dirk Van Hogendorp met zijn broeder Gijsbert Karel*, edited by E. du Perron and De Roos in the *Bijdragen tot de Taal- Land- en Volkenkunde van Nederlandsch-Indië*. The Hague, 1943. Vol. 102, pp. 125–273.
Interesting as showing the development of Hogendorp's liberal ideas and giving a picture of the Dutch East India Company's corruption and inefficiency which goes far to justify Raffles's subsequent strictures.

Levyssohn Norman, H. D. *De Britsche Heerschappij over Java en Onderhoorigheden (1811–1816)*. The Hague, 1857.
Written ninety years ago, this is still a standard work on the British interregnum in Java and is based on a careful study of English as well as of Dutch original sources.

Olivier, Jz. J. *Land- en Zeetogten in Nederlandsch Indië in 1817–1826*, 3 vols. Amsterdam, 1827.

———. *Tafereelen en merkwaardigheden uit Oost-Indië*, 2 vols. Amsterdam, 1836.
Interesting for his observations on the slave and Eurasian communities in the years immediately following the English interregnum.

Ottow, S. J. "*De Verwarring Raffles*," *De Oorsprong der conservatieve Inrichting*. Utrecht, 1937, pp. 35–64.
A trenchant criticism of Raffles's administration of Java, largely vitiated by the author's unwarrantable assumption that Raffles was a consummate hypocrite—an unjust characterization which he applies (equally mistakenly) to Dirk van Hogendorp.

Roo de la Faille, P. de. *Iets over Oud Batavia*. Batavia, 1919.
A good review of social conditions at Batavia at the end of the eighteenth and beginning of the nineteenth centuries.

Van der Kemp, P. H. Series of articles in the *Bijdragen van het Koninklijk Instituut van Taal- Land- en Volkenkunde van Nederlandsch-Indië* during the years 1897–1905:

1. "*De Sluiting van het Londensch Tractaat van 13 Augustus 1814.*" Vol. 47, pp. 239–339.

2. "*Fendall's en Raffles' opvattingen in het algemeen omtrent het Londensch Tractaat van 13 Augustus 1814.*" Ibid., pp. 341–497.

3. "*Het afbreken van onze betrekkingen met Bandjermassin onder Daendels en de herstelling van het Nederlandsch gezag aldaar op den 1 Januari 1817.*" Vol. 49, pp. 1–168.

4. "*Sumatra's Westkust naar aanleiding van het Londensch Tractaat van 13 Augustus, 1814.*" Ibid., pp. 205–306.

5. "*De Singapoorsche Papieroorlog.*" Ibid., pp. 388–547; compare 11 infra.

6. "*Raffles' bezetting van de Lampongs in 1818.*" Vol. 50, pp. 1–58.

7. "*De Commissiën van den Schout-bij-Nacht C. J. Wolterbeek naar Malacca en Riouw in Juli–December 1818 en Febr.–April 1820.*" Vol. 51, pp. 1–101.

8. "*Raffles' Atjeh-Overeenkomst van 1819.*" Ibid., pp. 159–240.

9. "*Palembang en Banka in 1816–1820.*" Ibid., pp. i–xii, 330–764.

10. "*Raffles' betrekkingen met Nias in 1820–21.*" Vol. 52, pp. 584–603.

11. "*De Stichting van Singapore, de afstand ervan met Malakka door Nederland, en de Britsche aanspraken op den Linga-Riouw Archipel.*" Vol. 54, pp. 313–476.

12. "*Benkoelen krachtens het Londensch Tractaat van 17 Maart 1824.*" Vol. 55, pp. 283–320.

13. "*Geschiedenis van het Londensch Tractaat van 17 Maart 1824.*" Vol. 56, pp. 1–244.

14. "*De Terruggave der Oost-Indische Koloniën in 1814–16.*" The Hague, 1910.

15. "*Oost-Indië's Herstel in 1816.*" The Hague, 1911.

16. "*Het Nederlandsch-Indisch Bestuur in 1817 to het vertrek der Engelschen.*" The Hague, 1913.

17. "*Het Nederlandsch-Indisch Bestuur in het Midden van 1817.*" The Hague, 1915.

18. "*Java's Landelijk Stelsel.*" The Hague, 1916.

19. "*Oost-Indië's inwendig bestuur van 1817 op 1818.*" The Hague, 1919.

20. *"Oost-Indies Geldmiddelen Japansche en Chineesche handel van 1817–18."* The Hague, 1919.

21. *"Sumatra in 1818."* The Hague, 1920.

This series of essays forms an invaluable supplement to Boulger and other English writers, for in addition to utilizing the Dutch and Batavian records, Van der Kemp has made use of numerous English documents in the India Office at London which were transcribed for the Netherlands Indies Colonial Institute in 1895–96, many of which escaped the notice of Boulger.

(cf. *Onderzoek van stukken in het India Office. Verslag van Mr. W. Roosegarde Bisschop. Bijdragen T. L. & V.*, Vol. 47, pp. 183–209.)

His later efforts of 1910–20 amount to little more than digesting the sources used in his earlier essays into narrative form.

Van der Wall, Victor Ido. *Figuren en Feiten uit den Compagniestijd.* Bandoeng, 1933.

An excellent account of various aspects of social conditions at Batavia during the Company's time and the English interregnum, based on contemporary sources including the *Java Government Gazette,* 1811–16.

Verhandelingen van het Bataviaasch Genootschap van Kunsten en Wetenschappen. Batavia, 1779–1941.

The first eight volumes of the transactions of this academy— the first of its kind in the tropics—were published at irregular intervals in the years 1779–1816, the seventh and eighth under the auspices of Raffles.

C. SOURCES NOT DIRECTLY CONSULTED

1. Collection of printed papers on the Gillespie affair. Bound in book form, small-folio, and printed at Batavia in 1815 on the order of Raffles, without a title; containing his answers to the accusations brought against him by Major General Gillespie.

2. *Official and secret papers relating to the sale of lands and other subjects during the British Administration of Java.* The Hague, 1883.

3. *Proceedings of the Lieutenant-Governor in Council, 1811– 1816.*

Resolutions of the British-Indian Government over Java and dependencies; only those in the "Public Department" still in the archives at Batavia (1912). Those in the "Secret Department" and other departments have disappeared.

4. *Java Government Gazette*. Batavia, 1811–16.

NOTE: None of the above works could be traced in the United States libraries, and lack of time, coupled with wartime restrictions and their aftermath, prevented copies being obtained from England. The Dutch historians, Levyssohn Norman, Van der Kemp, and De Haan, however, utilized them to a considerable extent and I have availed myself of their quotations where relevant.

INDEX

INDEX

Abdullah, Munshi, 124–27, 289, 459–60
  autobiography, 60, 124
  description of Lord Minto, 131–35
  description of Olivia Raffles, 60, 67–68
  on founding of Singapore, 458, 461–65, 466–70
  on his father, 124–25
  on Java campaign, 109
  on Major Farquhar, 460–61
  on Sir Stamford Raffles, 112, 113–14, 125–27, 139–45, 524
Acheen, 401, 452, 454–56, 462, 472
Adam, Mr., 470, 471
Addenbrooke, Colonel, 401, 472
Addison, George Augustus, 227, 289, 291, 293, 294, 296–300, 301–02, 405
Afterlenden (ship), 96
Ahmed Shah, Sultan, 94–96
Ainslie, Dr. Daniel, 262–66, 270, 271, 272, 278–79, 280, 281, 284, 285, 286, 294

Albuquerque, 85
Amboina, 242
Amboina Massacre of 1624, 450
America, 435; see also North America
American Embargo Act (1808), 106
American Revolution
  cause of, 6
  English attitude toward, 4
Amherst, Lord, 353
Anderson, Dr., 14
Anglo-Chinese College, 515
Ann (ship), 1, 2
Anthony Adverse (book), 211
Army Medical Officers, 291
Arnold, Dr. Joseph, 387, 389, 393–94, 405, 523, 533
  death of, 393–94, 404
Asia, 8, 80, 87, 150
Asiatic Annual Register, 28
Asiatic Journal, 41
Asiatic Society, 136, 232, 407
Assey, Charles, 172, 274, 291, 294, 300–01, 315, 427, 470, 479–80, 534
Atkinson, Brooks, 87

571

Auchmuty, Sir Samuel, 115, 149, 151, 152, 154, 337
dinner party for, 161, 217
Auspicious (ship), 338
Australia, 5
Autobiography of Munshi Abdullah, The, 60, 124

Badruddin, Mahmud, 168
Bagdad, 234, 309
Bali, 207, 324, 437
Banca, 164, 165, 167, 168, 329 434, 436, 439, 443, 449, 543
Banjermassin scandal, 449
Banjoewangi, 293
Banks, Sir Joseph, 405, 414, 522, 524
death of, 419, 522
Banner, H. S., 131, 161
Bannerman, Colonel, 473, 474, 476, 477, 478, 479, 480–86
Bantam, 96
Barrett, W., 291, 294–95
Basel, Maria Wilhelmina Engelhard-Senn van, 186, 190
Batavia, 52, 107, 108, 118, 139, 149, 150, 152, 154, 155, 160, 161, 165, 171, 262, 283, 290, 298–99, 313, 320, 459
Chinese quarter, 184
courts in, 238
crowded conditions, 371
description of, 183–84, 298–99
Dutch colonial life in, 225
food in, 190, 225–26
housing in, 184
mixed population of, 235

Portuguese songs, 194–95
slaves in, 204, 207, 208, 210, 212
social life in, 178–200, 217–23
unhealthy conditions in, 107, 154, 176–78, 227–29, 298
Batavian Society of Arts and Sciences, 229–33, 262, 514
Batta tribe, 408–12
Bawean, 293
Bay of Biscay, 364
Belgian Congo, 8, 245, 372, 386
Belgium, 359, 360
Bell, Dr., 530, 532
Beluwa, Prince, 500
Bencoolen, 130, 316–17, 326–27, 338, 339, 363, 364, 365–81, 413, 414, 435, 438, 442, 443, 452
Benevolus (Robert Tytler), 228
Bengal, 5, 11, 36, 89, 91, 101, 115, 119, 207, 239, 253, 273, 298, 306, 378
Raffles's visit to, 101
Bentan, 95
Bertie, Admiral, 128
Bertrand, Countess, 336
Bertrand, Marshal, 336
Běsar, Těngku Pěnglima, 139–45
Betel chewing, 186, 192, 198
Bible, 23
Billiton, 168, 436, 439, 449
Bintang, 434, 438
Biographical Dictionary of the Living Authors of Great Britain and Ireland, 63

Birds' Nest Rocks, 249
Bishopsgate, 9
Blagrave, Mr., 314, 315
Bleecker, 232
Blomhoff, Jan Cock, 285, 286, 288
Bloomfield, Sir Benjamin, 355
Boer War, 447–48, 450
Bombay, India, 224
Bonaparte, Josephine, 38, 221
Bonaparte, Louis, 108
Bonaparte, Napoleon, 51, 81, 105, 108, 160, 161, 221, 233, 273, 315, 323, 324, 332–36, 428, 525
Border Minstrelsy, 55, 91
Borneo, 145, 173, 207, 321, 437, 449, 533, 543
Borneo (ship), 424, 530
Bosanquet, 511
Boulger, Demetrius, 107, 359, 428–30, 448–50, 452
    on Bannerman, 478
    on Captain Benjamin Raffles, 15
    on founding of Singapore, 465
    on Java campaign, 109, 137, 138, 158, 310
    on Napoleon, 105
    on Olivia Raffles, 30–32, 64, 66, 67, 69, 318
    on Penang climate, 56
    on Sir Thomas Raffles, 14, 19, 21, 31, 102, 103, 121, 164, 170, 244, 251, 252, 307–08, 317, 319, 344, 354, 359, 366, 441, 485, 537
    on Sophia Raffles, 400
Bourbon, 82, 102, 104, 127–29
Braam, F. A. van, 442

"Brain Trust," 92
Breton, Mr., 270–71
British East Africa, 67
British East India Company. See East India Company
Broughton, Commodore, 148
Browne, Mr., 350
Browning, Robert, 63
Brussels, Belgium, 358
Buckinghamshire, Earl of, 324, 325
Buitenzorg, 107, 139, 155, 172, 183, 290, 301, 320–21, 326, 328
Bunbury, Mrs., 218
Byron, Lord, 61

Cabow, Menang, 444
Calcutta, Raffles's visits to, 101–02, 401, 404, 406, 451–53
Calcutta University, 57
Cambay, Gulf of, 224
Cambodia, 502
Canada, 260
Cannibalism, 408–12
Canning, George, 432, 435, 441, 479, 480, 511–12
Canton, 231, 262, 267, 272, 285, 286, 546
Capellen, Baron van der, 525
Cape of Good Hope, 8
Carimon Islands, 460–61, 465, 537
Caroline, Queen, 352, 353
Carteret, Captain, 180, 216
Cassa, 285, 286
Celebes, 207, 323, 494, 533
Ceylon, 51, 84
Chantrey, 37
Chapones, Mrs. Esther de, 186

573

575 ❧